The Blue Guides

Albania

Austria   Austria
Vienna

Belgium and Luxembourg
Bulgaria
China
Cyprus
Denmark
Egypt

Czech and Slovak Republics   Czech and Slovak
Republics
Prague

France   France
Paris and Versailles
Burgundy
Loire Valley
Midi-Pyrénées
Normandy
South West France
Corsica

Germany   Berlin and eastern Germany

Greece   Greece
Athens
Crete
Rhodes and the
Dodecanese

Hungary   Hungary
Budapest

Southern India
Ireland

Italy   Northern Italy
Southern Italy
Florence
Rome
Venice
Tuscany
Umbria
Sicily

Jordan
Malaysia and Singapore
Malta and Gozo
Mexico
Morocco

Netherlands   Netherlands
Amsterdam

Poland
Portugal

Spain   Spain
Barcelona
Madrid

Sweden
Switzerland
Thailand
Tunisia

Turkey   Turkey
Istanbul

UK   England
Scotland
Wales
Channel Islands
London
Oxford and Cambridge
Country Houses of
England

USA   New York
Museums and Galleries of
New York
Boston and Cambridge

D1424343

Please write in with your comments, suggestions and corrections for the next edition of the Blue Guide. Writers of the most helpful letters will be awarded a free Blue Guide of their choice.

Czech & Slovak Republics

Michael Jacobs

A&C Black • London
WW Norton • New York

BLUE GUIDE

2nd edition © Michael Jacobs, 1999
Published by A & C Black (Publishers) Limited
35 Bedford Row, London WC1R 4JH

Maps and plans drawn by Robert Smith, RJS Associates, © A&C Black

Illustrations © Jim Urquhart

A CIP catalogue record of this book is available from the British Library.

ISBN 0–7136–4429 X

Published in the United States of America by
WW Norton and Company Inc.
500 Fifth Avenue, New York, NY 10110

Published simultaneously in Canada by
Penguin Books Canada Limited
10 Alcorn Avenue, Toronto
Ontario M4V 3B2

ISBN 0–393–31932–6 USA

Cover photograph: Three Girls, Frantisek Muzika, from the Narodni Galerie, Prague.

Michael Jacobs studied at the Courtauld Institute of Art, where he received a Ph.D in 1982 for his researches into eighteenth-century Italian art. A full-time author and translator of Spanish and Latin American drama, he has written numerous books on art and travel, including *The Phaidon Companion to Art and Artists in the British Isles* (1980, with Malcolm Warner), *The Good and Simple Life: Artist Colonies in Europe and America* (1991), *A Guide to Provence* (1990). *Santiago de Compostela* (1991), *Between Hopes and Memories : A Spanish Journey* (1994), *The Painted Voyage: Art Travel And Exploration, 1564-1875* (1995), *Madrid Observed* (1997), *Andalucia* (1990; revised 1998) and *Budapest: A Cultural Guide* (1998). He is currently senior honorary research fellow in the Hispanics department at Glasgow University. He is also the author of *Blue Guide Barcelona* and *Blue Guide Prague*.

Printed and bound in England by Butler & Tanner Ltd, Frome and London.

Preface

The first edition of this book was commissioned in 1988, at a time when virtually the only available guides to the then communist Czechoslovakia were an officially-approved Czech work (with the obligatory information about housing estates and heavy industries), and a comparably uninspired English-produced guide that came with hand-drawn maps and a text whose main descriptive term was 'nice'. Given such competition, I responded eagerly to the challenge of writing a book that would impress upon travellers the exceptional wealth of cultural treasures awaiting them in the former Czechoslovakia. What other country of its size could offer so many uncannnily well-preserved old towns, squares and country houses, or indeed lay claim to an artistic and architectural legacy that included such original highpoints as the fantastical late medieval vaulting of Benedikt Ried, the viscerally dynamic statuary of Matthias Braun, the 'gothic-baroque' churches of Santini-Aichel, the idiosyncratic 'Cubist' designs and buildings by Gočár and others, and the pionering modernism achieved during the first years of the Czechoslovak Republic?

Events that have taken place in Central Europe since the time I began writing on Czecholsovakia have not only highlighted the difficulties facing guide-book writers in the late twentieth century but also given to my endeavours an absurd dimension that calls to mind the ironic musings of such contemporary Czech authors as Milan Kundera and the late Bohumíl Hrabal. When I embarked on the first edition of this book, the Czech Communist regime kindly sponsored a two-month tour of the country largely undertaken in a chauffeur-driven black Tatra. But by the time the text was nearing completion, the Communist government collapsed, thus bringing about the fall from power of many of those who had helped me, and the necessity of extensively revising what I had written, not least through altering a high proportion of the book' street names. The speed with which the country began changing after 1989, combined with the sudden surge of information that became more widely available, meant of course that any guide-book that appeared in the early 1990s would soon seem out-of-date. However, I had hardly imagined that the publication of *Blue Guide Czechoslovakia* in 1992 would be followed so shortly afterwards by the splitting of the country in two (did anyone consider the inconvenience this would cause to travel writers?). Inevitably, it was with a certain trepidation that I set about the long and protracted task of bringing out this present edition, the final touches to which were indeed accompanied by another, not altogether pleasant surprise. On 15 October, 1998, while returning by train from Prague to Budapest, I was briefly held in custody by the Slovakian police on the grounds that new visa regulations for British visitors—announced only the day before, and completely unknown to me—had come into force a few hours before my arrival at the Slovakian frontier. The day happened to be my birthday.

From the tourist's point of view, the changes that have occurred since the return to democracy in 1989 cannot be said to have been entirely beneficial. The great improvements in standards of food and hotels have to be set against the transformation of much of central Prague into a congested Disneyland, with buildings repainted in inappropriate (and at times damaging) pastel colours, and long queues preventing easy access to such popular sites as the Charles Bridge.

Romantic travellers, remembering the Czechoslovakia of old, will probably be shocked by what has been done to the once evocatively decayed town of Český Krumlov, and are likely to be dismayed by the way in which a giant Tesco's has almost superceded the cathedral as the dominant presence in the western Slovakian capital of Košiče.

This said, the Czech lands and Slovakia remain as a whole very much as I had first known them: remarkably little visited outside of Central Prague, and with a cultural history largely filled with names with which most Western visitors are unlikely to be familiar. In line with the new style of Blue Guides, I have included in this new edition more practical information than before, and have supplied a select list of hotels. None the less, this is still essentially a cultural guide partly written in the hope of promoting a greater knowledge of and enthusiasm for Czech and Slovak art, architecture, literature and music. In view of the nationalistic intolerance now growing in Slovakia, I have also tried to ensure that the major role played by the Hungarians in Slovakia's cultural history is not as forgotten as might sometimes seem today.

I would like to renew my thanks to all those who helped in the first edition of this book, notably Pieter Biely of Čedok, and my two wonderful guides Jaroslav Spíšek and L'udovít Haeberle. Jim Urquhart, Julia Borbély and Tony Worcester of Arts Europe have been lively companions on recent trips to the Czech and Slovak Republics, while Adam Yamey, as well as providing the learned notes on which much of this book's music section is based, has supplied me with much useful information culled from his own travels here. Zuzana Dančak of the Czech and Slovak Centre in London has been very patient and efficient in arranging places for me to stay, and has kindly read through the manuscript. Jackie Rae, with whom I visited Prague in the winter of 1987, has done much to prevent me from giving up in despair the revision of this work. My thanks also to Alexander Fyjis-Walker, Thomas Tuohy, Clare de Vries, my meticulous editors, Alison Effeny, Gemma Davies and Judy Tither of A&C Black, my agent David Godwin, and the many readers of the first edition who have written in with suggestions and corrections.

Michael Jacobs
March 1999

Contents

Preface 5

Practical information 9
  Planning your trip 9
  Getting to the Czech and Slovak
    Republics 12
  Where to stay 14
  Travelling around the Czech and
    Slovak Republics 15
  General information 17
  Food and drink 22
  Language 27

Background information 34
  Historical summary 34
  Art and architecture 48
  Music 66
  Literature and cinema 73
  Further reading 94

The Guide

The Czech Republic 97

1 **Prague** 97
  A. The Old Town ~ Staré Město 104
  B. The Little Quarter ~ Malá Strana 130
  C Prague Castle and the Hradčany 142
  D. The New Town ~ Nové Město 162
  E. Vyšehrad and Southern Prague ~ Zbraslav, Hlubočepy and Smíchov 177
  F. Eastern Prague ~ Vinohrady, Žižkov and Karlín 181
  G. Western Pargue ~ Střešovice and Břevnov 184
  H. Northern Prague ~ Letná, Holešovice-Bubeneč, Troja and Dejvice 186
2 **Excursions from Prague** 191
  A. Kutná Hora and Kolín 191
  B. Průhonice, Sázava, Český Šternberk and Konopiště 198
  C. Karlštejn and Křivoklát 200
  D. Lidice and Budeč 203
  E. Roztoky, Nelahozeves, Veltrusy and Mělník 205

East Bohemia 207

3 **Prague to Náchod** 209
4 **Prague to Harrachov** 222
5 **Harrachov to Trutnov** 225

North Bohemia 229

6 **Harrachov to Děčín** 232
7 **Prague to Děčín** 236
8 **Děčín to Karlovy Vary** 241
9 **Prague to Karlovy Vary** 246
  A. Via Louny and Žatec 246
  B. Via Lubenec 247

West Bohemia 249

10 Karlovy Vary to Mariánske Lázně 250
11 Mariánskee Lázně to Domažlice 264
12 Domažlice to České Budějovice 268
13 Prague to Plzeň 272

South Bohemia 278

14 Plzeň to České Budějovice 280
15 Prague to České Budějovice 282
 A. Via Příbram and Písek 282
 B. Via Tábor and Bechyně 285
16 Prachatice to Jindřichův Hradec via Vyšší Brod 289

Moravia 303

17 Prague to Brno 306
 A. By the motorway 306
 B. Via Žďár nad Sázavou and Pernštejn 308
18 Jindřichův Hradec to Brno 311
19 Telč to Brno via Vranov and Znojmo 315
20 Brno 320
 A. Central Brno 322
 B. Western Brno 327
 C. Northern Brno 329
21 Brno to Ostrava 332
 A. Via Olomouc 332
 B. Via Kroměříž 338
 C. Via Uherské Hradiště and Zlín 346
22 Hradec Králové to Ostrava 351
23 Hradec Králové to Olomouc 354
24 Brno to Bratislava 357

The Slovak Republic 361

25 Bratislava 365
 A. Central Bratislava 370
 B. Bratislava Castle and Devin 381
 C. Northern Bratislava and the northern environs 384
 D. Petržalka and Rusovce 388
26 Bratislava to Zvolen 389
 A. Via Komárno 389
 B. Via Nitra 393
27 Bratislava to Žilina 397
28 Trenčín to Banská Bystrica 402
29 Ostrava to Liptovský Mikuláš 410
30 Liptovský Mikuláš to Prešov 416
31 Poprad to Svidník 425
32 Svidník to Košice 431
33 Košice to Banská Bystrica 437

Index 440

Maps and plans

Banska Bystrica 408
Bratislava 368–369
Brno 321
České Budějovice 298
Český Krumlov 293
Hradec Králové 213
Karlovy Vary 252
Kutná Hora 195
Mariánské Lázně 263
Olomouc 334
Plzeň 274
Prague 106–107
Prague castle 144
Prague cathedral ~ St Vitus 149
Prague, days out 192

Practical information

by Clare de Vries

Planning your trip

Climate and when to go

The climate of the Czech and Slovak Republics is typically continental, with warm summers and cold winters, and the best time to visit is in spring or autumn. Spring can sometimes not show at all, but is the best season when it does. Average temperatures in March are between 1 and 7°C and in April and May between 9 and 15°C. Summer, when the average temperature is between 14 and 24°C, sees Prague abandoned to tourists and very crowded. Autumn is a close contender with spring for prettiness, with crisp air, clear skies and an average temperature between 6 and 15°C. Winter is long, cold and grey, with lots of shops, restaurants and sites being shut, but the romance of Christmas helps break it up. When it snows, Prague is charming, but the smog from coal heating is often bad. Average winter temperatures are between -4 and 3°C.

Passports and formalities

Czech Republic. Visitors from the US, the EC and most other European countries do not need a visa to enter the Czech Republic but do need a valid passport, with eight months to spare by the end of the visit. Canadians and New Zealanders no longer require a visa, but Australians do, although now it costs nothing. Visitors from other countries need to obtain a visa in advance from their local Czech embassy. Visas are also obtainable at three border crossings, at Waidhaus–Rosvadov, Wullowitz–Dolní Dvořiště and Klein Haugsdorf–Hatě, and at Prague's Ruzyně airport. For visa information once in Prague, ☎ (02) 61 44 11 19.

British, Canadian and Slovak nationals can stay for up to 180 days, New Zealanders, Irish and other EC nationals for up to 90 days and Americans for up to 30 days. If you wish to stay longer than your visa (or visa-free period) allows, you will need an extension which can be obtained from a police station or, if in Prague, from the Foreigners' Police Headquarters (Úřadovna cizinecké policie) at Olšanská 2, Žižkov, Prague 3. ☎ (02) 61 44 12 20.

Slovak Republic. US, EC and most other European nationals (except those from the UK) do not need a visa to enter the Slovak Republic but do need a valid passport, with six months to spare by the end of the visit. Visitors from elsewhere including the UK (since October 1998), need a visa from their local Slovak embassy. The cost of the visa (2000 Slovak Kč) combined with the trouble of obtaining one, is having the effect of greatly reducing British transit and short-term visitors to Slovakia.

If you wish to stay longer than three months, you need a visa extension obtainable from the Foreigners' Police Office (Oddelenie cudzineckej polície) in Bratislava at Záhradnická 93. ☎ (17) 51 21 111. Extension visas for the two Republics are incredibly difficult to obtain unless you have a job lined up. Many people avoid the issue by leaving the country for a few days and then re-entering, but the legality of this is doubtful. If you do this, make sure you get your passport stamped.

Technically you are meant to register with the local police within 30 days of arrival—hotels will do this for you—but many visitors do not bother.

National Tourist Boards

When planning your trip, the following **websites** have plenty of information on every aspect of life in the Czech Republic: **Czech Tourism Pages**: www.infotec-travel.com/CZGENERA.html; **Czech Info Centre**: www.muselik.com/czech/; **Czech Days**: www.netlink.co.uk/users/webman/czech/; **Czech Republic**: www.czech.cz/

UK. **Czech and Slovak Tourist Centre**, 16 Frognal Parade, Finchley Road, London NW3 5HG. ☎ 0171 794 3263/3264, fax: 0171 794 3265, website: www.czech-slovak-tourist.co.uk, email: cztc@cztc.demon.co.uk, free call ☎ 0800 026 7943. This is a tour operator for the Czech Republic and the tourist centre for the Slovak Republic, with information on everything except timetables for trains, which change constantly. It can help you in every instance, whether it be printing opera tickets or organising your wedding ceremony. It also sells the Prague card which allows travel for three days and entry to 40 museums free of charge (adult card 480Kč, child's card 380Kč). Generally you need to send a stamped and self-addressed envelope to the Centre to receive the card.

The **Czech Tourist Authority** in London, 95 Great Portland St, London W1N 5RA. ☎ 0171 291 9920, fax: 0171 436 8300. Open Mon–Fri 10.00–18.00. The Authority will send out free of charge tourist brochures on all regions in the Czech Republic, national accommodation details, road maps and advice for motorists, lists of camp sites, cultural events in Prague and other regions and information on tour operators and travel agents from the UK to the Czech Republic (send a stamped and self-addressed envelope).

US. **Czech Cultural Centre**, 1109 Madison Avenue, New York, NY 10028. ☎ (212) 288 0830, fax: (212) 772 0586 or 3200 Linnean Ave NW, Washington DC 20008. ☎ (202) 363 6315. Open Tues–Fri 09.00–17.00. The Centre has information on all subjects.

The **Slovak Info Center**, 406 East 67th St, New York, NY 10021. ☎ (212) 737 3971, fax: (212) 737 3454, email matica@inx.net. A walk-in centre that can also provide information by phone, fax or email.

Canada. **Czech Tourist Authority**, 130 King St W, Suite 715, Exchange Tower, Box 198, Toronto, Ontario, M5X 1A6. ☎ (416) 367 3432, fax: (416) 367 3492.

Slovak Culture and Info Center, 12 Birch Ave, Toronto, Ontario M4V 1C8. ☎ (416) 925 0008, fax: (416) 925 0009.

In the republics themselves, **tourist offices** (informační centrum) give out maps and pamphlets on local sights and can help with accommodation.

Prague. The **Prague Information Service** (Pražká informační služba or PIS) provides free information, maps and general help.

PIS, Na příkopě 20, Prague 1. ☎ (02) 26 40 22/general info 187/54 44 44. Metro Můstek or náměstí Republiky. Open Mon–Fri 09.00–19.00, Sat, Sun 09.00–17.00.

Bratislava. BIS (Bratislavská informačná služba). ☎ (17) 53 34 325/53 33 715.

Tour Operators

UK. **Martin Randall Travel**, 10 Barley Mow Passage, London W4 4PH. ☎ 0181 742 3355, fax: 0181 742 7766. Upmarket art and architecture tours.

Bohemian Promotions, 61 Mere Road, Erdington, Birmingham B23 7LL. ☎ and fax: (0121) 373 9107.

Czechbook Agency, Jopes Mill, Trebrownbridge, near Liskeard, Cornwall PL14 3PX. ☎ and fax: (01503) 240 629.

Czech and Slovak Tourist Centre Ltd, 16 Frognal Parade, London NW3 5GH. ☎ (0171) 794 3263, fax: (0171) 794 3265.

Czech Travel Ltd, 1 Trinity Square, South Woodham Ferrers, Essex CM3 5JX. ☎ (01245) 328 647, fax: (01245) 322 407.

Čedok Travel Ltd, 53–54 Haymarket, London SW1Y 4RP. ☎ (0171) 839 4414, fax: (0171) 839 0204

US. Abercrombie & Kent, 1520 Kensington Road, Suite 212, Oak Brook, IL 60521-2141. ☎ (630) 954 2944/800 323 7308, fax: (630) 954 3324, website: www.abercrombiekent.com. Deluxe tours.

Czech and Slovak Travel Service, 7033 Sunset Boulevard, Suite 210, LA, CA 90028. ☎ (213) 389 2157.

Travcoa, Box 2630, 2350 SE Bristol St, Newport Beach, CA 92660. ☎ (714) 476 2800/800 992 2003, fax: (714) 476 2538.

Maupintour, Box 807, 1515 St Andrews Drive, Lawrence, KS 66047. ☎ (785) 843 1211/800 255 4266, fax: (785) 843 8351.

ČEDOK, 10 East 40th St, Suite 3601, New York, NY 10016. ☎ (212) 689 9720, fax: (212) 213 4461, email: viktul@aol.com. Open Mon–Fri 09.00–17.00.

Fugazy Intl, 770 US-1 North Brunswick, NJ 08902. ☎ (800) 828 4488.

Ireland. Thomas Cook, 11 Donegall Place, Belfast BT1 5AJ. ☎ (01232) 554 455, fax: (01232) 550 029.

Thomas Cook, 118 Grafton St, Dublin. ☎ (1) 677 1721, fax: (1) 677 1258. website: www.thomascook.co.uk

Joe Walsh Tours, 8–11 Baggot St, Dublin. ☎ (1) 676 8915, fax: (1) 676 6572.

Budget Travel, 134 Lower Baggot St, Dublin 2. ☎ (1) 661 1866, fax: (1) 662 9388.

Prague. ČEDOK, Na Příkopě 18, Nové Město, Prague 1. ☎ (02) 41 97 203, fax: (02) 24 19 72 34. Metro Můstek or náměstí Republiky. Open Mon–Fri 09.00–17.00, Sat 09.00–13.00.

Martin Tour, Štěpánská 16, Prague 1. ☎ and fax: (02) 24 21 24 73. Open Mon–Fri 09.00–16.30.

PIS, Staroměstské nám 1, Prague 1. ☎ (02) 24 18 25 69 or (02) 24 48 23 80. Both companies offer guided tours for groups and individuals.

Tom's Travel Ltd, Ostrovní 7, 11008—Prague 1, ☎ (02) 22 939 72, or (02) 22 90 696 or (02) 22 993 49; fax (02) 22 918 66. Exceptionally helpful agency that can organise every aspect of your visit to the Czech Republic.

Bratislava. Tatratour, Bajkalská 25, B27 27 Bratislava. ☎ (17) 52 14 844/52 33 282, fax: (17) 52 12 722.

Lucky Tour, Obchodná 7, 811 06 Bratislava. ☎ (17) 53 33 520/53 35 008, fax: (17) 53 31 190.

Both companies organise sightseeing tours, spa treatments, sporting events, exhibitions, culinary festivals, hotel accommodation and all travel requirements within the Slovak Republic.

Getting to the Czech and Slovak Republics

By air

Several airlines fly **to Prague from the UK** at least once a day. **British Airways** (☎ (0345) 222 111, website: www.british-airways.com) and **British Midland** (☎ (0345) 554 554, website: www.iflybritishmidland.com) depart from Heathrow twice daily. **Czech Airlines** (České aerolinie or ČSA) (☎ (0171) 255 1898, website: www.csa.cz) departs from Heathrow twice daily and also from Stansted (daily except Sat) and Manchester (daily except Sun). Flights take 2 hours. A return flight by British Midland currently costs £185 for travel during the week and £205 at the weekends. British Airways costs £205 mid-week and £16 extra at weekends. Czech Airlines costs £195 in the low season and £310 in the high season.

There are no direct flights **to Bratislava from the UK**. The best way to get to the Slovak Republic is to fly to Vienna (every major carrier goes there) and then take the Bratislava bus, run by Eurolines Slovak Republic (SAD), which waits for flight connections. It takes about 1 hour and costs 100 Austrian shillings— about £5. There are signs to the bus in the airport. For the bus timetable, contact your local Slovak Tourist Centre. A much more expensive way is to fly to Prague and then on to Bratislava with ČSA or Air Ostrava, which also flies to other destinations within the country: ☎ (02) 67 15 54 71

Discount flights are advertised in the Sunday papers and are available from specialist agents: **Campus Travel**, 52 Grosvenor Gardens, London SW1. ☎ 0171 730 3402. **STA Travel**, 86 Old Brompton Road, London SW7. ☎ 0171 361 6161.

To those travelling **from the US**, all the major airlines offer plenty of flights from plenty of airports, but ČSA is the only non-stop carrier from the States, departing from New York and Chicago. All the others make stopovers in Europe. Flights from New York take 9–10 hours and from Los Angeles 16 hours. The cheapest flights can be bought from specialist agents, but these allow little flexibility, and the same applies to charter flights. Fares always depend on the season—the high season is the summer and around Christmas and Easter, and weekend flights cost about $50 more than those in mid-week. The cheapest flights are Apex tickets, but must be booked 21 days before your departure, and you must spend at least seven days abroad. Super Apex tickets limit your stay to between 7 and 21 days. Most cheap fares require you to spend a Saturday in the destination country. Useful numbers include: **ČSA (Czech Airlines)**, ☎ (212) 765 6022/6545, website: www.csa.cz ; **Continental**, ☎ (800) 231 0856, website: www.flycontinental.com; **Delta**, ☎ (800) 221 1212, website: www.delta-air.com; **American Airlines**, ☎ (800) 433 7300, website: www.aa.com; **United Airlines**, ☎ (800) 538 2929, website: www.ual.com; **KLM**, ☎ (800) 3 747 747, website: www.klm.nl; **Air France**, ☎ (212) 247 0100, website: www.air-france.com; ČSA also flies direct to Prague **from Canada**, with daily flights from Montreal and Toronto in the summer.

There are no direct flights to Prague **from Ireland**. Flying via London is the easiest way, and Aer Lingus, Ryanair and British Midland fly to London daily. Return flights to Luton/Stansted with Ryanair cost IR£60. Flights with Aer Lingus and British Midland are a little more expensive at IR£75, but fly direct to Heathrow, saving you time. Flights from Belfast to London on British Airways costs £95. Good deals and packages are obtainable from several travel agents (see above).

Useful numbers include **Aer Lingus**, ☎ (0645) 737 747. **Aer Lingus**, Dublin, ☎ (1) 844 4777. **Ryanair**, ☎ (0541) 569 569. **Ryanair**, Dublin, ☎ (1) 677 4422.

Prague's airport, Ruzyně, was built by British Aerospace and is small but brand new. Arrival and departure information, ☎ (02) 20 11 33 14. Other information, ☎ (02) 20 11 40 33.

The airport is about 20km northwest of the city centre, and is only served by buses, although some hotels will collect you if you book ahead. The **express airport bus** is quick and cheap. Two buses run into town: **Touristic Praha** (☎ (02) 29 06 40) goes to náměstí Republiky every half hour between 08.30 and 19.00 and costs 75Kč; **Cedaz** goes to náměstí Republiky (90Kč) and to Dejvická metro station (60Kč), the last station on the green line A, and runs every hour from 05.00 to 10.00 (☎ (02) 23 17 598).

Three **local buses** go from the airport to metro stations every 20mins between 05.00 and 24.00. The cheapest but slowest is bus No. 179, which goes to Metro Nové Butovice (yellow line B). Bus No. 108 goes to Metro Hradčanská (green line A) and bus No. 119 goes to Metro Dejvická (green line A). It costs 6Kč.

Special airport **taxis**—usually white limousines—also operate a service. Normal taxis are not allowed to park at the airport. The airport taxi will cost 400Kč if your hotel is in the centre, and about 600Kč if it is on the further side of town.

From **Bratislava's airport**, MR Štefánika, a bus goes direct to the centre every 10mins. It costs about 10Sk. A taxi will cost about 400Sk.

Airport information, ☎ (17) 52 23 00 36.

By rail

From London's Victoria station the train journey to Prague takes 24 hours. Trains leave at 08.00 and run via Ostend, Brussels, Cologne, Frankfurt and Nuremberg before entering the Czech Republic by the Schirnding–Cheb border crossing. The train arrives at Praha Hlavní Nádraží, off Wenceslas Square, Wilsonova 2, which is the city's main international railway station.

With **Eurotrain**, a standard return ticket from London costs £264. You can shorten your journey by taking the Eurostar to Brussels, which costs £79 return (as long as you are away a Saturday night), plus £185 for a return ticket from Brussels to Prague; couchettes cost an extra £10 each.

Students and those under 26 can get better deals: £160 to Prague (via Ostend). An **InterRail** ticket costs £209 a month if you are under 26 and over 65, £279 for others. This covers two zones of the European rail network.

To reach Bratislava, take a local train from Prague. The journey takes 5hrs and costs about £5 one way. There is also a service from London via Brussels and Vienna, from where you catch a local train to Bratislava.

Eurostar, Waterloo Station, London SE1. ☎ (0345) 881 881. **Le Shuttle**, information and ticket sales: ☎ (0990) 353 535. **British Rail European Travel Centre**, Victoria Station, London SW1. ☎ (0990) 848 848. **Eurotrain**, Campus Travel, 52 Grosvenor Gardens, London SW1. ☎ (0171) 730 3402.

By bus

This is the cheapest and most uncomfortable way of travelling. Do not forget to take a small amount of German and Belgian money to buy snacks. **Eurolines** departs from Victoria Coach Station, London, **to Prague** every day at 09.30 and arrives 09.00 the next day. Tickets cost £58 single and £89 return. Students pay £52 single and £84 return. **Kingscourt Express** leaves on Tues, Weds, Sat and Sun at 19.00 and arrives 18 hours later in Prague. Tickets are £50 single and £85 return. Under 26s pay £45 single and £79 return. During the high season (June to September) there are six departures a week (every day except Mon). All international buses arrive at and depart from Prague's main bus station, Florenc, on Křižíkova, except for Eurolines buses which arrive at Želivského bus station.

SAD (Slovenská Autobusová Doprava) goes **to Prešov** from London once a fortnight in the low season, and once a week in the high season. Adults pay £51 single and £95 return, students and over-65s pay £47 single and £82 return. **Bohemia Euroexpress International** goes **to Ostrava and Bratislava**, but you need to change in Prague. Superdirect goes straight to Bratislava, leaving on Sat at 12.30 and arriving on Sun at 13.00. Adults pay £90 return and £52 single. Students and under-26s pay £88 return and £49.40 single.

Eurolines, National Express, 164 Buckingham Palace Road, London SW1. ☎ (0990) 808 080 or (0345) 303 030. **Kingscourt Express**, 15 Balham High Road, London SW12. ☎ 0181 673 7500. **Bohemia Euroexpress International**, 16 Frognal Parade, Finchley Road, London NW3 5HG. ☎ 0171 794 3263/3264, fax: 0171 794 3265. **SAD**, 16 Frognal Parade, Finchley Road, London NW3 5HG. ☎ 0171 794 3264, fax: 0171 794 3265.

By car

The drive from the UK to Prague takes at least 20 hours, without an overnight stop. Paris to Prague is 670 miles, Brussels to Prague is 575 miles and Geneva to Prague is 590 miles.

It is best to use the Channel Tunnel at Folkestone, and take Le Shuttle (for information, see above) to Calais. Return fares cost £160–£220 per vehicle between April and September. There are discounts in the low season. At peak times, crossings leave every 15 minutes and every hour during the night. Throughout the continent, you have to pay motorway tolls. Prices vary from country to country, but make sure you have some money in the currency of each country you will be passing through.

To get to the Czech Republic from Calais/Dunkirk, follow signs to Lille, Brussels, Cologne, Frankfurt and Nuremberg. You can enter the Czech Republic at the Waidhaus–Rozvadov border crossing. The other border crossing is the Reitzanhain–Pohraniční which you reach by following signs to Lille, Brussels, Cologne, Hessen via Erfurt and Chemnitz. For the Slovak Republic, follow signs to Lille, Brussels, Cologne, Frankfurt, Nuremberg, Regensburg, Linz, Vienna and then enter at the Berg–Bratislava border crossing.

Where to stay

Finding a room used to be quite a challenge. Hotels in the Czech Republic were once poor compared to those in the West—you could easily find yourself in a high rise—and expensive. Service and accommodation have vastly improved now that entrepreneurs have finished their renovation schemes, and a law has been passed that prohibits charging foreigners more than locals. That said, accommodation is still over-priced and will be the most expensive part of your stay.

In the Slovak Republic, hotels are not as advanced. There are still some state-run monsters, many places are closed for renovation and the standard of service is generally lower. The prices are lower too, however.

Hotels should always be booked ahead, as most places are full months in advance during the high season. ČEDOK offices abroad (and other tour operators) will arrange accommodation for you, but will only contact the more expensive hotels. If you speak German, it is a good idea to telephone the hotel of your choice directly. Rooms can still be very expensive, especially in the high season (April–September) although tour groups receive discounts. If you are staying a while, say two weeks, you can get better deals. Most hotels have bars and restaurants and breakfast is included in the price of your room. **Pensions** are cheaper and often friendlier than hotels.

Choosing **private accommodation**, a room in someone's house, is a good way of paying less and feeling more of a local, but be sure you are not stuck in the outskirts. Check which facilities you will have to share with the owners, and what your proximity to them will be. It is probably best to stay one night and then decide if you want to stay longer. Private rooms can be booked through local tourist offices, but it can be cheaper to arrange this directly. Look out for signs saying *Zimmer frei* or *pokoje*. Breakfast is included in the price of the room but Czechs are very hospitable, so you may be invited to supper.

Youth hostels do not exist: the Youth Travel Agency (Cestovní kancelář mládeže or CKM) is affiliated to Hostelling International but is not much of a bargain. Unofficial youth hostels charge very little, for which you get very little in return, and are best avoided.

Campsites are plentiful. The large ones, *autokemp*, can have shops, swimming pools and other amenities. The smaller ones, *tábořiště*, just provide toilet facilities and cold showers. Some have bungalows (*chata*) which are as cheap as £4/$6 a night. Most are open from May to September.

Travelling around the Czech and Slovak Republics

By train

The Czech and Slovak train companies **ČD** (České dráhy or Czech Railways; information, ☎ (02) 24 22 42 00) and **ŽSR** (Železnica Slovenskej Republiky; **information**, ☎ (17) 54 24 703) together form one of Europe's most comprehensive networks. Their trains go everywhere and are a fun and romantic way of travelling, but journeys are also time-consuming, often involve several changes, and can be slow, overheated and crowded. The quickest and most expensive trains are the *expres* or *rychlík* trains. Fast trains (*spěšný vlak*) cost less but stop more often. Local trains (*osobní vlak*) stop everywhere and are very cheap. First class seats are 50% more expensive.

Train **timetables** are difficult to read, with crucial notes and explanations in Czech or Slovak: arrivals are abbreviated to příj. in Czech and prích. in Slovak; departures are respectively odj. and odch. To avoid confusion, write all the details of your journey on a piece of paper, including whether you want a return ticket, and hand it in at the ticket office.

Train stations in Prague: Praha Hlavní nádraží, off Wenceslas Square, Wilsonova 2. The main international railway station. **Nádraží Holešovice**, north of the centre in the district of Holešovice. Serves Budapest, Berlin and

Bucharest. **Smíchovské nádraží**, southwest of the centre in Smíchov. Serves West Bohemia. **Masarykovo nádraží**, on the northern edge of the centre in the district of Nové Město. Domestic trains only, usually to and from East Bohemia.

Train stations in Bratislava: **Hlavná želczničná stanica**, situated on Bajkalská, 4km north-west of the town centre.

By bus

Buses are the easiest and fastest way of getting around, and are cheap except in Prague, the ski resorts in the Tatra mountains and the spa towns of West Bohemia. Timetables are incredibly complicated: ignore them and talk to the clerk in the information centre instead. If travelling within a republic, you can buy your ticket on the bus, but if travelling between the two republics, you will need to buy a ticket ahead of time.

ČSAD (Česká automobilová doprava; ☎ (02) 20 32 11 11) serves the Czech Republic, and the private company **Čebus** (☎ (02) 24 81 16 76) also serves Prague, Brno, Karlovy Vary and Liberec. **SAD** (Slovenská autobusová doprava; ☎ (02) 24 81 16 76) serves the Slovak Republic.

In Prague, international buses arrive at and depart from Florenc (except Eurolines, which use Želivského). Other bus stations can be found at the following metro stops: Anděl, Hradčanská, Holešovice, Palmovka, Roztyly, Smíchovské nádraží. In Bratislava, the main bus station is a 20-minute walk east of the centre on Mlynské nivy. In smaller towns, buses usually depart from near the station.

By car

Driving in Prague cannot be recommended. The narrow streets are difficult to negotiate, and you must reckon with trams and the possibility of theft. Outside Prague driving is a much better option: you can see a lot more of the country and Czech and Slovak drivers are polite and friendly.

To drive your own car in the Czech and Slovak Republics, you need a driver's licence but no longer require an international insurance green card. You must carry your vehicle's registration documents with you. The wearing of seatbelts is compulsory and you must never drink and drive. You should carry a red warning triangle, replacement bulbs and a first aid kit. Children under 12 must always sit in the back. The **speed limit** is 55mph/90kph on main roads, 35mph/60kph in towns and 70mph/110kph on motorways. Drive on the right-hand side of the road. A yellow diamond sign means you have right of way, a black line through it means you do not have right of way. Give way to pedestrians at lights if turning left or right. Do not drive on tram lines; trams always have right of way.

To drive on any **motorway** you must have an authorisation disk (Czech, *dálniční známka*) or sticker (Slovak, *úhrada*). This costs around 880 Kč (valid for one year) and is available from petrol stations, post offices and border crossings. Failure to display the disk results in heavy fines.

There are three types of **petrol**: 96 octane (*super*), 90 octane (*special*) and lead-free (*natural*). Petrol stations close after 18.00. They do not accept credit cards, only Czech or Slovak currency. Petrol currently costs 18Kč a litre (£0.40/$0.60).

To **rent a car**, you must be over 21 and have a driver's licence. Insurance is arranged by the rental agency. If you hire from abroad, a small car for a week cost £130/$200. The well-known car hire companies charge much more than local Czech ones.

Car hire companies in the UK include **Avis** ☎ (0990) 900 500; **Budget** ☎ (0800)181 181; **Europcar** ☎ (0345) 222 525; **Hertz** ☎ (0990) 996 699; **Holiday Autos** ☎ (0990) 300 400.

Car hire companies in the US include **Avis** ☎ (800) 331 1212; **Budget** ☎ (212) 641 5700; **Hertz** ☎ (800) 654 3131; **Holiday Autos** ☎ (800) 422 7737.

Car hire companies in Prague include **Alamo**, Prague Airport, ☎ (02) 20 11 35 34; **Budget**, náměstí Curieových 5/43 (Hotel Intercontinental), Prague 1. ☎ (02) 24 88 99 95; **Rent Car**, Wenzigova 5, Prague 2. ☎ (02) 24 26 21 31; **Rent A Car**, Palace of Culture, 5.května 65, Prague 4, 5. ☎ (42 02) 61 22 20 79.

Car hire companies in Bratislava include **Auto Danubius**, Trnavská 31. ☎ (17) 27 37 54; **MM Car Rental Service**, Rovniankova 4,.☎ (17) 83 58 31; **Profit Car**, Hagarova 8. ☎ (17) 28 50 03.

By air

ČSA flies from Prague to the Czech cities of Brno and Ostrava, and to the Slovak cities of Bratislava, Poprad and Košice. **Tatra Air**, a charter company, flies to Bratislava, Košice, Poprad and Brno. **Air Ostrava** serves Prague, Brno, Ostrava and the Slovak Republic. A new destination is Žilina, which is useful if you want to get to the high Tatras.

Useful numbers include: **ČSA**, **Prague**, ☎ (02) 20 11 11 11. **ČSA**, **Bratislava**, ☎ (17) 31 12 05. **Tatra Air**, ☎ (17) 23 60 54. **Air Ostrava**, ☎ (02) 24 03 27 31.

General information

Communications

Post offices can be confusing because each window has a different service, and you may find yourself queuing up unnecessarily unless you are careful. The main post office in Prague is at Jindřišská 14, Prague 1, where you can buy stamps, send faxes and change money. You can also receive letters (at position 28) if they are addressed c/o Poste Restante Jindřišská 14. A central post office in Bratislava is at Bratislava 1 nám. SNP1, ☎ (17) 53 93 111. To collect your letters from another town, they must be addressed to Pošta 1, followed by the name of the town. **Stamps** for postcards to the UK cost 6Kč, to the US 8Kč. Sending letters to the UK costs 9Kč and to the US 12Kč. Stamps can also be bought at newsstands and tobacconists. Mail boxes are orange. Post takes up to 5 working days to reach the UK, 7–10 days to the US.

Most **public telephones** now run on cards (*telekart*) which can be bought from post offices, train stations, metro stations, kiosks, large department stores, hotels and anywhere displaying a blue-and-yellow Telecom sticker. They come in 50 units, 100 units and 150 units. Units cost 2Kč and for local calls last three minutes from 07.00 to 16.00 on weekdays, six minutes from 16.00–07.00 weekdays and all day weekends and Sundays. You need a more expensive card for international calls. The Slovak Republic uses different cards, which can't be used in the Czech Republic. In telephones which take cash, local calls cost 3Kč. Telephone numbers consist of 5, 6, 7 or 8 digits.

It can sometimes be a challenge calling AT&T, Sprint and other card companies. Persevere because some hotel operators may refuse to make the connection and when they do, will charge you premium rate. If you have problems, call the international operator.

Dialling codes are as follows (leave out the zero for local codes if dialling from outside the republics): Czech Republic country code: 420; Prague: 02; Slovak Republic country code: 421; Bratislava: 07.

Crime

Petty crime such as pickpocketing is more likely to affect you than anything more serious. Be sensible: make photocopies of your passport and note down the numbers of your travellers' cheques and credit cards. Carry your valuables in a money belt or leave them in the hotel safe. Report anything stolen to the police, as you will need documentation for your insurance company. *Byl jsem okraden* means 'I've been robbed.'

Currency

There are separate currencies for the two republics, both known as the crown. The **Czech crown** (*koruna čescá* or Kč) is made up of 100 *halérů*(h). Coins come in 10h, 20h, 50h, 1Kč, 2Kč, 5Kč, 10Kč, 20Kč and 50 Kč denominations. Notes come in 20, 50, 100, 500, 1000, 2000 and 5000Kč denominations. There are about 53Kč to £1 sterling and 35Kč to the US dollar (April 1998).

The **Slovak crown** (*Slovenská koruna* or Sk) is made up of 100 *halier* (h). Coins come in 10h, 20h, 50h, 1Sk, 5Sk and 10Sk denominations and notes come in 20Sk, 50Sk, 100Sk, 200Sk, 500Sk and 1000Sk denominations.

Customs

Visitors over the age of 18 can take 250 cigarettes or 100 cigars, 1 litre of spirits, 1 litre of wine and up to up to 3000Kč worth of goods into either country. On leaving, you can take 250 cigarettes, 2 litres of wine, 1 litre of spirits and up to 500Kč worth of consumer goods. These limits are liable to change so check before you go. You are not allowed to export antiques. To find out if your chosen *object* is an antique or not, contact the curator either at the National Museum in Prague, ☎ (02) 24 49 71 11, or in Bratislava, ☎ (17) 36 19 73/36 66 39.

Disabled travellers

The Czech and Slovak Republics are not the best place for disabled travellers, and very few allowances are made for them. Buses and trams are inaccessible for wheelchairs; trains are a little better, as some have been designed to take wheelchairs and several metro stations have lifts. There are no hand-control cars at all from car rental companies. Museums are also impossible to get into, but the National Theatre now has some chairs for disabled people. It is best to travel with a non-disabled partner. For more information, travellers could try the following organisations.

UK. **Holiday Care Service**, 2nd floor, Imperial Building, Victoria Road, Horley, Surrey RH6 9HW. ☎ (01293) 774 535. Information on all aspects of travel. **RADAR**, 12 City Forum, 250 City Road, London EC1V 8AS. ☎ (0171) 250 3222.

US. **Society for Advancement of Travel for the Handicapped**, 347 5th Ave, New York, NY 10016. ☎ (212) 447 7284. **Mobility Intl USA**, Box 10767, Eugene, OR 97440. ☎ (541) 343 1284 or fax: (541) 343 6812.

Europe. **Mobility Intl**, at 18 Boulevard Baoudouin, B-1000 Brussels, Belgium. ☎ (32 2) 201 5608, fax: (32 2) 201 5763.

Electricity

The supply in both republics is standard Continental 220 volts AC. Visitors from Britain and the United States will need adaptors for European-style two-pin round plugs for hairdryers, razors and other appliances. Americans will also need a transformer.

Embassies

Foreign embassies in Prague: **American Embassy**, Trzište 15, Malá Strana, Prague 1. ☎ (02) 57 32 06 63, fax: (02) 57 32 09 20. Metro Malostranská. Open Mon–Fri 09.00–12.00 and 14.00–15.30. **Australian Trade Commission and Honorary Consulate**, Na Ořechovce 38, Prague 6. ☎ (02) 24 31 07 43/(02) 24 31 00 71. Metro Dejvická. Open Mon–Thur 09.00–17.00, Fri 09.00–14.00. **British Embassy**, Thunovská 14, Malá Strana, Prague 1. ☎ (02) 57 32 03 55, fax: (02) 57 32 10 23. Metro Malostranská. Open Mon–Fri 09.00–12.00. **Canadian Embassy**, Mickiewiczova 6, Prague 6. ☎ (02) 24 31 11 08, fax: (02) 24 31 02 94. Metro Hradčanská. Open Mon–Fri 09.00–12.00 and 14.00–16.00.

Foreign embassies in Bratislava: **American Embassy**, Hviezdoslavovo nám. 4, 81102 Bratislava. ☎ (17) 53 30 861, fax: (17) 53 35 439. **British Embassy**, Panská 16, 81101 Bratislava. ☎ (17) 53 13 673 or (17) 53 17 688, fax: (17) 53 10 002. Open Mon–Fri 08.30–12.30 and 13.30–17.00. **Consulate of Canada**, Kolérska 4, 811 06 Bratislava. ☎ (17) 36 12 20.

Embassies of the Czech Republic abroad: **Australia**, 169 Military Road, Dover Heights, Sydney, NSW 2030. ☎ (02) 371 8878. **Canada** 541 Sussex Drive, Ottawa, Ontario K1N 6Z6. ☎ (613) 562 3875. **Ireland**, Confederation House, Kildare St, Dublin 2. ☎ (1) 671 4981. **New Zealand** (consulate) 48 Hair Street, PO Box 43035, Wainuiomata, Wellington. ☎ (04) 564 6001. **UK**, 26 Kensington Palace Gardens, London W8 4QY. ☎ (0171) 243 1115, fax: (0171) 727 9654. visa hotline: (0891) 171 267, email: london@embassy.mzv.cz **US**, 3900 Spring of Freedom St, NW Washington DC 20008. ☎ (202) 274 9100, fax: (202) 966 8540, email: washington@embassy.mzv.cz, website: www.czech.cz/washington

Embassies of the Slovak Republic abroad: **Australia**, 47 Culgoa Circuit, O'Malley, Canberra, ACT 2606. ☎ (06) 290 1516. **Canada**, 50 Rideau Terrace, Ottawa, Ontario K1M 2A1. ☎ (613) 749 4442. **UK**, 25 Kensington Palace Gardens, London W8 4QY. ☎ (0171) 243 0803, fax: (0171) 727 582, email: skemb@nepcomuk.co.uk **USA**, 2201 Wisconsin Ave NW, Suite 250, Washington DC 20007. ☎ (202) 965 516, fax: (202) 965 5166, email: svkemb@concentric.net, website: www.slovakemb.com

Health

Health care in the Czech and Slovak Republics is not quite up to Western standards, but is improving all the time. There are no major health problems in the two republics, and you will not need any vaccinations unless you are travelling in the forest areas, in which case you may want to be vaccinated against Central European encephalitis. The tap water is safe to drink, but does not taste great.

24-hour pharmacies in Prague. Belgická 37, Prague 2, ☎ (02) 24 23 72 07; Lékárna U Anděla, Štefánikova 6, Prague 5, ☎ 53 70 39; First Aid

Palackého 5, Prague 1, ☎ (02) 24 22 25 20. Open Mon–Fri 07.00–19.00 and 24 hours Sat–Sun.

24-hour pharmacies in Bratislava. Mýtna 9, ☎ (17) 49 65 15; Ružinovská 12, ☎ (17) 23 11 43; Lí'čle Odolle 57, ☎ (17) 65 42 25 962.

Pharmacies (*lékárna*) that are open 24 hours a day are listed in the front of the Yellow Pages under 'Lékány s nepřetržitou pohotovostní službou'. Other pharmacies are open until about 18.30.

The **emergency medical service** for foreigners is at U Nemocnice 2, Prague 2, ☎ (02) 24 96 11 11/24 96 30 56. American citizens will have to pay for this, British citizens do not. **Medical insurance** is a good idea wherever you have come from; do not forget to ask for proof of any expenses.

Medical centres in Prague: Canadian Medical Center, Veleslavínská 30/1. ☎ (02) 31 65 519. **Dental Emergencies**, Vladíslavova 22, ☎ (02) 24 22 76 63. **Na Homolce Hospital for Foreigners**, Roentgenova 2, Motol, Prague 5. ☎ (02) 52 92 21 46.

Hospitals in Bratislava: Fakultna nemocnica, Mickiewiczova 13. ☎ (17) 35 90 111. **Nemocnica Prievoz**, Krásna 22. ☎ (17) 29 11 21

Money

It is now much easier to use credit cards such as Visa, Mastercard and Amex in restaurants and shops, but you should carry travellers' cheques in sterling, US dollars or Deutschmarks—Thomas Cook and American Express are the best known. Eurocheques are not a good option. You can withdraw cash from cashpoints, but do not rely on this alone.

The Czech crown is fully convertible, but the Slovak crown is not. You can only buy the latter in the country and you should change your money once you are there: Czech bureaux are reluctant to do this and offer poor rates. Commission at banks (2%) is less than at the exchange bureaux (up to 6%), but the queues are longer and the opening times less flexible. If you are going to the Czech Republic, it is always a good idea to change some money before you arrive to avoid delays at the airport exchange counter.

Accommodation will take the largest chunk out of your money, but otherwise everything is still very cheap, though prices are creeping up. In the Slovak Republic, you should expect to pay £20/$30 a day for hotels and meals and on the Czech side, £30/$45 a day. This assumes you want to eat well and are not roughing it. You can easily double this if splashing out.

Opening hours

Banks are open Mon–Fri 18.00–17.00 with a break at lunch.

Government offices are open Mon–Fri 08.30–17.00.

Post offices open Mon–Fri 08.00–17.00 and Sat 08.00–12.00 in the Czech Republic and Mon–Fri 07.00–19.00 and Sat 08.00–11.00 in the Slovak Republic.

Restaurants generally open for lunch around 11.00, and stay open until 22.00 or 23.00; they are usually open on Sundays.

Shops open Mon–Fri 08.00 or 09.00 to 17.00 or 18.00. Many shops are open until 12.00 Sat. Some shops close for lunch and many close in August. 24-hour shops are called *vecerka*.

For museums, see **Tourist sites**, below.

Public holidays

Czech Republic	Slovak Republic
January 1 (New Year's Day)	January 1 (New Year's Day)
Easter Sunday and Monday	Easter Friday, Sun and Mon
May 1 (Labour Day)	May 1 (Labour Day)
May 8 (VE Day)	May 8 (VE Day)
July 5 (SS Cyril and Methodius Day)	May 11 (Religious holiday)
July 6 (Jan Hus Day)	July 5 (SS Cyril and Methodius Day)
October 28 (Independence Day)	August 29 (Slovak National Uprising 1944)
December 24–26 (Christmas)	September 1 (Founding of Slovak Constitution)
	September 15 (St Mary's Day)
	November 1 (All Saints' Day)
	December 24–26 (Christmas)

Time

The Czech Republic is one hour ahead of the UK and six hours ahead of US Eastern time. Times go forward one hour in the summer (usually April/May) and back one hour in the winter (usually September).

Tipping

In restaurants, round your bill up to a few crowns above the total: this may have been done for you already, so check (VAT at 23% is included in the price of your food). Don't leave the tip on the table, but pay it with the bill.

It is normal to tip 10 per cent in all the places you would tip in the West—taxis, hotels, and so on.

Toilets

Public conveniences are few and far between. Those that do exist are clean and have attendants, whom you pay for sheets of paper (2Kč). If desperate, you can always use the toilets in a restaurant or hotel.

Tourist sites

Some tourist attractions are only open in the summer. Many **museums** are closed from the end of October until Easter Monday. Opening hours tend to be 09.00–16.00 or later, closed Mon. Ticket prices are very low and students can gain admission for half-price. Most museums only have Czech labelling although they may provide English pamphlets. There are two types of museum outside Prague: a *krajské muzeum* is a regional museum with local history and a *městské muzeum* is even more provincial. Of generally greater tourist interest than these museums are the hundreds of castles and chateaux that can be visited throughout the Czech Republic, albeit in the obligatory company of generally dreary guides. After having experienced a surfeit of such tours, some visitors might find it a relief to visit Slovakia, where the castles and chateaux are fewer and further apart, and frequently ruined. Common to the two Republics—and perhaps the most enjoyable sight-seeing option if you are accompanied by children—are the outdoor museums of reconstructed folk architecture known as Skansens.

Large **churches** sometimes charge an entry fee for their cloisters or crypts. Most of the churches outside Prague are open only a couple of hours a day, probably just before or after a service. If you find the priest (*kněz*), however, he will be happy to show you around.

Useful addresses and numbers

Information

Directory Enquiries (Prague), ☎ 120

Directory Enquiries (rest of country), ☎ 121

Directory Enquiries (international), ☎ 149

Operator, ☎ 120

Speaking clock, ☎ 112

Emergency numbers

Police, ☎ 158

Ambulance, ☎ 155

Fire, ☎ 150

Emergency Medical Service, ☎ (02) 49 61 111

Emergency Road Service, ☎ 154

Money

American Express, Václavské nám 56, Prague 1. ☎ (02) 24 22 98 83

Eurocard/Mastercard, Na příkopě 14, Prague 1

Travel

M.R. Štefánika Bratislava airport, ☎ (17) 52 20 036

Bratislava bus terminal, ☎ (17) 52 67 231

Bratislava main railway station, ☎ (17) 20 44 484

Prague airport, ☎ (02) 20 11 33 14

Prague main railway station, ☎ (02) 24 22 42 00

Airlines in Prague

Air France, ☎ (02) 24 22 71 64

Austrian Airlines, ☎ (02) 20 11 43 24

British Airways, ☎ (02) 22 11 44 44

Czech Airlines, ☎ (02) 36 70 760

Delta, ☎ (02) 20 11 43 84

KLM, ☎ (02) 20 11 43 22

Lufthansa, ☎ (02) 20 11 44 56

Sabena, ☎ (02) 20 11 43 23

Swissair, ☎ (02) 20 11 43 24

Airlines in Bratislava

Aeroflot, ☎ (17) 53 35 192

Austrian Airlines, ☎ (17) 53 11 610

British Airways, ☎ (17) 39 9801

Czech Airlines, ☎ (17) 36 10 38

Delta, ☎ (17) 53 34 718

Lot, ☎ (17) 36 40 07

Lufthansa, ☎ (17) 36 78 14

Food and drink

by Michael Jacobs

Many people visit the Czech and Slovak Republics for no better reason than to drink their excellent beer, though it is unlikely that anyone would wish to come here simply for the food. Magdalena Dobromila Rettigová (1785–1845), Bohemia's answer to Mrs Beeton, was a key figure in the Czech 'national revival', and saw food as playing an important role in the renewal of her country. However, the food of Bohemia and Moravia did not emerge from centuries of Austrian dominance with an exciting and distinctive character of its own; nor did the food of Slovakia overcome the pervasive influence of Hungary. In the composite country that was Czechoslovakia, Slavic, Austrian and Hungarian influences were blended together to form an amorphous cuisine, a process greatly assisted by the years of Communist rule, when lack of fresh produce and private initiative significantly lessened the scope for regional flair. The cuisines of the Czech and Slovak Republics have strong peasant roots, though not in a way which would make them appeal to the fashionable, health-conscious tastes of today: their essential simplicity is frequently disguised by over-rich dressing, and there can be few national cuisines quite as fattening.

In contrast to places such as Italy, Spain or France, a rather hurried attitude to food predominates here, and eating in itself is undertaken less for pleasure than for filling the stomach, or as a means to maintain long bouts of drinking. Heartiness is the key note of Czech and Slovak food, and this is evident even in the local breakfasts, which normally comprise large quantities of ham, eggs, sausages or cheese, and often feature more substantial dishes such as goulash, washed down by large glasses of beer. It is perhaps significant that in the Czech and Slovak Republics, as in other Eastern European countries, restaurant menus usually state the exact weight of the food on offer, just as the pubs here always advertise the alcoholic content of the beer they serve. In short, these are countries where food is best enjoyed on a cold winter's day, fuelled by considerable quantities of alcohol. Under such circumstances the lavish descriptions of food with which the great drinker and gastronome Jaroslav Hašek larded his *Good Soldier Švejk* begin to sound appetising.

Bacon and above all caraway seed are the ubiquitous flavourings of both Czech and Slovak food and, as in Russian and Hungarian cooking, soured cream is an accompaniment to numerous dishes. The first thought which comes to mind at the very mention of Czech food, however, is of dumplings (*knedlíky*), which have the same role in Bohemia and Moravia as chips do in other countries. There are several types of dumpling, including potato dumplings (*Bramborové knedlíky*), plum dumplings (*Švestkové knedlíky*) and, most common of all, a type of dumpling known as *Houskové knedlíky*, which is made in the shape of a Swiss roll from a mixture of flour, eggs and cubes of white bread, and is served in slices that are invariably, though unintentionally, stale; some of the better restaurants will even provide you with a separate tray piled high with a selection of all of these. One of the pleasures of coming to Slovakia from Bohemia and Moravia is that dumplings are not so common here, boiled potatoes and rice being the more usual substitutes. The differences between Czech and Slovak food are otherwise not so great, though the latter tends to be spicier, with a liberal use of paprika as in Hungary. Many of the Slovak dishes of Hungarian origin such as goulash (*Segedinský guláš*), stuffed peppers (*Plnené papriky*) and paprika chicken (*Kuře na paprice*) have today been incorporated in milder form into Czech cuisine.

Starters

Shortly after you sit down in some of the fancier restaurants here you are likely to be offered aperitifs from a trolley followed by a tray of unappealing canapés, for which you will be charged individually; the canapés, of glazed, artificial appearance, invariably feature cream or cream cheese, one of the more popular ones being a ham roll filled with cream cheese and gherkin slices; others are coated with hard lumps of jelly, and should be avoided at all costs. A normal Czech meal, however, begins with a soup; two common varieties are potato soup (*Bramborová polévka*) and a thick white soup known as *Kmínová polévka*, both of which are heavily flavoured with caraway seed; a popular clear soup is *Polévka s játrovými knedlíčky*, which is beef broth with little dumplings made from liver, garlic, lemon rind, eggs and breadcrumbs.

Main courses

Main courses on restaurant menus are usually divided between *Minutky* and *Hotová jídla*, the former being dishes that are cooked to order, the latter being ready cooked ones in heavy sauces. The most typical main dish you can eat in Bohemia and Moravia is pork or Frankfurter-style sausage accompanied by dumplings and sauerkraut. Meat is consumed in vast quantities all over Czechoslovakia, and tends to be tough and overcooked. Pork is often served with eggs and ham on top and, like veal, is frequently dipped in a mixture of flour, breadcrumbs and eggs to form an escalope or *řízek*; a tastier dish is *Vepřová pečeně*, or pork roasted with caraway seeds. Thick fillets of beef piled high with cream and cranberries can be found in the more pretentious establishments, but beef is more commonly served as braised slices in a brown onion sauce (*Dušená roštěnka*) or else as boiled slices in a delicious dill-flavoured white sauce known as *Koprová omáčka*. There are far fewer poultry than meat dishes in the Czech and Slovak Republics: the most usual one is roast chicken (*Pečené kuře*); goose is becoming less common but is traditionally served roasted with sauerkraut (*Pečená husa se zelím*).

Not even Mrs Rettigova, in her standard book on Bohemian food, could find much to write on fish, which is little eaten here. Apart from in the international restaurants of Prague,the best places for finding fish are the Slovak capital of Bratislava—where a number of the restaurants serve pike and trout fished straight from the polluted Danube—and South Bohemia, which abounds in huge ponds where carp is bred. Carp is by far the most popular fish in the two republics, but even so tends to be eaten mainly as a traditional Christmas Eve dish, when it is served with a near indigestible black sauce made from fish stock, raspberry juice, beer, lemon rind, sugar, honey cake, raisins and almonds (*Kapr na černo*).

The great joy of the Czech and Slovak cuisines, if such an extreme term can be used, is its game, which is the particular speciality of Slovakia and is sometimes roasted over a wood fire and flavoured with juniper berries. Especially good, though difficult to find in restaurants, are roebuck and—if you can overcome ecological principles and childhood memories of favourite toys—brown bear.

'A smaller selection is usually possible when it comes to fresh vegetables (sterilised ones are often served even in summer),' wrote one of the authors of a government-sponsored guide to Czechoslovakia published in 1989. Fresh fruit and vegetables are now far more widely available than before, but for some reason are still only rarely found in restaurants, where tinned fruit (often served as a mixed compote known as a *Míchaný ovocný kompot*), sauerkraut (*zelí*) and pickled vegetable salads such as cucumber salad (*Okurkový salát*) predominate. Cheese tends to be processed and served in dried-out slices, though in Slovakia you can still find a delicious brine cheese called *bryndza*, which is comparable to the Greek *feta*.

Puddings are of the hearty kind, such as plum jam cake (*Povidlový koláč*) or, more commonly, *palačinky*, pancakes that are usually heaped with mountains of cream and chocolate sauce, and occasionally flambéd. The legacy of Austria is fortunately still apparent in the delectable range of cakes and pastries to be found in the countries' cafés and bakeries. The coffee itself, however, is mainly Turkish (*turecká káva*), while the so-called espresso—regarded by many as a more refined alternative—is more often than not tepid instant coffee of insipid flavour.

Spirits, wine and beer

Spirits and liquors tend to be drunk neat as an aperitif or as a beer chaser, one of the most famous being the greenish, herb-flavoured liquor known as *becherovka*, a speciality of the Bohemian spa town of Karlovy Vary (Carlsbad) and reputedly far more beneficial to the health than the town's waters. Most spirits, however, come from Moravia and Slovakia and include plum brandy (*slivovice*, one of the more renowned brands being *Jelínek*), and a juniper-flavoured gin known as *borovička*, a particular speciality of the Slovak town of Trenčín: according to popular tradition a glass of *borovička* drunk half an hour before eating is a considerable aid to the digestion, though its potential beneficial effects are sometimes cancelled out by the hors-d'oeuvres that often come with it.

The largest **wine-producing** area in the two republics is in southern Slovakia and includes a small part of the famous Tokay vineyard, whence come Hungary's sweet Tokay and Furmint wines; the other Slovakian wines also use the same grapes as those of northern Hungary, for instance, Muscat Otonel, Ezerjó, Veltiner, Müller-Thurgau, Italian Riesling and Leánkya. The adjoining Moravian vineyards, all of which are to be found south of Brno, are smaller in extent but have a reputation for slightly better wines and excellent Ruländer, Sauvignon, Traminer and Spätburgunder wines are made in places such as Velké Pavlovice, Mikulov, Musov and Znojmo. Bohemia's small number of wines are grown mainly around Mělník, an area which was planted with Burgundy grapes during the reign of Charles IV. Wines throughout the two republics are drunk principally in the setting of a *vinárna* or wine bar (see below), but there is a pleasant tradition common to both Slovakia and Moravia (in particular in Brno, Bratislava and Nitra) of friends and families coming together for bouts of intensive drinking in small private cellars.

Wine here is less commonly drunk than beer, which is by far the most popular local drink and the usual accompaniment to meals. When it comes to discussing Czech beer, superlatives can at last be used with complete honesty, for it is generally agreed to be the best in the world, and has a reputation going back to the Middle Ages.

Beer is made throughout the country, and dark as well as light beer can be found here, as can a number of small breweries, some of which are attached to their own pubs. However the general consensus of opinion is that the finest are the light and creamy ones from the Bohemian towns of České Budějovice (the original Budweiser) and, above all, Plzeň, where the *Prazdroj Urquell* brew served as the prototype for Pils-style beers throughout the world; the most famous of the Slovak beers is *Zlatý Bažant* (Golden Pheasant) from the small town of Hurbanovo.

Eating out in Prague

A few words should finally be said about the actual places where you can eat and drink in the Czech and Slovak Republics. The smartest of the restaurants, bars and night-clubs here prefer their clients to be formally dressed (this is particularly true outside Prague), and all of them have cloakrooms where you are obliged to leave your coats immediately on entering; booking is advisable in the large towns, and essential in Prague, particularly in the summer, when you often have to reserve a table up to one week in advance.

The wine-bars or *vinárna* are smart establishments generally situated in historic cellars, and always providing food, though they will never serve you with beer. The modest restaurants, pubs and beer-cellars are invariably the liveliest and friendliest of all the eating and drinking establishments here, and their smoke-filled atmosphere, dirty walls and floors, and portly waiters or waitresses who will slam a large glass of beer on to your table often without your asking for it, are an intrinsic part of their charm; food is served at most of the pubs and beer-cellars and is usually no worse, and certainly far cheaper, than in the more pretentious establishments. In such places you will often find yourself sharing your table with others. Your privacy will be respected, but it is customary to wish each other 'bon appetit' (*dobrou chut'*) when your food arrives.

The hurried tourist could snatch a bite at a *bufet*, a self-service establishment where you are generally obliged to eat standing up; an *automat* is the same but with cold rather than hot food. Even more time could be saved at one of the many outdoor kiosks, which specialise in *bramborák* (a type of potato pancake) and Frankfurter-style sausages (*klobása*), the latter served on a paper plate together with a mountain of mustard. A *cukrárna*, which is only open during the day, is a café specialising in cakes and pastries.

An eating establishment which originated in Slovakia in the early 1960s, but is now also found to a lesser extent in Bohemia and Moravia, is the *koliba*, a cosy wooden hut usually situated in a bosky setting and supposedly inspired by bandits' encampments of the last century. The gastronomic speciality here is meat grilled or barbecued over a wood fire, most notably 'Robber's steak', which comes accompanied with onions and peppers; to complete the whole macho experience you should drink *hriatô*, a warm mixture of alcohol, caramelised sugar and spices served with diced smoky bacon. Unique to Slovakia, and a more genuinely modest establishment than the *koliba* is the *salaš*, an imitation of a shepherd's hut and specialising in sheep products, in particular *Bryndzové pirohy s máslom* and *Bryndzové halušky*. These two simple but magnificent dishes, both of which are made from ewe's cheese and sprinkled with diced smoky bacon, feature respectively *tortellini*-like pasta and *gnocchi*-like dumplings; the traditional drink to accompany them is sour sheep's milk.

Menu

Polévky, Soups
Boršč, Beetroot soup
Bramborová, Potato soup
Čočková, Lentil soup
Fazolová, Bean soup
Hovězí, Beef soup
Hrachová, Pea soup
Slepičí, Chicken soup
Rajská, Tomato soup
Zeleninová, Vegetable soup
Chléb, Bread

Máslo, Butter
Vejce, Eggs
Sýr, Cheese
Niva, Soft blue cheese
Oštiepok, Smoked curd cheese
Pivný sýr, Beer-flavoured cheese
Tvaroh, Curd cheese

Maso, Meat
Čevapčici, Spiced meat balls
Hovězí, Beef
Játra, Liver

Kachna, Duck
Klobásy, Sausages
Kuře, Chicken
Salám, Salami
Sekaná, Meat loaf
Slanina, Bacon
Šunka, Ham
Telecí, Veal
Vepřové, Pork

Ryby, Fish
Kapr, Carp
Makrela, Mackerel
Pstruh, Trout
Zavináč, Herring

Zelenina, Vegetables
Brambory, Potatoes (*Hranolky*, Chips)
Cibule, Onion
Česnek, Garlic
Houby, Mushrooms
Hrášek, Peas
Květák, Cauliflower
Kyselé zelí, Sauerkraut
Lečo, Ratatouille
Mrkev, Carrot

Rajče, Tomato
Špenát, Spinach
Salát, salad
Zelí, Cabbage
Žampiony, Champignons

Ovoce, Fruit
Banán, Banana
Broskev, Peach
Citron, Lemon
Víno, Grapes
Hruška, Pear
Jablko, Apple
Meruňka, Apricot
Pomeranč, Orange
Třešně, Cherry

Nápoje, Drinks
Čaj, Tea
Káva, Coffee
Koňak, Brandy
Minerální voda, Mineral water
Mléko, Milk
Pivo, Beer
Víno, Wine

Language

by Elizabeth Brimelow

There is no such language as Czechoslovak. There is Czech, and there is Slovak, two distinct languages, though very closely related. Both are members of the western Slavonic group of languages. **Czech** is the language of Bohemia and Moravia. **Slovak** is the language of Slovakia. Czech speakers easily understand Slovak, and vice versa.

Czech and Slovak **grammar** is complex, in the manner of other highly inflected Indo-European languages: nouns and adjectives decline in seven cases; adjectives agree with nouns in number, case and gender; verb forms reflect both tense and aspect. No one will expect a visitor using a phrase-book, however, to have got to grips with all this.

Czech and Slovak uses the Latin alphabet. The Czech orthography, reformed by Jan Hus at the start of the 15C, provides admirable consistency in **spelling and pronunciation**. To English eyes it appears dense and prickly, but it is not as difficult as it looks. The following is a simplified guide. Approximate transliterations of Czech words are given in square brackets. Slovak equivalents are given in the righthand column.

Vowels

Czech		Slovak
a	Southern English 'u' as in 'cup', or Northern English short 'a' as in 'grass', eg, **ano** [u-no], yes	*ako* [u-ko], as
á	'a' as in 'half' eg, **dáma** [dah-ma], lady	
e	'e' as in 'mend', eg, **den** [den], day	*ten* [ten], this
é	no real equivalent in English: roughly like the first part of the vowel sound in 'there' or 'pear' eg, **léto** [leh-to], summer	*nové* [no-veh], new
ě	'ye' as in 'yet', eg, **pět** [pyet], five	no equivalent
i	'i' as in 'pit', eg, **pivo** [pi-vo], beer	
í	'ee' as in 'need', eg, **víno** [vee-no], wine	
o	'o' as in 'not', eg, **okno** [ok-no], window	
ó	'aw' as in 'claw', eg, **móda** [maw-da], fashion	
u	southern English 'u' as in 'put' or 'oo' as in 'book', eg, **ruka** [ru-ka], hand	
ů	'oo' as in 'school', eg, **dům** [doom], or house	only ú: *údolie* [oo-do-lie], valley
ú	eg, **údolí** [oo-do-lee], valley	
y, ý	exactly the same as i, í	
ô		'wo' as in worm, *stôl* [stwol], table
ŕ		'rrr', eg, *Vŕba* [vrrr-ba], willow
ä		open a as in that, eg, *Mäso* [ma-so]

The letters l and r can do duty as vowels and form a syllable when standing between two other consonants: eg, Brno [Br-no], the chief city of Moravia eg, **vlk** [vlk], wolf (cf. American pronunciation of 'missile' or 'turn')

Diphthongs

Unlike in English, both letters of a diphthong are pronounced equally clearly.

Czech		Slovak
au	'ow' as in 'now', eg, **auto** [ow-to], car	
ou	'o' as in a Northern English 'oh' eg, **houska** [hoh-ska], bread roll	Does not exist in Slovak language
eu	does not occur in any single English word; rather like the vowels in Northern English 'Eh up', eg, **pneumatika** [pneoo-ma-ti-ka], tyre	
		ie: like 'Pierre', eg, *Viem*, I know

Consonants

Generally the same or nearly the same as in English, but there are exceptions:

Czech	Slovak

c   'ts' as in 'oats', eg, **co** [tso], what   *oco* [o-tso], Dad

č   'ch' as in 'child', eg, **český** [che-skee], Czech

g   always hard as in 'get', never soft
    as in 'general', eg, **guma** [goo-mah], rubber

j   'y' as in 'you', eg, **jak** [yak], how, eg,   *ja* [ya], me
    kraj [krai], region (rhymes with 'try')
    eg, **olej** [o-lei], oil (rhymes with 'pray')

ch   Scottish 'ch' as in 'loch', eg, **chléb**   *chata* [khata], cottage
    [khlehb], bread

r   rolled Scottish 'r' as in red, eg, **ryba**
    [ri-ba], fish

ř   no equivalent in English; combines a   does not exist in Slovak
    rolled Scottish 'r' with the 'zh' sound   language
    as in 'pleasure', eg, **řeka** [rzhe-ka], river

š   'sh' as in 'she', eg, **šest** [shest], six   *šestˇ* [she-stj], six

ž   the 'zh' sound in 'pleasure',
    eg, **žena** [zhe-na], woman

d, t, and n, if followed by i or í, are softened, ie, pronounced as though there was
an (English) 'y' after the consonant:

eg, **divadlo** [dyi-va-dlo], theatre,

eg, **není** [ne-nyee], it isn't,   *nič* [ny-tch], nothing

These consonants may also occasionally be softened other than when followed
by i or í; this is indicated by an apostrophe after the consonant or, for the letter
n, a haček above it

eg, **loď**, boat   *matˇ*, mother

eg, **zbraň**, weapon

Stress and intonation. The main stress in Czech and Slovak always falls on
the first syllable of the word. Stressed syllables can be either long or short. So
can unstressed ones. The idea of unstressed long syllables may seem odd, but
they occur in English too: try saying 'always', or 'for his part' with the stress on
'his'. Unstressed syllables don't get reduced and distorted as they do in English;
eg, in the word **matka** [mat-ka] ('mother') the second letter 'a' is pronounced in
exactly the same way as the first. The word is not pronounced 'maht-ker' as it
probably would be in English.

   Intonation is roughly like English: down at the end of a sentence for a statement, up at the end for a question. In the following vocabulary Czech words are
given in **semi bold** type, Czech pronunciation follows in square brackets, and
Slovak words in *italic* type.

Useful phrases

Mluvíte anglicky? [mloo-vee-te ang-glits-ki]   Do you speak English?
Hovoríte po anglicky?

Nerozumím česky. [ne-ro-zoo-meem che-ski]   I don't understand Czech.
Nerozumiem po slovensky   I don't speak Slovak

Rozumíte? [ro-zoo-mee-te]   Do you understand?
Rozumiete?

Jsem Angličan(ka). [Y-sem An-gli-chan(ka)]   I am English (the 'ka' ending is used if the speaker is a woman).

Som Anglican(ka)

Ano [a-no]   Yes
Áno

Ne [ne]   No
Nie

Prosím [pro-seem]   Please
Prosím

Děkuji (mockrát) [dye-koo-yi mots-kraht]   Thank you (very much)
Ďakujem

Díky [dyee-kil]   Thanks
Vďaka

Dobrý den [do-bree den]   How do you do. (lit. 'good
                                                       day', general purpose
                                                       greeting)

Dobrý deň

Na shledanou [na-skhle-da-noh]   Goodbye, au revoir
Dovidenia

Dobrou noc [dob-roh nots]   Goodnight
Dobrú noc

Kdy? v kolik hodin? [gdi? fko-lik ho-dyin?]   When? At what time?
Kedy? O kol'kej?

Jak dlouho? [yak dloh-ho]   How long? (ie. time)
Ako dlho?

Kde? [gde],   Where?
Kde?

Kde mohu koupit...? [gde mo-hu koh-pit]   Where can I buy...?
Kde možem kúpit...?

Co? [tso]   What?
Čo?

Jak? [yak]   How?
Ako?

Jak se dostanu k...? [yak se do-sta-nu k]   How do I get to...?
Ako sa dostanem do...?

Smím...? [smeem]   May I...?
Môžem...?

Máte...? [mah-te]   Have you got...?
Máte...?

Chtěl bych (chtěla bych)...
    [khytyel bikh/khtye-la bikh]   I would like... (the 'a' on the
                                                       end is used if the speaker is a
                                                       woman)

Chcel(a) by som...

Kolik (stojí...)? [ko-lik sto-yee]   How much (does it cost)?
Kol'ko stojí...?

Prosím napište... [pro-seem na-pish-te]   Please write (may be helpful
                                                       if you are getting an answer

in Czech which is an address, a number, a date or time of day)

Prosím napište...
Promiňte [pro-min-te]

Excuse me. (As in English, this can be used either when accosting or interrupting someone, or as a mild apology.)

Prepáčte
Je mi (velice) líto [ye mi ve-li-tse lee-to]
Je mi (vel'mi) l'úto
Není zač [ne-nyee zatch]

I'm (very) sorry

Not at all (lit. 'there is nothing for which', a polite response to thanks or apologies)

Nieje za čo
Máte lístek v angličtině? [mah-te lees-tek van glitch-ti-nye]

Máte lístok v angličtine?

Have you got a menu in English?

Prosím, platit [pro-seem pla-tyit]

The bill please (lit. 'please, to pay')

Prosím platit'
Pane, Paní, Slečno [pa-ne, pa-nyee, sletch-no]

Mr, Mrs, Miss (Like 'Monsieur' or 'Madame' in French, they can be used with or without a proper name following. They are given here in the vocative case, which is used when you are talking *to* someone rather than about them.)

Pán, pani, slečna

Signs, notices and tourist glossary

Pozor, *Pozor!* Attention, warning, mind out for...
Vchod, *Vchod* Entrance
Východ, *Východ* Exit
Otevřeno, *Otvorené* Open
Zavřeno, *Zatvorené* Closed
Zakázán, *Zakázaný* Forbidden
Vstup zakázán, *Vstup zakázaný* No admittance
Kouření zakázáno, *Fajčenie zakázané* No smoking

Nešlapte (nevstupujte) potrávě, *Nešlapte po tráve/Nestúpajte na trávu* Keep off the grass
Vlevo, *Vl'avo* Left, to the left
Vpravo, *Vpravo* Right, to the right
Záchod, *Záchod* WC
Muži, *Muži* Men
Páni, *Páni* Gentlemen
Ženy, *Ženy* Women
Dámy, *Dámy* Ladies
Informace, *Informácie* Information

Volný, *Volný* Free (ie, vacant, not taken)
Obsazeno, *Obsadený* Reserved (table), full up (bus), taken (seat)
Pitná voda, *Pitná voda* Drinking water
Pokladna, *Pokladňa* Cash desk booking office
Plaťte u pokladny, *Palťte pri pokladni* Pay at the desk
Samoobsluha, *Samoobsluha* Self-service
Ulice, *Ulica* Street
Ulička, *Ulička* Alley
Náměstí, *Námestie* Square
Třída, *Trieda* Avenue
Silnice, *Cesta* Road
Cesta, *Cesta* Path
Kostel, *Kostol* Church
Chrám/katedrála, *katedrála* Cathedral
Kaple, *kaplnka* Chapel
Klášter, *Kláštor* Monastery
Svatý, *Svätý* Saint
Most, *Most* Bridge
Křižovatka, *Križovatka* Cross-roads
Nábřeží, *Nábrežie* Embankment
Trh, *Trh* Market
Tržište, *Tržnica* Market-place
Kašna, *Fontána* Fountain
Hrad, *Hrad* Castle
Zámek, *Zámok* Château
Palác, *Palác* Palace
Věž, *Veža* Tower
Radnice, *Radnica* Town hall
Město, *Mesto* Town
Vesnice, *Dedina* Village
Staré město, *Staré mesto* Old town
(Historická) čvrt˘, *(Historická) štvrt'* (Historic) quarter
Památky, *Pamiatky* Monuments, historic buildings
Hřbitov, *Cintorín* Cemetery
Zahrada, *Záhrada* Garden
Sady, *Sad* Park
Muzeum, *Múzeum* Museum
Galerie, *Galéria* Gallery
Šatna, *Šatňa* Cloakroom
Objížďka, *Obchádzka* Diversion
Silnice v opravě (se opravuje), *Cesta sa opravuje* Roadworks, Road up
Letiště, *Letisko* Airport
Nádraží, *Nádražie/(železničná) stanica* Railway station
Nástupiště, *Nástupište* Platform
Odjezd, *Odchod* Departure
Příjezd, *Príchod* Arrival
Občerstvení, *Občersvenie* Refreshments, snack-bar
Čekárna, *Čakáreň* Waiting room
Výstava, *Výstava* Exhibition
Národní, *Národné* National
Knihovna, *Knižnica* Library
Divadlo, *Divadlo* Theatre
Opera, *Opera* Opera
Socha, *Socha* Statue
Obrazy, *Obrazy* Pictures
Lesy, *Lesy* Woods, forest
Hory, *Hory* Mountains
Kopec, *Kopec* Hill
Vrch, *Vrch* Hill
Důl, *Baňa* Mine
Řeka, *Rieka* River
Pramen, *Prameň* Spring
Mlýn, *Mlyn* Mill
Jezero, *Jazero* Lake
Ostrov, *Ostrov* Island
Rybník, *Rybník* Man-made lake, fishpond
Přístaviště, *Prístavisko* Landing-stage
Loď, *Loď* Boat
Průvodce, *Sprievodca* Guide (either a person or a guidebook)
Kavárna, *Kaviareň* Café
Restaurace, *Reštaurácia* Restaurant
Hospoda, *Piváreň, Krčma* Inn, tavern
Pošta, *Pošta* Post office
Známky, *Zná mky* Stamps
Noviny, *Noviny* Newspapers
Nehoda, *Nehoda* Accident
Lékař, *Lekár* Doctor
Policie, *Polícia* Police
Pas, *Pas* Passport
Koruna, *Koruna* Crown (Czech/Slovak currency)
Haléř, *Halier* one-hundredth of a Crown
Porucha, *Porucha* Breakdown

Numbers

0 **nula** [nu-la], *nula*
1 **jeden** [ye-den], *jeden*
2 **dva** [dva], *dva*
3 **tři** [trzhi], *tri*
4 **čtyři** [chti-rzhi], *štyri*
5 **pět** [pyet], *pat'*
6 **šest** [shest], *šest'*
7 **sedm** [se-dum], *sedem*
8 **osm** [o-sum], *osem*
9 **devět** [de-vyet], *devät'*
10 **deset** [de-set], *desat'*
11 **jedenáct** [ye-de-nahtst], *jedenást'*
12 **dvanáct** [dva-nahtst], *dvanást'*
13 **třináct** [trzhi-nahtst], *trinást'*
14 **čtrnáct** [chtr-nahtst] *štrnást'*
15 **patnáct** [pat-nahtst], *pätnásť*
16 **šestnáct** [shest-nahtst], *Šestnást'*
17 **sedmnáct** [se-dum-nahtst], *šedemnást˘*

18 **osmnáct** [o-sum-nahtst], *osemnást'*
19 **devatenáct** [de-va-te-nahtst], *devatnásť*
20 **dvacet** [dva-tset], *dvadcat'*
30 **třicet** [trzhi-tset], *tridcat'*
40 **čtyřicet** [chti-rzhi-tset], *štyridcat'*
50 **padesát** [pa-de-saht], *pat'desiat*
60 **šedesát** [she-de-saht], *šest'desiat*
70 **sedmdesát** [se-dum-de-saht], *sedemdesiat*
80 **osmdesát** [o-sum-de-saht], *osemdesiat*
90 **devadesát** [de-va-de-saht], *devät'desiat*
100 **sto** [sto], *sto*
1000 **tisíc** [tyi-seets], *tisíc*

Intermediate numbers work like English, or, more precisely, like American English: 127 is said as 'one hundred twenty-seven', **sto dvacet sedm** (there is no 'and'). Czechs and Slovaks may, however, reverse the order of tens and units when saying or writing the words, eg, 'seven-and-twenty', **sedmadvacet** (the same words in reverse order, with an 'a' in the middle) as this avoids some grammatical complications. You may therefore hear '**sto sedmadvacet**' for 127. If in doubt, ask for the number to be written down.

Days and months

Sunday, **neděle** [ne-dye-le], *nedel'a*
Monday, **pondělí** [pon-dye-lee], *pondelok*
Tuesday, **úterý** [oo-te-ree], *utorok*
Wednesday, **středa** [strzhe-da], *streda*
Thursday, **čtvrtek** [chtvr-tek], *štvrtok*
Friday, **pátek** [pah-tek], *piatok*
Saturday, **sobota** [so-bo-ta], *sobota*
January, **leden** [le-den], *január*
February, **únor** [oo-nor], *február*
March, **březen** [brzhe-zen], *marec*
April, **duben** [du-ben], *apríl*

May, **květen** [kvye-ten], *máj*
June, **červen** [cher-ven], *jún*
July, **červenec** [cher-ve-nets], *júl*
August, **srpen** [sr-pen], *august*
September, **září** [zah-rzhee], *september*
October, **říjen** [rzhee-yen], *október*
November, **listopad** [lis-to-pad], *november*
December, **prosinec** [pro-si-nets], *december*

Note that days and months do not have capital letters in Czech or Slovak. For menu terms, see **Food and drink**.

Background information

Historical summary

'Confusion, blood and catastrophes' was how the French writer and politician Chateaubriand summarised the history of this complex part of Europe in 1833. Today, in view of all that has happened here since the Second World War, one is tempted to emphasise not so much the tragic aspects of this history as its absurdities. Milan Kundera's novel, *The Book of Laughter and Forgetting* (1979), opens with an image of the Communist leader Klement Gottwald stepping out onto a balcony in Prague's Old Town Square to proclaim to a vast crowd the coming of the Communists to power. 'It was', Kundera noted, 'a crucial moment in Czech history—a fateful moment of the kind that occurs once or twice in a millennium.' Standing behind Gottwald was one of his close associates, Clementis, who, as it was cold and Gottwald was bare-headed, solicitously gave the new president his own fur cap. The photograph of the balcony scene became an image known to every Czech schoolboy, with the difference that in later versions of the picture Clementis could no longer be seen, the man having been accused of treason and hanged only four years after it was taken. 'All that remains of Clementis', wrote Kundera, 'is the cap on Gottwald's head.'

Gottwald himself has now been largely erased from history, and the remains of his diseased corpse, which had once lain in glory below the largest equestrian statue in the world, are buried today in a mass grave after having been recently rejected by his family. His name and those of all other Czech and Slovak Communists (including, so unfairly, the brave journalist Julius Fučík, who was killed by the Nazis) have disappeared from all the streets and squares of a part of Europe whose street-signs have been altered repeatedly in the course of the 20C: in his novel *The Miracle Game* (1972), Josef Škvorecký wrote about a small town high street 'which over the past thirty years had been named after Eduard Beneš, Frederick the Great, Stalin, Lenin, Professor Nejedlý, Tomáš Garrigue Masaryk, and finally, once more, Lenin.'

Masaryk, the first president of Czechoslovakia, occupies today a more elevated position than ever in the Czech pantheon of heroes, while Andrej Hlinka, Jozef Tiso and other Fascist sympathisers have become, disturbingly, the object of a growing cult in the newly created Slovak Republic. In this absurd world of changing ideologies and ephemeral reputations, it is no wonder that Czechs and Slovaks have so often found both an escape and a sense of historical purpose in their medieval and ancient past, where fact and fiction can more freely be allowed to mingle.

Empires, martyrs and myths

The early history of the present-day territory of the Czech and Slovak Republics is scantly documented, and the first Czech chronicler, Cosmas, was himself to admit c 1120 that he had been unable to find much firm information dating from before the 9C AD. Greek and Roman sources refer to the Celtic tribe of the **Boii**, who came here probably around 400 BC and from whom the name 'Bohemia' almost certainly derives. The Boii were subjugated in about 10 BC by the Teutonic tribe of the Marcomanni, and by the 2C the Romans had penetrated as far as the Slovakian town known today as Trenčín. The Slavs only began moving into this part of Europe from about AD 450, those among them who ended up in Bohemia being led, according to legend, by a certain **Čech**, who decided to settle here after surveying the fertile countryside to be seen from the top of the hill of Říp. No less mythical a person than Čech was his descendant Countess Libuše, who ruled the Bohemians until about AD 800, when they tired of being subject to a woman and provoked her into marrying a ploughman (*Přemysl*).

Following the mythical emergence of the **Přemyslid dynasty** at the beginning of the 9C, Bohemia was eclipsed in importance by its Slavonic neighbour Moravia, which, after subduing the non-Aryan tribe of the Avars, was to forge alliances with the Slavs in both Bohemia and the County of Nitra (Slovakia) to form the **Great Moravian Empire**. The greatest threat to the Slavs at this time came from the north, where Charlemagne and the subsequent rulers of Germany coveted Bohemia and Moravia not simply for political reasons but also in the cause of spreading Christianity. Christianity did take root in these lands during the 9C, but it was in an attempt to lessen the influence from Germany that the Moravian leader Count Rostislav turned in 863 towards the Church in the East, and appealed to the Emperor Michael at Byzantium to send clergy capable of expounding the Christian faith in the language of the Slavs. The Emperor responded by sending the brothers **Cyril and Methodius**, whose enormous success at the Court of Moravia was doubtless facilitated by their apparent invention of the Cyrillic alphabet, a Greek-based script adapted to suit certain Slav peculiarities.

Rostislav was later deposed by his treacherous nephew Svatopluk, who has often been portrayed romantically as a Slavonic champion, though in fact he plotted with Charlemagne's grandson, Louis the German, and was responsible for the brief imprisonment of Methodius in Germany. Methodius was later summoned by the Pope to Rome, where he was able successfully to defend the Slav liturgy; none the less Moravia and Bohemia were soon to enter the sphere of Rome, and the Slav liturgy and script was to be driven eastwards. The collapse of the Great Moravian Empire, however, was brought about not by religious strife but by a completely unforeseen eventuality, which was to lead the Germans to side with the Slavs. Shortly after the death of Svatopluk in 894 hordes of **Magyars** began arriving in Europe and were crushingly to defeat the combined forces of the Slavs and Germans at a battle which took place near Posonium (Bratislava). The southern part of the empire, Slovakia, came to be incorporated into the new country which the Magyars created, and was to remain a part of Hungary until 1918. The Slavonic unity which the Great Moravian Empire had fitfully represented was in later centuries to fuel the dream of Panslavism.

After the collapse of its empire Moravia, which has never been separated from **Bohemia** by firm geographical boundaries, became absorbed into Bohemia, which from the early 10C onwards began developing into an important power in its own right. The history of Bohemia after c 860 was marked at first principally by the consolidation of Christianity in the country. Count Bořivoj, the first documented member of the Přemyslid dynasty, was converted to Christianity, probably by Methodius, and Bořivoj's widow, Ludmila, provided Bohemia with its first saint and martyr after she was murdered by her daughter-in-law in 874.

Ludmila's grandson was the equally pious **Wenceslas**, who was made Count of Bohemia in 921, and was later to be immortalised by the popular Christmas carol which wrongly designates him as 'Good *King* Wenceslas'. Politically the reign of Wenceslas was characterised by successful efforts to improve relations with Germany, and it was around this fact that certain 19C historians, aware of the necessity of a German orientation for Bohemia, promoted him as one of the greatest of all Czech heroes. His reign was to be a short one, however, for in 929, when he was only 22, he was murdered by his brother Boleslav, who became in consequence Boleslav I or 'the Cruel'. Boleslav broke off the cordial relations that his brother had established with Germany, but later in life sided with the German ruler Otto the Great, and shared in the latter's decisive victory over the Magyars at Lechfeld (near Augsburg) in 955. Germany played an increasingly important role in Bohemia's development in the Middle Ages, and growing numbers of **German merchants** came to settle here, receiving particular encouragement to do so from Soběslav II, who in 1178 granted them fiscal privileges and exemption from military service. A later ruler, Přemysl Otakar I, played a skilful game of shifting allegiances during Germany's civil war of the early 13C, and thereby won constant concessions for his country, culminating in 1212 when he extracted from the Holy Roman Emperor a Golden Bull granting to him and his descendants the title of king. The 13C saw Bohemia rapidly gaining both in political and economic power, and was the period when most of its major towns were founded: a particular boost was the discovery of silver mines in Kutná Hora and elsewhere, a discovery which was to make the Bohemian court one of the wealthiest in Europe.

The golden age

The Přemyslids, like the Hungarian dynasty of Arpád, died out at the beginning of the 14C, their last king, Wenceslas III, being murdered in 1306. As Wenceslas had no heir, the German king Henry VII, of the House of Luxemburg, managed to secure the throne of Bohemia for his own family by arranging that his son John marry the second daughter of Wenceslas II, Eliška. John, who became known as 'the Blind' after being wounded in the eye and treated by a quack doctor, showed little interest in Bohemia, and in 1344 entrusted its government to his son Charles, a small and ugly man whose rule was to bring about what is generally described as 'the Golden Age of Bohemia'. King of Bohemia in 1346, King of Germany in 1347, and Holy Roman Emperor in 1355, **Charles IV** made Bohemia the capital of his empire, and in so doing managed to place the country at the forefront both of European politics and culture. He enlarged the boundaries of his kingdom, reorganised the country's legal and administrative systems, founded both the city of Carlsbad (Karlovy Vary) and the New Town of Prague, built Prague's magnificent Charles Bridge and the enormous castle at Karlštejn, established the first university in Central Europe, and attracted to his court at Prague many of the leading artists, architects and intellectuals of the day. Though brought up in France and equally fluent in French, German and Czech, his particular preference was for Czech, and he refused official appointments in Bohemia to all Germans who could not speak this language. In addition he secured from the Pope permission to use Czech in all ecclesiastical services in certain monasteries. More importantly he gave support to a generation of reformist preachers—including Milíč of Kroměříž, Matthew of Janov and

Tomáš of Štítný—whose advocacy of the Czech language over Latin and calls for a return to the pious simplicity of the early Christians were to pave the way for one of the greatest figures in the early history of Czech thought and literature, Jan Hus.

Jan Hus and the religious wars

Charles died in 1378, and his son and successor, the quarrelsome and impulsive Wenceslas IV, inherited little of his father's greatness, succeeding in losing the crown of Germany to his brother Sigismund in 1400, and leading Bohemia into a great social and religious crisis, out of which the **Hussite movement** was to emerge. Jan Hus, who gave his name to this movement, was born in 1373 of peasant parents in the South Bohemian village of Husinec. After studying at Prague University, he entered the Church and rapidly earned for himself such a reputation as a priest that he was selected as confessor to Queen Sophie. He was at first unwavering in his devotion to the Church of Rome, but the papacy's corruption at the time of the Schism—as exemplified in its selling of indulgences in the streets of Prague—was to turn Hus into one of its most violent opponents. In 1402 he began denouncing the morals of the clergy from Prague's Bethlehem Chapel, a place which had been founded ten years earlier by a Czech patriot who had insisted that the preaching of the word of God be done in the mother tongue; two years later Hus was to find support for his views following the arrival in Prague from England of two disciples of the English reformer John Wycliffe, James and Conrad of Canterbury.

The preachings of Hus soon won him an enormous following among the Czech people and led to a great rift developing at Prague University between the Czechs and the Germans, the latter all taking the side of the Church of Rome. In 1409 a major victory was scored for Hus after he managed to persuade Wenceslas IV to impose the Decree of Kutná Hora, whereby the voting system in the university was changed greatly in favour of the Czechs, a decision which led to an exodus from Prague of 2000 German students and many professors, who went on subsequently to found the university of Leipzig in Saxony. The success of the Czech reform movement incited the new Pope at Rome, Alexander V, to authorise the archbishop of Prague to destroy all the writings of Wycliffe and to punish those who read and preached his doctrines. When Hus persisted in his preachings he was excommunicated: all those who supported him were threatened with the same fate, even if they only offered him food and drink; it was further stipulated that all religious services were to be suspended in every town that he entered. Wenceslas IV persuaded Hus to leave Prague for a while, in the hope that his absence from the city would help to calm the situation. In his 20 months of voluntary exile Hus produced most of his finest writings, but also continued to preach, finding his congregations in the villages and farms around his native Husinec. In the meantime Wenceslas's brother Sigismund induced the church authorities to call a Council at Constance to settle the dispute between the rival pontiffs. Sigismund also suggested that Hus should attend this council to refute the charges of heresy, promising him a safe-conduct and a free return to Bohemia whatever the outcome. Hus was burned at the stake at Constance on 6 July 1415.

The enormous popular support which Hus had enjoyed during his lifetime was vastly to increase after his death: many Czech historians have interpreted this support in terms of a great 'humanist' tradition in Bohemia, while Communist apologists have shown it as an example of the socialist and revolutionary tendencies of the Czech people. The Hussites did not in fact represent a united front, and came to be divided after Hus's death into two main camps, moderate and radical. The symbol common to both parties was the chalice, a reference to the Hussite belief that the Holy Communion should be administered to the laity both with bread and wine, an ancient practice which had been preserved in the Greek Orthodox Church, from which Bohemia had received Christianity. The moderate Hussites, drawn mainly from the Bohemian nobility and the more conservative nationalists, are sometimes referred to as the 'Calixtines' (after the Latin for chalice), though they are more usually known as the Utraquists (from the Latin phrase *sub utraque specie*). The more popularly based radical wing of the Hussites went far further in their views than the Utraquists, maintaining that the Holy Bible was the sole authority in all matters of religious belief, and rejecting the doctrine of the existence of Purgatory, all the Sacraments with the exception of Baptism and Communion, and many other of the teachings of the Church. The radicals enjoyed the leadership of one of the greatest of Bohemia's military commanders, **Jan Žižka**, a man whose early background is little known other than that he came from a family of the lesser nobility in South Bohemia, and had held a post at the court of Queen Sophia; he and his followers, the Táborites, were to establish as their principal base a stronghold in South Bohemia which they named Tábor after the biblical hill where Christ had been transfigured.

The widespread unrest resulting from Hus's death came to a head in 1419 when Wenceslas attempted to check the Hussite movement by allowing the return of all priests who had opposed Utraquism and granting the Utraquists the use of only three churches in Prague. On 29 July of that year, only one week after Táborites from all over the country had gathered in South Bohemia, a procession of Utraquists led by Jan of Želivský marched through the Prague streets, being greeted with stones as they passed underneath the New Town Hall. In anger the Utraquists stormed the building, and flung the mayor and several of his councillors out of the window and onto the square, where they were torn limb from limb. This was to be the first of the two so-called '**defenestrations**' in Bohemia's history, incidents that on both occasions were to bring the country to war. The news of what had happened at the Town Hall had the immediate effect of making Wenceslas so annoyed that he died of apoplexy; as he was without an heir, this in turn led to the thorny problem of succession. The principal claimant to the throne was his brother Sigismund, a man widely hated in Bohemia, particularly after his treacherous behaviour to Jan Hus; his only supporters were the Roman Catholics, most of whom belonged to the country's German communities. In the absence of a king, Queen Sophia was appointed regentess of the country, but shortly afterwards a Papal Bull was issued proclaiming a crusade against the heretics of Bohemia. By June 1420, Sigismund, at the head of crusading forces drawn from almost every European country, reached the outskirts of Prague, where he was defeated in battle by Jan Žižka, whose forces knelt upon the field of victory and intoned the Te Deum. Before fleeing to Moravia, Sigismund had himself crowned in Prague's St Vitus's Cathedral, but the ceremony was such a hurried and reduced one that his opponents considered it to be invalid. It was in any case to be a further 16 years before he would be able to take possession of his kingdom.

Jan Žižka died of plague in 1424, and was succeeded as Táborite leader by

Prokop, a married priest who was to earn himself the nickname of 'the Great' and prove himself almost as formidable a soldier as Žižka. He and his well-disciplined soldiers were to hold out as late as 30 May 1434, when they were brutally crushed at the Battle of Lipany near Kolín; this day was one of many to be described by later Czech historians as 'the saddest in Bohemian history'. Sigismund, by now an old man, was only to reign over Bohemia between 1436 and 1437, after which came the equally brief rule of his detested son-in-law Albert of Austria (1347–49). A period of confusion then followed, for Albert's only heir was born after his father's death, hence his nickname of Ladislav the Posthumous. A strong regent was clearly required during the minority of Ladislav and, following much fighting between the Utraquists and the Catholics, the young Utraquist leader **George of Poděbrady** was recognised by Ladislav's guardian—the Emperor Frederick III— as *de facto* ruler in Bohemia. Ladislav was crowned in 1453, but power in the country continued to remain in the hands of George who, after Ladislav's death from plague in 1457, was elected by the Bohemian Diet as King of Bohemia: to mark this triumph of Utraquism, a resplendent chalice was placed on the west façade of Prague's Týn Church. Another important moment in the religious history of Bohemia was the formal organisation, ten years later, of the Bohemian Brethren, whose true founder was Peter Chelčický. The most remarkable of George of Poděbrady's Czech contemporaries, Chelčický, carried the doctrines of Wycliffe and Hus one stage further and condemned the use of force in religious matters, emphasising the Christian teachings of humility and the equality of all men.

The Habsburg succession

George of Poděbrady, the most popular of Bohemia's kings after Charles IV, died in 1471, and his throne was sought by a number of candidates, including Matthias of Hungary, Albert of Saxony and George's own two sons, the Dukes of Münsterberg. In the end Prince Vladislav Jagiello of Poland was elected, partly because he was George's own designated candidate, and partly because of his maternal descent from the Luxemburg and hence Přemyslid dynasties. He proved to be a weak ruler, however, and was soon called King All-Right, owing to his habit of saying *Dobře* or 'Good' to everything that was said to him by his powerful barons; he was also a Catholic, and his reign was one of compromise between the rival Utraquist and Romanist factions. On the death of Matthias of Hungary in 1490, Vladislav inherited the throne of Hungary, and thereafter transferred the capital of his by now vast domains to Buda. The fates of Bohemia and Hungary were to be linked from this moment right up to 1918. Shortly before his own death in 1516, Vladislav had signed with the Habsburg Emperor Maximilian what has been described as one of the most momentous marriage contracts in history. The outcome of this was that Vladislav's daughter Anne was married to the Emperor's second grandson, Archduke Ferdinand, while his young son Louis became the husband of Ferdinand's second sister Mary; in the event of Louis dying childless, it was agreed that the Crown of Bohemia should pass to Anne's descendants. In 1526 the 20-year-old Louis drowned in a swamp while fleeing the Battle of Mohács, where the Hungarian army was virtually wiped out by the Turks. This was effectively the year when the **Habsburg monarchy** was born, a monarchy which would control the destinies of Bohemia and Hungary for the next 400 years.

The religious tensions that had beset Bohemia during the 15C intensified in the course of the 16C with the rapid spread of Lutheranism, a religion which was brought into Bohemia, ironically, by German merchants. Utraquists, Bohemian Brethren and Lutherans came easily to outnumber the Catholics in the country, but the Catholics had the support of the Habsburgs, who ruthlessly introduced the Counter-Reformation into Bohemia, beginning with the invitation of the Jesuits to Prague in 1556, the year that Ferdinand I inherited the additional office of Emperor of Germany. At first Ferdinand's son Maximilian prevaricated between Catholic and Protestant causes, but placed his allegiance firmly on the side of the former as soon as he succeeded his father in 1564. In contrast, Catholic hopes were to be greatly disappointed by Maximilian's own son and successor, **Rudolph II**, who had been brought up in the fanatical environment of Spain and had been expected to pursue the intransigent policies of his grandfather Ferdinand. Rudolph turned out to be a suspicious and withdrawn man who was so incapable of coming to decisions that he even hesitated for 20 years over whether to marry Philip II's daughter, Isabella, and decided in the end to remain a bachelor.

His interest in matters of state was minimal, but he had in compensation a mania for art, astrology and astronomy which was to result not only in his amassing one of Europe's finest art collections, but also in the transformation of his court at Prague into a haven for many of the controversial thinkers and scientists of the day, such as Giordano Bruno, Tycho Brahe and Johannes Kepler. Clearly he had inherited a streak of madness from his Spanish great-grandmother Juana la Loca, and this was to encourage Habsburg plans to limit his power and eventually depose him. Under attack from his cousin Leopold and his brother Matthias he turned for help to the Bohemian Estates, and in return was obliged to sign in July 1609 the momentous 'Letter of Majesty', whereby he surrendered the absolutist pretensions of the Crown, and assured freedom of religion in Bohemia. In May 1611 Rudolph was forced finally to surrender the throne of Bohemia to Matthias, but he was allowed to retain the imperial title and the possession of the castle in Prague; during the remaining eight months of his life he actively intrigued with the Protestant Union.

Controversy over the interpretation of the 'Letter of Majesty' was to lead to the **Thirty Years War**, which was sparked off on 23 May 1618 when a group of Protestants marched into Prague Castle and threw out of the window two councillors whom they had accused of influencing the anti-Protestant bias of Matthias's successor, Ferdinand II. The Protestant nobility were encouraged afterwards to rise up in rebellion against the Habsburgs, and in the following year they succeeded in deposing Ferdinand and replacing him with the Elector Frederick V of the Palatinate, a man whose short-lived rule was to earn him the name of the 'winter king'. At the Battle of the White Mountain, which took place outside Prague on 8 November 1620, Ferdinand, with the assistance of the Catholic League and Maximilian of Bavaria, managed in the space of a few hours to put Frederick to flight and demolish the Bohemian army. This put a definitive end to Bohemian independence and initiated a series of terrible reprisals against the Protestants, including the execution on Prague's Old Town Square of 27 leading members of their nobility in 1621. Ferdinand consolidated the Habsburg cause in Bohemia in 1624 by moving the Bohemian Court Chancellery to Vienna and by instituting four years later an Imperial Ordinance re-establishing the hereditary right of the House of Austria to the throne of

Bohemia and making Catholicism the only permitted religion. Czech schools were closed, the Czech language was suppressed, the university at Prague was turned into a Jesuit college, and thousands of Czech books were destroyed; one Jesuit priest, Andrew Koniáš, even boasted of having himself burned 60,000 books.

The misfortunes of Bohemia after the Battle of the White Mountain, as with Czechoslovakia in 1938, heralded a tragedy on a much larger scale when Ferdinand II was dragged into the protracted war between Protestant and Catholic factions in Northern Europe, where many Bohemian exiles had taken refuge. The excellently equipped armies of the Swedish ruler Gustavus Adolphus seemed certain to come to the aid of the struggling German Protestants and threatened to jeopardise Ferdinand's Counter-Reformation policies. Ferdinand had to enlist the support of the brilliant but devious **Duke of Wallenstein**, a man who had benefited enormously from the confiscation of property from exiled and executed Czechs. Wallenstein drove back the Swedes from Bohemia in 1631, but his constant treacheries led to his murder by British mercenaries at Cheb in 1634. By 1648, when peace was finally declared, the Swedes had occupied Prague's Little Quarter.

The Treaty of Westphalia, which had brought about the end of the war, represented a further blow to Bohemian hopes, for it excluded the return to Bohemia of those exiles who had fought with the Swedes; such had been the damage incurred by the war that neither party was willing to fight further over this issue. Bohemia had been decimated over these 30 years, its economy and political importance destroyed, its towns razed, and its population reduced to a fraction of what it had previously been. A symbol of Bohemia's loss during these years was the exile of one of its most outstanding intellectual figures, the pioneering pedagogue Jan Ámos Komenský (**Comenius**), who was to be described by the French historian Michelet as 'the Galileo of Education'. Comenius's concern for the plight of his nation was expressed most poignantly in his appeal of 1650 entitled *Bequest of the Dying Mother of the Unity of Czech Brethren*; the words of this appeal were to provide succour to a Czech exile of a much later generation, Tomáš Masaryk.

In the wake of the Thirty Years War opposition to Habsburg rule was to be concentrated in Hungarian lands, Slovakia playing an important part in the rebellions led in the late 17C and early 18C by the Hungarian aristocrats István Bocskay, Gábor Bethlen and Ferenc Rákóczy II: among those who fought with Rákóczy was Juraj Jánošík, a Robin Hood figure who was one of Slovakia's earliest and greatest popular heroes. Bohemia itself was not to become involved in any major conflict until 1750, when Frederick II of Prussia waged war on the new Habsburg Empress Maria Theresa, accusing her Jesuits of wrongly persecuting the Silesian Protestants (who, according to the terms of the Treaty of Westphalia, should have been allowed freely to practice their religion). In 1757 the Prussians were laying siege to Prague when Frederick's troops were defeated at the nearby town of Kolín. The outcome of the **Seven Years War** was the further devastation of Bohemia. Maria Theresa finally decided to expel the Jesuits from Bohemia in 1773, and further major reforms were to be carried out by her successor Joseph II, who in 1781, a year after his mother's death, abolished serfdom, introduced a decree of religious tolerance, and suppressed 700 monasteries. The rule of Joseph II is often described as one of 'enlightened despotism': another of his acts was to try to introduce compulsory education while insisting that all teaching be conducted in German; he vainly hoped by this to bring unity to his vast empire and diminish the many cultural and linguistic barriers that divided it. In 1809, four years after massively defeating the combined Russian and Austrian forces near the Moravian town of Slavkov (Austerlitz), Napoleon made a stirring appeal to the Bohemian people to rid themselves once and for all of the Austrian tyranny. The appeal was for the moment unheeded, and the Bohemians continued to support the Austrians during the Napoleonic wars. None the less the early years of the 19C saw the beginnings in both Bohemia and Slovakia of a great cultural and intellectual renaissance.

The nationalist movement

A key moment in the revival of Czech culture was the foundation in 1818 of the Society of the Bohemian National Museum, a society whose members comprised a remarkable group of both Bohemian and Slovak intellectuals, including Josef Dobrovský ('the patriarch of Slavonic studies'), Josef Jungmann (the founder of the modern Czech literary language) and the Slovak philologist Pavel Šafařík. Perhaps the most important member of all was the historian, poet and politician **František Palacký**, who was fundamental in the founding of a Bohemian national party and whose enormous *History of the Czech Nation* led to his being called 'the Father of the Nation': in this pioneering work, the first volume of which was published in 1836, Palacký saw Czech history in terms of 'the constant contact and conflict between the Slavs on the one hand and Rome and the Germans on the other'. Palacký declined an offer to become Minister of Education at Vienna and in 1848 turned down an invitation to appear as one of six delegates to be sent by the Habsburgs to a meeting of the Germanic Federation at Frankfurt: he based his refusal on the grounds that he was 'not a German but a Bohemian belonging to the Slav race'.

As an impressive counterblast to the Frankfurt meeting, Palacký and his friends convoked in Prague that same year a congress of all the Slav races under the monarchy. The opening speech was made by Šafařík while Ľudovít Štúr— the only Slovak representative in the Hungarian Parliament—made an impassioned appeal in favour of common action between Slovaks and Czechs. Rioting ensued in the streets of Prague at the end of the congress, and rebellion was brutally suppressed by the military commander Prince Windischgrätz, a believer in the return of absolutist rule in Bohemia.

In the second half of the century tensions greatly increased not only between Germans and Czechs but also between Slovaks and Hungarians, particularly in the wake of the Dual Compromise of 1867, an agreement between Austria and Hungary which snubbed Bohemia and led to a policy of brutal 'Magyarisation' in Slovakia. Yet the **nationalist movement** continued to grow and found its expression not only in a great surge of patriotic works of art, architecture, literature and music, but also in the foundation of numerous nationalist schools, cultural organisations and other institutions. Notable among these were the Slovakian cultural organisation known as Matica Slovenská—which was founded in Martin in 1867—and the Sokol movement, a gymnastic society which spread rapidly throughout Bohemia and Slovakia from the 1860s onwards, and had as its aim the 'revival of the fatherland, by the education of the body and the spirit, by physical energy, by art and science, by all moral means.'

The 'years of 8'

A curious phenomenon of Czech history in the 20C, and one which was to lead in recent times to a positive superstitious mania, is the way in which most of the key events in this history have taken place in years containing the figure 8. The most significant of what Václav Havel was to call 'the years of 8' was 1918, when the breakdown of the Austro-Hungarian Empire resulted in the creation of the **Czechoslovak Republic**. The new country was made up of three sections, the largest comprising the so-called 'Lands of the Crown of St Wenceslas' (Bohemia, Moravia and Silesia); next in size came Slovakia, and finally there was Ruthenia, which was composed of the districts of northeastern Hungary populated by Ruthenians or Ukranians. Such a conglomerate inevitably caused not only antagonism between the Hungarians and other ethnic minorities, but also among the Slovakians, who had been promised the status of a separate republic under a Czechoslovak federation: Slovak resentment was voiced loudest by the proto-Fascist priest Andrej Hlinka, whose activities as leader of the Slovak People's Party frequently got him into trouble with the Czechoslovak authorities.

None the less, for all these problems, Czechoslovakia survived to become, under the enlightened rule of the former professor of history at Prague University, Tomáš Masaryk, one of the most progressive European countries between the wars, as well as the only long-lasting democracy in a part of Europe falling increasingly under the shadow of Fascism. It was thus particularly inexcusable when in 1938, three years after Masaryk had been succeeded as president by Edvard Beneš, the Allies signed the **Munich Agreement** and thereby allowed the German-settled territories of northern Bohemia (the Sudetenland) to be taken over by Nazi Germany, and parts of eastern Slovakia to be reclaimed by Fascist Hungary. Explaining to the British public the reasons for this fatal decision, Neville Chamberlain made the famous pronouncement: 'How terrible, fantastic, incredible it is that we should be digging trenches and trying on gas masks here because of a quarrel in a far-away country between people of whom we know nothing.'

It was not long after the signing of the Munich Agreement that Hitler seized the whole of Bohemia and Moravia, turning them into a Nazi protectorate on the preposterous historical grounds that they had belonged to the German Reich for over a thousand years; the greater part of Slovakia, meanwhile, was made an independent country ruled by the Fascist priest Jozef Tiso (Hlinka's successor in the Slovak People's Party), who acted as a puppet to Hitler. After November 1941, 75,000 Bohemian Jews were taken to the specially created ghetto town of Terezín in northern Bohemia, and of these only 9000 were to survive; following the assassination in 1942 of the Nazi 'Protector of Bohemia and Moravia' Reinhard Heydrich, the whole country was to suffer reprisals that make those experienced after the Battle of the White Mountain seem minor in comparison. In the freeing of Czechoslovakia from Nazi rule a major role was played by Slovak partisans and soldiers, though in later accounts of the liberation the emphasis was to be on the Soviet army, which entered Slovakia in November 1944 and reached Prague on 5 May of the following year.

The third of the fateful 'years of 8' was 1948, when the Communists came to power and created the **People's Republic of Czechoslovakia**. The general mood was at first one of optimism, and most Czechs believed that Communism would assume in this traditionally enlightened country a much milder form than that which it had taken in Russia. The mysterious death later that year of Jan Masaryk, the son of the former president, provoked certain misgivings, as did the first of the great wave of purges that took place from 1950 onwards. A powerful account of these years of terror is given in *Prague Farewell* (1988), the autobiography of Heda Margolius-Kovály, a Jewish woman who survived Auschwitz only to see her husband—an idealistic and conscientious government worker—executed along with ten other Jews as a result of the notorious Slánský Trial of 1951. Klement Gottwald died in 1953, ironically as a result of catching a cold while attending the funeral of his beloved Stalin; it was also rumoured that his health had been undermined by a combination of syphillis and excessive drinking.

The victims of the Slánský Trial were later 'rehabilitated', and in the 1960s there were signs of renewed optimism that were to culminate in the **'Prague Spring'** of 1968, when the Communist Party's newly elected First Secretary, Alexander Dubček, tried to introduce 'Socialism with a human face', and proposed policies that included a democratic parliament, freedom of assembly and the abolition of censorship. The arrival of Soviet troops on 21 August 1968 brought these developments to a spectacular end, with Soviet tanks and soldiers being taunted by motorcyclists, flag-waving students and mini-skirted women. After a day in which 58 people were killed, Dubček and other reformers were arrested and flown to Moscow, from where they would return as broken men. For a short while Dubček remained impotently in power in a Czechoslovakia that continued to be disturbed by protests, including, most famously, the self-immolation in January 1969 of the philosophy student Jan Palach on the steps of Prague's National Museum. With Dubček's replacement by the Soviet-appointed Gustav Husák in April 1969, all remaining hope for immediate political change vanished and the exodus of the country's intelligentsia gathered momentum. Among the thousands who opted for exile was Milan Kundera, who recalled the Russian invasion as not only a tragedy but also 'as a carnival of hate filled with a curious (and no longer explicable) euphoria'.

The only one of Dubček's policies to be carried out in the immediate wake of the invasion was one that highlighted the divided nature of Czechoslovakia. Dubček, a Slovak, had laid the foundations for what became in 1970 the Federal Socialist Republic of Czechoslovakia, the government of which was divided between Prague and the Slovakian capital of Bratislava; this development was greatly welcomed by most Slovaks, and helps largely to explain the relatively positive mood experienced in Slovakia at a time when the rest of the country was suffering from the deep sense of hopelessness described by Václav Havel in his autobiographical reflections, *Disturbing the Peace* (1990).

The 'Velvet Revolution'

For all these regional tensions there emerged from Czechoslovakia in 1977 the most sustained charter of human liberties in the history of Communist Europe, **Charter 77**. This document, representing the first open challenge to the rule of ('the President of Forgetting'), had come about directly as the result of the banning of a rock group called ''. One of its first and most famous signatories was the dramatist Václav Havel, who later helped to found, as an offshoot of the Charter, the Committee for the Defence of the Unjustly Prosecuted (VONS); in

1979 he himself was to join the ranks of those he was defending, being sent to prison for the next four years. In the late 1980s, when Mikhail Gorbachev's reforms in Russia were leading to a mellowing of conditions elsewhere in Eastern Europe, the Czech government remained as intransigent as ever. Out of respect for the 'years of 8' tradition, hopes for major change were placed on 1988, though all that happened that year was a petition for freedom of the Catholic Church signed by no less than 440,000 people and organised, no less remarkably, by a Moravian peasant called Augustin Navrátil, who cleverly exploited a loophole in the law. Fortunately the Czechs did not have to wait until 1998 for the much-awaited political breakthrough. It came in November 1989, and with such speed and ease that it was called afterwards the 'Velvet Revolution'.

On 17 November a gathering of people commemorating a student killed by the Nazis was transformed into a massive demonstration which ended up at Prague's Wenceslas Square; a new political party, **Civic Forum**, was hastily formed, and in the following days the square was continually filled with growing crowds. On 22 November Václav Havel appeared to the crowd on a balcony, in the company of Alexander Dubček, and on 3 December a call for a general strike finally toppled the crumbling government. Four days after Christmas, following a concerted student-led campaign with the slogan of 'Havel na Hrad' ('Havel to the Castle'), the Federal Assembly unanimously voted in Havel as President of Czechoslovakia.

An inevitable euphoria characterised the first few months of Havel's rule, despite the equally inevitable errors of judgement made in the fledgling democracy. Though Havel was admired for the speed with which he organised the withdrawal of Soviet troops from the country, he was heavily criticised on other fronts: his apology to the Sudeten Germans for their post-war expulsion met with much resentment, as did his amnesty solution to the problem of overcrowded prisons (his release of hundreds of prisoners was held partly responsible for the sharply rising crime rate). More controversial still was his institution of the so-called *lustrace* law ('lustration' in English means purification by expiatory sacrifice), which, through barring from public office for five years anyone suspected of being a former 'collaborator' with the secret police (the names of 300,000 were eventually published), led to numerous unfair accusations and the destruction of many a career.

Despite its mistakes, the Civic Forum was a clear winner in the general election held in June 1990, after which Havel set about forming a broad coalition government whose most urgent task was to decide the most effective way of switching to a **market economy**. In the end the country was rapidly privatised, and a restitution law was introduced whereby small businesses and property were handed back to those from whom they had been appropriated after the Communist coup of 1948; this was later extended to Jews whose goods had been seized by the Nazis but not to those thousands of Sudeten Germans whose homes had been taken away from them by the Czechs. Economic issues engendered a split within the Civic Forum, which came to be divided between the left-of-centre Civic Movement (Občanské hnuti or OH), and the right-of-centre Civic Democratic Party (Občanská demokratická strana or ODS), which was led by the charismatic and Machiavellian finance minister Václav Klaus, a convinced monetarist and Thatcherite.

The 'Velvet Divorce' and after

Klaus became prime minister following the success of his party in the elections of 1992, which saw also the rise of the Movement for a Democratic Slovakia (Hnutie za demokratické Slovensko or HZDS). The latter, under the leadership of the boorish one-time boxer and Communist Vladimír Mečiar, advocated not only Slovak independence but also a more gradual approach towards economic reform than the one being carried out by Klaus. Slovakian feelings of being treated as the inferior half of the federal state were now compounded by the fact that the region's economy was declining at a time when that of the rest of the country was rapidly improving. Havel's humanitarian decision to put a halt to the country's arms industry was particularly damaging to the finances of Slovakia, where this industry was largely concentrated; furthermore, with the dissolution of the USSR and the Eastern Bloc, the region lost the main export markets for its other principle money-earners, agriculture and steel.

Although polls revealed that 85 per cent of the Czechoslovak Republic wanted (like Havel) to keep the federal state, Klaus, ever the pragmatist, saw the great economic advantages of having a Czech state unburdened by Slovakia. After failing to persuade Klaus even to have a referendum to decide the issue, and feeling unable to supervise the break-up of Czechoslovakia himself, Havel resigned a few months after the 1992 elections, leaving the country briefly without a president. The terms of what came to be known as the 'Velvet Divorce' were decided by the end of the year and, on 1 January 1993, Czechoslovakia, after 74 years of existence, was divided into the **Czech Republic** (Česká republica) and the **Slovak Republic** (Slovenská republica). Despite his critical attitude towards Prime Minister Klaus, Havel was happy to be re-instated as Czech president. Mečiar, meanwhile, became prime minister of the Slovak Republic, the president of which, Michal Kováč, is someone with whom he too has maintained an uneasy relationship—to put it mildly.

Of the two halves of the former federation, Slovakia is undoubtedly the one that has prospered least from the break-up, and indeed has been reduced, some might say, to an ultra-conservative provincial backwater of Europe. The nationalist fervour and chiming of bells that greeted Mečiar's cry of 'Slovakia is yours!' at the outset of the republic was one that struck particular fear into the heart of the country's large Hungarian minority, whose understandable worries about reprisals (given what their ancestors had done to the Slovakians) shortly proved not to have been groundless: parliament passed laws restricting the use of the Hungarian language on radio and television and banning Hungarian streetsigns, such as were once commonly to be found in the country's southern regions. But soon it was not only the Hungarians who began worrying about what was happening to Slovakia under Mečiar's increasingly autocratic leadership.

Not only did Mečiar forestall any possible economic growth by bringing privatisation almost to a halt, he also attempted to prevent all criticism of his leadership by gaining extensive government control over the national media, and by firing editorial boards who spoke out against him and his party. Dissatisfaction with Mečiar grew to such proportions that in March 1994 his one-time ally President Kováč (himself no angel) orchestrated his removal from office and had him replaced by the former HZDS foreign minister Jozef Moravčík, whose interim government succeeded in making some improvements to the country's economy. Mečiar, however, perhaps remembering his days as a boxer, determinedly fought his way back into the political arena and succeeded in being re-elected prime minister in September of that year. This achieved he set out openly to try and discredit Kováč, who has since refused to speak with him. Matters reached a head after August 1995, when Mečiar became implicated in the kidnapping of the president's son, on whom was then laid the possibly trumped-up charge of being involved in swindling $2.3 million from an import–export business based in Bratislava. The portly Mečiar survived in power until the autumn elections of 1998, when he even resorted to such desperate ruses as being photographed at the start of the voting alongside the German model Claudia Schiffer. On being defeated he bizarrely announced his departure from government by the singing of a Slovakian folk-song. Although this was probably and thankfully Mečiar's literal swan-song, hopes that Slovakia would improve both its foreign image and its chances of entering the European Comunity were set back shortly after the 1998 elections by conflict with Britain over the fate of Slovakia's large gypsy population, which led to the imposition of visa regulations on British citizens entering the Republic.

In comparison to the Slovak Republic, the Czech Republic has thrived since 1993, with inflation being kept relatively in check, and considerable profits being made from the extraordinary surge in tourism. The picture is not entirely rosy, however; the Czech Republic, too, has been beset by political corruption and has even experienced its own brand of officially condoned **racism**, with a new Czech citizenship law that has left an estimated 100,000 gypsies stateless within their own country. Despite all this, Václav Klaus managed to maintain his popularity until as late as November 1997, when his government was finally forced to resign in the wake of a series of allegations that included his party's access to a slush fund held in an unauthorized Swiss bank account.

Fortunately the Czech Republic still has an inspiring and enlightened figure-head in **Václav Havel** who, in the aftermath of the government crisis of November 1997 and while still recuperating from a spell in hospital, delivered a remarkable 'state of the nation' speech in which he confessed to the shortcomings of the current Czech democracy with an openess, eloquence and sophistication worthy of his country's long-standing humanist traditions:

'After eight years of trying to build a market economy, many people wonder why our economy is still doing so poorly that the government must frequently cobble together hastily arranged budget amendments to deal with shortfalls. They wonder why we are choking in smog when so much is apparently being spent on the environment, why prices, including rents and utilities, are rising faster than pensions and social benefits. They wonder why we should have to be afraid to walk at night in the centres of our cities and towns, why almost nothing but banks, hotels and mansions for the rich are being built, and so on. In short, more and more people are disgusted with policies they understandably and rightly hold responsible for all these unfortunate things, and although they freely elected us, they regard us all with suspicion, if not outright repugnance.'

Art and architecture

The sentimental traveller to the Czech and Slovak Republics, confronted by these countries' extraordinary wealth of little-spoilt towns, might well reflect nostalgically on what the rest of Central Europe must have been like before the Second World War. Yet, in comparison, say, to the towns of pre-war Germany, the towns of the two republics have retained relatively few intact examples of their medieval architecture. The religious wars of the 15C and 17C brutally interrupted the artistic and architectural development of this part of Europe, and devastated its medieval legacy. Furthermore, much of what has survived from the Middle Ages has been hidden under successive layers of remodelling and rebuilding, work which in many cases was carried out with the conscious intention of papering over a heretical past.

The medieval period

Among the earliest and most distinctive survivals of Czech architecture are a number of heavily restored **rotundas** scattered throughout Bohemia and Moravia, and ranging in date from c 900 to c 1225. Probably the oldest is that of Levý Hradec near Prague, which appears to have been founded by Count Bořivoj, the first of the Přemyslid counts to be converted to Christianity. Of particular interest is the Rotunda of St Catherine at Znojmo, a late 11C structure which was covered in 1134 with a remarkable fresco cycle containing scenes representing the lineage of the Přemyslids. Other rare remains of **Romanesque painting** in the Czech Republic are to be found in the early 12C Basilica of St George in Prague, a building in the shape of a Roman basilica but with heavy walls and small openings that suggest the influence of Ottonian Germany. A **French style** of art and architecture was introduced into Bohemia and Moravia with the arrival later in the century of the Cistercians, whose abbey church at Tišnov features one of the finest medieval portals in the country, the so-called Porta Coeli (1260): the jambs and voussoirs of this unmistakably French portal are richly carved with vegetal motifs, while in the tympanum is a representation of Christ in Glory flanked by the Virgin and St John the Baptist, and the kneeling figures of Přemysl Otakar I and his wife, Constance.

Most of the large Czech towns were founded during the 13C, many being laid out on regular **grid-plans** that have been kept to this day. A common feature of these plans is a central market square lined on all sides with arcaded houses, the actual arcading being generally all that has survived of the original buildings. The largest of the many outstanding town squares to be seen in the Czech Republic is that of České Budějovice, which measures 133 square metres and was designed in 1265 by the engineer to Přemysl Otakar II, Hrz of Zvíkov. The ecclesiastical architecture of this period is characterised by the stubborn persistence of a Cistercian Gothic style and a resistance to the French High Gothic, which was to have only a moderate influence here. Beginning with the enormous churches of St Bartholomew at Plzeň, St Nicholas at Kutná Hora and St Nicholas at Znojmo—all of which were founded in the 1320s—the predominant medieval church plan in Czech lands was to be derived from the German hall church, in which the aisles are the same height as the nave.

It was during the reign of **Charles IV** that Bohemia was to experience the first great flowering of its art and architecture. Charles had been brought up in France, and it was thus not surprising that for the first major commission of his rule—the rebuilding of St Vitus's Cathedral in Prague—he should have called in a French architect, Matthew of Arras (?–1352). Matthew, who had previously worked at Avignon under Charles's friend Clement VI, produced a plan with radiating chapels in the ambulatory which was closely based on the French cathedral at Narbonne. However, Matthew died only eight years after work had begun on the building, and in 1352 Charles summoned to Prague an architect of a very different background, **Peter Parléř**.

Parléř (1330–1405/6), one of the outstanding architects of the Middle Ages, had been born to a family of architects in Cologne in 1330, and had probably received most of his training in the Rhineland. Within the limits imposed by Matthew of Arras's plan, Parléř introduced into St Vitus's Cathedral elements that look ahead to the German Sondergotik or late Gothic. Among his achievements here was the creation of a bold, openwork staircase which was to be copied in the cathedrals at Ulm and Strasbourg; but his principal contribution was his exceptionally inventive vaulting, which included a dazzling star-shaped formation and a system of free-standing ribs spread out like a fan.

The age of Charles IV saw the development of an important local school of painting, to which much impetus was given by Charles's large collection of French and Italian illuminated manuscripts, and by the numerous foreign artists who were attracted to his court, such as the Italian painter Tommaso di Modena. Italian and in particular Sienese influence can be felt in the work of many of the early Bohemian artists, for instance in the Master of Vyšší Brod and in the anonymous painter of the *Votive Panel of Jan Očko of Vlašim*, a work which shows the Virgin and Child flanked by the donor and Charles IV in a way which recalls an Italian *sacra conversazione*. The leading and most idiosyncratic painter in Charles's circle was **Master Theodoric**, who is best known for a series of 129 panels painted between 1357–65 for the Holy Rood Chapel at Karlštejn Castle: his solid but softly modelled figures are set there against a background studded with semi-precious stones, an unusual feature—also to be found in the Wenceslas Chapel in St Vitus's Cathedral—which reflects Charles's passionate love of jewellery. At the end of the century, during the reign of Charles's successor Wenceslas IV, the dominant Bohemian painter came to be the **Master of the Třeboň Altarpiece**, whose art, with its strong sense of colour and feeling for linear rhythm, turned not to the south but to the west, and has strong affinities with contemporary Burgundian artists such as Melchior Broederlam.

The intense period of building and cultural activity which Charles IV had initiated was cut short in 1420 with the outbreak of the Hussite Wars, and was not to be renewed until the end of the century, when the kingdoms of Bohemia, Hungary and Poland were united under the rule of Vladislav Jagiello I. Vladislav's rule saw some of the more spectacular achievements of the late Gothic style, as well as a budding influence from Renaissance Italy. Exuberant late Gothic ornamentation can be seen in the fantastical Royal Oratory in St Vitus's Cathedral and in the structures associated with **Matěj Rejsek** (c 1450–1506), for instance, the public fountain at Kutná Hora and the Powder Tower in Prague.

The Renaissance

Later in his life Vladislav was to move his court to Buda and surround himself with Italian artists and architects, but before doing so he invited to Prague around 1480 a German architect of extraordinary originality, **Benedikt Ried** (c 1454–1534). Ried, who came probably from South Germany and soon was to supersede all other architects in Bohemia, was given the monumental task of extending the fortifications of Prague Castle and rebuilding the Royal Palace there. For the latter he constructed in 1493 the vast Vladislav Hall, in which Renaissance features (in the doors and windows) are to be found in Bohemia for the first time, but combined eccentrically with late Gothic vaulting of a fantasy and complexity virtually unparalleled in the rest of Europe. Similarly elaborate vaulting was created by him in St Barbora's Cathedral at Kutná Hora, which he took over in 1515 from Matěj Rejsek, whose own vaulting here, though complex, lacks the flowing energy of Ried's. Another style of vaulting, no less idiosyncratic, was evolved at this time in provincial Bohemia, the earliest documented example being in the Deanery Church at Soběslav (1499–1501). This style, known usually as 'diamond vaulting', reached its apogee in the Franciscan church at Bechyně (c 1515), where an elaborate, whitewashed vault is composed solely of faceted recesses, the overall effect resembling a cross between a stiffly pleated skirt and an Expressionist film set.

The main painter at Vladislav's court in Prague was the **Master of the Litoměřice Altarpiece**, who is sometimes identified with the German artist Hans Elfelder; he was at any rate someone who had been brought up in South Germany and might also have had a first-hand knowledge of North Italian art. The altarpiece from which he derives his name was painted around 1500 for the chapel adjoining the Vladislav Hall, and is characterised by its lively and detailed realism. Artists from his workshop are often said to have been responsible for the frescoes of c 1509 on the upper walls of the Wenceslas Chapel, which reveal an Italianate sense of composition and perspective, as do the slightly earlier frescoes in the Smíšek chapel at Kutná Hora. The outstanding sculptor of this period was another German, **Master Pavol of Levoča**, who was active not in Bohemia but in an area of Central Slovakia known as the Spiš. This region, which had been colonised by Germans in the late 13C, experienced during the reign of Vladislav Jagiello the greatest period in its cultural life, culminating in the great Wing Altar which Master Pavol executed between 1508 and 1517 for the Church of St James in Levoča. Within a gilded late Gothic framework of breathtaking intricacy, Master Pavol created scenes of a most powerful naturalism, which is evident above all in the predella panel of the Last Supper, the faces in which are said to have been based on members of the town's council.

With the coming to power of the Habsburgs in 1526, the art and architecture of Bohemia and Moravia came to be dominated by Italians, most of whom were from the Como region. From the time of Benedikt Ried, Classical detailing had sometimes been applied to Gothic structures, but it was not until the 1530s that work was begun in Prague on a truly Italianate building. This, the so-called Belvedere in the Hradčany, was commissioned by Ferdinand I from Paolo della Stella, and is surrounded by a most elegant arcaded loggia decorated with exquisitely carved mythological and Classical scenes. The only feature which singles the building out as a work executed outside Italy is its bizarre copper roof in the form of the upturned hull of a ship, an addition of the mid-16C by the

Bohemian court architect **Bonifác Wohlmut** (?–1579). Wohlmut's architecture represents a curious synthesis of Italian and Czech elements, and indeed he created for the same Belvedere an upper floor inspired by Bramante's Tempietto in Rome; another work of his is the organ loft in St Vitus's Cathedral, which seems at first wholly in the spirit of the High Renaissance and yet conceals Gothic vaulting behind its Classical arches. Such a synthesis was to typify the spirit of the Czech Renaissance, and even the many **Italian architects** and craftsmen who were to come to Bohemia in the wake of Paolo della Stella were to adapt to local building traditions.

Pietro Ferrabosco, Baldassare Maggi (Maio da Vomio) and Giovanni Battista and Ulrico Aostalli (Avostallis) are among the better known of this later generation of Italian Renaissance architects, and were responsible for a whole series of monumental country residences, most of which featured courtyards with three tiers of Classical arcading. Of these houses, that at Bučovice (designed by Ferrabosco in 1567) has a particularly fine interior and contains one room where you will find—surrounded by Classical grotesque work—a gilded and exuberantly ornate stucco figure of Charles V which seems to have come straight from some medieval pageant. Also remarkable are the Renaissance interiors at Telč, which include richly polychromed carvings attached to Classical coffered ceilings. Telč was one of several imposing buildings commissioned by the powerful Lords of Hradec, a Moravian family whose favourite architect was Baldassare Maggi. One of the last and most original works that Maggi designed for them was an enormous, round garden pavilion at Jindřichův Hradec (1591): to an otherwise wholly Italianate structure Maggi lent a touch of Bohemian fantasy through the addition of an extraordinary conical roof ringed by gabled dormer windows.

Dormer windows, as well as fantastical parapets and stepped gables of every conceivable shape and size, are among the main distinguishing characteristics of the Czech Renaissance, as is the tendency to cover the exteriors of buildings with what are known as **sgraffito** decorations: the latter, created by incising into the plaster, are generally of scenes from Classical history and mythology, but are sometimes wholly ornamental. This style of architecture was applied as much to grand palaces such as the magnificent Šternberk Palace in Prague's Hradčany as to modest burghers' dwellings, and was to be current in Czechoslovakia right up to the late 17C.

The last great period of court patronage in Bohemia took place under **Rudolph II**, at the turn of the 16C. Rudolph's mania for art, and his habit in later life of shutting himself up in his *Schatzkammer* to contemplate obsessively the accumulated treasures therein, gave him much in common with his Spanish cousin Philip II, with whom he also shared a taste for the bizarre and the erotic. However, unlike Philip II, the artists whom Rudolph admired tended to be precious and ultra-refined, the eroticism of Correggio's *Io*, for instance, being apparently preferred to the more full-blooded sensuality characteristic of Titian's mythologies. His favourite sculptor was the Flemish-born Italian Mannerist Giambologna, in whom he showed an interest which was one-sided and hardly subtle: after amassing almost all this artist's statuettes of Venus he wrote to him to ask for 'another naked female figure of the same size'. Rudolph tried unsuccessfully to lure Giambologna to Prague, but succeeded instead in attracting here from Italy the latter's pupil Adriaen de Vries (1546–1626), as well as two other Flemish-born artists, the painters Hans van Aachen

(1552–1615) and Bartolomaeus Spranger (1546–1611), both of whom could combine precious eroticism with the sort of allegorical subject-matter that appealed to Rudolph's love of the esoteric.

As for Rudolph's taste for the bizarre, this was amply satisfied by the Milanese artist, **Giuseppe Arcimboldo** (1527–93), who had first been summoned to Prague in 1566 by Ferdinand I, and who was so admired by Rudolph that in 1592 he was given the title of Count Palatine. Arcimboldo, who worked at Prague not only as a painter but also as an organiser of lavish festivities, developed a speciality in 'visual punning' which was to be dismissed after his death as a mere curiosity but was to be greatly appreciated in the 20C by the Surrealists: he portrayed members of the court with appropriate still-life objects, thus turning the royal gardener into a composite of flowers, or the court historiographer Wolfgang Lazius into an accumulation of books.

In comparison to Rudolph's patronage of the visual arts, relatively little has been written about the architectural commissions associated with him, though these were in fact considerable. Mention, above all, should be made of the Italian Chapel in Prague's Clementinum, which was designed in 1590 by Ottaviano Mascharino and was the first church in Bohemia with an oval ground-plan, a form which was to be much used by Bohemian architects of the Baroque period.

Bohemian Baroque

It is ironical that a country with such strong Hussite and Protestant traditions as Bohemia should have ended up as one of the great Baroque centres of Europe. The devastation caused by the Thirty Years War led to a rebuilding campaign on a vast scale, and most of Bohemia's old towns, in particular Prague, have a predominantly 17C and 18C look. A vital role in the artistic and architectural renewal of the country was played by the **Jesuits**, who were determined to create resplendent buildings and works of art that would embody the spirit of the triumphant Catholic Church. In many ways their propaganda was quite subtle, for in their attempts to give a fresh image to the country, they turned to Bohemia's past and formed out of this a new national mythology which they hoped would counteract the Protestant one. A particular stroke of genius was to have discovered an obscure prelate called John of Nepomuk who had fallen foul of Wenceslas IV in 1393 and been thrown into the river Vltava. In the course of the 17C legends about him began circulating—that he had refused to betray the queen's secrets in the confessional, that a constellation of stars had hovered above his floating body—and eventually in 1693 he was canonised as St Jan Nepomucký, thus inspiring the consecration of many new churches and providing the subject of much of the religious statuary to be seen around the Czech Republic.

A truly Baroque style of architecture was slow to develop in Bohemia, and was not in fact to emerge until the arrival of the Dientzenhofers towards the end of the 17C. The majority of 17C architects continued to be from the Como region, and were for the most part deeply conservative. Shortly after the Catholic victory at the Battle of the White Mountain, a former Lutheran church in Prague's Lesser Quarter was transformed into Our Lady of Victory, which was little more than a gloomy, impoverished version of the Mannerist Jesuit Church in Rome. During the same decade the Duke of Wallenstein commissioned for himself a building misleadingly referred to as Prague's 'first baroque palace', though it is actually a structure wholly in the spirit of the Florentine High Renaissance.

The two leading Como architects of the middle and late years of the century were Carlo Lurago (1615–84) and Francesco Caratti (?–1677/9), both of whom achieved their effects of splendour largely through the unsubtle means of repeating the same elements over enormously long façades, the masterpiece in this style being Caratti's façade of the Černín Palace in Prague (1679–88). The main architect to break the Comasque hegemony at this time was **Jean-Baptiste Mathey** (c 1630–c 1695), a Burgundian by birth who had trained in Rome not as an architect but as a painter. The elegance and low relief of much of the detailing of his work are very French, and at the Troja Château on the outskirts of Prague he broke away from the block-like or quadrangular Italian villa through the introduction of a French pavilion system and projecting wings. An admirer of Mathey was the outstanding Viennese architect **Johann Bernard Fischer von Erlach**, whose own work was none the less essentially Italian in inspiration. Though active mainly in Austria, he executed in this country two of his greatest works, the earliest being the Hall of Ancestors at Vranov (1683), a grand Bernini-inspired oval which brilliantly exploited a peculiarly dramatic cliff-top situation; the last of his Bohemian buildings was the Clam-Gallas Palace in Prague (1713), which reveals the influence of Palladio while at the same time accommodating statuary by the most dynamic of Bohemia's Baroque sculptors, Matthias Braun.

The major architects of the Bohemian Baroque were virtually all of foreign origin, and it seems possible that nationalist tensions within Bohemia led to difficulties being put in the way of indigenous Czech architects, whether Czech or German-speaking. Significantly, the greatest of these indigenous architects, Balthasar Neumann (who was born in 1687 in the Bohemian town of Cheb) worked entirely in Germany, while the foremost German architects active in Bohemia, **Christoph and Kilian Ignaz Dientzenhofer**, originated from Bavaria. Remarkably little is known about Christoph Dientzenhofer (1655–1722), other than that he settled in Prague at some time in the late 1670s, married there in 1685 and died there in 1722, at the age of 67; there is also a document of 1689 which refers to him as someone who 'understood his art very well ... despite an inability either to read or write'. It is not always easy to distinguish his works from those of his extraordinarily prolific son, Kilian Ignaz (1689–1751), but it is generally agreed that he was the more brilliant and innovative of the two. The two architects can at any rate claim together to have popularised in Bohemia a dynamic architectural style indebted to the work of both Francesco Borromini and, above all, Guarino Guarini, who himself had produced a design in 1692 for Prague's Theatine Church of Our Lady of Perpetual Succour. The hallmarks of the Dientzenhofer style include undulating façades and interiors, plans based on intersecting ovals, a rich play of convex and concave surfaces, piers that project diagonally into the nave, and Gothic-inspired cross-vaulting such as Guarini had advocated. The supreme expression of this style is the Church of St Nicholas in Prague's Lower Quarter (1703–55), the dominant landmark in this city after the castle, and as such a particularly eloquent assertion of resurgent Catholicism.

Though Guarini and in turn the Dientzenhofers had revived the use of a Gothic system of vaulting, it was left to Bohemia's most original Baroque architect, **Johann Santini-Aichel** (1677–1723), to devise a new style of church architecture which was later christened as 'Baroque Gothic'. This represented only one aspect of the work of Santini, who produced numerous churches in a wholly Baroque manner as well as a vast number of palaces, but it is the aspect by which he is best remembered today. Born in Prague in 1677, Santini was the crippled grandson of an immigrant mason from Como, whose family later added the name Aichel. As with Mathey, under whom his father had worked, Santini's training was as a painter, and he seems to have had no building to his credit when in 1702 he was chosen to replace the architect P.I. Bayer in the rebuilding of the Cistercian abbey church at Sedlec. Santini's adoption of a Gothic style for this and the later Bohemian monasteries that he was to rebuild can be linked to the same motifs which had led the Jesuits to create the cult of St Jan Nepomucký. Sedlec had been burned down by the Hussites, and by reconstructing it in a medieval manner Santini was looking back to a past as yet uncontaminated by Utraquism and later heresies. The brilliance of Santini's work at Sedlec lies above all in the vaulting, which was certainly inspired by that of Benedikt Ried at nearby Kutná Hora and combines the latter's elegance and complexity with Baroque dynamism. An even more remarkable interpretation of a late Gothic manner can be seen in Santini's reconstruction of the Benedictine abbey church at Kladruby (1712–16), a building which had been razed first by the Hussites and then during the Thirty Years War. In this building, dominated on the exterior by a crossing dome in the shape of the Bohemian crown, Baroque frescoes by the blend happily into a setting which features star-shaped vaulting of dazzling complexity, altars that burst into a forest of crocketed pinnacles, and, for the high altar, a pinnacled open-work frame supporting agitated Baroque marble statuary. No wonder that the abbot of the time remarked that the 'building was in a hitherto unseen Gothic style'. The bizarre climax of Santini's career, however, was reached not in this work but in a pilgrimage chapel which was commissioned from him by the abbot of Žďár in 1720, and intended to commemorate the miraculous rediscovery the year before of the tongue of St Jan Nepomucký in an undecayed state. Every detail of this extraordinary five-sided building is replete with symbolic significance: Nepomucký's tongue, the five stars that hovered above his dead body and his steadfastness in the confessional are everywhere referred to, the resulting structure being unlike any other building in Bohemia.

The great surge of building activity in Bohemia from the late 17C onwards was accompanied by a renascence of the local schools of painting and sculpture. Few artists of interest were active in the first half of the century, with the exception of **Karel Škréta** (1610–74) who, though not the genius that is often claimed by Czech art historians, was a painter of great energy and versatility, who led an intriguing early life. Born to a Protestant family in Záborice in 1610, he and his mother fled to Freiburg in Saxony in 1628. From there he went to Italy, and spent time in Venice and Bologna before completing an artistic training in Rome, where he met and did a portrait of the French painter Poussin in 1634. Whether out of genuine conviction or a longing to return to his native Bohemia, he converted to Catholicism shortly after leaving Italy, and eventually settled in Prague, becoming there a prolific painter of altarpieces. As a painter he owes nothing to Poussin, but embraces a whole spectrum of Italian Baroque artists from Caravaggio to Guercino and Annibale Carracci. His dark and dramatic canvases sometimes display an impressive realism, which is particularly evident in his portraits, of which the most famous is a lively and informal group portrait of the gem-cutter Dionisio Miseroni and his family. Two painters of a slightly later generation are Michael Willman (1630–1706) and the latter's stepson and pupil Jan Liška (c 1650–1712), the former working in a strongly Rubens-inspired manner, the latter evolving a loosely handled and vividly coloured style which is sometimes described as proto-Rococo.

The leading painter active in Bohemia at the beginning of the 18C was **Petr Brandl** (1686–1735), who, like the sculptor Matthias Braun, enjoyed the patronage of the eccentric and visionary Count Sporck. Brandl was an artist as varied in his style and subject-matter as Škréta, painting portraits in an heroic French manner one moment and the next dark religious canvases in which the paint is handled with an agitation reminiscent of the sculptural effects of Braun. A contemporary of Brandl was the portraitist **Jan Kupecký** (1667–1740), in many ways the greatest of all Bohemian painters, but who neither studied nor worked in his native country. An active member of the Moravian Bethren, he was born in Prague, but was forced to emigrate with his Protestant parents to Pezinok, in western Slovakia. When he was 15 he ran away from home to avoid being apprenticed to a weaver, and entered a painter's workshop in Vienna before going on to Italy. After suffering years of hardship he was finally able to establish a workshop in Rome and stayed there until 1729, when he accepted an invitation from Prince Adam von Liechtenstein to settle in Vienna. His friend the portraitist Johann Caspar Füssli (the father of the Swiss-born English painter Henry Fuseli) described Kupecký's portraits as combining 'the power of Rubens, the delicacy and spirituality of Van Dyck, the sombreness and magic of Rembrandt'. Another contemporary, Anton Graff, gave a better idea of Kupecký's pictures when he wrote that you found in them 'true nature, life itself'. The realism of his portraits is certainly remarkable and gave much inspiration to the Bohemian artists at the end of the century who were trying to get away from the pleasing but shallow Rococo manner of painters such as Norbert Grund (1717–60).

The great specialists in large-scale **decorative painting** in Europe were the Italians, but relatively few of these worked in Bohemia. At the end of the 17C two obscure Italians, Francesco and Giovanni Marchetti, were invited to decorate the Troja Château near Prague but suffered the humiliation of being replaced there by the Dutch artist Abraham Godyn, who covered its main hall with one of the most spectacular examples of Italian-inspired illusionistic painting to be seen in this country. One of the main Italian exponents of this heavily architectural style of decorative painting was Padre Pozzo, who moved in later life to Vienna, where he influenced a number of Bohemia's artists, for instance Johann Hiebel (1681–?) and the prolific V.V. Reiner (1689–1743). A more painterly and colourful style of ceiling painting was practised by the great Austrian decorators, all of whom were active at some stage in Bohemia and Moravia, including Johann Michal Rottmayr, Paul Troger and, above all, **Franz Anton Maulbertsch**, whose ceiling in the Philosophical Hall at Prague's Strahov Monastery (1796) is one of the culminating works of the Bohemian Baroque. Among the indigenous decorators to be influenced by the Austrians were Franz Xavier Karl Palko (1727–67) and Johann Lucas Kracker (1717–79), the latter being responsible for the masterly ceiling paintings in the Church of St Nicholas in Prague's Little Quarter.

Few countries in Europe have such a wealth of **public statuary** as Bohemia, and much of this was the creation of the Baroque period, when palace façades were embellished with struggling giants and atlantes, bridges such as Prague's remarkable Charles Bridge lined with gesticulating saints, and almost every town square in the country adorned with tapering piles of statuary that offered thanksgiving to the Virgin for protection during a plague. The earliest of the great Baroque sculptors working in Bohemia was **Johan Georg Bendl** (c 1620–80), who is sometimes thought of as the sculptural equivalent of Škréta, combining as he does Baroque drama with powerful realism; though intimate with the sculpture of the Roman Baroque, he seems to have been trained in his native South Germany, which perhaps explains his particular genius for limewood carving. All the other main sculptors of the Bohemian Baroque took part in the decoration of the Charles Bridge, including Jan Brokoff (1652–1718) and Matěj Václav Jäckel (1655–1738), both of whom were influenced by Bernini. Brokoff's son, **Ferdinand Maximilian Brokoff** (1688–1731), began his career collaborating with his father on the Charles Bridge, but soon surpassed him both in technique and imagination, evolving a heavy monumental style enlivened with vivid touches of realism.

Brokoff would have been without equal in Bohemia if his career had not coincided with that of **Matthias Bernard Braun** (1684–1738), one of the most brilliant sculptors of the European Baroque. Born in the Oetz Valley in North Tirol and trained probably in Italy, Braun came to Prague in about 1710. The *Vision of St Luitgard*, which he executed that year for the Charles Bridge, is a dynamic sculptural group of astonishing technical virtuosity, and so painterly in its approach to stone that you can well believe the tradition which ascribes its design to the painter Petr Bendl. In later years the agitated, almost hysterical energy of his art was to make the work of Bernini seem quite restrained in comparison. Fortunately he was to benefit from the enlightened patronage of Count Šporck, who gave him a freedom far greater than that enjoyed by most other sculptors of the day. Šporck's vision and Braun's genius came together at Šporck's country estate at Kuks to produce some of the most exciting sculpture to be seen anywhere in Europe, culminating in the works in the Bethlehem Wood, where, in the last years of his life, Braun carved biblical scenes directly onto great boulders scattered in the middle of a dark forest.

Braun had a large workshop, but his influence on the Bohemian sculptors of the late 18C was slight. The leading sculptor of this later generation was Ignác František Platzer (1717–87), whose art owes less to Braun than to the more Classical style of Austria's foremost 18C sculptor, Georg Raphael Donner (1693–1741). Donner deserves a brief mention in an account of the arts in Czechoslovakia, owing to his having spent much of the 1720s and 1730s in the Slovak capital of Bratislava. His main work there, a bronze group of *St Martin and the Beggar* (1733–35) is remarkable for showing the saint dressed as a Hungarian hussar, a feature which invests this heroic Baroque group with a character which looks ahead to the Romantic era.

The late 18C brought with it major changes in the structure of **patronage** in Bohemia. The expulsion by Maria Theresa of the Jesuits in 1775 and Joseph II's dissolution of most of the country's monasteries in the course of the 1780s greatly diminished the political and economic power of the Church. The country's artists and architects could thus no longer depend on what had once been their most stable source of income, and were forced to rely more on the nobility, who came to be based for much of the year in Vienna and would visit Bohemia principally for summer stays on their country estates.

From neo-Classicism to Art Nouveau

An elegant neo-Classicism of French derivation became the dominant architectural style in Bohemia and Slovakia from the 1770s onwards, to be followed after about 1800 by an '**Empire style**' inspired, not so much by France as its name would suggest, but by Viennese architects such as Georg Fischer. Bratislava was transformed in the late 18C into one of Central Europe's smartest and most fashionable towns, owing to the long periods in residence there of Maria Theresa and her court. In Bohemia, meanwhile, much of the building activity was centred on the many newly founded **spa towns**, which attracted a growing aristocratic clientele from all over Europe. Some of these, such as Mariánské Lázně (Marienbad) and Karlovy Vary (Carlsbad), were extensively rebuilt in the late 19C, but others—in particular Teplice and Františkovy Lázně(Franzensbad)—have remained to this day showpieces of neo-Classical and Empire architecture, filled with simple and elegant structures in pastel colours, with a predominance of the vivid yellow once evocatively known as *Kaisergelb* or 'imperial yellow'.

The greatest Bohemian patrons of this period were the Chotek family, one of whom, Rudolf, had become Austria's first Supreme Chancellor in 1760. Rudolf's son, Jan Rudolf, after having supervised the laying out of Prague's first boulevard, Na příkopě, commissioned in 1802 for his estate at Kačina one of the grandest of Bohemia's Empire-style houses. He also shared the passion of his father and other members of his family for gardens, and not only provided Prague with the large public park of Letná, but also created in his estates at Kačina and Veltrusy magnificent gardens in an English Romantic style. Romantic **gardens**, adorned with extraordinary follies ranging from minarets to fantastical Gothic chapels, indeed constitute one of Bohemia's greatest attractions from this period, other notable examples being at Krásný Dvůr, and Lednice.

A remarkable eclecticism characterises the architecture of Bohemia in the late 19C: some of its historical pastiches are wholly fantastical both in their scale and style, such as the Schwarzenbergs' country house at Hluboká, an Austrian-designed building said to be in an 'English Windsor' style but in fact more reminiscent of 'Mad King' Ludwig's Neuschwanstein in Bavaria. A virtual monopoly on the neo-Baroque was enjoyed by the Vienna-based architects Ferdinand Fellner (1847–1916) and Hermann Helmer, who produced monumental opera houses and theatres all over the Habsburg Empire, including at Karlovy Vary, Bratislava and Prague. Nationalist sentiments found a partial expression in the **neo-Gothic**, of which one of the principal Czech exponents was **Josef Mocker** (1835–99), Bohemia's answer to Eugène Emmanuel Viollet-le-duc, and a man known for his drastic restoration and rebuilding of many of this country's medieval monuments, including Karlštejn. The major buildings of this period associated with the nationalist revival were in a **neo-Renaissance style**, which was initiated in Bohemia by **Josef Zítek** (1832–1909). Zítek was trained in Vienna under the architects of the Vienna Opera House, E. van der Nüll and A. von Sicardsburg, and devoted much of his life to the building of Prague's National Theatre (1867–81); his style was perpetuated by his one-time collaborator Josef Schulz (1840–1917), who was the author of the city's equally grandiose, if rather less eloquent, National Museum (1881–83). A variant of the style was the neo-Czech Renaissance, which, at the turn of the century, brought back a fashion for stepped gables and sgraffito decorations.

Neither Bohemia nor Slovakia can boast Art Nouveau architects of the same calibre, say, as Hungary's Ödön Lechner or Austria's Otto Wagner, but there are numerous fanciful buildings in this style to be seen here, most notably Prague's Municipal House, which was built between 1903 and 1911 by Antonín Balšánek, Osvald Polívka and Josef Chochol. The later development of **Art Nouveau**, when decorative exuberance gave way to more rationalist tendencies, is represented in Bohemia principally by Jan Kotěra (1871–1923), a pupil of Otto Wagner and the Viennese Secessionists, whose works helped pave the way for the remarkable generation of pioneering architects active in Bohemia in the early 20C.

Nationalism and nineteenth-century Czech and Slovak art

The **nationalist revival** of the 19C in both Bohemia and Slovakia provided a great rallying point for painters and sculptors and gave them necessary encouragement at a time when the conditions for producing art here were generally unfavourable. The situation for Bohemia's artists at the end of the 18C could in fact hardly have been worse, thanks to a combination of the Church's diminished role as a patron and Prague's decline into a provincial backwater. Concern with the provincial nature of Prague's cultural life led finally in 1796 to a group of Bohemian nobles and rich Prague citizens founding The Society of Patriotic Friends in Art. To help compensate for the loss to Vienna of Prague's imperial collections, this society began amassing a collection of paintings and sculptures which would later form the basis of the Czech National Gallery. Of more immediate consequence to the city's art life was the foundation by the Society in 1796 of the **Prague Academy of Fine Arts**, an institution at which most of Bohemia's leading artists of the 19C were to receive their basic training.

The majority of Bohemia's painters in the early years of the 19C were highly conventional, including the academy's first director, Josef Bergler (1753–1829)—who painted stiff mythologies and Baroque-style portraits—and its first professor of landscape painting, Karel Postl (1769–1818), an artist in the Claude tradition. The portraitist Antonín Machek (1775–1844) delicately portrayed the leading figures associated with the nationalist revival, while the landscapist Antonín Mánes (1784–1843)—the father of a great dynasty of painters—is notable principally for his romantic landscapes of sites associated with Bohemia's past. A more remarkable painter than either of these was **Josef Navrátil** (1798–1865), who painted still-lifes of extraordinary freshness and realism that only came to light long after his death. But by far the most important painter of the first half of the century was Mánes's son, **Josef Mánes** (1820–71), an artist of great versatility, equally adept at portraiture, landscape painting, nudes, romantic historical works, and Classical allegories. His central position in Czech art is also due to his fascination with Slavic country-folk and close involvement with the nationalist revival. A tour around Silesia in 1846 first aroused his interest in traditional rural life, and this interest was further stimulated in the course of numerous stays after 1849 with the Silva Tarouca family on their estate in the Haná region, a region of Moravia known for its strong folk culture; in 1854 he undertook a long journey through Moravia, Slovakia and Silesia with the specific aim of recording folk costumes and traditions. He designed banners for patriotic organisations and, in the last years of his life, ensured his lasting popularity in Bohemia through his delightful scenes of the Czech and Slovak countryside for the astronomical clock on Prague's Old Town Square.

Vienna and Munich were the principal art centres to which Bohemian artists were attracted in the first half of the 19C. By the middle of the century, however, Paris had superseded these places in popularity, and a number of the leading artists of this generation spent a long period of their lives there, including the Courbet-inspired portraitist and still-life painter Karel Purkyně (1834–68), the landscapist and genre painter Soběslav Pinkas (1827–1901) and Viktor Barvitius (1834–1902), who abandoned an early career as a history painter to devote himself to the portrayal of urban life. The only painter of this period to gain an international reputation was **Jaroslav Čermák** (1830–78), who painted scenes from Czech history in a style indebted to French artists such as Eugène Delacroix and Eugène Fromentin; as well as spending many years in France, he travelled extensively around Dalmatia, and produced a large body of work documenting the struggle of the Montenegran people against Turkish domination.

From the 1870s onwards, the situation for artists wishing to work in Bohemia itself was greatly improved and, following a pattern widespread throughout Europe, many of the artists who had lived for a long time in France began returning to their home country. The ambitious buildings that were erected in Prague in the last years of the century, such as the National Theatre, involved the collaboration of virtually all the country's important artists, and indeed this whole generation is referred to today as the '**National Theatre Generation**'. Two of these painters, František Ženíšek (1849–1916) and Vojtěch Hynais (1854–1925), produced spirited interpretations of often ridiculous Classical subject-matter, involving numerous female nudes; another, Václav Brožík (1851–1901), after specialising in quiet landscape studies in France, made a name for himself in Bohemia with two large canvases representing *Master Jan Hus before the Council of Constance* and *The Election of George of Poděbrady as King of Bohemia* (1898). The major landscapists to have worked in the National Theatre were Julius Mařák (1832–99), famous for his romantic woodland scenes, and Antonín Chitussi (1847–91), who spent much of his early life working in and around the Fontainebleau forest near Paris, and later applied a Barbizon School manner to the depiction of his native Czech-Moravian Highlands. The central figure of this generation was **Mikoláš Aleš** (1852–1913), whose works can be paralleled with the historical novels of his contemporary Alois Jirásek. He endlessly depicted scenes from Bohemian history and folk-tales, and at the National Theatre collaborated with Ženíšek on a great patriotic cycle entitled *My Country* (now in Moravský Krumlov). Lively and very decorative, his style was ideally suited to book illustration and after 1882 he virtually abandoned oil painting to devote himself to graphic work, a move which may also have been connected with his constant financial difficulties.

Aleš today is little known outside the Czech Republic, in contrast to his contemporary **Alfons Mucha** (1860–1939), most of whose life was spent in Paris, where he gained enormous fame for his luxuriously flowing Art Nouveau posters, in particular a series of the 1890s featuring the actress Sarah Bernhardt. Though an essentially decorative artist he worked in fact in many different fields, and was sponsored by a Chicago industrialist and Slavophile, Charles Richard Crane, to paint a series of 20 enormous canvases entitled *Slav Epic*. An immensely wealthy and celebrated artist, he settled permanently in Czechoslovakia in 1922, taking up residence in a Renaissance palace in Prague's Little Quarter and continuing his varied career through such activities as designing stamps and banknotes.

To the end Mucha's art remained deeply rooted in the world of the turn of the century, as did that of the later artist **Max Švabinský** (1873–1962), another highly successful figure working in many fields, from oil painting to the design of stained-glass windows and mosaics. The strong Symbolist elements in Švabinský's paintings are also evident in those of J. Preisler (1872–1918), who executed decorative works reminiscent of those of Pierre Puvis de Chavannes and designed mosaics for a number of Art Nouveau buildings in Prague. The principal exponent in Bohemia of an Impressionist style of landscape painting was Antonín Slavíček (1870–1910), while Post-Impressionist tendencies can be seen in the work of **Jakub Schikaneder** (1855–1924), whose highly subtle paintings mark the transition between Czech art of the 19C and the experimental generation of the early years of the 20C. Schikaneder began his career painting peasant genre scenes in the tradition of the French painter Jules Bastien-Lepage, but ended it with haunting and almost abstract evocations of dusk scenes in Prague.

After a period of decline in the late 18C, **Bohemian sculpture** was to enjoy a gradual renewal in vitality during the following century which was to lead eventually to one of the livelier periods in its history. The Prague Academy of Fine Arts was not to have its own sculpture school until 1896, but a number of aspiring sculptors went there to study drawing from the Antique, including Václav Prachner (1784–1832), who evolved a robust Classicism. Romantic historical subjects were the speciality of the brothers Josef Max (1804–55) and Emanuel Max (1810–1901), artists of German origin who, while often portraying scenes from Czech history, did so in a stiff and linear manner which owes more to German rather than Czech sculptural traditions. A very sensual modelling, which was to be one of the main characteristics of later Czech sculpture, was shown instead in the early works of Václav Levý, whose bronze of the legendary Czech bard Lumír (1848) in the Klatovy Museum is sometimes regarded as one of the first eloquent manifestations in sculpture of Czech national consciousness. However, Levý was unable to compete successfully with the Max brothers in Prague and in 1854 settled in Rome, where he fell under the cold and sterile influence of the religious art of the Nazarenes.

The second half of the century was dominated by **Josef Václav Myslbek** (1848–1922), a sculptor whose richly worked bronzes were to be admired by Auguste Rodin. In Myslbek's work a romantic Slavonic fervour vied with a strong neo-Renaissance element, and in the course of the slow evolution of his Wenceslas Monument in Prague (1888–1923) a wild and romantic portrayal of the saint gave way to a statelier and more sober one. One of the greatest of Myslbek's pupils was **Stanislav Sucharda** (1866–1916), who displayed particular brilliance as a sculptor of Symbolist metal reliefs and was also responsible for one of the most exciting of Prague's monuments, the Palacký Monument (1898–1912), a work with a pictorial verve worthy of Matthias Braun. The other outstanding monument from turn-of-the-century Prague was the Hus Monument (1900–15) by **Ladislav Jan Šaloun** (1880–1946), one of the few sculptors of this period to have developed independent of Myslbek. This much-neglected and misunderstood work revealed a painterly approach to bronze which was anathema to Myslbek, who had instilled in his pupils a rigorous tectonic approach to sculpture and had encouraged them to avoid the more extreme forms of Art Nouveau. A comparably isolated artist who had rejected both Myslbek's training and principles was František Bílek (1872–1941), the author of elongated Art Nouveau works of great expressive power. The more mainstream Czech sculptors at the turn of the century were heavily influenced by Rodin, including two of Myslbek's more important later pupils, Josef Mařatka (1874–1937) and Bohumil Kafka (1878–1942). The former organised a major exhibition of Rodin's work in Prague in 1902, while the latter entered Rodin's studio in Paris in 1904; in later years Kafka was to devote himself to Romantic historical works, culminating in his statue of Jan Žižka on Prague's Žižkov Hill, which is claimed to be the largest statue in the world. Another of Myslbek's pupils was Jan Štursa (1880–1925), who achieved particular notoriety for his exceptionally sensual female nudes, executed in a great range of styles, from the Classical to the highly realistic.

In comparison to Bohemia and Moravia, the art of 19C Slovakia was relatively modest in quality and output. The awakening of Slovakian national consciousness at the beginning of the 19C, though encouraging a literary revival there, was slow to have any impact on the visual arts. The indigenous Slovakian artists who remained in their native region were of purely local significance, including the painter Jozef Czauczik (1780–1857), whose charmingly naïf landscapes and portraits are reminiscent of some of the early examples of the 19C American school. Scarcely more sophisticated are the portraits of Peter Michal Bohún (1822–79), who is sometimes regarded as one of the father figures of a native **Slovakian school** of painting, not least because of his involvement in the revolutionary activities of 1848–49. Right up to the end of the 19C the story of Slovakian art was to remain inseparable from that of Hungarian art, and several of the artists appropriated today by the Slovakians have equal claim to be considered as Hungarians. Such is the case with two of the finest painters of the turn of the century, **Baron Ladislav Medňanský** (1852–1919) and **Dominik Skutecký** (1849–1921). The former, after a training as an engineer, studied art in Munich and Paris and subsequently set up studios in Vienna and Budapest. A strange and restless man, who wrote his diary in a secret code and was fascinated by Oriental mysticism, Medňanský was the author of expressive and often anguished landscapes and figure studies, executed mainly in sombre tonalities and with hasty but suggestive brushstrokes. Skutecký, a slicker and more straightforward painter than Medňanský, had a cosmopolitan training but returned to his native Slovak town of Banská Bystrica in the 1880s and spent the rest of his life there, drawing his inspiration largely from local life, in particular scenes from the town's smithies. From about 1900 onwards the art life of Slovakia became increasingly integrated with that of Bohemia and the region's growing number of artists, including the group referred to as 'the Generation of 1909', veered more towards Prague than Budapest.

The twentieth century

The vital role which Czech and Slovak artists played in the art and architecture of the 20C has come to be recognised only recently, and is still not widely appreciated. The towering genius of the early years of the century was **František Kupka** (1871–1957), one of the pioneers of abstract painting in Europe, but someone whose work was grealy neglected in Czechoslovakia after the Second World War. After studying at the Prague Academy of Fine Arts, and later in Vienna, Kupka settled in Paris in 1895 and was thereafter to live mainly in

France. In his early years he painted a number of vividly coloured Symbolist canvases, but worked principally as a satirical artist and book illustrator. From the start he had been fascinated by spiritualism and the occult, and from this had grown an interest in the spiritual symbolism of colour. Soon he began experimenting with linear rhythms and colour schemes that attempted to approximate to the effects of music, and even started to call himself a 'colour symphonist'. Inspired by high-speed photography after 1909, he went on to portray effects of movement, and this was to lead in 1912 to the pure abstraction of *Amorpha: Fugue in Two Colours* (now in the new Museum of Modern Art in Prague), which created a sensation at the Salon d'Automne of that year. The lyrical abstraction of these years, which can be related closely to the work of Robert Delaunay and the Orphists, gave way in the 1920s to a more geometric abstract style. In 1923 he published in Prague an influential theoretical work entitled *Creation in Plastic Art* (*Tvoření v Umění výtvarném*), and in 1931 was one of the founder members of the French-based Abstraction-Création Group.

In the years immediately before the First World War, when Kupka had been engaged in his experiments in Paris, Prague had emerged as one of the main centres of the European avant-garde. The more modern tendencies in Czech art had been represented for many years by the **Mánes Association of Artists**, which had been founded in 1887 in opposition to the Prague Academy of Arts, and had organised several highly influential exhibitions in the early years of the 20C. One of these was an exhibition of the Norwegian artist Edvard Munch in 1905, which had been derided by both the public and critics alike and yet had been a decisive influence on the formation in 1907 of Czechoslovakia's first avant-garde group of artists, The Eight (Osma). Four years later members of the short-lived Eight group were to found the Association of Plastic Arts, the membership of which included all the painters, sculptors and architects who were to be associated with **Czech Cubism**. A knowledge of French Cubism among Czech artists was at first derived largely from visits to Paris, but an important part in its dissemination here was also played by the art historian and future director of the National Gallery, Vincenc Kramář, an avid collector of the works of Picasso and Braque. The main Cubist painters in Czechoslovakia were Vincenc Beneš (1893–1979), Josef Čapek (1887–1945), Emil Filla (1882–1963), Antonín Procházka (1882–1945), Václav Špála (1885–1946), and the appropriately named Bohumil Kubišta (1884–1918); most of these artists were to remain faithful to the principles of Cubism for the rest of their lives. Filla, the principal spokesman of this group, made two attempts at Cubist sculpture, but the leading artist in this style was **Otto Gutfreund** (1889–1927), perhaps the most outstanding Czech sculptor of the century. After evolving an idiosyncratic 'Analytical Cubist' manner by 1911, later in the decade Gutfreund moved closer to 'Synthetic Cubism' before abandoning Cubism altogether after 1920 and producing works in a style which came to be known as 'Objective Realism'. In these last years Gutfreund devoted himself to the realistic but dignified portrayal of the everyday world, which he represented with simple, stately forms, often making use of colour and terracotta; these works were to have an enormous influence on Czech sculptors of the 1920s, including Karel Dvořák (1893–1950), Jan Lauda (1898–1959), Karel Pokorný (1891–1962) and Bedřich Stefan (1892–1982).

A phenomenon unique to Czechoslovakia was the impact of Cubism on architecture. Believing that the ever more severe brick and concrete structures of the Secessionist architect Jan Kotěra had become far too rationalist, a group of architect members of the Association of Plastic Arts attempted to create a more self-consciously artistic architecture, using a simplified ornamental vocabulary comparable to the forms employed by Cubist painters such as Braque and Picasso. Pavel Janák (1882–1956) was the leader of this group, but some of the finest buildings in the style were those created between 1911 and 1914 by **Josef Chochol** (1880–1956) at the foot of Prague's Vyšehrad: the façades of these structures were covered in faceted diamond-shaped forms that owe a debt not only to Cubism but also to the diamond or 'cellular' vaulting of the Bohemian architects of the late Gothic period. Another of the Cubist architects was **Josef Gočár** (1880–1945), who was inspired instead by the ordering of Bohemian façades of the Empire period, and came to evolve in the 1920s an academic Cubist style made up of cylindrical forms, most notably in the former Legio Bank in Prague.

The optimism and excitement that followed the creation of the Republic of Czechoslovakia in 1918 led to a period of quite exceptional cultural vitality and experimentation. Thanks to its situation at the heart of Europe, Czechoslovakia became a meeting-point for all the conflicting cultural fashions of the time, and appropriated and transformed such influences as Constructivism and Productivism from Russia, Dadaism from Zürich and Berlin, Futurism from Italy, the Bauhaus from Weimar and Dessau, and Purism and Surrealism from Paris. The great focal point of the Czech avant-garde of this period was a left-wing group which was formed in Prague's Union Café in 1920, and given the mysterious name of **Devětsil**, which is both the name of an obscure flower and a composite of two words meaning 'nine' and 'forces', the forces in question probably being the nine Muses of Parnassus. It was a group which experimented with most of the 'isms' of the 1920s, and included progressive figures active in all cultural fields, from architecture and the fine arts to design, poetry, music, drama and film; honorary memberships were even given to Charlie Chaplin and Douglas Fairbanks, though it is unlikely that these two figures would have been aware of the honour. Its leader was the witty and charismatic **Karel Teige**, an experimental poet and collage artist, who believed in the integration of all the arts, and whose theoretical writings included an article on the work of art in the age of mechanical reproduction which anticipated by some ten years Walter Benjamin's famous essay on this subject. Teige's aesthetic was based essentially on the reconciliation of the opposing extremes of utilitarianism and lyrical subjectivity, a dichotomy which he described in terms of '**Constructivism and Poetism**': 'Constructivism', he wrote, 'is a method with rigorous rules, it is the art of usefulness. Poetism, its living accessory, is the atmosphere of life ... the art of pleasure.' The Marxist utopianism of Devětsil was not to survive the growing totalitarianism of the 1930s, but when the group finally folded, in 1931, it had managed to maintain its delicate unity longer than all the other European avant-gardes of the 1920s.

One of the principal ideals behind Czech avant-garde architecture of the interwar years was a belief in the beauty of the industrial age, and it is significant that several of the Devětsil architects, such as Jaromír Krejcar (1895–1949), were inspired by transatlantic steamers and other modern forms of transport, incorporating into their buildings such elements as portholes, the rounded windows of express trains, and terraces balustraded with railings as on a ship's deck: such conceits were typical of Devĕtsil, the geometry of the architecture being invested with a strong element of poetry, in this case derived from the glamorous associations of long-distance travel. However, with the rapid growth of Devĕtsil's architectural membership, the poetry of the buildings was made increasingly subservient to their utilitarian and purely abstract elements, Constructivism becoming replaced by an international **Functionalism** of a type promoted by Le Corbusier, Walter Gropius and Ludwig Mies van der Rohe: an important example of such a building was Prague's former Pensions Institute 1929–34, a gaunt concrete structure by Josef Havíček (1899–1961) and Karel Honzík (1900–60).

Outside Prague the main centre of Czech Functionalism was the Moravian capital of Brno, where **Modernist architecture** was promoted by the town's enlightened Jewish industrialists, and included Mies van der Rohe's pioneering Villa Tugendhat as well as numerous structures by Bohuslav Fuchs (1895–1972). Another Moravian industrialist, the visionary and megalomaniac shoe-manufacturer, Tomáš Bát̆a, sought the assistance of Le Corbusier in the creation at nearby Zlín of a revolutionary modern township for his workers, a task which eventually befell the local architect František L. Gahura (1891–1958).

An architect of these years whose work ran contrary to all the prevailing Modernist trends was **Josip Plečník** (1872–1957), a Slovenian architect who had been invited to Prague by Jan Kotĕra in 1911 to teach at the School of Decorative Arts. Later Plečník formed a close friendship with the President Tomáš Masaryk, who commissioned from him in the 1920s the restoration of Prague Castle. His interest in the architecture of the past, as well as in traditional craftsmanship and materials, has led him to be hailed in recent years as a precursor of Post-Modernism, though in reality his work was so idiosyncratic as to defy rigid categorisation. His Church of the Sacred Heart in Prague is certainly one of the more bizarre masterpieces of Czech architecture between the wars, taking elements from such diverse sources as an Early Christian basilica and an Egyptian temple, and treating them with a boldness which is thoroughly modern.

The artists of Devĕtsil, in common with the Dadaists, rejected the notion of high art, though in their case they expressed this disdain at first through taking an interest in popular culture, devoting themselves at the beginning of the 1920s to what they termed '**Poetic Naivism**'. Inspired by ex-votos and anonymous shop signs, but also by Henri Rousseau, the Czech Cubists, and the childlike figures in the paintings of the Czech artist Jan Zrzavý (1890–1977), several of the Devĕtsil members, such as the painter and art historian Adolf Hoffmeister (1902–73), created self-consciously naïf works. Soviet-style Constructivism had little impact on the painters of this generation, though it did influence one of the most original of the Devĕtsil sculptors, **Zdenĕk Pešánek** (1896–1965), who experimented with kinetic art and also made a number of works involving electric light. Constructivism was also an important force behind the works of the pioneering **photographers**, Jaroslav Rössler (1902–90) and Jaromír Funke (1896–1945), both of whom were technically adventurous and flirted with pure abstraction. Two other outstanding photographers of these years were František Drtikol (1883–1961) and the one-armed Josef Sudek (1896–1976), the former specialising in female nudes in disturbing, geometrical settings, the latter concentrating on the abstract qualities of everyday scenes and objects, and also creating some of the most evocative images ever produced of Prague. The Devětsil leader Karel Teige employed photographs in his spirited and mysterious collages, which he described as 'Pictorial Poems'.

The free rein given to the poetic impulse and to the subconscious in the work of Teige and other Devětsil members created effects of pure Surrealism, which was perhaps the lasting legacy of the Devětsil artists. Not surprisingly, when Devětsil eventually closed, many of its members went on to found the **Czech Group of Surrealists**. The French Surrealist, André Breton, described Prague as 'the magic metropolis of old Europe', and it was only fitting that this city should have become one of the main European centres of Surrealism between the wars. The Czech Surrealists included the sculptor Ladislav Zívr (1909–80), who devised a number of strange assemblages, and Zdeněk Rykr (1900–40), an artist remarkable above all for his delicate collages made out of thread, tissues and other ephemeral materials. Among the other Surrealists were the versatile Jindřich Štyrský (1899–1942), and the morphological painters Josef Šíma (1881–1971) and Toyen (1902–80). Another of the painters was Kamil Lhoták (1912–), who was to be one of the most interesting Czech artists active in the 1940s and 1950s, executing strange and sinister landscapes that beautifully evoked the uncertainty of the war years and their aftermath.

As a whole the art and architecture of Communist Czechoslovakia was unmemorable, and certainly cannot be compared in quality to the literature, theatre and cinema of those years. The revolutionary Functionalism of the 1920s and 1930s led under Socialism to the drabbest of housing schemes and civic buildings, while the visual arts of this period suffered from a lack both of imaginative patronage and of a true spirit of communal endeavour. Some of the finer examples of Socialist patronage are to be seen in Slovakia, a region which has never been a major centre of the avant-garde, but has produced in the 20C a number of charming and colourful painters of local life and landscape, most notably Ludovít Fulla (1902–80) and Martin Benka (1888–1971). The remarkable **Slovakian monuments** of the post-war period are the numerous war memorials scattered throughout the region, often occupying the most beautiful sites. Among the powerful if conservative sculptors who have collaborated on these structures are Július Bártfay (1888–1979), Frano Stefunko (1903–) and Rudolf Pribiš (1913–), all of whom were involved in the creation of the most imposing monument of them all, the Soviet memorial on top of Bratislava's Slavín Hill. This austere, Classical-inspired structure of soaring proportions is a very impressive if chilling expression of the totalitarian spirit.

Since the collapse of Communism, the legacy of monuments such as these, and of militarism generally, has led to numerous thoughtful commentaries from the present generation of Czech and Slovak artists. The Slovakian Stano Filko, banned under Communism, has emerged as one of the most important of these political artists, and is well known for the incorporation of military objects in his works. Wittier and more widely appealing is the Czech 'Situationist' artist **David Černý**, who achieved considerable notoriety in 1991 by painting the Soviet memorial tank in the Prague district of Smíchov a bright pink (which was, as he explained to journalists, the colour of an infant babe in arms, a symbol of innocence). More recently, Černý has placed a giant immobile metronome on top of the granite plinth in Prague that once supported a massive statue of Stalin. The novelist Bohumil Hrabal only regretted that the statue itself had not been around for Černý to have applied his pink paint to that as well: 'Can you imagine', he wrote, 'what a wondrous sight that would've been...? In one fell swoop this would've made Prague the world centre for pop art; a happening like this here in Prague would've set the crown on that American school initiated all those years ago by Allan Kaprow, Claes Oldenburg and the rest...'

Music

'The music claimed me there a long time', wrote the American traveller Bayard Taylor on a visit in 1846 to the exuberant Baroque Church of St Nicholas in the Little Quarter of Prague. Most visitors today to the Czech and Slovak Republics are likely to have a similar experience, and to find themselves transfixed by the sounds of classical music that seem to emanate from so many of these countries' churches and palaces. For this is a part of Europe that has not only given birth to an exceptional number of composers, but which has also enjoyed a reputation for its vibrant musical life since at least the late 18C, when the English musical historian Dr Burney came here and opined that 'Bohemia is the conservatory of Europe.'

Early Czech music and the Church

The early history of Czech music is centred around St Vitus's Cathedral in Prague, which is documented as acquiring a new organ as early as 1245, and as already extending its choral resources by 1250. With the flowering of the arts initiated by Charles IV in the following century, the cathedral choir came to possess up to 100 singers, and a richly varied tradition of liturgical music began gradually to develop. The course of Czech music would soon, however, be radically altered by the rise of the Hussite movement.

With their opposition to anything in religion that might detract from the primitive simplicity of early Christianity, the Hussites disapproved both of the 'decadent' art of polyphony and of the use in churches of organs and other instruments; they encouraged instead **congregational music** and the abandonment of Latin songs in favour of ones in Czech, a language previously forbidden in church music. In 1561, when the fashion for choral music was at its height, as many as 750 new Czech hymns were brought together in the *Samostatný Hymnal* by the future Bishop of the Hussite Church, Jan Blahoslav (d. 1561), who, three years earlier, had published the pioneering *Musica*, which was not only the first musical text-book in Czech, but also the first theoretical treatise of any description in this language. The powerful and often folk-influenced melodies of these songs—later a source of rich material for the 19C national school—would be perpetuated over the centuries by Bohemia's numerous **singing societies**, of which over 100 were still in existence near the end of the 18C, despite the ban after 1620 on all but Catholic ones. In few other countries were social singing societies to proliferate so early or to exist so long.

But the Hussite abolition of the Latin liturgy, and the partial and temporary ban on instrumental church music, had the additional effect in the early 16C of cutting off Bohemia from the innovatory developments of the Flemish school, whose impact was so enormous on the music of the European Renaissance. Bohemia had little contact with these developments until the reign of Rudolph II, who turned his court into a truly cosmopolitan centre by inviting to Prague such musical celebrities as the German Hans Leo Hassler (1564–1612), the

Italian Filippo di Monte (1521–1603) and the Slovenian-born Jacob Handl (1550–91), who, despite his place of birth, is sometimes regarded as Bohemia's first polyphonic composer of European standing. Though Rudolph's court orchestra (which numbered about 60 musicians) had little direct influence on Czech music generally, it seems to have served as a prototype to the many **domestic bands** that were established in the 17C and 18C in the châteaux and town houses of the Czech nobility.

Czech and Slovak music in the 18th century

The musicians employed by these aristocrats were usually liveried servants whose duties extended beyond music to hum-drum domestic activities, as was the case with František Václav Míča (1694–1744), who, while employed by Count Johann Adam Questenberg as valet at Jaroměřice, organised the other servants into an orchestra and composed in 1730 the first Czech opera—*The Origin of Jaroměřice*. The most famous employee of this kind was the Bohemian-born violinist and composer **Heinrich Biber** (1644–1704), who worked as a teenager in the orchestras founded by Prince-Bishop Karl von Liechtenstein-Castelcorno at Kroměříž and Olomouc. Biber was an extraordinarily original composer who retuned stringed instruments to produce unusual notes (an effect known as *scordatura*), and used these to great naturalistic effect in the evocation of battle scenes, or even—on one occasion—a gall bladder operation.

In 1670 Biber left Olomouc on a mission to collect violins from the Austrian town of Absam, and never returned to Bohemia. Most other, but by no means all, Czech and Slovak composers of the 17C and 18C followed Biber's example and spent the greater part of their careers working in German lands. Of those who stayed behind several made fascinating use of local folk motifs, one of them—the Bratislava-based Czech composer Jiří Družecký (1745–1819)—going even so far as to incorporate actual folk instruments in his *Parthia auf Bauerninstrumentem*. Edward Pascha (1714–72), a Moravian who worked in the Slovak Franciscan monasteries at Žilina and Prešov, was the author of a *Christmas Mass in F Major* that has a text in a curious mixture of Latin and Slovak, and a music which fuses classical elements and Slovak folk tunes. Better known today (at least in the Czech Republic) is the Czech composer **Jan Jakub Ryba** (1765–1815), whose delightful and unconventional *Christmas Mass* of 1796 is still regularly performed every Christmas Eve in churches throughout Bohemia and Moravia. This work, with its rich folk influences, is sometimes said to have paved the way for 19C nationalist composers such as Smetana.

In the meantime Czech and Slovak composers were making a considerable name for themselves throughout Europe. **Jan Dismas Zelenka** (1679–1745)—one of several distinguished composers to have studied at Prague's Clementinum (another was Christoph Gluck)—was employed for the last 35 years of his life as a musician at the Court of Dresden: the author of stunningly inventive works that made considerable demands on the instrumentalists (especially the wind-players), he acquired such a reputation at Dresden that he was invited in 1723 to compose music for the coronation in Prague of the Habsburg emperor Charles VI.

Two of the best known operatic composers largely active abroad were **Jiří Benda** (1722–95) and **Josef Mysliveček** (1737–81): the former—one of a large family of Bohemian musicians—worked in Berlin for 28 years as a Kappelmeister to the Duke of Gotha, pioneering during this period the dramatic use of the spoken word against a musical background (that is, 'melodrama', in the original meaning of this term); Mysliveček, meanwhile, settled in Italy aged 26 and wrote operas there that earned him the title of *Il divino Boemo*, or 'The divine Bohemian'.

A large number of Czech composers were inevitably drawn to Vienna, including the prolific Jan Křtitel Vaňhal (1739–1813)—the author of more than 100 symphonies and 90 masses—and Leopold Koželuh(1747–1818), who succeeded Mozart as chamber composer to the Viennese court. Slovakia's most famous 18C composer, the Bratislava-born and bred **Johann Nepomuk Hummel** (1778–1837) spent important periods in Vienna in the course of his itinerant career, and indeed studied there under both Mozart and Salieri. Mozart himself, a great admirer of Hummel, was particularly influenced by the family of Mannheim-based Bohemian musicians led by **Johann Stamitz** (1717–57), who was born as Jan Václav Stamic in the Czech town of Havlíčkův Brod. The symphonic compositions of Stamic and the 'Mannheim School', with their change in emphasis away from strictly observed counterpoint towards harmonic contrasting of attractive melodies, were fundamental to Mozart's musical development.

Mozart in Prague

Mozart's debt to Bohemian music would be amply repaid, for it was perhaps thanks above all to Mozart that the Czechs today are so famed internationally as a music-loving nation. Though Mozart went as a child to Bratislava, Olomouc and Brno, he did not have any real contact with Bohemia until as late as January 1787, when he came to Prague with his wife Costanza to attend the production of his **Marriage of Figaro**, a work that had been improperly understood in Vienna. His English biographer Edward Holmes, writing in 1845, said of this production that 'the success of Le Nozze di Figaro, so unsatisfactory at Vienna, was unexampled at Prague, where it amounted to absolute intoxication and frenzy.' All this proved understandably exhilarating to Mozart, whose rapturous response to the city and its people was evident in a letter he wrote describing to his Viennese friend Baron Gottfried von Jacquis his attendance at a ball where 'the cream of the beauties of Prague is wont to gather':

> '*You* ought to have been there my friend! I fancy I see you running, or rather, limping, after all those pretty girls and women! I neither danced nor flirted with any of them, the former because I'm too tired, and the latter arising from my natural bashfulness. I looked on, however, with the greatest pleasure while all these people flew about *in sheer delight* to the music of my 'Figaro' arranged for contredanses and German dances. For here they talk nothing but 'Figaro'. Nothing is played, sung or whistled but 'Figaro'. No opera is drawing like 'Figaro'. Nothing, nothing but 'Figaro'. Certainly a great honour for me!'

Shortly afterwards he composed, while still in the city, his **'Prague Symphony'**; and he returned here with Costanza later in the year to perform and compose his opera *Don Giovanni*, which he dedicated to the 'good people of Prague', who, it would seem, were equally taken by him. ('The people of Prague', wrote his contemporary biographer Niemetschek, 'were charmed by his affability of manner and unassuming behaviour.') On this second visit, in the autumn, he stayed at first at an inn called *The Three Lions* before moving on to the house of the Czech composer **František Xaver Dušek** and his wife Josepha (1753–1824), an accomplished singer. This house on the outskirts of Prague (it survives today as the Mozart Museum) proved almost an over-congenial setting for the composer, who found himself constantly distracted from his work by all the laughter, conversation and playing of bowls that took place in this most unusually warm of autumns. Finally, in the course of an animated party given here on the evening of 3 November, one of the guests is said to have reminded Mozart that the premiere of **Don Giovanni** was scheduled for the following night, and that the overture for this had still not been written. The story then goes that Mozart duly retired to his room at about midnight, ordered some punch and asked Costanza to try and keep him awake by talking. Though the overture was ready by the time the copyists came to collect it at seven in the morning, the copyists were not as quick as the composer had been, and the audience had to wait 45 minutes for the performance to start, at seven forty-five that evening. Whether this story is true or not, *Don Giovanni* was certainly composed at remarkable speed, and its overture must have been performed sight unseen.

'My opera Don Giovanni', recorded Mozart, 'was received with the greatest applause.' Some time later, Josef Haydn, replying to a letter sent to him by the director of the opera house, wrote that 'Prague ought to retain him, and reward him well too; else the history of great genius is melancholy, and offers posterity but slight encouragement to exertion ... I feel indignant that this *unique* Mozart is not yet engaged at some royal or imperial court.'

Mozart came back to Prague in August 1791, alone and in such poor health that he was observed continually taking medicine. Commissioned to compose an opera to accompany the coronation in the city of the Emperor Leopold, he had begun this work—**La Clemenza di Tito**—in the carriage in which he travelled, and completed it in Prague 18 days later. He stayed again with the Dušeks, where he was side-tracked this time not so much by any activity organised by his hosts but by the billiards in a neighbouring coffee-house. Yet even when playing billiards, Mozart's creative mind was busily at work, and he kept on interrupting the game to take out a pocket book and scribble down notes while humming away: he later astonished everyone at the Dušek household by performing here soon afterwards the quintet from the first act of what would be his last work, *The Magic Flute*.

The Prague public, worn out by all the revelry that the emperor's coronation had entailed, did not respond to *La Clemenza di Tito* with the same enthusiasm that had been hoped for by the composer, who died in Vienna later in the year. An enormous affection for Mozart has none the less been maintained in Prague over the centuries, and he has now come to be treated here not only as an honorary Czech, but also as a person integral to the stereotypical image of the city—a status enormously enhanced by the filming here in 1984 of Miloš Forman's film, *Amadeus*.

Mozart's visits to Bohemia have been given so much emphasis that it is easy to forget the important stays here made by other leading European composers from the late 18C onwards. The spa towns of Teplice, Mariánské Lázně and Karlovy Vary were especially lively musical centres, and attracted such figures as Ludwig van Beethoven, Frédéric Chopin, Johannes Brahms and Richard Wagner (who began conceiving *Tannhäuser* while staying at Teplice in 1843). Prague too had a great appeal to composers of the **Romantic generation**, beginning with

Beethoven, who paid at least four visits to the city between 1796 and 1812. From 1813 to 1816 the German composer Carl Maria von Weber was musical director of the German Opera House that was founded here in 1807; and from 1840 onwards Franz Liszt became a regular visitor to the city, meeting up here with among others Hector Berlioz, Robert Schumann and a Czech composer who drew heavily on Liszt's work and that of Wagner to formulate a truly national Czech style—Bedřic Smetana (1824–84).

Smetana and Czech nationalism

The eldest son of a successful brewer from Litomyšl, Smetana grew us as a German speaker, and was never fully to master the Czech language despite a life-long dedication to the Czech nationalist cause. Whereas Liszt and Chopin were only able to flourish in Western Europe, Smetana found in his homeland a perfect environment for the nurturing of his talents: here he could follow closely the great revival of interest in Czech culture and history while being exposed to the latest developments in European music. After attending schools in Jindřichův Hradec, Jihlava, Prague and Plzeň, he settled in Prague, where he immediately revealed his political sympathies by composing in 1848 a work entitled *The March of the Prague Students' Legion*. In that same year he composed his piano work *Six Characteristic Pieces*, which he dedicated to Liszt, who became a friend and mentor, and indeed advised him in 1856 to move to Sweden, where many other Czechs had taken taken refuge in the wake of 1848.

It was after his return to a more liberal Bohemia in 1861 that Smetana composed the works that would soon turn him into a national figurehead. The country's new mood of optimism was epitomised by the inauguration in 1862 of a provisional Czech National Theatre for the performance of opera, ballet and plays. Encouraged by this, and swearing allegiance to the school of Wagner, Smetana set himself the task of creating a repertory of **Czech operas**, starting off with *The Brandenburgers in Bohemia*, which, though composed in 1863 was not performed until 1866, when he was appointed director of the National Theatre. Later in that same eventful year he produced here the even more successful *The Bartered Bride*, which remains to this day the most popular of Czech operas.

Smetana's national consciousness was expressed not only in his subject-matter but in his lofty and monumental compositions, which attempted to merge the achievements of European pioneers such as Wagner, Liszt and Schumann with a highly personal language derived from Czech folk music: in contrast to other 19C Romantics, he never quoted nor imitated folk melodies but tried to capture instead their essential spirit. A stirringly patriotic climax to his work was reached with his cycle of six 'symphonic poems' collectively known as **My Country** ('Má Vlast';1874–79). *Vltava* and *The Fields and Forests of Bohemia* celebrated the beauties of the Bohemian landscape, while *Tábor* and *Blaník* evoked two of the greatest periods in Bohemian history. The two remaining works of the cycle, *Vyšehrad* and *Šárka*, turned to the same legendary past that inspired his opera *Libuše*, the premiere of which in 1883 was chosen to open the magnificent neo-Renaissance structure constituting the new National Theatre. Remarkably this last decade of critical triumph for Smetana was marked by rapid physical and mental deterioration: made suddenly deaf as early as 1874, he died insane ten years later.

Antonín Dvořák

After Smetana's death, the role of inspirational figure to the new generation of Czech musicians was inherited by a composer 17 years his junior, and with a notably different background and character—Antonín Dvořák (1841–1904). Born in the village of Nelahozeves, just to the north of Prague, he was the son of the village butcher and publican, and began his career as a butcher boy. Lacking the education and resources of the young Smetana, he gained his interest in music entirely through his zither-playing father, who conducted the village band. After becoming a violin-player in this band from the age of nine, Dvořák went to Prague when he was 16, and became a pupil of the organ school attached to the Bohemian Church Music Society. So poor that he had to keep himself by playing the viola in cafés and the organ in a mental home, he was even unable to afford to go to concerts ('As for Mozart and Beethoven', he later reminisced, 'I only just knew that they existed.'). In 1862, when he was 21, he was accepted as viola player in the provisonal National Theatre orchestra conducted by Smetana, and in 1875 he was awarded a grant for impecunious musicians by an Austrian government committee that included Brahms, who became thereafter a keen promoter of his music.

Dvořák's roots in Czech peasant culture, and his lack of early exposure to classical music, gave him far greater credentials than Smetana as a musician closely wedded to the Czech soil. And yet, ironically, his aims as a composer were more overtly international than those of Smetana, and the folkloric elements of his music more integrated still into compositions betraying strong influences from Beethoven, Schumann, Brahms, and, above all, Wagner. International success came with the publication in 1878 of his *Moravian Duets* and *Slavonic Dances*, the latter drawing on folk-dances from all the Slav countries but without ever borrowing actual tunes. Invited thereafter to England and the United States (where he held the post of artistic director of the New York conservatory between 1892 and 1895) he became known especially for his symphonic works. Though he even referred to his famous symphony in E minor, subtitled *From the New World*, as 'genuine Bohemian music', his symphonies at their best transcend personal and national sentiments to achieve a truly universal significance.

Working under the shadow of both Smetana and Dvořák, but likewise considered as one of the founders of Czech national music, was **Zdeněk Fibich** (1850–1900), who wrote Wagner-inspired operas and concert melodramas. Unlike his more famous Czech contemporaries, he took virtually no interest in folk music, and has since become virtually unknown outside the Czech Republic, where his works are still regularly performed.

Janáček's new musical language

Though barely four years younger than Fibich, the composer Leoš Janáček (1854–1928) was a late developer whose music belongs essentially to the 20C. Born in the North Moravian town of Hukvaldy, he became at the age of ten a choir-boy at the Augustinian monastery at Brno, where he was greatly influenced by the monk Pavel Křížkovský (1820–85), a Moravian composer of strongly nationalistic tendencies who was an ardent transcriber of folk-songs. Janáček went on to pursue his studies in Prague and Leipzig, but remained so attached to his native Moravia that he returned afterwards to Brno, where he stayed for the rest of his life.

Isolating himself in this way from Prague led to his being treated at first as a composer of essentially provincial importance; but it was also the avant-garde nature of his work that hindered its early appreciation. In addition to collecting and notating the folk-songs of Bohemia, Slovakia and Moravia, he embarked in the early 1890s on the far more unusual task of recording on paper the melodic and rhythmic characteristics not only of the spoken word but also the sounds made by animals and inanimate objects. Calling these musical descriptions of real sounds '**Speech Melodies**' or 'Melodic Curves', he later boldly announced that 'no-one can become an opera composer who has not studied living speech'. 'Speech Melodies' encouraged him to abandon verse for prose in his own operas, the most famous of which was written in 1903, just after the death of his daughter Olga, whose dying rattle he had naturally recorded. Known originally as 'Her Step-Daughter' (*Její pastorkyňa*), this was first performed in 1904 in Brno, where it was a complete failure. Not until 1916, when it was premièred in Prague under the catchier title of **Jenůfa**, was its greatness finally recognised and Janáček acknowledged as an avant-garde composer of the stature and originality of Claude Debussy, whose new musical language had much in common with his own independently created one.

Stimulated by this late success, the elderly Janáček went on to produce most of the other works for which he is best remembered today, including the operas *The Makropolous Affair* (1926), *The Cunning Little Vixen* (1923), and *The Journeys of Mister Brouček on the Moon in the 15th Century*, a proto-Surrealistic piece based on the tales of the 19C author Svatopluk Čech. Just one year before he died he wrote his most important choral work, the *Glagolithic Mass*, an exultant work of almost barbarous joy in which 'Melodic Curves' are combined with the old Slavonic rite.

Whereas Janáček managed eventually to achieve a reputation as both an avant-garde and a popular composer, the same was not true of the far more prolific **Bohuslav Martinů** (1890–1959), who, despite being the only other Czech composer this century of major international status, was heavily neglected during the Communist era, and is only now beginning to feature more regularly in the Czech classical repertory. The son of a Moravian bell-ringer, and indeed brought up in the village bell-tower of Polička, he was a largely self-taught composer much drawn in his mature music to the works of Debussy, Igor Stravinsky and Albert Roussel. Moving to France in 1923, where he came to be regarded as a leading light of the School of Paris, he was to spend almost all his remaining life away from Czechoslovakia, while continuing to write music that expressed both his yearnings for his homeland (most poignantly in his *Fifth Symphony* of 1946) and his deep attachment to its musical traditions (for instance, in his 1937 choral work *Kytice*, which has a text drawn from collections of Czech and Slovak folk songs).

The persistent influence of folk music on Czech classical composers in the 20C is also illustrated in the work of Martinů's contemporary Alois Haba (1893–1973), who was a professor of composition at the Prague conservatory from 1923 to 1953, and, like almost all the important Czechoslovakia-based musicians of the inter-war years, a member of the Přítomnost Society for Contemporary Music. Haba's main claim to fame is as one of this century's most convinced exponents of composing in semi-tones, quarter tones and sixth tones (**microtone music**). Interestingly, he was originally prompted to embark on his life-long study of 'micro-intervals' largely as a result of his encounter with the modified scales used by Czech and Slovak folk singers.

Jazz and dissent

A major new influence on Czech and Slovak music from the 1920s onwards was jazz, which soon developed into a national mania. One of the classical composers effected was **Erwín Schulhoff** (1894–1942), who, in addition to the challenge of composing an oratorio on the unpromising subject of *The Communist Manifesto* (1932), wrote a *Jazz Oratorio* and other jazz-related works. He was also a member of the Jazz Orchestra founded in 1936 at the celebrated avant-garde venue known as The Liberated Theatre (Osvobozené Divadlo), which was associated with the Devětsil actor-playwrights Jiří Voskovec and Jan Werich. The orchestra director was Jaroslav Ježek (1906–42), who wrote jazz music to accompany Voskovec's and Werich's absurdly satirical pieces.

The jazz-obsessed novelist Josef Škvorecký, in his books *The Bass Saxophone* (1980), *Talking Moscow Blues* (1989) and *Heading for the Blues* (1998), has beautifully recorded how jazz in Czechoslovakia was transformed from the Second World War onwards from a music of pure entertainment into a **music of protest**—'a sharp thorn in the sides of the power-hungry men, from Hitler to Brezhnev'. The Nazis, for reasons largely of misleading propaganda, allowed former Jewish members of the Jazz-Quintet Weiss to regroup at Terezín as ''. However, they generally considered jazz, with its African rhythms, as decadent music, as did their Communist successors, under whom musical life in Czechoslovakia reached its lowest point.

During the Stalinist era Czech composers were not allowed to stray far from an officially sanctioned Romantic style often incorporating folk music: the orthodox *Wallachian Symphony* (1952) by the previously experimental Hába is a typical example of this. A more liberal attitude to musical expression set in during the early 1960s, and a number of interesting classical composers emerged during the last three decades of Communist power, including the Slovaks Ilia Zelenka (1932–) and Vladimir Godár (1956–), the electronic specialist Mikoslav Kabeláč (1908–), and the jazz-inspired Alexej Fried (1922–).

But the role of music as a symbol of personal freedom was assumed principally by **popular music**, which acquired in the 1960s and '80s some of the same emotive, epoch-making qualities that had characterised the works of Smetana and other nationalist composers of the 19C. The spirit of the Prague Spring of 1968 was epitomised in the mini-skirted figure of the singer Marta Kubišová, whose impromptu planting of a kiss on Dubček's lips was one of the images of her generation. And it was, of course, the censoring of a punk group unpromisingly named '' that led to the creation of Charter 77.

Literature and cinema

The recent elevation of a dramatist to the presidency of Czechoslovakia highlighted the vital role which literature has played in the history of the Czechs and Slovaks, a people for whom the search for a national cultural identity has gone hand in hand with the political struggle.

Chroniclers and preachers: from medieval times to the 18th century

One of the oldest written documents in the Czech language is the hymn 'Lord have mercy on us' (*Hospodine, pomiluj ny*), which is known to have been sung at the installation of Bishop Dietmar of Prague in 973, and has sometimes been attributed to SS Cyril and Methodius. The first major work of prose in Bohemia was, however, a Latin chronicle written by Cosmas of Prague (1045?–1125), 'the father of Bohemian history'. Probably of noble descent, he became first a canon and then a dean of the Chapter of Prague, though this did not stop him from marrying one Božetěcha at the age of 41. It was not until after Božetěcha's death in 1117, when he was already in his seventies, that Cosmas embarked on his **Chronica Boëmorum**, a record of Bohemian history from the earliest times up to his own day, written with immense learning but also with objectivity and wit; its success is attested by the numerous manuscript copies in existence. Nearly two centuries later a rather more fanciful version of this history was given by an obscure nobleman from northern Bohemia called Dalimil (c 1312), who wrote not only in verse but also in Czech, thus earning for himself the distinction of being Bohemia's earliest known poet.

The first important body of Czech prose took a more serious form than Dalimil's chronicle and comprised the theological works of the famous **reformist preachers** active in Bohemia from the late 14C onwards, including Milíč of Kroměříž (1330?–74), Tomáš of Štítný (1330/1–1401) and Matěj of Janov. The adoption of Czech rather than Latin, the normal language of the clergy, was part of their reform programme and at least one of them, Tomáš of Štítný—the author, among other works, of a moralising tract entitled *Of Virgins, Of Widows, and Of Married People*—was heavily criticised for doing so. These thinkers prepared the ground for Jan Hus (1371?–1415), whose literary achievement rests both on his sermons and on a series of letters written mainly in captivity at Constance, and addressed, modestly, 'To the whole Bohemian nation': thus was initiated a Czech tradition of **prison writing** which was to be perpetuated in recent years by Václav Havel in his *Letters to Olga* (1983). One of the more interesting thinkers in the wake of Hus was Petr Chelčický (c 1390–c 1460), a pacifist whose writings were to be much admired by Tolstoy. A man of modest background who knew no Latin, Chelčický wrote in a direct and colourful style which was to have a great influence on the future development of Czech prose.

From the time of Jan Hus right up to the outbreak of the Thirty Years War in 1620, literature flourished in Bohemia, at least in terms of quantity, and received particular encouragement from the late 15C onwards with the spread of the **humanist movement** and the growing strength of the Bohemian Brethren. One of the main humanist poets of the 16C was Šimon Lomnický (1552–1623?), a man of little religious or political idealism, but a self-confessed 'lover of sweet venus', who brought sexuality into a number of his works, including the unpromisingly titled *Advice to a Landowner*, the best known of his longer poems. A great opportunist, he made a living writing poems flattering the nobility, and was so successful in this that he was even awarded a noble title himself by Rudolph II. Later he welcomed in verse the brief accession to the throne of the Protestant Frederick of the Palatinate, and saved his neck afterwards by writing a poem praising the execution in 1621 of the Protestant nobility who had taken part in the Battle of the White Mountain.

Among Lomnický's contemporaries were two writers of spirited **travel accounts**, Václav Vratislav of Mitrovic (1576–1635) and Krištof Harant (1564–1621). The former, a Catholic, was sent at the age of 15 on a mission to the Turkish Sultan in Constantinople, and was subsequently imprisoned by the Turks and forced to serve for four years on the galleys; he published an account of his experiences on his return to Bohemia in 1599. Krištof Harant, Lord of Polžice and Bezdružice, spent several years working as a diplomat for Rudolph II before deciding in 1598, after the death of his first wife, to fulfil his desire to see the Holy Land. Accompanied by his friend Heřman Černín and only one servant, he set off from Plzeň to the Holy Land by way of Venice, and later moved on to Egypt. His account of his journey, published in Bohemia in 1608, is long-winded and excessively learned in parts, but is filled with vivid descriptions of landscapes and of the people he met. After surviving all the many dangers which he relates in this work, Harant ended up as one of the Protestant nobles executed on Prague's Old Town Square in 1621. He himself seems to have been aware of this irony, for he is reputed to have said on the way to his death: 'Oh my dear God, through how many lands have I travelled, how many dangers have I encountered, for how many days have I not seen bread; once I have been buried in the sands. From all these perils God has rescued me, and now I must die guiltless in my own dear land.'

The writer who movingly recorded Harant's last moments was the greatest of the many historians active in Bohemia at this time, **Pavel Skála** of Zhoř (1583–c 1640), a man whom Palacký was to describe as 'not only the most voluminous but also the most valuable historian of Bohemia'. Educated at the Protestant university of Wittenberg, Skála held a government office during the reign of Frederick of the Palatinate, and later joined Frederick in exile before settling in the Saxon town of Freiburg. His major work is the colossal *History of the Church* (preserved in ten enormous volumes of manuscript), which, despite its name, deals as much with political as ecclesiastical history; of especial interest is his lively and exceedingly graphic account of Bohemian history from the Defenestration of 1618 up to the tragic aftermath of the Battle of the White Mountain.

The most famous and influential of this generation of Bohemian exiles was **Jan Ámos Komenský** (1592–1670), who is better known under his Latinised name of Comenius. Born in Moravia, he was educated at the Universities of Herborn and Heidelberg, and in 1616 was ordained a priest of the Bohemian Brethren. In the year following the Battle of the White Mountain his house and library in the northern Moravian town of Fulnek were burned down by Catholics, and he led an increasingly precarious existence before finally deciding to leave his native country in 1628. The rest of his life was spent travelling around Europe, staying for long periods in both London and Amsterdam, and gaining an international reputation for his revolutionary theories of education. His main literary achievement, however, is not well known outside the Czech Republic, and indeed was not translated into English until as late as 1901. This, *The Labyrinth of the World and the Paradise of the Heart* (1631), is an account of the author's pilgrimage through a city symbolising contemporary society. Everyone whom he encounters in his journey only convinces him of the vanity and futility of human endeavour, and in the end he turns to Christ as the sole haven of security in the universe. The ravages of the Thirty Years War undoubtedly prompted Comenius in these reflections, and in one passage of the book he gives a harrowing description of a meeting with fighting soldiers: 'Then suddenly the drums beat, the trumpet resounds, noisy cries arise. Then, behold, all rise up, seize daggers, cutlasses, bayonets, or whatever they have, and strike unmercifully at one another till the blood spurts out. They hack and hew at one another worse than the most savage animals.'

Czech, Panslavism and the national revival

The **Czech language** continued to be widely spoken in Bohemia after the Thirty Years War, and when Peter the Great came here in 1697, he was able to speak to the Bohemian nobility in his own language, which was so close to theirs. However, the massive book-burning campaign which the Jesuits had initiated as part of their reprisals against the Protestants had devastating effects on the development of a native literary language, and, after the death of Comenius, there was virtually no one writing in Czech. The beginnings of a revival in the literary language only took place at the end of the 18C, during the reign of Joseph II, who, though excluding Czech from all schools and institutions, allowed books and even a newspaper in Czech to be issued as an expression of his Enlightenment views. A key role in the rehabilitation of Czech culture was played by **Josef Dobrovský** (1753–1829), who both codified the modern literary language and reappraised Czech literature of earlier periods. He wrote exclusively in German and Latin, and was apparently only interested in Czech for academic rather than nationalistic reasons. In contrast, his younger contemporaries who were associated with the Czech 'national revival' studied the literature of their forebears with patriotic fervour, and many of them became actively involved in nationalist politics. One of these figures was the author and philologist **Josef Jungmann** (1773–1847), who brought out a Czech–German dictionary between 1835 and 1839, and translated numerous books into Czech, including Chateaubriand's *Atala* in 1805 and Milton's *Paradise Lost* in 1811.

The other protagonists of this pioneering generation included two Slovaks writing in Czech, **Ján Kollár** (1793–1852) and Pavel Josef Šafařík (1795–1861). The former, a close friend of Jungmann and the prominent Panslavist of his time, was the author of a cycle of sonnets entitled *Daughter of Sláva*, which was first published in 1824 and increasingly enlarged in subsequent editions. These poems, which bring together a wide range of themes, from the erotic to the patriotic, feature such stirring lines as 'Slavia, Slavia! Thou name of sweet sound but of bitter memory; hundred times divided and destroyed, but yet more honoured than ever.' Šafařík was a philologist and archaeologist, who published several learned works on early Slavic history, in one of which he collaborated with the historian **František Palacký** (1798–1876). Palacký became the leading force behind the 'national revival', first as a writer and editor of the important *Journal of the Bohemian Museum*, and then as the Chairman of the Slavonic Congress in Prague in 1848. Between 1836 and 1867 he published the major work of his career, a nine-volume history of Bohemia, which, though only covering the period from 1526 onwards, has had an enormous influence on his compatriots, both through its stress on the liberating role of the Hussite movement, and its conception of Czech history as one of 'contact and conflict' with the Germans.

A consequence of the enormous interest in Czech history and culture which had been generated by Dobrovský and his learned followers was the creation of a **literary hoax** comparable to the contemporary Ossian forgeries by James

Macpherson. The main perpetrator was the future librarian of the National Museum, Václav Hanka (1791–1861), who in 1817 'discovered' a manuscript which was claimed to be the work of a Czech Homer active at the very dawn of Bohemia's history. Hanka was himself a poet, but the works published under his own name had none of the impact of his forgeries, which were translated into many languages and became models for those writers who were beginning to revive Bohemia's literary tradition; they were not to be exposed until the 1880s. A scholar and poet of more honest leanings than Hanka was Karel Jaromír Erben (1811–70), the son of a farmer who graduated in law and philosophy to become archivist of the city of Prague. Erben was primarily important for promoting an interest in Czech folk-songs and Slavonic folk-tales, which he avidly studied and collected; the influence of such works is very evident in his own poems. Karel Hynek Mácha (1810–36), though relatively little appreciated during his own life and sometimes dismissed as a Czech imitator of Byron, was the author of the one truly outstanding Czech poem of the first half of the 19C, *May*. This lyrico-epic work, full of Romantic pessimism and metaphysical anguish, was to make Mácha so popular with later generations of Czechs that when the Germans took over the Sudetenland in 1938 the Czechs were successfully to apply for permission to have his corpse exhumed from there and brought in ceremony to Prague.

Czech drama was to have little encouragement until the opening of the city theatre in Prague in 1859, but the first half of the century saw none the less the emergence of the influential Czech dramatist and theatre director Josef Kajetán Tyl (1808–56), one of whose plays contained the song which would later be adapted as the Czech national anthem, 'Where is my home?' (*Kde domov muj?*).

Czech novelists of the 19th century

One of the earliest Czech novelists was **Božena Němcová** (1820–62), who was also the first eminent Czech woman writer. She was born in Vienna in 1820 to parents who worked in the domestic service of the Duchess of Zaháň, the owner of a large estate near Náchod in North Bohemia; a significant and memorably happy part of Božena's childhood would be spent with her peasant grandmother at Ratibořice, a hamlet on the edge of the Duchess's estate. Forced by her father into a marriage with a much older customs officer, she and her husband lived at first in Kostelec and then at Domažlice, where she contracted consumption in 1845. After further changes of abode, her husband was forced to retire in 1853 as a punishment for having allegedly taken part in the political activities of 1848–49. They settled subsequently in Prague, where she tried ineffectively to scrape a living through writing. A respite from poverty seemed to be offered in 1861, when a publisher from Litomyšl invited her to come to his town, where she was promised 12 florints for every three pages of manuscript, as well as free lodging. After she had moved on her own to Litomyšl, however, she did not receive the agreed fees, and was to find furthermore that the publisher had ordered the hotel-keeper not to provide her with any food. Making do with bread and water before receiving financial assistance from her husband, she soon returned to Prague, where she was to die shortly afterwards, destroyed physically and emotionally. She published numerous folk- and fairy-tales but is best remembered for her autobiographical novel, *Grandmother* (1855), which is essentially a portrait of the village where she had spent the happiest days of her childhood, and features characters based on her grandmother, on her childhood self (under the name of Barunka) and on the Duchess of Zaháň, who is referred to as 'the countess'. This book, combining a romantic vision of country life with realistic observation, was to have such an international reputation after the author's death that 'The Ladies of the American Club' in Prague were even to erect a monument to Němcová over her grave in the Vyšehrad. Though largely forgotten today outside the Czech Republic, she continues to inspire here a reverence which is reserved for few other writers.

Jan Neruda (1834–91), one of the greatest Czech writers of the late 19C, enjoyed much more recognition than Němcová in his lifetime, but suffered a very sad personal life, remaining a bachelor after experiencing several emotional disappointments. The son of a tobacconist and a charwoman, he lived all his life in Prague, and was brought up among the city's poor. After graduating at university, he worked as a teacher before joining the staff of the foremost Czech newspaper, *Národní listy*, where he was to be employed as a writer and editor up to the time of his death. His literary achievement is one of great variety, and includes poetry which ranges from intimate lyrics of a reflective and analytical kind to the visions of an ardent nationalist. He was also an outstanding writer of short stories, basing his tales on a realistic portrayal of contemporary society, for instance in his *Tales of the Little Quarter* (1878), which describe the area of Prague where he lived. The remarkable concision and ironic humour of these stories is a reflection of his work as a journalist, in which the limitations both of Austrian censorship and of having to write to the length of a *feuilleton* compelled him to rely heavily on satire, aphorism and allusion. Many other Czech writers, right up to the present day, have also worked as journalists, and have likewise developed a concisely ironic style as a way of exploiting restrictions both in length and freedom. One such writer was Neruda's immediate precursor, Karel Havlíček Borovský (1821–56), who had founded in 1848 the Czech newspaper *Národní noviny* and, after a spell in prison for his Panslavist views, had died young of tuberculosis. His most original work was *The Conversion of St Vladimir* (which was unfinished and only published in 1874), a brilliant satire on the two institutions that he most hated, the absolutist regime and the established Church.

A very popular satirist of Neruda's generation was Svatopluk Čech (1846–1908), whose most famous creation was a man called Matěj Brouček, who, under the influence of the beer served in the Vikárka ale-house in Prague Castle, undertook fantastical exploits, including journeys to the moon and back to the 15C. Yet Čech was also a poet who wrote such Romantic and nationalist works as his long allegorical poems *Evropa* (1878) and *Slávie* (1884). Two other neo-Romantic writers of this period were Julius Zeyer (1841–1901) and Alois Jirásek (1851–1930). The former, a poet, novelist and dramatist of Jewish and French German origins, was a writer of a very cosmopolitan outlook, and yet in many of his works he gave a glamorous treatment to Bohemia's history and legends, for instance in his celebrated epic cycle, *Vyšehrad* (1880). Jirásek, a history teacher by profession, took up the writing of historical novels at a time when the genre was in decline, and wrote works inspired by Bohemia's glorious past—in particular the Hussite period—which were to win him a wide readership and have great political influence.

Tomáš Garrigue Masaryk (1850–1937), the most important political and philosophical writer of his day, rose from being the son of a former serf to become Professor of Philosophy at Prague University and eventually first president of the

Czechoslovak Republic. His philosophy was one of rationalist humanism, and two of his greatest heroes were Comenius and František Palacký. Another of his mentors was the journalist Havlíček Borouský, whom he admired for having rejected the uncritical idealisation of the past which had characterised many of the writers of the Romantic era. Sentimental nationalism was falling out of favour generally with the Czech writers who came to fruition at the turn of the century, many of whom were signatories of a manifesto declaring in 1895 that 'Gloomy auspices have presided at the growth of the present generation. Suffocated by empty phrases, nauseated by Slavic mottoes and patriotic anthems, we have opened our eyes. With scepticism we have looked upon our fathers. A sorry sight.'

One of the most original of this rebellious, **Decadent generation** was the poet Karel Hlaváček (1874–98), who died young of tuberculosis and was the author of the gloomy epic, *Song of Vengeance* (1898), an ironic tale of revolt set in 16C Holland and written with a precise, musical style which was to have a great influence on later Czech poetry. The reclusive school-teacher Otakar Březina (1868–1929) turned for inspiration for his metaphysical dream world to the work of Charles Baudelaire, Indian sacred writings and the Christian mystics, while Josef Svatopluk Machar (1864–1942) expressed his abhorrence of contemporary society through the taking up of themes from Classical antiquity. An almost violent streak of hatred runs through the poetry of Petr Bezruč (1857–1958), who in several of his works posed as a rough and ugly miner speaking on behalf of the oppressed 70,000 Czechs from his native Silesia. Stanislav Kostka Neumann (1875–1947), a rebel from an old Prague family, was to graduate from Decadence and anarchy to naturalism and Marxism.

The emergence of a Slovak literature

Whereas in Bohemia by 1900 a remarkable body of literature had evolved in a relatively short period of time, in Slovakia literature was still in its infancy. A written Slovak language had barely existed before the 19C, and right up to 1918 was to be used largely by doctors and the judiciary. The first person to codify a Slovak literary language was the philologist Anton Bernolák (1762–1813), whose *Grammatica slavica* of 1790 was based on the dialects of western Slovakia. A number of writers employed this language in the early 19C—such as the poet Ján Hollý—but it was to be superseded after 1846 by a Slovak language which had been constructed from the dialects of central Slovakia. The leading personality in the development of this new literary language was **Ľudovít Štúr** (1815–56), who was not only a philologist but also a poet and statesman who was untiring in his efforts to publicise his creation, despite much opposition on the grounds that it would endanger the common political struggle of Bohemia and Slovakia. Two of the earliest important poets to write in the new language were Andrej Sládkovič (1820–72) and Janko Kráľ (1822–76). The former was the author of the lyrical, Pushkin-inspired epic *Marína*, while the latter, a political radical, wrote ballads and lyrics that express Panslavonic enthusiasm in a style which echoes popular verse; mention should also be made of Ján Botto (1829–81), whose main achievement was a Romantic lyrical epic of 1862 based on the gruesome death of one of Slovakia's most popular heroes, Juraj Jánošík, the Slovak Robin Hood.

A prolific and sophisticated writer who did much to raise Slovak literature from its provincialism was Pavol Országh (1849–1921), a professional lawyer who wrote poetry and drama under the name of Hviezdoslav; one of the main advocates of Czech–Slovak co-operation, he produced work marked both by patriotism and the principles of his Evangelical faith. The founder of the Slovak novel was **Svetozár Hurban Vajanský** (1847–1916), a great fighter for Slovak rights who was imprisoned several times by the Austrian authorities; he idealised contemporary Slovak life in his novels, and urged the Slovaks to turn towards Russia rather than the decadent West. Martin Kukučín (1860–1928), another novelist, spent most of his adulthood as an emigré doctor in Chile and Dalmatia, but continued to draw inspiration for many of his works from Slovak village life.

The early 20th century

One of the greatest poets to have written in the German language in the 20C, Rainer Maria Rilke, was born in Prague and spent here an important part of his youth, though he has as much claim to be regarded as Czech as have Sigmund Freud or Gustav Mahler, both of whom also came from what is now the Czech Republic. However, a different case is presented by a remarkable group of German-speaking Jewish writers who were central to Prague's literary life in the early years of the 20C, and without whom any account of literature in Bohemia would be incomplete. Indeed the best known writer of this group, **Franz Kafka** (1883–1924), has become in the eyes of most foreigners one of the most significant of all 'Czech' writers.

The depressing facts of Kafka's life are well known, and lend themselves only too easily to Freudian interpretation. The only son (he had three sisters) of a dominating self-made businessman, Kafka developed a life-long obsession with his parents which was reflected both in his writings and in his inability to marry, despite several engagements. Trained unwillingly in the law, he worked at first for the Prague branch of the Trieste-based Assicurazioni Generali, from which he resigned in 1908 on the grounds of 'nervousness and cardiac excitability'. From 1908 he was based at a fifth-floor office in the Workers' Accident Insurance Institute, but from 1917 spent an increasing amount of time in sanatoria. In 1922 Kafka was forced by ill health finally to leave his job, and died of tuberculosis two years later.

An obsessive diarist, and a prolific writer of letters, above all to his father and to Felice Bauer, a fiancée, and Milena Jesenská, his mistress, Kafka unflinchingly analysed in these writings his every mood, action and physical sensation, and was equally honest in his ever-changing assessment of his family and friends. The rest of his literary output, however, was relatively small, and all that he published in his lifetime was a number of short stories that can easily be contained in a single, modestly sized volume; as for his three novels, *America*, *The Trial* and *The Castle*, these were not completed to his satisfaction and were only to be published after his death. Kafka was a stylistic perfectionist, but it would seem that his talent was best-suited to the short story, for as that other master of concision, Jorge Luis Borges, has perceptively noted, Kafka was primarily interested in atmosphere, and not in the convolutions of story or in creating a psychological portrait of the hero. The meaning of his works has been the subject of much dreary analysis, but some idea of the general character of his fiction is given by the word 'Kafkaesque', which is used today mainly by people who have never read anything by him. The innocent individual caught up inexplicably in a nightmarish situation which is beyond his power to control recurs again and again in his work, as in his story *Metamorphosis*, which has one of the most memorable of his opening lines: 'Gregor Samsa woke from uneasy dreams one morning to find himself changed into a giant bug.' The claustrophobia of his family life deeply affected his perception of the world, as did the labyrinthine bureaucracy of the Austrian Empire, of which he had close experience as an insurance clerk. A Czech edition of *The Castle* did not appear until 1938, and had little success; perhaps the book's impact would have been far greater had it been brought out during the Stalinist years, the terrors of which it seems to prophesy. As it happens, all Kafka's works were banned in Czechoslovakia for much of the period of Communist rule.

One of the main meeting-places for Kafka's literary circle in Prague was the **Café Arco**, which reached the height of its popularity just before the First World War. Its leading associates called themselves the 'Arconauts', and represented for the Viennese writer Kaul Kraus a Jewish cabal besmirching the purity of the German language. Kraus named these associates in his untranslatable line describing the café: '*Es werfelt und brodet und kafkat und kischt.*' Franz Werfel (1890–1945) began his literary career writing Symbolist dramas of ideas and lyrical Expressionist poetry, but progressed to historical and political realism, both in drama and fiction; he escaped on foot to Spain in 1940 and died five years later in Beverly Hills, California. Max Brod (1884–1968), who emigrated in 1939 to Tel Aviv, was a novelist and critic, but is best known as an editor and biographer of Kafka, to whom he was deeply devoted. Kafka for his part came to the conclusion that Brod had little understanding of him, but none the less entrusted him with the job of being his literary executor, a job which entailed as its main duty the destruction of all his unpublished manuscripts: Brod had sufficient understanding of Kafka not to fulfil this duty, realising that anyone who genuinely wished his works to be destroyed would not hand them over to a devotee. Egon Erwin Kisch (1885–1948) was in many ways the most 'Czech' of these German writers, working all his life as a journalist, and wittily commenting on lesser aspects of Prague life, as in his *Tales from Prague's Streets and Nights*.

A highly individual German novelist in Prague who separated himself from Kafka's circle was Hermann Ungar (1893–1929), a Moravian-born Jew who worked after 1921 as a commercial attaché at the Czechoslovak Embassy in Berlin; hypochondria forced him eventually to leave his job, but he died shortly afterwards in Prague of acute appendicitis. His masterpiece is *The Mutilated* (1923), a novel about a mediocre bank clerk enslaved by a young widow; one of the work's great admirers was Thomas Mann, who thought that it revealed a 'deep understanding of vice, shame and misery'. Completely forgotten after his death, the works of Ungar are beginning again to attract attention, though they still await an English translator.

The German literary world in Prague was rigidly separated from the Czech one, and the Czech journalist Milena Jesenská infuriated many of her compatriots by her fascination with Kafka and his circle. A writer who belonged to neither of these worlds, and yet highlighted through his personality and writings the enormous differences between the Czech and German character, was **Jaroslav Hašek** (1883–1923). Certainly few greater contrasts can be imagined than that between Kafka and Hašek, both in terms of their lives and their works. The picaresque life of Hašek is almost as entertaining as what he wrote, and has been the subject of a superb biography by the former British ambassador in Prague, Sir Cecil Parrot (*The Bad Bohemian*, London, 1978). The son of an impoverished school-teacher who drank himself to death, Hašek was brought up in Prague and studied there at the recently founded Czechoslovak Commercial Academy, where he acquired his life-long tastes for writing and vagrancy.

Interrupting his studies periodically to wander penniless around different parts of Central Europe, he was eventually expelled from the academy, and decided to devote himself full-time to writing, having already managed to have accounts of his wanderings published in *Národní listy*. For a while he was a member of a literary club called Syrinx, which used to hold rowdy meetings at Prague's *U Fleků* ale-house and later at St Thomas's cavern, but even these proved too intellectual for Hašek. He took an increasingly active part in anarchist activities, and committed the ultimate anarchist act when he bartered for drink the office bicycle of the particular anarchist group to which he belonged. At the same time he developed a notorious line in practical jokes, attempting on one occasion to commit suicide from the same spot on the Charles Bridge from where St John of Nepomuk had been thrown, and on another signing himself in to a Prague hotel as a spy, an act which was to lead to the hotel being surrounded by the Austrian militia. In 1909 he became editor of the serious natural history magazine called *Animal World*, and perplexed its readers by his invention of several new species. His most sustained escapade, however, was his creation in 1912 of a new political party called The Party of Moderate and Peaceful Progress Within the Limits of the Law, the meetings of which gave ample scope for Hašek's exhibitionism, and also helped bolster the ailing finances of the pub where they were held.

Hašek's varied career in the First World War, from which he returned a bigamist after serving a spell in Russia as a deputy commandant in the Red Army, provided him with the material for the book which was to secure his future reputation, *The Good Soldier Švejk*. Published in instalments together with illustrations by his friend Josef Lada, the book was composed largely in pubs, where Hašek would write hastily at the corner of a table, sending off every so often one of his companions to deliver the newly completed parts of the manuscript to the publisher. Hašek's health, after a lifetime of bodily abuse, was now failing him, and he moved from Prague to a village in the Czech–Moravian Highlands where he died shortly afterwards, leaving his book unfinished; few of his old friends and none of his family attended the funeral. Despite the enormous and immediate popular success of the *Good Soldier Švejk*, the book was not taken seriously as literature for many years, and few people of the time would have predicted its importance for later Czech writers. Švejk himself may not represent the archetypal Czech as some foreigners insultingly like to believe, but the way that this little man is used by Hašek to reduce global events to human proportions can be singled out as a characteristically Czech device. To Hašek the outwardly insignificant Švejk was in his own way no less of a hero than Alexander the Great, for in his simplicity and congenital idiocy he succeeded in exposing the absurdity of all those around him, just like Hašek himself had done.

The Czech writer who best encapsulates the spirit of the First Czechoslovak Republic was **Karel Čapek** (1890–1938), who came to literary prominence at the republic's onset, and died just before its demise. A humanist, a pragmatist and a man of moderate political views, he had an enormous amount in common with President Masaryk, to whom Čapek was to become both a close friend and a sort of Boswell, recording the president's life and thoughts over a long series of interviews carried out from the mid-1920s onwards. The son of a country doctor, Čapek was born in a village in the Giant Mountains of northeastern Bohemia, and studied philosophy in Prague, Berlin and Paris before finally taking up a career in writing. His first stories were published in 1916, and in the following year he began practising journalism, which he would continue to do for the rest of his life, believing, as numerous Czechs have done, that this was a good way of fulfilling a writer's duty to a nation. His literary activities proliferated in the course of the 1920s and came to include essays, novels, children's stories, travel writing, and even a humorous book on gardening. But he made his reputation above all in the theatre, both as a director, and as a writer of such famous works as *R.U.R.* (1921), *The Makropolous Affair* (1922) and the witty morality play *From the Life of the Insects* (1921), which he wrote in collaboration with his painter brother Josef. A strong **science fiction** element runs through his work, and in *R.U.R.* ('Rossum's Universal Robots'), he was to give international currency to the Czech word 'robot'; two years later he was to write a novel, *Krakatit*, in which, prophetically, an atomic bomb was invented. In these and other works he expressed his fear of man being dominated by the machines he invents, but he treated such a weighty theme with a complete lack of pretentiousness. Even when dealing with the strange and the exotic, he never lost his characteristically Czech common sense and interest in ordinary life: his robots were given the failings of normal human beings, as were the newts in his famous novel *The War of the Newts* (1936). By 1936 Čapek was a strong contender for the Nobel Prize, but the Swedish Academy was wary of offending Nazi Germany by honouring an outspoken anti-Fascist. The Academy reputedly asked Čapek to write some new, blandly inoffensive work, but Čapek replied with his typical wit that he had already submitted his doctoral dissertation. He died two years later, literally heart-broken by Neville Chamberlain's betrayal of Czechoslovakia.

The avant-garde between the wars

The great centre of Czech literary and artistic life between the wars was Prague's **Union Café**, where there gathered a particularly brilliant galaxy of poets. At the very beginning of the 1920s the dominant poetic fashion was for realistic, socially committed verse, of which one of the earliest exponents was Josef Hora (1891–1945), a member of the Communist party until 1929, and a journalist by profession. František Halas (1901–1949), the self-educated son of a textile worker, was another poet associated in his early years with this so-called 'proletarian phase'. But the most prominent advocate of the style among the Union Café poets was Jiří Wolker (1900–1924), who was also the least likely candidate for 'proletarianism', being a trained lawyer from a privileged background who arrogantly prided himself on his supposed English descent, believing that his surname was a corruption of Walker.

'Enough of Wolker!' was to be the battle cry of the advocates of **Poetism**, which became the new fashion after 1923 and one of the main forces behind the avant-garde group known as Devětsil. **Devětsil**, which had been founded at a meeting at the Union Café in October 1920, was made up of leading figures in all the arts and even Wolker had been one of its members until his disagreement with its orientation towards Poetism. The leader of Devětsil was the versatile **Karel Teige** (1900–51), who defined Poetism as 'the rule of pure poetry', an expression of joy in which ideas and images freely mingle, unconstrained by the normal continuities such as narrative and a rigid ideological viewpoint; ultimately Poetism, with its belief in free association and the impulse of the subconscious, was to give way to **Surrealism**. **Vítězslav Nezval** (1900–58), who in 1934 was to be a founder member of the Czech Group of Surrealists, was Poetism's most significant poet, and the author in 1924 of what could be described as the movement's manifesto, *Pantomime*. With a layout and graphics by Teige, illustrations by J. Štýrský and numerous photographs, this was a book in which the visual presentation was as important as the text itself, and where you could find such diverse concepts as a 'photogenic poem', a film script in book form, a libretto for a mime show, and a picture poem. Devětsil, and Poetism in particular, aimed to break down the barriers between the various arts, and its literary associates were all people of a strong visual imagination, some, such as Nezval, even practising painters.

Quite apart from its impact on poetry, art and architecture, Devětsil had a major influence on the development of Czech theatre between the wars. In 1926 a group of Devětsil members, including the directors Jindřich Honzl (1894–1953) and Jiří Frejka (1904–52) and the actors Jiří Voskovec (1905–1981) and Jan Werich (1905–80), founded the **Liberated Theatre**, which soon became one of the main avant-garde venues of Europe. Employing many of the techniques of the circus, music-hall and cabaret, it put on plays, ballets and dramatised poems by Devětsil authors, as well as numerous Futurist, Dada and Surrealist works by foreign authors such as Marinetti, Alfred Jarry, André Breton and Jean Cocteau. These fantastical and lyrical works were always enacted against simple, functional and anti-illusionary stage sets in the tradition of Soviet directors such as Meyerhold, thus successfully realising Devětsil's programme of reconciling Poetism with a more utilitarian Constructivism.

The **cinema**, which was then in its infancy in Czechoslovakia, was another potentially ideal medium in which to express the theories of Devětsil, and in 1925 Karel Teige published a pioneering treatise of film aesthetics entitled *Film*, in which he put forward a case for 'pure cinematography', arguing that cinema should be an independent art with a self-sufficient poetic language of its own. His ideas, sadly, were not to be put into practice between the wars, but, in compensation, the avant-garde poetic humour and satire of the Liberated Theatre were to be taken up in the medium of film by the actors Voskovec and Werich. These two, whose partnership came to be known as 'the duo V&W', were associated in the 1930s with a number of films that greatly helped to raise the Czechoslovak film industry from its provincialism. Their second and best film, *Your Money or Your Life* (1932), represented the birth of the Czech film comedy, while later works of theirs took a more political direction, following a general trend in the arts in Czechoslovakia at the time of Hitler's rise to power. These latter films were directed by the prolific Martin Frič (1902–68), whose film *Jánošík*, based on the life of the Slovak Robin Hood, was one of the first works of the Czechoslovak cinema to gain international recognition.

Dada, slapstick and films were a great influence on the writings of the principal novelist associated with Devětsil, Vladislav Vančura (1891–1942), a virtuoso and experimental stylist who combined boundless fantasy with humour and satire, as in his story *Capricious Summer* (1926), which was to be the subject of one of the greatest Czech films of the 1960s. He evolved a more realistic style of novel in the 1930s, exploring social and political themes, but his involvement with left-wing politics led to his execution by the Nazis in 1942. Perhaps the best loved and most widely known writer to emerge out of Devětsil was the poet **Jaroslav Seifert** (1901–86), who was only narrowly to escape Vančura's fate during the Second World War. One of the few genuinely proletarian writers of this generation, Seifert was the son of a factory blacksmith from the Prague district of Žižkov, a strong working-class area of which Seifert was always to be intensely proud. His first volume of poetry, *Town in Tears* (1921), is considered one of the most 'proletarian' of all Czech works of poetry, but his subsequent collection, *Nothing but Love* (1923), marked the beginning of a long 'Modernist' phase, and has references to the circus, the cinema, skyscrapers and other subjects so typical of Devětsil. The euphonic, densely compressed and incantatory manner of his 'Modernist' works was to intensify from 1929 onwards, but in the last two decades of his life he developed a more 'conversational' style, directly addressing the reader in simple and unadorned free verse. Though his style changed, certain themes of his verse, such as his dual obsession with Prague and women, remained constant, and though his verse is at times intensely nostalgic and preoccupied with death, it is never morbidly introspective, and always retains a semi-humorous quality and a concern with the joys and pleasures of life.

Few other writers were so ideally suited to serve as spokesmen for the Czech nation, which is what Seifert virtually became from the late 1930s onwards, when he came to enjoy a popularity on a scale which no modern British or American poet could ever hope to achieve. From 1938, when Seifert mourned in verse the death of Masaryk, right up to the aftermath of 1968, the Czech public were anxiously to await his every word, whether expressed in poetry, or, as was the case with much of his writings during the war years, in journalism. Death nearly came to Seifert in 1945, when he was captured by the Germans and lined up against a wall to be shot, being reprieved only at the last moment. His later account of this Dostojevsky-like experience typifies not only the particular mentality of Seifert but also the approach to history of many of the finest Czech writers of a later generation: instead of dwelling on the horror and heroism of these potential last moments, Seifert relates how his mind was largely preoccupied with speculation about what the inhabitants of a neighbouring block of flats were cooking, and with a childhood memory of a nearby sidewalk toilet which had been defaced with a picture of a naked woman in a compromising position.

Communism, censorship and the literary renascence

An ironic humour and a sense of the absurdity underlying even the most tragic and oppressive situation were to provide Czech writers with the best means of coping with the limitations of freedom imposed by Communist rule. However, during the worst years of Stalinism, individuality of any sort was a dangerous commodity and a number of writers who had fought against Fascism now found themselves accused of anti-State activities, among them the Slovak poet Laco Novomeský (1904–), and the son of the artist Alfons Mucha, Jiří Mucha (1915–91), who was later to write an account of this period in his *Living and Partly Living* (1967). Seifert maintained a silence for much of the 1950s, but other contemporaries of his compromised their artistic integrity writing sycophantic poems to the new regime, Nezval even managing on one occasion to write a beautiful poem praising the distinctly unappealing wife of Klement Gottwald. Certain novelists, in particular the Slovak writer František Hečko (1905–60), fulfilled the demands of 'Socialist Realism' through detailed descriptions of village life; but the principal theme of Czechoslovak writing from 1945 right up to the end of the 1950s was the **Second World War** and the immediate period leading up to it, with especial emphasis on the heroic role of the Czech and Slovak partisans, and of the Soviet army.

Among the main novelists writing during this period were three Slovaks, Peter

Jilemnický (1901–49), Milo Urban (1904–), and the die-hard Stalinist Ladislav Mňačko (1919–), all of whom wrote novels about the Slovak involvement in the war. The Jewish experience of the war was dealt with memorably in the stories of Arnošt Lustig—which were based on life in the concentration camp at Terezín—and in an outstanding novel by **Jiří Weil**, *Life with a Star*, which was published during the period of relative freedom just before the Communist take-over, and was later denounced by the Communists as a 'decadent' example of 'pernicious existentialism'. Weil (1900–59), a journalist and former member of Devětsil, was expelled from the Czech Writers' Union early in the 1950s but, through the intervention of Seifert, later managed to be appointed as director of the Jewish State Museum in Prague, only one year before dying of cancer. *Life with a Star* is a highly autobiographical work, dealing with how a humble Jewish citizen of Prague copes with the increasingly tyrannical and ridiculous measures imposed on his race by the Nazis. Living in a house which has been stripped of everything, not allowed even to use public transport or enter certain shops, the protagonist is sustained in his loneliness through memories of his long departed mistress and through the companionship of a stray cat, but eventually the memory of the former fades and the latter is killed by a German soldier. The novel is saved from unrelenting bleakness by the author's ability to perceive the absurdity of the whole situation, and the conclusion is a curiously optimistic one, with the hero unafraid of anything else which might befall him.

The gradual improvement in the political and social situation in Czechoslovakia, leading in 1962 to the demolition of the monumental statue of Stalin which dominated Prague's Letná Hill, prepared the ground for a great **literary renascence**. The writers who emerged in the decade between 1958 and 1968 have gained for modern Czech literature an enormous international popularity, though it has to be said that foreigners continue to be ignorant of such interesting Slovak writers of this period as Ladislav Ballek (1941–), Ján Johannides (1934–) and Pavel Vilikovský (1941–). Ballek is the author of epic novels set in southern Slovakia, while Johannides made his name as an existentialist writer, many of whose works are preoccupied with guilt and the meaning of distinct national identity. Vilikovský wrote in the late 1960s one of the funniest novels in Slovakian literature, *Ever Green is...*, a book which poked fun at Slovakian nationalists and at everything which was held sacred in Slovakia under Communist rule; though accepted (with alterations) for publication in 1969, it was only issued 20 years later.

Of the new Czech generation of writers, one of the best known is **Josef Škvorecký** (1924–), who was born and brought up in the northern Bohemian town of Náchod, and acquired there a life-long passion for American literature and jazz. During the war years he was lucky enough to be able to remain in his home town through obtaining a job as an auxiliary worker in the local Messerschmitt engineering works: as with many Czech writers who were later obliged to take on factory and other manual jobs, the experience of working here was a formative one for his future development as a writer, for it enabled him to write sympathetically about Czechs from every walk of society. Of more immediate consequence, he met at the factory a working-class girl who deprived him of his virginity, and also spurred him on to try and sabotage one of the planes, a would-be act of heroism which was fortunately interpreted as incompetence. Shortly after the war he moved to Prague, where he worked for a while in a publishing house and became involved in one of the few circles of underground literature in the early 1950s.

In 1958 he committed what he described as artistic suicide by publishing a novel which he had written immediately after the war and had wisely decided to hold on to throughout the Stalinist years. Even in the marginally more tolerant climate of the late 1950s, this novel, **The Cowards**, was savagely denounced by the Communist party and later banned, thus greatly increasing the book's popularity; a new edition was to be allowed in 1962 and was to make Škvorecký one of the most fêted of Czech novelists. *The Cowards* was intended as a work of 'magic' as opposed to 'socialist realism', a work in which Škvorecký set out to write about events in his past life so that they would be 'etherialised by distance'. In contrast to the customary tales of Nazi atrocities and Soviet heroism, *The Cowards* gives a humorous and almost idyllic portrayal of life in a Czech town at the very end of the war, and centres around a group of youngsters whose primary interests are in girls and jazz rather than in the forthcoming glorious revolution. The work is almost completely autobiographical and would initiate a series of novels in which Náchod is referred to as Kostelec, and the young Škvorecký as Danny Smiřický. The girl known as Irena, the principal object of Danny's unrealised sexual fantasies, apparently never spoke to Škvorecký again after the publication of the first Kostelec novel, even though, as Škvorecký said, in his book he had straightened out her bandy legs; in later works her bandy legs were to return. The enormous popularity which Škvorecký enjoyed in Czechoslovakia following the second edition of *The Cowards* was much enhanced later in the 1960s with a series of droll and witty **detective stories** featuring the mournful-faced Lieutenant Borůvka. His critical reputation, however, was enhanced principally by his experimental novella *The Bass Saxophone* (1967), which is set in war-time Kostelec and adopts a prose-style which brilliantly emulates the rhythms of jazz, a form of music which was considered decadent first by the Nazis and later by the Communists. The last work which Škvorecký published in Czechoslovakia before becoming a banned author in 1969 was the delightful *Miss Silver's Past* (known in Czech as *The Lion Cub*), a tale of love set against the complexities of life in a Czech publishing house, influenced by Jewish experience in the Second World War.

Milan Kundera (1929–) was the first Czech novelist to have a large international success, though his popularity in his native country has never been as great as authors such as Škvorecký, not least because most of what he has written dates from after he went into exile in 1975. Born in Brno, his early career included work as a labourer, a jazz musician, and—in the mid-1960s, at the height of the Czech New Wave in film—a professor at the Prague Institute for Advanced Cinematographic Studies. His first and only novel published in Czechoslovakia before 1968 was **The Joke** (1967), the protagonist of which, a Communist student, commits the grave error of sending a teasing postcard to his earnest Stalinist girlfriend containing the lines: 'Optimism is the opium of the people! The healthy atmosphere stinks! Long live Trotsky!' The humour is not appreciated by those who intercept the card, and, despite the hero's protestations that 'it was only a joke', he is expelled from university and spends seven years consigned to an army penal corps, where he works in the coal mines. The novel contains in embryo most of the themes that Kundera was to explore in his later works, most notably the interconnected themes of 'lightness' and 'forgetting'. The 'burden of lightness' refers in this book's case to the way in which a joke deprives the hero 'of the right to tragedy', and condemns him to triviality. The absurd, inconsequential nature of history is further illustrated in Kundera's works by the process of 'forgetting', whereby the past, both personal and political, is rewritten; this theme was to have particular resonance after 1968, during the rule of President Husák, 'the president of forgetting'. *The Joke* was once described as a 'major indictment of Stalinism', but Kundera was quick to interject on this occasion, 'Spare me your Stalinism, please. *The Joke* is a love story!' An erotic element has always been central to Kundera's fiction, and the many graphic scenes of physical love that have featured in his works have been justified by him as a way of bringing out the essence of a character or a situation. These scenes have doubtless contributed to the vast sales of Kundera's works, sales that show him, in Britain at least, to be the most popular of all modern foreign authors.

Eroticism of a more playful and less pretentious kind featured in the novels and stories of **Bohumil Hrabal** (1914–97), who was thought of in the Czech Republic as the grand old man of Czech letters, and was in many ways the most influential of all Czech writers since the war. Though he graduated in law at Prague University, he was never able to practise as a lawyer after 1939, and worked from 1948 onwards in an astonishing variety of jobs, including as a clerk, a railway lineman, a train dispatcher, a stage-hand, a postman, a steel-worker, a travelling salesman, and as a dealer in scrap paper: it was while working in the latter capacity that he first came to know Škvorecký, whose duties at a publishing house included delivering obsolete galley proofs to the scrap-paper salvage centre. Hrabal, whose first novel was not published until 1963, was to remain in Czechoslovakia after 1968, though many of his works had to be adapted to meet the requirements of the censor. Notorious even up to his death as a habitué of Prague's pubs, he married a waitress who could have come straight out of one of his works, and preferred to refer to himself as a reporter of pub stories than as a writer. His down-to-earth humour, use of slang, and love of pubs have led to comparisons with Hašek, but his extraordinary fantasy, taste for 'Chaplinesque' slapstick, and special, almost untranslatable way of using Czech, made him closer in spirit to Vančura. Fame and a devoted readership came to him with the publication in 1965 of his novella, *Closely Observed Trains*, which, though a much tamer version of an earlier story of his called *The Legend of Cain*, displayed an irreverence towards war which far surpassed Škvorecký's. Set in a provincial railway station, it deals with an adolescent boy whose euphoria at overcoming a problem of premature ejaculation leads him to commit an unpremeditated act of patriotism. Perhaps Hrabal's greatest achievement was his novel **I Served the King of England**, which was the only one of his works which he resolutely refused to have altered in any way. To try and escape the attentions of the censor, he sneakily, and with typical 'Hrabalian' wit, allowed the work to be published as a special bulletin of the Jazz Section of the Czech Musicians's Union. Dedicated to the 'Readers of the Jazz Section so that they might have some fun', the work is a humorous and grotesquely distorted view of Czech history from the 1920s onwards as seen through the eyes of a diminutive waiter with a preternatural gift for survival and the giving of sexual pleasure. After distinguishing himself in the course of an extravagant banquet put on in a grand Prague hotel for the Emperor of Ethiopia, the waiter then goes on to marry a German woman who ends the war with her head blown off but still clutching in her hands a precious stamp album confiscated from a wealthy Jew. The sale of this album turns the protagonist briefly into a millionaire, but he finishes his life clearing remote forest roads in South Bohemia, possessing little more than his memories of the past, and an ability to contemplate the world with serene detachment.

Theatre and cinema in the 1950s and '60s

The 1960s were a golden age not only for Czech fiction, but also for Czech theatre and cinema. The exciting theatrical life of this period was concentrated on the many small theatres that grew up from the 1950s onwards and included such places as Semafor, **The Theatre on the Balustrade**, The Činoherní Klub and The Theatre beyond the Gate, the latter being run by the charismatic actor and present director of Prague's National Theatre, Otomar Krejča. The actor, singer, poet and writer Jiří Suchý (1931–) joined forces with the composer Jiří Šlitr to form the 'S&Š' duo, which carried on the tradition of 'the duo V&W' and the Liberated Theatre; another major theatrical figure of this time was Ivan Vyskočil (1929–), a writer of experimental prose who displayed eccentric brilliance but complete impracticality during his period as a director of The Theatre on the Balustrade. Semafor, under the creative domination of 'S&S', was the most popular and influential of the small theatres, but the Theatre of the Balustrade is today the most famous of these places owing to its associations with **Václav Havel** (1936–). The son of a distinguished civil engineer whose brother had been one of the creators of Prague's Barrandov film studios, Havel worked initially as an apprentice and later a laboratory technician at the Czech Technical High School at Prague. He published his first works of journalism in 1955, and was to continue writing for a number of periodicals, mainly literary and theatrical, up to 1969. From the start he showed a strong political bent, and made his first public appearance with a highly critical address given at a working party of new authors at the Dobříš Writers' Home near Prague. Hindsight has led some Czechs to suggest that Havel subsequently became involved in the theatre principally as a way of entering into politics. After being turned down as a student at both the Film and Drama Faculties of Prague's Performing Arts Academy, Havel joined The Theatre on the Balustrade in 1960, working initially as a stage-hand and later as a literary adviser and assistant producer; his first play, *The Garden Party*, was performed here in 1963. In common with the Liberated Theatre of the 1920s, The Theatre on the Balustrade developed a speciality in the drama of the Absurd, and in the course of the 1960s put on important productions of works by both Alfred Jarry and Samuel Beckett. Havel's own plays maintained this absurdist vein, but used it to comment on life under totalitarianism.

International interest in the great cultural developments that were taking place in Czechoslovakia from the late 1950s onwards was stimulated above all by the cinema of this period. The promising tendencies that had emerged in Czech cinema in the late 1930s had still been very much in evidence in the years immediately after the war, with Czech directors continuing to show poetic lyricism and an ability to transpose good literature to the screen. One of the more important films of these years was **The Strike** (1946), which was the first and only Czech film to win a Golden Lion award at the Venice Film Festival; this adaptation by Karel Steklý (born 1903) of a popular novel about a miner's life by Marie Majerová (1882–1967) combined social pathos with avant-garde poetics. The Second World War—which was to be the main theme of Czech and Slovak films right up to the end of the 1950s—was the subject of two other outstanding films of these years, *Silent Barricade* (1948) by Otakar Vávra (1911–), and *Stolen Frontier* (1947), which was the story of a Czech frontier village after the Munich agreement, and the first full-length work by Jiří Weiss (1913–). Alfréd Radok (1914–76), for whom Havel was to work in the 1960s at The Theatre on the Balustrade, was one of the more interesting directors to emerge during the Stalinist years, and made in 1953 the **first**

Czechoslovak musical, *The Magic Hat*; another pioneering work of his, *The Distant Journey* (1950), was an expressionistic tale of the Terezín ghetto inspired to a large extent by Surrealist poetics, but was immediately banned for being 'existentialistic'. One of the main outlets for the visionary and avant-garde imagination during this repressive period was the medium of **animated film**, the greatest practitioners of which were Jiří Trnka (1912–70) and Karel Zeman (1910–), both of whom worked at the celebrated animated studios that had been established in the 1930s by Tomáš Baťa at Zlín. The relaxation of censorship after 1956 saw the beginnings of a renascence in Czech cinema, as well as the emergence of the first major work of **Slovak cinema**, *Forty-four* (1957), a powerful work by Palo Bielik (1910–) based on a suppressed revolt of Slovak soldiers during the First World War. The attention of the world, however, was directed to Czechoslovakia at this time not by any one film but by a revolutionary new art form devised by Alfréd Radok in 1958 and involving a mixture of cinema and theatre. Known as **The Magic Theatre**, it enjoyed a great success at the Brussels World Exhibition of 1958, and introduced the world to one of the future protagonists of the Czech New Wave, Miloš Forman.

From the time of Devětsil, literature in Czechoslovakia had been closely associated with the cinema, but this was particularly true of the 1960s, when leading writers such as Škvorecký, Kundera and Hrabal played an important role in the history of the **New Wave**. The main characteristics of the films of this period were those that had informed some of the greatest works of Czech literature, notably a concentration on scenes of ordinary life and a transformation of reality through elements of fantasy and whimsical humour. Another feature of the New Wave was the extensive use of non-professional actors, a feature which had been common to British and Italian realist films of the post-war period, but had been frowned upon, curiously, by the advocates of 'socialist realism', who demanded both professional actors and theatrical acting: Jiří Weiss, in his film *The Last Shot* (1950), which showed the end of the war in a large steel mill, had been criticised for a lack of pathos and for giving leading roles to amateurs. The first key film of the New Wave was *Sunshine in a Net* (1963) by the Slovak director Štefan Uher (1930–), a work which did away with dramatic conventions of plot and with political opportunism to concentrate instead on the inner life of ordinary people and to show on the screen aspects of the true face of economic reality. Other Slovak directors of this decade included Elo Havetta (died 1975), a former graphic artist whose best known film was *Party in the Botanical Garden* (1969), a joyful and anarchical protest against pettiness, filled with Surreal images inspired by rural life in the Slovakian hill country. The creation of the New Wave, however, was essentially the work of Czech directors, one of whom was Jan Němec, whose *Report on the Party and the Guests* (1966) was a morality play dealing with the way 'ordinary' people can become indifferent to the fate of others and even willingly accept force and violence: this parable, set at a large outdoor banquet, and culminating with a pack of dogs chasing the one guest who decides to make his escape, was not allowed to be shown in Czechoslovakia until the Prague Spring of 1968, after which it was immediately banned once more.

The two Czech film directors of this period with the greatest international reputation were **Miloš Forman** (1932–) and Jiří Menzel (1938–). Forman's first feature film was the story of a boy informer, *Black Peter* (1963), but he came to international prominence with *A Blonde in Love* (1965), a charming comedy of small town life. The town in question, featuring a shoe factory employing hundreds of women, has a serious shortage of men, and asks the army to supply the missing 'male element', but, instead of receiving young soldiers, it is sent a unit of middle-aged reservists. This witty satire on bureaucracy's absurd ways of coping with emotional human needs is full of vivid observations of everyday life, as, for instance, in a famous scene when an idyllic erotic encounter between the eponymous blonde and a touring piano player is constantly interrupted by a malfunctioning blind. Forman returned to the absurdities of provincial life in the last film which he was to make in Czechoslovakia, *The Fireman's Ball* (1967), which, taking as its subject a dance and beauty competition organised by the dignitaries of a fire brigade, hilariously shows up bureaucratic stupidity, incompetence and dullness.

Fantasy, surreal comedy, and a poetic obsession with the absurd minutiae of everyday life, come together in the work of **Jiří Menzel**, one of whose most famous films, *Capricious Summer* (1967), is based on Vančura's novel about a circus troupe in the country. But of all the authors whom Menzel adapted, the one whose vision most closely corresponded to his own was Bohumil Hrabal. Menzel's version of *Closely Observed Trains* (1966), which Hrabal claimed to prefer to his own novella, was the most successful Czech film of this period, and won an Oscar for the Best Foreign Film. Its accumulation of detail builds up to a remarkably evocative picture of a provincial Czech railway station, but each of these details is loaded with suggestions, as for instance the waiting-room sofa which is torn in the course of the boy's momentous first sexual encounter. Or again, the bilingual rubber stamps of the stationmaster, which on one notorious occasion are pressed on a girl's naked bottom, a moment which is not only intensely erotic but also serves to ridicule bureaucracy, for the man who has used the stamps in this way is later accused not of a sexual offence but of abusing the German language; furthermore a pun was also intended, the Czech expression 'heading for the arse' meaning 'heading for disaster', a reference in this case to the German armies. Menzel, an actor who directed plays as well as films, was very keen to take on the part of the boy in *Closely Observed Trains*, though, as Škvorecký noted in his short book on the making of this film, this was probably less for artistic reasons than to have an excuse to go to bed with the girl, if only in the studio; in the end he had to content himself with the Freudian role of doctor-confessor. Škvorecký's own work provided Menzel with the subjects of two of his films, and in 1968 preparations were going ahead for Menzel's projected film version of *The Cowards*, which would have featured the daughter of bandy-legged Irena playing her own mother. The arrival of Soviet troops in August of that year sadly interrupted these whimsical plans.

The literary resistance and samizdat publishing

The impact of the **Soviet invasion of 1968** on the cultural life of Czechoslovakia was scarcely less dramatic than that of the Battle of the White Mountain in 1620, though fortunately the effects were not to be so long-lasting. Virtually all the main films of the Czech New Wave were immediately banned, as were most of the writers who come to prominence in this decade. Škvorecký emigrated in 1969 to Canada, where his wife was to found Sixty-Eight Publishers, which brought out much of the Czech and Slovak literature to be written during the 1970s and 1980s. Kundera remained in Czechoslovakia until 1975, deprived of his post as a teacher, and seeing all his books removed from public libraries; eventually he settled in Paris, where his combination of intellectual and sexual concerns, together with the mystique of being a banned writer, were soon to turn him into a hero for the French. One of those who stayed resolutely on in Czechoslovakia was Jaroslav Seifert, and Škvorecký was later to write that the one good consequence of the Soviet invasion was to have 'put the incapacitated old poet back on his feet'. The arrival of Soviet tanks so incensed him that he made his way soon afterwards on crutches to the Writer's Club on the Old Town Square and had himself elected the union's chairman, in the place of someone who had had to flee the country; he vigorously promoted the cause of writers for the remaining nine months of the union's existence, and was later to become a signatory of Charter 77. He was to cause further embarrassment to the government when in 1984 he was awarded the Nobel Prize for Literature.

Václav Havel, after suffering from bleak depression in the early 1970s, when he spent long periods of isolation in his country cottage in northern Bohemia, took an increasingly active part in the underground resistance after 1975, eventually becoming one of the main organisers of Charter 77, for which he was later to be sentenced to four years in prison. While in prison he was allowed to write one four-page letter a week to his wife Olga, but these had to refer only to 'family matters' and to conform to such other absurd rules as not having any deletions, underlinings, or quotation marks; these limitations forced Havel to write in a cryptic and abstract style which is at times barely comprehensible but was none the less to enhance his reputation as a thinker. The letters, which were eventually published in English as *Letters to Olga* (1988), circulated in Czechoslovakia in what is known as a *samizdat* edition, a typewritten edition of about twelve copies which were passed on secretly from one person to another. This form of publishing, born in this country at the beginning of the 1970s, had acquired a remarkably wide currency in the wake of Charter 77, and was the main means by which the principal Czech and Slovak writers continued to function within Czechoslovakia. The main *samizdat* organization was **Padlock Editions**, which published the most strictly forbidden authors, among whom were Pavel Kohout (1928–), **Ludvík Vaculík** (1926–) and **Ivan Klíma** (1931). All these authors were associated with the revival of the *feuilleton*, but it was Vaculík who perfected the genre, writing essays that are models of irony, wit and concision, as for instance in his collection *A Cup of Coffee with My Interrogator* (1986). However, the 'Padlock' author who is at present enjoying the most popularity is Klíma, a former journalist whose novels and short stories bring together that characteristically Czech mixture of amorous intrigue, ironic reflection, and a sense of the poetry and absurdity of everyday life. His ambitious novel *Love and Garbage* (1986), which adopts a narrative technique similar to that of Jiří Weil in *Life with a Star*, blends memories of a passionate, adulterous affair with philosophical reflections and descriptions of a writer working as a refuse collector. Another author who was banned for many years after 1968 was **Miroslav Holub** (1923–98), a practising immunologist who was also the greatest Czech poet of recent years. Associated at one time with a literary group called Poetry of Everyday, he used frequent medical analogies in his work and dissected human experience with the economy and precision of a pathologist.

The arts in the new republics

The inauguration of Václav Havel as president of Czechoslovakia was seen by some as this playwright's culminating achievement as a dramatist of the absurd.

It also seemed to presage a new era of intelligent state sponsorship of literature, film and theatre, particularly given Havel's belief in the central role of culture in the life of a country (a belief he strongly reasserted at the end of his 1997 'state of the nation' speech). However, with the change to a market economy, the problems of political censorship have now given way to ones of **commercial viability**, which has enormously reduced the number of Czech films being made, and led publishing-houses to dedicate much of their energies to the bringing out of cookery books and the like.

The Czech arts establishment is now mainly in the hands of the once controversial figures of Havel's generation, who, deprived today of any major target for their rebelliousness, have generally settled down to a nostalgic-looking late middle age. A particular case in point is the theatre and film-director Jiří Menzel, who, using scripts by contemporaries such as Hrabal and Havel, has produced enjoyable but worthy films largely lacking the anarchic and Surreal satirical bite of those he made in the 1960s. Neither has Menzel fostered any striking new talents, and indeed was such an indifferent director of the Czech national film school (the FAMU) that he was forced to resign by his students on the grounds of absenteeism. The one recent Czech film to have enjoyed both a commercial and critical success was the charming, sentimental and Oscar-winning *Kolja*, which deals with an ageing womanizer on whom is suddenly landed the burden of single fatherhood. The sole Czech director of today who still produces works of savage originality is **Jan Švankmajer**, who, after more than two decades of being banned, thwarted and misunderstood, has found foreign investors to back his surreal and bizarre creations involving animation and puppets.

Czech literature continues to be one of the most popular foreign literatures in translation, but only thanks to the continuing productivity of long-established writers such as Škvorecký, who, from his home in Canada, continues to dwell almost exclusively on the past—his own past, and that of his native country. Of the older Czech writers who were able directly to witness the 'Velvet Revolution' and its aftermath, Bohumil Hrabal was perhaps the one best suited to comment on the absurdities of sudden political change: 'The things that go on here in Prague,' he smiles, as he describes the tank-painting activities of the 'Situationist' artist David Černý in one of a series of published letters to a young woman called Alice. Ivan Klíma, meanwhile, has turned out to be a powerful chronicler of the disillusionment and sense of anti-climax and emptiness that inevitably accompanied the longed-for arrival of democracy. All this is expressed in the very title of his novel *Waiting for the Dark, Waiting for the Light* (1993), which is centred on the life of a television cameraman before, during and after 1989: having dreamt for many years of making a searing social documentary that the Communist authorities would never have allowed, he then finds himself unprepared for the new, supposedly unlimited freedoms, and ends up opting for lucrative short-term jobs such as working on a commercial and a porn film.

Now that the former Czechoslovakia has lost for foreigners the glamour of an oppressed country, the **new Czech writers** of today might well experience far greater difficulties than their predecessors in becoming widely known abroad. For contemporary Czech fiction, and Slovakian fiction generally, English readers have largely to make do with the short stories and extracts published in such excellent anthologies as Michael March's *Description of a Struggle: The Picador Book of Contemporary East European Prose* (1994), Paul Wilson's *Prague:*

A Traveler's Literary Companion (1995) and Elena Lappin's *Daylight in Nightclub Inferno: Czech Fiction from the Post-Kundera Generation* (1997). Among the new talents are Tereza Boučková (1957–) and Halina Pawlowská (1955–), both of whom provide a welcome female perspective on Czech history from the 1960s up to the present day, the latter in her novel *Thank You for Each New Morning* (1994), which was made into an award-winning film. Michal Ajvaz (1949–) carries on from both Kafka and Hrabal in his fantastical and at times nightmarish distortions of Prague, while Michal Viewegh (1962–) analyzes sex and contemporary life with a Kundera-like love of cryptic humour and philosophical whimsy. Jáchym Topol (1962–), a poet and one-time underground singer and lyricist as well as a novelist, earthily describes the current Czech scene with a rambling stream-of-consciousness prose that appears fuelled by drugs and alcohol. For all the recent changes to Czech society, these and other new writers show that Czech literature has not lost its ability to tackle serious contemporary themes with a combination of down-to-earth wit, surreal flights of fantasy, and a heavy dose of unfashionably unreconstructed erotic digression.

Further reading

General books and travel writing

Bailey, Anthony, *Along the Edge of the Forest: an Iron Curtain Journey*, London, 1983.

Brook, Stephen, *The Double Eagle: Vienna, Budapest, Prague*, London, 1988.

Bruce, G., *Wanderings in Czechoslovakia*, London 1930.

Irving, Washington, *The Journals of Washington Irving* (1822), ed. William P. Trent and George S. Hellman, Boston, 1919.

Klima, Ivan, *The Spirit of Prague*, London, 1994.

Leigh Fermor, Patric, *A Time of Gifts*, London, 1977.

Lützow, Count Francis, *Bohemia*, London, 1896.

Magris, Claudio, *Danube: a Sentimental Journey from the Source to the Black Sea*, London, 1989.

Piozzi, Hester Lunch, Observations and reflections. Made in the course of a journey through France, Italy, and Germany (1789), ed. Herbert Barrows, Ann Arbor, Michigan, 1967

Ripellino, Angelo Maria, *Magic Prague*, 1st English paperback edition, London, 1995.

Robson, E.I., *A Wayfarer in Czecho-Slovakia*, London, 1935.

Taylor, Bayard, *Views a-foot. Or Europe seen, with knapsack and staff*, New York, 1845.

Townson, Robert, *Travels in Hungary, in the year 1793*, London, 1797.

White, W., *A July Holiday in Saxony, Bohemia, and Silesia*, London, 1857.

History

Brock, P., *The Slovak National Awakening*, Toronto, 1976.

Brock, P., and Skilling, H.G., *The Czech Renascence of the nineteenth century*, Toronto, 1970.

Dekan, J., *Moravia Magna: the Great Moravian Empire*, London, 1979.

Demetz, Peter, *Prague in Black and Gold: scenes from the Life of a European City*, London, 1997.

Evans, R.J.W., *Rudolf II and his World: A Study in Intellectual History, 1576–1612*, Oxford, 1973.

Frankland, M., *The Patriots' Revolution: How East Europe Won its Freedom*, London, 1990.

Garton Ash, Timothy, *The Uses of Adversity: Essays on the Fate of Central Europe*, Cambridge, 1989.

Glenny, Misha, *The Rebirth of History: Eastern Europe in the Age of Democracy*, London, 1990.

Hillel, J.K., *The Making of Czech Jewry: National Conflict and Jewish Society*, Oxford, 1973.

Jarrett, Bede, *The Emperor Charles IV*, London, 1935.

Kaminsky, Howard, *A History of the Hussite Revolution*, Berkeley and Los Angeles, 1967.

Lettrich, J., *History of Modern Slovakia*, Toronto, 1985.

Mamety, V.S. and R. Luža, *A History of the Czechoslovak Republic 1918–1948*, Princeton, 1973.

Masaryk, Tomáš, *The Meaning of Czech History*, University of North Carolina, 1974.

Renner, Hans, *A History of Czechoslovakia since 1945*, London, 1989.

Seton-Watson, R.W., *The History of the Czechs and Slovaks*, London, 1943

Seton-Watson, R.W. (ed.), *Slovakia Then and Now*, London, 1931.

Shawcross, William, *Remember Dubček: Dubček and Czechoslovakia (1918–1990)*, London, 1990.

Wedgwood, C. Veronica, *The Thirty Years War*, London, 1992.

Wiskemann, Elizabeth, *Czechs and Germans*, London, 1985.

Zeman, Zbyněk, *The Break-Up of the Habsburg Empire*, Oxford, 1963.

Zeman, Zbyněk, *Prague Spring: A report on Czechoslovakia 1968*, Harmondsworth, 1969.

Biography and memoir

Buber-Neumann, Margarete, *Milena*, London, 1988.

Chateaubriand, Vicomte Francois René de Chateaubriand, *The Memoirs of Chateaubriand* (vol. 5), translated by Alexander Feixara de Mattos, London, 1902.

Dubček, A., *Hope Dies Last: The Autobiography of Alexander Dubček*, London, 1993.

Garton Ash, Timothy, *We The People: The Revolution of '89*, Cambridge, 1990.

Havel, Václav, *Letters to Olga*, London, 1988. *Living in Truth* (ed. by Jan Vladislav), London, 1987. *Disturbing the Peace*, London, 1990.

Levy, Alan, *So Many Heroes*, Sagaponach, New York, 1980.

Lützow, Count Francis, *Master John Hus*, London, 1909.

Margolius Kovaly, Heda, *Prague Farewell*, London, 1988.

Moricke, Edward, *Mozart's Journey to Prague*, (1850–51), translated by Leopold von Loewenstein-Wertheim, London, 1957.

Mucha, Jiří, *Living and Partly Living*, London, 1968.

Muir, Edwin, *An Autobiography*, London, 1980.

Parrott, Sir Cecil, *The Serpent and the Nightingale*, London, 1977. *The Bad Bohemian: the extraordinary life of Jaroslav Hašek, author of The Good Soldier Švejk*, London, 1978.

Pauel, Ernst, *The Nightmare of Reason: A Life of Franz Kafka*, London, 1988.

Škvorecký, Josef, *Talkin' Moscow Blues*, London, 1989.

Škvorecký, Josef, *Headed for the Blues: A memoir with ten stories*, London, 1997.

Vaculík, Ludvík, *A Cup of Coffee with my Interrogator*, London, 1987.

Zeman, Zbyněk, *The Masaryks: the Making of Czechoslovakia*, London, 1990.

Art and architecture

Bachmann, Erich, *Gothic Art in Bohemia: Architecture, Sculpture and Painting*, London.

Baroque in Bohemia, exhibition catalogue, Victoria and Albert Museum, London, 1969.

Bialostocki, Jan, *The Art of the Renaissance in Eastern Europe: Hungary, Bohemia, Poland*, London, 1976.

Blažíček, Oldřich, *Baroque Art in Bohemia*, London, 1968.

Buxton, D., *The Wooden Churches of Eastern Europe: An introductory survey*, Cambridge, 1981.

Cannon-Brookes, Peter, *Czech Sculpture, 1800–1938*, London.

Czech Functionalism, exhibition catalogue, Architectural Association, London, 1987.

Denkstein, V., and Matouš, A., *Gothic Art of South Bohemia*, Prague, 1955.

Denkstein, Vladimír (ed.), *Great Centres of Art: Prague*, London, 1979.

Devětsil: Czech avant-garde art, architecture and design of the 1920s and 30s, exhibition catalogue, Museum of Modern Art, Oxford, 1990.

Hempel, E., *Baroque Art and Architecure in Central Europe*, Harmondsworth, 1965.

Hořejší, Jiřina, *et al.*, *Renaissance Art in Bohemia*, London, 1979.

Kauffman, Thomas da Costa, *The School of Prague: Painting at the Court of Rudolph II*, Chicago, 1988.

Kauffman, Thomas da Costa, *Court, Cloister and City: The Art and Culture of Central Europe 1450–1800*, London, 1995.

Knox, Brian, *The Architecture of Prague and Bohemia*, London, 1962.

Laing, Alastair, 'Central and Eastern Europe' in Blunt, Anthony (ed.), *Baroque and Rococo: Architecture and Decoration*, London, 1978.

Margolius, Ivan, *Cubism in Architecture and the Applied Arts—Bohemia and France 1910–1914*, London, 1979.

Margolius, Ivan, *Prague: A Guide to Twentieth-Century Architecture*, London, 1994.

Mencl, Václav, *Czech Architecture of the Luxemburg Period*, Prague, 1955.

Mucha Jiří, *Alphonse Mucha*, London, 1966.

Petrová. S. and J.-L. Olivié, *Bohemian Glass*, Paris, 1990.

Sacha, Rostislav, *The Architecture of New Prague, 1895–1945*, Boston, 1997.

Teige, Karel, *Modern Czechoslovak Architecture*, London, 1947.

Vegesack, Alexander von, *Czech Cubism: Architecture, Furniture and Decorative Arts, 1910–1925*, Montreal, 1992.

Cultural studies and anthologies

Cincura, Andrew (ed), *Anthology of Slovak Literature*, Riverside, California, 1976.

French, Aldred (ed), *Anthology of Czech Poetry*, Ann Arbor, Michigan, 1973.

Lappin, Elena (ed), *Daylight in Nightclub Inferno: Czech Fiction from the Post-Kundera Generation*, North Haven, Connecticut, 1997.

Liehm, Antonín and Mira, *The Most Important Art: Soviet and Eastern European Film after 1945*, University of California Press, 1977.

Lützow, Count Francis, *A History of Bohemian Literature*, London.

March, Michael (ed), *Description of a Struggle: the Picador Book of Contemporary East European Prose*, London, 1994.

Naughton, James, *Traveller's Literary Companion to Eastern and Central Europe*, Brighton, 1995.

Němcová, Jeanne W. (trans.), *Czech and Slovak Short Stories*, London, 1967.

Newmarch, R., *The Music of Czechoslovakia*, Oxford, 1942 (repr 1969).

Osers, Ewald (trans.), *Three Czech Poets: Vitězslav Neval, Antonín, Bartušek and Josef Hanzlík*, Harmondsworth, 1971.

Pynsent, Robert, *Modern Slovak Prose: fiction since 1954*, London, 1991.

Wilson, Paul (ed), *Prague: A Traveller's Literary Companion*, San Francisco, 1955.

The Czech Republic

1 · Prague

Prague, a city spread over wooded hills on either side of the Vltava river, is a place that has always inspired superlatives and effusive prose. Spared by bombing in the Second World War and, until recently, scarcely defaced by billboards, brash neon and other attributes of the Western city, the old centre of Prague is so uncannily well preserved that at times the visitor seems to be walking not in a real place but in a stage set or fairy-tale illustration. Few dispute that Prague is a city unrivalled in its beauty in central Europe, but there are also many who would agree with Milan Kundera's assessment—reached in the course of a stroll one day up a deserted Petřín Hill—that Prague was 'the most beautiful city in the world'.

Evocations of Prague inevitably stress how the physical beauty of the city is matched by a haunting, almost disturbing quality. The British writer Patrick Leigh Fermor, whose indigestibly rich prose has conjured up images of a wholly fantastical Prague, is by no means alone in considering the city not just as one of the most beautiful he has known but also as the strangest. The word 'magical', so misused by travel writers, is literally applicable to Prague, a city where the Habsburg emperor Rudolph II immersed himself in alchemy and the occult to the extent that he was eventually deposed as insane, where Doctor Faustus sold his soul to the devil, and where the Surrealist poet André Breton discovered his 'magic metropolis of old Europe'. Few cities have so secretive a character, and none in Europe has so many covered passages, as Erwin Kisch pointed out in his curious book *Monograph of the Covered Passage*: here is, Kisch claimed, a city which you can cross without hardly touching a street. There exists an immensely sinister Prague, a city of dark and empty streets, of distorted gables from some Expressionistic nightmare, of crows hovering around the black silhouette of a medieval tower.

The writings of Franz Kafka might come to mind as you wander around the streets of Prague, and yet those of the contemporary author Bohumil Hrabal perhaps more faithfully convey the true flavour of the city. Hrabal is someone who combines an imagination which has been referred to as 'baroque' with earthiness and coarse humour: his is a mind nourished by the rough and dirty drinking establishments where many of the ordinary townspeople interrupt even their mornings downing great glasses of beer.

The beauty and 'magic' of Prague should not make you lose sight of the more down-to-earth place which exists beneath the often fantastical façade. The city so frequently described as 'Golden' is also a city of terrible pollution, blackened plaster and peeling paintwork, and where the vast number of buildings shrouded in apparently permanent scaffolding is the subject of continual outrage in the local press. The same view from the Petřín Hill which so enthused Kundera was described in the 1920s by the Scottish poet Edwin Muir as 'intensely dismal', the air filled even on the sunniest days with a 'fine, impalpable dust'.

Tourism has made its own unattractive contribution to Prague, and the situation is becoming increasingly worse, as rapidly growing numbers of western visitors have led to the congestion of present hotel facilities, the necessity of booking good restaurants sometimes at least a week in advance, and even to queues forming to walk across the incomparably beautiful Charles Bridge. In the spring and summer months the centre of the city rings with foreign and not Czech voices, and the streets are crowded with tourists ravenously collecting souvenirs at what for them are bargain prices, and getting drunk on the excellent and ridiculously cheap beer.

The tourist vision of Prague is an extremely limited one, and much of the tourism of the city is fortunately contained in and around the so-called 'Royal Road' which leads from the Powder Tower in the Old Town up to the Royal Castle on the Hradčany. Many of the buildings along this route have been renovated in recent years and have that pastel-coloured doll's house appearance which is to be found in many of the old town centres of present-day Germany. It is easy to come away from Prague with a nostalgic vision of an essentially medieval and Renaissance city overlaid with baroque and rococo tinsel. Yet there is much more to Prague than this, and you should be wary of seeing the place simply as a museum of the past. You should pay a visit to one of Prague's many small theatres to experience something of the city's continuing vitality as a cultural centre; and you need to wander into the side streets and suburbs to understand the vital role which Prague has played in the development of 20C architecture. Ideally too, you should come here both in the summer and winter, so as to see a city which can at one moment be greener than almost any other major city in Europe, and the next frighteningly and unforgettably monochrome. Prague makes an immediate impact on the first-time visitor, but its lasting appeal is only slowly appreciated, for it lies in the city's remarkable complexity.

History of Prague

Appropriately for a city of such fairy-tale appearance, there is a legend connected with the founding of Prague. In around AD 800, Princess Libuse, a woman with great powers of divination, sent her henchmen into the forest with instructions to found a town at the spot where they saw a ploughman (oráč) constructing the threshold (práh) of a house. She married the ploughman (thus establishing the Přemyslid dynasty) and from her palace at Vyšehrad, situated on a rocky outcrop above the right bank of the Vltava, predicted that the new town, later to be called Praha or Prague, would have a future so glorious that its fame would reach the stars.

The real origins of Prague are rather more prosaic and are connected with Slavic settlers occupying the left bank of the Vltava (to the north of Vyšehrad) about the beginning of the 6C AD. The citadel which was established here at the end of the 9C by the first documented member of the Přemyslid family, Count Bořivoj, became the first seat of the Přemyslid dynasty, and not Vyšehrad, as legend would have us believe. Prague was made a bishopric in 973, during the reign of Boleslav II, the Pious. In the course of the same century, numerous Jewish, German, Italian and French merchants settled on the right bank of the Vltava, at the meeting-place of several trade routes, and directly opposite the Slavic settlement on the left bank; the two areas were connected by a wooden bridge at the end of the century. The first known traveller's description of Prague dates from c 965, when the town was visited by Ibrahim ibn Ya'qub, an erudite Spanish Jew who had been sent by the Cordoban Caliph al-Hakam II as a member of a diplomatic mission to Emperor Otto I in Merseburg. He described in detail the lively international mercantile life of Prague, a town which belied its relative smallness by seeming to him to have been made 'richer by commerce' than all the other places he visited in Central Europe.

Count Vratislav II (from 1085 King Vradislav I) transferred his residence to Vyšehrad, which was to remain the seat of the Czech rulers until 1140, when the seat was moved back to its original location. The importance of Vyšehrad Castle greatly declined thereafter, but the area of the right bank to the north of it, where the merchants had settled, became an increasingly bustling commercial centre, particularly from the 1170s onwards, when the wooden bridge across the Vltava was replaced by a stone one—the so-called Judith's Bridge—and special privileges were granted by Count Soběslav II to encourage more Germans to stay here. This commercial settlement, featuring a walled merchant's court known as the Týn, formed a separate township which was granted a municipal charter in around 1230 and is called today the Staré Město or Old Town; the extensive Jewish community was contained from the early 13C within their own walled ghetto attached to the northern side of this settlement. Meanwhile on the left bank of the Vltava, in the sparsely populated outer bailey of the castle, King Přemysl Otakar II founded in 1257 the township later to be called the Malá Strana or Little Quarter, the population of which was originally made up largely of German colonists summoned by the king. In the early 13C the district of Hradčany was founded just to the west of the castle, and Prague emerged as one of the most important and densely populated cities in Europe.

But the highpoint of Prague's medieval development was to be reached during the reign of Charles IV (1344–78), who was to turn the city in 1355 into the capital of the Holy Roman Empire. Under Charles IV Prague became the 'Rome of the North', attracting scholars and artists from all over Europe, including the Italian poet Petrarch. Elevated to archbishopric in 1344, Prague became in 1348 the seat of the first university in central Europe, an institution which bears to this day the name of Charles University. In that same year Charles greatly increased the size of Prague by founding yet another township, the Nové Město or New Town, which incorporated the former horse and cattle markets (respectively today the Wenceslas and Charles Squares) and came eventually to extend from Vyšehrad all the way to the northeastern corner of the Old Town. Numerous churches and other monuments were founded by Charles, most notably the Gothic cathedral of St Vitus, on which there worked one of the outstanding medieval architects of Europe, Peter Parléř, who was summoned to Prague by Charles in 1353. In 1357, to replace the Judith's Bridge, another of Prague's great landmarks was created, the Charles Bridge.

With the succession of Wenceslas IV to the throne in 1348, social and religious tensions led to a period of cultural and economic decline. Urged by the religious reformer Jan Hus, Wenceslas curtailed the rights of the Germans at the Charles University, thus leading to the exodus of 2000 students and many professors. The peculiarly Czech tradition of throwing people to their deaths from high places—initiated by Wenceslas with the ejection of the prelate Jan Nepomucký from the Charles Bridge in 1379—continued in 1419 with the shoving of two Catholic councillors out of the window of the New Town Hall, an event which sparked off the Hussite Wars and was later dignified with the absurd and pompous name of First Defenestration. Renewed stability and building activity set in with the reign of George of Poděbrady (1458–71), but Prague's importance as a trading centre continued to decline. George's successor, Vladislav II Jagiello (1471–1516), brought the Renaissance to Prague by inviting here the outstandingly original architect Benedikt Ried, whose idiosyncratic Vladislav Hall in Prague Castle is the earliest example in Bohemia of the influence of contemporary Italian architecture. Vladislav also consolidated the political decline of Prague, however, by transferring his court in 1490 to the Hungarian capital of Buda.

Through most of the period of Habsburg rule, which began in 1526, Prague continued to play a secondary role in European politics, the city being now subservient to Vienna. It experienced a brief political and cultural revival during the rule of the Emperor Rudolph II (1576–1612), who established his court at Prague, and indulged here his passions for collecting, lavish festivities, astronomy and the occult. He attracted to Prague artists associated with the so-called Mannerist style (most notably Bartolomaeus Spranger, Adriaen de Vries and Giuseppe Arcimboldo), as well as such leading and controversial European scientists as the astronomers Tycho Brahe and Johannes Kepler, the alchemist Edward Kelley, the surgeon Jan Jesenius (who conducted the first public dissection in Prague) and the mathematician Jost Bürgi, the inventor of logarithms. In 1612 he was forced to abdicate in favour of his brother Matthias, who brought the court back to Vienna in 1617. On 23 May 1618, over 100 members of the Bohemian nobility rose up in revolt against the Habsburgs and made their way to Prague Castle, where they perpetrated the Second Defenestration, an incident giving rise to the Thirty Years War. After the defeat of the Protestants at the Battle of the White Mountain in 1620—which took place on the western outskirts of Prague, near the star-shaped hunting lodge of Hvězda—27 of the Protestant leaders were executed on the Old Town Square. Occupied by Saxons in 1631–32, Prague was later besieged by the Swedes, who managed to take possession of the Little Quarter just before peace was declared in 1648.

As with the rest of Bohemia, Prague was left in a state of devastation at the end of the Thirty Years War. Yet the process of rebuilding the city (beginning with the reconstruction from 1630 onwards of the Little Quarter), together with the spectacular reassertion of the Catholic Church following years of religious strife, led to the transformation of Prague into one of the great Baroque centres of Europe. The highpoint of the city's Baroque development was reached during the early 18C, during the period of architectural supremacy of the prolific Kilian Ignaz Dientzenhofer, who was responsible for the vast Clementinum and countless palaces and churches, most notably that of St Nicholas in the Little Quarter, which is comparable to Longhena's Church of the Salute in Venice in dominating the skyline of the city. This same century saw the burgeoning of palace gardens in the Little Quarter, the creation of the wooded parks of Letná, Troja and Petřín, and the extension, between 1753 and 1775 of Prague Castle into the complex of buildings and courtyards that is to be seen today. In place of the medieval fortifications around the Old Town there was laid out between 1760 and 1781 Prague's first boulevard, comprising Na Příkopě and its continuation, Národní třída. Prague's development into a bustling modern city was consolidated in 1784 with the bringing together into a single administrative unit of the four hitherto separate townships of the Old Town, New Town, Little Quarter and Hradčany.

The rapid industrialisation of Prague in the 19C, and the increase in the city's population from 80,000 to well over 200,000, went hand-in-hand with a mood of growing Czech nationalism, and ever greater tensions between the Czechs and Germans in the city. In 1848 a Czech national uprising centred on Prague was crushed, but in that same year there also took place here the first Panslavic Congress. Germans lost their majority in the Prague Municipal Parliament for the first time in 1861, and in 1882 the Charles University was divided up according to nationality. In the latter years of the century the city's skyline was enriched by two massive neo-Renaissance buildings that expressed the aspirations of the Czech people: one was the National Theatre at the western end of Národní třída, the other was the National Museum, situated above what was now emerging as the new focal point of Prague life, the Wenceslas Square. Other major urban changes occurring in Prague at this time included the demolition of the city's remaining ramparts in 1874–76, and the destruction of the Jewish quarter through the creation in the 1890s of a long street named after the city of Paris and lined, as its name would suggest, with pompous apartment blocks and fashionable shops. An important Industrial Exhibition held in Prague in 1891 confirmed the city's position as one of the main industrial and commercial centres of the Habsburg Empire.

By the early years of the 20C, Prague was already becoming a leading European centre of the avant-garde, and the visionary achievements of a writer such as Kafka were matched by the construction of exceptionally original 'Cubist' buildings by the likes of Gočár and Chochol. However, it was the establishment of the Czech Republic in 1918 which led to one of the richest and liveliest periods in the cultural history of Prague. Pioneering poets, painters, designers, photographers and architects were all brought together by the Prague-based group Devětsil, which was closely associated with the city's developing reputation as the European centre of Constructivism and Functionalism. Uncompromising structures in concrete and glass grew up in the very centre of the city, while suburbs such as Podbaba and Barrandov became showpieces of Modernist architecture.

The German occupation of 1939–45, followed by the repressive years of Communism, drove the city's cultural life underground, but by no means extinguished it, as became evident in the great burst of literary, cinematic and theatrical talent in the 1960s, culminating in the 'Prague Spring' of 1968. World attention was drawn once again to Prague, but admiration turned to horror in August of that year, when television cameras showed Soviet tanks entering Prague's Old Town Square. On 16 January 1969, at a spot near the Wenceslas Square, the student Jan Palach set fire to himself in protest against the Soviet invasion. The subsequent years, up to the signing in 1977 of Charter '77, were among the greyest in the city's history, though they were also ones of rapid urban growth: in 1974 the city's underground railway system was opened, and the city boundaries were greatly increased by the incorporation within them of 74 outlying communities, bringing the total population of Prague up to 1,200,000 inhabitants. The new architecture was generally drab and mediocre, reducing the exciting Functionalism of the 1920s to unimaginative uniformity; a lively literary culture, however, continued to exist in the city, thanks principally to *samizdat* publishing, typewritten articles and books that circulated from hand to hand within a wide illicit network. Leading dissident meeting-places included jazz clubs, the *Café Slavia* (opposite the National Theatre), and the back-rooms of the Magic Lantern theatre, the latter coming to play a vital role in the 'Velvet Revolution' of November 1989, a revolution which had begun on 17 November with a large student demonstration making its way from the Vltava down Národní třída and eventually settling in the Wenceslas Square. Among the first acts of the Civic Forum Government led by the playwright president Václav Havel was, in January 1990, to rename Red Army Square after Jan Palach. The renaming of numerous other squares and streets in Prague gathered momentum in the course of 1990, and in October of that year the remains of Jan Palach were brought back to Olšanské Cemetery in the Prague district of Vinohrady.

For more detailed coverage of Prague, see *Blue Guide Prague.*

❖ Practical information

For information on arriving in Prague see the relevant section in the practical information section.

Hotels and pensions

Expensive: over 4500Kč (£90); Moderate: 200Kč–4500Kč (£50–£90); Cheap: 1500Kč–2500Kč (£30–£50)

Malá Strana and Hradčany
Expensive

The Charles, Josefská 1, 100 00 Praha 1; ☎ (02) 5731 5491/4; fax (02) 5731 1318. Newly opened luxury hotel in elegantly restored 17C building, intimate in atmosphere, and with painted wooden beam ceilings in bedrooms.

Pod Věží, Mostecká 2, 118 00, Praha 1; ☎ (02) 533 710; fax (02) 531 859.

Soberly decorated bedrooms in pale grey in a wonderfully situated Baroque palace overlooking the Charles Bridge.

U Kréle Karla, Úvoz 4, 118 00 Praha 1; ☎ 53 88 05; fax (02) 53 88 11. Warmly restored Baroque palace of 1639, with grandly decorated rooms featuring murals, stained glass, wooden beam ceilings and elaborate wooden furniture.

U Páva, U Lužického semináre 32, 118 00 Prague 1; ☎ (02) 245 10 922; fax (02) 53 33 79. In the same ownership as the U Kréle Karla (see above), this similarly appointed and tastefully restored 17C palace on the northern half of the Kampa Island has a number of rooms with outstanding views.

U Raka, Cernínská 10, 118 00 Praha 1; ☎ (02) 205 111 00; fax (02) 205 105 11). This tiny former pension in a cottage-like building with a wooden log exterior, is located at the bottom of the quiet, toy-like district of the Novy Svét; it now forms part of the Romantik Hotels and Restaurants chain.

Moderate
Pension Dientzenhofer, Nosticova 2, 118 00, Praha 1; ☎ (02) 53 16 72; fax (02) 57 32. Hidden away in a quiet and attractive corner of the southern half of the Malá Strana, this is a simple and friendly pension occupying the birthplace of the architect Killián Ignac Dientzenhofer.

Kampa Hotel, Všehrdova 16, 118 00 Praha 1; ☎ (02) 5732 0508; fax (02) 5732 0262. Drably furnished and impersonal, but well situated.

Sax, Jánsky Vršek 328/3, 118 00 Praha 1; ☎/fax (02) 53 84 22. A bland modern conversion of an elegant early 19C building.

Hotel U Křízé, Újezd 20, 118 01 Praha 1; ☎ (02) 53 33 26; fax (02) 53 34 43. On a busy street next to the Petrín Park.

Cheap
Penzion U Kiliana, Všehredova 13, 118 00 Praha 1; ☎ (02) 561 81 40; (02) fax 73 41 10. A couple of rooms above popular eatery, directly in front of Kampa Hotel.

Staré Mesto and Josefov
Expensive
Casa Marcello, Řásnovka 783, 110 00 Praha 1; ☎ (02) 231 0260; fax (02) 231 1230. Hotel of character housed in a building of 13C origin once used as a dormitory by nuns of the adjoining St. Agnes Convent.

Maximilian, Haštalská 14, 110 00 Praha 1. Situated in an increasingly fashionable part of the Josefov, this is a smartly modernised hotel created out of a turn-of-the-century building.

Grand Hotel Bohemia, Královorká 4, 110 00 Praha 1; ☎ (02) 24 804 111; fax (02) 232 95 45. Not nearly as stylish as the nearby Paríz (see below), but with spectacular neo-Rococo ball-room in basement.

Paříž, U Obecního domu 1, 110 00 Praha 1; ☎ (02) 22 195 195; fax (02) 24 225 475. Turn-of-the-century elegance reinterpreted for the modern age.

Ungelt, Malá Stupartská 1, 110 00 Praha 1; ☎ (02) 248 11 330; fax (02) 231 95 05. Ten apartments sleeping up to four people in what looks like a modernised version of a grand country inn; just behind the Tyn Church.

Moderate
Betlem Club, Betlémské námestí 9, 110 00 Praha 1; ☎ (02) 242 168 72; fax (02) 242 180 54. The 13C cellar bar is the most appealing interior feature of this tackily furnished if well situated hotel.
U Klenotníka, Rystířská 3, 110 00 Praha 1; ☎ (02) 242 116 99; fax (02) 261 782. Distinguished by its offbeat decor and Surrealist works of art.
U Zlatého Stromu, Karlova 6, 110 00 Praha; ☎ (02) 242 213 85; fax (02) 242 213 85. Miniscule rooms behind attractive gabled façade on the 'Royal Way'.

Cheap
U Krále Jiřího, Liliová 10, 110 00 Praha 1; ☎/fax (02) 242 219 83. Basic but clean and excellently located bed and breakfast.

Nové Mesto
Expensive
Adria, Václavské námeští 26, 110 00 Praha 1; ☎ (02) 210 81 111; fax (02) 210 81 300. A restaurant dripping with stalactites is about the most imaginative feature of this otherwise unadventurously transformed late 18C building. However this is comfortable, efficiently run, and rather less sleazy than the other hotels on Wenceslas Square.
Ambassador Zlata Husa, Václavské námeští 26 110 00 Praha 1; ☎ (02) 241 93 111; fax (02) 242 23 563. Luxury at its most vulgar and depressing.
Esplanade, Washingtova 19, 110 00 Praha 1; ☎ (02) 2421 1715; fax (02) 2422 9306. Despite the major renovation programme carried out over the last few years, this newly re-opened hotel retains the same marbled, chandeliered magnificence of the original 1920s structure. Imposing yet friendly and intimate, this is in many ways the most appealing of Prague's grand hotels.
Palace, Panská 12, 111 21 Praha 1; ☎ (02) 2409 3111; fax (02) 24422 1240. Characterless recreation of a grand turn-of-the-century establishment.

Moderate
Atlantic, Na Poříčí 9, 110 00 Praha 1; ☎ (02) 2481 1084; fax (02) 2481 2378. Grim modern refurbishment of famous old hotel.
Europa, Václávské námeští 25, 110 00 Praha; ☎ (02) 242 281 17; fax (02) 242 245 44. Art nouveau splendour gone somewhat to seed, this will appeal to those who prefer architecture and atmosphere over comfort and cheerfulness.
Julius, Václavské námeští 22, 110 00 Praha; ☎ (02) 24 21 70; fax ()2) 24 21 8545. Functionalism that has become lacklustre, but with more pleasant bedrooms than the entrance lobby would suggest.

A. The Old Town ~ Staré Město

Along the Royal Route
The Staré Město, or Old Town, is bordered to the north and west by the river Vltava, and to the south and east by a long thoroughfare (comprising Národní třída, Na příkopě and Revoluční) marking the line of the medieval fortifications.

Powder Gate

The Powder Gate (Prašná brána) stands on the **náměstí Republiky**, which divides the pedestrian Na příkopě from its northern continuation, Revoluční.

History of the Powder Gate

Originally known as the New Tower, the dark and sinister Powder Gate, 65m tall, was commissioned in 1475 by Vladislav Jagiello on the site of one of the 13 gates forming part of the Old Town's defensive system, a system which had been made redundant following the founding of the New Town in 1348. The Gate, adjoining at one time the building which served from 1383 to 1484 as the seat of the Royal Court of Bohemia, was intended purely as a monumental entrance to the Old Town, and marked the beginning of the processional route used by the Czech kings on their way to be crowned in St Vitus's Cathedral. When in 1484 Vladislav Jagiello moved the Royal Court back to Prague Castle, work on the gate was abandoned, and the incomplete structure was given a temporary roof and put to use—until the end of the 17C—as a storehouse for gunpowder. Heavily damaged during the Prussian siege of Prague in 1737, it was left in a ruined state until the late 19C. Its present appearance is due largely to reconstruction work carried out between 1875 and 1886 by Josef Mocker, who provided the structure with its turreted upper gallery, steeply pitched roof and flamboyant Gothic decoration.

The profuse neo-Gothic ornament which covers the Powder Gate contains, alongside late 19C statues of Czech kings and other pseudo-medieval figures, fragments of the original sculptural decoration carried out by Matěj Rejsek of Prostějov after 1478; during the summer months you can climb up to the tower's upper gallery, the best point from which to study the layout of Prague's Old Town. **Open** daily 10.00–18.00.

Before entering the Old Town, you should take a look at two of the other monuments on the náměstí Republiky. Facing the gate, at the eastern end of the square (No. 3), is the house called **The Hibernians** (U Hybernů), which occupies the site of a former church and monastery belonging to the Hibernian Order (Franciscans of Irish origin). The monastery building, erected between 1637 and 1652, is a simple structure now used for offices; far more impressive is the adjoining former church, which was transformed by Georg Fischer in 1810 into a grandiose Customs House, inspired in its design by the former Mint in Berlin, and constituting one of the finest examples in Prague of the Empire style (the building now serves as a space for ambitious art exhibitions).

Municipal House

Meanwhile, flanking the northern side of the Powder Gate, and indeed dominating the whole square, is the Municipal House (Obecní dům), still the most remarkable Art Nouveau building in the Czech Republic, despite recent restoration that has made its beauty seem somewhat tawdry.

History of the Municipal House

The idea of erecting the Municipal House was that of the Czech Patriotic Society, which envisaged a building which would serve as a social and

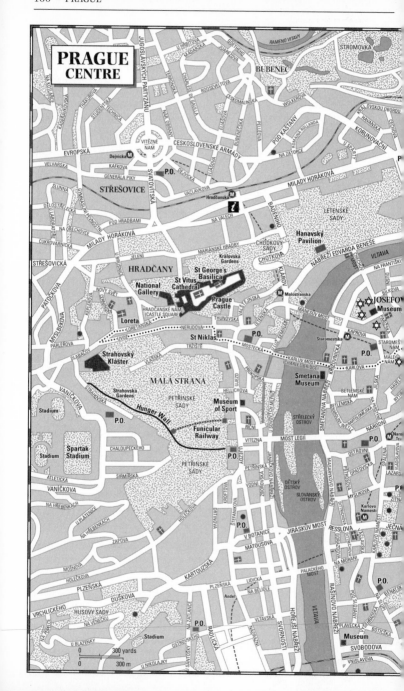

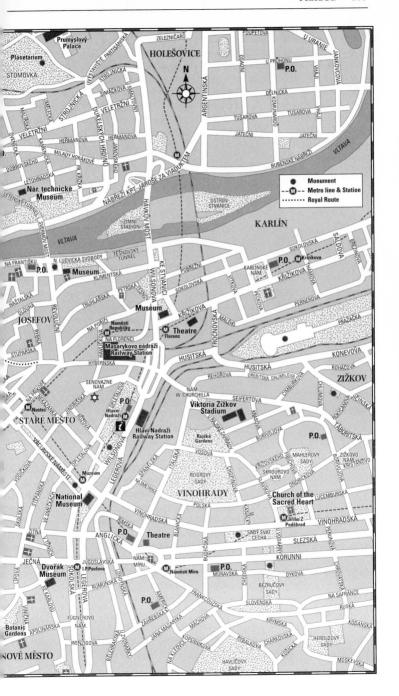

cultural centre for the Czech community in Prague, complete with café, restaurant, concert hall, and rooms for civic functions and assemblies. The architects chosen for the task, after a public competition which closed in 1905, were Antonín Balšánek and Osvald Polívka. Work on the building was undertaken between 1906–12, and involved the collaboration of many of the leading Czech painters and sculptors of the turn of the century, including Ladislav Šaloun (the sculptor of the Hus Monument in the Old Town Square; see below), Max Švabinský (who created the stained-glass windows in St Vitus's Cathedral), and Alfons Mucha, who had accepted the commission in the mistaken belief that he had been asked to carry out all the decoration (a protracted and heated correspondence in the press concluded that it would not be fitting for a single artist to assume responsibility for the whole work). The most important meetings to have taken place in the building were held at the end of the First World War, concluding with the proclamation here, on 28 October 1918, of the independence of Czechoslovakia, and the issuing of the new republic's Constitution. As for the concert hall, this continues to be one of Prague's most important cultural venues, hosting each year the inaugural concert of the Prague Spring Musical Festival; among the famous musicians to have performed in the hall are Sviatoslav Richter, David Oistrakh, Yehudi Menuhin, Mstislav Rostropovitch and Pablo Casals.

This large, irregularly-shaped building, once so wonderfully evocative of the city's turn-of-the-century splendour, now has the garish, artificial look of some modern pastiche. The restoration that was completed in 1997 has been rightly described by Daniel Špička, director of the Prague Centre for the Preservation of Architecture, as a textbook case of how not to renovate the city's buildings. Fortunately no amount of crude restoration can entirely diminish the genuine decorative brilliance of the structure, the exterior of which is impressive above all for its central **iron-work canopy**, which is coloured with stained-glass and topped by bronze figures of lamp-bearers executed by K. Novák. Above the canopy is a large lunette decorated by Karel Špillar with a mosaic, *Homage to Prague*; crowning this is a cupola, while on either side are sculptural groups by Ladislav Šaloun representing respectively the *Humiliation and Rebirth of the Czech Nation*. Numerous other sculptures adorn the exterior, including a statue by Čeněk Vosmík of the main architect of the adjoining Powder Gate, and a relief by Šaloun commemorating the first assembly in 1918 of the National Committee of the Czechoslovak Republic.

The Municipal House

Inside the building you find yourself in a vestibule adorned with bronze statues of *Flora* and *Fauna* by Bohumil Kafka. To the right a door leads into a **restaurant**, with large views of Prague by Josef Tomec and Antonín Záhel, and paintings by Josef Wenig representing *Hop-Growing, Viticulture*, and *Prague Welcoming its Visitors*; to the left of the vestibule is the similarly elegant **café**, featuring at one end a niche containing a statue of a nymph made of white Carrara marble by Josef Pekárek. A further restaurant and a late-night bar are situated in the basement, where you will find coloured drawings by Mikoláš Aleš and a folkloric fantasy by Jakub Obrovský entitled *Harvest Time*. The Concert Hall and Civic Rooms are to be found on the first floor, and can be visited during the day by guided tour (temporary exhibitions are also held in some of the newly renovated rooms). The large, ochre-coloured **Concert Hall**, named after the composer Smetana, has a central section domed in stained-glass, and two wide balconies flanked by large murals by Karel Špillar representing Music, Dance, Poetry and Drama. In between the stage and two prominent boxes at the front of the hall (the box on the left is that used by President Havel), are two dynamic stucco groups by Ladislav Šaloun portraying scenes from Dvořák's *Slavonic Dances* and Smetana's opera *Vyšehrad*. Among the other first-floor rooms are the small and exquisitely tasteful neo-Classical pastiche called the **Sweetshop**, the rather brasher **Oriental Room**, and the **Němcová Salon**, decorated all over with stuccowork inspired by folkloric themes. Other rooms on this floor have ambitious large-scale paintings, for instance the **Rieger Hall**, which has two long painted panels by Max Švabinský, *Czech Spring*, containing portraits of leading Czech writers, artists and musicians such as Jan Neruda, Božena Němcová, Josef Mylsbek, Josef Mánes, Mikoláš Aleš, Bedřich Smetana and Antonín Dvořák. Pride of place among the Civic Rooms must go to the **Hall of the Lord Mayor**, the windows of which occupy the central position on the building's façade. All the furniture and furnishings, and every detail of the decoration of this circular room are by Alfons Mucha, including allegorical murals on the walls and shallow ceiling, the pale blue stained-glass windows, the Lord Mayor's chair, and the elaborately embroidered curtains. **Open** Mon–Sat 10.00–18.00.

After leaving the Municipal House, turn left and then left again into the narrow side-street U Obecního domu, which flanks the northern side of the building. On the right-hand side of this street is another fine building of the turn of the century, the newly and brashly revamped **Hotel Paříž**, which was built in 1907 by Jan Vejrych and regarded in its time as a model of Art Nouveau architecture. There are colourful figurative decorations on the corner façade of its gabled, Gothic-inspired exterior, while inside are an attractively panelled café, and a mirrored restaurant with blue mosaics.

At the end of U Obecního domu turn left into the short U Prašné brány, where you will pass at No. 1 an Art Nouveau apartment block built by Bedřich Bendelmayer in 1903–04, and featuring inside an elegant semi-circular staircase. The street brings you back to the Powder Gate and to the eastern end of **Celetná**. Celetná, the pedestrian street at the start of the Royal Route, is one of the showpiece streets of the Old Town, and is lined principally with recently restored houses of medieval origin that were given pastel-coloured façades during the Baroque period. At No. 31, on the right-hand side of the street, is a palace built in 1750 by K.I. Dientzenhofer for the Master Minter Josef Pachta of Rájov; the Mint itself was situated up to 1784 in the palace at No. 36 on the opposite side of the street, a building which Pachta erected in 1759 on the site of the medieval Mint, and featuring atlante figures of miners by the Baroque sculptor I.F. Platzer.

At No. 34 Celetná, is one of the more interesting modern buildings in the Old Town, the corner department store known as the **House of the Black Virgin** (Dům U černé Matky Boží). Built as a department store in 1911–12 by Josef Gočár, this corner house is one of the masterpieces of Czech Cubism, and has two prominent cornices as well as heavy prism-shaped forms painted a dark maroon; its name is derived from a curious survival of the Baroque building it replaced—a 17C statue of the Virgin that inspired in 1921 Jaroslav Seifert's poem *Prayer on the Pavement* ('I raised my eyes towards the Black Virgin/ Standing there/and keeping her protecting hand over my head/and I prayed ...'). Major restoration carried out in 1993–94 attempted to bring back as much as possible the look of the original interior: partition walls and ceilings were demolished, revealing reinforced concrete beams reminiscent of Gothic vaulting. Although plans to recreate the original first-floor cafe have been abandoned, the building now houses the **Czech Museum of Fine Arts** (České muzeum výtvarných umění), which displays on the top two floors a collection of Czech Cubist paintings, sculptures and works of applied art culled both from its own holdings and those of the Museum of Decorative Art, the National Technical Museum, and various regional museums. **Open** Tues–Sun 10.00–18.00.

Opposite the building, at No. 23 Celetná, is to be found another statue of the Virgin, this one by a pupil of Matthias Braun and attached to the undulating Baroque façade of the palace built for the Schönpflok family. Continuing to walk on the right-hand side of Celetná, turn right just after No. 17 and walk through the covered passage leading towards the Malá Štupartská, on which stands the former **Monastery Church of St James** (sv. Jakub), which was founded by Minorites in 1232, and completely remodelled by Jan Šimon Pánek between 1689 and 1702. The tall twin-towered west façade has rich stuccowork by O. Mosto, executed in 1695 and featuring representations of SS James, Francis and Anthony of Padua. The enormously long and imposing interior, which has retained the medieval three-aisled plan and tall, Gothic proportions, is profusely whitewashed and gilded, and contains ceiling frescoes of the *Life of the Virgin* by F. Voget (1736), and 22 altars. The main altarpiece, supported by an exuberant gilded framework of angels high above the chancel, is a painting by V.V. Reiner of the *Martyrdom of St James*. Three of the altars on the right-hand side of the nave are by Petr Brandl, and were executed around 1710; another work by Brandl (the St Joseph Altar of 1708) is on the left-hand side of the nave, where an altar by J.K. Liška representing St Valburg can also be found. This side of the nave also boasts one of Prague's grandest funerary monuments, the *Monument to Jan Vratislav of Mitrovice*, designed by J.B. Fischer von Erlach in 1721 and containing sculpted figures by F.M. Brokoff.

Turning right on leaving the church and taking the first turning to the left, Tynská, you will reach (at No.6) the medieval **House of the Golden Ring** (dum U zlatého prstenu), which has now been taken over by the collection of 20C Czech art belonging to the **Prague City Gallery**. The long and rambling building, with its whitewashed vaulted rooms and views of the Týn Church, provides a characterful setting for a comparatively small selection of mainly early 20C Czech works, including Max Svabinsky's powerful *Destitute Land* (1900), sculptures by Bílek, boldly handled landscapes by Antonín Slavícek (among which is an unfinished view of Prague Cathedral of 1912), Indian-inspired paintings by Otakar Nejedly (who spent several years in Southern India and Ceylon at the beginning of the century), delicate fantasies by Zrzy, Sima, and Toyen, Cubist and other works by Filla, and Surrealistic photo montages by Jiří Kolar. The labelling and information panels are in Czech and English, and, as with the Museum of Modern Art in the Trade Fair Palace, the collection is arranged under such enigmatic and generally unhelpful headings as 'Rigid Unrestful'. **Open** Tues–Sun, 10.00–18.00.

Return to Celetná through the same covered passage, and you will find yourself directly in front of the spacious beer cellar at No. 22 known as **At the Vulture** (U Supa), which is housed on the ground floor of a pale green, late 18C building with a German inscription dating back to the days when the royal jeweller Gindle had his shop here. Continuing west on the left-hand side of Celetná, you will come, at No. 12, to the elegant **Hrzán Palace**, a building of Romanesque origin remodelled to a design by G.B. Alliprandi in 1702, and with sculptural decorations on the façade by pupils of F.M. Brokoff; Franz Kafka's father, Hermann, had a haberdashery shop here after 1882. Further down the street, No. 2, is where the Kafka family lived in 1888–89, and where Albert Einstein is said to have first explained his theory of relativity. Between 1896 and 1901 the Kafka family lived on the opposite side of the street, at No. 3, where the writer's street-facing bedroom inspired one of his earliest stories, *The Window onto the Street*. At the adjoining No. 5 is the 17C **Týn Presbytery**, occupying the site of a 12C hospice for foreign merchants; a short and narrow alley between the two houses leads to the south portal of the Church of Our Lady before Týn (see below).

Old Town Square

Celetná comes to an end at the spacious Old Town Square (Staroměstské náměstí), one of Europe's most beautiful squares.

History of the Old Town Square

Situated at what was formerly the junction of several trade routes, the Old Town Square served as the market-place of the Old Town in the 11C and 12C centuries. An important point on the traditional processional route of the Bohemian kings, and overlooked by the former Hussite Church of Our Lady before Týn, the square was later to witness some of the most significant—and tragic—events in the history of Prague, and came almost to symbolise the struggles and aspirations of the Czech people. Jan Želivský—the Hussite leader whose storming of the New Town Hall in 1419 had sparked off the Hussite Wars—was executed here in 1422; 56 other Hussites, including the officer Jan Roháč of Dubé, were executed on the square 15 years later. At the Old Town Hall, George of Poděbrady was elected King of Bohemia in 1458, and in 1621, 27 of the Protestant leaders who had taken part in the Battle of the White Mountain were beheaded outside the building. In 1945 large crowds welcomed the arrival here of Soviet troops, and three years later Klement Gottwald proclaimed from the balcony of the Kinský Palace the accession of the Communists to power. A rather different response to the Soviet army was shown in 1968, when, at the end of the 'Prague Spring', Soviet tanks advanced on the square, their arrival being greeted not by applause but by Molotov cocktails.

The square is surrounded by a picturesque jumble of medieval to Baroque buildings, to which recent restoration has given a toy-like cleanliness and cheerful range of light and vivid colours. Though most of the square is now traffic-free, it is the tourist heart of Prague, and you would be best advised to come here early in the day to appreciate the place before it fills up with a vast and noisy crowd in which buskers, street vendors and money-changers now jostle with the foreigners.

Jan Hus Monument

Rising on steps near its centre and dominating the whole space, is the extraordinary bronze monument to Jan Hus, a disgracefully undervalued work of the early years of the century, considered by some to be completely out of place in the square, but which is surely one of the most powerful public monuments in any European city, and one which brilliantly complements its surroundings.

History of the monument

Jan Hus Monument by Ladislav Šaloun

The monument was the masterpiece of the idiosyncratic sculptor Ladislav Šaloun, who began planning the work as early as 1898, and struggled with it for the next 17 years, making constant changes throughout this period of gestation. The monument was intended to be unveiled in 1915, on the occasion of the 500th anniversary of the burning of Jan Hus for heresy. The unveiling went ahead as planned, but few worse moments could have been chosen for the completion of a highly emotive monument symbolising the Czech national consciousness and the fight for Czech independence. The Austrian authorities did not permit any speech or ceremony of any kind to take place, but within a few days the work was completely covered with flowers, and all that showed of it was a solitary finger pointing menacingly to the sky. At this time there still stood next to the monument a Marian column erected in 1650 to commemorate the Peace of Westphalia—the treaty which brought the Thirty Years War to an end. In 1918, only five days after the declaration of independent Czechoslovakia, this symbol of Catholic and Habsburg dominance, with its sculpted angels trampling over devils, was pulled down, leaving only Jan Hus to preside over the square. The continuing power of the latter monument was attested in the wake of the Soviet invasion of August 1968, when it was shrouded in black drapes.

Šaloun's monument to Hus, which bears at its base the preacher's words 'The truth will prevail', features the figure of Hus rising above a struggling sea of gesticulating people in a defiant posture reminiscent of one of Rodin's *Burghers of Calais*; the power of this detailed yet unified composition lies to a large extent in the way in which—even on the brightest of days—it forms against the light and cheerful background of the square a dark and menacing profile, vividly reminding the spectator of the bleaker moments in Czech history.

Church of Our Lady Before Týn

The eastern end of the square is overshadowed by the most prominent building in the Old Town, and one of those most closely associated with the Hussite cause, the **Church of Our Lady Before Týn**. As with most medieval churches in Bohemia it does not rise directly above the square, but is set back behind a row of arcaded houses, comprising in this case a house of Romanesque origin with a tall late 18C façade (No. 15, at the southeastern end of the square), and the attractive **Týn School** (No. 14), which has a late 14C ground floor and a pair of stepped 16C gables recalling those of the Scuola Grande di San Marco in Venice; the architect Matěj Rejsek of Prostějov was a teacher at the school in the late 15C. Walking through the second of the school's four arches will take you to the west portal of the church (alternatively you could enter the church through its south portal by following the alley alongside the Týn Presbytery at No. 5 Celetná; see above). For many years much of the exterior of the Týn has been encased by scaffolding, and access to its very restricted site has been extremely limited; entry to the building can only be guaranteed at times of services, and this situation is likely to persist for several more years.

History of the church

The origins of the Týn church are in a Romanesque building first mentioned in 1135 as the property of the foreign merchants' hospice in Celetná. Work on the present structure was begun in 1365, and by the 1380s the north portal, the side aisles, the walls of the nave and much of the east end had been completed. The reformist preachers K. Waldhauser and Milíč of Kroměříž were already preaching in the building by the end of the 14C, and early in the following century the place was to become the main Prague church of the Hussites; it was to remain associated with the followers of Jan Hus until 1621. The nave was vaulted by 1457, a year before the accession to the throne of the Utraquist monarch George of Poděbrady, who was to be one of the church's greatest benefactors. Under George the northern of the west façade's twin towers was erected (the southern one dates from the early 16C), as was this façade's tall gable. The gable was adorned with a statue of George and a gold chalice symbolising the Utraquist cause, but these were removed after the Battle of the White Mountain in 1620, and replaced with an image of the Virgin, whose halo was made from the gold of the chalice. A severe fire in 1679 led to the rebuilding of the nave vault and extensive remodelling of the interior.

The twin-towered exterior of the church is a gloomy pile of exposed masonry, the principal decoration being concentrated on the north portal, where there is a late 14C tympanum of the Crucifixion from the workshop of Peter Parléř (the original is now in the National Gallery in Prague Castle). The north portal can be reached along the narrow Týnská, which runs along the northern side of the Týn School, and off which there is a gateway (just to the east of the church) leading into the merchants' courtyard which gave this area its name (*týn* means 'enclosure'); the courtyard, used from the 11C to 18C for the stocking and selling of goods, and as a customs house, retains only the ground-plan of the medieval structure, the oldest surviving part being the mid-16C loggia of the Granovský House.

The interior of the Týn church, in need of restoration, is a dark three-aisled hall space with crumbling, unadorned plaster from the Baroque period. At the western end of the north aisle is a Gothic baldachin by Matěj Rejsek (1493) which was originally situated above the tomb of the Hussite bishop A.L. Mirandola. The outstanding work of art in the building is the intricately carved *Baptism of Christ* by the Monogramist I.P. (c 1526) on the pier immediately to the right of the south portal. Attached to the south aisle pier directly in front of the main apse is the red marble tombstone of the Danish astronomer Tycho Brahe. The high altar of the Ascension (1649) is by Karel Škréta.

Returning to the Old Town Square, and continuing to walk north along its eastern side, you will come next to the **House at the Stone Bell** (Dům U kamenného zvonu) at No. 13, a narrow-fronted structure, the Baroque cladding of which was recently removed to reveal its original late 14C stonework; the interior, now used for concerts and small exhibitions, features a small chapel with fragments of 14C murals. Adjoining it, at No. 12, is one of the most elegant of the city's 18C palaces, the **Goltz-Kinský Palace** (1755–65), which was built by Anselmo Lurago to a design supplied by K.I. Dientzenhofer, and richly stuccoed by C.G. Bossi. The twin pediments of the façade are a clever solution to the building's position at the corner of the square, and show how the architects were anxious not to destroy the unity of the multi-gabled square by producing a single enormous pediment. **Open** Tues–Sun 10.00–18.00.

The northern side of the square was radically altered at the end of the 19C, at around the same time that the pompous Pařížská třída was built. At the northeastern corner of the square, adjacent to the Goltz-Kinský Palace, is the late 17C former Pauline Monastery (klášter Paulánu), but the space between here and Pařížská is now taken up by the enormous, neo-Baroque building housing the Ministry of Domestic Trading.

Church of St Nicholas

The Church of St Nicholas (sv. Mikuláš) was once tucked away at the very corner of the square, at the junction of Pařížská and U radnice but, since the destruction in the Second World War of the northern wing of the Town Hall, has now a prominent, exposed position, and indeed is one of the square's great glories.

History of the church

The original church of St Nicholas was founded by merchants in the late 13C, and served until the building of the Týn church as the parish church of the Old Town. The reformist preacher Jan Milíč gave sermons here in the 1360s, and in the following century the building was taken over by the Utraquists, who were to keep it for over two centuries. In 1635 the church was presented to the Benedictines, who had it rebuilt between 1650 and 1660. During the rule of Abbot Anselmo Vlach it was demolished and replaced by the present structure, which was built in 1732–35 by K.I. Dientzenhofer. The monastery was abolished in 1787, and for a while the church was used as a concert hall before being handed over to the Russian

Orthodox Church in 1871. Since 1920 it has been the property of the Czechoslovak Hussite Church, which was founded in that same year. A thorough restoration of the building was completed in 1990.

The church, which has recently been given a dazzling coat of white paint, is a centrally planned structure with an unusual design which was determined to a large extent by the once cramped nature of the site. Dientzenhofer, wishing to create a structure which would powerfully reaffirm the Catholic faith in the wake of the building's Utraquist past, was forced by the restricted site to put the emphasis on verticality. The twin-towered southern façade of the church, adorned with sculptures from the school of Braun, has an arrangement recalling that of Borromini's Sant' Agnese in Rome, but the architectural elements have been elongated in the creation of soaring proportions. The spectacular interior, now also a brilliant white, is dominated by the enormously tall central dome, and gives one the impression of being inside a wedding cake. There are ceiling frescoes by the Bavarian artist P. Assam of scenes from the Old Testament and the lives of SS Nicholas and Benedict but—unusually for Dientzenhofer—the painted decorations are subservient to the exceptionally rich stucco framework by Bernard Spinetti. **Open** Tues–Fri 10.00–12.00, Wed 10.00–12.00 and 14.00–16.00.

Adjacent to the west façade of St Nicholas, on Maislova, is the site of the house where Franz Kafka was born on 3 July 1883; not until 1965, when the Communist regime finally accepted Kafka as a 'revolutionary critic of capitalist alienation', was the present bronze commemorative bust by Karel Hladík attached to it. The house, known as **At the Tower** (U Věže), originally belonged to the Benedictines, but by Kafka's day had been turned into a warren of small apartments at the southernmost end of the Jewish ghetto; largely destroyed by fire in 1887, but replaced in 1902 with a new structure that retained the original Baroque portal, the building now features a small Kafka museum. **Open** Tues–Fri 10.00–18.00, Sat 10.00–17.00.

Old Town Hall

Immediately to the south of the Church of St Nicholas is a small garden laid out on the site of the demolished northern wing of the Old Town Hall. The heavily restored Old Town Hall (Staroměstská radnice), which projects into the southwestern corner of the Old Town Square, is the square's principal tourist attraction. Its history is a complex one, the place being an assemblage of several buildings, the earliest of which dates back to the beginning of the 14C.

To understand the Town Hall's genesis you should walk slowly around the exterior, beginning with the eastern end, which incorporates part of the ground floor of the original building—a private house which the civic authorities purchased from one Wolflin of Kámen in 1338. A tower was added to this in 1364, and a chapel—with an oriel window projecting east—built on its first floor by 1381; on the wall underneath the oriel is a plaque bearing the names of the 27 Protestants executed on the square in 1621, the exact place of the execution being marked on some nearby paving stones. The block which was attached to the northern end of Wolflin's house was a late 15C addition, rebuilt in the late 18C, and again in the early 20C; it was burnt down by the Nazis on the penultimate day of the

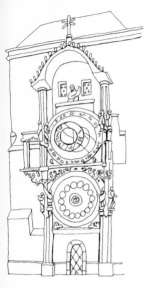

Astronomical Clock

Second World War, and plans to put up a modern extension on its site seem to have been abandoned. Walking the length of the southern side of the Town Hall, from east to west, you will come immediately to the famous **Astronomical Clock**, which was added to the south façade of Wolflin's house in 1410.

History of the clock

Installed originally by the master clocksmith Mikoláš of Kadaň in 1410, the clock was rebuilt in 1490 by a teacher at the Charles University, Master Hanuš of Růže. According to legend Hanuš was blinded to prevent him from creating another such marvel in Prague, but the blind man then climbed up the tower and stopped the clock. The true story is that the clock's mechanism was not to be perfected until Jan Táborský repaired it between 1552 and 1560, after which it required no further alterations. Only its decorations have been changed, the painted calendar on the lower level being executed by J. Mánes in 1865 (the original is in the National Gallery at the convent of St Agnes), and the coloured figurines on all three of its levels being carved by V. Sucharda in 1948. The middle level comprises the clock proper, which both tells the time and gives the position of the Sun and Moon.

Just before the striking of each hour a large crowd gathers in front of the clock to watch an impressive spectacle which begins with a skeleton (on the upper right corner of the clock) raising an hour glass and pulling a funerary bell; windows subsequently open on the upper level, and a macabre procession of Apostles and allegorical figures (such as a miser gloating over a sack of gold) files past.

West of the clock is a portal of 1470–80, attributed to Master Rejsek, and constituting the main entrance to the building. Further west is the former **Kříž House**, purchased by the civic authorities in 1360 and featuring a fine Renaissance window of 1520 bearing the Latin inscription *Praga caput regni* ('Prague, capital of the kingdom'). In 1458 the Town Hall was extended by the purchase of the now attached house to the west, a property belonging previously to Mikeš the Furrier and which was to be remodelled in a neo-Renaissance style in 1878 by the architect A. Baum. The complex was enlarged yet further in 1835 with the purchase of the adjoining house called **At the Cock** (U kohouta), an originally Romanesque structure given an Empire façade in 1830. Finally, in 1896, the Town Hall bought the splendid property adjacent to the western end of At the Cock, **At the Minute** (Dům U minuty), a house where the Kafka family had lived from 1889 right up to the time of its purchase. The exterior of the house is covered with among the finest sgraffito decorations in Prague; these monochrome works, representing Classical and biblical scenes and allegorical figures of the Virtues, were executed around 1611, and restored in 1919 by none other than J. Čapek, the brother of the writer Karel (they were to be restored again after the 1945 fire).

The interior of the Town Hall can only be visited with a guided tour, and these take place at irregular intervals throughout the day, and attract great crowds of tourists. Though it has been much altered over the centuries and was badly gutted in 1945, it retains on the second floor the late Gothic **Council Chamber** of 1470. The late 19C Assembly Room on the same floor was dominated until recently by two large canvases by V. Brožík, *Jan Hus at the Council of Constance* and *The Election of George of Poděbrady as King of Bohemia* (these are now in the Troja Château; see p 190); the Gothic vaulting in the vestibule of the building has a mosaic decoration of 1937, executed after designs by M. Aleš, and representing the story of the mythical Countess Libuše. A visit to the Town Hall is complemented by a climb up its 70m-high tower, from where an excellent view can be had. **Open** Tues–Sun 09.00–17.00, Mon 11.00–17.00.

Before leaving the Old Town Square, you should walk along its southern side, which is lined with an especially attractive row of arcaded houses. The neo-Gothic one at No. 16 (at the entrance to Celetná) has sgraffittoed decorations by M. Aleš, most notably a representation of St Wenceslas on horseback. Further west, at No. 20, is the **House at the Golden Unicorn** (Dům U zlatého jednorožce), which has an 18C façade with a Gothic portal; the cellar is a Romanesque structure of the 13C, while the late Gothic vaulting in the vestibule was designed by Master Rejsek in 1496. A plaque on the outside of the building records that in 1848 the composer Bedřich Smetana established here his first music school.

Along Karlova

The Old Town Square leads at its narrow southwestern corner into the quieter and triangular-shaped **small square** (Malé náměstí), which is centred around a small **fountain** surrounded by a Renaissance ironwork grille of 1560. One of the oldest spaces in the Old Town, this was inhabited in the 12C by French merchants; fruit markets were held here during the Middle Ages. Though a number of the houses have Romanesque cellars, the present appearance of the square is due mainly to 18C and 19C remodelling. One of the most prominent of the buildings is that at No. 3, which was rebuilt in a neo-Renaissance style in 1890 for the ironmongery firm of V.J. Rott; the name of Rott appears on the recently repainted façade, which is covered all over with figurative and ornamental motifs based on designs supplied by M. Aleš. An excellently preserved neo-Baroque pharmacy of the last century is incorporated into the late 18C house at No. 13.

Although this reception centre has now gone, Americanisation of the worst kind has done much to destroy the character of the neighbouring **Karlova**, along which you can continue heading west following the processional route of the Bohemian kings. As much of a showpiece as Celetná, but narrower and more winding, and with houses that are picturesquely askew, this street has sadly lost much of its former fairy-tale charm through its recent encrustation of competing neon signs, brash eateries and other tourist establishments.

At the junction of Karlova and **Husova**, the first street which you cross, are three interconnected buildings forming the **Czech Museum of Fine Arts** (České muzeum výtvarných umění), where temporary art exhibitions are put on. The part of the gallery on Karlova is an elegant 18C structure, but the building where the gallery's main entrance is situated, at No. 21 Husova, is a

Renaissance house crowned by an attractive pair of stepped gables; the interior of the gallery, featuring a Romanesque cellar, successfully incorporates the surviving medieval elements into a bright modern setting. Just to the south of the entrance, at No. 19 Husova, is the beer cellar called **At the Golden Tiger** (U zlatého tygra), a popular haunt of the writer Bohumil Hrabal.

One of Prague's raunchiest Bohemian meeting-places of the early 20C, the **Cabaret Montmartre**, was situated around the corner from here, at No. 7 Řetězová (the first turning to your right as you continue south down Husova).

Returning to Karlova along Husova, and deviating this time to the north, you will reach one of the most celebrated of Prague's Baroque palaces, the **Clam-Gallas Palace**. Built between 1713 and 1719 for Count J.W. Gallas, it was the work of the great Viennese architect Johann Bernard Fischer von Erlach, aided by two of the leading artists of his day, the sculptor Matthias Braun and the Italian painter Carlo Carlone. The main façade, hemmed in on the narrow Husova, is in many ways remarkably Classical, with its large central pediment, simple fenestration, and largely undecorated walls. At the same time, however, it is given a dynamic Baroque quality through Braun's sculptural additions—the row of figures (replaced mainly by copies) along the attic, and, above all, the powerful, struggling atlantes who support the two portals, which are situated, unusually, at the sides of the façade. The dramatic elements of the exterior are continued inside in the exciting Grand Staircase, where there are further works by Braun in addition to sumptuous stucco-work by Santino Bussi and an exhilarating ceiling painting by Carlone representing *The Triumph of Apollo*. The whole building, boasting a number of other ceilings by Carlone, and beautifully restored in the 1980s, now houses the city archives, and is officially closed to visitors.

The northern side of the palace abuts into the náměstí Primátora Dr. Vacka, where you will find, immediately on turning right into the square, a **fountain** attached to the palace's garden wall. Within its niche is a famous sculpture executed in 1812 by the Romantic artist Václav Prachner (the original has now been taken to the National Gallery at Zbraslav): entitled *Vltava* but popularly called Terezka, it is a vigorous portrayal of a female nude, and tradition has it that an old man living in the neighbourhood fell in love with this image and left all his money for her in his will. The rest of the square is taken up by the northeastern corner of the vast Clementinum (see below), the grim Municipal Public Library (1924–28) and, on the eastern side of the square, the **New Town Hall** (Nová radnice). The latter, built in 1908–11 by O. Polívka, is a grey and heavy Art Nouveau structure enlivened by some fine and prominent statuary: the allegorical figures and reliefs around the main portal are by S. Sucharda and J. Mařatka, while the niche figures at the two corners of the façade are by L. Šaloun, and include a wonderful sandstone representation of Rabbi Löw (1910).

The short Seminářská, at the southwestern corner of the square, will take you back to Karlova. Continue walking west along this street and you will find, at No. 18, at the junction with the next street, Liliová, a pink Renaissance house named **At the Golden Serpent** (U zlatého hada), with a 19C plaque of a snake on the outside. In the early 18C the house was occupied by the Armenian coffee-merchant Deodatus Damajan, who sold coffee in the streets of Prague before opening here the first coffee-shop in Prague (later he opened another shop, At the Three Ostriches—U tří pštrosů—on the other side of the river); the place today is an unappealingly decorated restaurant. Further west along the southern side of Karlova, at No. 4, is a plaque marking the house where the German astronomer J. Kepler lived between 1607 and 1612, formulating during this period his first two laws concerning the movement of the Earth around the Sun; the tower within the courtyard of the house is said to have been used by Kepler as an observatory.

The Clementinum and its churches

The whole northern side of the Karlova, from Seminářská right up to the end of the street, is lined by the former Jesuit College of the **Clementinum**, the largest complex of buildings in Prague after the Castle, and covering an area of two hectares. **Open** Mon–Fri 08.00–22.00, Sat 08.00–19.00.

History of the Clementinum

As part of his campaign to strengthen the Catholic faith in Bohemia, the Habsburg Emperor Ferdinand I summoned the Jesuits in 1556 to Prague, where they took over the former Dominican church and monastery of St Clement. At the western end of Karlova, overlooking Knights of the Cross Square, the Jesuits began building in 1593 the Church of the Holy Saviour, the construction of which was later to involve two of the leading architects of the early Baroque in Bohemia, Anselmo Lurago and Francesco Caratti. By the middle of the 17C the teaching establishment which the Jesuits had founded alongside the church had been turned into a university college endowed with an important library. From 1653 onwards F. Caratti began work on the university buildings, a task which was to entail the pulling down of much of the Old Town and was not to be completed until 1748, under the direction of F.M. Kaňka. With the expulsion of the Jesuit order in 1773, the Clementinum was given over to the Charles University, which shortly afterwards transferred here its own library. This library has now been amalgamated into the Czech National Library, which takes up most of the complex and boasts such precious works as the Vyšehrad Codex of 1085.

Walking down Karlova from Seminářská you skirt the southern side of the former Dominican **Church of St Clement** (sv. Kliment), which is incorporated into the southern walls of the Clementinum. The church was rebuilt in 1711–15 by F.M. Kaňka, and is now used by the Greek Catholic Church. The recently restored interior, which is rarely open, is covered with ceiling paintings of the life of St Clement by J. Hiebel, who was also responsible for the illusionistic framework in the chancel, a work clearly inspired by the Italian *quadratura* specialist Padre Pozzo. More remarkable are the outstanding and emotionally charged series of statues of the *Evangelists and Fathers of the Church* by Matthias Braun and his workshop, decorating the niches of the piers.

Adjacent to the western end of the Church of St Clement, and attached to the apse of the Holy Saviour, is the **Italian Chapel** (Vlašská kaple), the rounded exterior of which affects the course of Karlova and gives drama to the street; built around 1590 (but with an interior redecorated in the 18C), it is the earliest example in Central Europe of an elliptically planned structure. The grandest of the churches associated with the Clementinum is that of the **St Salvator**, which was begun in 1593 and not completed until 1714. The Italianate west façade, facing Knights of the Cross Square, is inspired by that of the Jesuit's mother church in Rome, but has a three-arched portico which was added by Francesco Caratti in 1653–59; the sculptures on the portico's balustrade, as well as those on the pediment above, were executed by Jan Bendl in 1659. The interior, with alterations by both C. Lurago and F.M. Kaňka, has rich stucco decorations by Bendl, and also a ceiling painting of *The Four Continents* by K. Kovář (1748); among the furnishings is a confessional (1675) which Bendl decorated with sculptures of the Apostles.

Running north of the church of St Salvator along Křižovnická is the earliest and most grandiose of the Clementinum's façades, begun by F. Caratti in 1653 and featuring stucco medallions of Roman emperors by Antonio Cometa. An arch by the side of the church will lead you inside the complex, where you will find four large and greying courtyards, one of which has a statue by Emmanuel Max of a *Prague Student* (1847), a work commemorating the role played by students in defending the Charles Bridge during the Sack of Prague by the Swedes in 1648; in another of the courtyards is an 18C **observatory tower** crowned by a bronze of *Atlas* (1722). The interiors of the Clementinum, which can only be visited with special permission, are remarkable for their Rococo rooms by F.M. Kaňka, most notably the **University Library** of 1727, a sumptuous gilded space with a ceiling painting by J. Hiebl of *The Temple of Wisdom*, and walls enlivened by salomonic columns.

The small and busy **Knights of the Cross Square** (Křižovnické náměstí) derives its name from the hospice brotherhood to which the protection of the Judith's Bridge, the predecessor of the Charles Bridge, was entrusted in the 13C. The former **Monastery and church of St Francis** (sv. František), which once belonged to this order, stand adjacent to the Church of the St Salvator, and were rebuilt in the late 17C. Designed by Jean-Baptiste Mathey, and carried out by Carlo Lurago, the centrally-planned church has a dome based closely on that of St Peter's in Rome. The interior is ringed with dark Slivenec marble altars, and adorned with a ceiling painting of the *Last Judgement* by V.V. Reiner (1722–23); in the crypt are the foundations of the original three-aisled structure of the 13C. Just outside the church is a cast-iron memorial to Charles IV, designed by A. Hähnel in 1848 to commemorate the fifth centenary of the foundation of the Charles University. The western end of the square is marked by the **Tower of the Old Town Bridge**, a late 14C structure which served as a model for the Powder Gate, and has rich sculptural decorations from the workshop of Peter Parléř, including, above the gate, representations of St Vitus (the bridge's patron saint) flanked by St Wenceslas and Charles IV; the structure was heavily restored and considerably embellished by Josef Mocker in the 1870s. The view from the top is in many ways the finest in all Prague, embracing the Old Town, the Little Quarter and a grand sweep of the Vltava. Viewing gallery **open** daily 10.00–18.00 June–Sept; 10.00–17.00 Oct–May.

The southern Old Town

The arch of the tower leads on to the Charles Bridge (see Chapter 1C), along which the coronation processions would pass on their way to St Vitus's Cathedral. Leave the Royal Route and head south from the square along the **Smetana Embankment** (Smetanovo nábřeží) to visit the southern half of the Old Town. The first turning to the right is the short Novotného Lávka, which takes you on to a tiny spit of land jutting out into the Vltava and dominated by the former **municipal water tower,** a structure of 1489 reconstructed at the end of the 19C. The furthermost building, originally a part of the municipal waterworks, was built in 1885 in a Czech Renaissance style, and is covered with sgraffito decorations representing the *Siege of the Old Town by the Swedes*, and executed after designs by M. Aleš, F. Ženíšek and J. Koula. Inside is the crammed café/bar/theatre/nightclub called **Lávka**, which is perhaps best appreciated during the summer months while sitting at its shaded riverside terrace.

Across the Smetana embankment from Novotného lávka is Anenská, which leads after a few metres into the intimate **Anenské náměstí**. Immediately to your right on entering the square (at No. 4) is a Rococo palace built c 1765 by Jan Josef Wirch for Count Hubert Karel Pachta of Rájov; the Pachtas were great patrons of music, and Mozart, his wife Costanza, and Beethoven were among those who stayed here. Attached to this building, at No. 5, is an early 19C building which was transformed in the late 1950s into one of Prague's most influential small theatres, **The Theatre on the Balustrade** (divadlo na Zábradlí).

On the opposite side of the square to the theatre is the former **Convent of St Anne** (klášter sv. Anny), which was founded by Dominican nuns in 1313 inside a monastery which has an imposing main façade of 1676. The church—where Christoph Willibald Gluck used to play the organ in the early 18C—survives to this day, though it has been put to other uses since the abolition of the convent in 1782; the whole complex, for many years the centre of the printing works of Schönfeld, is used today partly as lithographic studios, and partly as rehearsal rooms for the National Theatre.

The former convent extends east of the square all the way to the continuation of Anenská, Řetězová, on which stands, at No. 3, the **House at the Stork's** (Dům U Čápa), one of the more remarkable survivals in Prague of Romanesque domestic architecture, containing a ground floor which has remained little changed since around 1200; the building, which can be visited, belonged in the 15C to George of Poděbrady.

Return along Anenská to the Smetana Embankment, and walk south by the side of the Vltava. Shortly you will come to a small garden containing Prague's answer to London's Albert Memorial—a neo-Gothic **Monument to the Emperor Franz I**, who died in 1846. Erected in 1844–46 by J.O. Kranner, it features at its base a series of allegorical figures by Josef Max, executed in a style which owes nothing to Czech art, but much to German sculpture and engravings of the late 15C and early 16C; the equestrian statue of Franz I which once crowned the monument was taken down in 1918, and now languishes in that sculptural mortuary comprising the Lapidarium of the National Museum.

Due east of the garden, along Konviktská, is the tiny **Rotunda of the Holy Rood** (rotunda sv. Kříže), one of Prague's oldest buildings. Dating back to the early 12C, it was well restored by Vojtěch Ullmann in 1862–65, and ringed by an attractive iron-work grille designed by Josef Mánes; the interior, restored again in the late 1970s, contains fragments of 14C wall-paintings, including a scene of the *Coronation of the Virgin*.

Head south from the Rotunda down Karolíny Světlé and turn left along Krocínova into Bartolomějská. Towards the end of the latter street, you will pass on your left the former Jesuit **Church of St Bartholomew** (sv. Bartoloměje), which was built by K.I. Dientzenhofer in 1726–31, and has a richly decorated west façade and ceiling paintings by V.V. Reiner; next to it is a former Jesuit College intended for young noblewomen, and built in 1660 on the site of a centre for reformed prostitutes. Turn left at the end of the street into Pruchodní, which leads into **Bethlehem Square** (Betlémské náměstí). On the western side of the square, at No. 1, is the **House at the Hálaneks**, which was formed of three 15C houses that were remodelled at the end of the 16C. An extension to this was built in 1886 to house the anthropological callections now forming the **Náprstek Museum of Asian, African and American Cultures**. Open Tues–Sun 09.00–12.00 and 13.00–17.30.

Bethlehem Chapel

The north side of the Betlémské náměstí is dominated by the austere twin-gabled Bethlehem Chapel (Betlémská kaple), which gives the square its name.

History of the Bethlehem Chapel

In 1391, followers of the reformist preacher Milíč of Kroměříž decided to build a church where the Mass would be said in Czech. The Catholic authorities agreed only to the construction of a chapel, which, however, turned out when completed in 1394 to be large enough to contain a congregation of 3000. Jan Hus preached here between 1402 and 1413, and the place— called the Bethlehem Chapel—was to remain the spiritual centre of his followers long after his death. His friend, Master Jakoubek of Stříbro, succeeded him as preacher here from 1414–29, and in 1521 the German peasant leader Thomas Münzer proclaimed from the chapel's pulpit his Utopian social views; from 1609 up to the Battle of the White Mountain in 1620, the chapel belonged to the Union of Czech Brethren, one of whose preachers was the future father-in-law of Comenius, J.A. Komenský. Taken over subsequently by the Jesuits, the building was destroyed three years after the expulsion of the Jesuit Order in 1773, and a private dwelling put up in its place. In 1919 part of the chapel was unearthed under the house, and further archaeological excavations in 1949 revealed that all except the southern wall of the chapel had been used in the construction of the later building. The decision was then taken to reconstruct the Bethlehem Chapel in its original state, the idea being to create a memorial to the Hussites, who, according to remarks made at this time by Klement Gottwald, were already 'fighting for communism' 500 years ago.

The box-like interior of the chapel, which was reconstructed in 1950–52 by Jaroslav Fragner, has pseudo-medieval wall-paintings and wooden furnishings, and is focused on the pulpit rather than the altar. A door on the eastern side leads into the house where Jan Hus and other preachers lived: inside you will find a partial recreation of a domestic interior of the early 15C, and displays relating to the Hussite movement. **Open** daily 09.00–18.00.

After leaving the building turn left and then left again into Husova, on which stands—shortly to the north on the right-hand side—the **Church of St Giles** (sv. Jiljí). Founded in the 13C and rebuilt between 1310 and 1371, this church has a sturdy, twin-towered west façade which has been little altered since the

14C, when the building was the principal base of the reform preacher Milíč of Kroměříž; the tall interior, however, was remodelled by F. Špaček after 1733, and has been cloaked with massive gilded capitals, rich stucco decoration by B. Spinetti, and ceiling frescoes by V.V. Reiner comprising a central panel of the *Celebration of the Dominican Order*, and two flanking ones representing the legends of St Giles and St Thomas Aquinas.

Head east of the church along the tiny Zlatá, turn right into Jilská, and then immediately left into Vejvodova; this will take you into Michalská, where you turn right again, and then first left into **Havelská**. At its northeastern end Havelská widens into a narrow square, enlivened today by Prague's last surviving open-air market, and dominated by the **Church of St Gall** (sv. Havla). The latter, a 13C foundation, was remodelled around 1722 by Pavel Bayer and Johann Santini-Aichel, who gave the church its powerful, undulating façade. Between here and the former Fruit Market (Ovocný trh) to the northeast is the **Estate Theatre** (formerly Tyl) an elegant neo-Classical building designed by Antonín Haffenecker in 1781, and famous as the place where Mozart's opera *Don Giovanni* had its premiere in 1787.

Adjoining the theatre, at No. 9 Železná, is the **Carolinum**, the original building of the oldest university in Central Europe. Founded by Charles IV in 1348, the university building is also claimed to be the oldest still in use in Europe, though in fact very little of the medieval structure remains, the principal survival being the charming oriel window on the southern side, facing the Fruit Market. The structure was extensively rebuilt by F.M. Kaňka after 1718, at the time when the university was in the hands of the Jesuits; further major reconstruction took place after the Second World War.

Continue north up Železná, and turn left into Kožná, where, at **No. 1**, is a house with a beautiful Renaissance portal featuring two bears. A plaque indicates that the house was the birthplace of the journalist Egon Erwin Kisch (1885–1948), who devoted much of his writing to accounts of his native Prague, including *Prague Adventures* and *Tales from Prague's Streets and Nights*. Another of his works was dedicated to the city's covered passages, and it is singularly appropriate that from No. 10 Kožná you can walk through such passages all the way back to Jilská. Kisch's birthplace stands at the corner of Melantrichova, where you turn right to rejoin the southern side of the Old Town Square.

The Jewish Town ~ Josefov

Walk to the opposite side of the square and enter **Pařížská**, a good starting-point for a tour of the northern half of the Old Town. This long, straight avenue, built at the end of the 19C, is lined with large, oppressively ornamented blocks featuring fantastical corners composed of irregularly shaped balconies and openings piled up one on top of each other. Its creation constituted one of the few major plans of urban renewal within the Old Town of Prague, cutting a great swathe through a slum area crammed with picturesque but decayed old houses inhabited largely by the city's Jewish population. Before reaching the main monuments of Jewish Prague, take the first turning to the right, and then turn right again into Salvátorská, on which stands, at No. 8 an innovative brick building constructed for the Stenc Fine-Arts Publishing House by Kotěra's student Otakar Novotný in 1908–11; exposed brickwork is uncommon in

Bohemia, and reveals here Novotný's great interest in the works of Frank Lloyd Wright and the Dutch architect Hendrik Petrus Berlage.

Return to Pařížská, and continue walking north until you reach a sudden interruption in the line of Pařížská's turn-of-the-century blocks. Just below the pavement level on the left-hand side are three of the main survivals of Jewish Prague—the Jewish Town Hall, and the Old-New and High Synagogues. The first two buildings, together with several other neighbouring monuments, form part of the Jewish Museum (Židovské muzeum), which since 1994 has been administered by the city's Jewish community. The Jewish Museum is today one of the city's obligatory tourist sights, and the throngs of visitors who descend upon this restricted area lead to unpleasant congestion and long queues to enter some of the monuments. An extremely expensive entrance ticket covering all the various parts of the museum can be purchased from any of the quarter's ticket offices (male visitors both to the Old-New Synagogue and the Jewish Cemetery are also provided with the small cap known as a yarmulka).

History of the Jews in Prague

Jews began settling in Prague from at least the 10C onwards, though it was not apparently until the mid-13C that they began forming a ghetto in the district around the Old-New Synagogue; in accordance with the Third Lateran Council of 1179 this ghetto was separated from its Christian surroundings by a wall. Despite fires, pogroms and even a law of 1541 banishing Jews from the whole of Bohemia, the ghetto flourished, and by the 17C an estimated 7000 people were crowded into the area. Two of its most influential figures were active during the reign of Rudolph II, one being the Emperor's finance minister, Mordechaj Markus Maisel, who was responsible for the paving of the ghetto and the building of the Maisel Synagogue and the Jewish Town Hall. The other great Jew of this period was the Rabbi Löw, a man much respected by Rudolph II and the leading aristocratic families of the time, and under whose influence the Jewish community in Prague enjoyed the most privileged period in its history. A prominent theologian, Löw was the author of many writings that became an inherent part of Hasidic teaching, such as his homily *On the Hardening of Pharaoh's Heart*. But Löw was to be remembered above all for his reputed supernatural powers, a reputation doubtless enhanced by his being a passionate devotee of the Cabbala, whereby he believed that the whole of human history, past, present and future, could be read in the Torah.

The law requiring the Prague Jews to be contained in the ghetto was abolished in the 1781 by Emperor Joseph II, whose ultimate intentions were to assimilate Jews fully into the rest of the population and destroy their language and culture by forbidding Hebrew and Yiddish for business transactions, and forcing the Jews to Germanise their names (it was not until 1867 that Jews were assured all civil rights equal to those guaranteed to Czechs and Germans). In 1850, when the ghetto had been almost entirely infiltrated by outsiders and only 10 per cent of the former Jewish population was left, this area of Prague was turned into a municipal district known as Josefov in honour of Joseph II. The emperor would not perhaps have entirely appreciated the honour, for this district was by now a festering slum, more over-populated than any other area in the city, without water-supply or drainage, and with a notorious reputation for its low life: decrepit smoke-filled bars, and brothels marked by poles hung with red lanterns, stood provocatively alongside the houses of the remaining Orthodox Jews, whose sabbath chants would sometimes be interrupted by the shouts and songs of drunken revellers and prostitutes.

Despite the protests of poets, students, architects and others, this whole area was largely razed in 1895, leaving only the buildings of historical interest still standing (the 21,700 waggonloads of rubble were used as land-fill to protect a district that was still constantly under the threat of floods). Later the Nazis, far from wishing to destroy these surviving monuments, planned to turn them into a 'Museum of Jewry', so as to record for posterity the culture of what they believed would soon be an extinct race. A museum of Jewish art had existed since the beginning of the century but, as a result of the Nazis' confiscation of Jewish property, the holdings were swelled to become the world's largest collection of synagogical art. The museum's growth coincided with the dwindling of the Jewish population of Bohemia and Moravia to a tenth of its former size: a memorial in the Pinkas Synagogue in Prague records the names of 77,297 Jews killed during the Nazi occupation of the country. Today only a small community of Orthodox Jews remains in the traditional Jewish quarter of Prague.

Architecturally and historically the most important of the Jewish Museum's monuments is the **Old-New Synagogue** (Staronová synagoga), which is also Prague's most outstanding early medieval building. The oldest functioning synagogue in Europe, it dates back to the middle of the 13C, and owes its unusual name to the fact that it was originally called the 'New Synagogue' until another 'new' one was built in the vicinity. After noting on the exterior the unusually tall, stepped brick gables (a 15C addition), you enter a narrow, barrel-vaulted vestibule that was originally the main hall of the synagogue until the present one was added after c 1270 (it later became the women's gallery); in the 17C metal boxes were placed in this vestibule for the collection of Jewish taxes. The actual main hall, one of the finest examples in Central Europe of the Cistercian Gothic style, is reached through a 13C portal with an exquisitely carved vine tree bearing 12 bunches of grapes that refer to the 12 tribes of Israel. There are numerous further references to the figure 12 both in the decoration and the plan of the hall itself, a harmonious double-aisled vaulted hall-nave. Leaf ornament of the 13C decorates the tympanum of the shrine on the east wall containing the Torah (a parchment scroll of the five Books of Moses, or Pentateuch). In the middle of the hall stands a pulpit or almenar, surrounded by a beautiful Gothic grille of the late 15C; above this hangs a flag donated to Prague's Jews in 1648 by the Emperor Ferdinand, who wanted to thank them for helping him fight off the Protestant Swedes. The benches lining the walls are early 19C, while on the walls themselves are traces of medieval frescoes and inscriptions of 1618 recording certain sections of the Psalms.

Directly facing the south portal of the building is the entrance to the **High Synagogue**, which was built in 1568, extended at the end of the following century, and remodelled and given its present façade in the 19C; used until recently for the display of synagogical metalwork and textiles, this has now become once again a functioning synagogue, and is closed to the public.

Adjoining the synagogue, and until the 19C connected to it by a door, is the picturesque **Jewish Town Hall**, founded by Maisel in the late 16C, but completely rebuilt in 1763 when it was given its toy-like wooden turret, complete with a Hebraic clock which tells the time backwards ('The hands of the clock in the Jewish quarter are turning backwards /And you are passing slowly backward through the history of your life', wrote Apollinaire in his visionary poem *Zone*).

Walking south from here down Maislova, and crossing Široká, you will come to the **Maisel Synagogue** at No. 10, which was commissioned and paid for by Maisel in 1590, later rebuilt in a Baroque style, and then given a wholly neo-Gothic appearance by A. Grotte from 1893 to 1905; at present the newly restored building contains an uninspiring display relating to the history of the Jews in Bohemia and Moravia from the 10C up to the period of their emancipation in the 18C. Heading instead north along Maislova from the Old-New Synagogue you will find at the end of the street (at No. 21) an elegant and beautifully decorated Art Nouveau apartment block, built by František Weyr and Richard Klenka in 1911; facing its northern side, at No. 2 Břehová, is another fine building of this period, designed by Bedřich Bendelmayer.

Returning to the Old-New Syagogue and heading due west along U hřbitova you will shortly reach the **Klaus Synagogue**, which dates back to 1694 and has a stuccoed, barrel-vaulted interior containing today a large collection of Hebraic manuscripts and prints. Next to this is the entrance to the Old Jewish Cemetery, which is flanked on its western side by the former **Ceremonial Hall**, which was designed by F. Gerstl in 1906 for the Jewish Burial Society: taking the form of a tiny neo-Romanesque castle, it features a display of children's and other drawings depicting conditions at the Terezín ghetto and concentration camp (see Chapter 7).

Within the **Old Jewish Cemetery** (Starý židovský hřbitov)—the Jewish Museum's most popular attraction—are 20,000 tombstones jumbled together among trees in a manner which, until recently, echoed at times the visiting conditions (today's tourists are obliged to walk single-file along a designated trail). Though established in the late 15C, it contains tombs transferred from an earlier cemetery, the oldest being that of the Rabbi Abigdor Kar (d. 1389); the last person to be buried here was Moses Beck in 1787.

Today's designated trail through the cemetery will lead you to the **Pinkas Synagogue**, which is attached to the cemetery's southern wall. Founded by Rabbi Pinkas in 1479, this was rebuilt in 1535, and enlarged and remodelled by Juda Goldsmid de Herz in 1625. The hall, turned after the Second World War into a memorial to the Jewish victims of the Nazis, was closed in 1968 for restoration that was interminably and suspiciously protracted by the Communists. Only recently completed, the restored walls are once again entirely blanketed with the names, personal data, and home towns and villages of the 77,297 Jews killed by the Nazis in Bohemia and Moravia (of this number, 36,000 were from Prague). The sites in the Jewish Museum are **open** (with some variations) Sun–Fri 09.30–18.00 Apr–Oct; 09.30–17.00 Nov–Mar.

Continuing east along Široká you will come, at the end of the cemetery wall, to the large riverside square which since 1989 has been named after the 1968 'martyr' Jan Palach, to whom there is a small memorial containing a bust made from a death mask. The four-span concrete bridge (the Mánesuv most) that leads from here to the Little Quarter, dates back to 1911–14 and includes reliefs by such leading sculptors of the time as František Bílek and Jan Štursa. On the northern side of the square stands the imposing late 19C **Rudolfinum**, built in 1875–84 by Josef Zítek and Josef Schulz, it functioned originally as an art gallery and concert hall before serving from 1918 to 1939 as the seat of the Czech parliament; after the war it was used again for cultural purposes, and is now one of the main venues of the annual music festival known as the Prague Spring.

Turning right as soon as you enter the square from Široká, and walking north from it along 17. listopadu, the next building which you come to is the **Museum of Decorative Arts** (Umělecko-průmyslové muzeum), a French-style neo-Renaissance structure rising up above the western side of the Old Jewish Cemetery. The museum, founded in 1885 with a largely didactic purpose, was housed at first in the Rudolfinum while awaiting its eventual transference to the present building, which was completed by Josef Schulz in 1900; the façade is covered with reliefs by Bohuslav Schnirch and Antonín Popp representing the different branches of the decorative arts in Bohemia, and the coats of arms of the Bohemian towns most renowned for these arts. The museum itself, frequently empty, and looked after by a particularly charming group of elderly women, is one of the great little-known attractions of Prague. Its collections, ranging from the Middle Ages up to the present day and with the main emphasis on Bohemia and Moravia, include glass, ceramics, porcelain, woodwork, furniture, metalwork, clocks, textiles, costumes, prints, posters and photographs. **Open** Tues–Sun 10.00–18.00.

Continuing north along 17. listopadu will take you to the náměstí Curieových, a riverside square standing at the northern end of Pařížská, and bordered to the south by the fussy modern block of the luxurious *Hotel Intercontinental* (1968–74), and to the west by the Law Faculty of Charles University, an Art Deco structure designed by J. Kotěra in 1919. Head south of the square along Pařížská, and turn left beyond the *Hotel Intercontinental* to reach, on the eastern side of a small garden, the ulice Elišky Krásnohorské, where, at Nos 10–14, is a remarkable 'Cubist' block, built by Otakar Novotný in 1919–21 as the **Prague Teacher's Co-operative**.

Continuing south along this street, you will shortly rejoin Široká, passing on your left just before doing so the **Church of the Holy Ghost** (sv. Duch), a single-aisled structure of 1346 remodelled after a fire in 1689; in front of the building stands a statue of St John of Nepomuk (1727) by F.M. Brokoff. Turn left along Široká, and then turn left into Dušní, where, directly facing the eastern end of the Church of the Holy Ghost, is the **Spanish Synagogue**, a neo-Moorish structure designed by J. Niklas in 1882 for the city's Sephardic Jews; the interior, with its elaborate stucco decorations inspired by those of the Alhambra in Granada, was due to reopen in late 1998 with a permanent exhibition documenting the history of Czech Jews from the late 18C up to 1945. Walk north along Dušní until you reach the 17C–18C **Church of SS Simon and Jude** (Sv. Šimon a Juda), the choir of which has an organ on which both Mozart and Haydn played.

Convent of St Agnes

U milosrdných, which runs east of the church, will take you to the present entrance of the former Convent of St Agnes (Anežský klášter), a large and important medieval complex.

History of the convent

The convent, which is sometimes known by the ridiculous name of the 'Bohemian Assisi', was founded for the Poor Clares by Wenceslas I in 1233, probably on the request of his sister, Agnes of Bohemia, who became the first abbess (beatified in 1874, Agnes was only canonized on 12 November 1989, four days before the outbreak of the Velvet Revolution). The complex was virtually complete by the end of the 13C, and relatively few changes were to be made to it over the next four centuries, even after 1555 when the place was taken over by the Dominicans. A certain amount of new building work and remodelling was to be carried out in the wake of the Old Town fire of 1689, but with the dissolution of the convent in 1782, the whole complex fell into decay, its buildings being used as crafts workshops and poor people's homes. Extensive restoration work was begun in the 20C, and in the course of this the foundations of a neighbouring Minorite monastery of the early 13C were discovered. Restoration is finally nearing completion.

The museum installed in the convent is centred around a large cloister, which has largely retained its mid-13C appearance, apart from the upper level of the eastern side, which features a Renaissance arcade built by the Dominicans. At the cloister's southeast corner is a door leading into the convent's two adjoining churches: the earliest of the two was dedicated to St Francis and completed by the mid-13C; however only its presbytery has survived, and this is known today as the **Mánes Hall** and is used for concerts. Projecting east of this structure is the spacious and elegant Church of St Saviour, which dates from the 1280s, and is a fine example of French Gothic influence.

The building now contains the 19C Czech paintings belonging to the National Gallery. The works displayed in the well-modernised upper rooms are arranged chronologically, beginning with classical landscapes by Procházka and ending with the rural genre scenes and cityscapes by Jakub Schikaneder, with whose late works Czech art is brought into the 20C. **Open** Tues–Sun 10.00–18.00.

Among the more important Czech artists working in the early 19C were the painter of Romantic Gothic interiors, **Ludvík Kohl**, the portraitist **Antonín Machek**, the mythological painter **František Tkadlík**, and the landscapists **August Piepenhagen** and **Karel Postl**, the latter being the first professor of landscape painting at the Prague Academy. Two other major names are **Josef Navrátil**—the author of a stunningly simple and realistic series of still-lifes—and **Antonín Mánes**, who is represented here by a number of Romantic landscapes imbued with nationalist sentiment, most notably his view of the ruins of Kokořín Castle (1839). Two of Mánes's sons were painters, the most famous being the elder one, Josef, whose work dominates Czech 19C art. The paintings of his on show here reveal his extraordinary variety, and range from such academic canvases as *Petrarch and Laura* (1845–46) to a series of remarkably fresh landscapes painted in the 1850s and 1860s (for instance *Gmunden, and the Mountain Hut*); among his other works here are lively portraits of Luisa Bělská

(1857) and Anna Václavíková (1862), detailed drawings of national folk costumes, a pair of mysteriously lit nudes (*Dawn* and *Evening*, 1857), and two large-scale oil studies for banners (one for the Říp Association at Roudnice, 1863–64, and the other for the Smíchov Lukes Choir, 1868).

Of Mánes's younger contemporaries, the only one to achieve an international reputation was **Jaroslav Čermák**, who specialised in ambitious scenes of Czech history, such as *The Hussites Defending the Pass* (1857); Čermák, a Byronic figure with the painterly pretensions of a Delacroix, became an active witness to history by going off to record the war between Turkey and Montenegro—the subject of several scenes in the museum. Academic landscapists of this period include **Bedřich Havránek**, **Alois Bubák** and **Adolf Kosárek**, while one of the finest of the genre painters was **Soběslav Pinkas**, who did numerous scenes of Prague life, such as his *Children on Kampa Island* (1854).

From the 1850s onwards an increasing number of Czech artists spent long periods in France, including Pinkas himself, **Viktor Barvitius**, **Karel Purkyně** and **Antonín Chitussi**. Barvitius was the author of the delightfully detailed and atmospherically lit genre scene, *Thursday in Stromovka Park* (1865); Purkyně meanwhile was an artist who fell strongly under the influence of Courbet, as can be seen in his powerful portrait of *Jech the Smith* (1860), and in the boldly painted still-lifes, *The Snow Owl* (1862) and *Onions and Partridges* (1862). Chitussi painted many landscapes while staying in and around Paris and, on his return to Czechoslovakia, did numerous Barbizon-inspired scenes in the region where he was born—the Czech Moravian Highlands.

Towards the end of the 19C many of the leading Czech artists were engaged in the decoration of the Prague National Theatre, including the landscapist **Julius Mařák**, and the specialists in allegorical and Classical scenes involving female nudes, **Vojtech Hynais** and **František Ženíšek**. The most important of the artists of the so-called National Theatre Generation was the prolific **Mikoláš Aleš**, among whose works in the museum is a series of cartoons for his series, *Legend of My Country*, which he painted for the National Theatre; many other of his drawings and decorative designs are to be seen here, as well as numerous historical canvases such as *The Meeting of George of Poděbrady with Matthias Corvinus* (1877), *Milica and the Yugoslavs* (1876) and *Hussite on the Baltic* (1877), a bleak, snow-covered landscape featuring a lone rider on horseback in front of the tomb of one of his comrades.

The turn-of-the-century Czech artist best known outside the Czech Republic, **Alfons Mucha**, is represented here only by very slight works. In compensation there is a superb group of paintings by **Jakub Schikaneder**, ranging from the Bastien-Lepage-inspired *Autumn* (1884) to the large, suggestive and almost monochromatic city scenes of the first and second decades of this century, such as *Winter Evening in the Town* (1907–09) and *Embankment* (1916–18).

After leaving the Convent of St Agnes head south down the short Anežská (passing, at No.2 the charming *U Červeného Kola Restaurant*), at the end of which you will come to the **Church of St Castullus** (sv. Haštal), which dates back to the early 14C. Though the main nave and chancel were remodelled following the fire of 1689, the south aisle has been preserved in its medieval state, as has the remarkable twin-aisled extension which was added to the north side of the church in 1375; the extension features a fine net vault with bosses decorated with masks and leaves. The walls of the sacristy meanwhile are covered with medieval murals, comprising a series of Apostles' heads of c 1400 and scenes of the Crucifixion and the Last Supper of c 1500.

Running along the southern side of the church is the Haštalská třída, where at No. 4 is an Art Nouveau house (1905) with a beautiful tree decoration on its façade; next to this is a portal of the same period incorporating an elegant rose window. Parallel to this street to the south is the Dlouhá třída, which follows the early medieval route connecting the Old Town Square with the colony of German merchants at Poříčí (see Chapter 1D). Turn left along Dlouhá, passing, at No. 37, the **House at the Golden Tree** (Dům U zlatého stromu), which has a late 16C courtyard dating from the time when the house belonged to the Mayor of the Old Town, Václav Kročín. At the eastern end of Dlouhá you will come to Revoluční, where you turn right, rejoining shortly afterwards the náměstí Republiky.

B. The Little Quarter ~ Malá Strana

Across the Vltava

The Little Quarter or Malá Strana, founded in 1257 by Přemysl Otakar II in the outer bailey of Prague Castle, was known up to the early 14C as the New Town below Prague Castle. Later in the century Charles IV considerably extended this town with the creation of new fortifications incorporating the Petřín Hill to the south. Today this hill forms part of a large wooded park, the northern sides of which are fringed by lush gardens attached to Baroque palaces. Gardens and palaces, many of which now serve as embassies, are the dominant feature of the Little Quarter, the most genuinely picturesque area of a city steeped in the picturesque, and the one which can most truly be compared to a stage set. Although overprettified in parts in recent years, and largely lacking today the romantically decayed corners of old, it has so far escaped the worst of the commercialisation now affecting the Old Town. Furthermore, in comparison to the flat Staré Město, this steeply pitched district offers from afar an enticingly variegated profile. Despite the now almost oppressive congestion of pedestrians that can mark the Royal Route as it crosses the Charles Bridge, it is difficult not to feel an acute sense of drama and expectation while being drawn by the bridge's gesticulating statuary towards the Little Quarter's turreted entrance gate, behind which rises the massive dome of the Church of St Nicholas, and, higher still, the dramatic silhouette of Prague Castle.

Charles Bridge

The Charles Bridge (Karlův most), one of Europe's most beautiful bridges, is not simply the visual centrepiece of Prague, but has also played a central role in the life and history of the city.

History of the Charles Bridge

In 1357 Charles IV entrusted the architect Peter Parléř with the construction of a new bridge, which was to be known as the Stone or Prague Bridge up to 1870, and only thereafter as the Charles Bridge. Built out of sandstone blocks, this 16-arch structure runs a slightly irregular course due to the fact that, while the bridgeheads of the Judith's Bridge were retained, new piers were constructed in the middle of the river, just to the south of the old ones. The new structure, which was completed in the early 15C, has been damaged a number of times by floods, and two of its arches had to be rebuilt in 1890, but it has never collapsed.

As well as serving as part of the processional route of the Bohemian kings, the Charles Bridge was a place where business transactions took place, tournaments held, custom dues collected, law suits settled, criminals executed, and delinquents punished by being dipped in the Vltava in wicker baskets. The most famous incident in its history occurred on 20 March 1393 when the future St John of Nepomuk was bound hand and foot and thrown from its parapet into the river, where, according to legend, his body floated for an unnaturally long time, a group of five stars hovering above it. In 1683, at a time when the Jesuits were beginning to promote the Nepomuk cult, a statue to him by J. Brokoff was placed on the bridge, near the supposed point from where he was flung. This led to several religious orders commissioning other statues for the bridge, from J. and F.M. Brokoff, M.V. Jäckel, Matthias Braun, J.O. Mayer, and M.B. Mandl. The Baroque statues, which were all in place by 1714, were joined in 1857–59 by works by Emmanuel Max; between 1908 and 1937 a number of other statues were added, and some of the more worn ones removed to the Lapidarium of the National Gallery and replaced by copies.

The bridge, which is closed to traffic, is overwhelmed by day by lingering tourists and street artists, and at night functions additionally as a meeting-place for singing and guitar-playing students, whose appearance and behaviour are little different to those of their hippy predecessors who gathered here in the late 1960s. The views on all sides are uninterruptedly beautiful, and the place becomes especially evocative on a winter's night when, in the dim light of lanterns, a freezing mist rises from the river, and isolated groups of pedestrians glide past and disappear into the gloom.

Another of the bridge's attractions are of course its statues, which turn the whole structure into a museum of Bohemian sculpture. On the first pier to the right immediately beyond the Old Town Bridge Tower (see Chapter 1A) stands the *Madonna and St Bernard* (1709) by Matěj Václav Jäckel, a sculptor who introduced to Bohemia the dynamic high-flown style of the Italian artist Bernini. This style was used to far more expressive effect in the work of Matthias Braun, an Austrian-born sculptor who first came to Bohemia in 1710, invited by the Cistercians of Plasy to execute statues for the Charles Bridge; a copy of the second statue which he did here, representing *St Ivo* (1711), can be seen on the left-hand side of the bridge, directly facing Jäckel's Madonna. The other outstanding Bohemian sculptor of this period was Ferdinand Maximillian Brokoff, an artist noted for his realism, who carried out several works for the bridge, including the sculptural group of *SS Barbara, Margaret and Elizabeth*, which adorns the second pier on the left-hand side. The first monument to be placed on the bridge was a gilded bronze *Crucifix*, cast by J. Hilger in 1629, and set up on the third pier to the right in 1657; the two stone figures were executed by E. Max in 1861, while the Hebrew inscription on the cross, dating from 1696, is said to have been paid for by a Jew as a fine for mocking this Christian symbol.

Continuing to cross the bridge, you will pass between the sixth and seventh piers a relief marking the supposed spot where St John of Nepomuk was thrown into the Vltava in 1393; the bronze statue of the saint which was placed on the bridge in 1683 stands on the eighth pier to the right, and was executed by Johann Brokoff after a bozzetto by Matthias Rauchmüller. Towards its western end the bridge crosses the picturesque Kampa Island, which is separated from the left bank by a narrow canal, and is sometimes referred to as the 'Venice of Prague' (see below). Above the steps leading down to it, on the twelfth pier to the left, is a sculpture of *The Vision of St Luitgard* (1710), which was the first work that Matthias Braun made in Prague, and in many ways the most powerful and emotionally compelling on the bridge; tradition has it that the work was based on a design by Peter Brandl, and there is certainly something very painterly in its wildly agitated drapery. Two piers further along to the left is another of the sculptural masterpieces of the bridge, a group by F.M. Brokoff of 1714 featuring *SS John of Matha, Felix de Valois, and Ivo*, with a Turk guarding a group of captured Christians, the whole carved with Brokoff's characteristic realism (note, in particular the face of the Turk); the work was commissioned as a gesture of thanks to the Trinitarian Order for having redeemed Christians from Turkish captivity. Directly opposite this group is a statue by F.M. Brokoff of *St Vitus* (1714), the only marble work on the bridge, the other stone sculptures being all of sandstone.

The bridge ends picturesquely at a gate of 1410 flanked by two **towers**, the taller of which was built in 1466 at the behest of George of Poděbrady, and is closely similar to the Tower of the Old Town Bridge and Powder Gate; the shorter tower, a survival of the Judith's Bridge fortifications, dates back to 1166 but was remodelled in 1591. Once through the Little Quarter gate the royal processional route headed west along **Mostecká**, today a busy shopping street featuring a number of fine Renaissance and Baroque palaces, most notably, at No. 15, the **Kaunic Palace**, which was built in 1773–75 by Anton Schmidt, and has a façade richly decorated with stuccoes by Ignác Platzer.

Little Quarter Square

The street leads into the Little Quarter Square (Malostranské náměstí), which is divided in two by the massive Church of St Nicholas and adjoining buildings.

History of the square

The square, surrounded today by buildings of largely 17C and 18C appearance, formed originally the nucleus of Prague Castle's outer bailey, and in the middle there once stood the Romanesque Rotunda of St Wenceslas; the site of a market and Town Hall for many centuries after the foundation of the Little Quarter in 1257, the square remains to this day the lively heart of this area, with an important tram junction at its lower, eastern end.

The latter half of the square, known as the Lower Square, features on its eastern side (at No. 21) the former **Town Hall** (Radnice), which was founded in the late 15C, and where in March 1575 a group of Habsburg opponents comprising neo-Utraquists, Lutherans and members of the Union of Czech Brethren formulated the so-called Czech Confession, a plea for legal recognition of Evangelical trends.

Dominating the northern side of the Lower Square is the imposing **Smiřický-Montág Palace**, which dates back to 1606 but was rebuilt in a late Baroque style by J. Jäger c 1763; the building is famous as the place where, on 22 May 1618, Albrecht Smiřický and an invited group of leaders of the anti-Habsburg opposition hatched the plot which was to lead the following day to the 'Second Defenestration', the incident which sparked off the Thirty Years War.

Walking up from the southeastern corner of the Little Quarter Square to the square's upper, western half, you will skirt to your right the southern side of the Church of St Nicholas and to your left a group of tall, narrow-fronted houses of Renaissance and medieval origin, where you will find several long-established places for eating and drinking. No. 10, At the Golden Lion (Dům U zlatého lva), is the only building in the whole square to have completely retained its Renaissance appearance, and houses one of Prague's better-known restaurants, *U mecenáše*; this restaurant, serving good food in intimate, Renaissance-style dining-rooms, is on the site of a tavern dating back to the reign of the Emperor Rudolph.

Church of St Nicholas
The upper and quieter half of the Little Quarter Square is known as the Upper or Italian Square, and has in its centre a **plague column** put up by Alliprandi in 1715 in place of a fountain. Its western side is taken up entirely by the neo-Classical façade of the Liechtenstein Palace (1791), while facing this is the west façade of the Church of St. Nicholas (sv. Mikuláš), one of the outstanding Baroque buildings of Central Europe, and rivalled only by Prague Castle as the dominant element in the city's skyline.

History of the church
The present church occupies the site of a 13C three-aisled structure which was handed over to the Jesuits shortly after the Battle of the White Mountain of 1620. Later in the 17C the Jesuits built a college alongside the old church, and in 1673 laid the foundations of a new church, the construction of which was not begun until 1703, under the direction of Christoph Dientzenhofer. The church was roofed by 1705, but work was subsequently interrupted through lack of funds, and was only continued between 1709 and 1711, when the west façade was completed and the nave vaulted. Further financial difficulties led to the east end being closed by a provisional, illusionistically painted wooden screen until 1737, when work was resumed under the direction of Dientzenhofer's son, Kilian Ignaz, who between 1737 and 1752 built the chancel and domed crossing; the tower alongside the dome was added by Anselmo Lurago in 1755.

Despite the protracted history of its construction, the Church of St Nicholas has an impressive unity, and its undulating west façade, with its remarkably rich play of concave and convex surfaces, is a powerful preparation for the dynamic interior. Once inside the single-aisled building you are astonished by an array of pinks and pastel greens, and exhilarated by an extraordinary sense of movement. The nave walls, with their undulating balconies and giant, obliquely set pilasters, positively ripple and create a flowing line which culminates in the enormous oval of the crossing. The originality of the nave vaulting, with its intersecting ribs as in a Gothic building, is obscured by the vast ceiling painting by Johann Lukas Kracker representing *The Apotheosis of St Nicholas* (1760–61); the dome, meanwhile, is covered by *The Celebration of the Holy Trinity* (1752–53) by Franz Xavier Palko, who also executed, along with Josef Hager, the wall-paintings in the chancel. The magnificent statuary was largely the work of Ignác Platzer the Elder, who was responsible for the statue of St Nicholas on the high altar, the agitated saints along the nave, and the four overblown figures of the Church Fathers in the corners of the crossing. The remarkable pulpit (1765), a gilded Rococo confection in pink marble, is by Richard and Peter Prachner. Of the paintings, special mention should be made of the first chapel to the left, where there is an altarpiece of the Holy Rood by K. Škréta, and one of St Barbara by L. Kohl; a painting of St Michael by the Neapolitan painter F. Solimena is in the second chapel to the left, while in the third chapel to the right is *The Death of St Francis* by F.X. Balko.

After leaving the church, head to the northern end of the Upper Square, turn right, and just before entering once again the Lower Square, turn left into the narrow **Sněmovní**. Among the old palaces and houses on this street, which lies almost in the shadow of Prague Castle, is the gabled and well-preserved Renaissance structure at No. 10 called **At the Golden Swan** (Dům U zlaté labutě), which was built by Ulrico Avostalis in 1589 for one Michal Lagrand. At its upper end the street is continued in the once picturesquely shabby cul-de-sac with the exotic name of U zlaté studně (At the Golden Well); the recently restored end house, at No. 3, is known as At the Painter's (Dům U malíře), for it belonged to the turn-of-the-century artist Karel Klusáček, who painted on its façade a decoration featuring St Methodius.

The gardens of the Malá Strana

After turning back at the end of the street, take the first turning to the left, which leads you into **Wallenstein Square** (Valdštejnské náměstí). This narrow square is named after the **Wallenstein Palace** at No. 4 on its eastern side, which was built in 1623–30 for the great Albrecht of Wallenstein. It was to remain the family seat until 1945.

Built by Giovanni Pieroni to designs supplied first by Andrea Spezza and then by Niccolo Sebregondi, it was the earliest of the many grand palaces erected in Prague in the 17C and 18C. Its interior, open to the public for occasional concerts (but currently closed for restoration), features a splendid main hall with a stuccoed ceiling incorporating a fresco by B. Bianco representing Wallenstein himself dressed as Mars and riding a chariot; the work was executed in 1630, only four years before Wallenstein's ignominious murder at Cheb (see Chapter 10). Architecturally the finest feature of the building is the loggia overlooking the palace's wonderful gardens, the entrance to which is on Letenská (see below).

Before making your way to Letenská a number of other important palaces and gardens remain to be seen to the north of the Wallenstein Palace, beginning with the **Ledebour-Trauttmansdorf Palace**, on the northwestern corner of the Valdštejnské náměstí. This late Baroque palace, designed by I.J. Palliardi in 1787, is remarkable above all for its gardens, which were laid out by Santini-Aichel in 1716 and rise steeply in terraces from a *sala terrena* up to a belvedere, the whole enlivened by fountains and a statue of Hercules. The gardens, recently restored thanks to help from the Prague Heritage Fund, today form part of a public park known as **the Palace Gardens Below Prague Castle** that also comprise the terraced gardens of two adjoining palaces to the north, on Valdštejnská. The first of these palaces, at No. 14, is the early 18C **Pálffy Palace** (now a music academy with an excellent and very atmospheric student-run restaurant), the gardens of which feature three terraces linked by a covered staircase and a loggia; on the middle terrace is a sundial bearing a Latin inscription and the date 1751. The entrance to all the gardens is to be found alongside the next palace, the **Kolowrat-Černín Palace**, situated at No. 10. The building was designed in 1784 by Ignác Jan Palliardi, who was also responsible for laying out its gardens, which are perhaps the finest of them all and comprise a luxuriant Rococo complex of staircases, terraces, fountains, loggias, balustrades and pools. The last of the great palaces along Valdštejnská is the **Fürstenberg Palace**, which was built in 1743–47 by an unknown architect clearly under the influence of K.I. Dientzenhofer; it is now the Polish Embassy, and its attractive 18C gardens are closed to the public.

Return to the Valdštejnské náměstí and continue south along **Tomášská**, where you will pass on the left-hand side, just before rejoining the Little Quarter Square, one of Prague's best known beer-cellars, U Schnellů; this long-established and recently revamped tourist bar and restaurant has décor dating back to 1787. Turn left at the end of the street into **Letenská**, where you will find immediately to your left the dazzlingly restored **Church of St Thomas** (sv. Tomáše), which was founded in 1285 for the Order of Augustinian Hermits. The medieval church, partially rebuilt in the 16C and 17C, was remodelled by K.I. Dientzenhofer between 1722 and 1731. The main façade, featuring a portal of 1617 and a sandstone statue of St Thomas by Hieronymus Kohl (1684), was given by Dientzenhofer a dramatic Borromini-inspired appearance through the addition of massive, projecting forms intended both to strengthen the structure and to make the most of the restricted site; the interior, with a presbytery retaining some of the medieval masonry, has ceiling paintings by V.V. Reiner representing scenes from the lives of SS Augustine and Thomas and (on the dome) *The Four Continents*. In the first chapel on the right is a painting of St Thomas (1671) by K. Škréta, by whom there are two further paintings in the presbytery (an *Assumption* and a *Holy Trinity*, both of 1644). Paintings by Rubens of St Augustine and the *Martyrdom of St Thomas* were recently transferred from here to the National Gallery and replaced by copies.

The former friary attached to the church is now an old people's home, but its cellar (entered at No. 8 Letenská) continues to function as the celebrated ale house known as **U Tomáše**, which was founded here in 1348, its dark beer having originally been made by the monks. This establishment is today a tourist attraction which tends to be booked up in advance by large groups; earlier this century, however, it was the place to which the rowdy literary club known as Syrinx transferred its allegiance after tiring of the now equally spoilt U Fleků in the New Town (see Chapter 1C).

Across Letenská from the Church of St Thomas is the entrance to the short Josefská, on which stands the former **Church of St Joseph** (sv. Josefa), an oval structure which was built by Jean Baptiste Mathey in 1682–92 and modelled on Flemish and Roman patterns.

Continuing to walk north along Letenská, you will skirt to your left the walls of the **Wallenstein Palace Gardens** (Valdšteinska' zahrada) and eventually come to the entrance. The gardens, now partly restored and open throughout the year, were laid out in the early 17C and have at their centre an avenue of bronze statues copied after works by Adriaen de Vries that were stolen from here by the Swedes in 1648 and have been standing since then outside the Swedish royal palace at Drottningholm. The avenue leads to a tall and magnificent loggia built by G. Pieroni in 1623–27, and decorated inside with painted scenes by B.

Bianco of *The Trojan Wars* (1629–30), set in a stucco framework. Elsewhere in the gardens are an aviary, grottoes, and a long fishpond which was used in 1816 for the testing of a model of a steamboat designed by J. Božek; the bronze of Hercules standing in the middle of the pond is an original by de Vries. On summer weekends the gardens are used by artists for the display of their works, while the former riding-school here houses occasional temporary exhibitions organised by the National Gallery.

Letenská comes to an end at the broad and busy **Klárov**, which marks the northwestern edge of the Little Quarter. Turning left here will bring you immediately to the Malostranská Metro Station, the most elegant in Prague; erected in 1978, it has a small forecourt with fountains and statuary copied from 18C models, and a vestibule containing copies both of Rococo vases and of Matthias Braun's statue of *Hope* from Kuks (see Chapter 3). In the square in front of the station there is a plaque commemorating a student, Marie Charousková, who was killed during the protests of 1968.

Turning right at the end of Letenská will bring you into U lužického semináře, which was named after a seminary (at No. 13) built in 1726–28 for Lusatian–Serbian students. To your right you will skirt the walls of the large **Vojanovy Gardens**, which were founded in the 17C and contain near their entrance (which is also on this street) a statue by I.F. Platzer of St John of Nepomuk standing on a fish. Near the southern end of the street turn right into Mísěňska', where you will find at Nos 1 and 12 two appealing corner houses designed respectively by Kilian Ignaz Dientzenhofer and his brother Christoph.

The continuation of Misěňska', Dražického, will bring you back to the Charles Bridge, next to the main entrance of the celebrated **The Three Ostriches** (U tří pštrosů), the exterior of which has fragments of mural decorations of ostrich feathers, as well as a house-sign with ostriches, all dating back to 1606. The building owes both its name and decoration to a merchant called Jan Fux, who rebuilt the house after 1597, and made a living partially by selling ostrich feathers, then a fashion novelty. Functioning already as a tavern in Fux's time, the building was acquired early the following century by the Armenian coffee-salesman Deodatus Damajan, who in 1714 opened here the first coffee-shop in the Little Quarter. Between 1972 and 1976, the place was restored and transformed into a luxury restaurant and tiny, exclusive hotel.

The southern Little Quarter

After returning to Mostecká you should turn left immediately into **Lázeňská** to begin a tour of the southern half of the Little Quarter. On this short street were once situated the workshops of Adriaen de Vries and other foreign sculptors who came to Prague at the time of Rudolph II. Later in the 17C the street came to have a hotel, *At the Baths* (Vlázni) at No. 6, which until the early 19C was to host some of the most distinguished visitors to Prague, including Peter the Great of Russia in 1698, the pioneering balloonist Jean-Pierre Blanchard in 1790–91 and, in 1833, the French writer Chateaubriand; two years after the latter's visit (which is commemorated by a plaque), the hotel was rebuilt in an Empire style. In 1796 Beethoven stayed at the fine late Baroque palace **At the Golden Unicorn** (Uzlatého jednorožce) at No. 11.

At the southern end of the street begins a small area of town originating in plots of land that in 1169 were given over by Vladislav II to the Order of the Maltese

Knights (the Johannites). The church which formerly belonged to this order, **Our Lady under the Chain** (Panny Marie pod řetězem), dominates the area, standing at the junction of Lázeňská and the narrow, connected **Malta Square** and **Square of the Grand Priory** (Maltézské náměstí and Velkopřevorské náměstí). The original three-aisled Romanesque structure of the 12C, the oldest church in the Little Quarter, was pulled down in the middle of the 14C, and work was begun on a new building. The latter was abandoned by the end of the century, the only parts to be completed being the western vestibule and its two austere and fortress-like towers, which form such an incongruous presence in the middle of this intimate part of town. The former nave of the Romanesque church serves now as a forecourt to a Baroque church built largely by Carlo Lurago between 1640 and 1660; within the latter is a high altar of the 1660s by Karel Škréta, representing the Virgin Mary and St John the Baptist coming to the assistance of the Knights of Malta during the Battle of Lepanto of 1571.

Facing the church, at No. 11 at the northeastern end of the Maltézské náměstí, is a building dating back to 1531, and known as **At the Painter's** (Dům U malířů) after the painter Jiří Šic, who lived here in the late 16C, and whose name, when pronounced in English ('Shits'), was an unfortunate one in view of the place's later function: the building, remodelled in around 1690, and restored in the 1930s, now houses Prague's most exclusive French restaurant, with fresh produce flown in daily from France, and an entirely French wine list. A number of fine 17C and 18C palaces line the rest of the square, at the centre of which is a sculptural group by F.M. Brokoff featuring St John the Baptist, erected as a plague memorial in 1715. On the eastern side of the square, at No. 14, is the arcaded **Straka Palace** of c 1700 (with fresco decorations inside by the early 18C Swiss painter J.R. Byss), while at No. 6 on the western side is Jäger's **Turba Palace** of 1767–68, a beautiful Rococo structure articulated with giant pilasters and serving today as the Japanese Embassy. Giant pilasters also feature on the façade of the large **Nostitz Palace** at No. 1, today the Dutch Embassy, which takes up all of the southern side of the square, and was built in 1660–70 by Francesco Caratti, who was later to perfect such an ordering of a façade in his Černín Palace on the Loreta Square (see Chapter 1C); the main portal is a Rococo addition of 1760 attributed to A. Haffenecker, while the attic was decorated in 1720 with sculpted vases and emperors by M.J. Brokoff (the originals have now been replaced by copies).

Make your way back to Our Lady under the Chain, and turn right into the Velkopřevorské náměstí. Immediately to your left on entering the square is the main façade of the **Grand Prior's Palace**, which was rebuilt to a design by Giuseppe Bartolomeo Scotti in 1726–28, and has a fine portal with vase decorations from the workshop of Matthias Braun; torchbearers and vases from the same workshop adorn the grand staircase of the richly stuccoed interior. The building, which once housed the Museum of Czech Music, was reclaimed after 1989 by the Knights of Malta, who are currently restoring it, together with the church of Our Lady under the Chain.

On the southern side of the square, facing the Lennon Wall, are the late 16C **Small Buquoy Palace** at No. 3 and the adjoining **Buquoy-Valdstejn Palace** at No. 2, now the French Embassy, the present façade of which dates back to 1719. At the eastern end of the square, also on the right-hand side at No. 1, is the **Hrzán Palace**, which despite remodelling carried out in 1760 still retains a largely Renaissance appearance, complete with extensive sgraffito decorations. Another Renaissance structure at No. 7, directly facing the palace, is the picturesquely gabled **Grand Prior's Mill** or Stepan's Mill, which was functioning up to 1936, and is one of several mills built on the narrow branch of the Vltava called the Čertovka or the Devil's Stream. This stream, separating the Little Quarter from Kampa Island, was first referred to simply as 'The Ditch', and only acquired its present, more romantic name towards the end of the 19C, when the Straka Palace on the nearby Malta Square came to be known as 'The Devil's House' after an eccentric woman owner.

Beside the Grand Prior's Mill is a bridge leading over the Čertovka stream to **Kampa Island**, an area once taken up entirely by vineyards, gardens and fields, and which only acquired buildings from the late 16C onwards. Successive floods changed the shape of the island over the centuries, and the narrator of Jiří Weil's novel *Life with a Star* (1964) even recalls frequent arguments with his mistress when she 'claimed that Kampa was a peninsula and I said it was an island'. Most of the houses on this so-called Venice of Prague are concentrated in the northern half of the island, on either side of the quiet and tree-lined Na Kampě, where, at No. 11, there is a bronze plaque and bust marking the house where the composer Bohuslav Martinů lived. At its northern end the street broadens out into a picturesque square from which steps lead up to the Charles Bridge. A pottery market was regularly held here up to 1936, and this tradition has recently been revived; the square, like the Charles Bridge itself, also attracts numerous singing, guitar-playing students, who seem to have stepped straight out of the 1960s.

Walk south down Na Kampě to the southern half of the island, which largely comprises a public park. Leave the island at its southernmost point and turn right into Říční, where you will soon pass on your right the **Church of St John at the Wash-House** (sv. Jana Na prádle). The homely name of the church is entirely appropriate to this structure of rustic simplicity, which dates back to the 13C, and contains fragments of late 14C wall-paintings. On the opposite side of the street, at No. 11, a plaque marks the turn-of-the-century building where the brothers Josef and Karel Čapek moved to after settling in Prague in 1907.

From the Church of St John at the Wash-house head northwest along Všehrdova, passing at No. 14 the **Works Mill** (Mlýn), another of the old mills on the Čertovka. The narrow and slightly run-down Všehrdova will take you to the long and busy **Újezd**, where you will find, immediately to the right at No. 40, the **Michna of Vacínov Palace**, a large complex dating back to the late 16C, and with a Baroque wing built by Francesco Caratti in 1640–50. This wing, with a grimy, peeling façade overlooking Újezd, is covered both on the outside and inside with Italianate stucco decorations by Domenico Galli. The interior, which is occupied today by the sports faculty of Charles University, is also worth seeing for its small but very evocative **Sports Museum** (Muzeum tělesné výchovy a sportu), with old bicycles, sports trophies, photographs, and other objects relating to the history of sport in Prague, all incongruously displayed under Galli's stuccoes, in rooms that appear to be as little visited as they are dusted. **Open** 09.00–17.00 Tues–Sun.

Walk north along Újezd into its northern continuation, **Karmelitská**, on which stands, on the left-hand side, the former **Carmelite Church of St Mary the Victorious** (Panny Marie Vítězné). Built originally for the German Lutherans between 1611 and 1613, it came into the possession of the

Carmelites in 1624, who subsequently had it rebuilt as a thanksgiving for the Habsburg victory at the Battle of the White Mountain. Though generally referred to as the first Baroque church in Prague, it would be better described as one of the many dreary European imitations of the Gesù in Rome, and has little of architectural interest. Its singularly dark and depressing interior, however, is much visited on account of a tiny votive image of the Infant Christ (the Bambino di Praga) displayed in a chapel on the right of the nave.

Of greater artistic interest than the Bambino di Praga itself is the gilded wooden altar on which it has been placed, a Rococo structure carved by Petr Prachner in 1776; elsewhere in the church are a number of dramatic canvases of saints by Petr Brandl.

Continuing north up Karmelitská, you will pass on your left, at No. 25, the **Vrtba Palace**, which František Kaňka remodelled around 1720 and endowed with some of the most beautiful if also most hidden gardens in Prague. The **Vrtba Gardens**, reached by way of a passage running through the palace, today form a small and quiet public park at the edge of a great sweep of verdant parkland covering the Petřín Hill. After passing through a courtyard adorned with statues by Matthias Braun of Atlas and two female allegorical figures, you will come to a *sala terrena* decorated with painted mythological scenes by V.V. Reiner. Further works by Braun, of Bacchus and Ceres (c 1730) are followed by a balustraded double staircase where mythological figures alternate with Greek vases; from the highest of the gardens' terraces there are wonderful views of Prague Castle and the Church of St Nicholas.

The approach to Prague Castle

Karmelitská will bring you back at its northern end to the Little Quarter Square (Malostranské náměstí), from where you begin the steep walk up to Prague Castle, passing through what is in many ways the most attractive part of the Little Quarter. There are three main ways of climbing up to the castle from the square.

The shortest and steepest route, and the one offering the finest roof-top views, is the ascent up the **Castle Steps** (Zámecké schody). From the northwestern corner of the Lower Square turn right into Sněmovní, and then immediately left into Thunovská, off which stands at No. 14 the large **Thun Palace**, a building of 17C origin with a façade of 1716–27 by Antonio Giovanni Lurago; at this palace, now the seat of the British Embassy, Mozart and his wife Costanza stayed during their first visit to Prague in 1787.

Further west up Thunovská, on the right-hand side of the street, the Castle Steps begin, passing to the left, at No. 25 Thunovská, the greyish-white and recently restored **Palace of the Lords of Hradec**, which dates back to the late 16C and is crowned by a group of small, Renaissance gables; this building, now connected to the Italian Embassy on Nerudova (see below) was from 1911 to 1928 the house of the artist Alfons Mucha, who is commemorated here by a plaque. The steps, which lead directly up to the Hradčany Square, were built originally in the 15C on the site of a path of 13C origin. A number of small buildings grew up alongside them, and in the 16C and 17C artists and craftsmen used to sell their wares here (the wide stone ledges of some of the windows were once used for display purposes).

The tourist shops today are not to be found on the Castle Steps but are concentrated instead along **Nerudova**, which is the main and most traditional approach to the castle, and the one which was favoured by the royal coronation processions. Nerudova begins at the upper western end of the Little Quarter Square, and is lined its whole length with 16C to 18C buildings, many of which have shop fronts displaying crafts products and souvenirs. The first building on the right (at No. 2) houses the once lively pub *At the Cat* (*U kocoura*), a famous haunt of the city's pre-1989 underground musicians, writers and hangers-on; it is still a good place to drink Pilsner and Purkmistr beer. Further up the street, on the left-hand side at No. 5, is the **Morzin Palace** (now the Romanian Embassy), which was built by Santini-Aichel in 1713–14 and has magnificent sculptural decoration by F.M. Brokoff on its façade: its two portals are surmounted by statues of Day and Night, while in between these is a balcony supported by figures of Moors, executed with Brokoff's customary realism. The Italian Embassy, slightly higher up Nerudova on the opposite side of the street at No. 20, occupies another splendid Baroque building by Santini-Aichel, the **Thun-Hohenstein Palace**: built between 1716 and c 1725, its portal was decorated around 1730 with two deeply and vigorously carved eagles by Brokoff's great and dynamic rival, Matthias Braun. Santini-Aichel seems also to have been responsible for the portal of the adjoining **Church of Our Lady of Unceasing Succour at the Theatines** (Panny Marie ustavičné pomoci u kajetánu); the rest of the church, built in 1691–1717, has been attributed to J.-B. Mathey.

Further up the street at No. 34, also on the right-hand side, is the **House at the Golden Horseshoe** (Dům U zlaté podkovy), where you will find the beautifully preserved wooden interior of an early 18C pharmacy, one of the oldest surviving pharmacies in Prague. At the top of the street, at No. 47 on the left-hand side, is the **House at the Two Suns** (Dům U dvou slunců), a building of Renaissance origin with attractive late 17C gables. Attached to its façade is a large memorial plaque—executed in 1895 by F. Houdek after a design by V. Oliva and a model by V.R. Smolík—recording that in this house there lived between 1845 and 1857 the poet and journalist after whom the street is named, Jan Neruda; the everyday life of this part of Prague provided Neruda with the subject matter of his delightful short-stories, *Tales from the Little Quarter* (1878). To complete the journey up to the castle, you should turn sharp right at the end of Nerudova and walk up the street named Ke Hradu, which means 'Towards the Castle'. Turning instead to the left you enter Úvoz , which climbs up slowly towards the Strahov Monastery and Loreto Square (see Chapter 1C); the street is bordered to the right by another fine succession of 16C–18C houses, and to the left by a shaded balustrade commanding excellent views of the Petřín Park.

A third way of climbing up towards the castle and the Hradčany from the Little Quarter Square is to follow the streets running parallel to Nerudova to the south, beginning with Tržiště, which starts at Karmelitská, by the side of the Vrtba Palace (see above). By far the grandest palace on this dark and quiet street is the **Schönborn-Colloredo Palace** (now the American Embassy) at No. 15, which was built in the mid-17C on a site previously occupied by five houses, and remodelled in around 1715, probably by Santini-Aichel.

Tržiště veers to the right after the palace, and after tunnelling through a group of houses, joins up with Nerudova, at a point directly in front of the Thun-Hohenstein Palace (see above). Alternatively, you could turn left at the Schönborn Palace on to Vlašská, or take the second turning to the left, and walk up the narrow street parallel to Vlašská, Břetislavova. The building at No. 2 Břetislavova is an early 18C structure known as **At the Child Jesus** (U Ježíška) and attributed to Santini-Aichel.

Břetislavova leads into Jánský vršek, where, on turning right, you will reach the upper end of Nerudova. Turning instead to the left you will come to Vlašská, at a point just below this street's most important building, the **Lobkowicz Palace** (at No. 19, now the German Embassy). Begun by G.B. Alliprandi in 1703 and completed by I.J. Palliardi in 1769, this palace took as its main inspiration Bernini's unrealised plan for the Louvre in Paris, and features an entrance hall leading to a large oval vestibule projecting out on to the palace's gardens.

From the palace you can reach the upper end of Nerudova by walking due north along the narrow Šporkova, which curves around a picturesque group of houses before ending up at Jánský vršek (see above). Continuing instead to walk west along Vlašská you will pass to your left the northern walls of the Lobkowitz Gardens and, to your right (at No. 34), a hospital and chapel founded in the early 17C by Prague's Italian community, which was centred in this area.

Petřín Hill

At the western end of Vlašská you enter the large area of parkland covering the Petřín Hill, and can either turn right in the direction of the Strahov Monastery (see Chapter 1C), or else turn left and make your way to the top of the hill, which is crowned by trees. Peering up above the summit is a slightly decrepit imitation of Paris' Eiffel Tower; this **observation tower**, closed at present for much-needed restoration, was erected for the Jubilee Exhibition of 1891 and commands a remarkably extensive panorama of the city, with particularly fine views towards the Castle. Immediately to the south is another structure created for the Jubilee Exhibition, a crenellated neo-Gothic building (also closed at present) containing a hall of mirrors and a large tableau with waxwork figures representing Czech students defending the Charles Bridge against the Swedes in 1648: the hall of mirrors is recalled in Josef Škvorecký's novel, *The Cowards* as the place where the book's hero, Danny Smiřický, asks to be kissed by the girl he loves so that 'it would be like a thousand kisses all at once'.

Just to the south, and also among trees, is the **Church of St Lawrence** (sv. Vavřince), a Romanesque structure remodelled in the 18C. Further south still is the upper station of a **funicular railway** which was built in 1891 and has recently been opened following a long period of closure; it descends down to the long Újezd (see above), towards the bottom of the hill passing through the so-called **Petřín Gardens**, where there is a statue to the poet Jan Neruda.

South of the funicular the green and wooded slopes of the Petřín Hill are interrupted by the so-called **Hunger Wall** (Hladová zed'), which was erected by Charles IV in 1360–62, and marks the southeastern boundary of the Little Quarter; it derives its curious name from the fact that the poor of the city were employed in its construction, and were thus able to secure a livelihood. On the bosky slopes that stretch south of the wall into the district of Smíchov can be seen the charming, if rather neglected, wooden **Church of St Michael** (sv. Michal), an 18C structure brought here in 1929 from a remote Carpathian village near the Ukranian town of Mukačevo (Mukatehevo).

C. Prague Castle and the Hradčany

Prague Castle

'A spell hangs in the air of this citadel', wrote Patrick Leigh Fermor in *A Time of Gifts*, 'and I was under its thrall long before I could pronounce its name.' The enormous Prague Castle (Pražský Hrad) rises up above the Little Quarter like a town in its own right, its elegant Classical casing holding together a veritable architectural treasury from which project the fantastical Gothic spires of St Vitus's Cathedral.

History of the castle

The complex history of Prague's citadel goes back to around AD 870 when Count Bořivoj, founder of the Přemyslid dynasty and first Count of Bohemia, erected on top of a hill a modest but strategically situated fortified settlement. This became the seat of the Přemyslid counts, replacing the previous one at Levý Hradec, further north along the Vltava. In the early 10C the Church of St George and the Rotunda of St Vitus were founded here, and in 973, when the citadel became also the seat of the Prague bishopric, Bohemia's oldest convent was established alongside St George's. A devastating fire in the early 11C led in 1041 to Count Břetislav I replacing the former earthen ramparts of the citadel with stone ones, but 26 years later the Counts of Bohemia were temporarily to abandon the citadel in favour of Vyšehrad, where they were to remain until 1139. In preparation for the return here of the Přemyslids, Soběslav I constructed a new palace and rebuilt the fortifications, the line of which is largely preserved in the citadel of today.

The importance of the citadel was to reach its zenith in the 14C, during the reign of Charles IV, when the place was transformed into an imperial residence and work was begun on the great Gothic cathedral of St Vitus. Later in the century, though the citadel was to remain the seat of Bohemia's government, its role as a residence of the country's rulers was to be greatly diminished as a result of Wenceslas IV's decision to move to the Royal Court in the Old Town. King Vladislav Jagiello turned the place once more into a royal residence in 1484, and brought Benedikt Ried to Prague to rebuild and extend the castle's palace and fortifications; however, later in his reign, he and his court were to be based mainly in Budapest.

Bohemia's first Habsburg rulers, beginning with Ferdinand I, renewed the building activity in the citadel, and in the course of the 16C the place was to become an impressive Renaissance complex, with pioneering Italianate structures such as the Summer Palace (Belvedere), and the Great Ball-Game Court. With Rudolph I, and the international group of scientific and artistic luminaries that he gathered around him, the castle was once again, if only briefly, the seat of one of Europe's most brilliant courts. His successor, Matthias, vaunted the glories of the Habsburgs through the commissioning in 1614 of the imposing triumphal arch known today as the Matthias Gateway. Yet it was only four years later that the Habsburgs were to suffer here a profound humiliation when two of their councillors were ejected from one of the palace windows. Following this incident, which sparked off the Thirty Years War, the rebelling Czech Estates made the castle the seat of their government, though they were only to remain here for two years, their cause being momentously defeated at the Battle of the White Mountain in 1620. Reduced subsequently to the status of secondary residence the castle declined, and little important work was to be carried out here until the reign of Maria Theresa, who initiated a major rebuilding campaign which was to give to the complex the late Baroque and neo-Classical framework which it has largely kept to this day.

The last important building campaign in the castle took place after 1918, when Tomáš Masaryk turned the complex into the presidential seat of the newly created Republic of Czechoslovakia. St Vitus's Cathedral was finally brought to completion, and the lively and idiosyncratic architect Josip Plečnik was entrusted with the relaying of gardens, and the remodelling of courtyards and interiors. Plečnik's additions are bright and cheerful, but in the 20C the castle has acquired sinister connotations, thanks partially to the popular identification of the place with the novel of this name by Franz Kafka, who indeed worked here after 1916 in a house rented by his sister on Golden Lane. Kafka's vision of faceless tyranny and monstrous bureaucracy seem at any rate to have been prophetic of the years when the castle served as the seat of Czechoslovakia's Communist rulers.

A more human image for the whole complex has been acquired during the presidency of Václav Havel, who at one time could be seen riding around here on his scooter. The once drab costumes of the castle's guards were replaced by a colourful garb designed by a friend of Havel's whose previous most important job had been as the costume designer for Miloš Forman's film *Amadeus*. More importantly, areas of the complex once rigorously closed and guarded by machine-gun-carrying soldiers, have now been opened up to the public.

There is so much to see in the castle that the better part of a day is required to begin to do justice to the complex. To conserve their energy, many people prefer to reach the castle by public transport and save the beautiful walks through the Little Quarter for the late afternoon descent (see Chapter 1B). The easiest access by public transport is to take the underground to the Malostranská station, and from there catch a No. 22 bus to the junction of Mariánské hradby and U Prašného mostu, where you are left with a 5min walk, arriving eventually in the citadel's second courtyard. If you decide to walk all the way up the hill to the castle, the quickest ascent is up the **Old Castle Steps** (Staré zámecké schody), which begin the climb at a point just to the north of the Malostranská station, and enter the citadel at its narrow eastern end.

First and Second Courtyards

Whichever way you reach the castle, a tour of the place is best begun at its western end, which faces the Hradčany Square. Railings and a gate flanked by copies of two overblown sculptural groups of *Battling Giants* by Ignác Platzer (1786) mark the entrance to the **First Courtyard**, which is guarded by soldiers who perform a Changing of the Guard ceremony at 12.00 and 15.30 every day.

On the other side of the courtyard to the gate is the **Matthias Gateway**, a large Roman-style triumphal arch inspired, if not actually designed by, the Mannerist architect Vicenzo Scamozzi and executed by Giovanni Maria Philippi

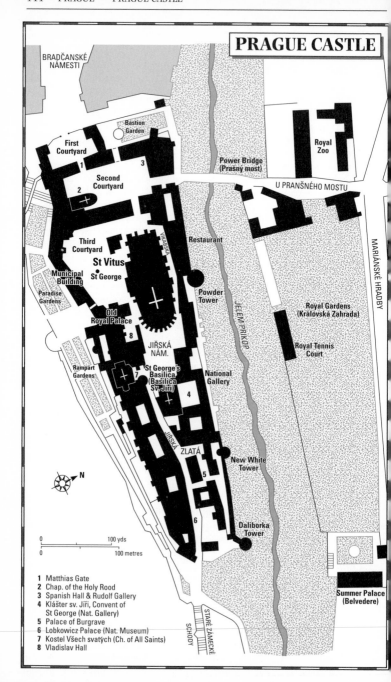

PRAGUE CASTLE

BRADČANSKÉ NÁMĚSTÍ

Bastion Garden

First Courtyard

1

3

Second Courtyard

2

Third Courtyard

St Vitus

• St George

Municipal Building

Paradise Gardens

Old Royal Palace

8

VIKÁŘSKÁ

JIŘSKÁ NÁM.

Rampart Gardens

7

St George's Basilica (Basílica Sv. Jiří)

4

National Gallery

JIŘSKÁ

ZLATÁ

5

New White Tower

6

Daliborka Tower

Power Bridge (Prašný most)

Restaurant

Powder Tower

JELENÍ PŘÍKOP

Royal Zoo

U PRANŠNÉHO MOSTU

Royal Gardens (Královská Zahrada)

Royal Tennis Court

MARIÁNSKÉ HRADBY

N

0   100 yds

0   100 metres

STARÉ ZÁMECKÉ

SCHODY

Summer Palace (Belvedere)

1 Matthias Gate
2 Chap. of the Holy Rood
3 Spanish Hall & Rudolf Gallery
4 Klášter sv. Jiři, Convent of
   St George (Nat. Gallery)
5 Palace of Burgrave
6 Lobkowicz Palace (Nat. Museum)
7 Kostel Všech svatých (Ch. of All Saints)
8 Vladislav Hall

in 1614. Originally a free-standing structure rising directly above the ramparts of the citadel, it was later incorporated into the palace's monumental west façade, which was built to designs by the court architect N. Pacassi in 1763–71. Further modifications to the courtyard were devised in 1920–22 by Josip Plečnik, who designed the two 25m-high flagpoles (tapering structures made out of pine trees taken, symbolically, from the Czechoslovak frontier), pierced the main block with openings on either side of the Matthias Gateway, and ingeniously planned to reduce the importance of the latter—a symbol of Habsburg dominance—by laying across the courtyard two paths of darker coloured paving stones that direct the eye to the new side entrances.

To the right of the gate is a staircase climbing up to the presidential reception rooms, while to the left is a recently installed glass opening affording a view of Plečnik's greatest work for the castle—an enormous hall built in 1927–31 and named today after the architect: featuring a ceiling of copper panels and walls articulated by three superimposed rows of Ionic columns, this room looks ahead to many of the 'Post-Modernist' structures of the 1970s and 1980s. Havel, as befitting a true follower of Masaryck, is a great enthusiast of Plečnik's work, and is anxious to make as much of it as possible accessible to visitors.

To enter the castle's Second Courtyard you can go through either the Matthias Gateway or else the arch just to the left of the First Courtyard; adjacent to the latter, at the northern end of the castle's west façade, is the small **Bastion Garden** laid out by Plečnik in 1927, and arranged on two levels that are joined by an ingenious circular stairway. The **Second Courtyard**, dating back to the late 16C, and given its present unified appearance in the late 18C, is centred around a Baroque fountain adorned with statues by Jeronym Kohl (1686). The southern side of the courtyard comprises the western end of a long building known as the **Municipal Building**, which extends all the way up to the Old Palace in the Third Courtyard; its monotonous, uniform façade shields a series of rooms (closed to the public) dating back to 1534. Attached to the southeastern corner of the Second Courtyard is the **Chapel of the Holy Rood** (sv. Kříže) which was built in 1756–63 by Anselmo Lurago after a plan by Pacassi, and remodelled in 1852–56. Now brashly transformed into the castle's ticket office, it previously housed for many years the greater part of the treasury of St Vitus's Cathedral.

The main rooms on the northern side of the Second Courtyard comprise the **Spanish Hall** and the **Rudolph Gallery**, two mirrored and richly stuccoed halls dating back to the late 16C but remodelled in a neo-Baroque style by Heinrich von Ferstel in 1866; generally closed to the public (except for the occasional concert) they are used today mainly for governmental meetings and receptions. The Rudolph Gallery originally housed the extraordinary art collection belonging to Rudolph II, the sorry remnants of which can once again be seen in the Prague Castle Gallery in the ground-floor rooms below.

History of the collection

Rudolph II ranked with his cousin Philip II of Spain as one of the greatest of the Habsburg collectors, but many of his pictures were transferred after his death to Vienna, and others were seized by the Swedes in 1648. In the mid-17C Ferdinand III built up a new collection at Prague, the nucleus of which was made up of works acquired from the Collection of the Duke of Buckingham, which was auctioned at Antwerp in 1648–49. The new gallery remained intact until 1721, when Charles IV began removing many of the better works to Vienna; later in the century Maria Theresa sold off many more of the paintings, as did her son Joseph II in 1782. The dispersal of the collection continued throughout the 19C, and by the end of the First World War it was thought that all the paintings had gone from Prague. Investigations carried out in 1962–64 by the art historian Jaromír Neumann revealed that in fact much had remained in the city, and in 1965 the surviving works were brought together to form the Prague Castle Gallery.

The **Prague Castle Gallery** occupies a series of beautifully modernised rooms, and there are few other collections in the Czech and Slovak Republics that are quite so well displayed. The works on show, however, are largely minor ones, and a panel of photographs reconstructing Rudolph II's original collection only emphasises the general mediocrity of what has survived. Works by artists of Rudolph's time include paintings by Bartolomaeus Spranger, Hans von Aachen, Cornelisz von Harlem, and an excellent wooden relief of the *Adoration of the Kings* by Adriaen de Vries. There are works by the Bohemian artists Petr Brandl and Johann Kupecký, and a painting by Rubens of the *Council of the Gods*, executed probably in Mantua in 1602. The bulk of the collection is of the Italian 16C and 17C, including a *Flagellation* by Tintoretto, a *Young Woman at her Toilet* by Titian (a version of a painting in the Louvre), *St Catherine and the Angel* and *Christ Washing the Feet of His Disciples* by Veronese, *The Centaur Nessus and Deianeira* by Guido Reni, and a peculiarly erotic *St Sebastian* by Saraceni, with a single arrow placed directly in the groin; among the other Italian paintings are works by Bernardo Monsú, Viviano Codazzi, Orazio Gentileschi, and Leandro, Jacopo and Francesco Bassano. **Open** Apr–Oct daily 09.00–17.00, Nov–Mar 09.00–16.00.

Third Courtyard and St Vitus's Cathedral
Entering the third and principal castle courtyard you find yourself directly in front of the west front of St Vitus's Cathedral, one of the finest and most richly endowed in Central Europe. **Open** Apr–Oct daily 09.00–17.00, Nov–Mar 09.00–16.00. Tower **open** daily 10.00–16.00.

History of the cathedral
The cathedral has its origins in a rotunda founded by Prince Wenceslas c 925, and transformed in 973 into the cathedral church of the Prague bishops; in 1060 this was replaced by a three-aisled Romanesque basilica. On the occasion of Prague's elevation from bishopric to archbishopric in 1344, Charles IV ordered the construction of the present Gothic building, for which he summoned from the papal court at Avignon the architect Matthew of Arras. Matthew had laid the foundations of the building and completed its east end up to the triforium level by the time of his death in 1352. In search of an architect to complete Matthew's work, Charles IV turned this time to Germany, and found there Peter Parléř, who had been born in about 1330 to a family of Cologne builders and whose father had been responsible for the great town church at Schwäbisch-Gmund. From 1353 up to his own death in 1399 Parléř was to be engaged on the building,

completing the east end, doubling the size of the chapel of St Wenceslas on the southwestern corner of the ambulatory, constructing the south portal and its adjoining open staircase, and beginning the nave; his work was to be continued by his sons Václav and Jan, who began work on the south tower. When the Hussites occupied the castle in 1421 the cathedral was greatly damaged and many of its furnishings destroyed; building activity was subsequently suspended for many years, the completed east end being closed off by a temporary wall.

Work on the cathedral was only to be resumed towards the end of the 15C, during the reign of Vladislav Jagiello: the strange Royal Oratory was put up on the south side of the ambulatory in the 1480s, the upper walls of the Wenceslas Chapel were painted in 1504, and the foundations of the north tower were laid in 1509–11. At the same time Vladislav Jagiello's principal architect, the great Benedikt Ried, formulated grandiose plans for the completion of the nave but, sadly, lack of funds led to their having to be abandoned in 1511. The main additions to the cathedral later in the century were the work of Bonifác Wohlmut, who was responsible in the 1560s for the Renaissance organ loft in the north transept and for crowning the Gothic south tower with a Renaissance gallery and bulbous domes (the top part of the tower was later destroyed by fire and rebuilt by N. Pacassi after 1770). A new attempt to complete the nave was made by Domenico Orsi in 1675, but this too was thwarted, and it was not until after the formation in 1861 of the 'Union for the completion of the Cathedral' that work was begun in earnest to try to finish the building. This new campaign was begun by Josef Kranner, and taken over by Josef Mocker, who was Czecho-slovakia's answer to Viollet-Le-Duc and someone responsible for the 'restoration' and pseudo-Gothic remodelling of many of Prague's other medieval monuments, such as the Powder Gate. The last architect to work on the cathedral was Kamil Hilbert, who finally completed the fabric of the building in 1929.

The most recent and dullest part of the cathedral is the twin-towered west façade, which features a large rosette window with stained-glass by F. Kysela and three portals with tympana containing carved reliefs executed in 1948–52 to designs by K. Dvořák and L. Pícha. The high point of the exterior is undoubtedly the **south façade**, thanks to Peter Parléř, who wanted to give particular emphasis to the side of the building which both housed St Wenceslas's tomb and faced the city. This façade is dominated by its 96m-high **tower**, the tapering Gothic part of which was begun by Parléř's sons in the early 15C and has a main window protected by a wonderfully intricate Renaissance grille; the arcaded gallery above this is a mid-16C addition by Bonifác Wohlmut, while the crowning steeple was designed by Palassi in 1770.

Immediately to the right of the tower are the three arches of Peter Parléř's South Porch or **Golden Portal**, which is decorated on the outside with a much-restored mosaic decoration of the Last Judgement executed in the late 14C by Venetian artists; in the spandrels of the central arch are the work's donors, Charles IV and his wife Eliška Pomořanská. One of Peter Parléř's main contributions to the cathedral was his inventive vaulting, as can be seen inside the porch, where a skeletal system of ribs is spread out like a fan. Above the porch is a further example of Parléř's structural daring—a complex, openwork staircase which was to be imitated in the cathedrals at Ulm and Strasbourg.

Entering the church through the south porch you should note how Parléř creates an ingenious progression from three arches to a double doorway and, finally, to a single portal. Once inside you will find yourself in the south transept, from where one of the best views of the interior can be had. The plan and proportions of the building clearly reflect the work of a French architect, and indeed the arrangement of the east end, with its radiating chapels, seems to have been inspired by that of Narbonne Cathedral, which was completed early in the 14C by Jean Deschamps. Peter Parléř provided the choir with its elegant vaulting system of parallel diagonal ribs, and also began the triforium, which runs round the whole building and has inside it a celebrated series of **portrait heads** representing all those involved in the building of the cathedral, including Parléř himself and members of Charles IV's family. Twenty-one of these busts— which are so high up that they can scarcely be seen—were executed by members of Parléř's workshop, but the rest (mainly in the nave) are modern works portraying recent figures such as the sculptors Bohumil Kafka and J. Štursa. The whole west end of the nave is a lifeless imitation of the east end, and bears little relation to the ambitious structure which Benedikt Ried would have created. The finest of the modern contributions to the building are the **stained-glass windows**, executed mainly by F. Kysela, K. Svolinský and Max Švabinský, the latter's largest work here being the Last Judgement window in the south transept.

To your right, immediately on entering the church from the south portal, is the **Wenceslas Chapel**, which Parléř enlarged by pushing out its southern and western walls, the latter at the expense of the transept. Visitors today are no longer allowed inside the chapel, and have to content themselves with the views from the railings. The chapel, containing the much-restored 14C tomb of St Wenceslas (d. 929 or 935), has a door of 1370 incorporating a Romanesque lion's-head knocker to which Wenceslas is said to have clung when he was attacked and murdered by his brother Boleslav. The interior, reflecting perhaps Charles IV's love of jewellery, is studded on its lower level with around 1372 precious stones. On this same level are also to be found a series of paintings of the Passion by an anonymous Czech artist of 1372 (identified variously as Master Theodoric and Master Oswald). The story of St Wenceslas is portrayed above these, in elaborately detailed works of 1504 generally attributed to the Master of Litoměřice; the room is further enhanced by Parléř's splendid ceiling, comprising parallel diagonal ribs springing from eight corbels to form a star-shaped dome.

In the middle of the long east end of the cathedral stands the **Royal Mausoleum**, a large memorial in white marble, executed between 1571 and 1589 by the Netherlandish sculptor Alexander Collin, and surrounded by a Renaissance grille by J. Schmidthammer: on its upper slab are reliefs of the Emperor Ferdinand I, his consort Anne of Jagiello, and his son Maximilan II, while on the sides are shown Charles IV and his four consorts, and the kings Wenceslas IV, Ladislav Pohrobek and George of Poděbrady. The actual tombs of these monarchs, as well as those of Rudolph II and members of the Přemyslids, can be seen in the **Royal Crypt**, the entrance to which lies just to the right of the mausoleum; within the crypt are also displayed the excavated remains of the

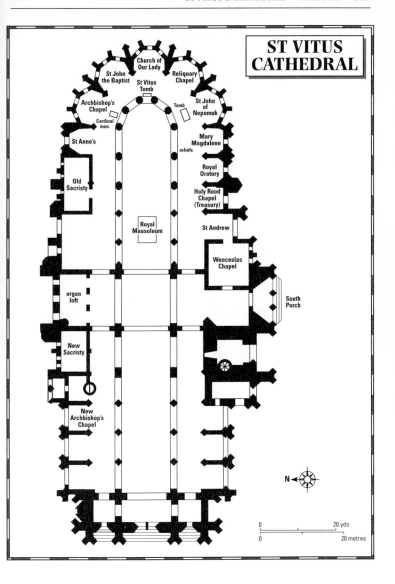

St John
the Baptist
Church of
Our Lady
Reliquary
Chapel
St Vitus
Tomb
Archbishop's
Chapel
Tomb
St John
of
Nepomuk
Cardinal
mon.
St Anne's
Mary
Magdalene
reliefs
Old
Sacristy
Royal
Oratory
Holy Rood
Chapel
(Treasury)
Royal
Mausoleum
St Andrew
Wenceslas
Chapel
organ
loft
South
Porch
New
Sacristy
New
Archbishop's
Chapel

ST VITUS CATHEDRAL

N

| 0 | | 20 yds |
| 0 | | 20 metres |

cathedral's foundations, including masonry of the 10C and 11C. Behind the mausoleum is the uninspired high altar, a neo-Gothic work of 1868–73, designed by J. Kranner and later altered by J. Mocker.

Walking around the ambulatory from its southwestern end, you will find next to the Wenceslas Chapel the Chapel of St Andrew, containing the tombstone (to the left, under the window) of Jaroslav von Martinic (d. 1649), one of the two Habsburg councillors thrown out of the Old Royal Palace window in 1618 (see below). The subsequent Chapel of the Holy Rood, with fragments of 14C murals, is followed by one of the more remarkable additions to the ambulatory, the **Royal Oratory**—a balcony decorated with characteristic late Gothic fantasy and naturalism, the architectural members imitating the branches of a tree; this highly entertaining work, dating back to the early years of Vladislav Jagiello's reign, is sometimes attributed to the Frankfurt sculptor Hans Spiess.

Next comes the Chapel of the Mary Magdalene, containing the wall tombs of the cathedral's two main architects, Matthew of Arras and Peter Parléř; fragments of late 14C wall-paintings can be seen here, as they can in the following Chapel of St John of Nepomuk, which also contains the marble tomb of Jan Očko of Vlašim, a work of 1370 from the Parléř workshop. The actual **Tomb of St John of Nepomuk** stands in the ambulatory passage in front of the last chapel, and is unquestionably the finest of the Baroque furnishings in the cathedral: an elaborate silver structure under a canopy hung with draperies supported by angels, the tomb was made in Vienna in 1733–36 to the designs of the great J.B. Fischer von Erlach.

Tombs from the Parléř workshop (1370s) of prominent members of the Přemyslid family are to be found in the next three chapels: the tombs of Kings Přemysl I (d. 1230) and Přemysl Otakar II (d. 1278) are in the Reliquary Chapel; those of Counts Břetislav I (d. 1055) and Spytihněv II (d. 1061) are in the Chapel of Our Lady, where work on the cathedral was probably begun in 1344; and those of Counts Břetislav II (d. 1100) and Bořivoj II (d. 1124) are in the Chapel of St John the Baptist, where there can also be seen a statue by J.V. Myslbek of St Methodius (1869–70) and the so-called Jerusalem candelabrum, a fine example of Rhenish craftsmanship of the early 12C. Behind the high altar, and directly in front of the Chapel of Our Lady, is the **Tomb of St Vitus**, with a statue of the saint by J. Max of 1840. The northernmost of the five radiating chapels of the apse is the Archbishops' Chapel, featuring the plain brown marble tomb of Vratislav of Pernštejn, a work of the late 16C by J. Vredemann de Vries.

In the ambulatory passage in front of this chapel is J.V. Myslbek's over life-size bronze statue of the kneeling Cardinal Bedřich Schwarzenberg (1891–95), the most important of the 19C sculptures in the cathedral. South of this is St Anne's Chapel, displaying on its altar a silver reliquary of 1266, decorated with enamels and precious stones. Further south you come to the **Old Sacristy**, the vaulting of which (begun in 1356) shows Peter Parléř at his most daring, featuring as it does a dramatically suspended boss supported by four skeletal ribs.

Attached to the north wall of the north transept is Bonifác Wohlmut's **Organ Gallery** (1557–61), which curiously combines a harmonious Renaissance front taken from the pages of Serlio with Gothic vaulting inside; the stained-glass window above this is the work of Max Švabinský and contains scenes of *The Holy Trinity*, *The Madonna with Count Spytihněv II*, and *St Wenceslas with Charles IV* (1939–49). The finest of the chapels in the nave is the third on the left-hand side, the **New Archbishop's Chapel**, which has been the burial place of Prague's archbishops since 1909, and also houses the tomb of the art historian bishop Antonín Podlaha, whose researches played an important part in the last phase of the cathedral's construction. The chapel is adorned with a vivid stained-glass window by Alfons Mucha of the *Lives of SS Cyril and Methodius*, and has next to it a powerful wooden sculpture of the *Crucifixion* (1899) by F. Bílek.

Leave the cathedral by its western door and turn right, touring the rest of the castle complex in a clockwise direction. Skirting the northern side of the cathedral is the narrow Vikářská, where at No. 2 is the former Deanery, which was remodelled after 1705 by Santini-Aichel. The congested tourist eateries crammed into this street have replaced a famous beer-cellar in which the 19C writer Svatopluk Čech set his very popular tale about Mr Brouček—a man who, under the influence of beer, goes on a series of imaginative adventures, including to the moon and back to the 15C.

A nearby alley leads from the street to the castle's northern bastions, which were renewed by Benedikt Ried in 1485 and include the round tower known as the **Powder Tower** (Mihulka). A small exhibition relating to the castle's fortifications is housed on the ground floor of this building, while on the upper floors (from where there are good views north towards the Summer Palace) are exhibits relating to the scientific and cultural life at the Renaissance court of Prague: the emphasis is on the time of Rudolph II, of whom there is an elaborately detailed bronze bust by Adriaen de Vries.

National Gallery

Vikářská leads to **George's Square** (Jiřské náměstí), which faces the apse of the cathedral and is named after the former Basilica of St George and its adjoining convent. The **Convent of St George** (Klášter sv. Jiří), in the northeastern corner of the square, was founded in 937 by Count Boleslav II and his sister Princess Mlada, who became its first abbess; rebuilt several times—including, most recently, between 1657 and 1680—it was turned into a barracks after its dissolution in 1782 and then converted between 1962 and 1972 into the branch of the **National Gallery** containing Czech art from the medieval to Baroque periods.

The **basement** and the **ground floor** contain the early holdings (up to around 1530), the first important sculpture being the bronze equestrian statue of *St George and the Dragon* (1373) by the brothers George and Martin of Kolosvar, a copy of which stands in the Castle's Third Courtyard. An adjoining room is dedicated to the first major Bohemian painter, the anonymous Master of the Vyšší Brod Altarpiece. This altarpiece of the mid-14C, originating from the former Cistercian monastery at Vyšší Brod in South Bohemia, was probably commissioned by Petr I of Rožmberk; it comprises nine panels of scenes from the life of Christ and the Virgin.

A more distinctive personality of slightly later date, and one of the earliest Bohemian artists known by name, was **Master Theodoric**, who is most famous for his panels and murals painted in the Holy Rood Chapel at Karlštejn Castle in 1357–65; he is represented here by six large and luminously modelled heads of saints. A work of great historical interest is the votive picture of John Očko of Vlasim, which portrays the enthroned Madonna flanked by what are sometimes considered as the earliest examples of Bohemian portraiture—remarkably realistic representations of Charles IV, Wenceslas IV and the panel's donor himself, John Očko, Archbishop of Prague. The main sculpture from this period in the gallery is the tympanum of the Crucifixion, which was taken from the north portal of the Týn Church in Prague.

The last years of the 14C are dominated by the **Master of the Třeboň Altarpiece**, whose principal work, from which he derives his name, is to be found here. Only three panels of this work—which was painted c 1380 for the former Augustinian church of St Giles in the South Bohemian town of Třeboň—have survived: these panels, painted on both sides with the most vivid colours and charming naturalistic detail, represent Christ on the Mount of Olives, SS Catherine, Mary Magdalene and Margaret, SS Augustine, Giles and Jerome, the Resurrection, and SS James, Bartholomew and Philip. Of the many anonymous sweetly smiling madonnas of the early 15C the finest is the famous Vyšší Brod Madonna of 1420.

The last of the outstanding Bohemian painters represented in the lower rooms of the gallery is the anonymous **Master of the Litoměřice Altarpiece**. The altarpiece itself is in the North Bohemian Gallery at Litoměřice (though it seems originally to have come from St Vitus's Cathedral in Prague), but the National Gallery has a number of other impressive works associated with him, most notably a series of panels from the Strahov Monastery in Prague (c 1505) and a triptych of the Holy Trinity of 1515–20. Of the later sculptures, special mention should be made of the expressive relief of the *Lamentation of Žebrák* (early 16C) and a series of five intricately carved reliefs by the artist known as the Monogramist IP, who seems to have come from the Passau or Salzburg region.

The collections of Renaissance and Baroque art on the first floor begin with works by artists of the Rudolph Circle, including a bronze of Hercules (1625–26) by **Adriaen de Vries** and an outstanding painting by **Bartolomaeus Spranger** of the *Risen Christ* (c 1590), which was intended for the tomb of the artist's father-in-law, the Prague goldsmith **Nicholas Müller** (who appears, together with other members of his family, at the bottom of the work). The 17C collections feature an especially large number of paintings by **Karel Škréta**, of which the most striking are the portraits, in particular a bust of the French painter Nicolas Poussin (whom Škréta met in Rome in 1634–35), an informal group portrait of the gem-carver *Dionysio Miseroni and his Family* (1653), and a delightful full-length portrait of *Maria Maximiliana of Sternberg dressed as a Shepherdess* (1665).

Among the later paintings of the 17C are the very Rubenesque *Liberation of St Andromeda* (1695) by **M. Willmann**, and a number of rapid oil sketches by **Jan Liška**. Baroque sculpture is represented most notably by **J.G. Bendl**'s *Archangel Raphael* of c 1650, which was taken from the demolished plague column on the Old Town Square, several works by **F.M. Brokoff**, in particular two *Moors* of 1718–19 from the gates of the mansion at Kounice, and a polychromed statue of St John of Bohemia, and **Matthias Braun**'s hysterically posed St Jude Thaddeus (1712), originally forming part of an altarpiece from the now-demolished Church of Our Lady in Prague's Old Town. From the latter dismantled altarpiece there is also a painting of St Jude Thaddeus by **Petr Bendl**, one of the most successful and prolific Bohemian artists of the early 18C: in addition to this and numerous other religious works by him, the gallery has an extensive collection of his portraits, including two self-portraits dating from 1697 and 1703.

A more remarkable portraitist than Bendl was **Johann Kupecký**, who is represented here by two of his greatest works, a seated portrait of the ostentatiously dressed miniaturist Karl Bruni and a portrait of *The Artist with his Wife*: the latter, a work of uncompromising realism, was painted, unusually, as a token of reconciliation with his wife, whom he had found to be unfaithful and whom he portrayed here in the guise of a penitent. Among the other 18C works are **V.V. Reiner**'s *Orpheus with Animals in a Landscape* (before 1720), **A. Kern**'s *St Augustine* (c 1735), **N. Grund**'s *Gallant Scene with a Lady on a Swing* (c 1760) and oil sketches for frescoes by **F.A. Maulbertsch**.

The plain white rooms arranged around the convent's simple cloister provide a perfect setting for the paintings and sculptures, through which you are directed chronologically by arrows. **Open** Apr–Sept Tues–Sun 09.00–18.00; Oct–Mar 10.00–17.00.

The **Basilica of St George** (Basilika sv. Jiří), attached to the southern side of the convent, is the oldest church in the citadel, having been founded in 905. Transformed into a three-aisled structure in 973, it was rebuilt following a fire in 1142, and then again in 1657–80; restoration campaigns undertaken in 1897–1907 and 1959–62 brought back many of the building's 10C–12C features, making the church one of the best-preserved Romanesque structures in Bohemia. The main Baroque survival is the vivid ochre west façade (facing George's Square) and the adjoining **Chapel of St John of Nepomuk** (sv. Jan Nepomucký), which was built by F.M. Kaňka and the Dientzenhofer brothers in 1718–22, and is adorned on the outside with a statue of the saint by F.M. Brokoff. The south portal of the basilica, facing Jiřská, is an early 16C coffered Classical structure by Benedikt Ried incorporating in the tympanum a late Gothic relief of *St George and the Dragon*, the original of which is in the National Gallery. The principal Romanesque features of the basilica's exterior are the twin white towers rising up at the eastern end of the church.

The cold and heavily restored interior, which is now deconsecrated and used only for the occasional concert, retains in its nave the original arcades of the 10C and 11C. At the end of the nave, in front of the raised choir, are the tombs of Count Boleslav II (encased by a Baroque grille of 1730) and Count Vratislav I (in painted wood), the founder of the church. In between the two flights of the Baroque staircase which leads up to the choir is the entrance to the remarkable **crypt** of 1142, featuring columns with cubic capitals, and a particularly grim and realistic sculpture of a decomposing female corpse (executed in 1726). The vault of the choir has scant fragments of wall-paintings of c 1200 representing the Celestial Jerusalem; fragments of 16C painting decorate the vault of the adjoining **Chapel of St Ludmilla** (sv. Ludmila), which was added in the late 14C and houses the tomb (from Peter Parléř's workshop) of the murdered Ludmilla, one of Bohemia's patron saints.

The eastern citadel

Jiřská or George's Street, which runs due east of the basilica and slowly descends through the tapering eastern half of the citadel, is the main and oldest street of the citadel, and is lined with a number of Renaissance and Baroque buildings. Before reaching the finest of these, you should take the first turning to the left to visit the celebrated **Golden Lane** (Zlatá ulička). This row of tiny houses dating from the end of the 16C runs directly underneath the northeastern ramparts of the citadel, in between the New White Tower and the Daliborka Tower, both of which formed part of the new fortifications designed by Benedikt Ried for Vladislav Jagiello. The name of the lane is sometimes romantically connected with the alchemists at Rudolph's court, though in fact it derives from the gold-smiths who once lived here alongside the castle's guards. In the 18C and 19C the dwellings here were inhabited by the very poor, and it was only after 1960 that they were to receive their cheerfully coloured doll's-house appearance and tiny shops selling artefacts for the thousands of tourists who daily throng this restricted area. The **New White Tower** (Bílá věž) at the western end of the lane served after 1584 as a prison, among its most famous inmates being the English alchemist Edward Kelley and the leaders of the anti-Habsburg uprising of 1618.

Returning to Jiřská and continuing to walk east you will pass to your left, at No. 4, the former Palace of the Burgrave of Prague Castle, which was built in 1541 by Giovanni Ventura and adapted in the early 1960s to serve as the House of Czechoslovak Children; today, it maintains its association with children by housing the deeply disappointing **Toy Museum** (Muzeum hraček), an unimaginative display of objects such as toy robots, cars, and even Barbie dolls (not even the most undemanding of today's children could possibly enjoy this). **Open** Tues–Sun 09.30–17.30.

More interesting (at least for its setting) is the hotch-potch of drably arranged objects making up the **Historical Museum** on the other side of the street. This documents the history of Bohemia from the arrival of the Slavs up to 1848–49 and occupies the **Lobkowicz Palace**, which was rebuilt in 1651–68 to the designs of the Italian architect Anselmo Lurago and retains several 17C and 18C ceilings, including, in Room 19, a heavily stuccoed 17C ceiling incorporating a clumsy if amusing painted panel of *The Triumph of Caesar*. **Open** Tues–Sun 09.00–17.00.

A little below the palace Jiřská reaches the citadel's eastern gate, on the other side of which you will come out at the top of the Old Castle Steps (Staré zámecké schody; see above).

Old Royal Palace and gardens

Make your way back to George's Square and bear left, passing to your left immediately on re-entering the square the Church of All Saints (Všech svatých), which was rebuilt after a fire at the end of the 16C and attached after 1755 to the adjoining Theresian Convent for Noblewomen.

On the western side of the Church of All Saints is the Old Royal Palace, parts of which date back to the 12C but which owes its present appearance largely to the rebuilding campaign undertaken by Benedikt Ried in the late 15C for Vladislav Jagiello. Occupying the site of the 9C palace of the Princes of Bohemia, it served from the 13C to the 16C as the palace of the Kings of Bohemia. After the Habsburgs moved their quarters to the western end of the citadel and up to the end of the 18C the building functioned as the central offices of the Bohemian state. Thereafter it was neglected and partially used as storage space until 1924, when it was thoroughly restored and taken over for governmental purposes; its main rooms, which have only been open to the public since the 1960s, are still the scene of the occasional important political assembly.

The palace is entered from the castle's Third Courtyard, and as you make your way there from the Church of All Saints you will pass to your left a parapet overlooking the palace courtyard, above which rises the **Vladislav Hall**, which is adorned on the outside by elegant Renaissance windows that give no hint of the late Gothic fantasies to be found within. When you eventually enter the hall after crossing a dark and austere antechamber adjoining the palace's main entrance, you are confronted with what is architecturally one of the most exciting spaces to be seen in Europe. The vast hall, which is by far the largest room in the palace, was built by Benedikt Ried in 1493–1502 and is dominated by vaulting of breathtaking elaboration: the ribs, likened frequently to the intertwined branches of a forest, have largely ceased to play a structural role, but snake their way around the ceiling in an essentially decorative way, drawing the visitor into the room through their powerful movements, and creating dynamic effects that look ahead to the Baroque period. The vaulting, representing an extreme development of the late Gothic style, contrasts markedly with the innovatory Renaissance windows, yet even when handling Classical forms, Ried often did so in a highly idiosyncratic fashion, as can be seen in his famous door at the northeastern end of the room, where a Renaissance arch is supported by twisted pilasters, which are almost a mockery of all that the Renaissance stood for.

Before crossing to the eastern end of the hall, you should go through the door in its southwestern corner to visit the room of the **Bohemian Chancellery**, which is famous as the place where the 'Second Defenestration' took place in 1618.

After returning to the hall walk across to its southeastern corner, where there is a door leading to a **terrace** offering a magnificent view of Prague; the helical staircase which descends from here to the gardens below was built by Otto Rothmayer in 1951. Back once more in the hall, and crossing over to its northeastern corner, you will pass to your right a balcony looking down into the Church of All Saints (see above), which has mainly 17C and 18C furnishings. The extraordinary door with twisted pillars at the northeastern corner of the hall leads into the **Diet Hall**, which is covered with another late Gothic vault of fascinating complexity. The room, built by Ried in 1500, was destroyed by fire in 1541, and reconstructed nine years later by Bonifác Wohlmut, who provided it with the Renaissance tribune once used by the Supreme Scribe.

Returning to the Vladislav Hall, and turning right, you will come immediately to a double Renaissance portal. Through the arch on the left is a spiral staircase climbing up to the rooms of the **New Land Rolls**, where there is a ceiling decorated with the heraldic shields of the clerks of the Land Rolls; the right-hand arch leads directly to the **Riders' Staircase**, which horses had once climbed on their way to joust in the Vladislav Hall. Built by Ried in around 1500 it is vaulted in a way which almost surpasses in complexity this architect's achievement in the Vladislav Hall, with ribs that intersect, interrupt and are suddenly truncated, the overall effect being one of suspended movement, a sense of playful abandon being controlled by a rigorous geometrical discipline in a way which would have impressed the Baroque architect Borromini.

Walking down the Riders' Staircase you reach the palace's northern door, where you can either leave the building or else continue your visit by going first to the ground-floor rooms of Charles IV's palace, and then to the gloomy cellar below, a survival of the 12C palace of Count Soběslav; these Romanesque and Gothic chambers are largely bare, but there are copies of some of Parléř's triforium sculptures from St Vitus's Cathedral in the large **Charles Hall**—a space currently ear-marked to house the cathedral's famous treasury. **Open** Apr–Sept Tues–Sun 09.00–17.00; Oct–Mar 10.00–16.00.

After walking back to the western end of the palace, you should take a closer look at the southern half of the Third Courtyard, in the middle of which stands the famous bronze statue of *St George and the Dragon* by the brothers George and Martin of Kolosvar (the original is in the National Gallery at the Convent of St George). Between 1928 and 1932 the whole courtyard, which at one time was slightly sloping, was relaid and straightened by Josip Plečnik, who also designed for it a granite monolith commemorating the dead of the First World War.

At the same time Plečnik pierced the eastern end of the monotonous Municipal Building on the southern side of the courtyard with a portal and ingenious staircase leading down to the gardens which had been laid out originally in the late 17C over the notorious ditch into which the two councillors had been thrown in 1618. The gardens, commanding a magnificent panorama of Prague, were also relaid by Plečnik, who divided them into the **Rampart Garden** and the **Paradise Garden**, thus breaking up the monotony of the original formal plan. One of the more welcome recent changes has been the opening up of these gardens to visitors, who might well find them a refreshingly quiet place to get away for a while from the crowds of fellow sightseers. From the Paradise Garden, where Plečnik placed a 40-ton granite basin on two small blocks, there is also a monumental staircase leading back to the Hradčany Square. **Open** May–Oct Tues–Sun 10.00–18.00.

North of the citadel

From the Third Courtyard you should make your way back to the Second Courtyard, which you should leave through the arch on its northern side. This will take you to the **Powder Bridge** (Prašný most), which spans the so-called **Stag Moat** (Jelení příkop), where red deer were kept from the 16C to 18C. After crossing the bridge and continuing to walk north, you will pass on the left an elegantly simple building designed by J.-B. Mathey in 1694 as the **Royal Riding-School** (Jízdárna), and then restored by Pavel Janák in 1948–54. On the other side of the path are the gates to the beautifully maintained and azalea-laden **Royal Gardens** (Královská zahrada), which have been largely re-opened to the public following years of closure during the Communist period.

Walking east inside the garden you will come shortly to the much-restored **Great Ball-Game Court** (Míčovna), an harmonious Renaissance structure built by Bonifác Wohlmut and Ulrico Avostalis in 1565–69, and covered all over with Renaissance sgrafitto work. More impressive still is the **Summer Palace** (Letohrádek královny Anny) at the gardens' eastern end. Popularly and wrongly known as the Belvedere, the Summer Palace is one of the purest examples in Central Europe of the Italian Renaissance style, the proportions of its arcaded lower level strongly recalling the architecture of Brunelleschi. Begun in 1537 to a design by Paolo della Stella (who executed as well the exquisite mythological and ornamental reliefs on the arcade), it was completed in 1552–69 by Bonifác Wohlmut, who provided it with the one feature which reveals it as a work situated in Central Europe rather than Italy—the curious copper roof shaped like the inverted hull of a ship. The interior, remodelled in the mid-19C, was restored after the Second World War by Pavel Janák, and again in recent years. The tiny Renaissance garden on its western side contains a celebrated bronze fountain known as the **Singing Fountain** on account of the sounds made by the water dropping from its two basins: the finely detailed work was designed in 1563 by Francesco Terzio. The Royal Gardens are **open** May–Oct Tues–Sun 10.00–17.45. Belvedere **open** Tues–Sun 10.00–18.00.

On the eastern side of the palace is the small **Chotěk Park**, which was founded in 1833 by the Supreme Burgrave K. Chotěk, and was Prague's first public park; in an overgrown bosky setting at its eastern end stands a delightful memorial by Josef Maudr to the 19C poet Julius Zeyer, whose bronze bust is placed on top of a grotto enclosing a group of white marble figures from his poems.

West of Prague Castle

Return to the castle's Second Courtyard, and from there make your way back to the Hradčany Square to begin a tour of the former township that grew up to the west of the castle's walls. Made a township in 1320, and enlarged 40 years later by the construction of the Hunger Wall (see p 141), this became the scene after 1541 of intensive rebuilding work; the place was raised to the status of royal town in 1598, and remained as such until the creation of a unified Prague in 1784.

The district covers a relatively small area, but is crowded with important monuments, beginning with those on the **Hradčany Square** (Hradčanské náměstí) itself. This sloping, wedge-shaped square, lined with imposing palaces, features at its centre a **Marian column** of 1726 ringed by eight statues of saints by F.M. Brokoff. Adjacent to the western façade of the castle, behind a fine ironwork lampholder, is the **Archbishop's Palace** (No. 16), which dates back to a building by Wohlmut of 1562, but was rebuilt by J.-B. Mathey at the end of the 17C and given an Italianate Baroque façade, with a crowning pediment and statuary, by J.J. Wirch in 1763–65; the interior, closed to the public, is rich in 18C furnishings, including a set of eight Gobelin tapestries of 1753–56.

Šternberk Palace ~ National Gallery

On the left-hand side of the palace is an alley descending to the **Šternberk Palace** (No. 15), a gloomy but impressive structure which is completely hidden from the square. Designed by D. Martinelli, and executed between 1698 and 1707 by G.B. Alliprandi and J.B. Santini-Aichel, it is particularly remarkable for its courtyard, which is dominated on its western side by a large oval pavilion. However, the building is visited less for its architecture than for its paintings, for it houses the pre-modern Foreign School holdings of the **National Gallery** (the modern ones have now been transferred to the Trade Fair Palace in Holešovice; see Chapter 1H).

The rooms of the Šternberk Palace, featuring a number of fine stuccoed and painted ceilings of the early 18C, make an elegant setting for the Old Master Foreign School paintings (which have been housed here since 1945), but the display is crammed, old-fashioned and poorly lit. The dingy main staircase adjoining the ticket-office leads up to where the bulk of the collection is shown. **Open** Tues–Sun 10.00–18.00.

On the **first floor** are the Italian 14C to 16C paintings, which include among the primitives works by **Nardo di Cione** and **Bernardo Daddi** and an expressive *Lamentation* by **Lorenzo di Monaco**; the quattrocento is represented only by four works, the finest of which are by **Benozzo Gozzoli** and **Pasqualino Veneto**.

It is on the second floor that the true quality of the gallery is felt, beginning with an excellent group of German 15C to 16C paintings, including **Hans Schücklin**'s *Beheading of St Barbara* (1470), monochrome fragments of an altarpiece of 1509 by **Hans Holbein** the Elder, a portrait by his son of Elizabeth Vaux, **Altdorfer**'s *Martyrdom of St Florian*, **Baldung Grien**'s *Beheading of St Dorothy* (1516), and a variety of works by **Lucas Cranach** the Elder, most notably a delightful *Adam and Eve* of 1537, a *Judith and Holofernes* of 1550, and fragments from an altarpiece in St Vitus's Cathedral which was taken down by Protestants in 1619 (the main survival is a panel of the Assumption surrounded by angels and saints). Especially powerful are two large panels by **Hans Süss of Kulmbach** which originally decorated the organ loft of the Church of Our Lady in the Snows in Prague's New Town; they are vigorous and near life-sized representations of the Emperor Henry II and the Empress Chunegunda.

Süss was an artist greatly influenced by **Albrecht Dürer**, who is represented here by one of his most famous works, *The Feast of the Rose Gardens*, which was painted in Venice in 1506 for the church of San Bartolomeo. It was acquired by Rudolph II in 1606, and is the most important of his pictures to have remained in Prague.

A small room tucked away behind the room with the Dürer contains the small and unimpressive holdings of 17C and 18C French and Spanish art, featuring works by **Bourdon**, **Charles le Brun**, **Boucher** and **Mignard**, and an indifferent portrait by **Goya** of *Don Miguel de Lardizabal* (1815). The best of the French paintings—a dramatically coloured *Suicide of Lucretia* (1625–26) by **Simon Vouet**—was painted in Rome under the influence of Caravaggio and is thus displayed in the rooms devoted to the 16C–18C Italian School. The Italian cinquecento contains good portraits by **Lotto** and **Bronzino**, and the so-called *Madonna of the Veil*, a Holy Family group painted c 1519 by **Sebastiano del Piombo**, and on loan from the cathedral at Olomouc. The 17C and 18C Italian paintings include **Domenico Fetti**'s *Christ in the Garden of Gethsemane*, **Magnasco**'s *Mary Magdalene in a Landscape*, **Piazzetta**'s *St Joseph and Child*, an enormous view of London by **Canaletto**, a head of an old man by **G.D. Tiepolo** (erroneously attributed to his father Giambattista), a *St Jerome* by **Ribera**, and small oils by **Pittoni** and **Sebastiano Ricci**.

Of the Netherlandish holdings of the 15C and 16C, **Jan Gossaert**'s *St Luke Drawing the Virgin and Child* (1513–16) and **Pieter Brueghel** the Elder's *Haymaking* (1565) stand out; the former was hung on the main altar of St Vitus's Cathedral from 1618 up to the end of the 19C, while the latter formed part of a famous series of panels of the months painted for the artist's Antwerp friend Nicolaes Jonghelinck (the other surviving panels from this series are in the Kunsthistorisches Institut in Vienna). Among the 17C Flemish paintings are a *St Bruno* (1615) by **Van Dyck** and several works by **Rubens**, including a *Cleopatra* of c 1615, and two large canvases of *St Augustine* and *The Martyrdom of St Thomas* which the artist painted between 1637 and 1639 for the former Augustinian Church of St Thomas in Prague's Little Quarter.

The Dutch 17C holdings are extensive and feature genre scenes by **Dou**, **Ter Borch**, **Ochtervelt**, **Metsu** and **David Teniers**, still-lifes by **Pieter Klaesz** and **Willem Kalf**, and landscapes by **Jan van Goyen**, **Salamon Ruisdael** and **Aert von der Meer**; the two outstanding works in this section are **Rembrandt**'s *Scholar in his Study* of 1634 and the half-length portrait by **Frans Hals** of the rather cocksure Jasper Schade van Westrum (c 1645).

Leaving the gallery and continuing to tour the Hradčany Square, you will find on its southern side, at No. 2, the **Schwarzenberg-Lobkowicz Palace**. This large, gabled palace, built by Augustín Vlach for Jan of Lobkowicz in 1543–63, is one of the finest examples in Prague of Bohemian Renaissance architecture, and is covered with restored sgraffito decorations, including on its wide projecting cornice; the interior, featuring 16C painted ceilings on the second floor, now houses a beautifully displayed **Military Museum** (Vojenské muzeum), with exhibits relating to early military history throughout the world. **Open** May–Oct Tues–Sun 09.30–16.30.

The wide, western end of the square is largely taken up by the **Thun-Hohen-**

stein Palace (No. 5); though known sometimes as the 'Tuscan Palace' (the Duke of Tuscany owned it after 1718), this is in fact a Roman-inspired building, built by J.-B. Mathey in 1689–91, and with an upper balustrade crowned by statues by F.M. Brokoff. At the northwestern corner of the square, overlooking Kanovnická, is the gabled Martinic Palace of 1618–24, its façade sgraffitoed with biblical and mythological scenes.

Walking north along Kanovnická you will come at the end of this street to the **Church of St John of Nepomuk** (sv. Jana Nepomuckého), which was built by K.I. Dientzenhofer in 1720–28 and is the first known church by this architect; its newly repainted exterior is unremarkable, but the Greek Cross interior, with ceiling paintings of the life of the saint by V.V. Reiner (1728), is richly decorated and stuccoed, and full of movement.

Turning right at the end of Kanovnická, and then immediately left, you will come to the top of what is perhaps the most picturesque of the Hradčany's streets, **Nový Svět** or 'The New World' (a name which is also applied to this whole corner of town). This narrow, cobbled street, originating in a path leading from Prague to Střešovice, was lined at the end of the 16C with a number of modest houses; the latter, crumbling away over the centuries, came to be occupied by the very poor, but have now become some of Prague's most exclusive addresses. At No. 1, on the left-hand side, is the house which belonged first to the astronomer Tycho Brahe and then, after 1600, to his successor as court astronomer, Johann Kepler; at No. 25, further down on the same side, is a memorial plaque by O. Španiel commemorating the house where the violinist František Ondříček was born in 1857.

After turning around at the last house and retracing your steps for a few metres, take the first turning to your right, Černínská, and climb up to the quiet and sloping **Loreto Square** (Loretánské náměstí) at the narrow northern end of which, immediately to your right, is the former **Capuchin Church of Our Lady**, the monastery of which is the oldest Capuchin institution in Bohemia and was founded in 1600; the mid-17C church is very plain in its architecture and decoration, in accordance with the ideals of this order, but is worth visiting during the Christmas period to see the famous crib which is assembled here.

Rising above a terrace, and occupying the whole western side of the square, is the **Černín Palace**, which was designed and begun by Francesco Caratti in 1669 for Humprecht Jan Černín of Chudenice, the imperial ambassador to Venice. Domenico Rossi, G.B. Alliprandi and F.M. Kaňka were among the later architects to play a part in the construction of the palace, which would fall seriously into disrepair by the beginning of the 19C. In 1928–34 the whole structure was extensively restored and remodelled by Pavel Janák. However, the main façade overlooking the Loreto Square remains, in its overall conception if not in its detailing, essentially as Caratti had planned it, and is not only one of the most monumental façades in Prague, but also the first truly Baroque structure in the city, being articulated the whole of its great length (150m) by a giant order of Corinthian columns. Since 1918 the building has served as the Ministry of Foreign Affairs, and in 1948 was the scene of a notorious incident when one of Beneš' ministers, Jan Masaryk (the son of Czechoslovakia's first president), experienced the peculiarly Czech fate of falling out of the window.

Sanctuary of Our Lady of Loreto

Facing the Černín Palace on the eastern side of the square is the Sanctuary of Our Lady of Loreto, an important place of pilgrimage as well as one of the Hradčany's main tourist attractions. The sanctuary dates back to 1626 when Benigna Kateřina of Lobkowicz, anxious to revive the Marian cult, commissioned a replica of the Virgin's House at the Italian town of Loreto, a house which, according to a 15C tradition, had been transported there miraculously from the Holy Land; at least 50 other copies of this house have been made, but the one in Prague remains the most famous. The Virgin's House is encased by a Baroque complex, the main, western façade of which was begun by Christoph Dientzenhofer in 1716 and completed by his son Kilian Ignaz in 1722; in front of it is a balustrade decorated with statues of cherubs by O. Quittainer. The elegant tripartite façade has a frontispiece crowned by a tall tower enclosing an elaborate **carillon** which was made by Petr Neumann in 1694 and plays various melodies by means of a keyboard, including—at the stroke of every hour—the Marian hymn, *We Greet Thee a Thousand Times*.

After passing through the main portal you come to the cloisters, in the middle of which stands the Virgin's House, which was built by G.B. Orsi in 1626–31, and shrouded in 1664 with a heavy stuccoed decoration featuring Old Testament figures and scenes from the Life of the Virgin; the simple, barrel-vaulted interior in unfaced brick has traces of 17C frescoes. The cloisters themselves date back to 1661 but were raised by a storey by K.I. Dientzenhofer in the 1740s. They are surrounded by small and elaborately decorated 18C chapels, and feature off their eastern side the **Church of the Nativity** (narození Páně), which was designed by J.J. Aichbaurer in 1734, and has a sumptuously gilded interior with ceiling paintings by V.V. Reiner and J.V. Schöpf.

After having walked around the cloisters in a clockwise direction you complete your tour of the sanctuary by climbing up to a room off the cloister's western side, where you will find—displayed under a modern ceiling hung with a glass decoration in questionable taste—a **treasury** comprising chalices, monstrances and other liturgical objects from the 16C to 18C. Its spectacular highpoint is the so-called **Diamond Monstrance** (known also as 'the Prague Sun'), which was designed by the great Viennese architect J.B. Fischer von Erlach and executed in 1699 by the Viennese court jewellers Matthias Stegner and Johann Kanischbauer. **Open** Tues–Sun 09.00–12.15 and 13.00–16.30.

Strahov Monastery

At the foot of the Sanctuary's main entrance is a flight of steps leading up to the southern end of the Loreto Square. Turn right at the top of the square and you will come almost immediately to **Pohořelec**, a square which has its origins in a suburb of the Hradčany founded in 1375; it is lined today with 17C and 18C buildings that, after long years of grime and decay, now sparkle under their pastel coats of paint. Climbing up the dark and narrow passage through the house at No. 8 (on the southern side of the square) will lead you into the peaceful and newly restored courtyard of the Strahov Monastery (Strahovský klášter); alternatively you could reach this courtyard by walking to the southwestern corner of the square, and then turning left, entering the monastery through its elegant gate of 1742, and passing on your left the early 17C Church of St Roch (now a private art gallery).

History of the monastery

The former Premonstratensian monastery of Strahov was founded by Vladislav II in 1140 on the instigation of the Bishop of Olomouc, Jindřich Zdík, who had first come into contact with the Premonstratensian Order on a visit to Palestine. The monastery, endowed with a formidable library, soon became one of the great centres of learning in Bohemia, and many of the leading personages of the day were educated here. Devastated and plundered by the Swedes in 1648, the place prospered once again after the subsequent Treaty of Westphalia, and acquired so many more books that in 1671 G.D. Orsi began building a new library hall, known today as the Theological Hall. Between 1682 and 1689 the rest of the monastery was remodelled and extended by J.-B. Mathey, and towards the end of the following century a further library hall, the Philosophical Hall, was commissioned from I.J. Palliardi by the enlightened abbot Václav Mayer (1734–1800). Mayer was also responsible for the founding of the abbey's Cabinet of Curiosities, and it was during his abbacy that the man known as the 'patriarch of Slavic philology', J. Dobrovský, used to stay here. In deference to the monastery's literary traditions, a Museum of Czech Literature was established in the monastery buildings in 1953. Archaeological investigations carried out here during this same decade uncovered extensive remains of the 12C monastery. Since 1989 the place has become occupied again by monks (there are currently 32 of them), and they have made the complex more commercially viable than it was during the Communist period: the monastery's brewing traditions have been revived, two of its buildings have been profitably leased out, and the place's tourist potential has been exploited to the full.

On the southern side of the courtyard is the functioning **Monastery Church of Our Lady** (Nanebevzetí Panny Marie). This church, which retains its 12C Romanesque basilica plan, was remodelled in the early 17C and again in the middle of the following century; the mid-18C interior has a ceiling decorated with stucco cartouches designed by J. Palliardi, and an organ on which Mozart played. The finest of the Baroque additions to the monastery are its two library halls, the entrance to which is adjacent to the church's west façade. The grander of the two is the first one you come to, the **Philosophical Hall**, which was built at the end of the 18C around richly gilded and carved walnut furnishings by J. Lahofer that were brought here from the dissolved Premonstratensian monastery at Louka outside the South Moravian town of Znojmo (see Chapter 19). In 1794 one of the greatest fresco painters of Central Europe, the Austrian A.F. Maulbertsch, covered the entire vault of this hall with a vast ceiling painting representing the modest theme of *The Struggle of Mankind to Know True Wisdom*.

The **Theological Hall** has kept its original wooden shelving and is adorned in its centre with 17C and 18C globes as well as tables displaying a select few of the library's incomparable collection of illuminated manuscripts and incunabula, among which is the Strahov New Testament, an Ottonian work of the 9C–10C constituting one of the oldest written documents surviving in the Czech Republic; the magnificent ceiling is decorated with late 17C stucco cartouches by Silvestro Carlone framing frescoes by Siard Nosecký, also celebrating human knowledge. In the short corridor between the two libraries are glass cabinets displaying some of the natural history 'curiosities' (including a whale's penis) amassed by Abbot Mayer and others.

The once rambling and delightfully chaotic **Museum of Czech Literature** (Památník národního písemnictví), of interest largely to Czech speakers, has now been streamlined and relegated to some ground-floor rooms off the church's adjoining cloisters. Above them is the small and recently opened **Strahov Art Gallery**, which features some of the works of art acquired by the monks over the centuries and now returned to them after being confiscated by the Communists (until 1989 a few of these works hung in the Šternberk Palace; see above). The paintings range from the mid-14C *Strahov Madonna* to a number of fine Baroque and rococo oils by Skřeta, Brandl, Sebastiano Ricci, Maulbertsch and Antonín Kern; in between are some striking works of the Rudolphine period, notably Spranger's *Resurrection of Christ* (c 1576), Hans von Aachen's portrait of Rudolph II (1604–12) and, more interesting still, Dirck de Quade van Ravesteyn's *Allegory of the Reign of Rudolph II* (1603), a good example of the erotic use of allegorical figures. **Open** Tues–Sun 09.00–17.00.

A gate through the monastery's eastern wall brings you out into the extensive parkland covering the Petřín Hill, and an enjoyable short walk, with beautiful views towards Prague Castle, can be made from here to the observatory tower at the top of the hill (see Chapter 1B). To return instead to the Hradčany Square, go back to Pohořelec and from there head east down Loretánská, which has a number of fine palaces at its eastern end, including, at No. 4, the **Martinic Palace**, which was built by G.B. Scotti in 1700–05 for Jiří Adam II of Martinic— the imperial ambassador to Rome—and was closely modelled on the buildings of the Roman architect Carlo Fontana. At No. 1 is the former Hradčany Town Hall (Hradčanská radnice), which dates back to shortly after the raising of the Hradčany to the status of a Royal Town in 1598, and has early 17C sgraffito decorations by Marian de Marianis.

D. The New Town ~ Nové Město

The New Town, which was founded by Charles IV in 1348, lies to the south and east of the Old Town. Formed by the construction of a great line of outer fortifications stretching from the foot of the Vyšehrad hill in the south all the way to the Vltava in the north, it constituted one of the most ambitious examples of town planning in 14C Europe. The largest of the four original townships of Prague, it was to begin with the main home of the city's craftsmen and poor, and was later to emerge as the commercial, administrative and social centre of Prague. The medieval street plan has been largely retained to this day, but rapid urban development from the late 19C onwards led to the pulling down of the fortifications in 1875, and the demolition of most of the surviving old houses to make way for large apartment blocks and imposing civic buildings. There are a number of medieval churches to be seen in the district, and numerous Baroque monuments; but the appeal of the New Town to the sightseer lies essentially in its great range of exciting monuments from the late 19C and early 20C.

Wenceslas Square

The heart of the New Town, and indeed the bustling centre of the whole city, is the Wenceslas Square (Václavské náměstí), a thoroughfare 60m wide and

750m long, which slopes down from the National Theatre to the long boulevards marking the boundary of the Old Town.

History of the Square

Originally a place where horse markets were held, the Wenceslas Square was known as the Horse Market (Koňský trh) up to as late as 1848, when it acquired its present name. The principal thoroughfare of Prague, the square has also been since 1848 the stage of some of the key historic moments in Czech history. A national mass held here in 1848 heralded the revolutionary disturbances of that year, while in 1918 crowds gathered here to celebrate the downfall of the Habsburgs. On 25 February 1948, a popular demonstration in support of the Communist Party of Czechoslovakia took place in the square, and on 16 January 1969, the student Jan Palach set fire to himself near here to draw world attention to the plight of the Czech people. The square also played a major role in the great events of November 1989, beginning with the 17th of that month, when a group of students, officially commemorating the fiftieth anniversary of a Czech student's murder by the Nazis, made their way here from Prague's second district, their numbers greatly swollen in the course of the journey. Greeted by riot police, they burst into chants of 'Freedom' and began singing the Czech version of 'We Shall Overcome', but the police reaction was brutal, and one person was killed and many more injured. This was to spark the whole country into action, and over the next few days crowds gathered in their thousands at the square, chanting 'Freedom', 'Resign' and 'Now is the time'; the statue of Wenceslas was papered with posters and protest leaflets, and in front of it flowers and candles were placed in commemoration of Jan Palach. To the utter disbelief of the crowd, on 24 November, Alexander Dubček, followed by Václav Havel, appeared on the balcony of the Socialist Publishing House to proclaim the imminent success of the 'Velvet Revolution'.

The present-day character and appearance of the Wenceslas Square belie its glorious history, the whole place having something of the tackiness and seediness of London's Leicester Square or Berlin's Kurfürstendamm. Shopping-arcades, hotels, cinemas, cheap eating establishments and bars and nightclubs with a distinctly dated look surround the square, and at night the place teems with drunken tourists and other, more sinister types; muggings have greatly increased here since the 'Revolution', and many Czechs now like to warn you of the dangers of the square late at night, though these dangers remain slight in comparison with those of many Western cities.

National Museum

Tall buildings dating from the late 19C onwards line the whole length of this long thoroughfare and flank a central row of gardens which were laid out in the 1980s and lead up to the vast National Museum (Národní muzeum), a pompous neo-Renaissance structure rising up on ramps at the very top of the square, and dominating the whole vista.

History of the Museum

The National Museum was founded in 1818 by a group of Czech intellectuals headed by the botanist, geologist and palaeontologist Count Kašpar Šternberk and including Josef Dobrovský, the pioneer of modern Slavonic studies. Thanks largely to the particular interests of Šternberk, the emphasis of the collections was largely on science, but the museum was greatly broadened in its scope from the 1830s onwards, when it became increasingly the focus of Czech cultural life and national endeavours; a very important role in developing the scope of the museum was played by the celebrated historian František Palacký, who became the museum's secretary in 1841, and envisaged a place which would reflect every aspect of his country. The involvement of the institution in nationalist political movements, culminating in the insurrections of 1848–49, inspired a growing hostility towards the place on the part of the Austrian authorities, yet the museum was soon to occupy one of the most prominent sites in Prague. The collections were housed at first in the refectory of the Minorite monastery attached to the Church of St James, but the demolition of the New Town fortifications in 1875 and the consequent removal of the Horse Gate led to a site becoming available at the top of the Wenceslas Square. The opportunity to use a site of such patriotic associations was immediately seized upon by the museum authorities, and in 1883–84 a competition was held for the design of the museum building to be erected here. The competition was won by Josef Schulz, and work on the structure was completed in 1890; its extensive sculptural embellishment involved most of the prominent academic sculptors of the day.

The main façade of the museum features a tall rusticated basement supporting a giant order of Corinthian columns, in the middle of which is a pedimented frontispiece crowned by a gilded dome. The sculptural decoration, like the architecture itself, is very conventional, and includes, at the top of the double ramp which climbs up to the main entrance, a dull group by Anton Wagner representing Bohemia between the Rivers Labe and Vltava. The principal component of the dauntingly large, red marbled interior is the Pantheon, a room decorated all over with ambitious historical and allegorical murals by Václav Brožík, František Ženíšek and Vojtěch Hynais; in the centre of the room are six statues and 42 busts—mainly executed between 1898 and 1901—of distinguished Czechs from the 14C onwards, the work of A. Popp. A. Procházka, J.V. Myslbek, M. Havlíček, B. Vlček, L. Šaloun, J. Štursa and K. Dvořák. The National Museum's collections have now been shared out between various buildings throughout Prague, the ones on show in this building comprising those devoted to geology, archaeology, prehistory and coins and medals (all of which are to be found on the first floor), and to zoology and palaeontology (on the second floor). The display is gloomy and unimaginative, and the layman might well agree with the writer Stephen Brook's assessment (voiced in his book, *The Double Eagle*) that the main emotion which the museum inspires is a sense of awe at the sight 'of so many display cases exclusively devoted to the cockroach'. **Open** Mon, Fri 09.00–16.00, Wed, Thur, Sat, Sun 09.00–17.00.

Walking down the Wenceslas Square from the National Museum, the first monument you come to, in the middle of the thoroughfare, is the **St Wenceslas Monument**, the masterpiece of J.V. Myslbek and comprising an equestrian statue of Wenceslas surrounded by four other patron saints of Bohemia—SS Ludmilla, Procopius and Adalbert and the Blessed Agnes. Originally conceived in 1887, the work was to occupy much of Myslbek's life up to his death in 1922; in the course of the monument's long gestation, the artist's vision of the saint significantly changed, so that the initial romantic representation of a spiritual and temporal leader of the Slavic people became transformed into a sturdy, tightly modelled portrayal of a man embodying the power and authority of the Czech state.

Walking down the left-hand side of the square, you will pass, after the junction with Štěpánská, the Lucerna Palace, an ugly block of 1907–10 featuring a gallery with shops, a cinema and sleazy restaurants and, in the basement, a large hall used for concerts and dances; Václav Havel's father, also called Václav, was one of its architects and owners, and joined this establishment with his restaurant at Barrandov to form the lucrative Barrandov-Lucerna Enterprises. The next building of interest on this side of the square is the **Melantrich House** (No. 36), from the balcony of which Alexander Dubček and Václav Havel appeared in November 1989 to address a vast protesting crowd.

The adjoining building at No. 34 is a gabled structure in a Bohemian Renaissance style designed by A. Wiehl in 1896 and covered with restored sgraffito decorations by Mikoláš Aleš. Facing this, on the other side of the square (at No. 25/27) is a far more remarkable turn-of-the-century building, the **Grand Hotel Europa**. Built in 1903–06 by Bedřich Bendelmayer and Alois Dryák, it features a beautifully ornamented façade crowned by a large ceramic lunette; but its great joy is its perfectly preserved interior, above all that of its bar and restaurant, both boasting stained-glass windows and elegant panelling. Further down on this same side, at No. 19, is a neo-Baroque building of 1895–96 now housing the Polish Cultural Centre but originally the Prague headquarters of the Trieste-based insurance company, Assecurazioni generali. This is famous as the place where the 24-year-old Franz Kafka began his first job, in October 1907; a medical certificate attesting to 'nervousness and cardiac excitability' allowed him to leave the company the following year, but he continued a career in insurance by joining in July 1908 the Workmen's Accident Insurance Institute, where he was to remain for the rest of his life.

Most of the square's remaining buildings of architectural interest are to be found on the left-hand side, beginning with the Alfa Palace (No. 28), a large Functionalist apartment block with shops and a cinema, designed by L. Kysela and J. Jarolím in the late 1920s, and featuring shop-windows of Cubist inspiration. The adjoining *Hotel Adria* at No. 26 is housed in the oldest surviving building on the square, dating back to the late 18C; just below it, at No. 22, is a hotel of radically different character, the *Hotel Juliš*, a Functionalist work of 1931–32 by Pavel Janák. Further down, at No. 12, is the Peterka House, an Art Nouveau former bank built by Jan Kotěra in 1898–1910, when greatly under the influence of the Viennese architect Otto Wagner; the façade is adorned with stucco decorations by J. Pekárek and S. Sucharda. Below an Art Nouveau building at No. 8 is the recently restored **Báťa Department Store** at No. 6, which was built by Ludvík Kysela in 1926–28 for the visionary shoe-manufacturer Tomáš Báťa.

The Báťa store on the Wenceslas Square, a Functionalist building of striking simplicity, comprises a reinforced concrete frame with minimum numbers of corridors in the sales areas, floor slab zones covered with translucent white glass (once used for advertising), and some of the earliest bands of continuous glazing uninterrupted by architectural supports to be seen in Europe. Restoration work carried out in 1990–92 removed later unattractive additions but also substituted the original tubular steel furniture and fittings with some half-hearted modern imitations; the place is at its best at night, when it is turned into a glowing apparition dominated by the neon sign promoting the name of Báťa The store's architect, Kysela, was also responsible for the adjoining and slightly-fussier Lindt's House at No. 4, which was built two years earlier and was indeed one of the first examples of Functionalism in Prague.

Immediately north of here the square broadens to form a large pedestrian area featuring the metro station Můstek and extending into the adjacent boulevards of 28. října and Na příkopě. The last building on the right-hand side (at No. 1) is the **Koruna Palace**, a fine Art Nouveau structure by Antonín Pfeiffer of 1910–14 with a futuristic corner tower and decorative detailing which looks ahead to the Art Deco period.

The northern and eastern New Town

The southern façade of the Koruna Palace overlooks the busy pedestrian thoroughfare of **Na Příkopě**, which is lined with banks, bookshops and department stores, including the British stores Marks & Spencer, Mothercare and Next. Turning into this boulevard from the Wenceslas Square you will pass immediately to your left, at No. 1, one of the better examples of recent architecture in Prague: built by Jan Šrámek and Alena Šrámková between 1974 and 1983, it is crowned by a glass-and-steel gable incorporating the clock of the department store which once stood here. Also to your left, at No. 3, is the former Wiener Bankverein (now the Czech National Bank), which was built by Josef Zasche in 1906–08 and is faced with polished granite. Prague's oldest department store, known originally as Haas, is on the opposite side of the street at No. 4, and was built in a North Italian Renaissance style by the Viennese architect T. Hansen in 1869–71.

The oldest surviving building on the street, and one of the most elegant Baroque palaces in the New Town, is further down on the right-hand side at No. 10. This, the **Sylva-Taroucca Palace** (1743–51), was built for Prince Ottavio Piccolomini by K.I. Dientzenhofer with the assistance of A. Lurago, and is a pedimented structure with a rusticated basement and a main floor articulated by giant order pilasters; the attic is decorated with sculptures of mythological figures and vases by F.I. Platzer, who was also responsible for the putti and vases on the balustrade of the staircase inside. Despite the atmospheric potential of the setting, the Swedish-run café-restaurant that can now be found here (*Segafredo*) is disappointingly lacking in character. On the building at No. 14— the Česká obohodní banka (1930)—a bust and plaque by B. Neužil records the site of the house where the writer Bozena Němcová died in 1862. Facing this, across the narrow Panská, is the **Church of the Holy Rood** (sv. Kříže), a massively built neo-Classical structure designed by G. Fischer in 1816.

A short detour down Panská could be made to see Prague's latest attraction, the **Mucha Museum** at No. 7, which opened in 1998 in the late 19C Kaunický Palace. This is a popular but disappointingly bland and threadbare museum devoted to the Moravian late 19C artist Alfons Mucha, who is best known abroad for his fin-de-siècle posters designed and executed in Paris. **Open** daily 10.00–18.00.

Continuing northeast down Na příkopě, you will pass at No. 18 the former Provincial Bank (now the headquarters of Čedok), an Art Nouveau building of 1911–12 by O. Polívka, attractively decorated on the outside with mosaics by J. Preisler and sculptures by C. Klouček and L. Šaloun. The same architect and sculptors collaborated on the adjoining former Savings Bank (No. 20; now the Živnostenská), a building of 1894–96 in a Czech Renaissance style, and incorporating a Baroque portal from a palace of 1757; the entrance vestibule is covered with wall-paintings of 1896 by Max Švabinský.

Next to the Slavonic House, at No. 24, is the Czech State Bank, which was put up in 1929–38 on a site that was occupied in the 19C by two hotels, *At the Blue Star* and *At the Black Horse*; a number of distinguished people were guests at these hotels, including the Russian anarchist Mikhail Bakunin, and the composers Chopin (to whom there is a plaque) and Liszt. Across the street, in a site now occupied by the grim 1930s administrative building at No. 33, there once stood Prague's most elegant café, the *Café Français*, where Liszt was frequently to be seen.

Na příkopě comes to an end at the Powder Gate and the náměstí Republiky (see Chapter 1A), where you should turn right into **Hybernská**, a narrow but busy street of 18C and 19C buildings, many in a decrepit condition, and others covered permanently with scaffolding. The first building to your right, at No. 20, was formerly a hotel where Tchaikovsky stayed in 1888 when he came to conduct the Prague première of his opera *Eugene Onegin*. Further down on the right-hand side, at No. 10, is the former and newly restored **Hotel Central** (now a theatre), a narrow-fronted but lavishly ornamented Art Nouveau structure built by F. Ohmann, B. Bendelmayer and A. Dryák in 1899–1902.

On the other side of the street the late 18C Sweerts-Špork Palace (at Nos 3/5) is followed by the beautiful and recently restored **Kinský Palace**, which was designed by Carlo Lurago after 1651 and given a new façade at the end of the 18C.

Further down the street Hybernská reaches an intersection formed by Havlíčkova to the north and Dlážděná to the south; at No. 15 on the corner of Hybernská and Dlážděná is the **Café Arco**, latterly a down-market and unremarkable-looking establishment (and currently closed), but at one time one of Prague's famed literary meeting-places, and with an elegant interior designed by Jan Kotěra and decorated with paintings by Kysela.

The **Masaryck Railway Station** (Masaryckovo Nádraží), at the corner of Hybernská and Havlíčkova, was Prague's first railway station, and was opened on 20 August 1845. The building, which has a main hall covered with an interesting roof in iron, wood and glass, is in a most depressing condition and attracts numerous loiterers of seedy and sinister appearance. Walk to the northern end of Havlíčkova and turn right into Na poříčí, where you will find immediately to your right, at No. 24, the former **Legio Bank** (now the Ministry of Consumer Goods), an extraordinary structure of Cubist inspiration built by Josef Gočár in 1922–25. In this highly sculptural building, featuring a heavy, projecting attic and a giant order of cubic columns crossed by deeply cut bands, Gočár enjoyed a most successful collaboration with the sculptors Jan Štursa and Otto Gutfreund; above the shop-front Jan Štursa placed four enormous consoles of workers (1922–23) to support a long frieze by Gutfreund (*The Return of the Legionaries*, 1921), a work of great stateliness and power which is considered by many to be one of the key landmarks in 20C Czech sculpture.

Further along the street, at No. 40, is the *Hotel Axa*, a fine Constructivist building of 1935 by V. Pilec. Just before the hotel, you should cross the street and head north along the short Biskupská, which was where the Merchants' Court of Poříčí's German community was situated up to 1235. At the end of the street is the late Gothic tower belonging to the former German **Church of St Peter na Poříčí**. The latter building, just to the north of the tower, is a triple-aisled structure which dates back to the mid-12C and was originally the parish church of the German Poříčí district; in 1235 the church and surrounding area fell into the hands of the Knights of the Cross. Fragments of the original Romanesque church survive in the west façade and south wall of the main nave, but the rest of the building was much altered over the centuries, and was subject to neo-Gothic remodelling by Josef Mocker in the 1870s.

Running behind the church is Petrská: walking west along this street you will come to the small Petrské náměstí, off which runs Soukenická. There you will find on the house at No. 13 a plaque marking the site of the birthplace of the topographical artist Wenceslas Hollar, who is best known for his views of London, where he died in 1677. Walking instead east along Petrská and then taking the first turning to the right you will rejoin Na poříčí at the point where it disappears under the large flyover which marks **Wilsonova Února**, the eastern boundary of the New Town.

On the other side of the flyover is the tiny and unpromisingly situated **Šverma Park** (Švermovy sady), which was founded in 1875 on the site of the recently demolished New Town fortifications. On this park's southern side, adjoining today a noisy area occupied by tacky market stalls, stands a grand neo-Renaissance structure built by A. Balšánek in 1896–98 to house the newly formed **Museum of the City of Prague** (Muzeum hlavní města Prahy). On the ground floor of this slightly run-down museum is a fine display of artefacts and works of art from the 6C onwards relating to the early history of Prague, and including Slavonic pots, fragments of 13C frescoes, old Bohemian glass, and Renaissance and Baroque furnishings; the second floor, at present being rearranged to take in recent developments in the city's history, is reached by a grand oval staircase, and features an enormous plaster model of Prague made by Antonín Langweil between 1826 and 1834. **Open** Tues–Sun 10.00–18.00.

Only a short distance south of the museum along the Wilsonova února is the magnificent Art Nouveau **Central Station** (Hlavní nádraží), but the journey is complicated on foot and best undertaken by taking the metro from Sokolovská (directly in front of the museum) to the following stop, Hlavní nádraží. The metro will take you to the station's modern extension, which dates from the 1970s and is built underneath the Wilsonova and the narrow Vrchlického Park to the west. The original station (once called the Franz Josef Station) stands above the eastern side of the wide Wilsonova února, and was built by Josef Fanta in 1901–09; its most exciting feature is its twin-towered façade, featuring an ironwork central canopy and large-scale carvings of nudes and other allegorical figures by S. Sucharda, H. Folkmann and Č. Vosmík.

Central Station interior

Further south along the Wilsonova in the direction of the nearby National Museum are the reconstructed late 19C Smetana Theatre (originally the main German theatre in

Prague) and the modern glass building of the **Federal Assembly**. At the south-western corner of the Vrchlického Park is another of the old luxury hotels of Prague, the *Hotel Esplanade* (with a neo-Baroque gilded interior), while directly across the park from the Central Station begins Jeruzalémská. Walking down the latter street, you will pass at No. 5 to your right the Jubilee Synagogue, a neo-Moorish building of 1906 with a vividly coloured façade. At the end of the street turn left on to **Jindřišská**, where you will find to your left the **Church of St Henry** (sv. Jindřicha), which was founded in 1350 but much altered in later periods and given a neo-Gothic exterior by Josef Mocker in 1879; Mocker was also responsible for the neo-Gothic remodelling of the late 15C **belfry tower** on the other side of the street. Continuing to walk down Jindřišská you will soon reach its intersection with Panská and Politických vězňů. At the corner of Panská is the *Palace Hotel*, a lavishly refurbished hotel dating back to the turn of the century. At the end of Jindřišská you will come back to the lower end of the Wenceslas Square.

The southern and western New Town

You can begin a tour of the southern half of the New Town from the bottom of the Wenceslas Square, where you should turn left into the quiet **Jungmann Square** (Jungmannovo náměstí), which runs parallel to the pedestrian thoroughfare of 28. října. The square epitomises the city's architectural richness, featuring the back façade of the pioneering Báťa Building (see p 165), a gabled late 14C Gothic gateway, and—as its centrepiece—a beautiful and highly eccentric **Cubist lamp-post** of 1913; this last monument, though recently re-attributed to the minor architect Emil Králíček (it was previously thought to be by the much better known Vratislav Hofman), is a work of great originality anticipating by many years Brancusi's *Endless Column*. The Gothic gateway, at the square's southeastern corner, opens out on to a courtyard leading to the former **Carmelite Church of Our Lady of the Snows** (Panny Marie Sněžné).

Cubist lamp-post

History of the church

Founded by Charles IV in 1347 on the occasion of his coronation as King of Bohemia, the Church of St Mary of the Snows was intended as a vast triple-aisled structure which would have extended right into the present Jung-mann Square. However, work on the building was interrupted during the Hussite wars, in which this church played an important role.

The radical Hussite speaker Jan Želivský preached here between 1419 and 1422, and it was from here that on 30 July 1419 a procession set out to the New Town Hall to carry out the 'First Defenestration' in Prague. Želivský was buried in the church in 1422, but the building was later left to decay and its steeple demolished. The abandoned church and convent came in 1603 into the hands of the Franciscans, who embarked on a campaign of restoration and rebuilding.

On entering the church you are immediately struck by its great height and size, though in fact what you are seeing constitutes only the chancel of the triple-aisled structure which was originally conceived. The furnishings are Baroque, but the building has otherwise a completely Gothic look, despite the fact that the net-vaulting and much of the masonry dates back only to the time of the Franciscan restoration. The former monastery gardens on the south side of the building were relaid in the 1950s and form today a pleasant public park, shaded by trees.

At its western end the Jungmann Square leads to the busy junction of 28. října, Jungmannova třída and Národní třída. The white corner building at the end of 28. října, at No. 1, is a fine Functionalist department store of 1927–31, while at No. 30 Jungmannova třída (almost immediately to your left on reaching the street from the square) is one of the earliest Modernist buildings in Prague, the **Urbánek House** (1912–13). The latter, with its large triangular gable and grid of brickwork squares encased within a deep rectangular frame, is a structure of great geometrical purity that reveals Kotěra's debt to his master Otto Wagner. Built for the music and arts publisher Mojmír Urbánek, it was intended to house apartments, offices, a small concert hall (the Mozarteum) and, on the ground floor, flanked by caryatid figures by Jan Štursa, an art gallery. This gallery, the Havel Gallery, was an important if brief-lived centre of the avant-garde, and organised as its inaugural show an exhibition of Futurist art that divided the Prague Cubists.

The corner of Jungmannova třída and Národní třída is taken up by the bizarre and colossal **Adria Palace**, a heavily ornamented structure built by Pavel Janák and Josef Zasch in 1923–25 and featuring an attic level made up of square, crenellated towers that give the whole building the look of some futuristic urban fortress; the sculptural decoration on the façades was carried out by J. Štursa, Otto Gutfreund and K. Dvořák. This fantastical building appropriately hosted for many years the theatrical spectacle known as the Magic Lantern, which has recently transferred to a specially built venue next to the National Theatre (see below). Performances of the Magic Lantern were still taking place here in November 1989, when its theatre became the meeting-place of the newly formed Civic Forum, which in a matter of days succeeded in ousting the Communist government of Czechoslovakia and hoisting Havel to the presidency of the country.

Národní třída (National Street) is Prague's most important street, and is vibrant with cars and people, and lined its whole length with department stores and monumental civic buildings. As you walk down it in the direction of the Vltava the first major building which you will pass to your right is the **Plateÿz House** at No. 37, which was rebuilt and enlarged by Henri Hausknecht after 1813 and turned into the first tenement building in Prague; the main wing contains a hall where concerts were once held, one of the musicians who performed here being Franz Liszt in 1840 and 1846 (a marble bust of the composer has been placed on the building's back entrance).

Continuing to walk west, you will pass almost immediately on the left-hand side of the street at No. 20 the **Reduta**, a famous and tourist-loved jazz club, which has photographs and a bronze plaque recording its most recent moment of glory, the visit in 1994 of President Clinton, who played his saxophone here.

Just after crossing Voršilská, the late 17C former convent Church of St Ursula (sv. Voršily), which was designed by Marcantonio Canevale. Facing this on the other side of the Národní třída are two remarkable and adjoining Art Nouveau buildings, both designed by Osvald Polívka. The first of these, at No. 9, is the former Topic Publishing House (1910), a richly stuccoed building which is now used by the Union of Czech Writers; the second building, at No. 7, is the former headquarters of the Praha Assurance (1905–07) and, though a less decorative structure than its neighbour, has superlative reliefs on its façade by Ladislav Šaloun. Much of the remaining right-hand side of the street is taken up by the Czech Academy of Sciences (at Nos 5 and 3), a grimly impressive neo-Renaissance structure built by V.I. Ullmann in 1858–61 as the headquarters of a bank. The last building on the right, at No. 1, is the recently reopened **Café Slavia**, a popular tourist haunt which is also one of the oldest of Prague's surviving literary cafés.

The two end buildings on the left-hand side of the street are the **New National Theatre** (Nová scéna) at No. 4 and the National Theatre at No. 2. The former, one of the boldest and most distinguished examples of recent Czech architecture, is arranged around a small square and comprises three shaped blocks coated in glass, the one facing the street resembling a translucent honeycomb; the complex was built in 1977–83 by Karel Prager. The building is used almost exclusively for drama productions organised by the National Theatre Company, the present director of which is Otomar Krejča, who achieved international fame as actor and director in the 1960s, when he ran the Theatre Beyond the Gate (divadlo Za Branou).

The southern block has now been taken over by the **Magic Lantern,** which was created originally for the Brussels World Exhibition of 1958 by Alfréd Radok. Once a brilliant illusionistic spectacle involving stage-sets, actors and film, it is now an anodine and at times embarrassingly bad tourist attraction booked up weeks in advance by large groups.

As a result of recent privatisation Prague opera is now divided between the more innovative State Opera and the National Opera, the latter having as its premises the superb **National Theatre** (Národní divadlo), one of the great landmarks of Prague and by far the most eloquent architectural expression of Czech nationalist aspirations in the late 19C.

History of the theatre

In 1845 a group of prominent Czech patriots, including František Palacký, Josef Jungmann, Josef Kajetán Tyl and Jan Evagelista Purkyně, sent a petition to the Emperor Ferdinand V asking for permission to build an independent Czech theatre in Prague. The proposal was also supported by the writers Jan Neruda, Vítězslav Hálek and Karel Havlíček Borovský, the latter making the practical suggestion that the money for the building should be raised through voluntary contributions. A fund-raising campaign with the slogan 'the Nation for Itself' was subsequently begun, but it was not until 1868 that the foundation stone of the building was laid. The architect chosen was Josef Zítek, who was supervising the final details of his work in 1881 when a fire broke out, destroying the auditorium and much of the building's decorations. Within the remarkably short space of six weeks enough money had been raised to rebuild the theatre, a task which was given to Josef Schulz. The theatre was finally opened on 18 November 1883 with a production of Bedřich Smetana's opera *Libuše*. The painters and sculptors involved in the decoration of the building include almost all the leading Czech artists of the late 19C, a generation which is in fact referred to as the 'National Theatre Generation'; among these artists were the sculptors J.V. Mylsbek, Bohuslav Schnirch and Anton Wagner, and the painters Mikoláš Aleš, Václav Brožík, Vojtěch Hynais, Josef Tulka and František Ženíšek. In 1977–83 the building was extensively restored by Karel Prager, and can be appreciated today at its resplendent best.

The grand exterior of the building, which has echoes of the Vienna Opera House and rather more distant ones of Renaissance Italy, is crowned by a Palladian-style roof highlighted by gilding. Some of the finest statuary of the main façade is concentrated on the attic level where there is a row of statues of Apollo and the Muses by B. Schnirch, who also modelled the flanking bronze chariot groups; on the side façade overlooking the Masaryk Embankment is a portal decorated with reclining figures by J.V. Myslbek of *Opera* and *Drama*.

A bronze figure by Myslbek representing *Music* presides over the profusely embellished main foyer, where can be seen allegorical ceiling paintings by Ženíšek, fourteen lunette paintings by M. Aleš of scenes from Smetana's symphonic poem *My Country* (*Má Vlast*) and a gallery of bronze busts by different artists of the leading figures in the history of Czech theatre and opera. Of the many other decorations in the building special mention must be made of the works of Vojtěch Hynais. He decorated the stairs leading up to the presidential box with a painted allegorical frieze, painted vivid representations of *The Four Seasons* for the ladies' boudoir of the presidential box (note in particular the female figure floating over a snow-covered landscape), and provided the stage with its superlative and celebrated back-cloth; the latter, portraying the unpromising theme of *The Origin of the National Theatre*, is full of references to Raphael and Renaissance painting and yet is saved from the absurder excesses of academic art through the sheer energy of the composition and execution.

The Národní třída comes to an end by the Vltava river, where you should head south down the Masaryk Embankment passing alongside the **Slavonic Island** (Slovanský ostrov) which is now taken up by a wooded public park laid out in 1931.

Straddling the narrow stretch of water between the island and the southern end of the Masaryk Embankment is the **Mánes Gallery**, the seat of the Mánes Society of Artists, which was founded in 1898 in opposition to the Czech Academy of Arts. Their present headquarters, a simple, white Functionalist building erected by Otakar Novotný in 1923–25, is curiously but picturesquely linked to a Renaissance water tower which once formed part of the Sitka Mills; the gallery puts on exhibitions by contemporary artists.

The Mánes Gallery is a favourite building of Václav Havel, despite the one-time presence there of agents from the Czech Secret Service, who used to spy on him from the top of its water tower when he was living at No. 78 Rašínovo nábřeží, immediately to the south of the Masaryck embankment. His riverside apartment there, designed by his grandfather, adjoins today a controversial new building that has proved especially popular with the city's foreign tourists. Popularly known as the '**Fred and Ginger**', on account of its vague resemblance to a dancing couple, this was built in 1993–94 by the American architect Frank Gehry, currently at the height of his international fame following the opening in 1997 of his Guggenheim Museum in Bilbao. Although this gloriously topsy-turvy, inebriated-looking structure is intentionally at variance with its sombre, neighbouring buildings, it seems perfectly in tune with the more expressionistic and fantastical side to the Central European spirit. The interior, sadly, is rather less interesting than the exterior, and is partly occupied by the singularly unfriendly French-run café and restaurant pretentiously calling itself *La Perle de Prague*.

Retrace your steps towards the Mánes Gallery and then head east down Myslíkova, turning off on to the third street to the left, Křemencova, to visit at No. 11 on the left-hand side Prague's most famous beer-cellar, **U Fleků**.

History of **U Fleků**

The origins of *U Fleků* go back to at least 1499, when the brewer Vít Skřemenec acquired the house which stood on the site of the present building and founded the beer-cellar and small brewery which came to be known for the next 250 years as 'Na Skřemenici' (hence the name of the street). The name *U Fleků* dates back to after 1762, when the establishment was bought by the Flekovsky family from Počenice, who, during the short time that they owned the place, became celebrated throughout Prague for the quality of their beer. The present neo-Gothic appearance of the interior is due to renovations carried out in 1898–1905, under the direction of the architect F. Sander; the pseudo-medieval wall-paintings were the work of L. Novák. The newly restored ale-house soon became a popular literary haunt, and for years afterwards there would always be a section reserved for writers.

A picturesque old clock, hung like a tavern sign, marks the entrance to *U Fleků*, which has a number of attractively panelled rooms, with wooden tables and neo-Gothic vaulting; the dark beer which is made and served here is excellent. Unfortunately, however, the place today has mainly been taken over by loud-mouthed carousing tourists (mainly German coach groups), and this is not an establishment where many Czechs would be proud to be seen.

Returning to Myslíkova turn left until you reach the lower end of Spálená, where, on turning left again, you will find shortly on the right-hand side the wonderful Cubist corner building known as the **Diamond House** (Diamant), which was built in 1910–12 by Ladislav Skřivánek and Matěj Blecha; an amusing feature is the Cubist arch (designed perhaps by Antonín Pfeiffer) which joins the building to the neighbouring 18C Church of the Holy Trinity and frames a statue of St John of Nepomuk by M.J. Brokoff (1717).

Retracing your footsteps and heading south down Spálená you will soon reach the northern end of the long **Charles Square** (Karlovo náměstí), a square which is even larger than that of Wenceslas, but with a much more sober and less energetic character. Originally Prague's biggest market square, and known as the Cattle Market until 1848, it was transformed in the middle of the 19C into a wooded public park, complete with statues to famous Czechs such as the poet Vítězslav Hálek and the botanist Benedikt Roezl; the buildings that surround the park are set back from it by wide and busy streets and have largely a stately but unremarkable 19C character.

The main building at the square's northern end is the **New Town Hall** (Novoměstská radnice), which dates back to 1367 but has kept little of its medieval structure apart from the tower of 1425–26, the cellars and the double-aisled entrance hall (now used for marriages); the gabled façade overlooking the square is a reconstruction of 1905 of the building as it appeared in the 16C. The Town Hall is famous as the place where on 30 July 1419 an irate mob led by the reformist preacher J. Želivský demanded from its councillors the release of certain reformist prisoners; after refusing these demands the councillors were thrown out of the windows and killed, thus sparking off the Hussite revolution and inaugurating a long Czech tradition of 'defenestration'.

Adjacent to the Town Hall, on the northeastern corner of the square at No. 24, is the late 18C **Salm House**, which marks the site of a Renaissance home (of which the portal has survived) owned in the early 18C by the leading Baroque sculptor Matthias Braun, who died here in 1738.

Cross over to the western side of the square and walk half-way down it to Resslova, where you turn right, heading back in the direction of the river. On the right-hand side of the street at No. 9 is a former priest's home designed in 1736 by K.I. Dientzenhofer, who was also responsible for the adjoining **Church of SS Cyril and Methodius** (sv. Cyrila a Metoděje) to which this institution was attached. This impressive church, built in 1730–36 and originally dedicated to St Charles Borromeo, is a tightly-composed structure with symmetrically treated pedimented façades and a powerful entablature tying the whole building together; the interior is stuccoed by M.I. Palliardi and decorated with frescoes by K. Schöpf depicting the life of St Charles Borromeo. In 1942 the parachutists responsible for the assassination of the German Protector of Bohemia, Reinhard Heydrich, took refuge in the church's crypt but were killed here while making a last stand against the Nazis. Crypt open Mon–Sat 09.00–11.00. Further down the street, on the left-hand side, is the **Church of St Wenceslas** (sv. Václava), which was founded in 1170 but rebuilt at the end of the 14C, during the reign of King Wenceslas IV. The building has been much altered over the centuries, though fragments of the medieval masonry are to be seen in the façade, and there survives inside a late Gothic vault of 1586–87; the distinguished Art Nouveau sculptor F. Bílek executed the pews and the altar of the *Crucifixion* (1930).

At the end of the street head south down the Rašínovo nábřeží until you come to the **Palacký Square** (Palackého náměstí). The late 19C **Palacký Bridge**, which spans the river at this point, was once crowned at its corners by large and imposing sculptural groups by J.V. Myslbek representing mythical figures from Prague's early history, but these were transferred in 1945 to the park at Vyšehrad. Their absence is amply compensated for by the presence in the middle of the square of the **Palacký Monument**, one of the most exciting examples of public statuary in Prague, and the masterpiece of Stanislav Sucharda, assisted by the architect Alois Dryák. As with the near-contemporary Hus Monument in the Old Town Square, its gestation was a long one, being first planned in 1898, and not unveiled until 1912, by which time it was to seem rather dated and its outstanding qualities not fully appreciated; a romantic and deeply poetic work, it shows an ingenious use of different materials, the real world—including the heavy, seated figure of Palacký himself—being depicted in stone, the allegorical one in bronze, the whole composition culminating in a magnificent, asymmetrically placed bronze group soaring up above the central stone plinth.

From the square head east up Na Moráni, which will bring you back to the Charles Square, at its lower end. The southern side of the square is taken up by a hospital wing of the Charles University, the large building at its western corner being romantically known as the **Faust House**. This late 18C structure marks the site of a house where Edward Kelley—the English adventurer at the court of Rudolph II—carried out his alchemical experiments in the hope of producing gold; later alchemists also worked here, and in the 18C, when a chemist occupied the building, the legend was born that the imaginary Doctor Faust had been another of its occupants until he was carried off through its laboratory ceiling after having sold his soul to the devil. Whether out of a sense of humour or in respect of the building's tradition, the Medical Faculty of Charles University has installed here its own pharmacy.

Walking south from the Faust House down **Vyšehradská**, you will soon see, picturesquely rising above a great double-ramp staircase on the left-hand side of the street, the **Church of St John on the Rock** (sv. Jana Na skalce), which was built between 1729 and 1739, and is one of the more remarkable buildings by Kilian Ignaz Dientzenhofer. Extracting the maximum dramatic potential from the restricted site, the architect canted the twin towers of the west façade to create a powerful sense of movement which is continued in the interior, the nave of which comprises an octagon with concave sides. Floating above the white walls inside are ceiling frescoes by K. Kovář depicting the *Glorification of St John of Nepomuk* (1745), while on the high altar has been placed a wooden statue of the saint by J. Brokoff (1682), a work which served as the model for the bronze of this subject on the Charles Bridge.

On the other side of the street to the church is the former Na Slovanech Monastery (popularly known as the **Emmaus Monastery**), which was founded by Charles IV in 1347 for the Croatian Benedictines. Extensively remodelled and rebuilt during the 18C and 19C, the whole complex was heavily damaged by bombing in 1945, and thereafter restored for the use of the Czechoslovak Academy of Sciences. The finest medieval survival, though heavily restored after 1960, are the frescoes of 1370–75 preserved in the vaulted monastery cloister and representing scenes from the Old and New Testaments; these were the work of three painters, M. Wurmser, Master Osvald and the painter known as the Master of the Emmaus Cycle. The Gothic walls of the monastery church now support a daring but very elegant modern superstructure built by František Černý in 1965–68 and comprising two interlaced sail-like forms soaring up into the sky.

The southern continuation of Vyšehradská, Na slupi, skirts the **University Botanical Garden** (Botanická zahrada; **open** daily Apr–Aug 10.00–18.00; Sept–Oct and Jan–Mar 10.00–17.00; Nov, Dec 10.00–16.00) and passes to the left, as it nears the Vyšehrad Hill, the **Church of Our Lady Na Slupi** (Panna Maria na Slupi), a building of late 14C origin which was restored by Bern Grueber in 1858–63; a notable feature of the interior is the way the 15C vault is supported by a single pillar. Immediately south of the church turn left into Horská and head east until you reach the large monastic complex known simply as the **Karlov**. This former Augustinian monastery was founded by Charles IV in 1351, and has a most exciting church, the nave of which is octagonal in emulation of Charlemagne's burial chapel at Aachen. The church was completed in 1377, but its nave was covered by Bonifác Wohlmut in 1575 with an astonishingly bold star-shaped vault. The furnishings and other elements of the building are additions of the Baroque period, including the steep, triple-flighted staircase which leads up to the Chapel of the Holy Steps on the southern side of the church; this Scala Santa, up which pilgrims are meant to climb on their knees, was built in 1708–09 and is often attributed to Santini-Aichel. A visit to the church is completed by descending into the crypt, where you will be surprised and delighted to find yourself in an early

18C grotto imitating the cave in Bethlehem where Christ was born; the walls are covered with pastel-coloured stucco decorations by R. Beier, representing Classical buildings and giving you the impression that you have taken a wrong turning and stumbled from the Holy Land into Arcadia. **Open** Sun 14.00–17.15.

Heading north from the Karlov up **Ke Karlovu**, the third street which you will pass to your right is Na Bojišti, where, at No. 12, is a large beer-house that owes its fame to being mentioned in Jaroslav Hašek's book *The Good Soldier Švejk*. To this establishment, known as **U kalicha** (*The Chalice*), the congenital idiot Švejk decides to come on the day that the Sarajevo assassination is announced in Prague.

Returning to Ke Karlovu and continuing north, you will come almost immediately to the elegant summer pavilion which was built by K.I. Dientzenhofer in 1715–20 for Jan Václav Michna (at No. 20 on the right-hand side), and is generally known as the **Villa America** on account of a hotel which existed nearby. This jewel-like building, painted outside a vivid red, is set in a small garden adorned with sculptures from the workshop of Matthias Braun; the main room on the first floor is covered with a delightful illusionistic ceiling painting (c 1730) by J.F. Schors. Since 1934 the building has housed the **Dvořák Museum**; the composer lived in the vicinity (see below) and his writing-desk, piano and other personal belongings are exhibited here. **Open** Tues–Sun 10.00–17.00.

On the other side of the street to the building is a small and rather neglected wooded park, off which stands the former Augustinian **Church of St Catherine** (sv. Kateřiny). This building and its adjoining convent were founded by Charles IV in 1354 in thanksgiving for his victory at the battle of San Felice in Italy. Destroyed by the Hussites in 1420, the church was rebuilt in 1518–22, and then again by K.I. Dientzenhofer and F.M. Kaňka in 1737–41. The one survival of the medieval church is its enormously tall tower, which, thanks to its octagonal upper floors, is sometimes known as 'the Minaret of Prague'. The outside of the building is remarkably dilapidated, but the magnificent Baroque interior, with ceiling frescoes by V.V. Reiner, has been given added magic and drama through housing the sculpture collections of the Museum of the City of Prague, including works by J. Platzer and Matthias Braun, and J.J. Bendl's wonderful statue in polychromed wood of the *Archangel Rafael* (c 1650).

At its northern end Ke Karlovu emerges at the wide and busy **Ječná**, which you should cross and then turn left and enter the first street to your right, Štěpánská. Walking north up Štěpánská you will pass to your right Na Rybníčku, on which stands the much-restored and altered Rotunda of **St Longinus**, which dates back to the beginning of the 12C and is the smallest of Prague's Romanesque rotundas. Further north Štěpánská joins **Žitná**, another busy thoroughfare, where, if you turn left, you will find on the left-hand side at No. 14 the building where the composer Antonín Dvořák lived from 1877 up to his death in 1901; he stayed at first in a now ruinous house in the courtyard, but later moved to a more salubrious location at the front of the building (where a plaque to him has been placed high up on the façade). On the opposite side of the street begins Školská, where at No. 16 you will find a plaque recording the house where the writer Jaroslav Hašek was born on 30 April 1883; ironically for the birthplace of the future *enfant terrible* the house belonged at that time to a respected advocate and Prague alderman, Dr Jakub Škarda, a family relative. Near the eastern end of Žitná you will come to the Wilsonova, where, on turning left, you will soon return to the National Museum on the Wenceslas Square.

E. Vyšehrad and southern Prague ~ Zbraslav, Hlubočepy and Smíchov

The Vyšehrad citadel

Below the southern end of the New Town is a great wooded outcrop of rock rising above the Vltava river and supporting the citadel of Vyšehrad ('The Castle on the Heights'), the history of which is tied to the mythical origins of Prague.

History of the citadel

According to legend the castle at Vyšehrad was the home of Countess Libuše, who foresaw from this site the future glories of Prague, and married here the ploughman founder of the Přemyslid dynasty. The truth, however, was that this was not the first seat of the Czech princes, and was preceded both by Prague Castle and Levý Hradec. Founded probably in the early 10C, at the end of the century it became briefly the seat of Boleslav II. In the late 11C the Přemyslid princes once again abandoned Prague Castle in favour of the Vyšehrad, and founded here in 1070 a Collegiate Chapter. The latter, headed by a dean whose role came to be analogous to that of Chancellor of Bohemia, was to remain here for centuries afterwards, but the princes themselves returned permanently to Prague Castle in 1140. The importance of the Vyšehrad declined, though it was to be renewed once more during the reign of Charles IV, who rebuilt the royal palace, erected new fortifications, and established the castle as the starting-point of the Czech coronation processions. In 1420, during the Hussite Wars, almost all the buildings on the Vyšehrad were destroyed, and in their place there subsequently built up a small town of craftsmen and tradesmen. This town, known as the Town of Mount Vyšehrad, was destroyed in the mid-17C to make way for a Baroque fortress, which was to be abolished in 1866, just under 20 years before the Vyšehrad was to be incorporated into the city of Prague.

The Vyšehrad's mythical early history, its nationalist associations and, not least, the romantic beauty of its site, combined to make the place in the 19C a great source of inspiration to artists, writers and musicians, notably Smetana, whose opera *Libuše* was chosen appropriately for the inauguration of the Prague National Theatre in 1883. At the height of all this romantic adulation of Vyšehrad, two deans, V. Šulc and M. Karlach, proposed to convert the original parish cemetery of the Chapter into a national cemetery, a scheme which took root in the 1880s and culminated in the building between 1889 and 1893 of a great pantheon of celebrated Czechs, the Slavín. The rest of the citadel was laid out in 1927 as a public park.

The easiest approach to the Vyšehrad from the centre of Prague is to take the metro to the Vyšehrad station, where you will find yourself on the southern side of a long bridge—a masterly piece of engineering of the late 1960s—which connects the hill with the New Town and the Vinohrady. On the eastern side of the station stands one of Prague's most recent luxury hotels, the bland, American-style *Hotel Forum* (opened in 1989), which overlooks a large prison, the courtyard of which had to be roofed over so that the hotel guests would not be offended by the sight of exercising inmates. On the other side of the bridge is the similarly characterless **Palace of Culture** (1969–81), which none the less enjoys a wide terrace with extensive views to the north, a panorama dominated by the Karlov church (see Chapter 1D).

Walking west along this terrace you will come to Na Bučance, a quiet street which will take you to the western entrance of the Vyšehrad citadel in a few minutes. You enter through the mid-17C **Tábor Gate**, and, after passing to your right the scant ruins of part of the 14C fortifications erected by Charles IV, reach the monumental **Leopold Gate**, the most impressive survival of the 17C citadel, and protected by a deep ditch once spanned by a drawbridge; it was built before 1678 by C. Lurago. On the other side of this gate you will see to your right the oldest surviving structure in the Vyšehrad, the **Rotunda of St Martin** (sv. Martina), which dates back to the late 11C but was heavily restored in 1878–80: the earliest of Prague's Romanesque rotundas, it is also the only one to have kept its original shape. Walking west from here along the lane called K. rotundě, you will pass to your left the former late 18C **Deanery**, which was built on the site of the Romanesque basilica of St Lawrence; the foundations of this church (which was destroyed by the Hussites in 1421) can be seen at the back of the building, while inside there is a small display relating to the history of the Vyšehrad.

Further west, on the right-hand side of the road, is the **Church of SS Peter and Paul** (sv. Petra a Pavla), which, though founded by Vratislav II in 1070 in conjunction with the Collegiate Chapter, owes its present appearance to neo-Gothic rebuilding carried out by J. Mocker and F. Mikeš between 1885 and 1903. Besides the twin-towered western façade of the church is the entrance to the **Vyšehrad Cemetery**, which is surrounded by a neo-Renaissance arcade designed by A. Wiehl in 1887, shortly after it was decided to convert the former parish cemetery into the resting-place of great and famous Czechs. **Open** daily May–Sept 08.00–19.00; Mar, Apr, Oct 08.00–18.00; Nov–Feb 09.00–16.00.

To the south of the church is a shady **park** entered through a Baroque gate taken from a 17C armoury; standing forlorn and neglected in the middle of this area are J.V. Myslbek's large sculptural groups of mythical Czech figures such as Libuše and Přemysl, which once proudly stood on the corners of the Palacký Bridge in the New Town. The most enjoyable feature of the park is the dramatic view down to the Vltava from the western ramparts, from where you will also see, clinging to the rock face, the ruins of an early 15C watch-tower which was given in the 19C the romantic name of Libuše's Baths. After leaving the park turn right down K rotundě, and then immediately left, skirting the eastern wall of the cemetery. You will soon reach the citadel's 19C northern gate, from where you begin the sharp descent to the heavily built area comprising the former outer bailey of the castle.

Cubist House

Most of the buildings are apartment blocks of the 19C and 20C, and at the bottom of the first street to the right, Přemyslova, you will find at No. 98 (on the corner with Neklanova) a tall, angular and exceedingly graceful building articulated by prismatic forms. This remarkable apartment building of 1911–13 is the earliest and largest of three **Cubist buildings** erected by Josef Chochol at the foot of the Vyšehrad. Turning left at Neklanova, and walking around the hill in an anti-clockwise direction you will come after Vnislavova to Libušina, on which stands, at No. 3, a building by Chochol of 1912–13 intended for single family occupancy and featuring a beautiful façade built up of diamond shapes. At its southern end the short Libušina joins the Rašínovo nábřeží (the former Engels Embankment), where, on turning left, you will shortly find on the left-hand side of the street at No. 6 the third of Chochol's buildings in the area, a house intended for three families, also dating from 1912–13.

The southern districts

South of the Vyšehrad extends a vast area of suburbs with little of architectural or scenic interest until you reach the outlying district of Zbraslav, which lies on the other side of the Vltava and was not incorporated into Prague until 1974. From the Rašínovo nábřeží you could take trams No. 3, 17 or 21, which go under the Vyšehrad Tunnel of 1902–03 and follow the right bank of the Vltava all the way south to Prague-Braník Station; a No. 245 bus runs from there to Zbraslav.

Zbraslav, 12 kilometres from the centre of Prague, will give you a first taste of the Czech countryside, and indeed continues to be a popular place for weekend excursionists, accessible in the summer months by a pleasure boat departing from below the Palacký Bridge: it was on a boat outing to Zbraslav organised by the Mánes Association of Artists in 1926 that Kafka's former mistress, Milena Jesenská, met and fell in love with the man who was to become her first husband, the architect Jaromír Krejcar. The beauty of the place lies essentially in the wooded riverside parkland attached to its former **Cistercian monastery**, one of the best views of which is to be had from the bridge which the No. 245 bus crosses. The monastery, founded in 1292 on the site of a Royal hunting-lodge, was entirely rebuilt in the early 18C, first under the direction of Santini-Aichel (from about 1700) and later under that of F.M. Kaňka (from 1724–32). The building was reopened in October 1998 to show off the National Gallery's extensive and outstanding **Collection of Asian art**, which contains some 12,000 pieces that had not been seen by the general public for forty-six years.

The relative remoteness of Zbraslav (in fact it is only a fifteen minutes bus journey from the Smíchovské nádraží metro station) should not deter anyone from visiting the new Asian museum, which is surely one of the finest of its kind in Europe, not simply for the high quality of the exhibits but also for the sensational nature of the actual display. Information panels of exemplary clarity and informativeness in both Czech and English guide you through a museum that can also be enjoyed as a purely aesthetic and, at times, theatrical experience: imaginative lighting, and coloured timbers arranged to suggest bridges, temples, tea-rooms and so on, convey an oriental context and atmosphere with the most stunningly simple of means.

The **ground floor** rooms are taken up almost entirely by the Japanese holdings, which range mainly from the 16C–19C, and feature superlative examples of laquerwork, enamelling, sword hilts, porcelain, metalwork and Buddhist sculptures, as well a regularly changing selection of screens, prints and painted scrolls. But the museum's greatest strength are the Chinese works on the **first floor**: largely amassed by Czech archaeologists and collectors travelling in China between the wars. These objects had an enormous influence on leading Czech artists of those years such as Emil Filla and Ludvík Kuba, who is represented here by a self-portrait in front of Chinese porcelain. The Chinese holdings, dating from the Bronze Age right up to the 19C, comprise works in a great variety of media (with even some wonderful fragments of 6C AD wall painting), and reveal the extraordinary degree of naturalism attained by Chinese artists during Europe's Dark Age; for instance, in the funerary ceramics of animals and other figures from the Six and Tang dynasties. A highpoint of the collection is the darkened room showing a series of 11C–14C Buddhas against a dark blue ramp, which gives the viewer a strong sense of being inside in a cave temple. Moving on from the Chinese collection to the relatively small holdings of Islamic and South-East Asian art comes inevitably as a slight disappointment, but there is the consolation of a large and dramatically-lit group of painted Tibetan scrolls from the 17C.

Several buses (Nos 129, 241, 243 and 245) head back north from Zbraslav along the left bank of the river, following a dual carriageway which in its later stages runs directly alongside a train line and other roads to create a polluted thoroughfare of inhuman proportions. To your left, as you enter the suburb of **Hlubočepy**, there rises above all this a wooded hill crowned by the spacious residential district of Barrandov, which was laid out by Max Urban, Václav Havel and Josef Barek in 1927–37. To walk up to this district you should descend from the bus just before the Antonín Zápotocký Bridge, and bravely make your way across the road and train line until you reach the pleasant path which ascends to the **Barrandov Tower**, at the northern end of the narrow Barrandov.

This fine Constructivist building, surrounded by trees and with a terrace commanding an excellent panorama of the Vltava, was created by the father of President Havel (with the assistance of Max Urban); originally a restaurant forming part of Havel's Lucerna-Barrandov Enterprises, it is now a nightclub. Numerous Functionalist villas built for the wealthy and enlightened middle classes of the 1930s can be seen in the course of a walk to the upper, southern end of Barrandov, three particularly interesting ones being situated at the junction of Skalní (No. 10), Barrandovská (No. 60) and Lumiérů (No. 41). Lumiérů, a straight street running along the top of the ridge, leads at its southern end to the greying buildings of the **Barrandov Film Studios**, which were founded by President Havel's uncle Miloš in 1933. Outside the studios you can catch a No. 248 bus, which will allow you to rejoin your route north along the river.

North of the great 'spaghetti junction' which surrounds the Barrandov Bridge you will reach one of Prague's most heavily industrialised areas, **Smíchov**. Most of the buses stop at the Smíchov Station, which, though modernised and enlarged after the war, is one of the oldest of Prague's main railway stations, having been founded in the 1860s. The actual district of Smíchov, despite its largely bleak look, has several places of interest, but these are all to the north of its station, from where it would be best to take the underground to the following stop, Anděl, which is in itself worth a visit, at least if you are a lover of Soviet kitsch: formerly known as Moskevská (there is an identical station in Moscow called Prashkaya or Prague Station), Anděl might have lost its Russian name but it has kept its Utopian murals of Soviet workers marching into a future in which thrusting towerblocks rise alongside St Basil's Cathedral.

From Anděl you can walk west along the busy Plzeňská for about 1.5 kilometres, and then turn left on to Mozartova, where you will find, at No. 169 at its upper end, the main tourist attraction of Smíchov, the **Bertramka**. This modest and recently restored 18C villa, with a wooden gallery and a quiet, bosky garden, was the home in the late 18C of the composer F.X. Dušek and his wife J. Dušková, a famous singer. They were close friends of Mozart, who stayed with them on his visits to Prague in 1786, 1787 and 1791. The house has now been done up as a delightful small **Mozart Museum**, with appropriate 18C furnishings, unobtrusive background music, and several mementoes of the composer's stay in Prague: these include a piano on which he allegedly played and a curious German painting of c 1800 showing the interior of a former beer-cellar near the Powder Tower, and bearing the inscription: 'This is where Mozart ate, drank and composed *Don Giovanni* in 1787.' Casanova, who was also staying in Prague at this time, later claimed responsibility for forcing Mozart to write this opera. **Open** Tues–Sun 09.30–18.00.

On your way back to Anděl metro station you could make a short detour to your left at the bottom of Mozartova to visit the house at No. 2 Duškova where the Communist journalist and Nazi victim Julius Fučík was born in 1903.

Back at Anděl metro station head north along Štefánikova (the former S.M. Kirova), where you will pass shortly to your right a large and dark neo-Renaissance church by Antonín Barvitius (1881–85). In the decayed garden on its northern side is the **Portheimka**, a small summer villa built by K.I. Dientzenhofer for his own family, but now in a crumbling condition; this toy-like building, with a first-floor room covered by a ceiling painting by V.V. Reiner, is used today for avant-garde art exhibitions that often clash violently with the faded setting. Due east of here is the small Lesnická, where there is a plaque at No. 7 marking the house where the physicist Albert Einstein lived while teaching at the German university in Prague from 1911–12. Continuing north along the busy shopping street of Štefánikova you will pass to your left **The Realistic Theatre**, the drab appearance of which belies the lively nature of its productions (a liveliness which dates back to the 1920s, when J. Čapek was a director) and the important part which it has played in Czechoslovakia's recent history. For it was here, following a strike of actors and students on 19 November 1989, that a hastily convened late-night meeting led to the creation of the Civic Forum Party, which was soon to replace the Communist regime.

Just to the north of the theatre the street emerges at the **Kinský Square** (náměstí Kinských), which, until only a few years ago, was named Sovětských Tankistů, and had at its centre a plinth supporting one of the first Soviet tanks to reach Prague in May 1945.

On the western side of the square is the entrance to the **Kinský Gardens**, which form part of a vast area of parkland stretching up the Petřín Hill and into the Little Quarter (see Chapter 1B). Turning left immediately on entering the gardens and following the path parallel to Holečkova, you will reach the early 19C **Kinský Villa**, where you will find the ethnographic collections of the National Museum, with costumes, pottery and other exhibits relating to Czech and Slavonic folk culture.

F. Eastern Prague ~ Vinohrady, Žižkov and Karlín

Vinohrady

East of the Wenceslas Square extends the district of Vinohrady, a large area of long, straight streets lined with dirty 19C and 20C apartment blocks and offices, some with a decayed splendour. The places of specific interest here, as throughout eastern Prague, are widely scattered, making a walking tour practicable only to the most dedicated sightseer. The main civic buildings of Vinohrady are around the large náměstí Míru, which lies one metro stop from the southern end of the Wenceslas Square. In the middle of the square stands the brick neo-Gothic **Church of St Ludmilla** (sv. Ludmily), which was built by Josef Mocker in 1888–93 and has a west tympanum decorated with a relief by J.V. Myslbek of *Christ with SS Wenceslas and Ludmilla*. The northern side of the square is dominated by the grand façade of the recently restored **Vinohrady Theatre**, a neo-Baroque building with Art Nouveau elements, built in 1903–06 and crowned by winged allegorical groups by M. Havlíček.

East of here begins one of the longest streets of Vinohrady, Slezská, where, on the left-hand side at No. 7, is an interesting red-brick building by Josef Gočár, built in 1924–26 as an agricultural college. Nearby, on the parallel Vinohradská, stands the former School of Commerce, which is decorated around its entrance by four sculptural groups of workers by Karel Dvořák (1925), a very lively example of so-called Objective Realism.

Further east down Vinohradská, adjoining the Jiřího z Poděbrad metro station (one stop east from náměstí Míru), is one of the greatest and most original monuments erected in Czechoslovakia between the wars. This, the **Church of the Sacred Heart** (Nejsvětějšího Srdce Páně), was built by Josip Plečnik in 1929–33, and looms massively over the bleak gardens that have been laid out in the middle of the George of Poděbrady Square (náměstí Jiřího z Poděbrad). Inspired by a combination of an Early Christian basilica and an Egyptian temple, it handles its eclectic borrowings with a boldness which is uncompromisingly modern. Its glazed-brick exterior, studded all over with what seem to be overblown guttae, has walls that project diagonally near the top to form a massive cornice; a great pedimented clock tower, as wide as the building itself, rises high above the east end of the building and supports an enormous clock, glass-fronted on both sides and resembling a rose window. The wide, single-aisled interior, with coffered ceiling, unfaced brick walls and marble floors, has an altar made with marble from the Šumava Mountains and impressive statuary at its east end by D. Pešan. The whole building, which acquires a particular magic when spot-lit at night, looks ahead to 'Post-Modernist' architecture of the 1960s and 1970s, but has a grandeur and individuality which is quite unique to Plečnik. There are few other modern churches in Europe which are quite as powerful as this one.

At its bleak, easternmost end, Vinohradská Street passes next to three of Prague's largest cemeteries. Beyond the Flora metro station the street skirts the southern side of the **Olšany Cemetery**, which was founded during the big plague in 1680, and soon became the main burial place serving the communities on the right bank of the Vltava. One of the most honoured occupants of the cemetery is the student 'martyr' Jan Palach, whose tomb (just to the right of the main entrance) is usually shrouded with flowers and candles; his body was immediately placed here after his dramatic death in 1969, but then was removed in 1974 to his country village, and only brought back here in November 1990.

Immediately to the east is the **New Jewish Cemetery** (Židovské hřbitovy), the entrance to which is adjacent to the Prague-Strašnice metro station: arrows here will direct you to its most visited tombstone, that of the writer Franz Kafka (the monument is a symbolical Cubist crystal designed in 1924 by Leopold Ehrmann). Slightly further east Vinohradská skirts the northern side of the

Vinohrady Cemetery, which was founded in 1885 and has in its centre the neo-Gothic Chapel of St Wenceslas. One of the greatest Czech painters of the turn of the century, Jakub Schikaneder, is buried here, as is the most influential and original Czech sculptor of the 20C, Otto Gutfreund, who died from drowning in 1926, and is commemorated here by a bust by his close friend Karel Dvořák. In the Functionalist crematorium to the east of the cemetery lie the ashes of the journalist and writer Egon Erwin Kisch. Olšany and Vinohrady cemeteries open daily dawn to dusk; New Jewish Cemetery **open** Apr–Aug Sun–Thur 08.00–17.00; Sept–Mar 08.00–16.00.

Žižkov

North of Vinohrady is the district of Žižkov, a traditional working-class area with a long history of revolutionary activity that once earned it the name of 'Red Prague'. It also has strong associations with poetry, being the birthplace of both the German poet Rainer Maria Rilke and of the Nobel-Prize winning poet, Jaroslav Seifert, who was born here in 1901 and was recently honoured by changing of the name of the district's main street from Kalininova to Seifertova. Seifert once referred to this place where he spent his childhood and adolescence as 'my beautiful and adored Žižkov', though this is not a reaction which is going to be shared by most of the casual visitors here, the majority of whom come simply to climb up to the Jan Žižka Monument. The traditional approach to this monument from the centre of Prague is to walk from the Powder Gate to the eastern end of Hybernská (see Chapter 1D), and then turn left on to Husitská.

From a path off this street's western end you climb up a wooded hill, passing to the right a grey block containing the post-1918 holdings of the **Military Museum** (the earlier holdings are in the Schwarzenberg-Lobkowicz Palace; see p 158): howitzers, armoured tanks and other grim weaponry guard the entrance to the building, while inside is an exhibition covering such subjects as the Czech contribution to the Second World War, the invention of Semtex, and even the anti-chemical unit prepared for the Gulf War of 1991. **Open** Apr–Oct Tues–Sun 08.30–17.00; Nov–Mar 09.30–16.30.

The monument to the Hussite hero Jan Žižka occupies the site where he defeated the troops of King Sigismund on 14 July 1420. The monument, known officially as the **National Monument**, features a granite-faced building dating back to 1929–30, adorned inside with mosaics by M. Švabinský and J. Obrovský, and relief carvings by K. Pokorný. This building was enlarged and adapted after the Second World War to contain the Grave of an Unknown Soldier from Dukla, together with the tombs of prominent Communists such as Klement Gottwald, Antonín Zápotocký, and Ludvík Svoboda. Since 1990 the monument has been closed pending a decision about its final fate.

In front of the building stands an enormous equestrian bronze of Jan Žižka by Bohumil Kafka, a work of 1950 which is certainly impressive from a great distance, but is largely of interest for featuring in the Guinness Book of Records as the world's largest sculpture. The greatest reward of a walk up to the monument is the magnificent panorama of Prague to be had from here, a panorama which used to inspire the young Jaroslav Seifert, who was later to write some of the finest poetry ever dedicated to this city.

East of the monument a monotonous tree-lined avenue runs the whole length of the hill's ridge, at the eastern end of which you can turn left and descend a steep path down to the railway line and across to U Invalidovny. You have now entered the district of **Karlín**, and will see to your right the impressive if rather dilapidated block of a great hospital (now the Invalid War Veterans' Home), which was built in 1730–37 by Kilian Ignaz Dientzenhofer; though of enormous size, what you see today represents only a corner of a projected complex of truly monumental proportions. Sokolovská stretches west from here all the way back to the Jan Šverma Park, at the entrance to the New Town (see Chapter 1D).

G. Western Prague ~ Střešovice and Břevnov

Střešovice

Střešovice, which lies immediately to the west of the Hradčany (see Chapter 1C), is traditionally the most luxurious of Prague's suburbs, and is a quiet area of attractive modern villas, spaciously laid out. The district had sinister connotations for Prague's Jewish community during the Second World War, for it was in one of these villas that the Central Office for Jewish Emigration was situated. This office was directly subordinate to the Gestapo and was responsible for the organisation of the notorious 'transports' to the ghetto at Terezín and elsewhere: accounts of the compulsory visits to Střešovice are included in Jiří Weil's disturbing novel, *Life With a Star* (1964), which was based on the author's war-time experiences.

Examples of the sort of tram used by Weil's protagonist can be seen in the enjoyable **City Transport Museum** (Muzeum městskó hromadné dopravy) at Patoćkova 4, which has shiningly maintained examples of every type of city tram and trolley-bus that ever ran through the streets of Prague; during the summer months it runs a tram service to and from the city centre. **Open** Apr–Oct Sat, Sun 09.00–17.00.

West of the museum extends the large area of Střešovice known as the Ořechovka Villa Quarter, which was planned by J. Vondrák and J. Šenkýř in 1920–23 on the model of England's 'garden suburbs'. In the course of the 1920s this quarter was greatly expanded and, between 1929 and 1931, there was built on its outer southern limits (at No. 14 Nad hradním vodojemem) by far the most distinguished of Střešovice's villas, the **Maison Muller**. This cube-like structure, with large expanses of bare masonry discreetly pierced by small, irregularly placed openings, is the work of the revolutionary Moravian-born architect Adolf Loos (assisted by Josef Fanta), and is the only one of his buildings to be seen in the Czech Republic; the interior, characterised by its every space being of different height and shape, may be opened as a museum in the near future.

Břevnov

The district of Břevnov, which extends to the south of Střešovice and to the west of the Petřín Hill (see Chapter 1B), begins at its eastern end with the largest sports stadium in the world, the **Spartakiáda Stadium**. Designed by Alois Dryák in 1926 for a seating capacity of over 200,000, this ungainly complex looks for most of the time like some stranded folly of megalomaniac scale, but comes to life every five years with an internationally renowned gymnastic display known as the Spartakiáda; the next such event is planned for the millennium. Running west from near here is the long Bělohorská, which passes though an area of large housing estates, including one of 600 apartments dating from the late 1930s. Further west along the street, at No. 28, is the elegant Empire-style hostelry known as **At the Chestnut** (Dům U kaštanu), where on 7 April 1878, a secret meeting headed by J.B. Pecka and L. Zápotocký led to the formation of the Czech Social Democratic Workers' Party, an event marked by a plaque.

Just beyond the building the street turns into a wide thoroughfare which is bordered on its northern side by a neglected corner of countryside surrounding the **Monastery and Church of St Margaret** (sv. Markéty), accessible by trams No. 8, 22 and 23, which run the whole length of Bělohorská. Though recently restored, and reclaimed by monks, this unfairly neglected place, with its isolated situation in a generally grey Prague suburb, may induce a sense of great pathos in the visitor, particularly in those who come here in the knowledge that they are visiting the oldest monastery in Bohemia and one of Prague's finer Baroque complexes. Founded for the Benedictine Order in 993 by Boleslav II and the Prague bishop, St Adalbert, the monastery and church were completely rebuilt by Christoph and Kilian Ignaz Dientzenhofer in the early 18C. The monastic buildings, with fine ceiling frescoes by C.D. Assam of 1727, are not open to the public. But the interest of the complex lies essentially in its church, which was built by Christoph Dientzenhofer between 1700 and 1715, and has a powerful and tightly composed exterior with a giant order of pilasters and columns running around its whole length, and a dynamic attic level of gables crowned by undulant pediments. The single-aisled interior is composed of a series of inter-secting tranverse ovals, with giant piers projecting diagonally into the nave as in Christoph Dientzenhofer's comparably majestic Church of St Nicholas in the Little Quarter; the ceiling frescoes, by J.J. Steinfels, represent the founding of the monastery by St Adalbert. The crypt, open on Sundays only, is that of the original Romanesque building of the late 10C. Within the orchard garden behind the church is a Baroque pavilion surrounding a well where St Adalbert is said to have met Boleslav II at the time of the monastery's foundation. Guided tours Sat 10.00 and 14.00, Sun 10.30 and 14.00.

At the westernmost end of Břevnov is the limestone hill associated with one of the most famous and tragic battles in the history of Bohemia, the Battle of the White Mountain (Bílá hora). It was here, on 8 November 1620, that the Protes-tant army led by Count Matthias von Thun was defeated by the Habsburg troops under Maximillian of Bavaria; Elector Frederick of the Palatinate, who had been elected King of Bohemia by the Protestants the previous year, was forced to flee, and Bohemia was not to regain its independence until after the First World War. Much of the site is taken up by an English-style **park** which was laid out in 1797 on a game reserve founded by Ferdinand I in 1530 (to reach its main gates you can continue along Bělohorská on trams No. 8 or 22, and get off at Na Vypichu).

Within the park long alleys of trees lead to the remarkable Renaissance building known as the **Star Castle** (letohrádek Hvězda). This star-shaped structure of 1555–58 was built by Hans Tirol and Bonifác Wohlmut as a hunting-lodge for Ferdinand of Tyrol, and later became the residence of the latter's future wife, Philippine Welser. The exterior, restored by Pavel Janák after the Second World War, is austere and rather dilapidated, but the interior features outstanding stucco ceiling decorations of mythological scenes and grotesques by Italian artists. The building was turned into a powder-magazine after the 16C but now houses on it upper floors a **museum** devoted to the 19C writer of historical romances, Alois Jirásek, and to his painter contemporary, Mikoláš Aleš (who is represented here largely by his book illustrations). In the basement is a large model of the Battle of the White Mountain. **Open** Tues–Sat 09.00–16.00, Sun 10.00–17.00.

The western continuation of Bělohorská is Karlovarská, on which stands, at No. 6, the early 18C **Church of Our Lady of Victory** (Panny Marie Vítězné), which replaced a 17C chapel commemorating the Habsburg victory at the Battle of the White Mountain; the interior has ceiling paintings by V.V. Reiner and C.D. Assam.

H. Northern Prague ~ Letná, Holešovice-Bubeneč, Troja and Dejvice

Letná

Rising above the Vltava immediately to the east of the Little Quarter is the large **Letná Park** (Letenské sady), which was laid out after 1858. Occupying an excellent vantage point at its western end, with beautiful views across the river to the Old Town, is the **Hanavský Pavilion**, an exuberantly eclectic structure mingling the neo-Baroque with tentative Art Nouveau forms. Built by Otto Prieser for Prague's Jubilee Industrial Exhibition of 1891, it was admired in its time (and later by Le Corbusier) for its innovative use of cast iron—a material promoted in Bohemia by the man who commissioned the building, Prince William of Hanava, the owner of ironworks at Komárov near Hořovice. The building proved so popular with those who attended the exhibition that it was rebuilt in its present location seven years later; now brightly restored, it functions as an elegant restaurant.

On the opposite end of the park to the Hanavský Pavilion is the similarly well-located *Praha-Expo 58 Restaurant*, which originally formed part of the Czech Pavilion for the Brussels World Fair of 1958; the indifferent quality of the food served here is partially compensated for by the dining-room's panoramic, semi-circular window.

Holešovice-Bubeneč

To the west and north of the restaurant extends the district of Holešovice, which was annexed in 1869 to the village of Bubeneč, and incorporated into Prague in 1884; the place today is now experiencing new life thanks to its popularity with the city's expatriate communities, and the recent opening of its extraordinary modern art museum (see below). A large and grim Functionalist block immediately behind the restaurant houses the **National Technical Museum** (Národní technické muzeum), which includes among its extensive collections sections devoted to astronomy, metallurgy and horology. Of particular interest to children is the guided tour of a reconstructed coal-mine in the basement; also entertaining is the section labelled in English 'the Centre for Noise Ecology', where you can play around with numerous objects for making and recording sounds. But, above all, you should visit the Hall of Transport at the back of the building, a tall space crammed to capacity with every conceivable form of transport from the early 19C onwards; the exhibits are arranged in three superimposed galleries around the hall and also in the centre of the room, where old bi-planes and even a hot-air balloon hover above a traffic-jam of old cars and trains, including the luxury train carriage in which the Emperor Franz Joseph travelled in 1891. **Open** Tues–Sun 09.00–17.00.

Trade Fair Palace

A grid of streets lined with blackened apartment blocks of the 19C and 20C begins behind the museum. Head east on Letohradská and, at the end of this street, turn left on to F. Křižka, which crosses the busy shopping street of Milady Horákové and comes to an end at the wide Veletržní, near the 1960s block of the luxury *Park Hotel*. Directly in front of this hotel, at 45 Dukelských hrdinu, is the enormous former Trade Fair Palace, which was built in 1926–28 by Oldřich Tyl and Josef Fuchs, and was the first Functionalist building of its scale in Europe. It has now been stunningly adapted to house the modern holdings of the National Gallery.

With the opening of the **Museum of Modern Art** (Galerie moderního umění) in the Trade Fair Palace, Prague has gained not only an attraction rivalling any of its older monuments, but also one of Europe's most exciting new galleries. As yet attracting a relatively small stream of tourists, this spacious and peaceful gallery is worth a visit as much for the architecture as for the collections: the building shows that Functionalism in its early stages was far from being the drab and pedestrian style that it so often became in the hands of its later imitators. The vitality, originality and exhilarating freshness of the building is exemplified above all in the pristinely white Great Hall, which offers an architectural thrill as intense as the Vladislav Hall in the Hradčany. This luminous sky-lit hall, situated at the eastern end of the palace, near the entry to the actual museum (the palace's main western door leads to a part of the building still used for trade exhibitions) is surrounded by balconied galleries that, on one side, form an inwardly sloping wall of railings reminiscent of the hull of some futuristic ocean liner of *Titanic* proportions. **Open** Tues, Wed, Fri–Sun 10.00–18.00, Thur 10.00–21.00.

Inevitably, in view of how little is known about Czech art outside the Czech Republic, most foreign visitors head directly for the second floor, where, in a long suite of interconnected small rooms, the gallery's foreign holdings are displayed, beginning with a large and celebrated selection of French art from the Impressionists to the Cubists. Among the artists represented are **Pissarro** (an excellent view of Pontoise, before 1870), **Renoir**, **Manet** (a head of Proust, 1855–56), **Degas** (*Portrait of Lorenza Payese*), **Van Gogh** (*Green Rye*, 1889–90), **Sisley**, **Cézanne** (*House in Aix*, 1885–87, and a superlative portrait of the Pontoise doctor, patron and friend to the Impressionists, Joachim Gasquet, 1896–97), **Gauguin** (a wooden relief done in Tahiti, and the famous Pont-Aven parody of Courbet, *Good-day Mr Gauguin*, 1889), **Rodin** (a bronze maquette of his Balzac monument), **Toulouse-Lautrec** (*Moulin-Rouge*, 1892), the **Douanier Rousseau** (this artist's only known self-portrait, 1890), **Signac**, **Van Dongen**, **Matisse**, **Bonnard**, **Chagall**, **Utrillo** and **Dufy**.

Many of these works were amassed by Vincenc Kramář, the enlightened director of the Prague National Gallery during the 1920s, who donated his collection to the gallery in 1960, a few months before his death at the age of 83. Kramář's greatest contribution to the arts in Czechoslovakia was his early championing of Cubism, buying in Paris in the first and second decades of this century works that would profoundly influence a whole generation of avant-garde Czech artists and architects. Thanks to Kramář, the National Gallery has a collection unrivalled in Central Europe of the works of **Picasso** and **Braque**. The Picassos begin with two paintings belonging to his so-called Negro Period (a *Self-Portrait* of 1907 and a *Female Head* of the same year) and continue with a large group of 'analytical Cubist' works of 1910 and 1911; there are also some 'synthetic Cubist' works of 1912 and 1913, and later purchases such as his monumental *Standing Nude* of 1921. The paintings by **Braque** trace his career from the analytical Cubist period of 1910–11—when his works were virtually identical to Picasso's of these years—to the development of his very lyrical and painterly still-lifes of the 1920s. Among the other Cubist paintings are some early works by Derain, most notably a view of Cadaqués of 1910; Derain's later manner is represented by a sturdy and very Classical *Seated Woman* of 1921.

The rest of the foreign school holdings are particularly notable for their fine German and Austrian works dating mainly from the first three decades of the 20C. Among the former are three paintings by **Liebermann**, a self-portrait by **Corinth** showing the plump and manic artist naked to the waist, Expressionist canvases by **Schmidt-Rottluth** and **Pechstein**, and a disturbing work by the undeservedly little known **Max Oppenheimer**, entitled *The Operation*: it shows an hysterical group of hands and scalpels.

The Austrian holdings are dominated by superb paintings by Schiele, Klimt and Kokoschka. Schiele is represented by a small townscape of 1911 (a view of Český Krumlov; see Chapter 16) and a haunting tall canvas of a monk and a woman; the sole painting by Klimt is a large decorative composition in vivid blues and purples, entitled *The Virgin* and showing an entwined group of female nudes (1913). Kokoschka lived in Prague in 1934–35, and there are several works by him from this period, of which pride of place must go to three large and expressively painted views of Prague from the river, constituting possibly the finest landscapes ever made of this city.

The Russians **Repin**, **Mikhail Nesterov** and **A.V. Lentulov**, the Italians **Severini**, **Guttoso** and **Carlo Carrà**, and the Spaniards **Oscar Dominguez**, **Miró** and **Tàpies**, are among the other foreign artists whose works are owned by the National Gallery. But an artist whose work was more relevent to the development of early 20C Czech art was **Edvard Munch**, who is represented here by a single but highly atmospheric painting of a group of women dancing by a moonlit shore (1900).

The foreign school holdings on the second floor are abruptly succeeded by a series of rooms devoted to Czech art of the 1950s and '60s. Before seeing these, you should go up to the third floor, where the bulk of the gallery's Czech holdings are displayed, in a roughly chronological sequence. Confusingly for those new to Czech art and unfamiliar with most of the names, the works of a particular artist are rarely shown altogether but are instead divided up according to the perceived artistic preoccupations of specific decades—preoccupations that are sometimes categorised in the accompanying catalogue with such unhelpful titles as 'The Mythology of the Mundane' and 'Primitivism, Civilism and Spiritual Realism'.

The earliest of the Czech paintings provide a natural sequel to the atmospheric, darkly coloured works by **Schikaneder** that bring to a close the 19C collections in the St Agnes Convent (see Chapter 1A). An almost Scandinavian degree of introspection is evident in the penumbral landscapes of **Antonín Hudeček**, which feature the small lake at Okoř (20 kilometres northwest of Prague off the Kralupy road), where the artist Mařák had a small painting school: especially haunting is the work entitled *Evening Silence* (1900), in which a woman with her back to the spectator stares down towards the fading light of the distant lake. Another lake, the imaginary Black Lake, is an obsessive motif in the works of Hudeček's contemporary **Jan Preisler**, an artist of strong Symbolist orientation whose paintings betray the influence of Puvis de Chavannes and Gauguin. The third outstanding painter of this generation is **Antonín Slavíček**, who created landscapes and cityscapes of extraordinary emotional intensity and pictorial expressiveness, including a number of rain-swept views of Prague and its surroundings, for instance, *The Mariánské náměstí* of 1906.

Munch (whose influential exhibition held in 1905 in Prague's Mánes Gallery was partly organised by Preisler) became a seminal early influence on the subsequent generation of artists, notably Václav Špála, Emil Filla and Bohumil Kubišta. Works such as **Špála**'s fiery *Self-Portrait with Palette* (1908), **Filla**'s spiritually tormented *Reader of Dostoyevsky* (1907) and **Kubišta**'s sinisterly green *Cardplayers* (1909), are pure *hommages* to the Norwegian artist. These three painters, together with **Otakar Kubín**, **Antonín Procházka** and **Josef Čapek**, later embraced no less whole-heartedly the Cubist works of Picasso and Braque: many of their Cubist paintings would be virtually indistinguishable from the art of their French peers were it not for the occasional Czech lettering and landscapes (as in, for instance, Kubišta's *Quarry in Braník* of 1910–11, and Filla's *Still Life with Art Monthly*, 1914).

A far more idiosyncratic painter than any of these was the deeply spiritual artist **Jan Zrzavý**, some of whose early works (such as *The Anti-Christ*, 1909) display a powerfully expressive use of colour and brushstroke. At the same time he began developing a completely different style characterised by strange doll-like figures and an almost naively simple handling of paint and composition: one of the earliest such paintings was his *Valley of Sorrow* (1908), which he later described as being imbued with all his sense of 'sadness and hopelessness'.

But the most original and truly outstanding Czech painter of these years was **František Kupka**, whose works on show here reveal his development from a Fauve-like manner (for instance, his *Actress from the Cabaret*, 1909–10) to the pioneering abstract compositions of 1911 onwards, such as the fluently lyrical blue and red *Fugue in Two Colours* (1912). A sensational transitional work—and one which first reveals the influence of music on his art—is *Piano Keys–Lake* (1909), in which reflections on water are effortlessly transformed into the keys of a piano. With his creation of pure abstraction two years later, Kupka experimented with what he called 'cosmic architecture', which is demonstrated here in a series of ambitious canvases begun in 1911–13 and reworked at the beginning of the 1920s, some of which resemble coloured and fractured organ pipes, such as his *Perpendicular and Transverse Areas* (1913–23). A literal climax to his art is reached in the magnificent *Story about Pistils and Stamens, 1* (1920), which has been described as a 'depiction of a cosmic sexual act'. From the 1930s onwards, his art becomes more academic and rigorously geometric, in particular his *Abstract Painting* of 1930, which comprises a white canvas marked with one vertical and two horizontal black lines: not even Mondrian could match such minimalism.

The gallery's early 20C Czech paintings are interspersed with a superbly representative selection of Czech sculpture, beginning with three famous nudes by **Jan Štursa**—a standing bronze of *Eve* (1908–09), a limestone carving of strong Oriental influence entitled *Melancholy Girl* (1906) and the elongated, daringly poised *Wounded Man* of 1921. Dominating Czech 20C sculpture in the same way that Myslbek had presided over the preceding century was **Otto Gutfreund**, who began his career in a Cubist vein (for instance the bronze *Cubist Bust*, 1912–13), and later went on to develop a very realistic yet highly personal style devoted to the portrayal of the everyday world. These latter works, characterised by their simple, stately forms and complete lack of sentimentality (as in the bronze *Family*, 1925), often made use of colour, for instance in the terracotta *Self-portrait*, 1919, and in the groups of *Industry* and *Commerce*, both executed in 1923, in wood and plaster respectively. They represent a truly Czech style of sculpture and their so-called Objective Realism was to be emulated by numerous other artists such as **Karel Pokorný** (*Earth*, 1925 and *Ostrava*, 1936), **Josef Jiříkovský** (*Girl Brushing Hair*, 1923) **Jan Lauda** (*The Potter*, 1923), **Karel Kotrba** (*Portrait of the Painter Miloslav Holý*, 1924), **Bedřich Štefan** (*Girl Drinking Grenadine*, 1924), **Otakar Švec** (*The Motorcyclist*, 1924) and **Karel Dvořák** (*The Girl Friends*, 1924).

Much of the remaining space on the third floor is taken up with the delicate dream-like Surrealism of painters who came to the fore in the 1920s such as **Toyen**, **Jindřich Štyrský** and **Josef Šima**. More arresting and memorable examples of the influence of Surrealism are the 1930s assemblages of **Zdeněk Rykr** and **Ladislav Zívr**: Rykr used glass boxes in which to assemble a mixture of treated paper and unorthodox (and often ephemeral) materials such as pebbles, silver paper, cotton wool, wood and silver foil (as in his *Orient* series, 1935); Zívr also improvised from random materials but in a more three-dimensional and morbid way, as in his *Heart Incognito* (1936), in which a heart-like object is trapped in netting above a black vase. But the prize for originality must be awarded to the kinetic light sculptures of **Zdeněk Pešánek**, whose principle work on this floor is the *Torso* that formed part of a fountain exhibited at the World Exhibition of Art and Technology in Paris in 1937: this luminous, welded-together blend of plastic, glass, neon and lightbulbs is like an avant-garde response to the Venus of Milo. Sadly, the Second World War intervened before the artist was able, as he intended, to reassemble the whole fountain on a site between Prague's Rudolfinum and the Vltava.

Surrealism continued to dominate the work of the avant-garde (and often censored) Czech artists of the '40s and afterwards, such as **Mikuláš Medek**. But the works on the second floor that have perhaps the greatest appeal today fall into the 'Mythology of the Mundane' category, for instance the haunting urban landscapes of **Jan Smetana** (*Last Stop*, 1944), **František Gross** (the ironically titled *Garden of Eden*, 1943), and, above all, **Kamil Lhoták**, whose works are a perfect blend of realism, poetry, colouristic subtlety and arresting imagery, notably *Officer's Mess in Paris* (1947), *Baseball Player* (1947) and *Meteorological Station after a Storm*.

Troja

North of Holešovice-Bubeneč, on the other side of the Vltava, is the suburban district of Troja, which was named after a large Baroque country house known generally as the **Troja Château** (the easiest access by public transport is by bus No. 112 from the Praha-Holešovice metro station). This magnificent house, brashly restored in the late 1980s and early '90s, was built in 1679–75 for Count Václav Vojtěch of Šternberk; the architect was Jean-Baptiste Mathey, who introduced a French pavilion plan with projecting wings. Its principal façade is its southern one, dominated by a monumental oval staircase profusely decorated with statues of gods and goddesses battling with Titans. The rooms on the main floor boast one of the most extensive cycles of Baroque frescoes to be seen in the Czech Republic, including, in the side rooms, some amusing allegorical ceiling paintings by Francesco and Giovanni Francesco Marchetti, and illusionistic landscapes on the walls; the enormous Grand Hall is covered all over with frescoes by Abraham Godyn set in an ambitious illusionistic framework featuring fictive architecture and tapestries, one of which is marked by the shadow cast by a Moor plunging head forwards into the room.

The building now houses the collections of the **Prague Municipal Art Gallery**, which is composed almost exclusively of 19C Czech painting. Most of the leading Czech artists of this period are represented, though largely with minor works: among these artists are Viktor Barvitius, Alois Bubák, František Ženíšek, Jakub Schikaneder, Maximilian Pirner, Max Švabinský, Jan Preisler, Luděk Marold and Mikoláš Aleš. Particularly numerous are the works of Jaroslav Čermák and Václav Brožík, the latter being the author of the gallery's two most celebrated pictures, *Master John Hus Facing the Council of Constance* and *The Election of George of Poděbrady as King of Bohemia*. The garden below the building's southern façade is one of the earliest examples in Bohemia of a French formal garden, and has terraces adorned with eccentric ornamental vases by Bombelli. **Open** Apr–Oct Tues–Sun 10.00–18.00.

Next to the house is the entrance to Prague's **Zoo**, which was founded in 1931, and can only be recommended to those who might enjoy the experience of riding over an aviary in a chair-lift. **Open** daily June–Sept 09.00–19.00; May 09.00–18.00; Apr 09.00–17.00; Oct–Mar 09.00–16.00.

2 · Excursions from Prague

Almost everywhere in Bohemia and even Moravia is within a relatively short distance of Prague, making the possibilities of day excursions from the capital almost endless. Included below are the major sights that fall within the administrative region of Central Bohemia; other, lesser sights within this same region, not meriting a special journey, are included in the longer itineraries described elsewhere in the guide.

A. Kutná Hora and Kolín

Total distance 137km: Prague • 34km Kostelec nad Černými Lesy • 31km • Kutná Hora • 16km Kolín • 56km Prague.

Transport
Buses depart regularly to Kutná Hora from stand 56 at Praha-Florenc or from Metro Želivského (1hr 15min).

Direct **trains** to the town all leave from Prague's Masarykovo nádraží (1hr by the very occasional express service, and 2hrs by the normal one); if you travel from Prague's main station (Praha Hlavní nádraží) you have to change trains at Kolín. The main station at Kutná Hora (Kutná Hora hlavní nádraží) is near the outlying township of Sedlec; to get from here to the centre you have either to take a No. 2 or 4 bus, or else the shuttle train service to the Kutná Hora město station.

The fastest route to Kutná Hora from Prague is by way of Kolín, but a quieter and more attractive approach is to take the road which runs parallel to the south, passing through Říčany (20km southeast of Prague) and Kostelec nad Černými Lesy.

Kutná Hora

Picturesquely situated above the northern banks of the narrow and meandering Vrchlice river, Kutná Hora is a place that had until very recently a melancholic,

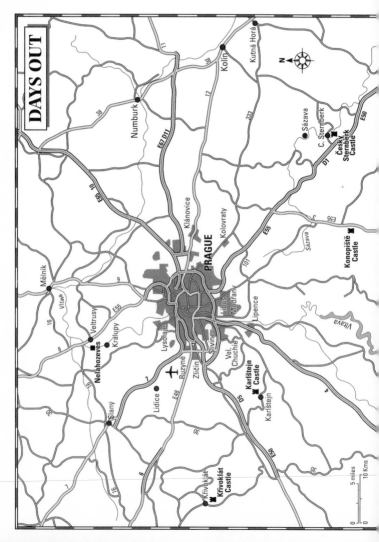

decayed beauty. Major restoration is now rapidly turning the town into a pedestrianised showpiece, and bringing back some of the splendour of its medieval heyday, when it was the second most important town in Bohemia.

History of Kutná Hora

The rapid development of Kutná Hora in the Middle Ages is due to the discovery here, in the late 13C, of rich silver deposits, a discovery which was soon to make the Czech monarchs among the richest in Europe. Wenceslas II invited Florentine mintners to found a Royal Mint at Kutná Hora, and by the 1380s work was begun here on one of the greatest of Bohemia's cathedrals. At the end of the century the town became the favourite residence of Wenceslas IV, but it was to suffer greatly in the course of the Hussite Wars, the retreating Hungarian troops under Sigismund of Luxemburg even setting fire to the place in 1421. Kutná Hora experienced a brief renewal of prosperity during the late 15C and early 16C, when the townspeople were able to secure for the completion of their cathedral two of the most outstanding architects of the time, Matěj Rejsek and Benedikt Ried. By the middle of the 16C, however, the local silver deposits were exhausted, a crisis resulting in the cathedral being left unfinished in 1558, and the town entering a long decline which was to be consolidated by the Thirty Years War and a severe fire in 1771. Kutná Hora is today a district capital, with engineering works and a tobacco factory on its outskirts, but with an essentially unspoilt historical centre reflecting the town's many years of stagnation. Today new life is being given to the local economy both by renewed tourism and by a huge injection of cash from the American tobacco giant Philip Morris.

Approaching Kutná Hora from the Prague road, you will find, at the western end of the old town, fragments of the original fortifications, in front of which you should take the turning to the right marked Černiny. The Cathedral of St Barbara, occupying a verdant southwestern corner of the town, will appear shortly to your left, but, if you were to continue for a further 1km on this road, you would find to your right a turning leading to the **Church of the Holy Trinity**, a late 14C to early 15C structure standing in isolation in a field; this small, triple-aisled hall church, usually closed, has a most elegant interior, its vaulting supported by four slender columns.

Cathedral of St Barbara

You can park your car facing the west façade of the Cathedral of St Barbara (sv. Barbora), to which you descend on steps from the road.

History of the cathedral

The building, founded in 1388, was initially conceived on the model of a French Gothic cathedral, in emulation of Peter Parler's cathedral at nearby Kolín; by 1421, however, when work was suspended, only the eight chapels in the apse and part of the aisles had been vaulted. Work on the building was not to be resumed until 1481, first under the direction of Master Hanuš, and then, after 1489, under that of the great Matěj Rejsek, who was responsible for the vaulting of the chancel. Six years after Rejsek's death in

View of Kutná Hora

1506, the burghers of Kutná Hora, anxious as always to employ the most fashionable and prestigious architects of the time, called on the services of the royal architect Benedikt Ried, who had only recently completed his remarkable work for Prague Castle. The possibility that funds might run out before the massive structure originally envisaged could be finished may have encouraged Ried drastically to change the plan of the building and transform it into a three-aisled hall church, the side aisles becoming galleries, and flying buttresses being used to support sheer walls pierced with enormous, traceried windows. The vaulting of the nave was completed to his design in 1547, but just over ten years later work on the cathedral was abandoned, and the west end left as a blank wall; the present west façade is a dreary, compromise solution of the late 19C.

The Cathedral of St Barbara represents one of the most extreme developments of the late Gothic style in Europe, and has a most bizarre and exotic skyline comprising three massive tent-like forms that from the distance give the impression that some fabulous Turkish sultan has encamped here. The fantastical character of the light and spacious interior is due largely to the extraordinary **vaulting**, comprising stiff rib patterns of exceptional complexity in the chancel and, in the nave, flowing lines of endlessly fascinating geometrical inventiveness, spreading out like tree branches from the piers before bursting out in the centre into six-petalled flowers. The furnishings of the cathedral include a pulpit of c 1560 decorated with stone reliefs of the Evangelists, 17C confessionals, and an exuberant Baroque organ. The most interesting additions to the interior are the anonymous late 15C frescoes to be found in the **Smíšek Chapel** on the southern side of the ambulatory. Jan Smíšek of Vrchoviště—a rich mine owner and the Administrator of the Royal Mines—acquired this chapel in 1485 and was buried here in 1512. The decorations on the walls, executed c 1496, include a *trompe-l'oeil* recess in which Smíšek can be seen dressed as a sacristan and preparing for a mass with the assistance of his two sons; the other scenes are of the *Crucifixion*, *Trajan's Justice*, the *Arrival of the Queen of Sheba before Solomon*, and *Augustus with the Tiburtine Sibyl*. The figurative style of these works and their perspectival illusionism suggest a knowledge of North Italian painting of the early Renaissance.

The cathedral once stood isolated from the rest of the town, but in the late 17C the Jesuits built immediately to the north of it their largest **seminary** outside Prague.

The attractive **Barborská** runs in between the long eastern façade of this building and a Baroque balustrade adorned with statues by Baugut; from here can be had one of the best views of Kutná Hora, with some of the town's finest

KUTNÁ HORA

Church of the Holy Trinity & TÁBOR

buildings—including the distant Church of St James—standing huddled around the edge of a curving slope which is covered in gardens and falls steeply down to the Vrchlice river. Just to the north of the seminary, on the right-hand side of the street, is the **Hrádek**, a structure of 13C origin with a charming late Gothic oriel window, originally forming part of the fortifications but later adapted as the home of the Administrator of the Mines, Jan Smíšek; it now houses the town's **Mining Museum** (Muzeum střbra a středověké důlní dílo), from where you can pick up a white coat, helmet and torch and walk through gardens to the entrance of the medieval mines, into which you descend to a depth of 50m. **Open** Apr–Oct Tues–Sun 09.00–12.00 and 13.00–17.00.

From the First World War Memorial just to the north of the Hrádek a charming, cobbled lane called Ruthardská heads east towards the Church of St James (see below). Continuing instead north on Barborská, at the end of the street you will reach the Komenského náměstí, where you should turn left and walk up Rejskova until you come to a remarkable 12-sided **Gothic fountain** (Kašna), which was created in 1493–95 to provide the town with a supply of drinking-water uncontaminated by the mine workings: designed probably by Matěj Rejsek, this is an extensively rebuilt structure ringed with finials and blind ogee arcading.

Head east of here along Husova, and take the first turning to the left, which joins up with the Radnická. Directly facing you, on the northern side of the street, is the so-called **Stone House** (Kamenný dům), a late 15C structure with a much-restored gabled façade dominated by a box-shaped oriel covered all over with lively carvings; inside is a dreary local museum. Just to the east of this is the Václavské náměstí, where you should head south on Šultysova, a beautiful short street which is lined with decayed 17C and 18C buildings and leads to a Marian **plague column** of the early 18C; at the end of the street, on the left-hand side, is an excellent old beer-cellar.

The exceedingly narrow Vysokokostelecká, which runs south from here, is hemmed in by narrow houses, above which rises the impressively tall Gothic tower of the **Church of St James** (sv. Jakub). When this triple-aisled hall church was begun in the 1330s, it was conceived on a scale comparable to that of deanery churches such as the one at Plzeň, but work was brought to a halt by the Hussite Wars, leaving even the south tower unfinished; the interior, completed at a much later date, is Gothic in structure, but entirely Baroque in its furnishings, which include a high altar of *Christ and St James* by Petr Bendl.Leaving the church by its south portal you will find immediately to your left the most important secular building in town, the former Royal Mint or **Italian Court**, which was built in 1300 for the Italian mintners invited to Kutná Hora by Wenceslas II; in around 1400 the place was enlarged and remodelled as a residence for Wenceslas IV and, following the closure of the mint in 1727, was converted into a Town Hall, which it remained until very recently. The interior, which can be visited on a guided tour, features a ground-floor room where a selection of coins are displayed, including the most famous ones to have been minted at Kutná Hora—the Prague silver *groschens*, the last of which was made in 1547. The most important room is the early 15C **Session Hall**, which has a panelled ceiling of 1400 and two large wall-paintings of the late 19C, representing *The Election of Vladislav Jagiello* and *The Decree of Kutná Hora*—a decree passed by Wenceslas IV in 1409 whereby the rights of Czechs at Prague University were greatly improved; these late Romantic works were painted by the Spilar brothers in collaboration with K.J. Klusáček. Another room, The Hall of Revolutionary Traditions, has a bombastic canvas of around the same date by Adolf Liebscher, depicting *Jan Žižka outside Kutná Hora*. The chapel which Wenceslas IV founded in 1400 was completely redecorated early in the 20C. **Open** Apr–Sept daily 09.00–17.00; Oct–Mar 10.00–16.00.

At the Havlíčkovo náměstí, which lies on the eastern side of the Italian Court, turn left to reach the large **Palackého náměstí**, the town's main square, where there are a number of fine old houses as well as a rather bleak modern hotel, the *Medínek*.

Heading east from here on Tylova, you will pass immediately on the right-hand side, at No. 507, the 18C house where the pioneering Czech dramatist and theatre director J.K. Tyl was born in 1808; inside is a small commemorative museum to him.

Continuing east on Tylova, and taking the third turning to the left, Brandlova, you will reach the late Gothic **Church of Our Lady** (Panna Maria), where the great Baroque painter Petr Brandl was buried in 1735. Return to the Palackého náměstí, and head north on Na Sioně, which will take you to Jiřího z Poděbrad, where there stands a former **Ursuline convent**, begun by K.I. Dientzenhofer on a pentagonal plan in 1734 and never finished.

One of the outlying residential districts to the east of the convent is **Sedlec**, which you can reach by No.1 or 4 bus, or else pass through on your way to Kolín. The first monument you will see as you head there from the town's ring road is the imposing church of the former **Cistercian abbey of Sedlec**.

History of the abbey

The abbey was founded in 1142, but the present church dates back to around 1300, when work was begun on a building modelled on a French cathedral, with a five-sided apse and seven radiating chapels in the chevet. This church, which was more or less complete by the 1320s, was gutted during the Hussite Wars, and was not to be rebuilt until 1702. This task was first entrusted to the German architect P.I. Bayer, but he was soon replaced by an architect at the very beginning of his career, Santini-Aichel. The new building, completed by 1706, is a masterly example of the 'Baroque-Gothic' manner peculiar to this architect, and features vaulting which is as complex as Ried's in the Cathedral of St Barbara in Kutná Hora (to which it clearly owes a debt), but treated with dynamic, Baroque fluency.

At present, unfortunately, you can neither visit the church—which has been closed for many years for restoration—nor the adjoining monastic buildings (now a tobacco factory partly owned by Philip Morris), which feature a vast refectory of 1752–57, decorated with 16 enormous frescoed scenes by the Moravian painter with the appropriate name of Juda Tadeáš Supper. What you can see, however, is the nearby **Ossuary** (just to the north of the church, along Zámecká), which was formed initially of the bones of 30,000 people killed in a plague of 1318; the chapel to house these was remodelled in the 18C by Santini-Aichel, and again in the 19C. In 1870 the Schwarzenberg family, who had acquired the chapel following the dissolution of the monastery in 1783, commissioned one František Rinta to arrange the skulls and bones in a decorative manner, a task which had first been undertaken in the early 16C by a half-blind monk. The results of Rinta's endeavours, which were to occupy him and members of his family for four years, are morbidly fascinating, and include chandeliers, bones hung like Christmas paper chains, and even the coat of arms of the Schwarzenberg family. **Open** May–Sept Tues–Sun 08.00–12.00 and 13.00–17.00; Oct–Mar 09.00–12.00 and 13.00–16.00.

One and a half kilometres east of Sedlec along Road 33 you reach the intersection with Road 38, which will take you after a further 12km to Kolín. Continuing instead east along Road 33, after 4km you will come to the country house of **Kačina**, which was built between 1802 and 1822 for Count Johann Rudolf Chotek. Designed by the Dresden architect Ch.F. Schuricht, this is a Palladian exercise on a megalomaniac scale, and features an enormous pedimented frontispiece, flanked by exceptionally long Ionic arcades. The excellently preserved interior contains outstanding Empire furnishings, and there is a fine English-style park, with lakes and long avenues of trees.

Kolín, which has been described as 'Bohemia's Crewe', is a heavily industrialised town and one of the main railway junctions of the Czech Republic. You should come here, however, if only to see the Deanery **Church of St Bartholomew** (sv. Bartoloměje), which rises on a small hill just to the south of the main square. Begun in the late 13C, it seems to have been damaged by fire in

1349, and was partially rebuilt after 1360 by the great Peter Parléř, who had been called in by the building's patron, the Abbot of Sedlec. The dark and broad nave—built around 1280, and the earliest example in Bohemia of a German Hall structure—is joined awkwardly by steps to Parléř's light and elegant chancel. The large main square was rebuilt after a fire in 1734, and features on its western side a group of extraordinary gabled houses by the local Baroque architect, Josef Jedlička. From Kolín you can return to Prague on the busy Road 12, which passes through flat and dreary countryside.

B. Průhonice, Sázava, Český Šternberk and Konopiště

Total distance 140km: Prague • 13km Průhonice • 34km Sázava • 17km Český Šternberk • 31km • Konopiště • 45km Prague.

Transport
Weekday **buses** to Průhonice (15min) leave every 30 to 60min all morning from the ČAD stand at Prague's Opatov metro station, on Line C.

The other places described above are most enjoyably reached by **train** (from Prague's Central Station), which will take you right to the heart of the beautiful forested scenery extending immediately to the southeast of Prague. For Sázava (1hr 30min) and Český Šternberk (2hrs) change trains at Čerčany, and alight at Sázava Černé Budy and Český Šternberk zastávka respectively. For Konopiště take the train to Benešov (1hr, via Čerčany), and walk the remaining 2 kilometres (15min).

Heading southeast of Prague on the Czech Republic's main motorway, the D1, after 13km you will reach the suburban district of **Průhonice**. Its castle, which dates back to the 13C, was rebuilt in a neo-Gothic style at the end of the last century for Count Ernest Emmanuel Silva-Tarouca; it has retained, however, an old chapel with much-restored 13C frescoes. Next to the chapel is an entrance to a small and enjoyable art gallery, largely composed of French-inspired landscapes by Czech artists of the first half of this century, including works by Antonín Slavíček, among them the delightful *Veltrusy Park* (1897), Josef Ullman, Josef Hubáček, Otakar Nejedlý, Jan Slavíček, Vilém Nowak, Otakar Kubín, Josef Kilián, Oldřich Blažíček and Václav Špála. Of special interest are the castle's extensive gardens, which were laid out at the end of the last century, and bought by the Czech state in 1927. The gardens, which are now administered by the Botanical Institute of the Czech Academy of Sciences, are informal in their layout and filled with rare and exotic plants. **Open** daily Apr–Oct.

Returning to the D1 and continuing to drive south, you should leave the motorway at Ostředek (25km), and head north through forest to the former **Monastery of Sázava** (9km), which is situated by the Sázava river, in an area popular as a summer resort.

History of the monastery
The monastery was founded by Prince Oldřich in around 1032, supposedly as a result of a chance meeting in the forest with the hermit priest St

Procopius. Procopius, a Slavonic scholar, became the first abbot of the monastery, which belonged initially to the Basilian order, a Slavonic order founded by Basilius the Great in the late 4C. Sázava became a great centre of Slavonic culture, and it was here that the Slavonic liturgy was used for the first time in Bohemia; this liturgy was to be banned after 1096 following the expulsion of the Slavonic monks by Břetislav II. The abbey church was rebuilt after 1315, and the whole complex greatly altered in the 17C and 18C. Shortly after its dissolution by Joseph II in 1785, the monastery was sold at auction and converted into a private residence for Emmanuel Tiegel, Knight of Lindenkron. Archaeological excavations carried out after 1940 have revealed fragments of the medieval monastery.

A visit to Sázava is more of historical than of architectural or artistic interest. The interminably protracted guided tour around the monastery buildings is devoted to the ground-floor rooms around the former cloisters, beginning with displays relating to the history of the Great Moravian Empire, and including a collection of archaeological finds from the site.

The richly stuccoed early 18C **refectory** is decorated with frescoes by Jan Kovář, representing the story of the founding of the monastery. The highpoint of the tour is the **chapter house**, where 14C frescoes of the *Life of the Virgin* were discovered in 1943. The upper rooms of the monastery have a collection of locally made glass.

The Gothic **church**, begun in 1315, was left incomplete, and its western tower and the arches of its nave stand today exposed in front of the present church, which comprises an 18C remodelling of the 14C east end. The white interior has a high altar of 1755 featuring a dynamic and elaborate sculptural surround by Richard Prachner; the semi-circular crypt with Gothic rib vaults in brick was restored in the 17C and again in 1950. Nearby can be seen the excavated foundations of the original 11C church. **Open** Apr–Oct Sat, Sun 09.00–16.00; May–Sept Tues–Sun 08.00–12.00 and 13.00–17.00.

Further south along this beautiful, forested stretch of the Sázava river is the impressive castle of **Český Šternberk**, which rises above the trees on a great outcrop of rock. The easiest approach to the castle from Sázava is to return to the D1, which you then leave after 8km, and drive for a further 2km. The castle was founded in around 1240, but rebuilt and strengthened in the late 15C and early 16C. Crenellations and battlements from the medieval structure can still be seen, though the present appearance of the building is due largely to further remodelling carried out in the 17C and 18C; the interior is remarkable above all for the heavy and extensive stucco decorations executed between 1660 and 1667 by the Milanese artist Carlo Brentano. **Open** Apr, Sept, Oct Tues–Sun 09.00–12.00 and 13.00–16.00; May–Aug Tues–Sun 08.00–12.00 and 13.00–17.00.

From Český Šternberk retrace your way back to the D1, but instead of rejoining the motorway, drive under it and follow the road to Divišov (2km), from where you continue driving west to the small town of Benešov (16km). The castle of **Konopiště** lies 2km west of the town, and is set high in a hilly wooded park, with Baroque statuary and strutting peacocks adorning the upper lawns. Dating back to 1300, the castle has prominent medieval features such as tall, crenellated round towers and a moat where bears were kept until very recently.

The whole place was in fact completely remodelled after 1889, when it came into the possession of the ill-fated successor to the Austro-Hungarian throne, the Archduke Franz Ferdinand d'Este. Ferdinand, who was married to a member of the Bohemian Chotek family, stayed regularly at Konopiště right up to the time of his assassination in 1914, and held here in his last year secret meetings with the German Emperor Wilhelm II: Mrs Müller, from Hašek's novel *The Good Soldier Švejk*, refers to him as 'our Ferdinand ... the fat churchy one, from Konopiště'. The heavy panelled interior of Konopiště is immensely evocative of the last days of the Habsburgs, of whom there are numerous photographs and other mementoes, including portraits of Ferdinand and his family by František Dvořák. You are shown not only Ferdinand's bedroom but also his magnificently appointed bathroom; in addition you will see a school painting by Botticelli presented to Ferdinand by the Kaiser Wilhelm, fine collections of Meissen and armoury (including an exquisitely wrought arm-piece of 1598 made for Gesualdo da Venosa by Pompeo della Cesa), and some of the earliest radiators in the Austro-Hungarian Empire. But the lasting impression of the building is of a veritable forest of antlers and other hunting trophies, of which there are an estimated 300,000. **Open** Apr and Oct Tues–Sun 09.00–12.00 and 13.00–15.00; May–Aug 13.00–17.00.

Drive north from Benešov along the E55, and leave the road after 5km to visit the village of **Poříčí nad Sázavou**, where there are two Romanesque churches of the early 13C; one is the tiny cemetery Church of St Peter, while the other is the parish church of St Gall, which was remodelled inside during the Baroque period but has kept its original crypt with cubic capitals. Eleven kilometres further north along the E55 you will rejoin the D1 at Velké Popovice, a 27km drive from Prague.

C. Karlštejn and Křivoklát

Total distance 125km: Prague • 31km Karlštejn • 14km Beroun • 21km Křivoklát • 25km Lány • 34km Prague.

Transport
There are regular **buses** from Prague to Křivoklát at weekends, leaving from Dejvice metro station (about 1hr 30min).

Trains to Karlštejn depart hourly (40min) from Prague's Smíchov Station; from Beroun (50min by express train from Prague), you can take the less regular Rakovník-bound train (every 2 hours) to Křivoklát (a further 50min). There is a direct train to Křivoklát from Prague's Smíchov Station on Saturday mornings.

Karlštejn
From Prague head south for 10km on the dual carriageway of Road 4, then take the turning to the right marked Radotín and Černošice, and follow the Berounka river until you reach Karlštejn, a small wine-growing village lying under the shadow of one of the largest and most fantastically shaped castles in Bohemia. Karlštejn **castle**, which projects high above the steep and densely forested slopes

behind the village, is by far the most popular sight near Prague, and attracts daily great coachloads of tourists.

History of the castle

The castle was built by Charles IV in the mid-14C to house the imperial crown jewels, the Bohemian royal insignia and a large collection of relics. Designed by the great French architect, Matthew of Arras, the building was begun in 1348, and completed in the remarkably short space of seven years. The imperial jewels were removed to Prague by Sigismund of Luxemburg in 1420, shortly before the castle was besieged for seven months by the Hussites; the jewels were eventually to end up at the Hofburg in Vienna. As for the Bohemian royal insignia, these were to be returned at the outbreak of the Thirty Years War to St Vitus's Cathedral, where they can now be seen in a room above the Wenceslas Chapel. Extensively rebuilt in 1575–97, the castle complex later lost its importance, and was in a ruinous state when, in 1887, F. Schmidt and Josef Mocker embarked on a restoration campaign which was to be no less drastic than that of Viollet-le-Duc at Carcassonne.

You cannot drive up to the castle from the village, but have to make the arduous ascent on foot, sharing the narrow, winding road with a queue of other tourists. Your spirits are at first maintained by the castle's extraordinarily romantic and picturesque profile, but begin to sag the more you realise that what you see is largely a medieval sham, which seems almost to have been devised for the tourist market. Gloomy, insensitively restored rooms await you, as well as a guided tour of numbing boredom; however, a visit to the castle is made worthwhile not only by the magnificent forest views to be had from the top, but also, and more importantly, by the outstanding 14C decorations to be found within.

After passing through two gates you will find yourself in the **Burgrave's Courtyard**, beyond which to the west steps descend to a narrow stretch of battlements containing an 80m-deep well which was built in the 14C by mining experts from Kutná Hora. You should return to the courtyard (where the castle's ticket office is to be found) to begin a tour of the main part of the castle complex, which is built up on the slope to the north of here, its highest and furthest point being the keep.

The first part of the castle which you visit is the **Imperial Palace**, where you will find displays relating to the Bohemia of Charles IV as well as a diptych by Tomaso di Modena, which is kept at present in what was once the imperial bedroom. Next you come to the **Tower of Our Lady**, which features on its second floor the Chapel of St Mary, the walls of which are covered with dark and faded murals—attributed to Nikolaus Wurmser and painted in the 1370s—representing the Apocalypse, scenes in the history of the castle's creation (including the gift from the King and Dauphin of France of two thorns from the Crown of Thorns) and Charles IV himself, who is portrayed with unflattering realism, stooped before a gilded cross. The Emperor's own, private chapel was the adjoining **St Catherine's Chapel**, where he would shut himself up for hours in deep meditation, important documents being passed to him through a hole in the west wall. This tiny chapel can literally be described as jewel-like, for Charles had the walls embellished all over with gilded plaster and a dazzling array of coloured, polished stones, leaving uncovered only some murals of saints, of slightly earlier date.

The highpoint of the castle tour should be the **Keep**, which is joined to The Tower of Our Lady by a covered, wooden gallery. Sadly, however, this has been closed for many years for restoration, and you are thus prevented at present from seeing the remarkable **Chapel of the Holy Rood**. This chapel, consecrated in 1360, and divided in two by a gilded iron screen, has a gilded ceiling set with glass stars, and walls encrusted with no fewer than 2200 semi-precious stones as well as 128 painted wooden panels by one of the greatest Bohemian painters of the 14C, Master Theodoric. The relics were once to be found behind the panels, while the jewels and insignia were kept in a niche behind the altar, over which Tomaso da Modena's diptych was originally placed. **Open** Jan–Mar and Nov–Dec daily 09.00–15.00; Apr, Oct 09.00–16.00; May, June, Sept 09.00–17.00; July, Aug 09.00–18.00.

Křivoklát

From Karlštejn you should head west along the river Berounka to the small town of Beroun (14km), after which you continue to follow the river for much of the way to the castle of **Křivoklát**, a further 21km. The landscape after Beroun becomes densely forested, and Křivoklát itself is hidden among trees above a tiny tributary of the Berounka. It is another of Bohemia's royal castles, but a less spoilt one than Karlštejn, and with a pleasantly ramshackle character.

History of the castle

Founded in 1109, the castle was acquired in the mid-13C as a royal residence by Přemysl Otakar II, and was later inherited by Charles IV. Charles spent little of his time here, in contrast to his son Wenceslas IV, who was a passionate huntsman, and came frequently to hunt around Křivoklát; the place provided him with respite from the duties of kingship, and he even burnt down the comfortable dwellings in the castle's outer bailey so that he would not be too troubled by emissaries coming to visit him here. He strengthened the fortifications and undertook much rebuilding at Křivoklát, but the present appearance of the castle is due largely to work carried out at the end of the 15C by Vladislav Jagiello. The Habsburg Emperor Rudolph II stayed here several times, but in 1658 the Habsburgs were obliged first to pawn the castle to John Adolph of Schwarzenberg and then to sell it to the Counts of Wallenstein. After 1685 the building came into the possession of the Fürstenbergs, who were to be responsible for much rebuilding and restoration work in the 19C and early 20C, work which was partially to be supervised by the leading neo-Gothicist Josef Mocker.

The castle at Křivoklát comprises a picturesque and slightly run-down assemblage of structures, dominated at the narrow, eastern end by a tall, round tower. The central building is the royal palace, which features on its south façade a delicately carved oriel window, adorned with relief carvings of Vladislav Jagiello and his son Louis.

The interior, which has been gutted several times by fire, is remarkable above all for the chapel attached to the eastern end of the palace. Begun in the 13C but altered in the late 15C, it has elaborate late Gothic vaulting to which have been added wooden and brightly coloured skeletal ribs supporting a pendulant boss; the stalls are of the late 15C, as is the splendidly intricate altarpiece, a structure in polychromed wood dedicated to the life of the Virgin and attributed to a Litoměřice artist. The 13C library, once one of the most important in Bohemia, has today a largely 19C appearance. Some rooms off the outer bailey house today a large collection of hunting guns. **Open** July, Aug daily 09.00–17.00; June Tues–Sun 09.00–18.00; May, Sept 09.00–16.00; Mar, Apr, Oct–Dec 09.00–15.00 .

The fastest way back to Prague from Křivoklát is to return to Beroun and from there take the D5 motorway. Alternatively you can head northeast to join the E48 at Kačice (19km), passing after 14km the village of **Lány**, which has a former Fürstenberg castle which was used this century by both Presidents Masaryk and Beneš; Masaryk, together with his American wife and their son, lie buried under a simple tombstone in the cemetery on the outskirts of the village. Kačice, a 32km drive from Prague, is situated in the middle of a large coal-mining area incorporating Kladno and Lidice (see Chapter 2D below).

D. Lidice and Budeč

Total distance 54km: Prague 20km • Lidice • 9km Budeč • 25km Prague.

Transport
By **bus** Lidice is a short journey from Prague on the line from the Dejvice metro station to Kladno (30min); buses to Kladno leave every 30 to 60 minutes, but do not take the direct one (*přímý spoj*), which does not stop at Lidice.

Few places in Europe testify so poignantly to Nazi atrocities as **Lidice**, a village and memorial situated 20km northwest of Prague in a grim and flat coal-mining area (2km west of the dual carriageway of Road 7). The present village, a characterless grid of the post-war years, lies just to the west of the extensive memorial marking the site of the previous village, a place which the Nazis had hoped to obliterate completely from all maps, but which is now, ironically, one of the most visited of Czechoslovakia's war monuments.

History of Lidice
The destruction of the village of Lidice on 10 June 1942 was the most notorious of the many Nazi reprisals that followed the assassination of the German Protector of Czechoslovakia, R. Heydrich. Lidice appears to have been chosen for no apparent reason other than that it belonged to a coal-mining region with a strong Socialist tradition. The official Nazi explanation was that the villagers were all partisans who had supported Heydrich's assassins, though it was later to transpire that the Nazis themselves had compromised the place by hiding a large cache of weapons in a mill outside the village. On the evening of 9 June 1942, shortly after placing these weapons, members of the Gestapo and the SS surrounded Lidice, rounding up all the village men into a farmyard, and taking the women and young children to the village school. In the course of the night 173 men were executed, the oldest being a man of 84, the youngest being not yet 15; 11 more were killed early the following day after returning from night-shift in

the mines. The women were all sent to concentration camps, as were most of the children, the majority being eventually gassed in Poland; the more German-looking children were given German names and placed in German homes. The village was razed to the ground, buried under soil and its name obliterated. The only male villager later to return was a murderer who had been kept in a Prague prison, and went back to Lidice one day hoping to surprise his mother and ask her forgiveness for his crime. The decision to rebuild the village and erect a commemorative memorial to the old Lidice was taken almost immediately after the Soviet 'liberation' of Czechoslovakia in May 1945. An architectural competition was subsequently held, the winners of which were the architects, V. Hilský, Z. Jirsák, F. Marek, R. Podzemný and A. Teuzer; the foundation stone of the new village was laid in June 1947. In the summer of 1954, the Chairman of the British Committee 'Lidice Shall Live' proposed to enlarge the memorial with the creation of a 'Rose Garden of Friendship and Peace'; opened in 1955, this was created from rose seedlings sent from all over the world.

Despite being in the middle of an ugly, built-up area, the memorial itself is spread over a pleasant green slope fringed with distant pines. At the higher end of the hill are the **Rose Garden of Friendship and Peace** and a large and austere arcaded memorial centred around an eternal flame. At the end of the eastern arcade is a **museum** containing photographs of the murdered villagers, and other sad mementoes, such as identification cards pierced by bullet-holes. A path below the museum leads down the green slope to the mass grave of the murdered men, adjoining which is the reconstructed wall of the farm where they were shot. Further down are the foundations of the village church and school, the latter once bearing the inscription, 'School, My Happiness'. Museum **open** daily Apr–Sept 08.00–16.00; Oct–Mar 08.00–17.00.

The only other place of interest in the immediate vicinity of Lidice is the site of the Slavonic hill-fort of **Budeč**, which can be reached by returning to Road 7 and driving north to Stehelčeves (2km), where you take the turning to the right; the site, which is situated 4km east of Road 7, in between the villages of Kováry and Zákolany, is marked by an isolated church rising above fields. The fort at Budeč, which features in the early Czech legends, seems to have been founded around 900 by Prince Spytihněv, the second earliest known prince in Czech history. It was he who was probably responsible for the building of the much-restored rotunda which forms today the apse of the Budeč church; to this rotunda, the oldest surviving in Bohemia, a Romanesque tower was attached in the 12C, and a nave in the 17C.

E. Roztoky, Nelahozeves, Veltrusy and Mělník

Total distance 79km: Prague • 8km Roztoky • 15km Nelahozeves • 5km Veltrusy • 19km Mělník • 32km Prague.

Transport
If you do not have a car, the best way of seeing this attractive stretch of the

Vltava north of Prague is by a combination of **bus and train**. Trains depart regularly from Prague's Masaryk Station to Nelahozeves (30min; alight at Nelahozeves zastávka); one stop further on is the bridge leading over the river to the château at Veltrusy. There are hourly buses from Veltrusy to Mělník (25min), which can also be reached directly by bus from Prague (45min). Buses depart both from the Florenc bus station and the Holešovice metro station.

A pleasant excursion north along the river Vltava can be made from Prague's Dejvické náměstí, from where you head north along Jugoslávských partyzánu (see Chapter 1H) and then follow the banks of the river all the way to Mělník. In the outlying township of **Roztoky** 8km away is a small round castle dating back to the 13C but rebuilt in the 16C, and used in 1945 as a factory for making penicillin; the former moat has been covered over and turned into gardens, while the castle itself has now a modest but interesting historical museum. Standing on top of a ridge just to the north of the town, with views over a railway line down to the river, is an isolated medieval church marking the site of the 9C Slavonic hill-fort of Levý Hradec, the first seat of the Přemyslid princes.

The small industrial town of **Kralupy**, 13km further north along the river, features in the poetry and recollections of Jaroslav Seifert, who had happy childhood memories of the place before the Second World War, and paid a nostalgic return trip there shortly after the town was badly damaged by an Allied air raid in March 1945; on this visit he re-met by chance one of the girls of his childhood dreams, and discovered that she was the sole survivor from her Jewish family, and was on the point of emigrating to Canada.

Two kilometres further north is the quiet and attractive village of **Nelahozeves**, where the composer Antonín Dvořák was born in 1841, in an early 19C house marked today by a plaque. Dvořák's father was the local butcher and, at the back of the house, an outdoor toilet has been built in what was once the slaughter house; the house itself is now a commemorative **museum** containing mementoes and furniture from the composer's childhood.

Crowning the hill which rises immediately to the south of the house is the village's impressive Renaissance **castle**, which was built in the 1550s, possibly by Bonifaz Wohlmut, for Florian Griespek of Griespach, a wealthy Bavarian nobleman employed in the service of Rudolph I; the place, now back in the possession of its pre-Communist owners, the Lobkowicz family, has been extensively restored by the Boston-bred William Lobkowicz, who puts on dinners for visiting tourists. Sgraffito decorations extensively cover the exterior of the building, while inside is a large hall with elegant Renaissance fireplaces as well as painted and stuccoed scenes of Classical history and mythology.

The greater part of the enormous interior is taken up today by Old Master paintings and sculptures from the former Lobkowicz Picture Gallery at Roudnice (see Chapter 7). The gallery is particularly strong on Spanish works, and though the supposed Velázquez painting is obviously a school work, there are fine portraits by Juan Pantoja de la Cruz and Sánchez Coello; the other works are mainly by 16C–18C Flemish and Italian artists, including Conrad Wiertz, Frans Francken, Cornelis van der Voort, Antonio Molinari, G.M. Preti, G.P. Panini and Canaletto (a large view of a *Carnival on the Thames*, 1748). The 19C is represented principally by a romantic evocation of a monastery by Granet, suggestive nocturnal scenes by Jakub Schikaneder, and a view of Nelahozeves in 1841 by Carl Robert Croll.

On the other side of the Vltava to Nelahozeves is one of the most beautiful country houses near Prague, **Veltrusy**, a place which inspired the setting of Dvořák's opera, *The Jacobins*. This former residence of the Chotek family was built in the 1720s on a marshy, wooded site known as 'the island'. The house, comprising four small wings radiating from a domed cylindrical hall, was inspired by the pleasure palace designs of Fischer von Erlach. The interior was extensively remodelled after 1760 when the then owner, Rudolf Chotek, was made Austria's first Supreme Chancellor; it contains fine collections of porcelain and 18C furniture, much Rococo stuccowork, and several painted ceilings including, in the main hall, an ambitious composition described in the English brochure to the house as 'an allegory of the four periods'. The main façade of the house, featuring a great staircase adorned with statuary, overlooks a French formal garden of the early 18C. Behind the house, however, extends a vast wooded park which was begun shortly after a great flood in 1764, and came to be one of the greatest examples of romantic landscaping in Bohemia, with numerous splendid follies, including a mock medieval mill, a Doric pavilion, a Chinese pheasantry, a Greek rotunda, and a bizarre Egyptian structure erected during the wake of publicity following Napoleon's Egyptian campaign of 1816–19. The park today, more romantic than ever for being in a slightly dilapidated state, attracts numerous weekend excursionists from Prague.

Nineteen kilometres north of Veltrusy along Road 9 is the small town and wine-growing centre of **Mělník**, which is beautifully situated on a vine-covered hill rising above the confluence of the rivers Vltava and Labe; the vines were brought originally from Burgundy by Charles IV. The dominant landmarks are the tall steeple of the 15C–16C Church of SS Peter and Paul and the imposing bulk of the adjoining **castle**. The castle, which dates back to a Slavonic hill-fort of the 10C, was the occasional residence of the Bohemian queens up to 1475. The present structure—the result of rebuilding and remodelling carried out in the 16C and 17C—houses both a small viticultural museum and a well and spaciously arranged art gallery devoted to Czech painters of the 17C and 18C, including Willman, Kupecký, Jan Liška, Václav V. Reiner, Jan Jiří Heinsch and Karel Škréta. Also to be found here is the *Zámecká Wine Bar and Restaurant*, where you can try the local wines while enjoying a steep view over vines down to the river. From Mělník, the direct route back to Prague (32km) is to head south along Road 9.

East Bohemia

Bordered to the south by the broad lowlandzs of the Labe (Elbe) basin, and to the north by the highest massif in the Czech Republic, this is perhaps the Bohemian region with the greatest diversity of scenery. The main artistic and architectural attractions are concentrated in Chapter 3, which follows the Labe right up to the Polish frontier: Matthias Braun's statuary at **Kuks** is one of the most exciting Baroque sights of Central Europe, while the large town of **Hradec Králové** should not be missed by anyone with an interest in Czech culture during the innovative early years of the 20C.

Scenically, the region's greatest curiosity are the picturesquely twisted sandstone peaks of the **Český ráj** (the highpoint of Chapter 4), which became understandably popular in the Romantic era. Chapter 5 covers the forested **Krkonoše** or **Giant Mountains**, which, though badly affected by acid rain and not nearly as spectacular as their name suggests, draw large numbers of skiers and summer excursionists, mainly from Germany and the Czech Republic.

Transport
Trains
Connections with Prague: Jičín (2 daily; 1hr 50min); Pardubice (1–2 hourly; 1hr 10min–2hr 20min); Trutnov (1 daily; 4hr); Turnov (11 daily; 2hr–2hr 40min); Hradec Králové (5/6 daily; 2hr 30min).
From Hradec Králové: Častolovice/Doudleby nad Orlicí (5–6 daily; 50min/1hr 50min); Chlumec nad Cidlinou (13 daily; 20–40min); Dvůr Králové (9 daily; 40min–1hr); Hořice (12 daily; 30–50min); Jaroměř (hourly; 20–30min); Kuks (6 daily; 40 min); Pardubice (1 or 2 hourly; 30min); Třebechovice pod Orebem (10–15 daily; 15min).
From Turnov: Hradec Králové (12 daily; 1hr 50min–3hr); Jičín (10 daily; 50min–1hr 10min); Železný Brod (8 daily; 20min).

Buses
Connections with Prague: Harrachov (up to 5 daily; 3hr); Jičín (5 daily; 2 hr); Litomyšl (up to 6 daily; 3hr 30min); Náchod (up to 6 daily; 3hr); Špindlerův Mlýn (up to 6 daily; 2hr 40min); Vrchlabí (up to 8 daily; 2hr 30min); Hradec Králové (8 daily; 2hr 30min).
From Hradec Králové: Jaroměř (hourly; 25min); Kuks (up to 10 daily; 30–40min); Litomyšl (5 or more daily; 1hr 10min); Náchod (up to 6 daily; 1hr); Nové Město (up to 5 daily; 1hr 20min); Pec pod Sněžkou (up to 8 daily; 2hr); Trutnov (up to 14 daily; 1hr 10min).

Hotels and pensions
Český ráj
Hotel Lázně Sedmihorky, 516 62 Karlovice u Turnova. ☎ (04396) 916 112. Neo-Gothic château at the centre of this famous beauty spot.
Hradec Kralové
Penzion U Jana, Velké náměstí 137, 500 01 Hradec Kralové. ☎ (049) 241 55. Luxury modernised pension overlooking the old town square.
Krkonoše
Hotel Nechanický, Bedřichov 43, 543 51 Špindleruv Mlýn. ☎ / Fax: (0438) 932 63. One of the older and more rustic of the Giant Mountains' resort hotels, this was built in 1929 and tastefully modernised in 1993.
Pardubice
Zámecká, Zámecká 17, 530 02 Pardubice. ☎ (040) 515 893, Fax: (040) 516 925. Pretentiously restored Baroque mansion adjoining castle.
Turnov
Hotel Korunní Princ, náměstí Českého ráje. ☎ & Fax: (0436) 242 12. Beautifully situated in attractive turn-of-the-century building on main square.

3 · Prague to Náchod

Total distance 170km: Prague (leave by the D11/E67) 48km Poděbrady •
22km Chlumec-nad Cidlinou • 28km Hradec Králové • 72km Náchod.

This, the main route between the Czech Republic and Poland, will soon be
entirely covered by the D11 motorway, which at present has only been
completed up to the junction with Road 32 to Jičín. It heads due east through
what is at first flat and dreary agricultural countryside, after 37km passing near
the tiny spa town of **Sadská**, which was where Mozart stayed for three weeks on
his second visit to Bohemia in 1787; his stay was paid for by Czech friends who
were anxious about the impoverished musician's health.

The Czech Republic's youngest spa town, **Poděbrady**, lies 11km further on, by
the banks of eastern Bohemia's largest river, the Labe. In the main square is an
equestrian statue by B. Schnirch to the town's most famous son, George of
Poděbrady, who was Regent of Bohemia before becoming king of the country in
1453; his brilliance as a statesman was comparable to that of his Hungarian
contemporary, Matthias Corvinus, who was likewise elevated from regent to king. A
museum to George is to be found in the town's ochre-coloured **castle**, which stands
off the square and projects over the Labe. This much-restored building, dating back
to the 13C, was rebuilt between 1545 and 1582, and further altered in the mid-
18C. In its large austere courtyard is a plaque to a German farmer, Bülow, who,
searching for new sources of drinking water for the town, uncovered in 1905 a
mineral spring within the castle grounds. The curative properties of the water were
soon afterwards recognised by a local physician, Dr Bohumil Bouček. Poděbrady's
spa, founded in 1908, is especially favoured by those suffering from heart diseases;
its buildings lie scattered around a great park just to the north of the main square.

Further east along the D11/E67 the landscape becomes hillier and more
wooded. Outside the village of Chlumec nad Cidlinou, 21km from Poděbrady, is one
of Bohemia's most original Baroque mansions, **Karlova Koruna**. Commissioned
by František F. Kinský to commemorate a visit by Charles VI, it was begun in 1721
to one of the last designs by Johann Santini-Aichel, and completed in 1723 by F.M.
Kaňka; comprising three wings arranged in star-like fashion around a circular
block, it was probably inspired by the fantastical 'pleasure house' designs of the
Austrian architect J.B. Fischer von Erlach. The interior, gutted in 1947, now houses
a permanent collection of masters of the Bohemian Baroque, including Karel
Škréta, Jiří Heerman, Jan Liška, Michael Leopold Willman, Antonín Kern, Johann
Kupecký, Václav Reiner and Matthias Braun; plastercasts of Braun's monumental
works at nearby Kuks (see below) take up much of the ground-floor saloon.

The village of **Chlumec** itself is of purely historical interest, the place having
been the centre in 1775 of one of the largest peasant uprisings in Bohemia's
history: after its suppression, nearly 3000 serfs were brought to a farm near
Chlumec and burned to death. On the outskirts of the village, in the direction of
Hradec Králové, is a statue of a rebel peasant by J. Obrovský.

The direct road from Chlumec to Hradec Králové passes 6km south of the
castle of **Hrádek u Nechanic** (3km before reaching Hradec turn left on to the

Nechanice road, and then turn left again at Stěžery). The castle was built between 1839 and 1857 for Franz Ernst von Harrach, who had hoped to enlist the services of Franz Beer, the architect of the extraordinary neo-Gothic pile at Hluboká (see Chapter 15B); in the end the building was designed in a Tudor Gothic style by the Viennese architect Karl Fischer, who supposedly was inspired by Edward Buckton Lamb's designs for Crewe Hall in Cheshire. Many of the castle's original furnishings survive, though a large part of the interior is also devoted to contemporary Czech history; there is a large deer park in an English style.

Pardubice

An alternative route from Chlumec to Hradec Králové is by way of Pardubice, which is reached by leaving the D11/E67 3km east of Chlumec, and then driving 27km southeast along the D36. Ten kilometres before Pardubice is the small spa resort of **Lázně Bohdaneč**, which has innovative spa buildings in a 'Cubist' style by Josef Gočár, designed in 1911 when the architect was 31. Pardubice, a large industrial town on the river Labe, has an important history and a small but attractive old quarter.

History of Pardubice

First mentioned in 1295, Pardubice was elevated to the status of town in 1340; but its greatest period was from 1491 to 1581, when it was owned by the Pernštejn family, among the most important Bohemian patrons of the Renaissance. Heavily damaged by fire in 1507, the town was rebuilt at remarkable speed, with Italian masters working alongside native craftsmen. A Master John from Olomouc was called in to create a unified town plan comparable to those of Renaissance Italy. Sadly, most of 16C Pardubice was destroyed during the Thirty Years War, in particular as a result of a siege carried out by the Swedish army in 1645. From the late 19C the town developed as one of the major industrial centres of Bohemia, with extensive chemical and engineering works. The town's best-known product, manufactured in the outlying district of Semtín, is the explosive known as Semtex, a particular favourite with terrorists owing to its being undetectable by electronic means.

The surviving monuments of old Pardubice are concentrated on the small yet excellently preserved **Pernštejn Square** (Pernštýnské náměstí), which comprises almost entirely buildings of the 16C and 18C. The square can be entered through the arch of the Renaissance **Green Tower** (Zelená brána) of 1540, a tall structure rivalled only by the nearby castle as the dominant element in the old town's skyline. **Open** May–Sept Tues–Sun 09.00–12.00 and 13.00–17.00.

Pernštejn Castle itself, built between 1512 and 1543 to replace an earlier Gothic building, has been badly damaged over the years, though it still retains an exquisitely carved Renaissance gateway and bridge, and some interesting painted panels of this period, including an allegory of Fortune which is considered to be the earliest painting of a nude in Bohemia; the interior also contains a regional museum, and—in what was once the castle brewery—the **East Bohemian Gallery** (Východočeská galerie), featuring works mainly by 19C artists including A. Machek, A. Kosárek, Julius Mařák and A. Chitussi. Castle **open** Tues–Sun 10.00–18.00; gallery **open** Tues–Sun 10.00–17.00.

The **Church of St Bartholomew** (sv. Bartoloměj) on Pernštejn Square dates back to 1295 but was rebuilt after 1515 by the Pernštejns, who displayed here their characteristic love of rich sculptural decoration. A house on the south-western corner of the square has a tablet of 1511 recording the legendary encounter of the first Pernštejn with a bison. For an actual representation of a monster you should turn to the house known as **U Jonáše** on the opposite end of the square, which has an extraordinary stuccoed façade of 1797 by Jakub Teplý representing Jonah and the Whale.

In the suburban district of Pardubice known as Pardubický, near the so-called 'Small Château' or Zámeček, is a small **memorial museum** to those killed by the Nazis in 1942 in retaliation for the town having harboured the parachutists implicated in the assassination of Reinhard Heydrich (see p 174).

Eight kilometres south of Pardubice along the D37 is **Chrudim**, a dull industrial town but with remains of its medieval fortifications, and with a number of old houses, including the Mydlář house (Mydlářský dům) of 1573–77, which contains a museum of puppetry; in addition the town boasts a puppet theatre and an annual international puppet festival. The main tourist attraction near Pardubice is the stud farm at Kladruby nad Labem, 14km west of the town in the direction of Kolín (see Chapter 2A); here you can hire horses or go riding in horse-drawn carriages.

North of Pardubice the D37 follows the quiet and attractive Labe Valley, 3km outside the town passing the rebuilt Hussite castle of **Kunětická Hora**, which rises above the river Labe on a wooded hill of volcanic origin.

Hradec Králové

After 22km, at the confluence of the rivers Labe and Orlice, you come to Hradec Králové, the administrative, cultural and economic centre of East Bohemia.

History of Hradec Králové

One of the oldest towns in Bohemia, Hradec Králové was already a fortified settlement and the leading centre in eastern Bohemia before the establishment of the Czech state in the 10C. Turned in the 14C into the seat of the widowed queens of Bohemia (hence the name 'Hradec Králové' or 'Castle of the Queens'), the town soon became one of the most imposing in the country. Badly damaged during the Thirty Years War, the place was extensively rebuilt during the late Baroque period. An imposing new fortress was constructed between 1766 and 1789, but this was destroyed shortly after the crushing defeat of the Austrians by the Prussians at the battle which took place at Chlum Hill, on the eastern outskirts of Hradec Králové, on 3 July 1866. Between 1900 and 1930 the town was considerably enlarged, a new quarter growing up on the right bank of the Labe. The architects responsible—most notably, V. Rejchl, O. Liška, J. Kotěra and J. Gočár—were leading exponents of the avant-garde, and helped transform Hradec Králové into one of the foremost centres of modern Czech architecture. The town has continued to grow at a rapid pace since the Second World War, but with rather less original results. It is now a major industrial town, specialising in such diverse products as chemicals, timber, diesel engines for ocean-going vessels, and musical instruments.

The **Old Town** (Staré Město) of Hradec Králové, surrounded by the extensive remains of its fortifications, stands on high ground in between the Labe and Orlice rivers. Quieter and less vital than the new town, this has now become a grand if slightly sombre showpiece, filled with imposing Renaissance and Baroque build-ings, many of which have been recently restored. The vast, lozenge-shaped **Velké náměstí**, attached to the smaller **Malé naměstí**, is lined at its western end by the **Town Hall** (dating back to the Gothic period but heavily remodelled first in the Renaissance and then in 1850), the impressively tall **White Tower** (Bílá věž) of 1574–80, and the twin-towered **Cathedral of the Holy Spirit** (sv Duch). The latter was begun in 1360, and much restored after fires in 1484, 1509 and 1536; the brick exterior is virtually unornamented, while the white and similarly austere interior has a very tall nave, low aisles and simple vaulting.

In complete contrast is the 18C **Jesuit church** on the southern side of the square: built in 1654–66 to designs by the Italian architect C. Lurago, this has a resplendent Baroque interior in white and gold, and a main altarpiece by Petr Brandl framed by painted architecture. Adjoining the neighbouring Jesuit college is an 18C bishop's palace, which until recently was the setting of the finest collection of modern Czech art outside Prague

The **Gallery of Modern Art** (Galerie moderního umění) has now been relocated to the square's eastern corner, and is more appropriately housed in a black-faced, five-storeyed Secessionist building designed by Osvald Polívka in 1910–12. Dynamic sculpted figures by Ladislav Šaloun flank the main entrance, which leads into a foyer illuminated by a stained glass ceiling. Further stained glass decorates the stairs and corridors surrounding a glazed oval atrium, around which are a series of small rooms with newly placed and luridly coloured carpets. The earlier works are on the first floor and include wood carvings by **František Bílek**, bronze reliefs by **Sucharda**, sculptures by **Jan Štursa**, and two fine paintings by **Jan Preisler**: a large lunette (recalling the art of Puvis de Chavannes) from the dining room of the Hotel Bystrica (see below), and a Klimt-like painting of a woman in a landscape entitled *Spring* (1901–2). **Mucha**, best known for his flowing decorative art nouveau posters, is shown here at his most pompous and ambitious in his early *Nero Observing Rome on Fire* (1887), while the future pioneer of abstract painting, **František Kupka**, is featured by a charming if wholly conventional symbolist oil painting of a woman with her hair tied in a bun (1897). The mystical and idiosyncratic **Josef Václav**, a dabbler in Satanism, provides this floor with two of its more curious highpoints—the powerful *Invocation of the Devil* (a work of 1909 steeped in turn-of-the-century decadence), and the even more curious portrait of *Jindry Imlaufa* (1924), whose diabolical features are framed by a red and yellow confusion of Orphist-like circles.

Czech Cubism is well represented in the museum, beginning on the first floor with works by **Bohumil Kubista**, notably his amusing *Harlequin and Columbine* (1910), a boldly painted double portrait of *Mr and Mrs Pospíšil* (1908), and a superb *Café* scene of 1910. Works by Cubist and other Czech artists of the early years of the 20C also take up much of the second floor, where you will find paintings by **Čapek**, **Kubín** and **Špala** (a vivid blue *Mill on the Otava River*), **František Janoušek**'s Picasso-like *A Woman* (1934) and **Emil Filla**'s delightful *The Painter* (1934)—an original interpretation of Synthetic Cubism, with the world of the painter's imagi-nation contrasted with a drab and unmistakably Czech reality (red bricks, a railway bridge, factory chimneys and a telegraph pole). Two curiosities on this floor are **Miloslav Holý**'s portrayal of Prague's famous *Union Café* (1925), and **Alois Wachsman**'s powerful *Hide, War!* (1935), a disturbing surrealistic work featuring crutches, columns, a tin bath, and a blood red background.

The third floor, dedicated to **post-war art** up to 1968, is memorable principally

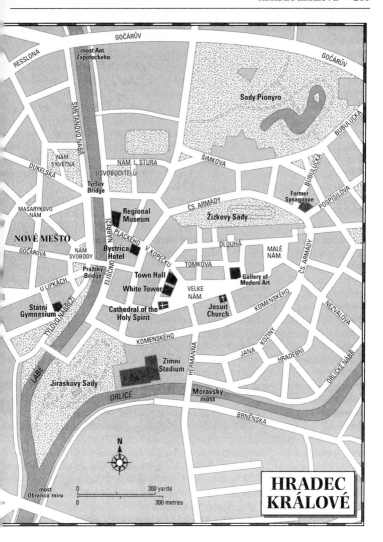

for its haunting landscapes and cityscapes by artists such as **Jan Smetana** (*A View of the Town*, 1945), **Václav Tikal** (*Construction of a Bridge*), and, above all, **Kamil Lhoták**, a painter whose grey, devastated scenes of the post-war years give way in later life to works combining bright patches of pure colour with strange, realistically observed detail, for instance *A Car* (1968), and *Helicopter* (1964). The story of Czech art after 1968 is illustrated by a small and largely uninteresting selection of works displayed under a skylight on the top floor (one of the more notable works is **Jiří Kolář**'s *Rollage*), where there is also a terrace café with panoramic views over the main square. **Open** Tues–Sun 09.00–12.00 and 13.00–18.00.

Turning left on leaving the museum you will come to the Malé náměstí, at the north-eastern corner of which is a street which descends down to the ring of boulevards marking the site of the town's battlements. Immediately facing you, at Nezvalova 1, is a pleasingly simple Lutheran church by Kotera's pupil Oldřich Liskou, while, just to the north of this, at the junction of Pospíšilova and Československé armády, is the curious, massive bulk of the former **Synagogue**, a Secessionist structure with oriental features built by V. Weinzettel in 1904–5.

Returning to the main square and heading north-west along V Kopečku, you will reach the **New Town** (Nové Město), which was begun along the leafy eastern banks of the Labe. At first the dominant architect was Jan Kotěra, who was responsible for the grand but crumbling and currently closed **Hotel Bystrica**, which you will pass to your left as soon as you enter the northern continuation of V. Kopočku, Palackého: this magnificent building, which has been awaiting restoration for many years, was famous for its restaurant featuring stained glass by František Kysela and murals by Jan Preisler. Another, earlier work by Kotěra can be seen in the riverside gardens at the other end of Palackého: built in 1909–11 as the **Regional Museum** (Krajské muzeum), it has a superlative Secessionist exterior in red brick and concrete, with two enormous polychromed sphinxes by Stanislav Sucharda guarding the main entrance. The comparatively restrained interior is worth visiting primarily for the beautiful stained glass windows by Kynsela on the staircase, and (under the dome) the mosaic panels designed by Preisler, one of which is a Matisse-like scene of naked female figures by a Mediterranean coast. The rag-bag collections, largely displayed on the top floor, are mainly composed of domestic objects from the 18C onwards, among which are a faded glass cabinet and other Cubist pieces of furniture by Gočár (the better pieces are now on show in Prague's House of the Black Madonna; see p 110); also to be seen here are Sucharda's maquettes for his remarkable sculpted figures on the museum's exterior. **Open** Tues–Sun 09.00–12.00 and 13.00–17.00.

Gočár's development as an architect and designer after the war—when he succeded Kotěra as the guiding figure behind the new Hradec Kralové—can be observed on the opposite, western side of the Labe, where there extends the greater part of the New Town. Kotěra's Secessionism paved the way both for 'Rondo-Cubism' (so-called because of its extensive use of semi-circular shapes) and for Functionalism, a severe example of the latter being Gočár's **Státní Gymnasium**, which you will come to after crossing Kotěra's stylish Pražský Bridge and walking southwest from the river down V. Lipách. A lively and elegant bronze nude by Jan Štursa stands on a column directly in front of the building, while adjoining it is Gočár's even more forbidding **Ambrožův sbor**, a Protestant church built on a boldly angular site.

A more widely appealing aspect of Gočár's later work, his 'Rondo-Cubism', is seen at its best in what is undoubtedly the architectural jewel of the New Town—the **Masaryk Square** (Masarykovo náměstí), two blocks due north of the Ambrožu sbor. Centred on a recently returned statue of Masaryck, this fan-shaped and very theatrical space is backed by buildings with high and richly articulated attic levels, for instance the former Anglo-Czechoslovak Bank of 1922–23 at the corner of Čelakovský, which is topped by a row of exciting concave forms that could be described as 'Rondo-Cubist gables'.

Ten kilometres north-west of Hradec Králové, off the Jičín road (D35/E442), is the **1866 Battle of Chlum Memorial**, which commemorates an exceptionally bloody battle (supposedly the second biggest in the history of the 19C) that was fought on 3 July 1866 between the Austrians and the Prussians, and is now annually re-enacted; there are several evocative neo-gothic monuments arranged around the site, as well as a 25 metre high tower erected in 1901, and a small military museum created in 1936. Museum **open** daily, Apr–Oct, Tues–Sun 09.00–12.00, 12.30–16.00.

Retracing your steps to the village of Všestary (4km to the south), you can take the side road marked Předměřice nad Labem to join after a further 4km the D33/E67, which heads north-east of Hradec Králové in the direction of Jaromer. 8km north of the junction (and 14km from Hradec Králové) is the village of **Smiřice**, the original home of the Smiřický family. Their former mansion, in the bosky southern outskirts of the village, has a large chapel, begun in 1696 or 1699, and consecrated in 1713; its undulant oval plan has something of the dynamism of Christoph Dientzenhofer's architecture, but the Gothic-inspired vaulting recalls the work of Johann Santini-Aichel. **Jaroměř**, 10km further north, has a 15C church with a Baroque belfry and a row of late Gothic and Renaissance burghers' houses, but its principle interest is the fortress known as the **Josefov** in the southern half of the town: founded by the Emperor Josef II in 1780, this was a complex of considerable structural strength and sophistication, but one which never had to withstand a single siege.

Leave the D33/E67 at Jaroměř and take Road 299 to Dvůr Králové. After 6km the road passes through the tiny and pretty village of **Kuks**, outside which you will find the remains of what was once an ambitious **Baroque Complex**. These remains, comprising a chapel and a hospital, dominate the verdant slopes on the other side of the river Labe to the village. Though only fragments of a once magnificent whole, and themselves in a lamentable condition, they—and the nearby and similarly ruined statuary in the so-called Bethlehem Wood—constitute some of the greatest Baroque attractions of Central Europe.

History of Kuks

The creation of the Kuks spa was due to Count Franz Anton Graf von Sporck, a man of fascinating contradictions and one of the most enlightened patrons of the European Baroque. Sporck came from a recently ennobled family of German origin, his father being from a line of modest Westphalian freeholders. The father had been raised to the nobility and given an extensive estate in Bohemia as a reward for the active part which he had played both in the Thirty Years War and in the wars against the Turks. In 1662, at the age of 65, he had increased his Bohemian domain through the acquisition of a large property now known as Choustníkovo Hradište, in the vicinity of Kuks. Franz Anton Sporck was born that same year, and was to spend much of his youth on his father's new estate. After studying law and philosophy, when only 17 he inherited all his father's properties and vast wealth, estimated at more than 6000 guilders. Subsequently he travelled around Western Europe, spending much of his time at the court of Louis XIV. The sight of Versailles under construction must undoubtedly have nourished Sporck's plans to create something on a comparably megalomaniac scale in his native Bohemia. He was only too conscious of being from an aristocratic family of little standing, and was anxious to astound the Bohemian nobility through a spectacular act of patronage.

It says much about his character, however, that he seems to have despised the very nobility whom he wanted to impress. He was to lead the life of an autocratic nobleman, determined to have control over every aspect of his subjects' lives, while at the same time remaining at heart a life-long rebel. A champion of the poor against feudal exploitation, he was even to be discovered at one large ball in Prague at three o'clock in the morning debating social injustices in Bohemia. Though a former law student, he was to hold all lawyers in contempt, and was even to commission at Kuks an enormous symbolical sculpture of Herkomanus, the patron of dishonest lawyers. Both Sporck's rebelliousness and the perverse, contradictory nature of his character are also reflected in his attitude towards religion: schooled at a Jesuit college, he was to have constant disputes with the Jesuits, attempt to liberate Catholicism from the rigid influence of the Vatican, belong to a circle of free-thinkers who advocated religious tolerance, regularly attend the sermons of the Lutheran preacher Christian Voight, and become involved with Jansenism to the extent of sympathising with numerous Czech exiles. And yet he was to support the Catholic authorities in Bohemia and, to their approval, to commission for near Kuks some of the most moving and powerful religious statuary in the history of Baroque art, works that were perfectly in accordance with the Jesuit ideal of emotional directness in religious representation.

The history of Kuks goes back to the early 1690s when Sporck discovered near his estate at Hradiště a mineral spring reputed to have healing powers. In 1694 these powers were verified by a group of professors from Prague University, and Sporck decided to turn the place into a spa, the fame of which he hoped would soon eclipse that of Karlovy Vary. A number of spa buildings, guest houses and places of entertainment were constructed on the left bank of the Labe, on a site now occupied by the village of Kuks; alongside these structures Sporck also built for himself a large mansion intended to replace his family seat at Hradiště.

After 1707 construction work was extended to the right bank of the Labe, where there were laid out in ascending order a racecourse, a summerhouse and garden (complete with maze and fountains), a chapel and hospice, a further garden, a cemetery, and a windmill pumping water to the whole area. The architect of the chapel, and probably of the Sporck mansion as well, was the Italian-born G.B. Alliprandi, one of the pioneering Baroque architects of Bohemia and at that time very much in demand in the Bohemian capital. But Sporck's greatest coup was in securing in 1712 the services of the Tyrolean sculptor Matthias Braun, then fresh from his triumphant first commission in Bohemia—the sculptural group of St Luitgard for the Charles Bridge in Prague. The first biographer of Braun, M. Pelc, suggested that it was Sporck who had had this sculptor brought to Bohemia in the first place. Though this is unlikely, there was clearly a very close understanding between the two men, and at Kuks Braun was allowed a freedom which he would have found in few other places in Europe.

By 1712, construction work at Kuks was nearing completion, and attention could be devoted more fully to the decorative embellishment of the place. So far the main sculptural work carried out at Kuks had been by an artist of Flemish descent, Bartholomew Zwengs, and had consisted of a number of dull and mannered works for the hospice garden. Braun's first task was the bizarre one of executing a series of grotesque dwarfs to surround the racecourse; but even in these minor works he showed himself to be an artist far more suited to convey Sporck's dynamic ideas than was the staid Zwengs. Afterwards he was commissioned to produce a group of Beatitudes to be placed on the terrace in front of the hospice chapel. Whereas for these works he was considerably helped by his workshop, for the flanking allegorical figures of the Vices and Virtues—his subsequent commission—he appears to have been largely unaided. Braun's final works for Sporck were his biblical scenes for the nearby New Grove at Žireč ('the Bethlehem Wood'), a series of chapels, statuary and hermitages that were brought to completion around 1733 and constituted the last and in many ways most personal of Sporck's plans for the area.

During Sporck's lifetime, Kuks was indeed the thriving social and cultural centre which he had intended. There were great hunting expeditions, fairs in which wells would be filled with wine, Venetian nights on the Labe involving music and cannon salvoes, and knighthood ceremonies for the Order of St Hubert, a hunting order founded and led by Sporck himself and boasting the Emperor Charles VI among its members. Sporck was a man of enormous culture, and his house at Kuks attracted numerous artists, writers, musicians and philosophers, including the painter Petr Brandl, the lyric poet Matthias Gunther, and Johann Sebastian Bach. At Kuks Sporck amassed an important library of philosophical works, and set up his own printing press, which brought out numerous tracts of the French Enlightenment. He had a particular love of music, acquiring a private orchestra, and developing a specialist interest both in popular religious songs and—much to Bach's approval—the French horn, with which he had fallen in love in Paris: thanks to Sporck, Kuks became the first place in Bohemia to hear this instrument. It was perhaps fortunate that Sporck died in 1738, at the height of Kuks' fame, for it was only two years later that a tragedy was to befall the place from which it was never to recover.

On 22 December 1740, the Labe overspilled its banks, washing away the three bridges, the racecourse, the summer pavilion, and a number of other structures; more importantly, it destroyed for ever the healing spring, thus bringing to an end Kuks' days as a spa. The later history of Kuks is a depressing tale of decay, insensitive alterations and wilful destruction, culminating in 1901 in the pulling down of Sporck's mansion. Not even the Bethlehem Wood was spared, the buildings and statuary becoming so overgrown and neglected that in the late 18C much of the stone was taken away to be used in the construction of the Josefov fortress at Jaroměř. Thoughts on the transience of earthly glory might easily come to the visitor to Kuks today, and yet the sense of pathos which the place emanates is also integral to its haunting and unforgettable appeal.

Virtually nothing of the Kuks known to Sporck is to be seen on the left bank of the Labe, with the exception of the **village school**, which was formerly the *Sun Inn*. On the outskirts of the village there has also survived one of a number of timber-roofed cottages built for craftsmen, workers and servants; this particular one was once the home of the engraver M.J. Rentz. The hospice and chapel on the other side of the river are reached by a pleasant if steep path through meadows. Finally you come to a grand flight of steps built around the entrance of the chapel crypt, and leading to the **terrace** which Braun adorned with his statues of Beatitudes and Vices and Virtues (the latter group has recently been replaced by copies, the originals having been taken inside). These wildly gesticulating statues, together with Alliprandi's dynamic and richly modelled chapel façade, enliven the otherwise dreary silhouette of the hospice, the work mainly of Petr Netola.

The whole complex is at present being thoroughly and slowly restored, and only a small part of the interior can now be visited. The guided tour which you are obliged to follow takes you first inside the deconsecrated oval **chapel**, where a number of paintings have been placed, including a hunting portrait of Sporck by Jozef Ignaz Capon. Of the adjoining **hospice rooms** that you can at present visit, the most interesting is the apothecary, which is claimed to be the oldest surviving in Europe after that at Dubrovník. Another room contains a fascinating anonymous painting representing Kuks in 1724, featuring the bizarre racecourse as well as the many splendid buildings on the left bank of the Labe.

A number of statues by Braun and his workshop, including some of the 12 surviving dwarfs from the racecourse, are to be seen in the corridors and derelict courtyard of the hospice; others are in the overgrown garden (closed to visitors), together with works by Zwengs. The intention is eventually to display the choicer pieces in the renovated parts of the hospice, but as yet only the remarkable **Vices and Virtues** from the terrace are on show in the new setting.

Occupying the whole of a long dormitory on the other side of the courtyard to the chapel, these 24 figures, weathered though they are, have a quite overwhelming impact. The influence of the Roman Baroque sculptor Bernini is evident, but the pathos of Braun's figures, and the hysterical rendering of their draperies, make Bernini's works seem quite restrained in comparison. Similarly the allegorical details are taken largely from Cesare Ripa's *Iconologia* (a source book for Baroque artists), and yet Braun is remarkably free and inventive in his interpretation of them. He is perhaps at his best in his figures of the Vices, for in these he combines drama with savage and satirical naturalistic detail, some of it clearly intended to parody the nobility: the strutting woman representing Pride, for instance, is evidently some society hostess at a ball. Two further works by Braun are shown at the end of the tour, when you are taken outside and down into the chapel crypt. This austere chamber, where Sporck lies buried, has a main altar featuring a stone relief by Braun of the *Resurrection*, and a freestanding *Crucifixion* by the same artist. This latter work, Braun's only known one in wood, portrays the twisting body of Christ with extreme emotion.

A visit to Kuks is not complete without a trip to the nearby **Bethlehem Wood** (Betlém), where the most moving of all Braun's works are to be found. At one time there was a clearly marked forest path connecting the place with the hospice, but today it is best reached by car from the village of Kuks. Follow the side road in the direction of Dvůr Králové, and after 3km turn left at Žireč; after 2km you will come to a car park, from where it is about a 20min walk to the site. The various chapels, hermitages and sculptures that Sporck built in the forest here were partly intended as an alternative religious attraction to a large Jesuit college at Žireč; their site was also a reflection of Sporck's hunting interests, and indeed one of the commissioned sculptures was of the patron saint of the hunting order which Sporck had founded, St Hubert. The end result was like a mixture of a Calvary and some fantastical Renaissance garden such as Bomarzo near Viterbo. All that remains today are some heavily worn carvings and sculptures chiselled directly into boulders and rock formations found in the forest. They are disposed on either side of a long path, and recent sign-posting and tidying of the site have threatened to give the whole the bland character of some nature trail; one of the sculptures has already been protected by a ridiculous wooden roof, and the day might not be far off when all the works will have to be covered in this way. None the less there can still be few places in Europe where art of the highest quality merges so closely with Nature as it does here.

The first work to which you come is a near indecipherable *Flight into Egypt* by Petr Brandl. The following works are all by Braun, beginning with a dramatic freestanding sculpture of the hermit *Garinus*: this, the only known representation of an obscure Egyptian who chose to live like an animal as an act of penance, portrays the hermit emerging from his cave with a terrified expression (opposite there was once a sculpture of a hound rushing towards him); the life-like quality of this work was originally enhanced by the figure being painted. Next come sculptures of the Czech saint *Jan Krstu*, the Egyptian hermit *Onufrius* (1731) and *Mary Magdalene*. The latter is attached to a large rock on which are to be found the most important works on the site, including the one which gave the area its name. Adjoining the Magdalene is a powerful and deeply cut relief representing *The Vision of St Hubert* (1726); on the collar of a dog can be seen the inscription FAGUS, a reference to Sporck's name (Franz Anton Graf von Sporck). Excellently preserved reliefs of the *Nativity* and the *Journey of the Magi* (both of 1731) come next, divided from the St Hubert scene by a cave where there was originally a spring which flowed into a quadrangular pool. Further along the path is the last of the surviving monuments, *Jacob's Well* (1732), a pond once filled with water around which are the ruined figures of Christ and the women of Samaria; the water for this came from a powerful spring behind, which also supplied water for seven nearby fountains, including one which spouted up to a height of 8m. Opposite the well is a stone seat on which Braun supposedly sat while at work here. **Guided tours** May–Sept Tues–Sun until 17.00; Apr, Oct Sat, Sun 09.00–12.00 and 13.00–15.00.

To Náchod and beyond

Returning to Žireč you can continue 3km to **Dvůr Králové**, which was once the favourite residence of a Bohemian queen. Its main tourist attraction is its zoo, which was founded in 1946 by the African explorer Josef Vágner, who was concerned to save various African species from extinction; the open layout of the place is on the lines of England's Whipsnade. In the centre of the town is an elegant if much-restored hall church of c 1400 and, on the main square, a former Town Hall (now a restaurant), designed by U. Avostalis in 1572 but much modified in recent years.

Take the main road back to Jaroměř, and rejoin the D33/E67 in the direction of Náchod. Twelve km from Jaroměř is the small town and health resort of **Česká Skalice**, well known in the Czech Republic for its associations with the much-loved writer, Božena Němcová (1820–62). Němcová, Bohemia's first important woman writer and a pioneering novelist in the Czech language, attended the wooden village school here between 1824 and 1830 (this much-altered building, behind the main square, is now a memorial to her). In 1837 she married in the town, the wedding taking place in *The Golden Lion Inn* (U Českého lva), which has now been converted into a museum to her; outside is a statue of her by M. Kucová-Uchytilová. Němcová was brought up in a valley 4km to the north of Česká

Skalice, in a tiny valley now known as Grandmother's Valley (Babiččino údolí) in honour of Němcová's most famous novel, *The Grandmother*. Many of the places described in this simply written tale of country life can be recognised in the valley, such as the Úpa river, Vitorka's sluice-gate, and the charming, isolated cottage named the Old Bleaching Place. A naturalistic sandstone group of *Němcová's Grandmother* (1922) by Otto Gutfreund stands in front of an old mill, while at the nearby Baroque mansion of **Ratibořice** (remodelled in an Empire style c 1800) are kept souvenirs of Němcová's life; the mansion was the property of the Countess of Zaháň, who employed Němcová's parents in her domestic service.

The poet Jaroslav Seifert (1910–86), a self-confessed urbanite who was rarely happy while staying in the countryside, confessed in his memoirs to have spent in the Grandmother's Valley 'a few dazzling moments, which one apparently can experience only in this country and in this region, hallowed by the reality which we respect and the legends which we love ... The little Ratibořice château in the distance radiated so much artistic colourfulness that it reminded us of the best etchings by Mr Vincent Morstadt ... In a remote valley people were mowing hay, and when the warm wind was blowing gently, we smelled the mingled odours of hay, of freshly cut grass, and of the ripe meadow, from which the sun was drinking morning dew and all the hidden nectars. As we walked slowly along the meadow path, our eyes could not absorb all the colours, the white and yellow daisies, the blue veil of sage and the red poppy. There was also the tenderly pink sainfoin, not to speak of all the constantly shifting and trembling greens...'

Náchod, 8km east of Česká Skalice, is a border town with Poland and a centre of the textile and rubber industries.

History of Náchod

Náchod was the birthplace in 1924 of one of the greatest Czech novelists of today, Josef Škvorecký, who lived here until moving to Prague after the Second World War. During the war Škvorecký worked at the local Messerschmitt factory, and came to know the future film director Miloš Forman, who was staying at Náchod with his uncle. Memories of the town and of his upbringing here are the subject of his charming essay, 'I Was Born at Náchod', which is included in his collection of prose, *Talkin' Moscow Blues* (1988). A visit to the town will also be very much appreciated by anyone who has read Škvorecký's so-called 'Smiřický' novels, highly autobiographical works in which the town is thinly disguised as 'Kostelec'. Škvorecký cheekily gave to the narrator of these works the name of Danny Smiřický, whose family is supposed to be distantly related to the famous and powerful owners of Náchod's castle; Škvorecký's adoption of this aristocratic name for his fictional persona seems to have been inspired by his uncle's discovery that a 17C ancestor had managed the estates of Count Czernin. The first of these books was *The Cowards* (1958), and later ones include *The Swell Season*, *The Engineer of Human Souls* and *The Miracle Game*.

Rising on a wooded hill above Náchod's small main square is a huge Renaissance **castle** built for the Smiřický family; they had to forfeit the building following their involvement in the Battle of the White Mountain in 1620, and it came into the hands of the Piccolominis, who extended the house to the north and laid out a formal French garden; inside is a richly stuccoed chapel of 1654 and collections of Baroque and Empire furniture, and Dutch tapestries. **Open** May–Sept Tues–Sun 09.00–12.00 and 13.00–17.00; Apr, Oct Sat, Sun 09.00–12.00 and 13.00–16.00.

Four kilometres to the south of Náchod, along Road 14 to Rychnov, is the small and attractively situated town of **Nové Město**, founded in 1501 on a spur locked in a bend of the river Metuje. After a fire in 1526, the lords of the town, the Pernštejns, decided to rebuild the place in a uniform Renaissance style. The main survival of this period is a row of houses on the square, all featuring identical arcades and vaulting. The castle built by the Pernštejns was completely remodelled during the Baroque period and then re-altered between 1909 and 1911 by D. Jurkovič; the same architect was responsible for the Art Nouveau 'Ribbed Hall'.

The most important castle in the area is that of **Opočno**, 13km further south (continue on Road 14 until you reach Dobruška, and then turn right). This castle, occupying an impressive site above a lake and a ravine, is famous as the place where the treaty of the Anti-Napoleon Coalition between the Russian Tsar Alexander I, the Prussian Chancellor Hardenberg and the Austro-Hungarian Chancellor Metternich was signed in 1813. The present-day appearance of the building is due mainly to construction work carried out between 1560 and 1569 for William Trčka of Lípa, a diplomat who had recently taken part in an important mission to Genoa in Italy. The highpoint of the architecture is the magnificent three-storeyed courtyard, inspired in its detailing by contemporary Italian examples, but with tall proportions that are more characteristic of Czech Renaissance architecture. The much-altered interior contains a wide variety of collections, from Venetian and Neapolitan paintings of the 16C to 18C to hunting trophies, Flemish tapestries and African and American ethnographical objects. **Open** May–Sept Tues–Sun 09.00–18.00; Apr, Oct Sat, Sun 10.00–17.00.

Northeast of Náchod you enter an enclave of Bohemia which juts out into Polish Silesia. At **Hronov**, 6km from Náchod in the direction of Broumov, is the wooden cottage where the writer Alois Jirásek was born in 1851. Jirásek, one of the most famous Czech writers of historical novels and plays, wrote often of his native region, most notably in his chronicle U nás (In Our Country). He is commemorated at Hronov by a statue to him by Q. Kocián outside his birthplace, and an annual amateur dramatic festival called Jirásek's Hronov. **Police nad Metují**, 9km further north, has a small convent church remodelled by the great Baroque architect Kilian Ignaz Dientzenhofer, who worked extensively in this area.

Crossing the modest Falcon Mountains, you come to a broad valley which opens out to the southeast into the Polish plain of Klodzko. **Broumov**, in the centre of this valley, is a dull town but has an interesting **Benedictine monastery** (Benediktínský klášter) founded in 1322, but rebuilt by K.I. Dientzenhofer between 1728 and 1738. Only the church of the monastery is readily accessible, the rest of the complex now being occupied by several orders of nuns; you should try to persuade the nuns to allow you into the splendidly decorated library, and into the inner courtyard, each side of which has a dynamically projecting centrepiece crowned by a pediment. Othmar Zinke, the abbot who commissioned from Dientzenhofer the reconstruction of Broumov, was also responsible for providing him with work in numerous other places in the area, the intention being to promote the glories of the Catholic Church in traditionally Protestant Silesia. There are churches designed or altered by Dientzenhofer in the surrounding villages of Verneřovice, Ruprechtice, Heřmánkovice, Bezděkov, Vižnov, Šonov and Křinice. But the finest of the commissions obtained for Dientzenhofer by Zinke was that of the abbey church of Swieta Jadwiga at Legnickie Pole (Wahlstatt), which lies some 20km to the north and is now in Polish territory.

4 · Prague to Harrachov

Total distance 127km: Prague (leave by the D10/E65) 19km Brandýs nad Labem–Stará Boleslav • 35km Mladá Boleslav • 31km Turnov (Český ráj) • 42km Harrachov.

The popular resorts of the **Bohemian Paradise** (Český ráj) and **Giant Mountains** (Krkonoše) are easily accessible from Prague by way of the D10/E65, which is a dual carriageway almost as far as Turnov. Until just after Mladá Boleslav the landscape is flat and of little interest.

Brandýs nad Labem, 19km north of Prague and 2km west of the motorway, is a town dating back to the 14C and formerly had a large Jewish population. It was greatly favoured by the Emperor Rudolph II, who frequently hunted on the game reserve here. The medieval castle on the left bank of the Labe was transformed by the Emperor Ferdinand I in the early 16C into a four-wing Renaissance mansion; the building was further embellished by Rudolph II, who employed Italian craftsmen and architects in the creation of a fine series of terraces and gardens.

The once separate township of **Stará Boleslav** on the other side of the river is a smaller and generally more attractive place than Brandýs. Its quiet main square is entered through a Gothic gateway, the only survival of the town's fortifications, which were constructed originally in the 10C by the brother of King Wenceslas, Boleslav. Jealous of Wenceslas's popularity with the Czech people, Boleslav killed his brother in 929, supposedly outside the church on the opposite side of the square to the gateway (this church, now named after the murdered king, was rebuilt in the Baroque period). A statue of Wenceslas of 1894 stands in the middle of the square.

Seventeen kilometres further north along the D10/E65 is the exit to **Benátky nad Jizerou**, a village rising on an isolated wooded hill above the river Jizera. The place is dominated by its Renaissance castle, which belonged for many centuries to the Thun family. In the late 16C the Thuns were patrons to the astronomers Tycho Brahe and Johannes Kepler, both of whom stayed and worked at Benátky immediately after their arrival in Bohemia; an imaginary account of life in the castle at this time is featured in the novel *Kepler* (1981) by the Irish writer John Banville. A later guest at the castle was the composer Smetana, who was put up here while working as a music teacher to the Thuns in the early 1840s. The castle is now an old people's home, and only its courtyard and overgrown gardens can be seen. The main features of the exterior are a tall tower used by Tycho Brahe and Kepler as an observatory and, in the courtyard, some extensive and remarkable Renaissance sgraffito work featuring scenes from the Old Testament and hunting scenes; from the gardens there are panoramic views over the fertile Jizera Valley.

Back on the D10/E65, after 13km you will reach **Mladá Boleslav**, a town of 13C origin which has grown into a large industrial centre since the construction in 1895 of the Laurin and Klement factory; this factory, built at first to produce bicycles, later developed into the Škoda automobile works, the most important car manufacturers in Czechoslovakia. The dirty and poorly maintained old part of town is spread along a ridge, encircled by fragments of 13C walls; at its southern end is a medieval castle which was remodelled in the 16C and unhappily restored in recent years to house a regional museum. North of the castle is a main square containing a Gothic church heavily altered in the Baroque period, and a 16C Town Hall distinguished on the outside by sgraffito decorations of allegorical figures. On the northern outskirts of the old town is the small Baroque Church of St John (sv. Jana), with an altarpiece of 1727 by V.V. Reiner, while further north, beyond the enormous Škoda factory, you will come to the pleasant wooded suburb of Kosmonosy; in the middle of a bosky public park is an imposing Renaissance mansion which was rebuilt in the 18C and is now a school building in an advanced stage of decay.

The town of **Mnichovo Hradiště**, 10km further north, is associated with the Czech partisan Jan Šverma, who was born there, at 38 Palacký, in 1901; he was killed by the Nazis in 1944. Exhibits relating to Šverma's life are contained in the municipal museum which is housed in the 17C mansion on the town's northern outskirts. This enormous and austerely decorated building, at present closed for much-needed restoration, is preceded by an elegant though little cared-for formal garden, which in turn is enveloped by a large English-style park. Begun in the early 17C on the site of a 13C fortress, it belonged at first to Kryštof Budovec, one of the Protestant leaders who fought against the emperor Ferdinand II at the Battle of the White Mountain of 1620. The place was subsequently confiscated from him and, like many such properties, ended up in the possession of General Albrecht von Wallenstein, who by 1725 could boast of being the owner of over 50 castles and villages in Bohemia. Wallenstein himself was by no means consistent in his loyalty to the emperor, and his opportunism and scheming eventually led to his murder in Cheb at the hands of four English mercenaries. His body was afterwards brought to Mnichovo Hradiště, and now lies in a 17C Capuchin chapel to the north of the house. **Open** May–Sept Tues–Sun 09.00–12.00 and 12.45–16.00; Apr, Oct Sat, Sun 09.00–12.00 and 12.45–15.00.

The Bohemian Paradise

As you continue north towards Turnov, you will have your first glimpse to the right of the stone monoliths and dense forest that comprise the area known as the 'Bohemian Paradise'. **Turnov**, a popular centre for exploring this area, is a small and unremarkable town, but has a pleasant forested setting and a centuries-old reputation for jewellery and semi-precious stones (in particular for red Bohemian garnets); a large collection of such stones, together with panels devoted to the local jewellery industry, are contained in the municipal museum. In the northern outskirts of the town is the castle of **Hrubý Rohozec**, a late Gothic structure remodelled in a Renaissance style and containing much of its original decoration, as well as a large collection of weapons.

The bizarre sandstone rock formations of the Bohemian Paradise (Český Ráj) constitute one of several such curiosities in eastern and northern Bohemia, most notably in the Adršpach–Teplice area and near Hřensko. During the early

Mesozoic era deposits of sand and calcium clay were created here by the sea; when the water receded there remained chalk tables that were later eroded by rain water to form honeycombs, hollows, and fantastical phallic-like projections. It was during the Romantic period that these rocks protruding through the pines came to exert a widespread fascination, those in the Bohemian Paradise having the added Romantic attraction of ruined castles in the vicinity. The first attempts to scale the rocks were made in the early 19C, but it was not until the 1960s that climbers were drawn here in large numbers. The Bohemian Paradise, a relatively small area, is criss-crossed today with footpaths, and it is possible to walk its entire length, from Turnov to Jičín, in a long day.

For those visiting the area by car, from Turnov take the D35 southwest towards Jičín. Just outside the town, hidden among trees to the right of the road, stands the ruined castle of **Valdštejn**, 13C in origin but much altered in the 15C, 18C and early 19C; abandoned later in the 19C, its picturesque wooded setting helped to maintain its popularity with landscape painters and poets, among whom were K.H. Mácha.

Five kilometres further on you pass through the village of **Hrubá skála**, notable for its castle and nearby rock formations, the latter being among the most extensive in the area and sometimes described as forming a 'rock town' or 'ghost city'; to see them you should leave the main road and take the turning to the right marked Vyskeř. Back on the D35 continue for 2km and then turn right towards the hamlet of Troskovice; before reaching the hamlet you will come to a car park, from where there is a steep forest path ascending to the ruins of **Trosky Castle**, a landmark visible from far around and one of the most romantic sites in East Bohemia. Of this late 14C building (the name of which means 'Ruins'), only two towers survive, both implausibly perched on soaring pinnacles of rock. The pointed, jagged outline of the towers merges almost imperceptibly with the twisted forms of the rock, creating structures resembling those in the fantastical pen sketches of the Romantic writer and artist Victor Hugo. The taller of the two rocks can be climbed up to the base of the tower and is known as 'Grandmother Rock' (Věž Bába) to distinguish it from 'Girl Rock' (Věž Panna). The view from the top is quite magnificent and extends well beyond the surrounding trees of the Bohemian Paradise to embrace an endless undulating patchwork of meadows, cultivated fields and distant woods. **Open** May–Aug Tues–Sun 08.00–17.00; Sept Tues–Sun 09.00–16.00; Apr, Oct Sat, Sun 09.00–16.00.

Returning to your car, continue past Troskovice and rejoin the D35 at Újezd, from where it is a 12km drive to Jičín. Alternatively you can turn right at Újezd towards Mladějov and then take the first side road to the left, 3km before Jičín passing the **Prachovské Skály** rock formations. The latter include not only pinnacles but also a number of rocks perforated so as to form dramatic bridges and gateways; recent archaeological evidence shows that the site was inhabited in prehistoric times and that there was also a Slav settlement here.

An even longer detour from Újezd is to continue on the Mladějov road for 10km, all the way to the small town of **Sobotka**, on the northwestern outskirts of which is a curious conical hill supporting a bizarre 17C hunting-lodge: built for the eccentric aristocrat Jan Humprecht Černín, it contains a windowless central dining-room with echoing acoustics. Three kilometres further northwest in the direction of Žďár is the well-preserved 14C castle of **Kost**. From Sobotka you can continue a further 13km to Jičín on the main road from Mladá Boleslav.

The town of **Jičín** is well worth a visit for its arcaded main square, the best-preserved in this part of Bohemia, and lined almost entirely with Renaissance and 17C houses. Its dominant building is the **palace of Albrecht von Wallenstein**, occupying the site of a medieval castle and transformed between 1630 and 1634 into a ducal residence; the interior now houses a regional art gallery of little interest, but the elegant Italianate courtyard should be seen. The architect, the Italian Nicolo Sebregondi, was also commissioned by Wallenstein to undertake the replanning and reconstruction of much of the town, but building work was terminated after Wallenstein's murder in 1634. Assisted by his compatriots Spezza and Pieroni, Sebregondi was none the less able to complete, in a very short space of time, a relatively large number of buildings, including the **Church of St James** (sv. Jakub) in the new town, one of the first centrally planned structures of its type in Bohemia. The same team was also responsible for the large Carthusian monastery at nearby Valdice (this is now a prison and inaccessible).

Return to Turnov along the D35 and continue 42km on the D10/E65 to **Harrachov**, a popular centre for touring the Krkonoše (Giant Mountains); see Chapter 5.

5 · Harrachov to Trutnov

Total distance 60km: Harrachov (take the D14 to Trutnov, then side-roads) • 31km Vrchlabí • 29km Trutnov.

The Giant Mountains (Krkonoše) mark the northernmost frontier of East Bohemia, and are by far the most popular tourist attraction of this region, drawing large numbers of Czech and German visitors both in summer and winter. The mountains are not as spectacular as their name suggests, having gently rounded summits and being largely obscured by dense forests. Yet they include the highest mountain in Bohemia, Mt Sněžka (1600m), and give birth to one of the main rivers of Europe, the Labe (Elbe). Though mild in appearance, the mountains are also famous for their extreme and very changeable weather conditions, and indeed have average temperatures and snowfalls comparable to those of much higher peaks in the Alps.

History of the Giant Mountains
Dating back to the Palaeozoic age, 400 million years ago, the Giant Mountains seem to have acquired more or less their present shape in the Tertiary era. Their first mention in history is in a Slav document of 1110 referring to them as Krkonoše. Already by the 13C their natural resources were being exploited: gold and other metals were mined, trees cut down, and glassworks founded. In the 15C and 16C the activity of the area was greatly increased by the arrival of prospectors from Italy, who went further and further afield in their hunt for minerals and metals.

The population of the area was at this date still concentrated almost entirely along its four river valleys, the only other habitations being isolated wooden huts used occasionally by shepherds. The prospectors, with characteristic Italian exaggeration and fantasy, appear to have given colourful accounts of their excursions into the mountains, and the area soon developed a reputation for its wild aspect and supernatural occurrences. It was not so long after the arrival of the Italians that the mountains came to be known by the Latin name of 'Montes Gigantum', a reference not to their size but to a mysterious giant on whom responsibility was placed for the sudden and violent storms that are typical of this area. This giant, now called Krakonoš (Rübezahl in German), is today the tourist mascot of the area, and features in countless postcards and other souvenirs, resembling not so much a terrifying monster but rather an elderly and hirsute German hiker, complete with green jacket, hunter's hat, pipe and wooden stick.

Mining activity in the Giant Mountains declined with the Thirty Years War, and was soon superseded by cattle breeding and pasturing: the primitive shepherds' huts, known as *boudas*, were transformed by the 18C into large farmsteads. With the rapid development of tourism here after 1800, the word *bouda* came to be applied to tourist chalets and eventually to hotels—an idiosyncrasy of the area. Skiing was first practised in the Giant Mountains in the 1880s, and today the whole range has more ski-tracks and chair-lifts than any other part of Bohemia. The interests of tourism have frequently run counter to those of ecology, and the fate of the area arouses growing concern in the Czech Republic. It is an area famed for its botanical life, and is often regarded as a transitional zone between the vegetation of northern and southern Europe. Alpine plants grow in the ravines, rare flora dating back to the post-Ice Age are to be found in the upper peatbogs, while on the meadows on the middle slopes are endemic plants such as the bell-flower (*Campanula bohemica*).

In 1963 an area of 40,000 hectares was turned into the Krkonoše National Park, the first and as yet only such park in Bohemia, and—together with the park on the Polish side of the mountains—the largest natural reserve in Central Europe. However, though this has done something to check commercial exploitation of the area, there still remains the daunting problem of pollution, coming not only from nearby industrial works in Bohemia but also from others in Poland and Germany. Acid rain has affected the Giant Mountains more severely than any other part of Europe, and large stretches of forest have a pitiful desiccated look.

Harrachov, the main resort in the western half of the Giant Mountains, is a long, sprawling place which was formed in the early 18C by the joining together of three separate settlements along the Mumlava Valley. The name of the town is derived from that of the former lords of the area, one of whom, Count Ferdinand Bonaventura of Harrach, founded a glass factory here in the early 18C which is still functioning; the art of the Harrachov glass manufacturers can be seen in the showroom of the factory, in a chandelier in the Church of St Wenceslas, and in the modest **Museum of Glass** (Sklářské muzeum) which is situated at the very centre of the town. **Open** Mon–Fri 09.00–17.00, Sat 09.00–13.00.

Harrachov has the largest ski-jump platform in the Czech and Slovak Republics. One of the finest walks in the vicinity is up to the tourist chalet of *Vosecká bouda* (2hr 30min). This walk follows for most of its length the narrow, wooded banks of the Mumlava, and after 20min passes a small waterfall, a popular beauty spot; shortly before the river's source the path divides into two, the path to the right taking you to *Labská bouda* (see below), the one to the left to *Vosecká bouda*. At *Vosecká bouda*, you will find yourself above the tree level and just below the western end of the **Path of Czechoslovak–Polish Friendship**. This latter path, swerving in and out of Polish and Czech territory, follows the ridge of the Giant Mountains for 28km, up to the *Pomezní boudy* chalets. It is certainly the best introduction to the area, though until recently was out of bounds to Westerners.

Most of the main viewpoints in the Giant Mountains are accessible either by car or chair-lift. To reach these you have to make a number of turnings off the D14, which runs parallel to the entire range of the mountains while never affording any extensive panorama of them. You join the road 3km to the south of Harrachov, and follow at first the pleasantly wooded upper valley of the Jizera.

After 21km you come to the hamlet of Hrabačov, where there is a crossroad: turning right here you will soon reach the village of **Jilemnice** (outside which is a museum of folk costume housed in a mansion of 18C origin), while on turning left you will begin the steep 18km climb up to the tiny tourist chalet of **Vrbatova bouda**, on the ridge of the Giant Mountains. The views from this lonely spot are among the most dramatic in the area, and include, to the east, the rounded, forlorn peak of Mt Sněžka. You will also find around here a number of bunkers that were put up in the 1930s with the intention of warding off a Nazi invasion. Another sorry memorial—and one which serves as a salutary reminder of the potential dangers of the Giant Mountains—is to Bohumil Hanče and Václav Vrbata, two champion Czech skiers who were killed here in 1913 while skiing in adverse conditions. Northwest of this monument an unasphalted track leads to *Labská bouda*, a large, isolated and dramatically-situated modern hotel, almost literally hanging over Poland.

A short walk to the west of *Labská bouda* brings you to the source of the Labe, around which are placed the coats of arms of the major towns through which the river later passes, including the one at its estuary, Hamburg. To the east of *Labská bouda* runs a beautiful footpath which follows the Labe down to the resort of Špindlerův Mlýn (2hr 30min; see below), passing on the way a couple of waterfalls. To reach this resort by car from *Labská bouda*, you have to return all the way to the D14, and then follow this for 7km to **Vrchlabí.** This quiet town is worth a short stop to see its regional museum, which is taken up almost entirely by a permanent exhibition pretentiously called 'Stone and Life'. This didactic exhibition, displayed in a former Augustinian convent founded in 1705 by Count Maximilian Morzin, is devoted largely to the ecology of the Giant Mountains National Park, and features a taped commentary, slide projections and illuminated panels: the ground-floor rooms deal with the main vegetation belts of the mountains, while in the basement is a tank representing a cross-section of a typical mountain brook, including live birds and fish. Open Tues–Sun 09.00–12.00 and 13.00–16.00.

Leaving the D14 at Vrchlabí head north for 17km to **Špindlerův Mlýn**, the most central of the Giant Mountains' resorts, and in many ways the most pleasant. Laid out among trees and meadows sloping down to the Labe, it has a wide range of hotels: among these are the expensive *Hotel Savoy*, the cheap and humble *Starta* and the privately-owned *Hubertus*, three timber-framed structures dating from the turn of the century, the last one having originally been a pub. Špindlerův Mlýn has the additional advantage of being virtually traffic-free, as all visitors' cars have to be left in the car park on the southern outskirts.

A special permit is needed by those intending to drive from the resort up to the ridge of the Giant Mountains (8km), where there is a large tourist chalet, *Špindlerova bouda*. Two kilometres along this road is the *Koliba Myslivna*, where you can eat excellent game. Three kilometres further up is a track to the right leading precipitously down to what must be among the most attractive of the Giant Mountains' tourist chalets: these, the *Jelení boudy*, include a number of timbered 19C farm buildings with views over woods and mountain meadows.

It is possible to walk from Špindlerův Mlýn to the summit of Mt Sněžka in 3hr 30 min. To make the ascent by a combination of road and chair-lift, you have to drive back to Vrchlabí, drive east for 20km along the D14, and then turn left towards Pec pod Sněžkou. Eight kilometres before the turning is a road marked to **Hostinné**, a leading paper-making centre; in a former monastery church here, you will now find the Museum of Antique Art, a collection of casts from famous Greek and Roman statues. An alternative route to Pec pod Sněžkou is along the side-road through Janské Lázně (turn left 8km after Vrchlabí).

Janské Lázně, hidden among trees on the lower slopes of **Mt Černá** (1290m), is a small spa resort with a number of elegant buildings from the mid-19C; the popularity of the spa greatly increased after the First World War, with the discovery that its waters were beneficial for those suffering from polio. The main tourist attraction of the place is the funicular climb up Mt Černá; the funicular, completed in 1928, is the oldest in Czechoslovakia. Three kilometres beyond Janské Lázně you come to the main road connecting the D14 with Pec.

Pec pod Sněžkou, the main resort on the eastern side of the Giant Mountains, is dominated by a tall hotel block inappropriately named the *Hotel Horizont*. Those intending to take the chair-lift to the summit of Mt Sněžka, Bohemia's highest mountain, are obliged to leave their cars outside the hotel and walk from here to the chair-lift station (1.5km). The popular ascent up to **Mt Sněžka** is made in two stages (near the half-way point is an excellent small restaurant serving local specialities). The chair-lift is a very old one and inadequate for the large number of people who daily queue to use it; a new one is planned, but this is being strongly opposed by environmentalists, who are worried that the unique ecology of the mountain will be damaged even further. Crowds have been attracted to Mt Sněžka since at least 1880, when the first Czech guidebook to Bohemia described the scene as 'comparable to an ant hill: tourists with their rucksacks, salesmen with half barrels of beer or water, sedan chair porters to carry delicate ladies or stern people up and down ...' The bare summit of the mountain is not for lovers of sublime, solitary places, and is covered with a dense accretion of ugly, decaying structures: the oldest of these is a circular 16C stone building which has served both as a chapel and a pub. Matters are not helped by the summit being on the Polish border: menacing signs warn you not to cross a particular line, and there are soldiers with machine guns to reinforce these instructions.

Nine kilometres east of the junction of the Pec road with the D14 is **Trutnov**, a district capital sometimes referred to as 'the Gateway to the Giant Mountains'; its imposing main square features a number of recently restored Renaissance and Baroque houses. Trutnov is a popular centre for excursions both to the Giant Mountains and to the curious rock formations in between Adršbach and Teplice, 14km northeast of the town (follow the side-road to the Polish frontier, turn right to Chvalec, and then left to Adršbach). These rocks, comparable to those of the Bohemian Paradise (see Chapter 4), were visited by Goethe in 1770.

North Bohemia

Vast deposits of brown coal from the mountains known as the **Ore Mountains** (Krušné hory) have helped feed the industries of this now notoriously polluted region, which was developed in the 19C as the industrial epicentre of the Austro-Hungarian Empire. Devastated by bombing during the Second World War (when a large part of it became infamous under the German name of Sudetenland), and massively scarred today by factories, acid rain, and open-cast mines, this is a region that might seem to offer little of conventional tourist appeal. And yet it is a region rich in cultural and historical interest, with tantalising surviving fragments of the days when the steep, castle-crowned banks of the Labe, which runs through its centre, made it one of the great pilgrimage-places of Romantic Europe, and led the American traveller J. Bayard Taylor to exclaim in 1846: 'There is every thing which can gratify the eye—high blue mountains, valleys of the sweetest pastoral look and romantic old ruins ...'

Most of the remaining areas of natural beauty will be found in the course of following Chapter 6, which covers the region's eastern half, and includes the forested **Jizera Mountains**, the picturesque wooded gorges of the **České Švýcarsko** or 'Czech Switzerland' (a name coined by 19C Czech artists), and the large lake named after the Czech Romantic poet Karel Mácha, who found much inspiration here. Chapter 7, though winding its way along the banks of the Labe, is of interest today less for its landscape than for the former Jewish ghetto and concentration camp at **Terezín** (the region's principle attraction for tourists coming from Prague) and for the adjoining town of **Litoměřice**, which has a wonderful Baroque centre and a museum containing Bohemia's most celebrated 16C altarpiece.

The spa of **Teplice**, once one of the smartest in Europe, is visited in Chapter 8, which also goes to the Baroque château at **Duchcov**, where Casanova spent the last sad years of his life. Other sites in the western half of the region, including the delightful late 18C landscape gardens at **Krásný Dvůr**, are featured in Chapters 7A and B, which take you away from industrial pollution and into the agricultural lowlands that stretch between Prague and the spa towns of West Bohemia.

Transport
Trains
Connections with Prague: Bohušovice (9 daily; 1hr 10min–2hr); Chomutov (7 daily; 2hr 30min); Děčín (18 daily; 1hr 40min–3hr 30min); Kadaň (4 daily; 2hr 50min); Liberec (2 daily; 2hr 45min); Louny (3 daily; 1hr 50min); Most (3 daily; 2hr); Teplice (3 daily; 2hr); Žatec (5–6 daily; 2hr).
From Česká Lípa: Benešov nad Ploučnicí (12–14 daily; 25–30min); Děčín (11–12 daily; 40–50min); Liberec (11 daily; 1hr 10min–1hr 30min); Litoměřice (10 daily; 1hr 10min).
From Chomutov: Karlovy Vary (8 daily; 1hr–1hr 15min); Kadaň (hourly; 30–45min); Klášter nad Ohří (8 daily; 30min); Most (every 30min; 30 min); Plzeň (4 daily; 2hr 30min); Ústí nad Labem (hourly; 1hr 15min); Žatec (hourly; 30–45min).

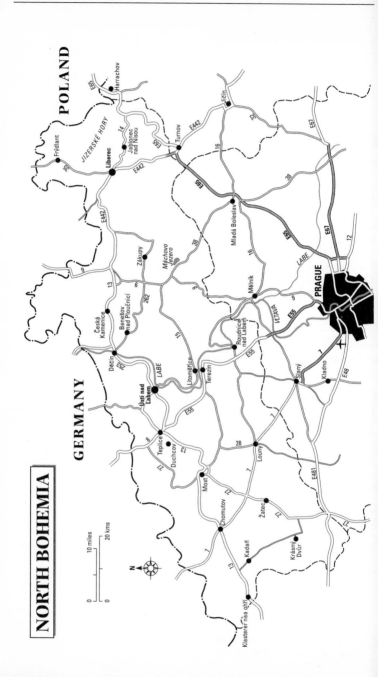

From Děčín: Benešov nad Ploučnicí (20–22 daily; 15–20min); Česká Kamenice (11 daily; 35–40min); Liberec (5 daily; 2hr–2hr 30min); Mezná (up to 8 daily; 35 mins); Teplice (8 daily; 1hr 15min).
From Liberec: Frýdlant (8–10 daily; 35min); Jablonec nad Nisou (14 daily; 30min); Ústí nad Labem/Teplice (3 daily; 2hr 30min/2hr 45min); Turnov (16 daily; 50min).
From Litoměřice: Děčín (5 daily; 1hr 10min); Liberec (7 daily; 3hr 15min); Mělník (9 daily; 30–45min); Ploskovice/Úštěk (11 daily; 12/35min).
From Louny: Libochovice (9 daily; 45min); Litoměřice (2 daily; 1hr 20min); Most (13–16 daily; 30–45min).
From Most: Děčín (4 daily; 1hr 15min–1hr 40min); Duchcov (1–2 hourly; 15–25min); Teplice (1–2 hourly; 30–40min); Ústí nad Labem (1–2 hourly; 45min–1hr).

Buses

Connections with Prague: Chomutov (up to 9 daily; 2hr 30min); Liberec (hourly; 1hr 40min); Litoměřice (hourly; 1hr 15min); Terezín (up to 12 daily; 1hr 10min).
From Děčín: Liberec (up to 3 daily; 2hr 10min); Mezná (up to 8 daily; 35 mins).
From Liberec: Hradec Králové (up to 5 daily; 1hr 50min); Vrchlabí (up to 6 daily; 2–3hr).
From Teplice: Děčín (up to 6 daily; 1hr 20min); Litoměřice (7 daily; 1hr 10min).

Boat

From Děčín: (2 daily in summer months, at 09.00 and 12.00; 30mins)

Hotels and pensions

České Švýcarsko
Hotel Mezní Louka, Mezní Louka 76. ☎ / Fax: (0412) 912 89. This old, gabled, rustic-style hotel makes a good base from which to explore the area.
Děčín
Hotel Česká koruna, Masarykovo náměstí 60, 405 01. ☎ (0412) 220 93; Fax: (0412) 266 24. Pretentiously and unappealingly furnished, but with the advantage of a good location in attractive Baroque house on the main square.
Liberec
Hotel Praha, Železná 1/1, 460 01. ☎ (048) 289 53; Fax: (048) 265 11. An imposing Art Nouveau hotel in a good location on the town's main square.
Hotel Ještěd, Horní Hanychov, 460 08. ☎ (048) 340 21; Fax: (048) 402 05. Perhaps the Czech Republic's most bizarrely situated hotel, this occupies the space-age capsule comprising the television and radio transmitter that dominates the skyline to the north of the town.
Litoměřice
Hotel Salva Guarda, Mírové náměstí 12, 412 01. ☎ / Fax: (0416) 3296. Occupies a newly restored Renaissance building on the main square.
Hotel Roosevelt, Rooseveltova 18, 412 01; ☎ (0416) 8061. Fax: (0416) 8062. Luxurious but charming hotel occupying one of the many grand turn-of-the-century mansions that make up this outlying, hill-side area of town.

6 · Harrachov to Děčín

Total distance 120km: Harrachov (leave by the E65, then Road 14) 23km Jablonec nad Nisou • 13km Liberec • E442 45km Zákupy • 30km Benešov n. Ploučnici • 9km Děčín.

South from Harrachov (see Chapter 5) the E65 descends sharply through forests for 10km to Tanvald, where you turn right on to Road 14 towards **Jablonec** 13km away. A small, industrial town set in the valley in between the Giant and Jizera mountains, Jablonec is today a place of bland and exclusively modern appearance, but it has had an international reputation over the centuries for its glass and costume jewellery.

History of Jablonec

Documents attest to glass being made in the Jablonec area as early as the 14C, but it was not until the second half of the 16C that the trade became firmly established here, the then virtually untouched surrounding forests providing the large amount of wood necessary for the furnaces. The Renaissance glass-makers of this area improved on the greenish 'sylvan' glass of the preceding period, but as yet were unable to emulate the clear glass produced at this time in Venice; the shape and decoration of the vessels created here were distinctly German, with crudely painted and engraved heraldic motifs and genre scenes.

By the late 17C extensive experimentation had led to the creation in northern Bohemia of a new type of glass involving potash and a high proportion of chalk. This glass was not only of far greater brilliance than that of before, but also had many of the properties of rock crystal and thus made possible intricate and sophisticated engraving—the hall-mark of 'Bohemian glass'. The fame of Bohemian glass spread widely, helped by the efforts of itinerant traders from the area, whose journeys established trade links with places as far apart as Moscow, Constantinople and Stockholm. However, from c 1725 the main centre for the manufacture of such glass shifted from Bohemia to Silesia, where most of the finest glass of the German Rococo was produced. The one unrivalled speciality of the Jablonec area from the early 18C onwards was the manufacture of costume jewellery, an industry which developed after c 1711 with the invention of the so-called 'Turnov paste', a pot metal of special composition which was capable of imitating many types of precious stone. Despite a serious slump in the 1930s, costume jewellery has become once again the main industry of Jablonec, and one of Czechoslovakia's most important exports.

An interest in glass and costume jewellery is the only good reason for stopping at Jablonec, which is a town almost devoid of architectural or historical monuments. The only buildings worth remarking date from the early years of the 20C, and the largest and finest of these—in the very centre of the town—houses the **Glass and Costume Jewellery Museum** (Muzeum skla a bižuterie). This tentative Art Nouveau construction of c 1900, dark and dirty on the outside, but with a completely modernised interior, was originally the export house of a large fashion jewellery company. Its clearly arranged collections have an excellent chronological display of glass and jewellery from the Middle Ages right up to modern times, including exquisite examples of Bohemian cut glass and bizarre Art Nouveau works; among the jewellery on display is 'ebony glass', which enjoyed a particular popularity in Victorian England owing to the mourning fashions of that time. **Open** Tues–Sun 09.00–16.00.

Fashion and costume jewellery is made today at the Jablonex factory on the outskirts of the town. The work produced here might not be to everyone's taste, but should you want to see it, you should visit the export showrooms, at 2777 Opletalova. The setting is at least pleasant—a handsome if over-restored Art Nouveau building.

Liberec and the Jizera Mountains

A short drive west of Jablonec, along Road 13/E442, leads you shortly into **Liberec**, the largest town in North Bohemia. This sprawling, amorphous place, dating back to the early Middle Ages, rapidly expanded in the late 19C, thanks largely to its thriving textile industry. Its most impressive monuments are largely of this period, including the eclectic former **Town Hall** (now the seat of the local council), which rises to an extraordinary height above the large and pompous central square. It was built in 1893 by the Viennese architect Neumann, who was also responsible for the rebuilding of the Altes Rathaus in Vienna. The most salient features of its exterior are its tall and steeply pitched roofs, its pointed Flemish-style gables, and its three remarkably elongated towers with complex piles of ornament tapering out to needle-like spires; beautiful stained-glass windows adorn the staircase well inside.

Southeast of the square, across the newly replanted gardens of a 16C château, is an art gallery founded in 1873, the **Oblastní Gallerie**, which has an extensive collection of 17C Dutch and Flemish paintings and 19C French landscapes, all of which reflect the conventional tastes of the German industrialist who bequeathed them, Johann Liebig; far more exciting are the Czech paintings of the 19C and 20C, most notably a group of Cubist works that include Kubišta's *Kiss of Death* and Josef Čapek's much-reproduced *Woman over the City*. **Open** Tues–Sun 10.00–14.00.

For sheer grandeur of architectural setting, the finest of the town's museums is the **North Bohemian Museum** (Severočeské muzeum) which was built at the same time as the Town Hall but in an extravagant German Renaissance style: situated northeast of the main square, along a shaded avenue exuding turn-of-the-century pomposity, it has objects relating to local history and natural history, as well as a fine collection of applied arts objects, most notably glass and porcelain; one of the lively highpoints is a Cubist tea set by Pavel Janák. **Open** Tues 12.00–17.00, Wed–Sun 09.00–17.00.

Dominating the skyline to the west of Liberec is **Mt Ještěd** (1012m), which is crowned by an enormous spaceship-like object which functions as a hotel, revolving restaurant and television tower. Another excursion can be made to the **Jizera Mountains** (Jizerské hory), which stand to the north of the town, occupying a narrow wedge of land between Germany and Poland.

The outstanding monument in this area is the castle at **Frýdlant**, 23km due north of Liberec on the main road to Poland. The castle, projecting romantically above a dense forest of pines, dates back to the mid-13C, but was largely rebuilt in a Renaissance style by the late 16C Lombard architect Marco Spazzio. One of the many Czech properties appropriated by Albrecht von Wallenstein at the beginning of the 17C, it was later acquired by the Clam-Gallas family, under whom extensive rebuilding was carried out in the 19C. The courtyard is distinguished by its extensive sgraffito decoration, while inside are a series of 19C panelled rooms of pseudo-medieval appearance. There is a gallery of works by the leading Czech Baroque artists, including a portrait of Count Sporck by P. Brandl. **Open** Apr–Oct Tues–Sun 09.00–16.00.

The village below the castle has a faded charm of its own, with a quiet main square on which can be seen (at No. 7) a pale blue 18C house decorated with stuccoed scenes of an amorous nature. Nearby stands the 16C **Church of the Holy Rood**, containing the *Sepulchre of Melchior, Catherine and Christopher of Redern* (1605–10). This work, the masterpiece of Gerhard Heinrich from Amsterdam, is one of the finest tombs to be seen in Czechoslovakia outside Prague. Though closely similiar to Venetian altar tombs of the Renaissance, it has elements that look ahead to the Baroque, such as the dynamic poses of some of its figures, and the clustering of columns in its centre.

You can continue a tour of the Jizera district by heading east from Frýdlant 10km to Hejnice, and from there take the turning to the right to nearby **Lázně Libverda**, a tiny spa-town in a verdant valley. Known for its healing springs since at least the 16C, in the 19C this pleasantly old-fashioned place attracted a number of famous visitors, including the writer Božena Němcová, the scholar and Czech nationalist Josef Jungmann, and the composer Carl Maria von Weber, who conceived here part of his opera *Der Freischutz*. The present spa buildings are of the early years of the 20C, and include a delightful promenade overlooking a small garden. A curiosity behind the village is the *Obří sud*, a restaurant taking the form of a gigantic beer barrel. The road east of Hejnice will take you into the heart of the Jizera Mountains: sadly, the devastation caused by acid rain resulting from unchecked industrial development in the Czech Republic, Poland and Germany is pitifully apparent in the burned-out forested landscape through which you have to pass.

West of Liberec

Continuing your journey west from Liberec along the E442, turn south at Lvová (26km) until you reach Mimoň (12km). The small town of **Zákupy** lies 7km to the west, along the road to Česká Lípa. The parish church is of the 16C, but the main interest is the sprawling castle on the outskirts, a construction with a mainly Baroque exterior and a formal terraced garden in a French style. Napoleon's son was made Duke of Zákupy in 1818, but never took up residence here. In 1850–53, the castle was adapted as a residence for Archduke Ferdinand, and the interior was redecorated by artists such as Josef Navrátil, who painted some rooms with Rococo motifs; the castle can today be visited on a guided tour, but the place has suffered greatly from a recent fire. **Open** May–Sept Tues–Sun 09.00–17.00; Apr, Oct Sat, Sun 09.00–16.00.

From Zákupy you can make a short detour south to what is now known as **Mácha's Region** after the Czech Romantic poet of the 19C, Karel Hynek Mácha. Take the side-road from Zákupy to Road 38, and then head south for 4km in the direction of Mladá Boleslav. You will then come to **Lake Mácha** (Máchovo jezero), a large lake used for swimming and sailing, and with densely forested hills coming directly down to the water's edge. Mácha, a native of northern Bohemia, was enamoured of the lake and its surroundings and found inspiration here for his most popular poem, *May* (1836).

From the village of Doksy, on the southern shores of the lake, you can retrace one of the poet's favourite walks by following the 8km path to the ruined medieval castle of **Bezděz** (those wishing to do the journey by car can continue south along Road 38 for a further 7km and then turn off to the left). Built in 1264–78 by King Přemysl Otakar II, Bezděz was made a royal residence in 1350 by Emperor Charles IV. After the Thirty Years War the castle, once one of the most important in Bohemia after Karlštejn (see Chapter 2C), fell into ruins. The combination of ruins, pine trees and a formidable history later made it a great place of pilgrimage for Romantics and nationalists, attracting the likes not only of Mácha but also of the composer Bedřich Smetana, who set here one of the scenes in his opera *The Secret* (*Tajemství*).

Driving west from Zákupy in the direction of Česká Lípa, you come shortly to the banks of the river Ploučnice, which you follow all the way northwest to Děčín. Twenty-two kilometres after Česká Lípa is the very attractive small town of **Benešov nad Ploučnicí**, which has a sloping and toy-like main square surrounded by old buildings. Among these are the upper and lower castles, both built by Friedrich de Salhausen in the early 16C. The lower of the two, intended for Friedrich's oldest son, is the only one which can be visited at present (the upper one is undergoing extensive restoration). Recorded early music accompanies you as you walk around its simple and tastefully restored Renaissance rooms, one of which is a well-preserved kitchen; there are collections of armoury from the Thirty Years War, 16C and 17C furniture, and—in a room above the entrance gate—a group of mainly Empire clocks.

The large industrial town of **Děčín** is attractively situated at the junction of the rivers Ploučnice and Labe, hemmed in by wooded hills. On its southeastern outskirts, dwarfed by flyovers, is a small and neglected Baroque footbridge with a sculptural group in the middle by J.M. Brokoff; these sculptures are shortly to be sent to the Lapidarium in Prague, and replaced by copies. Dominating the centre of the town, and occupying a lofty position above the Labe, is a vast castle dating mainly from the Baroque period, and preceded by formal, terraced gardens; Chopin was a guest here in 1835. Though the beautiful gardens can be visited, the building itself is currently closed for restoration, having been left in a pitiable state after being used for many years as a Soviet army barracks. Garden **open** May–Sept Tues–Sun 10.00–17.00.

Immediately to the north of Děčín begins one of the most beautiful remaining areas of natural beauty in North Bohemia. From the town right up to the German border at Hřensko, 12km away, the road follows one of the more picturesque and unspoilt stretches of the Labe (the journey can also be done by boat in the summer months), after which you should head east 5km to **Mezná**. This small village is a good base from which to explore the 35km strip of densely forested mountains and precipitous gorges that 19C painters named the **Czech Switzerland** (České Švýcarsko). A steep green-marked path leads down from the village to the river Kamenice, where a popular boat trip can be made through the river's gorge. Among the many places you can walk to in the area is to the natural sandstone bridge of **Pravčická brána**, which, at 30m long and 21m high, is the largest such bridge in Europe.

7 · Prague to Děčín

> Total distance 116km: Prague (leave by the E55) 45km Roudnice nad Labem
> • 19km Terezín • 2km Litoměřice • 26km Ústí nad Labem • 24km to Děčín.

The most direct route to North Bohemia from Prague is along the E55, a road which takes you through a predominantly flat landscape. The one prominent natural landmark comes into view a few kilometres north of Veltrusy (see Chapter 2E). This, the **Říp Mountain**, is a basaltic cone rising in isolation to a height of 459m above the surrounding fields. According to legend, Čech, the first Bohemian to arrive in the country, stood on top of this hill and was so impressed by the beauty of the surrounding landscape and abundance of game that he decided to found Bohemia. On top of the hill is a chapel founded by the 12C king Soběslav I in commemoration of a victory over the German emperor Lothair.

North of the Říp Mountain, and a 4km drive east of the E55, is the town of **Roudnice nad Labem**. This small town, built on a bend of the river Labe, is huddled around its monumental Baroque **castle**. Erected between 1653 and 1665 over the foundations of a 13C fortified residence belonging to the Archbishops of Prague, the castle was designed by the Italian-born architect Francesco Caratti. This 16-bay structure, articulated by giant Doric pilasters, is impressively grand, though it seems a tentative work in comparison with Caratti's subsequent Černín Palace in Prague, where the pilasters are replaced by a giant order of columns. The building has served for a long time as a military musical academy, and its art collections—amassed by the Pernštejns and the Lobkowicz—have been taken to Prague and Nelahozeves.

In the former stables near the palace, however, a small but select **Gallery of 20C Czech Art** (Galerie výtvarného umění) has been tastefully installed. There are Cubist works by Emil Filla and Jaroslav Král, but the highpoint of the museum is a large collection of Impressionist-style works by Antonín Slavíček: the latter were acquired by a friend of the artist, August Švagrovský, who came from Roudnice and of whom there is a portrait here by Miloš Jiránek.

Among the other attractions of Roudnice are two buildings by Octaviano Broggio, an Italian Baroque architect who settled in Litoměřice and produced much work in North Bohemia. One of his buildings at Roudnice is his reconstruction of the 14C **church** belonging to the former Augustinian monastery: this is of interest largely for its decorative detailing, in which he gives a Baroque interpretation to Gothic forms. His small **Chapel of St William**, built in 1720, is decorated by colourful frescoes by V.V. Reiner, painted in 1729 and representing the Holy Trinity surrounded by Virtues.

Regaining the E55, you could make a detour 17km to the west (on Road 246 to Louny) to visit the small village of **Libochovice**, which lies underneath the dramatic ruins of the Rožmberk fortress of Hažmberk. Within the village itself is another château, which, though still retaining many of its medieval features, was extensively remodelled in 1683–90 after passing into the ownership of the Lobkowicz family; the Baroque work was carried out by Antonio della Porta, who was assisted by fellow North Italians in the interior decorations, which include splendidly rich Renaissance-inspired stuccowork and some entertaining illusionistic frescoes. A bust over the main entrance reminds the visitor that the building was the birthplace in 1787 of the pioneering Czech doctor and leading member of the Czech national revival, Jan Evangelista Purkyně. **Open** May–Sept Tues–Sun 08.00–12.00 and 13.00–17.00; Apr, Oct Sat, Sun 09.00–12.00 and 13.00–16.00.

Back on the E55 and continuing to head north, you will soon pass on the left the former convent of **Doksany**. Founded as a Premonstratensian nunnery in 1144 by Vladislav II's queen, Gertrude, it was the scene in 1619 of a peasant revolt against the absolute authority of the Church; completely rebuilt after 1679, it was dissolved at the end of the 18C and converted into a château. The entrance gate to this vast complex is of undulating design, while inside the church is a painting by Petr Brandl of the *Birth of the Virgin Mary* and—in the dome—illusionistic frescoes by a Bohemian follower of A. Pozzo, Jan Hiebel; there are biblical frescoes by F.A. Palko in what was originally the refectory of the convent.

Terezín

Some 9.5km beyond Doksany, on the banks of the river Ohře, is the so-called **Small Fortress** (Malá pevnost) of Terezín, the sturdiest and best-fortified section of a defensive complex founded in 1780 by Joseph II and which included the adjoining town of Terezín. This grim and once impregnable complex is a fascinating example of neo-Classical military architecture, but it is essentially its terrible history, first under the Austrians, and then the Nazis, which draws visitors to the place today.

History of the Small Fortress

The Small Fortress of Terezín, known originally as Theresienstadt, was one of the more notorious political prisons in the Habsburg Empire, acquiring special fame after 1914 when Gavrilo Princip was imprisoned here for his part in the assassination of Archduke Ferdinand at Sarajevo. At the end of the First World War he was joined here by 560 soldiers who had participated in an anti-military rebellion in the North Bohemian town of Rumburk.

Though Theresienstadt was a place with a frightening reputation, conditions under the Habsburgs were as nothing in comparison to what they were to be under the Nazis, who in 1940 established in the Small Fortress a police prison headed by the infamous Heinrich Jöckel. The following year the townspeople in Terezín itself were cleared, and the town turned into a ghetto numbering c 250,000 Jews, of whom 80,000 were eventually deported to Auschwitz, Treblinka and Majdanek; many others died of hunger. For 'crimes' committed in the ghetto Jews were imprisoned in the Small Fortress, which, though officially a place for political prisoners rather than for extermination, assumed the character of a concentration camp. In April 1945 an epidemic of both enteric and spotted fever broke out here, and spread quickly owing to the appalling conditions. Soon afterwards the advancing Russian army forced the Nazis to abandon the place and its prisoners. Jöckel fled to Bavaria, but was eventually caught and himself imprisoned in the Small Fortress before being tried at Litoměřice and sentenced to be hanged.

The Jewish ghetto at Terezín occupies an important place in the history of Czech culture, owing to the large number of musicians, artists and writers who were interned here. Probably for propaganda reasons, the Nazis permitted a flourishing cultural life at Terezín, and the scores of at least 50 musical pieces composed here have survived, including works by Pavel Haas(1899–1944), Egon Ledec (1889–1944) and Hans Krasa (1899–1944); there was even an active jazz band known as 'The Ghetto Swingers', the members of which were largely drawn from the Jazz Quintet Weiss, a celebrated group from Prague. The internees were also allowed a studio for drawing, and a powerful group of drawings portraying ghetto life has been preserved in the Jewish Museum in Prague; the two men in charge of this studio were Bedřich Fritta (1906–44) and Karel Fleischmann (1897–1944). Some of the writers who survived the ghetto later wrote vivid fictionalised accounts of their experiences here, most notably the short-story writer Arnold Lustig; one author, J.R. Pick, even managed to write a humorous novel about Terezín called *The Society for the Prevention of Cruelty to Animals*, the plot of which involves a group of Jewish youngsters who catch and eat the pets of SS guards to protect the beasts from exposure to their masters. The opening story of *My First Loves* (1985) by Ivan Klíma (1931–) is a childhood impression of life in the ghetto, while both the ghetto and the Small Fortress feature in the novel *A Change of Skin* by the Mexican writer Carlos Fuentes, who visited Terezín in 1961 and 1963.

The Small Fortress is today a memorial to Nazi atrocities, and a symbolic ceme-tery commemorating those whom they murdered has been laid out in front of its main entrance. There are excellent and very informative English-speaking guides to accompany you on the harrowing visit to the fortress, which has been little altered since Nazi times, even to the extent that the chilling and ironic words *Arbeit Macht Frei* ('Work Makes Free', the slogan of the concentration camps) have been left above the entrance gate to one of the yards. Among the many cells that you are shown is one intended originally for 40 prisoners but which was filled with over 100 people by the Nazis; grimmer still is a small damp cell into which 60 Jews were crammed and forced to sleep standing up. You are shown too the cell in which Princip was incarcerated, a space containing today mementoes both of him and the Sarajevo assassination; Princip was condemned to 20 years imprisonment, but died here of tuberculosis after only four years. **Open** Apr–Sept daily 09.00–18.00; Oct–Mar 09.00–16.00.

A 10 minute walk west along the main road will take you from the Small Fortress to the **Main Fortress** (Hlavní pevnost), which lies on the western side of the Ohře river, and comprises a grid of drab, colourless buildings set within a star-shaped line of multiple red-brick fortifications, the grimness of which has today been tempered slightly by the planting of gardens within the former moats. This is now the actual town of Terezín, part of which is taken up by a small garrison, and the rest by a declining population of around 1500, three-quarters of whom are over retirement age, and the rest gypsies. In 1939, prior to being expelled to make way for the Jewish ghetto, 3500 Czechs had been living here. The main attraction for tourists today is the recently established **Ghetto Museum** (Muzeum ghetta), which documents the history of Terezín in a lively and informative way, and with the use of chilling video clips. **Open** Apr–Sept daily 09.00–18.00; Oct–Mar 09.00–17.30.

Around the corner, at 130 Pražská, is a restaurant and coffee-house called *Sabra*, which promotes itself as the 'first Jewish Restaurant in Terezín', and occu-pies a former nursery for soldiers' families that was later converted into an overcrowded block for Jewish inmates of the Ghetto; the park which it overlooks, once flanked by a hotel and casino used by the SS, had been out of bounds for the Jews.

Litoměřice

The large industrial town of Litoměřice, once the third or fourth city in Bohemia, rises 2km to the north of Terezín on the right bank of the Labe and just above its confluence with the Ohře. Founded in 1230, it has kept parts of its mighty original fortifications to this day. Much of the medieval town was destroyed in the Thirty Years War, however, and most of the old buildings that survive today are of the Baroque period. Polluted and with an overall covering of grey, Litoměřice might not be one of the most cheerful places in Bohemia, but it has much of architectural interest, as well as an excellent art gallery; and, as throughout so much of the Czech Republic, it is slowly being improved by much-needed restoration work. The architects who left the greatest mark on the town were Giovanni Broggio and his son Ottavio: the former, an Italian immigrant, settled in around 1668 at Litoměřice where his son—the more important of the two—was born that same year.

At the southeast corner of the large and dirty main square, the **Mírové náměstí**, is the **Church of All Saints** (Všech svatých), a late Gothic foundation remodelled by O. Broggio in 1718, and containing rich stucco decorations inside. The narrow Jesuitská leads south from here to the **Jesuit Church of Our Lady** (Panny Marie), a large red ochre building built by O. Broggio between 1704 and 1731; a bridge connects the church with the former Jesuit college where the leading Czech nationalist and compiler of the first Czech–German dictionary, Josef Jungmann, taught between 1799 and 1815. Heading off from the northeastern corner of the main square is the Velká Dominikánská, on which stands O. Broggio's **Church of St James** (sv. Jakub), distinguished by a tall and powerful façade now in a deplorable condition.

The main monuments of Litoměřice lie west of the main square, beginning with the **North Bohemian Gallery of Fine Art** (Severočeská galerie výtvarného umění) on the Michalská. Housed in the former Renaissance Town Hall, it was founded in 1874 and is one of the oldest museums in northern Bohemia. On the ground floor is to be seen the museum's greatest treasure, indeed one of the finest and most famous cycles of Renaissance painting in Bohemia—the six remaining panels of the so-called **Litoměřice Altarpiece**.

The Litoměřice Altarpiece

The panels, representing scenes from the Passion and the Life of the Virgin, were probably painted around 1500. The unknown artist, sometimes identified with the German Hans Elfelder, is always referred to as the Master of Litoměřice, and is also thought to have been responsible for the celebrated frescoes in the upper level of the St Wenceslas Chapel in St Vitus's Cathedral, Prague. The artist, who was a far more sophisticated painter than his contemporaries in Bohemia, was almost certainly a court painter to Vladislav Jagiello, and probably executed the Litoměřice Altarpiece for the Church of All Saints attached to the Royal Palace in Prague Castle. It is likely to have been removed from that church after 1541, when the building was damaged by a severe fire; the surviving panels are generally identified today with a group of scenes of the Passion documented as being presented in 1633 to the Church of All Saints in Litoměřice by the imperial magistrate of this town, Herold of Stod.

In the same room as the powerfully realistic panels by the Master of Litoměřice is an expressive *Crucifixion* by Wolfgang Katzheimer (d. 1508). The rest of the ground floor mainly comprises mediocre local works of recent times, but upstairs is a good representative collection of Czech art from the 15C to 20C, including works by Brandl, Škréta, Braun, Mánes, Slavíček and Mucha. **Open** Apr–Sept Tues–Sun 09.00–12.00 and 13.00–18.00; closes Oct–Apr 17.00.

You can ask one of the staff of the museum to take you to the **Mácha memorial room** at Máchova ul. 10 (a good 5 minute walk away to the south): this small museum to the poet Karel Hynek Mácha has been set up in the house where the popular Romantic poet died in 1836. In 1938, when this part of Bohemia was seized by the Germans, the Czechs were allowed to move the tomb of their beloved Mácha from Litoměřice to Prague's Vyšehrad.

If you turn north at the western end of Michalská you will reach the scant ruins of the town's castle, converted in the 19C into a brewery and now being made into a cultural centre. Turning instead to the south you begin the climb along the quiet Dómské up to the cathedral, passing as you do so the small, jewel-like church of **St Wenceslas** (sv. Václav): built in 1714–16 by O. Broggio, this oval structure with a lively undulating profile is similar to Christoph Dietzenhofer's chapel at Smiřice (see Chapter 3). This whole area of town has the quality of a sleepy suburb, and the cathedral itself stands on a large shaded and overgrown square surrounded—as in a cathedral close in England—by houses that once all belonged to the clergy. The **Episcopal Cathedral of St Stephen** (sv. Štěpán) was founded in 1057 but rebuilt after 1655 to designs supplied by J.D. Orsi and G. Broggio. The light and simple interior contains several fine works of art, including an altarpiece of St Peter by K. Škréta in the second chapel to the right, and two paintings by Cranach in the third chapel to the right. The high altar has a splendid gold-and-black frame encasing a dark and warped canvas by Škréta representing *The Stoning of St Stephen*.

From Litoměřice a short excursion can be made to the large country house of **Ploskovice**, 6km northeast of the town (take Road 15 to Žitenice). This building, the secular masterpiece of O. Broggio, was designed in 1720, but extensively redecorated inside in the 19C. The interior, featuring an amusing grotto flanked by atlantes, has various rooms in a Rococo style by Josef Navrátil; the gardens were laid out in 1850.

The journey from Litoměřice to Děčín can be made by winding your way along the banks of the Labe. The valley narrows shortly after leaving Litoměřice, and steep verdant hills roll down directly into the river, calling to mind certain stretches of the Rhine Valley. High above the river, on the southern outskirts of Ústí nad Labem, looms a castle which appealed to the Romantic generation with the same fervour as did the famous Rhineland sites, and which had a name in German which could have been taken from a Gothick novel—Schreckenstein.

Střekov, as this place is more prosaically known in Czech, was begun in the 14C, rebuilt two centuries later and destroyed at the end of the 18C. The castle's Romantic appeal, based partly on the beauty of its site, was certainly heightened by the numerous legends attached to the building, such as the story of Mathilde of Schreckenstein being discovered here with her lover by the dreaded huntsman Kuba: the enraged Kuba had her thrown from the battlements, and her cries are still said to echo around the ruins on dark summer nights. Many of the great Czech Romantics, such as the poet Mácha, visited the site, but the most famous visitor was Wagner, who came here in 1842 and was inspired to begin work on his opera *Tannhäuser*. Today the beauty of the place is somewhat marred by the ever-encroaching town of **Ústí nad Labem**, a river port and large chemical centre. Ústí was one of the North Bohemian towns to suffer most during the Second World War, but it has kept its Gothic cathedral—a hall-church rebuilt in around 1500 with star-vaulting. The town was the birthplace in 1728 of one of Europe's leading neo-Classical painters, Anton Rafael Mengs. A less attractive reason to remember the town, and indeed one that caused an international outcry in 1998, was the construction here in that year of a 5-metre high wall to segregate the local gypsies from the Czech residents. The town council defended this shockingly racist action on the grounds that it was for the gypsies own good.

Děčín (see Chapter 6) is 24km to the northeast, on the E455.

8 · Děčín to Karlovy Vary

Total distance 146km: Děčín (leave by Road 13/E442) • 34km Teplice • 8km Duchcov • 22km Most • 25km Chomutov • 15km Kadaň • 42km Karlovy Vary.

The E442 extends the whole length of North Bohemia, from Jablonec (see Chapter 6) to Karlovy Vary (see Chapter 10). After Děčín (see Chapter 6) it runs in between the now polluted Central Bohemian Highlands and a series of mining towns and industrial centres that make this whole area one of the most built-up in the Czech and Slovak Republics.

Teplice

It was not so long ago that this area was renowned for its great beauty, the spa town of Teplice being once the most popular of all Bohemia's spas, and inspiring Wagner to write to his sister: 'Oh this town of Teplice with its endless vistas; it is really the most beautiful place I know.'

History of Teplice

The spa at Teplice was founded by King Vladislav II's queen, Judita, as early as the 11C, and its curative waters had supposedly been discovered three centuries earlier by a shepherd. The fame of the spa was well established by 1793 when a disastrous fire destroyed much of the town. In the end, however, the disaster turned out to be beneficial, for, on the instigation of the local aristocrat Prince Johann Nepomuk von Clary und Aldringen, a major building programme was begun which soon was to turn Teplice into one of the smartest spas in Europe. Wagner, Chopin, Liszt, Pushkin and Ibsen were among the many celebrities who took the waters here in the 19C, though the two whose names are most closely associated with the place are Goethe and Beethoven. In 1812 both found themselves together at Teplice, and Beethoven described one of their meetings in a letter to the writer Bettina Brentano, an account which throws much light on the respective personalities of the two men. Apparently they were both walking in the park when the young third wife of the Austrian Emperor Franz I passed by. Goethe politely bowed and stood aside, but Beethoven walked resolutely on, later reminding Goethe of their own superiority in relation to the royal party.

If 1812 was a cultural landmark in the history of the town, 1813 was a political one, with Franz I, Alexander I of Russia and the Prussian king Friedrich Wilhelm III signing at Teplice a famous treaty against Napoleon. The spa continued to prosper until the 1880s, when the flow of the spring waters was badly affected by flooding in the nearby Döllinger mine. Since that time the waters at Teplice have had to be pumped, but it was only in recent years, with the digging of wells over 1000m deep, that the curative waters have come to be available again in significant quantities. The reputation of Teplice with foreign visitors has never recovered, however, due largely to the rapid industrial growth of the town since the end of the last century.

The extensive, noisy and polluted modern town of Teplice should not deter visitors from coming here for it shields a quiet and delightful spa town, spaciously arranged and with numerous fine old buildings, in particular from the neo-Classical period. At the centre of the old spa town is the **Castle Square** (Zámeké náměstí), dominated by a 20m-high **plague column**, one of the finest in Bohemia, and the work of Matthias Braun. The **castle** itself, of medieval origin, was completely transformed during the neo-Classical period, and has housed since 1897 a regional museum featuring period rooms, archaeological, historical and natural history collections, and rooms devoted to Beethoven and Pushkin; its enormous gardens, now a public park, contain two lakes and various temples and other follies. **Open** Tues–Sun 10.00–12.00 and 13.00–17.00.

The **chapel** adjoining the castle is one of the earliest examples in Bohemia of the neo-Gothic style, while adjacent to this is the Baroque **parish church** of c 1700. Directly in front of the castle, on the opposite side of the square, is Lázeňská, a narrow pedestrian street running between the buildings that comprise today the former J. Fučík Sanatorium. The pale blue building with the Palladian-inspired double colonnade is a reconstruction of the **Municipal Baths** (Městské lázně) of 1838–39; opposite is the yellow Zlatá harfa house, where a plaque commemorates Beethoven's stay in 1811.

Plague column of the Holy Trinity (1718) by Matthias Braun

The road north from Teplice leads after 15km to the nearby German border, from where it is a short drive to Dresden. Five kilometres after leaving the town, and immediately before climbing into the forested mountains marking the border, is the long village of Dubí, which is now the centre of a roadside red-light district full of luridly lit windows, and bars with names such as *Sexi Tropicana*; hundreds of Germans now cross the border in search of the cheap sex on offer from Czech and Romany prostitutes.

Duchcov

Travelling instead west of Teplice, after 8km you will reach the small mining town of Duchcov, which is built around a château formerly owned by the Wallenstein family. The château, which once formed part of a great complex featuring a theatre, riding-school, and a hospice, has frequently been compared with the eastern Bohemian castle of Kuks (see Chapter 3), an analogy reinforced by its important picture gallery founded in 1723, and its once incomparable collection of statuary by Matthias Braun. However, if Kuks today is only a shadow of its former self, Duchcov is a paler reflection still, and its present dilapidated condition and shabby surroundings testify to an especially poignant history of decline.

History of Duchcov

The original castle at Duchcov was a late 16C structure belonging to the Lobkowicz family and designed by the Italian architect U. Aostalli. The property was acquired by the Wallenstein family in 1642, and remained in their hands until 1921. Between 1675 and 1685 the property was rebuilt and extended by the French architect J.B. Mathey, whom Jan Bedřich of Wallenstein had summoned from Rome. In 1722 Jan Ferdinand Schor laid out the castle garden in a Baroque style, and six years later Ottavio Broggio brought to completion in the garden's western half a large hospice containing frescoes by V.V. Reiner and statuary by Matthias Braun.

Braun was summoned again to work at Duchcov in 1735–38, when he created almost 60 sculptures for the garden, many of which were placed—as at Kuks—along the terrace in front of the hospice. The château was remodelled between 1812 and 1818, and the garden relaid in an English style, a transformation which led to the selling off of many of Braun's statues; those that remained rapidly fell into ruin. A fire in May 1945 gutted the large castle chapel, destroying an altarpiece featuring a painting by Reiner and statues by Braun; the hospice was pulled down in 1959 to make way for a coal mine. The sad history of Duchcov was compounded in 1988 with the robbery of most of its important paintings, a fact of which you are not informed when purchasing your tickets for the obligatory guided tour.

The castle forecourt, facing the town's main square, contains the surviving statuary executed by Braun for the garden and hospice; the rebuilt castle chapel stands adjacent to the main block of the château. The tour of the interior is long and tedious, and the most impressive of the rooms that you are shown is the first one, its ceiling decorated by Reiner with scenes representing the military glories of the Duke of Wallenstein. The other rooms have a stripped, desultory quality, and display odd pieces of furniture on loan from the Museum of Decorative Arts in Prague, a collection of porcelain, and the sad remains of the Wallenstein picture gallery, most notably a curious picture by Paul Troger of *Adam and Eve and their Children*, and a painting attributed to G.D. Tiepolo of the *Rape of Europa*; the missing pictures include works by Spranger, Cranach, K. van Mander, Škréta and Liška. The rooms scarcely evoke the atmosphere of the house in former times, and it is difficult to imagine that such luminaries as Schiller, Goethe, Beethoven, Chopin and Tsar Alexander I were once guests here. The one person whose stay at Duchcov is remembered here today is **Giacomo Casanova**, whose life is the subject of a series of historical panels arranged in the rooms in the wing where he lived from 1785 to his death in 1798. A visit to Duchcov will be appreciated by anyone seriously interested in Casanova's life, for though the building has changed greatly since his day, the whole place highlights in its starkness and shoddiness the sense of desolation and abandon which the celebrated lover is known to have experienced in his last years.

A tour of Duchcov is completed by wandering into the gardens, which have now been turned into a public park; a hideous modern pavilion has been erected to

---

Giacomo Casanova

Born in Venice in 1725, Giacomo Casanova was brought up virtually as an orphan, and learnt from an early age how to live off his wits, in particular from the gullibility of the aristocracy. As a lover his career began when he was 16 or 17, reputedly initiated by two girls in the same bed; his passion for sexual intrigue soon equalled that of his other life-long loves, gambling and eating macaroni. By 1755 news of his increasingly scandalous sexual doings reached the ears of the Inquisition, and he was thrown into the notoriously damp and rat-infested prison of Venice's Ducal Palace; his remarkable escape from this was to provide him with a dinner-party story which was to win him invitations from many of the leading aristocratic families of the time. After 1757 his life and sexual adventures became ever more complex and took him to every corner of Europe. Eventually, in 1785, he befriended Count Wallenstein, who offered him token employment as librarian at Duchcov.

While at Duchcov, Casanova published various unreadable books on history and philosophy, and also wrote his delightful *Memoirs*, for which he was to be best remembered after his death. In one passage of these he referred to the continual mist which appeared to hang over Duchcov, and how he longed for some rays of sunshine to break through it and cheer him up. Elsewhere in this book he referred to his writing as 'the only thing which has kept me from going mad, or dying of grief in the midst of the discomfort and pettifogging annoyances daily caused me by the envious wretches who live with me, in this castle of Dux [Duchcov]...' His particular enemy at Duchcov was the house steward, Master Faulkircher, to whom he addressed a series of acrimonious letters at the back of the *Memoirs*. Matters came to a head on 11 December 1791, when Faulkircher supposedly arranged for one of his men to beat up Casanova in the streets of the town. Casanova died in the château in 1798, reputedly saying on his deathbed, 'I have lived as a philosopher and die as a Christian.'

display the frescoes by Reiner that decorated the dome of the destroyed hospice. **Open** May–Sept Tues–Sun 09.00–18.00; Apr, Oct 09.00–16.00.

From Duchcov an excursion could be made to the important convent of **Osek**, which lies 8km to the west, directly under the shadow of the wooded hills that mark the border with Germany. Osek was a Cistercian community founded at the end of the 12C. Its earliest surviving part is its chapter house of c 1240, joined by steps to a 14C cloister and featuring richly carved columns and other detailing that suggest links with the Cistercian architecture of Burgundy. The present convent church was begun in 1712 and is the ecclesiastical masterpiece of Ottavio Broggio. Its dynamic ground-plan, a variant of one by J.B. Fischer von Erlach, is matched by a tall and superb undulating façade, profusely decorated, and with a rich play of contrasting shapes and surfaces. **Open** Apr, Sept Tues–Sat 10.00–12.00 and 13.00–16.00, Sun 13.00–16.00; May–Aug closes 17.00 .

West of Duchcov

Regaining Road 13/E442 south of Duchcov, you will soon reach the small spa and mining town of **Bílina**, which has a 17C castle and late Gothic parish church. **Most**, 10km further west, lies at the very centre of North Bohemia's coal mines, and has a modern and largely unappealing look; the town is so polluted that the local school children have been provided with respiratory masks since November 1990. The place has retained a magnificent parish church, which was built in the form of a Saxon hall-church by Jakob Heilmann of Schweinfurt in the early 16C; the great Benedikt Reid is known to have been invited here in 1519 to settle a dispute over Heilmann's work, and he might well have had an influence on the graceful and elaborate vaulting.

West of Most the road turns briefly into a dual carriageway before reaching, after 25km, the town of **Chomutov**, a large mining town and centre of iron and steel industries, but with a number of buildings from the late Gothic, Renaissance and Baroque periods; late Gothic cellular or diamond vaulting, a peculiarity of Bohemia, can be seen in the parish church (in the space under the tower) and in a room of the Town Hall.

After Chomutov the landscape becomes hillier and more wooded, and continues to do so all the way to Karlovy Vary. At Verněřov, 15km west of Chomutov, turn left to **Kadaň**, a quiet town raised above the Ohře river, and with perhaps the best-preserved old centre in North Bohemia. A thriving town in the Middle Ages, Kadaň was destroyed by the Swedish army during the Thirty Years War but rebuilt in the 18C, and has not much changed since then. The long main square, with its arcaded houses and central plague column, has a particularly harmonious appearance. From here a wide pedestrian street, J. Švermy, leads to the tall Mikulovická Gate, the oldest remaining part of the town's fortifications.

You can regain Road 13/E442 by taking the road which follows the Ohře to Klášterec nad Ohří. Suspended above the river, in a wooded, isolated spot on the outskirts of Kadaň, is a former **Franciscan monastery** dating from the end of the 15C; the small complex, at present boarded up and rapidly decaying, has in its cloisters and chapter house what is reputed to be some of the earliest cellular vaulting in Bohemia (c 1480).

The tree-lined stretch of the Ohře valley west of Kadaň is especially attractive and can be appreciated to the full from the terrace of the small Baroque château at **Klášterec nad Ohří**. The surrounding gardens, now a public park, were once adorned with statues by J. Brokoff. The ones that have survived have been haphazardly assembled outside the château, the interior of which now contains a collection of porcelain made in the local Thun factory, which was founded in 1794. The village Church of the Holy Trinity was built in 1665–70 to the designs of C. Lurago.

Road 13/E442 snakes its way along the Ohře almost all the way to **Ostrov** (22km), a small town in the administrative region of West Bohemia. A plaque on the town's former monastery (now a school) records that the first concentration camp in Czechoslovakia was established here; nearby, in a wooded park, is an 18C château serving as a small art gallery and local museum.

For Karlovy Vary see Chapter 10.

9 · Prague to Karlovy Vary

A. Via Louny and Žatec

Total distance 147km: Prague (leave by Road 7/E442) • 59km Louny • 23km Žatec • 65km Karlovy Vary.

Leaving Prague on Road 7 to Slaný you pass through featureless built-up countryside. After Panenský Týnec, with its ruins of a Clarissine convent begun in 1532, the landscape improves, and you are offered a sweeping vista over the valley of the middle Ohře and across to the distant hills marking the Saxon frontier.

Louny, 10km further west, is situated on the Ohře and has retained sections of its fortifications as well as a number of medieval and Renaissance buildings. Its chief treasure is the **Deanery Church of St Nicholas** (sv. Mikuláš), built after 1518 in replacement of an earlier structure which had burned down the year before. The architect was the great Benedikt Ried, whose hand is immediately apparent in the triangular tent-shaped roof which dominates the exterior. But the great joy of the church is its wide and elegant pale yellow interior, which takes the form of a great hall divided into three naves of four bays each. From slender concave-sided piers ribs are sprung in tree-like fashion to form the playful and elaborate vaulting characteristic of Ried's work. The one incongruous element in this light and harmonious space is the heavy Baroque high altar of 1700–08.

Continue west along Road 7 for another 13km and then turn south to **Žatec**, a further 10km drive. This is famous hops country, and everywhere you look there are poles supporting what is sometimes referred to as 'green gold'. Žatec, the main hop-growing centre in the Czech Republic, rises on a spur of land above the Ohře, and has an excellently preserved centre, with a chain of old squares lined with Gothic, Renaissance and Baroque buildings; the Renaissance Town Hall was rebuilt in 1770 and given its onion-shaped dome. From Žatec you can either head straight to Kadaň 22km to the west and join up with Chapter 8 to Karlovy Vary, or else make a loop to the south to take in the country house at Krásný Dvůr (see Chapter 9B).

B. Via Lubenec

Total distance 123km: Prague (leave by Road 6/E48) • 47km Řevničov • 38km Lubenec • 38km Karlovy Vary.

The direct road from Prague to Karlovy Vary, Road 6/E48, runs through dull, gently rolling countryside and goes through no town or village of any great interest. At **Lubenec**, however, it is worth making a detour 17km to the north to visit the country house at **Krásný Dvůr** (take Road 226 to Podbořany, and, just before reaching there, turn left towards Buskovice and then take the first road to the right). Nearing Krásný Dvůr you enter the flat hop-growing landscape which extends towards Žatec (see Chapter 9A). Your first view of the property is of a wooded hill from which peeps what seems like a Gothic spaceship: this is not the house itself but one of the many follies in the extraordinary park.

Though the park is the main attraction of Krásný Dvůr, the house itself is by no means without interest. The present structure, commissioned by František Josef Czernin, was built in 1720–24 by František Maximilian Kaňka; it remained the property of the Czernin family until 1939, when it was commandeered by the Nazis. The pale yellow exterior, altered slightly in the late 18C, has an elegant French look. The interior is excellently preserved and is filled with fine 18C furniture, porcelain, stoves and clocks; among the paintings are works by Brandl, Škréta and Elisabeth Vigée-Lebrun, and a curious set of pictures of dogs by the Baroque artist P.V. Berger.

The park at Krásný Dvůr, laid out between 1783 and 1793 by the forester Jan Wachtl and the gardener Franck of Červený Hrádek, was the brainchild of Jan Rudolf Czernin. Czernin, a keen botanist, respected the existing trees in the grounds (such as an oak reputed to be over 1000 years old), and insisted also that all the new trees and shrubs to be planted were indigenous or semi-indigenous. As for the park's eclectic range of follies, this might well reflect the interests formed by Czernin in the course of a Grand Tour of Europe undertaken in 1779. Many hours could be spent wandering around the huge park and coming across unexpected delights at every corner, such as lakes, a rotunda, an obelisk, temples, a red house in a Dutch style, and a Chinese pavilion. The highpoint, both literally and architecturally, is the neo-Gothic belvedere, a soaring octagonal structure with an upper room supported by buttressing, and from which a good view can be had over the park and out towards the surrounding plains and distant Ore Mountains.

WEST BOHEMIA

GERMANY

GERMANY

0   10 miles
0   20 kms

N

Jáchymov   E442

Karlovy Vary

Sokolov   Loket   Bochov   E48

Frantriškovy Lázně

Cheb

E48   E49   E49

21

24

Mariánské Lázně   Teplá

Plasy   27

Planá   201   Konstantinovy Lázně

Tachov   198   21   E49

Žebráky   199   Stříbro   E50   Plzeň   E50

E50   Kladruby

200   26   Stod   E53   E49

Horšovský Týn   21   Nepomuk   E49   Lnáře

Klenčí Pod Cherchovem   Domažlice   Švihov

26   22   Klatovy   188

E53   22   187

Sušice

Kašperské Hory

Železná Ruda

West Bohemia

In pleasant contrast to northern Bohemia, this is a relatively unpopulated region with a land area nearly half-covered by dense forests, and with beautiful, little-spoilt mountain scenery marking its border with Germany. But its fame as a tourist area is due essentially to its northern spa towns of **Karlovy Vary**, **Mariánské Lázně** and **Františkovy Lázně**, which are still redolent of the days when they formed Austro-Hungary's answer to France's Côte d'Azur. They form the backbone of Chapter 10, which also includes the quiet and very German-looking small towns of Cheb and Loket.

At the opposite, southern end of the region are the now extensively protected **Šumava Mountains**, which can be reached from the spas by following Chapter 11, passing on the way Santini-Aichel's spectacularly original 'Baroque Gothic' church at **Kladruby**, and the well-preserved small town of **Domažlice**, which lies in the heart of a region well-known for its folklore traditions—the **Chod Region**. The Šumava Mountains themselves, together with their gateway town of Klatovy, with its lively main square and gruesome catacombs, are the main subject of Chapter 12, while Chapter 13 deals principally with the region's industrial capital, **Plzeň**. The latter town, though mainly visited on account of its world-famous beer, has a sensational Gothic cathedral in the middle of an important historical centre laid out in the shape of a chessboard.

Transport
Trains
Connections with Prague: Domažlice (2 daily; 2hr 40min); Karlovy Vary (6 daily; 3hr 20min–4hr); Mariánské Lázně/Cheb (8 daily; 2hr–3hr 30min); Plzeň (12 daily; 1hr 35min).
From Cheb: Františkovy Lázně (13–16 daily; 10min); Karlovy Vary (15 daily; 50min–1hr 10min).
From Domažlice: Klatovy (6–7 daily; 1hr).
From Karlovy Vary: Kadaň (8–9 daily; 50min–1hr 15min); Teplice (15 daily; 2hr).
From Mariánské Lázně: Teplá/Karlovy Vary (6–8 daily; 35min/1hr 30min).
Plzeň: Domažlice (12 daily; 50min–1hr 45min); Klatovy (10 daily; 1hr–1hr 20min); Plasy (9–13 daily; 30–45min); Stříbro/Mariánské Lázně/Cheb (14 daily; 30–50min/1hr 40min/1hr 35min–2hr 30min); Železná Ruda (3–6 daily; 2hr 10min–2hr 45min).

Buses
Connections with Prague: Jáchymov (2 daily; 3hr); Karlovy Vary (10 daily; 2hr 30min); Plzeň (18 daily; 1hr 20min–2hr).
From Karlovy Vary: Děčín (up to 4 daily; 3hr 45min); Jáchymov (up to 18 daily; 50min); Loket (up to 15 daily; 25min).
From Plzeň: Horšovský Týn (7 daily; 1hr); Karlovy Vary (up to hourly; 1hr 30min).

Hotels and pensions
Cheb
Hotel Hvězda, náměstí Krále Jiřího z Poděbrad 4–6, 351 01. ☎ (0166) 225 49; Fax: (0166) 225 46. Externally attractive hotel in 18C building with long hostelry traditions.
Františkový Lázně
Hotel Slovan, Národní třída 5, 351 01. ☎ (0166) 942 841; Fax: (0166) 942 843. A faded, and reasonably-priced hotel dating back to 1808.
Karlovy Vary
Grandhotel Pupp, Mírové náměstí 2, 360 91. ☎ (017) 310 9111; Fax: (017) 322 4032. This is the place to stay for those with a lot of money and a sense of history.
Hotel Embassy, Nová Louka 21, 360 01. ☎ (017) 322 1161; Fax: (017) 322 3146. A small family-run hotel occupying a pastel-coloured Baroque mansion, with each room individually decorated in a 19C style.
Villa Basileia, Mariánskolázeňská 4, 360 01. ☎ (017) 322 4132; Fax: (017) 322 7804. Modestly priced and characterful small pension in turn-of-the-century riverside villa.
Mariánské Lázně
Villa Butterfly, Hlavní třída 655, 353 01. ☎ (0165) 484 100; Fax: (0165) 762 10. Housed in an extravagantly reconstructed building at the centre of the town, this is a 1920s pastiche complete with two-tiered marble lobby.
Hotel Helga, Třebízského 428/10, 353 01. ☎ / Fax: (0165) 762 41. Occupying an Art Nouveau mansion in a quiet location away from the main street, this is a family-style hotel with mahogany furniture and other tasteful furnishings.
Plzeň
Hotel Continental, Zbrojnická 8, 305 34 Plzeň. ☎ (019) 723 6479; Fax: (019) 722 1746. A hotel with a curious history, recently restored to its early 20C splendour.
Penzion V Solní ulici, Solní 8, 305 31. ☎ (019) 723 6652. A cosy three-bedroomed pension housed in a 16C building off the main square.

10 · Karlovy Vary to Mariánské Lázně

Total distance 84km: Karlovy Vary (leave by Road 6/E49) • 46km Cheb • 38km Marianské Lázně.

Karlovy Vary

Karlovy Vary, lying picturesquely along a deep forested valley at the confluence of the rivers Teplá and Ohře, is perhaps the most visited town in the Czech Republic after Prague. Described since at least the 19C as the 'Queen of the Spas', it is better known under its German name of Carlsbad, a name which conjures up memories of a vanished aristocratic Europe.

History of Karlovy Vary

The town of Karlovy Vary, founded in 1370, grew up around a series of 12 hot mineral springs lined along the banks of the narrow river Teplá and discovered, according to tradition, by the Emperor Charles IV while on a hunting expedition. For over two centuries the place had little more than 100 buildings, but by the end of the 16C it had already begun to attract a distinguished aristocratic clientele; the international reputation of its curative waters spread rapidly after the Thirty Years War. The first bathing establishment was erected in 1704, bathing being at first the only way in which the waters were used: a popular treatment of the day was to be immersed in the hot water until the skin was sore, a barbaric practice which gave rise to the term *Hautfresskur* ('flaying-baths'). By around 1766 the fashion for bathing was temporarily abandoned, to be replaced by a scarcely more appealing drinking cure which involved the taking of between 50 to 70 cups of the hot, sulphurous liquid every day. Such excessive drinking was later to be heavily criticised by the local physician, Dr David Becher, who in 1789 carried out the first scientific analysis of the waters.

Building activity at Karlovy Vary intensified in the early 19C, and the town spread up into the surrounding hills as well as northwards towards the Ohře river, where it gradually merged with the villages of Bohatice, Drahovice and Tuhnice. The opening up of the railway to Karlovy Vary in 1870–71 increased yet further the flow of visitors to the town and led to the construction of majestic turn-of-the-century apartment blocks with names such as Venezuela, Brasilia and America that served to emphasise the international character of the place.

The full list of famous people who have visited Karlovy Vary over the centuries could extend for pages, but among the most celebrated visitors are Albrecht von Wallenstein (1630), Augustus of Poland (1691), Peter the Great (1711 and 1712), Frederick I of Prussia (1732), Leibnitz (1712), Maria Theresa of Austria, Goethe (14 seasons), the Prussian Field Marshal General Blücher (1812–13), Schiller (who spent his honeymoon here), Bismarck and Karl Marx (1874–76). The town has played an especially important role in the history of music, and its distinguished musical visitors have included Bach, Beethoven (who delighted the public by the playing of a free fantasia at a charity concert here), Liszt, Brahms, Paganini, Smetana, Janáček and Dvořák (who conducted here the first performance of the *New World Symphony*). A guidebook to the town of 1871 recorded that 'there is scarcely a piece of classical music of any recognised merit which does not figure in the programme at some concert during the seasons.' The practice of regularly performing classical music in the town's colonnades continues to this day, and in recent years a number of other important musical activities have been instituted, most notably the annual Dvořák Music Festival held in the autumn. The local symphonic orchestra is one of the oldest in Europe, and in 1984 celebrated its 150th anniversary.

In terms of sheer numbers of visitors, Karlovy Vary is perhaps more popular now than ever, though it is customary among travel writers to look back nostalgically to bygone days and bemoan the decline of the place today. Certainly the present-day visitors are neither as aristocratic nor as international as before, and are taken to a great extent from the German

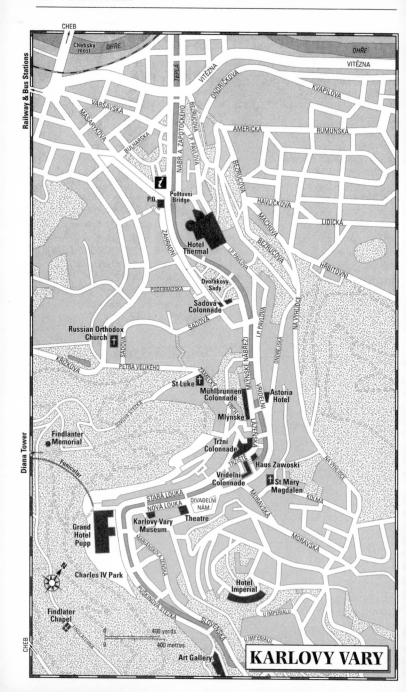

KARLOVY VARY

middle classes, whose presence here in large numbers have made Karlovy Vary one of the more expensive Czech towns in which to stay. The spa cure today—considered to be effective for the treatment of diabetes, duodenal ulcers and digestive and intestinal diseases—is based largely on a combination of bathing and drinking. As at Mariánské Lázně, one of the more bizarre sights at Karlovy Vary is that of hundreds of people slowly walking up and down the colonnades with specially shaped porcelain jugs that allow the water to be sucked through a long spout.

In addition to remaining an active spa town, Karlovy Vary has had an extensive industrial quarter along the banks of the Ohře since the beginning of the last century. Two of the traditional industries are porcelain and glass-making, the most famous factories being the Pirkenhammer Porcelain factory (founded in 1803) and the Moser Glassworks (founded in 1889). Another traditional industry (established in 1807) is the making of the popular herb-flavoured liquor known as *becherovka*. Bearing the name of the great Dr Becher, it is often jokingly described as the town's thirteenth spring, and the only one which works.

By far the most attractive approach to Karlovy Vary is from the south, along the side road which branches off the Mariánské Lázně road and winds its way along the Teplá. A more usual approach, however, is from the adjoining train and bus stations, situated in the drab and industrialised northern half of the town, where turn-of-the-century gloom competes with Socialist Functionalism of the 1950s and 1960s.

The beauty of Karlovy Vary is concentrated around the banks of the Teplá, which can be reached from the stations by walking the whole length of the broad Masarykova. You will end up at the Poštovní bridge, which marks the northern entrance to the spa town, and from which point onwards Karlovy Vary takes on the verdant picturesque aspect so familiar from photographs and paintings. The narrow, steep and restlessly winding valley in which the spa town is set is covered in its upper reaches with a dense covering of firs, pines, oaks and beeches, rising above which are numerous splendid monuments of the *belle époque*. The way in which the town snakes around the river creates an ever-changing sky-line and is liable also to make you lose your sense of direction, an experience known even to those who have stayed in the town for a long time.

When you reach the Poštovní bridge head south along the Teplá, keeping the river always to your left. As you walk towards the Dvořák Park you will note on the other side of the river a large modern complex: this is the **Thermal Sanatorium** (1975), a concrete monstrosity with a pleasant outdoor swimming-pool, and a useful box-office that will provide you with information about the town's cultural events (including the important annual film festival that has been held in Karlovy Vary since 1958). On the southern side of the small but elegant Dvořák Park (Dvořákovy sady) is the **Sadová Colonnade** (1881–82), an elaborately decorated wrought-iron work in white and grey by the prolific Viennese architects Fellner and Helmer.

Further to the south is the **Mühlbrunnen** or **Mill Colonnade** (Mlýnská kolonáda), a long and sober Classical structure designed in 1871 by the Prague architect Josef Zítek. It overlooks a square adorned with potted palms, beyond which is a diverse row of buildings standing on the opposite side of the Teplá (which at this point disappears briefly under the pavement). Directly in front of the northern section of the colonnade, where concerts are held, is a half-timbered and very Germanic-looking building housing a bar and restaurant called *Petr*: this was originally the House of the Golden Peacock, where Peter the Great is said to have stayed. Further south along the same row is the popular *Café Astoria* and the adjoining hotel of that name, a 1920s construction with a splendid ceramic decoration.

Lázeňská, the busy pedestrian street running between the Mühlbrunnen Colonnade and the Teplá, was once named after Karl Marx, who stayed several times in Karlovy Vary towards the end of his life, signing himself in at the hotel as Mr Charles Marx from London: though under continual police surveillance, the local police had little to report on him other than that he took the waters regularly at 6am and loved walking. Marx's stay here used to be commemorated by what was, surprisingly, the only Marx Museum in the Communist world; this has now been replaced (at No. 3 Lázeňská) by the bland Golden Key Museum, which has a dull collection of paintings and prints of Karlovy Vary over the centuries.

Further down the street, and overlooking the river, is the Art Nouveau **Haus Zawojski** (now the Živnostenská Bank), one of the finest buildings in this style in West Bohemia. Designed by the Viennese architect Karl Haybäck, the Haus Zawojski was built between 1899 and 1901 under the supervision of the local architect Karel Heller. The man who commissioned it, Felix Zawojski, was a successful tailor who had trained in Paris and Vienna and had worked in India, North America and on the French Riviera before deciding to settle at Karlovy Vary; his social prestige had been enhanced by marrying an academic Hungarian painter called Marie Stennpier. On the ground floor was a luxury glove shop, while above was a tailor's workshop, a doctor's surgery and—in the attic—a chemical laboratory. The building was sold to a bank in 1911, and divided into flats after 1945. After a long period of restoration it is now once more a bank.

On the opposite side of the street to the Haus Zawojski is the entertaining **Tržní Colonnade** (1883): this elaborate wooden structure by Fellner and Helmer, recently reopened after restoration, resembles the casing of a Swiss cuckoo clock. The colonnade is at the very centre of Karlovy Vary, facing the oldest and most important spring in town, and underneath the town's **castle**—a Baroque structure which replaced Charles IV's hunting-lodge, and is now joined to the lower town by an old lift. The Teplá is once again covered at this point, and over it has been built a square supporting on its eastern side a colonnade incorporating the famous Sprudel spring. The original structure, another work by Fellner and Helmer, was dismantled in 1939 by the Nazis, who used its copper roof for making armaments. It was replaced in 1975 by the fussy and uninspiring **Vřídelní Colonnade**, which was originally named after the Soviet cosmonaut Yuri Gagarin, who stayed in Karlovy Vary in 1961 and 1966. The **Sprudel spring** is not only the oldest in town, but also the hottest and most productive, attaining temperatures of 72°C, and producing daily over two million litres of water; at regular intervals throughout the day it spurts up to a height of over 10m, watched by an admiring crowd.

At its southern end Tržiště joins the Stará Louka, which runs alongside the now exposed Teplá, and was thought of in its heyday, when it was called the Alte Wiese, as a luxurious shopping street rivalled only by Vienna's Kärntnerstrasse. It is still lined—all the way down to the *Grand Hotel Pupp*—with restaurants, shops (including, at No. 40, the main outlet of the Moser Glass Factory), and cafés, notably the marbled *Elefant Café*, the best place for cakes and coffee.

Retracing your steps to the Vřídelní Colonnade, you should now walk south along the other side of the river, beginning at the **Church of St Mary Magdalene**, which stands on a raised site to the east of the colonnade. This important work by Kilian Ignaz Dientzenhofer, built in 1732–36, takes the form of an elongated oval, and has an exterior featuring a convex west façade and concave sides. South from here is Divadelní náměstí, on the southern side of which is the town's imposing **theatre** (1884–86), a neo-Baroque edifice by Fellner and Helmer and closely similar to their theatre at Odessa: it was here that Dvořák gave in 1893 the première of the *New World Symphony*, and it was also here that Hitler made a speech in 1938; the interior is well worth visiting if only to see the extensive painted decoration by a team of artists that included the young Gustav Klimt (whose self-portrait, playing the flute, stares at the audience from the bottom right-hand corner of the marvellous main curtain).

Further south, and almost opposite the *Grand Hotel Pupp*, is the **Karlovy Vary Museum** (Karlovarské muzeum), containing collections relating to the history and geology of the town, as well as a large collection of local porcelain and glass. Before crossing the river and visiting the *Grand Hotel Pupp*, you could continue heading south until you cross the Charles IV Gardens and reach the former **Kaiserbad** or Bathhouse I, as it is less glamorously known today, another grandiose structure by Fellner and Helmer (1892–95). Inside this oppressively marbled building there was installed during the late 1980s the first casino in Communist Czechoslovakia. The interior is memorable largely on account of its wall decorations by Wilhelm Schneider (1914), one of which is a gigantic representation of all the celebrated visitors to have come to Karlovy Vary.

The vast, dazzlingly white **Grand Hotel Pupp** represents the ultimate in wedding-cake architecture, and is surely one of the most impressive-looking Grand Hotels in Europe. The longest-running hotel establishment in town, after the 1989 Revolution it reverted back from *Grandhotel Moskva* to its original name, by which it has always been affectionately known.

History of the hotel

Founded by the (Konditorei) Johann Georg Pupp in 1793, the hotel was rebuilt in the late 19C, the principal architects involved being the ubiquitous Fellner and Helmer. It was shortly before the First World War that the infamous Colonel Redl—the subject of John Osborne's play *A Patriot for Me* and of a film by the Hungarian director István Szabó—handed over Austrian military secrets to the Russians. In 1938 the hotel was extended, and further additions and modernisation were carried out in questionable taste in the 1970s. Though renovated in 1981, further restoration is intended, and it is hoped eventually to remove the modern additions and bring back as much as possible of the building's turn-of-the-century character.

A remarkable amount of the original interior has survived, for instance, the mirrored and exuberantly stuccoed **Small Hall** (Malá dvorana), and the adjoining French restaurant, an elegant neo-Rococo space. But the great surprise of the interior is the unexpectedly large **Concert Hall**, a white and neo-Baroque stucco concoction constituting the most heavily ornamental work by Fellner and Helmer in Karlovy Vary. On its stage—flanked by busts of Smetana and Dvořák—is an organ comprising 66 keys and 4788 pipes, while on the staircase leading up to the upper gallery are two large paintings by Willhelm Schneider (1907). Before leaving the hotel you should ask to see Room 167, a large suite built for the Emperor Franz Josef (who never came here) and which has been left virtually unchanged since then: reserved today for important guests or honeymoon couples, it contains a huge bathroom equipped with all the most up-to-date appliances of the turn of the century.

Continuing walking south along the Teplá from the *Grand Hotel Pupp*, you will find yourself skirting extensive and densely wooded parkland which spreads up the hilly ground behind the hotel. As you walk along the riverside Puškinova stezka towards the town's art gallery—the last sight of importance on the western banks of the Teplá—you will see high on the hill on the other side of the river the *Hotel Imperial*, an establishment even more monstrous in size than the *Grand Hotel Pupp*, and intended when built to supersede the latter in luxury. Constructed just before the First World War by the French architect Ernest Hebrard, it never recovered from being converted into a hospital during the Second World War. The **art gallery** (galerie umění) is devoted exclusively to 20C Czech art, and has works by Jakub Schikaneder, Jan Preisler, Antonín Slavíček, Václav Špála, Otakar Kubín and Emil Filla; of particular interest is a *Cubist Circus* by Bohumil Kubišta, and a *Cubist Head* (1914) by Josef Čapek, the brother of the writer Karel. **Open** Tues–Sun 10.00–12.00 and 13.00–18.00.

The paths on either side of the gallery will lead you up into the wooded hills above the town, where numerous fine and celebrated walks can be taken. It is in the upper reaches of Karlovy Vary, away from the main tourist thoroughfare along the Teplá, that the most poignant memories of old Karlsbad are to be found. Within the vast forested park into which you climb you will come across numerous memorials to celebrities who have stayed in the town, as well as several chapels now mainly in an abandoned state. One of the latter is the wooden **Findlater Chapel**, paid for by the Earl of Findlater, a great benefactor of the town. Behind this is a look-out tower, now called the **Diana Tower** (Diana rozhledna): an extensive panorama can be had from the top. Nearby is an obelisk to the same Earl of Findlater ('Nature's Friend'), from where you can make your descent back into the town by way of the Sovova stezka. This will take you to Zámecký, next to the Evangelical **Church of St Luke** (sv. Lukáše), a red brick, neo-Gothic relic of Victorian England.

From here you could descend directly down to the Tržní Colonnade, passing on your left at No. 41 the former *Hotel Germania* (now the spa hotel *Olympie*), where Marx was put up on his visits to Karlovy Vary (this is marked by a plaque). Alternatively, you could turn left at the church on to Petra Velikého, and then, after passing a miraculously surviving statue to Marx, turn right into the splendid but shabby Sadová, which is lined by an impressive group of residential buildings. Steps at the top of the street lead up to the recently restored Russian Orthodox **Church of SS Peter and Paul** (sv. Petra a Pavla) of 1897, a gilded, bulbous-domed apparition. Descending the street you will pass in turn (respectively at Nos 729/32, 956/28 and 239/4) plaques recording the visits to Karlovy Vary of Janáček, Karel Čapek and Dvořák. Eventually you will find yourself back at the Sadová Colonnade.

Leave Karlovy Vary on Road 6/E48 to Cheb. Just off the road, on the western outskirts of the town, is the **Moser Glassworks**, a building dating back to the late 19C, and with a much-visited showroom, where you can not only buy modern examples of Moser ware but also look at the models made for distinguished clients of the past. At its most extravagant Moser ware features a deli-cate combination of gold and glass, examples of which are the models prepared for such monarchs as Alfonso XII of Spain, Victor Emmanuel of Italy, King Carol of Romania, and Edward VII of England.

Shortly before Nové Sedlo, you should briefly leave the E48 to visit the small town of **Loket**, romantically situated above a green and wooded bend of the Ohře river. Its impressively fortified castle, dating mainly from c 1400, is best seen from the old bridge across the Ohře, perched as if in some illustration of the picturesque above a steep and verdant bank. On the other side of the building is a small town resembling an ageing toy, with a narrow main square lined with old buildings. One of these is the *Hotel Bílý kůň*, where a plaque records numerous visits by Goethe. When in his seventies, Goethe met here the last great love of his life, Ulrike von Lewetzow; she was 17 at the time, and refused his marriage proposal. Goethe's stay in the town is also documented in a small museum installed within the castle, where you will also find displays of local porcelain and glass. **Open** Apr–Oct Tues–Sun 09.00–12.00 and 13.00–17.00; Nov–Mar 09.00–16.00.

You can regain the E49 by following the Ohře river in the direction of Sokolov, a modern town happily bypassed: the billowing smoke from its chemical indus-tries helps to explain much of the pollution both at Loket and Karlovy Vary.

Cheb

Cheb, raised on a spur of land above a flat, wide stretch of the Ohře valley, is an industrial and agricultural centre which has also managed to keep over the centuries a large and evocative medieval quarter.

History of Cheb

Since earliest times Cheb has occupied a border position between Bohemia and Germany. Archaeological evidence has been used by the Czechs to show that the original settlement was a Slavic one, but the first document to mention the place—of 1061—indicates a large and growing German popu-lation in the area. In 1167 the town became an eastern outpost of the Holy Roman Empire after Friedrich Barbarossa founded a fortress here. It was not until 1322 that the town was definitely acquired by the Czech crown, but even so the German element in the population was to remain a large and powerful one. Significantly the place remained a strongly Catholic town during the Hussite Wars, and had several bloody conflicts with the Hussites. The strategic position of Cheb at the entrance to Bohemia led to a highly insecure period during the Thirty Years War, with both sides using it as an important base for their military operations. Taken by the Saxon armies in 1631, it was retaken the next year by Albrecht of Wallenstein, and then occupied by the Swedes in 1647. In Czech history Cheb is known above all as the place where the great Wallenstein lost his life, murdered in 1634 after having been betrayed by his colonels.

Cheb took many years to recover from the devastation of the Thirty Years War, and a full recovery was not to take place until the 19C, thanks to the wealth brought in by the newly founded spa resort at Františkovy Lázně, and to rapid industrialisation. After the First World War the Germans in the town had sufficient influence to make Cheb part of the ill-fated Deutsches Böhmen province, an independent region which managed to survive for only one month. The fate of the German population in Cheb was sealed once and for all after the Second World War, when most of the Germans fled, leaving the town for many years seriously underpopulated.

Cheb was the birthplace of one of Germany's greatest Baroque architects, Balthasar Neumann (1687–1753). The son of a local cloth-maker, Neumann rose from his humble origins to become the favourite architect of the Schönborn Prince-Bishops of Würzburg and the consultant to virtually every prince in southern Germany.

As with Karlovy Vary, Cheb does not appear at its best when approached from the railway station, an ugly red-brick structure situated in an area of the town filled with large and grimy buildings. The attractive part of town is its northern half, beginning with the outstanding **George of Poděbrady Square** (náměstí Krále Jiřího z Poděbrad), which is named after the Czech king who did most to secure the political and financial security of the town. The sloping wedge-shaped square, which widens as it descends to the north, is lined on all sides with a superlative series of 15C to 18C houses. Near the top of the square, at the crossing with Březiny Ova, is the yellow, 18C **House of the Two Archdukes** (U dvou arcivévodů), who are depicted on a medallion. This is Cheb's oldest surviving inn, and an establishment much-vaunted in pre-First World War guides (it is now a clothing shop). Lower down, on the opposite side of the square, is the Baroque former Town Hall (1728), a building designed by G.B. Alliprandi and with a fine interior recently converted to house the regional **art gallery** (galerie výtvarného umění), which contains Czech 20C works. **Open** daily 09.00–17.00.

Attached to a gabled Gothic house further down on the same side is an 18C palace grandly decorated with a giant order of pilasters and exuberant Rococo stucco. But the buildings that leave the most lasting impression are a group of tall, free-standing and tightly packed houses at the lower end of the square: known collectively as the **Špalíček** ('block'), these half-timbered structures, used by Jewish shopkeepers in the 16C, give to this square a predominantly medieval and Germanic character. A large Renaissance house behind them, at the very end of the square, is famous as the place where Wallenstein was stabbed to death by a soldier acting under the orders of the Irish commander of the town garrison. The building now has the more placid function of regional **museum** (Chebské muzeum), where, in addition to the usual collections of local history, is displayed a large and rare group of old bicycles. **Open** Tues–Sun 09.00–17.00.

Immediately to the north of the square is the large parish **Church of St**

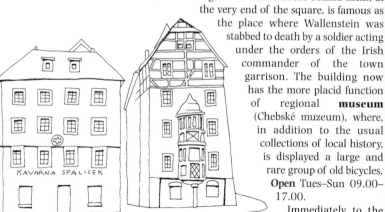

The Špalíček, a group of 16C merchants' houses

Nicholas (sv. Mikuláš), a 13C foundation rebuilt as a hall-church in the 15C, and much altered and restored since then, including by Balthasar Neumann in the 18C. A medieval church of more genuine appearance is the nearby **Church of St Bartholomew** (sv. Bartoloměj), which you will pass to your left as you walk north from the square down Kamenná, the street immediately to the west of St Nicholas; this 15C hall-church, containing fragments of wall-paintings, now serves as a small museum of Gothic statuary. The street on which it stands leads down to the river, through a bosky, and rather neglected, part of town. Projecting above the river's wooded banks is the **castle** founded by Friedrich Barbarossa in 1167, the entrance to which can be reached by turning left from Kamenná into Křížovnická, and from there into Dobrovského. It was at a banquet given here on 25 February 1634 that Wallenstein's loyal officers were killed, an event which immediately preceded the murder of Wallenstein himself. The castle and this tragic occasion were featured in Schiller's drama *Wallenstein* (1799), for which the author came to Cheb to research in 1791. Schiller's contemporary, Goethe, a frequent visitor to the town, befriended the castle's executioner.

The castle, strengthened in the 13C and again in the Baroque period, is now in a ruinous state, but has kept extensive sections of the early medieval walls. Of particular interest is its much restored late 12C **chapel**, a two-storeyed structure in a transitional Romanesque style with a crypt featuring crudely carved capitals and corbels. The surrounding overgrown forecourt is now used as an outdoor cinema, while in the rooms adjoining the sturdy entrance gate is a museum containing prehistoric finds and other items of local interest. **Open** Apr–Oct Tues–Sun 09.00–12.00 and 13.00–16.00; May, Sept till 17.00; June–Aug till 18.00.

Continuing to walk up Dobrovského you will soon come to Dlouhá, which heads back towards the upper end of the town's main square, passing on the way the town's two remaining churches of interest. One is the **Monastery Church of St Francis** (Františkánský kostel), remarkable above all for its 14C cloister. The other is the **Church of the Poor Clares** (sv. Klára) of 1707–11, a work generally attributed to Christoph Dientzenhofer, and featuring this architect's characteristic system of intersecting vaults: inside the latter building has now been installed a small museum relating to the life and work of Balthasar Neumann. Behind the Franciscan church is the town's modest neo-Classical theatre of the early 19C.

Františkovy Lázně

The spa town of Františkovy Lázně (Franzensbad) lies just 4km to the north of Cheb and was only made an independent township in 1852. The second oldest of West Bohemia's three most celebrated spas, it does not enjoy the beautiful surroundings of its two rivals: instead of being hemmed in by a densely wooded valley, it is encircled by marshes and flat parkland. None the less it is by far the quietest of the three places, and has been little disturbed by modern development. To Goethe, the place was a 'paradise on earth'.

History of Františkovy Lázně

The curative effects of the local water—initially called 'Cheb water'—were known back in the Middle Ages, and it is even said that in 1196 the water was drunk for medicinal purposes by Prince Jindřich Břetislav, brother of the Czech king Přemysl Otakar I. Cheb mineral water was recommended in the 16C by the great scientist and physician Paracelsus, and in the following century was exported to Saxony. Profits from the sale of the water helped pay for the restoration of Cheb's fortifications in 1670.

The decision to create a spa community around the mineral springs was not taken until 1793, the main person behind the scheme being the local doctor Bernhard Adler. The first season was inaugurated later that year, and in the following year the place was named 'Village of Emperor Francis' in memory of a visit paid by Francis II of Austria; in 1803 it was renamed 'Francis's Spa'. Twenty-four boarding houses had been constructed by 1810, and from 1829 onwards the surroundings of the spa were landscaped by Martin Soukup and his son Antonín. Among the distinguished visitors in the 19C were J.G. Herder, Goethe, Beethoven (1812) and Božena Němcová (1846–47), the latter staying here at the same time as Goethe's last great love—Ulrica von Lewetzow.

The spa treatment, involving both a drinking cure and mud baths, is used for limb, heart and circulatory disorders, but is especially renowned for its success with female sterility and other female problems.

Františkovy Lázně is a small place, having as its nucleus a square grid of streets surrounded by parkland on all sides. The main spring, the **Francis spring** (Františkův pramen), is on the southern end of the grid and encased in a 1963 reconstruction of one of the spa's original neo-Classical buildings. This small and engagingly simple Greek Doric rotunda of 1793 reflects the clean and peaceful character of the town. Inside are shiningly bright bronze pipes carrying what might possibly be one of the world's largest supplies of free mineral water—the townspeople of Cheb frequently come here to take it away in large jerry cans. Next to the building is a Doric colonnade of 1844, equally modest in its architecture, and also coloured—as are so many of the buildings here—the deep yellow known once as *Kaisergelb* or 'imperial yellow'. In the gardens in front of the spring is a hideous modern bronze of a seated naked boy holding a fish, a work which for some reason has come to be regarded as a symbol of the spa: the penis shines like a holy relic thanks to the popular belief that those who touch it will become pregnant, presumably a desperate last resort if the spa waters fail.

North of the spring runs the town's main street, Národní, where you will find what little there is of animation in Františkovy Lázně. The first building which you come to on the left is the former casino, a late 19C structure in the style of a Palladian basilica; a street behind it leads towards the **Luisa spring**, which is covered by a round and wide arcaded structure of c 1800 resembling an open umbrella. Continuing northwards up Národní, the next building on the left is the *Hotel Slovan* (formerly the *Three Lilies*), which dates back to 1808 and has attractive 19C furnishings. Further up the street at No. 4 on the same side is the house where Beethoven stayed in 1812 (a plaque commemorates this). The avenue leads into a small park with a lake and turn-of-the-century bandstand. Turning right before the park into Ruská you will come after a few minutes to the **Božena Němcová Theatre,** a good example of Czech 'Cubist' architecture of the 1920s. The street which runs south of the theatre, Dr Podhoreckého, represents the eastern side of the town's grid, and skirts the Smetana Gardens (sady Bedřicha Smetany) in the middle of which is the grand, turn-of-the-century *Hotel Imperial*. On the other side of the street, at No. 8, is the local **museum**, which has exhibits relating to the history of Františkovy Lázně, including a group of old bath-tubs. **Open** Tues–Fri 10.00–12.00 and 13.00–17.00, Sat, Sun 10.00–16.00.

In the gardens to the south of the Francis spring are the **Glauber springs** (Dvorana Glauberových pramenů), discovered in 1919 by Dr Glauber and housed in a building representing a wonderful Art Deco interpretation of the Classical style; the bright interior is particularly fantastical and appealing, with its ceramic-tiled floor, bronze and marble furnishings, and ethereally light colonnade. A building in a similar style covers the **Natalia spring**, a good 15min walk to the east, in a wooded setting on the edge of marshland.

Mariánské Lázně

After returning to the outskirts of Cheb on Road 21, you continue following this road for another 27km to Mariánské Lázně. Better known as Marienbad, this was the favourite spa of the British monarch Edward VII, and is idyllically set in a landscaped valley hemmed in by pine-clad slopes.

History of Mariánské Lázně

The local cold springs—of which there are 40—have been known since at least the 16C, but the wooded area in which they are situated remained wild and barely disturbed up to the beginning of the 19C. The land belonged to the Premonstratensian Monastery of Teplá (18km to the east), and it was an abbot of this institution, K.K. Reitenberger, who, together with a doctor called J.J. Nehr, was eventually to found the spa of Mariánské Lázně in 1809. Its popularity grew rapidly, and by the second half of the century its hitherto neglected site had been transformed into a complex of some 90 hectares of parks and gardens, laid out mainly by the landscape architect Václav Skalník (d. 1861). As with all the main Bohemian spas, the list of famous people who stayed here in the 19C and early 20C is formidable, and there are monuments to many of them scattered around its parks. Goethe, inevitably, was one of them, and it was while staying here that he paid his fateful trip to Loket and fell in love with 17-year-old Ulrike von Lewetzow, the muse behind his *Marienbad Elegy*. Gogol wrote *Dead Souls* here, and Wagner composed *Lohengrin*. Chopin came here, as did Weber, Goncharov, Turgenev, Ibsen, Lehár, Mark Twain, Maxim Gorky, Jan Neruda and Franz Kafka. But the final seal of approval was the popularity which the place enjoyed among monarchs, in particular Edward VII of England, a frequent visitor. Mariánské Lázně was not simply a centre of convalescence and entertainment, but also the scene of much diplomatic activity, culminating in a famous meeting in which Edward VII attempted to persuade Franz Josef to sever Austria's alliance with Germany.

The formidable, nostalgic associations of the name Marienbad lived on well after the collapse of the Austro-Hungarian Empire and were exploited by the French film-maker Alain Resnais in the title of his pioneering, hallu- cinatory film, *Last Year in Marienbad*. Needless to say, this film has absolutely nothing to do with the real spa, but its repeated image of static, isolated figures in a formal French park has strongly influenced the perception of Mariánské Lázně among those who have never come here. The lush and informal English gardens to be found instead might come as a surprise to many.

The side-road which descends into Mariánské Lázně from the wooded hills to the north brings you directly into the spa section of the town, and shows off the place and its surroundings to their best advantage. However the more usual approach is from the south, where the bus and railway stations, as well as the main parking area, are to be found. It is an exceptionally elongated town, and from the two stations you would be best advised to take a No. 5 trolley bus, which will lead you along Husova and into the **Hlavní Třída**. This long avenue constitutes Mariánské Lázně's main thoroughfare and runs along the whole north–south axis of the town. Bordered to the east by parkland incorporating the Ušovický river, it is lined on its western side by grand and now largely restored late 19C residential blocks and hotels.

Shortly after crossing Dykova, you will note rising behind the buildings to your left the gaudily painted **Russian Orthodox Church** (Pravoslavný chrám) of 1901, the interior of which has an unusual iconostasis made with ceramics from Loket. Just to the north of this building along Ruská (a street parallel to the Hlavní třída) is the neo-Gothic **Anglican Church**, a red-brick structure now restored and used as an exhibition space: its previous decrepit state had inspired the former *Times* correspondent Richard Bassett to write in his nostalgic *Guide to Central Europe* (1987): 'Where once a monarch [Edward VII] and his entourage regularly worshipped, there remains only dust and decay.' **Open** Tues–Sun 09.00–16.00. Near the northern end of the Hlavní třída is a small and sparse museum relating to Chopin's stay at Mariánské Lázně.

Turning right at the end of the Hlavní třída you will find yourself in the historical centre of town. The original spring, the **Cross spring** (Křížový pramen), is surrounded by a rectangular neo-Classical colonnade of 1818 and surmounted by a dome crowned by a cross—a reference to the spring's original ecclesiastical owners. Adjacent to it to the south is the long **Colonnade** (Kolonáda), formerly named after Maxim Gorky, a grandly embellished and recently restored cast-iron work of 1889 cast in the Blanské ironworks. At the other end of the Colonnade is the modern '**Singing Fountain**' (Zpívající fontána), a wide fountain with jets syncopated at every odd hour of the day with music (and with coloured illumination at night) to create popular water spectacles.

East of here is the náměstí J.W. Goethe, containing on its southern side a large and ungainly neo-Byzantine Catholic church of 1844–48. Among the pompous turn-of-the-century buildings on the upper side of the square is the thermal *Hotel Weimar*, once named the *Hotel King of England* in honour of the stays here of King Edward VII. The hotel which it replaced was owned by the mother of Ulrica von Lewetzow, whom the aged Goethe met and fell in love with while staying here in 1821–22. When Goethe returned to Mariánské Lázně in 1823, he moved into the adjacent 18C house which is now the town **museum** (in Goethe's day it was a hotel known as *At the Golden Grape*). The ground floor of this museum is devoted to local history, while on the upper floor is a suite of 18C rooms restored to the state in which they were when Goethe used them. **Open** Tues–Sun 09.00–16.00.

Following the Karlovarská east of the Náměstí J.W. Goethe you will reach a street which climbs up to the *Hotel Esplanade* (Wagner stayed in a house just below this hotel). In the wooded hills higher up is the turn-of-the-century *Krakonoš Hotel* where there is a terrace with broken statuary representing fairy-tale figures, including a statue of the giant Krakonoš; at one time there were statues lining the whole length of the attractive woodland path which descends from the hotel straight down into the town. The nearby and luxurious *Golf Hotel*, on the side-road

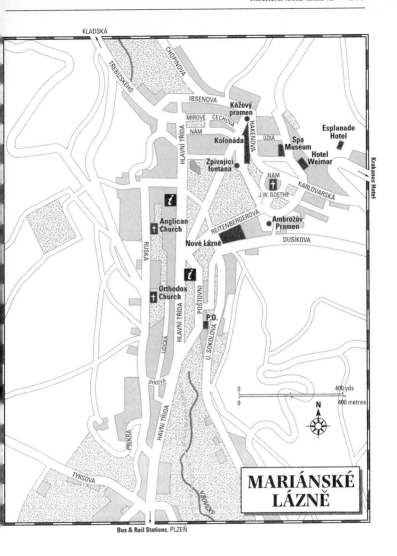

KLADSKÁ

TŘEBÍZSKÉHO

CHOPINOVA

IBSENOVA

Křížový pramen

MIROVÉ NÁM CECHOVA

HLAVNÍ TŘÍDA

Kolonáda

HAKENOVA

ÚZKÁ

Spa Museum

Esplanade Hotel

Hotel Weimar

Zpívající fontána

NÁM

J.W. GOETHE

KARLOVARSKÁ

Krakanos Hotel

Anglican Church

RUSKA

REITENBERGEROVA

Ambrožův Pramen

DUSÍKOVA

Nové Lázně

Orthodox Church

HLAVNÍ TŘÍDA

POŠTOVNI

P.O.

U. SOKOLOVA

LIDICKÁ

DYKOVA

HAVNÍ TŘÍDA

PRIKRA

TYRSOVA

VSOVICKÝ

0   400 yds
0   400 metres

N

MARIÁNSKÉ LÁZNĚ

Bus & Rail Stations, PLZEŇ

leading to Prameny, is popular with foreign golfers and even has a head porter—the charming Tunkl Boris—who was one of the leading Czech golf players. The hotel's celebrated golf course, one of the best in this country, was founded in 1905 by Edward VII, who is commemorated here by a plaque attached to one of the trees; the club pavilion is a half-timbered English-style building of 1908. Beyond the hotel is a side-road to the left which descends through the forest to the tiny spa of **Lázně Kynžvart**. The lords of the village were the Metternichs, and it was the famous Chancellor Metternich who in 1833 had the Baroque ancestral home rebuilt as a three-winged neo-Classical construction by the Vienna-based Italian architect Pietro Nobile; the building, now re-opened after nearly a decade of restoration, stands in the middle of a large English park, and has fine Empire furnishings, as well as a collection of gifts presented to the Chancellor.

Another excursion from Mariánské Lázně can be made to the former Premonstratensian monastery of **Teplá**, on the outskirts of the village of that name (take the Karlovy Vary road for 6km and then turn off to the right).

History of the monastery

The monastery was founded in 1193, and soon rose to become one of the wealthiest in Bohemia. However, from the late 14C onwards it was troubled by a series of misfortunes, beginning with plagues, and culminating in the looting and razing of the monastery following the excommunication of its monks in 1467. Rebuilding was begun in the early 16C, but the monastery was soon to suffer further extensive damage as a result of a series of fires, local peasant uprisings, and the Thirty Years War. At the end of the 17C Kilian and Christoph Dientzenhofer were brought in to rebuild much of the complex, and further work was carried out here in the early years of the 20C. Dissolved after the Second World War, the place served until recently as a barracks.

Today the monastery has a sad and shabby look, its buildings lining an unkempt forecourt. The church, which was consecrated in 1232, is by far the oldest part of the surviving complex, and has kept its original Cistercian Gothic fabric, even if heavily disguised by later restorations and a series of Baroque altars. The important library of the monastery, containing numerous illuminated manuscripts produced here from the 16C onwards, occupies a neo-Baroque building of 1902–10, the large interior of which has a stuccoed and frescoed ceiling in the manner of the great artists of the Bohemian Baroque. **Open** May–Oct Tues–Sun 09.00–16.30; Feb–Apr, Nov, Dec closes 15.00.

11 · Mariánské Lázně to Domažlice

Total distance 73km: Mariánské Lázně (leave by Road 21) • 36km Stříbra • 27km Horšovský Týn • 10km Domažlice.

From Mariánské Lázně, take Road 21 to Stříbro and then the side road south from there to the village of Kladruby, pleasantly situated on the peaceful river Úhlavka. Looming fantastically above the wooded, hilly banks on the other side of the river to the village—off the road which leads towards Ostrov u Stříbra—is the former Benedictine **Monastery of Kladruby**, containing one of Central Europe's most striking and original Baroque churches.

History of the Monastery

The monastery was founded by the Czech Prince Vladislav I in 1115 on an ancient merchant route linking Prague with Bavaria. Generously endowed by Vladislav and subsequent members of the Přemyslid family, the place became in the 14C Bohemia's richest monastery. On the death of Abbot Racek in 1393, King Václav IV attempted to use the monastery's vast revenues to create a new episcopal see in Bohemia, the idea being to undermine the power of his chief political adversary, Jan of Jenštejn, Archbishop of Prague. The Archbishop thwarted this plan by encouraging the monks at Kladruby to elect a new head, an appointment which was later endorsed by the Archbishop's Vicar-General, Jan of Pomuk (Jan Nepomucký). Eventually the enraged king had the latter tortured, and flung into the Vltava river.

Though badly damaged during the Hussite Wars and again during the Thirty Years War, the monastery regained its former importance in the course of the 17C. The emergence at the end of the century of John of Nepomuk as patron saint of Bohemia and the centre of a flourishing Jesuit cult coincided with the magnificent Baroque reconstruction of the monastery. The main architect involved was Johann Santini-Aichel, who brought the monastery church to completion in 1726. In 1765 reforms instituted by the Emperor Joseph II led to the dissolution of the monastery, which later passed into the hands of the Austrian Field-Marshal Prince Windisch-Grätz; it remained the property of this family until 1945.

In his pioneering architectural guide to Bohemia and Moravia, *The Architecture of Prague and Bohemia* (1962), Brian Knox described Kladruby as a 'dream made stone', but wrote that it 'is hardly mentioned in the guides, and the organised parties pass it by. It is a little damp; a few windows have been broken. But I do not feel that it can ever be forgotten.' His comments held true right up to the early 1990s, and though today much of the complex has been brightly restored, the place remains undeservedly little visited.

Turning right after going through the monastery gate you enter an inner courtyard bordered to your left by the **New Monastery Building**, which was built by Kilian Ignaz Dientzenhofer between 1729 and 1739 and later adapted for use as a library by Prince Windischgrätz: featuring a main portal flanked by atlantes, it was in a lamentable state until very recently; though now well restored, it remains closed to visitors.

The official tour of the monastery begins with the Winter Refectory in the adjacent **Old Monastery Building**, where a small art collection has been assembled, including a portrait of Count Nostic by Škréta and a painting by Tischbein. Along the north side of the large cloister has been placed a group of statues by Matthias Braun and his school, taken from Valeč château near Karlovy Vary. On the east side, meanwhile, leading to the church entrance, can be seen four 16C wooden reliefs from southern Germany.

As soon as you reach the **church**, all the other attractions of the monastery, interesting though they are, become of incidental significance. An extraordinary example of the adaptation by a Baroque architect of the Gothic style, the church was begun by Santini-Aichel in 1713 and made to incorporate the ground-plan of the original three-aisled Romanesque basilica, the longest in Bohemia and completed and consecrated in 1233. From the outside the church has a largely conventional Gothic appearance, with the exception of the bizarre crossing lantern—a ring of exuberant ogee-arched windows with a pinnacled superstructure supporting the crown of the Prince of Bohemia (the abbot of the time, Abbot Finzguth, described it as being *more Gottico nondum viso*, 'in a hitherto unseen Gothic manner'). A less spectacular but no less original feature is the glazed staircase well attached to the north side of the apse.

The exhilarating interior of the church, in vivid pistachio green, is notable above all for its elaborate, fantastical vaulting—worthy in its complexity of Benedikt Ried's at Kutná Hora—and for its furnishings. The latter, designed also by Santini-Aichel, include an inlaid wooden pulpit in the form of the prow of a ship and culminate in a quite remarkable high altar situated at the end of an undulating chancel. The altar, a perfect synthesis of Baroque movement and Gothic fantasy, comprises white and dynamic marble figures by Matthias Braun set against an openwork Gothic structure spiked with nodding crocketed pinnacles. Below the crowning sculpture of the Crucifixion are the symbols of the Evangelists, while lower down is a statue of the Madonna (the only work not by Braun) flanked to the left by St Benedict and to the right by St Wolfgang. Of great iconographic interest is Braun's tiny statue of Christ in the golden tabernacle underneath the Virgin: this is unique in showing the crucified Christ with only one hand attached to the cross, the other one touching instead his right thigh. The frescoes in the lantern vault and along the sides of the nave are by the celebrated Bavarian artist Cosmas Damian Assam, and feature scenes from the lives of the Benedictine saints. **Open** June–Aug Tues–Sun 09.00–12.00 and 13.00–18.00; May, Sept till 17.00; Apr, Oct till 16.00. Group tours hourly.

After leaving the monastery continue on the Ostrov road for a further kilometre, then turn right to Zhoř and a drive another 23km to **Horšovský Týn**. Commanding extensive views over flat wooded and agricultural countryside, Horšovský Týn is an attractive small town centred around a sloping square lined with colourful and recently restored Gothic, Renaissance and Baroque houses. A bridge links the upper part of the square with a large castle dominating a wooded public park comprising the former moat and castle gardens.

The **castle** itself was built originally between 1260 and 1270, and after a fire in 1547 was extended into a four-winged mansion by John the Younger of Lobkovice and his son Christopher, major-domo to Rudolph II. Confiscated from the family in 1623 after Vilém of Lobkovice had been sentenced to death for his part in the Battle of the White Mountain, the estate was then acquired by Count Maximilian Trauttmansdorf, whose family were to keep it until 1945. Behind the gabled Renaissance façade and entrance gate is a courtyard with fine Renaissance sgraffito decoration. A surprising amount of the original medieval interior has survived, and the highpoint of the obligatory guided tour is the chapel of c 1275, a tall rib-vaulted structure containing fragments of Renaissance frescoes. Later in the tour you come to a series of Rococo rooms, some of which are hung with paintings optimistically described as being by Canaletto. **Open** May–Sept Tues–Sun 09.00–12.00 and 13.00–16.00; June–Aug closes 17.00; Apr, Oct Sat, Sun 09.00–12.00 and 13.00–15.00.

The Chod Region

Horšovský Týn marks the northern boundary of a small region famed for its folklore and quaintly called in English the Chod Region (Chodsko). The capital of the Chod Region, and the scene every August of the Chod Folk Festival, is **Domažlice**, a well-preserved town in verdant surroundings which has a long,

The Chods

The Chods, an ancient ethnic group, were entrusted in the Middle Ages with guarding the Bohemian border with Germany. In 1325 the Bohemian monarchy rewarded them with special privileges, the loss of which after the Thirty Years War was to result in 1692 in a Chod uprising led by Jan Sladký-Kozina. In the 19C the history and strong folkloric traditions of this people came to have a Romantic attraction to a number of leading Czechs—most notably the composer Jindřich Jindřich and the novelist Božena Němcová. Until comparatively recently the women of the region could be seen on Sundays dressed in their traditional folk costumes featuring low black shoes, brilliant red hosiery and elaborately decorated bodices and silk aprons; the men meanwhile had white shirts and broad-brimmed black hats. Ceramics and other craft objects in a traditional Chod style continue to be produced today, but in factories rather than in the typical wooden houses of old, of which few survive.

narrow and particularly beautiful arcaded main square. The houses date back mostly to the Gothic and Renaissance periods, but have Baroque or Empire gables. One of the houses at the western end of the square has a plaque to Božena Němcová, who worked here as a teacher. Half-way down the square stands the town's most prominent landmark, the round and slightly leaning 13C tower attached to the **Church of St Mary** (Panny Marie); an excellent panorama of the town and its surroundings can be had from the top. **Open** Apr–Sept daily 09.00–12.00 and 13.00–17.00.

The church itself was rebuilt in the early 18C to the designs of Kilian Ignaz Dientzenhofer, and has frescoes inside by the Baroque painter F.J. Lux. Opposite the church is the neo-Renaissance Town Hall of 1891, while at the eastern end of the square is a tall, heavily restored and steeply gabled gatehouse of c 1270, the main survival of the town's medieval fortifications. The town's castle, just to the south of the main square, was founded in 1284, but was completely transformed in the 18C; it houses today the drearily old-fashioned Chod Museum, devoted to local history and folklore. Further folkloric items, collected by the composer Jindřich–Jindřich, can be seen in the museum named after him just below the town's medieval gatehouse.

A 28km tour around the Chod Region could be made by driving 5km south along the main road to Germany, and then turning right to **Újezd** (a further 5km), the birthplace of the leader of the 1692 Chod uprising, Jan Sladký-Kozina; there is a small museum to him at the so-called Kozina's farm, and a tall statue of him in traditional Chod costume on top of the hill of Hrádek, behind the village. Eight kilometres further west, at the foot of hills popular with skiers, is the small town of **Klenčí pod Čerchovem**, known for its ceramics (which can be bought at the Chodovia Cooperative) and for being the birthplace of the Chod Region's most famous native writer, J.S. Baar (1869–1925), who is commemorated here by a memorial room. From here you can return to Domažlice via Draženov 5km away, where there are three rare surviving examples of traditional Chod farmsteads (Nos 2, 5 and 8).

12 · Domažlice to České Budějovice

> Total distance 168km: Domažlice (leave by Road 22) • 37km Klatovy •
> 30km Sušice • 38km Vimperk • 20km Prachatice • 43km České Budějovice.

The southwest frontier of Bohemia, bordering with Germany, is marked by the **Šumava Mountains**, a range of about 120km which you follow for almost its entire length while driving from Domažlice to České Budějovice by way of Sušice. Gently contoured, relatively little populated, and covered with one of the largest and most dense forests in Bohemia, the area is popular both as a summer and winter resort, and since 1963 has formed a protected landscape region of 1630 sq km. The river Vltava—the longest river in the Czech Republic and the inspiration of innumerable poems—has its source in these mountains, as does its tributary, the Otava. The route described here is roughly that of the medieval trading route known as the Golden Path, along which malt was exported and salt imported.

Klatovy and its environs

Head east from Domažlice on Road 22, after 11km passing the village of **Kdyně**, dominated by the ruins of the 13C Rožmberk Castle, destroyed by Ferdinand III in 1655. **Klatovy**, 21km further east, is sometimes known as the gateway to the Šumava region, and is one of the most important towns in the area. Founded in 1260, it had become by 1547 the seventh wealthiest town in Bohemia.

Though retaining its medieval chessboard plan, sections of its fortifications and a number of fine monuments, the town centre never lives up to the expectations aroused by the magical silhouette of spires and towers which the place presents from a distance. Almost everything of interest is to be found around the lively main square, **náměstí Míru**, where Renaissance and Baroque monuments vie with uninspiring development of more recent years.

At the southwest corner of the square stands the town's tallest and most distinctive monument, the **Black Tower** (Černá věž), begun in 1547 by one Master Antonín and restored in 1925; you can climb up to the gallery to enjoy a wonderful view south over the Šumava range. **Open** May–Sept Tues–Sun 09.00–12.00 and 13.00–17.00; Apr, Oct Sat, Sun 09.00–12.00 and 13.00–16.00.

Adjoining it is the Renaissance Town Hall of 1557–59, decorated with modern sgraffiti. Adjacent to the tower on the western side of the square is the twin-towered **Jesuit church**, begun to designs by Giovanni Domenico Orsi in 1656, but rebuilt by Kilian Ignaz Dientzenhofer in 1703–22 following a severe fire. The interior is interesting primarily on account of the Pozzo-inspired illusionistic frescoes over the east end, the work of the Jesuit painter Ignaz Raab and František Palko.

The most popular tourist attraction in Klatovy lies underneath the Jesuit church, but can only be reached from a door outside the building. This, the Klatovy **catacombs**, was used as a burial place from 1676 up to 1783, when the Emperor Joseph II forbade the practice of church burial. Thanks to a system of ventilating air-holes that allow dry air to circulate freely within the crypt, the 40 corpses that remain here (out of an original 200) are in a mummified condition. A taped commentary in English, beginning jovially with the words

'Welcome to Klatovy', provides an historical distraction while you gape morbidly at the corpses, most of which are of people associated with the Jesuit college to which the church was attached. Among the mortal remains you can admire are those of one of the founders of the college, Albert Chánovský, the mathematician Benjamin Schleier, and a certain foreigner named Jok Fabricius, whose career began auspiciously as a bachelor of philosophy, but ended as college shoemaker. **Open** May–Sept Tues–Sun 09.00–12.00 and 13.00–17.00; Oct–Apr Tues–Fri 09.00–12.00 and 13.00–16.00.

A more cheerful sight is that of the neighbouring **Baroque pharmacy**, situated on the west side of the square, at No. 149. It was originally to be found inside the Jesuit college, but following the suppression of the Jesuit Order in 1773 was acquired by a local apothecary and transferred to his own premises; it functioned as a pharmacy up to 1964, but now forms part of a small museum. The beautiful Rococo panelling was completed in 1733 by John Geschwent, a cabinet-maker who was born in Allgau in Schwaben in 1701 and died in Silesia in 1745. A carved unicorn's horn (the apothecary's trademark) hangs in the room, though unquestionably the most spectacular work here is a Baroque centrepiece featuring a statue of St Michael, the patron of apothecaries, trampling over the devil, the symbol of disease; below these figures are two black men holding vessels which probably once contained 'Therial' and 'Mythridatum'. In a backroom can be seen 18C distillation and grinding equipment. **Open** Apr–Oct Tues–Sun 09.00–12.00 and 13.00–17.00.

Off the northeast corner of the square stands the **White Tower** (Bílá věž), which was built in 1581, redecorated in 1687, and again in 1898. Behind this is the **Archdeacon's Church**, which conceals behind a 19C west façade an attractive hall-church with a chancel of c 1400 and a nave completed by Master Antonín in the 1550s; the nave has elaborate net vaulting.

Eleven kilometres to the north of Klatovy on the Plzeň road is the impressive castle of **Švihov**, begun c 1480 by Puta of Rýzmberk, chief justice of Bohemia, and completed in around 1520 following the intervention of Benedikt Ried. The eastern half of this once massive castle was razed on the orders of the Habsburgs, and the remaining parts suffered much damage after being transformed into a granary in the 18C. The most eloquent survival is the late Gothic chapel of 1515, decorated with an amusing painting of *St George and the Dragon*; also of interest is the hall, which has a a fine coffered ceiling of 1578 taken from the château at Dobrovice. **Open** May, Sept Tues–Sun 09.00–12.00 and 13.00–17.00; June–Aug closes 18.00; Apr, Oct Sat, Sun 09.00–12.00 and 13.00–16.00.

Those intending to stay a while in the Šumava could drive 39km south along Road 27/E53 from Klatovy to **Železná Ruda**, passing through a landscape which becomes progressively hillier and more forested. Železná Ruda, the most popular of the Šumava resorts, is 2km from the German border, just to the north of the highest peak in the range, Grosser Arber (1456m), the summit of which is in Germany. Two kilometres to the north of Železná Ruda on the road to Nýrsko is the resort of **Špičák**, from where you can take a chair-lift (in three stages) to the summit of **Pancíř** (1214m). From the car park at Spičácké sedlo, 1km further north along the road, a bus will take you up to the Black Lake (Černé jezero), a beautiful if often crowded spot encased in a wooded mountain hollow.

Continuing east from Klatovy, you should stay on Road 22 for a further 13km, then head south on Road 187 for another 17km to **Sušice**. Sušice is a tiny indus-

trial town with the slightly incongruous reputation of being the leading manufacturer of matches in Central Europe; this industry was established here in the
early 19C, and soon gave the place an international renown. The main tourist
attraction is the **Šumava Museum** (muzeum Šumavy), situated in the beautiful
Veprchovský House on the main square. The house itself, of medieval origin,
immediately attracts attention with its Renaissance façade, featuring an extraordinary gable made up of superimposed rows of blind arcading, the end result
looking more Indian than European. As for the museum, this is one of the oldest
in the Czech Republic, having been founded in 1879 on the instigation of a local
schoolteacher with a passion for preserving the relics of the past: at the time of its
foundation there were only 26 other museums in Bohemia and Moravia. The
collections are small but excellently displayed in a homely and lovingly restored
interior, including rooms in Renaissance, Baroque and Beidermeier styles. Apart
from items relating to local history, ethnography and archaeology, there is a good
collection of traditional Šumava glass, a 15C woodcarving of the Madonna and
Child, and a superlative set of pewter which had been hidden for three centuries
in the masonry of a local house, where it had been left by one Adam Cech, a local
citizen who had fled the country after the Battle of the White Mountain. **Open**
Tues–Sat 09.00–12.00 and 12.45–17.00, Sun 09.00–12.00.

From Sušice you could make a short detour to see the ruined castle of **Rabí**,
which lies 10km to the north in the direction of Horaždovice. Belonging to the
powerful Rožmberk family and one of the largest castles in Bohemia, Rabí was
besieged and conquered in 1421 by the Hussite leader Jan Žižka, who lost here
his second eye; the complex, of 14C origin, was rebuilt in the 1520s with the
assistance of Benedikt Ried.

The eastern Šumava

Returning to Sušice, continue driving in a southeasterly direction towards
Vimperk, on Road 145. A winding drive of 17km through an attractive forested
valley will take you to **Kašperské Hory**. A gold-mining town in the Middle
Ages, this is now little more than a large village with a cheerful looking main
square, one side of which is taken up by the Baroque Town Hall, a three-gabled
structure in dazzling white and yellow. Peering over a pine-forested hill to the
north of the village are the extensive ruins of the castle erected by Charles IV in
1356 to guard the local gold mines. These romantically set ruins can best be
reached by driving east out of the village, and then taking the turning to the left
marked Nezdice; after 2km you come to two houses, alongside which is a path
leading up into a forest; follow the green markings, and after 1.5km you will
arrive at the castle (only the exterior can be seen).

East of Kašperk castle you cross into the administrative region of South Bohemia.
The village of **Vimperk**, 21km further on, lies in the shadow of a 13C castle reconstructed in the 19C and used today as a local museum with documents relating to
local history and industries, and to the flora and fauna of the Šumava Mountains;
at Sudslavice, 4km to the north, is a 600-year-old lime tree, one of the oldest in the
Czech Republic and measuring nearly 12m in diameter. Twenty kilometres to the
east of Vimperk, in the direction of České Budějovice, is **Husinec**, the birthplace of
Jan Hus (1369–1415), who is commemorated by a statue by Karel Lidický (1958)
in the village square, and a small museum in the house where he was born.

As a youth Hus frequented the market at **Prachatice**, situated high on a hill

4km to the south and encircled by extensive surviving sections of its medieval walls. It is the most attractive town in the Šumava region, and a foretaste of the so-called Rose Towns to the east.

History of Prachatice

Founded as a trading post in 1325, at the end of the century Prachatice received a royal charter from Wenceslas IV which gave it the Bohemian monopoly on the salt trade. The town prospered as never before, though its golden age is generally considered to have been the 16C, when it came into the possession of the Rožmberk family. A severe fire in 1507 led the Rožmberks to rebuild most of the town, and the old centre today has an essentially Renaissance character.

The town is especially rich in sgraffitoed Renaissance buildings, many of which are to be found on the beautifully preserved main square. At the top of the square is the **Old Town Hall** (c 1571), with monochrome scenes by both Czech and Italian artists of the *Dance of Death*, and allegories of Justice; the New Town Hall (1903), further down on the same side, is in a neo-Renaissance style, and covered with sgraffiti. At No. 169 is the **Princes' House** (Knížecí dům), built by the Rožmberks in 1572 and decorated with much-worn biblical scenes. Among the finest of the sgraffiti decorations are the battle scenes on the 16C **Rumpál House** (Rumpálův dům), a house owned by the Rumpál family up to 1671 which later became for a while a brewery and pub.

Towering behind the northeast corner of the square is the imposing, fortress-like mass of the 14C **Church of St James** (sv. Jakub), the interior of which has net-vaulting of 1410. The picturesque narrow street which leads down to it from the square is lined the whole length with old buildings including—just below the church—the richly decorated Hejdlův House. The street ends at the sgraffitoed Písek Gate, which is attached to the longest surviving section of the town's 14C and 16C fortifications and features a faded scene of Vilém of Rožmberk on horse-back, as well as the Rožmberk rose emblem; a long and narrow park lies below them, offering a fine view of the town rising above its defensive walls.

Leave the town on Road 141 to Vodňany, and 4km to the north you will regain the main road to České Budějovice. Ten kilometres along this is the exquisite Renaissance summer palace of **Kratochvíle**, situated at the western end of a marshy lake, and with its moats now silted, and gardens planted with vegetables rather than flowers. Commissioned as a pleasure retreat by Vilém of Rožmberk (the brother of Petr Vok), it was built between 1583 and 1590 by Baldassare Maggi da Vomio. This same architect was responsible for the extensive stucco decorations that—together with the much damaged frescoes by Jiří Widman of 1589—constitute the chief artistic interest of the interior: the greatest of the rooms, the Golden Hall, runs along the whole western side of the house, and has a remarkable ceiling stuccoed all over with scenes from Classical history. Bizarrely, the rest of the interior has now been given over to an albeit lively and enjoyable **Museum of Animated Film** (Muzeum animovaného filmu), which records the pioneering achievements in this medium of Czech directors such as Jiří Trnka, Karel Zeman and Hermína Týrlová, all of whom were active between the wars in the Moravian town of Zlín (where a museum of this kind would surely be more appropriate). **Open** May–Sept Tues–Sun 09.00–12.00 and 13.00–17.00; Apr, Oct Sat, Sun 09.00–12.00 and 13.00–16.00.

After Netolice, 2km to the east, continue driving east for a further 13km, until you join the E49, which will take you after 12km to České Budějovice (see Chapter 16).

13 · Prague to Plzeň

Total distance 78km: Prague (leave by the D5/E50) • 18km Beroun • 44km Rokycany • 16km Plzeň.

The main road from Prague to Plzeň runs through gently rolling countryside with dense areas of forest. A dual carriageway for the first 28km, the D5 bypasses the town of Beroun, and 14km later goes through **Žebrák**, where there is a ruined royal castle dating back to c 1280; remodelled by Wenceslas I at the end of the 14C, the building was further altered during the Renaissance period. The more important royal castle of Točník, founded by Wenceslas IV c 1400, stands 2km north of the road, but is closed to visitors. The town of Rokycany, 26km further west, is one of the oldest in Bohemia, though the few surviving traces of its past—such as remains of its medieval fortifications—have now been surrounded by iron foundries and other industries.

Plzeň

More extensive industrial development awaits you at Plzeň, known for its Škoda works but, above all, for its beer.

History of Plzeň

Founded in 1295 by the banks of the river Radbuza, Plzeň enjoyed many royal privileges and soon flourished as a commercial centre, its drapers acquiring an international reputation. Commercial prosperity continued into the 17C, and many foreign merchants, craftsmen and artists settled here, in particular from Germany and Italy. A strong bastion of Catholicism since Hussite times, Plzeň suffered terribly during the Thirty Years War, the ravages of war being also compounded by a series of plagues. However, the town began to revive at the end of the 17C, with a new wave of immigrants and the establishment here of the iron, steel and textile industries. The industrialisation rapidly intensified in the course of the 19C, with the creation in turn of the first tannery (soon to be the third largest in Bohemia), the Burgher Brewery (which was to make the name of Plzeň perennially linked with beer), and the Škoda engineering works. At the same time Plzeň emerged as an important centre of the Czech National Movement, and many important theatrical productions in the Czech language were brought here from Prague by the famous playwright and director J.K. Tyl, who died in the town in 1856.

In recent years Plzeň has been able to celebrate an aspect of its 20C history that was completely denied during the Communist period: the liberation of the town by the US Third Army under General Patton on 6 May 1945. The official Soviet story, omitting all reference to the Americans in

Plzeň, was finally put right in May 1990, when, in the presence of numerous US war veterans, a memorial to the Americans was erected in the southern half of the city, on the Chodské náměstí. Later the major thoroughfare formerly known as Moskevská (just to the south of the old town) was renamed Americká, and given a granite monument planned in 1945 and inscribed with the words 'Thank you, America'.

Plzeň is not one of the Czech Republic's more beautiful towns, its industrial growth having led in the last century to the destruction of many of its older houses, and to the pulling down after 1828 of the remaining sections of its medieval walls; further devastation was caused by heavy bombing in 1944–45. None the less a number of interesting monuments have survived, as well as the town's original chessboard layout.

The greatest concentration of old buildings is on the blackened and enormous main square, **náměstí Republiky**, which takes up two large blocks of the chessboard. Occupying an isolated position on the northern half of the square is the **Cathedral of St Bartholomew** (sv. Bartoloměj), built between the 14C and 16C, and crowned by the tallest steeple in Bohemia (103m); you can climb up to the gallery. **Open** daily, 10.00–18.00.

The interior of this recently restored triple-naved hall-church has vaulting sprung from massive round piers; there are traces of wall-painting, and a delicately poised marble Madonna and Child of the 14C. The late Gothic Šternberk Chapel (Šternberská kaple), attached to the south side of the chancel, has interesting vaulting with pendulant bosses supported by free-standing ribs.

Adjacent to the cathedral's west façade is a **plague column** of 1681 with sculptures by K. Widman, while behind this, on the north side of the square, is the Renaissance **Town Hall**. Built in 1555–58 by the Italian architect Giovanni Stazio, this building, with its rusticated ground floor, has elements of a Tuscan cinquecento palace; however, the gabled attic storey—probably an addition of the 1570s—gives the structure an unmistakably Central European look. The pseudo-Renaissance sgraffito work dates from the time of the building's restoration in 1907–12; elsewhere in the square are late 19C sgraffito decorations by M. Aleš.

Among the other surviving old houses on the náměstí Republiky is the Baroque Archdeacon's House (1710) directly opposite the cathedral's west façade. North from here runs Dominikánská, where, at No. 25, stands the modest but elegant early 18C Mestl house. The finest of all the town's secular Baroque buildings is that at No. 251 on the parallel street to the west, Sedláčkova. Crowned by a gable in the form of a broken Borrominesque pediment, it is named after the architect who built it, Jakub Auguston (d. 1735), the son of Italian immigrants to the town. Another of Auguston's works can be seen by walking to the southern end of Sedláčkova, and then turning left into Bezručova. This work, the Dominican **Church of St Anne** (sv. Anny), is at the junction of Bezručova and B. Smetany, and was Auguston's major Plzeň commission; the convent to which it was attached was converted in 1804 into a school (now the State Science Library), where the composer Bedřich Smetana was to study between 1840 and 1843.

The old centre of Plzeň is surrounded today by a series of gardens marking the site of the medieval walls. In the Smetana Gardens, immediately to the south of the former convent of St Anne, is a memorial to Smetana (1874), as well as an

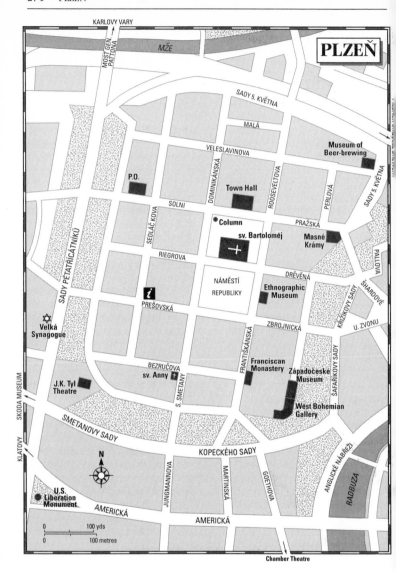

imposing turn-of-the-century theatre named after J.K. Tyl (Divadlo JK. Tyl). Northwest of the theatre, on the adjacent Sady Pětatřicátníků, looms the massive bulk of the **Great Synagogue** (Velká Synagóga), which is now being restored after years of having been left as a blackened ruin: built in 1892 in a neo-Romanesque style, it is the largest synagogue in the Czech Republic (and one of the largest in Central Europe), a surprising fact given that the town's Jewish population never amounted to more than 3000.

The Tyl Theatre stands at the southwest corner of the old town, and from here a detour could be made into an ugly modern district to see the **Škoda Museum** at Korandova 4, a good 20min walk to the west (or take a No. 34 bus along the busy Tylova to Husovo náměstí, then head south).

History of Škoda

The history of the Škoda works goes back to the foundation in 1859 of the Waldstein engineering works, a company which was purchased by the Plzeň-born Emil Škoda ten years later. Under Škoda the company rapidly expanded, particularly after 1890, when it began manufacturing arms. Today the name Škoda is generally associated with cars that in Western Europe once had a reputation as bad as the Russian Ladas, and were likewise the subject of many English jokes, for example: *Question*: 'What is a Škoda without a roof?'. *Answer*: 'A skip.' The $1 billion dollar investment loan placed in the company by the German firm Volkswagen in 1989 undoubtedly played its part in making these jokes no longer so pertinent.

The museum has much photographic documentation relating to the history of the Škoda works, as well as many working models of engines, cars, and other products.

Returning to the old town head east of the Church of St Anne to the Františkánská, where you will find a former **Franciscan church and monastery** (Františkánský klášter s kostelem) dating back to the late 13C; the church itself was rebuilt in the Baroque period, but the former chapter house, now the Chapel of St Barbara, has not been altered since medieval times, and is extensively covered with interesting frescoes of c 1460. Behind the monastery, at the southeast corner of the old town, is a grand neo-Baroque structure of 1886, designed by Josef Škorpil and housing today both the **West Bohemian Museum** (Západočeské muzeum) and the more recently formed **West Bohemian Gallery** (Západočeská galerie). The former has historical, natural history and applied arts collections, while the latter specialises in Czech art of the 19C and 20C, including works by M. Aleš, J. Navrátil, K. Purkyně, J. Preisler (the Symbolist triptych, *Spring*), A. Slavíček, B. Kubišta, E. Filla, V. Špála, J. Čapek and J. Šíma. **Open** Tues–Sun 10.00–18.00.

Immediately to the north of the museum building (but with a main entrance on the adjacent Zbrojnická, is the early 20C *Hotel Continental*, which enjoyed a reputation in the inter-war years as one of Czechoslovakia's most luxurious hotels, frequented by the likes of Marlene Dietrich, Ingrid Bergman and Jack Benny. Owned after 1929 by Emanuel Ledecký and his young wife Eugenie, it was hit in December 1944 by a stray American bomb that killed 100 people including Emanuel but not Eugenie, who was out of town at the time visiting her dying mother. As soon as the Americans had left Plzeň—where they had used the *Continental* as their headquarters—Eugenie began slowly rebuilding the hotel but, with the advent of Stalinism in Czechoslovakia, fled to America with a new husband. Recently, as a result of the Czech Republic's restitution laws, Eugenie was able to reclaim the *Continental*, the ownership of which she immediately handed over to a son by her second marriage, George Janaček. Janaček, a photographer from Salt Lake City, Utah, is currently undertaking a major renovation of the hotel, and has already brought back to some of the rooms their former mirrored and damask splendour, complete with Art Deco furniture and other original works of art.

Continuing to walk north along the gardens that border the eastern edge of the old town, you will pass on your left (in between Dřevěná and Pražská) a curious long building known as the **Meat Hall** (Masné krámy): though dating back to the founding in the early 14C of the Plzeň Guild of Butchers, the oldest guild in the city, it was much altered in the 19C, and is now used for concerts and temporary exhibitions. Opposite it, on the northern side of Pražská, is a tower of 1532 which served both as a water-tower and as part of the town's fortifications. The parallel street to the north of Pražská is Veleslavínova, where at No. 6 a building of 14C origin houses the **Brewery Museum** (Pivovarské muzeum), a fascinating collection relating to the history of beer-making in the town, and incorporating the building's medieval beer-cellars and malt-house. Nearby, at No. 65 in the adjacent Perlová, you can descend (by guided tour) down to some extensive underground tunnels built for defensive purposes in the 14C but later used for the storing of beer.

After retracing your footsteps south, head east along Pražská and cross the river Radbuza. The continuation of Pražská on the other side of the river is the wide and bleak u Prazdroje, off the left-hand side of which you will come after a short walk to the entrance to the **Pilsner Urquell Brewery** (Plzeňský Prazdroj), the major tourist attraction of the town. Visits to the brewery are now held every weekday at 12.30 (advance booking is no longer necessary); the weekends are reserved exclusively for tour groups.

History of the Brewery

The rights to brew beer were granted to the Burghers of Plzeň from the time of the town's foundation in 1295; these rights, later restricted to those who had houses within the old fortifications, were to be kept right up to the 19C. The beer was brewed in the cellars of the burghers' homes and then sold after having been stringently tested by inspectors appointed by the Town Council: beer of low quality could be sold at a lower price only to the poor of the town, while beer considered a complete failure was publicly disposed of in front of the Town Hall, this being the biggest disgrace a burgher-brewer could suffer. The way in which the beer was tested is not known, though there is a popular and fanciful tradition which has it that the inspectors sat with their leather trousers on an oak bench on which the brew was poured: if, on rising, the beer stuck to the trousers, it was thought to be of sufficent density and thus a good brew.

In 1842 the Plzeň citizens holding the beer-brewing right decided to pool their resources into a single enterprise, so as to profit from new and improved methods of production. The success of the Burgher Brewery was immediate, the taste for the beer produced here catching on immediately in Prague, and then spreading by the 1850s to Vienna and the West Bohemian spas; by the 1860s the beer was being exported to Paris and London, and in 1873 the first shipment of it was made to the United States of America. In 1898 the beer was given the label 'Pilsner Urquell' (in Czech, 'Prazdroj Plzeň'), meaning 'the ancient spring of Plzeň'. The original 'Pils', and as such the prototype of pale beer throughout the world, its popularity continues to increase, and there are many who regard it as the finest of all beers. The key to its success lies partly in the care taken in the proper drying of the malt, in the use of the excellent hops around Žatec in northwest Bohemia, and in the maturing of the beer in the traditional oak wood casks.

Beside the entrance to the brewery is a lively turn-of-the-century **beer-hall** (*Na Stílce*), where you can drink the beer to the accompaniment of suitably copious and hearty fare. The entrance itself takes the form of a triumphal arch erected in 1898, and celebrating 56 years of the brewery's existence. Beyond it extends an industrial landscape which can have changed little since the beginning of the century, with red-brick chimneys, ageing rails and pseudo-medieval towers. The interesting guided tour starts off with a short film show, and then takes you down into the cold and evocative 19C cellars, where warm clothing is advisable. At the end of the tour you might finally get round to tasting the beer (in today's capitalist climate this is much less of a certainty than before), and do so in a gabled turn-of-the-century building with a delightful white stucco façade decorated with scenes of beer-making; the intimate interior has an Impressionist-style painting by Blažíček representing a *Beer-Garden* (1924).

From the brewery it is a 20 minute walk south along Nádražní and Mikulášská to the **Church of St Nicholas** (sv. Mikuláš); the same journey could be undertaken in a No. 1 or 2 tram. This simple, modest building dates back to 1410 but was remodelled during the Baroque period; in its shaded cemetery you will find the graves both of Emil Škoda and J.K. Tyl, the latter commemorated by a statue of an angel mourning over a representation of the masks of comedy and tragedy. In the northeastern suburb of Doubravka, and best reached from the brewery by car, is the **Church of St George** (sv. Jiří). Standing isolated among fields in a bend of the river Berounka, this church dates back to the Ottonian period, and though extended in the Gothic and Baroque periods, has retained a much-restored 9C apse.

A short excursion 24km due north of Plzeň on Road 27 takes you to the former monastery of **Plasy**, which was founded in 1144 by Vladislav II and then transformed in the late 17C and early 18C into the present huge and slightly chaotic complex: the early Baroque architect Jean-Baptiste Mathey was involved, as was Johann Santini-Aichel, who designed, off the brilliant white cloisters, the subtley-realised St Bernard Chapel, which has an undulating outer wall encasing an oval. After the dissolution of the monastery in 1826, the place fell into the hands of the Austrian Chancellor Metternich, who turned the cemetery church across the road into his family mausoleum. The monastery itself is largely taken over today by a gallery of contemporary art which—during the arts festival held here in June/July—attracts avant-garde artists from all over Europe. **Open** June–Aug Tues–Sun 09.00–17.00; May, Sept 09.00–16.00; Apr, Oct. 09.00–15.00.

South Bohemia

Although developed only recently as a major tourist destination, this is the part of Bohemia that best lives up to idyllic foreign preconceptions of the Bohemian countryside—forests, lakes, and rolling hills, dotted with toy-like castles and medieval towns that seems straight out of some fairy-tale vision of old Europe. Nowhere else in Bohemia has been so unaffected by industries, or left so untouched by the Second World War.

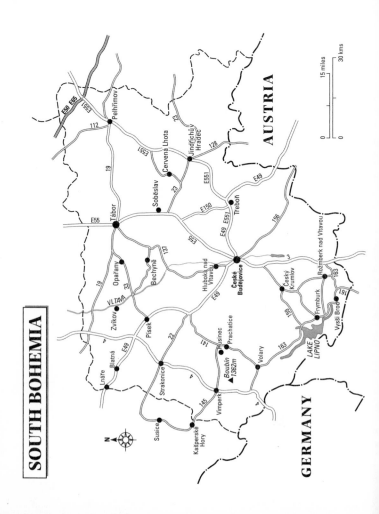

One of this region's many characteristic features are its 'water-castles' (castles built in the middle of lakes), two fine examples of which are those at **Blatná** and **Strakonice**, which can be seen in Chapter 14. A romantic backdrop to many of the region's architectural monuments is provided also by the Vltava river, which you can follow all the way from Prague in Chapter 15A, passing at **Zvíkov** a major medieval castle thrust high above the confluence of the Vltava and the Orava. An alternative route from Prague is Chapter 15B, which will take you to the lakeside town of **Tábor** (an essential stop for anyone interested in the Hussite movement), as well as to the extraordinary neo-Gothic fantasy at **Hluboká nad Vltavou**.

The region's greatest concentration of architectural riches is to be found along Chapter 16, which begins at the important early medieval monastery of **Vyšší Brod**, and goes on to include all of the celebrated 'Rose Towns', the name of which is derived from the emblems of this region's two most powerful families—the red rose of the Rožmberks and the black rose of the Lords of Hradec.

Transport
Trains
Connections with Prague: České Budějovice (9 daily; 2hr 30min–4hr 20min); Písek (2 daily; 2hr 30min); Strakonice (1 daily; 3hr); Sušice (1 daily; 3hr 45min); Tábor (every 1–2hr; 1hr 30min–2hr 20min).
From České Budějovice: Český Krumlov (8 daily; 1hr); Horní Planá/Černý Kříž (6 daily; 2hr 15min/2hr 30min); Jindřichův Hradec (9 daily; 1hr–1hr 30min); Plzeň (9 daily; 1hr 45min–3hr); Strakonice (12 daily; 50min–1hr 20min); Volary (5 daily; 3hr).
From Tábor: Bechyně (9–10 daily; 50min); České Budějovice (12 daily; 1hr–1hr 40min); Jihlava/Brno (1 daily; 1hr 50min/4hr); Milevsko/Písek (9 daily; 40min/1hr 30min); Pelhřimov (8 daily; 55min–1hr 20min); Třeboň (3–4 daily; 30min).
From Volary: Prachatice (8 daily; 40min); Vimperk/Strakonice (6 daily; 1hr/2hr).

Buses
Connections with Prague: České Budějovice (up to 12 daily; 2hr 25min–3hr); Český Krumlov (up to 3 daily; 3hr 20min); Orlík/Písek (up to 6 daily; 1hr 30min/2hr 10min); Strakonice/Prachatice (up to 4 daily; 2hr/3hr); Tábor (hourly; 1hr 20min); Volary (up to 2 daily; 3hr 30min).
From České Budějovice: Hluboká nad Vltavou (1–2 hourly; 20min); Holešovice (2–5 daily; 40min); Prachatice (up to 10 daily; 1 hr 15min).
From Český Krumlov: Rožmberk/Vyšší Brod (3–9 daily; 30/40min); Lipno nad Vltavou (1–4 daily; 1hr 15min).
From Jindřichův Hradec: České Budějovice (12 or more daily; 1hr 10min); Slavonice (up to 8 daily; 1hr 30min).
From Pelhřimov: Humpolec (up to 10 daily; 30 min); Jihlava (up to 8 daily; 45min); Kámen (up to 7 daily; 30min).
From Tábor: Bechyně (up to 14 daily; 40min–1hr 15min); Kámen (up to 6 daily; 30min).

Hotels and pensions
České Budějovice
Hotel Zvon, náměstí Přemysla Otakara II. ☎ (038) 731 1383. Recently renovated luxury hotel occupying three of the colourful old houses surrounding one of the most spectacular squares in the Czech Republic.
Český Krumlov
Hotel Růže, Horní 153, 381 01. ☎ (0337) 5481; Fax: (0337) 3881. A superb sgrafittoed Renaissance structure built as a Jesuit college in the early 17C and then turned into a hotel as early as 1889, this has a number of spacious rooms with the original wood ceilings, and cheaper alternative accomodation (without baths) in the former Jesuit cells.
Pension Ve věži, Latrán 28, 381 01. ☎ / Fax: (0337) 5287. Romantically cramped into a Renaissance guard tower.
Hluboká nad Vltavou
Hotel Bakalář, Masarykova 69, 373 41. ☎ / Fax: (038) 965 516. Tastefully simple hotel situated in a curious 19C building.
Tábor
Hotel Kapitál, 9. Května 617, 390 01. ☎ (0361) 256 096; Fax: (0361) 252 411. Centrally located small hotel in pink 19C house.
Třeboň
Hotel Zlatá Hvězda, Masarykovo náměstí 107, 379 01 Třeboň. ☎ (0333) 2661; Fax: (0333) 2604. Faded, overpriced, but excellently located on the main square.

14 · Plzeň to České Budějovice

Total distance 141km: Plzeň (leave by Road 20/E49) • 36km Nepomuk • 24km Blatná • 25km Strakonice • 56km České Budějovice.

Leave Plzeň on the E49, if you wish making a short detour at the southeastern suburb of Černice to visit the Church of All Saints, a pre-Romanesque rotunda heavily restored over the centuries, at **Starý Plzenec** 3km to the east of the road. Continuing along the E49 you will shortly pass on the left, 10km south of Plzeň, the ruined hill-top castle of Radyně, a 14C structure largely hidden by pines.

Nepomuk, 20km further to the south, is famous as the birthplace of Jan Nepomucký, the insignificant 14C prelate who was to be transformed 300 years after his death in 1393 into the patron saint of Bohemia. This quiet hill-side village, just off the main road, has a parish church with a Gothic façade of c 1380 shielding a Baroque structure built by Kilian Ignaz Dientzenhofer between 1733 and 1738; the interior, undecorated by frescoes, is notable for its simplicity. At **Lnáře**, 15km further on, is an early 17C château preceded by a bridge adorned with 18C statues.

You are now officially in South Bohemia, and beyond Lnáře pass the first of the small lakes that are so characteristic of this region. **Blatná**, 9km further east, has a celebrated example of one of South Bohemia's many 'water-castles'. Fringed by trees and surrounded on three sides by a great expanse of water, Blatná was the principal seat of one of the most important Bohemian families, the Rožmitáls. It was Zdeněk Leo of Rožmitál, Supreme Burgrave of the Kingdom of Bohemia, who between 1523 and 1530 had the medieval castle transformed into a formidable Renaissance residence, with a modern system of water defences; Benedikt Ried is known to have been involved in the planning. The picturesque profile of the castle today, complete with steeples, turrets and a half-timbered tower, is largely the result of extensive remodelling carried out in the early 19C. The interior—at present closed for restoration—contains some late 15C wall-paintings featuring naïf views of Blatná and Rožmitál, and exhibits relating to the 19C Czech physicist J.E. Purkyně, who was a tutor here to the Hildprant family between 1810 and 1813. The village church has an elegant two-aisled interior of 1515 covered with the curious cellular vaulting peculiar to Bohemia.

Rising directly above fields outside the tiny village of **Paštiky**, 2km northeast of Blatná, is the undulating west tower façade of the Church of St John the Baptist (1747–51), a late work by K.I. Dientzenhofer. The plan of this single-aisled church is longitudinal, though the rounded corners inside give the impression of a centralised one.

Nine kilometres southeast of Blatná, leave the E49 and head south along a side-road to Osek and **Strakonice** (16km). On the river Otava, the town derived its wealth initially from gold found in the river; from the 18C onwards it developed into a small industrial centre which from 1812 mysteriously concentrated on the making of fezzes, in which field it has—perhaps, not surprisingly—few rivals in Europe. Another of its curious traditional industries is the making of bagpipes: the dramatist Tyl wrote a play entitled *The Bagpiper of Strakonice*, and every August a bagpipe festival (attracting large contingents of Scots) is held in the grounds of its castle. The castle, one of the first in Bohemia to be surrounded by water, stands on a verdant island in the middle of the Otava. Founded in 1260, it comprises an attractive jumble of medieval buildings, including a machiolated round tower, several half-timbered burgher houses, and a church. There is a small museum with tools and other objects relating to the gold-sifting industry.

East of Strakonice follow Road 22 to Vodňany (23km), where you will regain the E49; a drive of 33km though a landscape of lakes and marshes will take you to České Budějovice (see Chapter 16).

15 · Prague to České Budějovice

A. Via Příbram and Písek

Total distance 235km: Prague (leave by Road 4) • 62km Příbram • 17km Březnice • 18km Orlík • 18km Zvíkov • 16km Písek • 52km České Budějovice.

The main route from Prague to České Budějovice by way of Příbram and Písek runs parallel to the river Vltava, though, after Zbraslav (see Chapter 2) always at some distance from the river. There is a small road which follows the Vltava from Zbraslav to Štěchovice, 16km to the south, but afterwards the river winds unaccompanied through dense forest; pleasure boats from Prague also turn back at Štěchovice, for between here and Zvíkov lie a series of major dams that have turned the river into a sinuous series of connected lakes, the shores of which are popular with swimmers, anglers and campers.

Road 4, the main road running southwest of Prague, is dual carriageway almost all the way to Příbram (62km). After 54km the road passes next to the industrial town of **Dobříš**, where there is an important Rococo château designed by the French architect Jules Robert de Cotte in 1745, and completed in 1765; the large English garden once attached to the house is now a public park, but the house itself, together with its surrounding French garden (containing statuary by I.F. Platzer), is reserved for members of the Czech Union of Writers, and cannot be visited; it was at a meeting of young writers held in Dobříš in the autumn of 1956 that the future playwright and Czech president Václav Havel (1936–) first drew attention to himself, making a controversial speech on the ambiguous relationship between official and suppressed literature.

One of the most famous of all Czech writers this century, Karel Čapek (1890–1938), acquired in 1935 a country cottage 3km southeast of Dobříš at **Strž**. He and his wife (whom he had married that year following a long friendship dating back to the early 1920s) devoted an enormous amount of energy to improving and looking after the 22ha of land which came with the house. However, he was to die only three years later, literally heartbroken by Chamberlain's betrayal of Czechoslovakia. He was in Prague at the time, and had been eagerly awaiting the spring, when he hoped to return to Strž; as he lay dying he reputedly asked the doctors, 'What's the weather like outside? Is there ice on the ground? In ninety-one days we'll go to Strž together. All of us. In Strž the trees and the grass will be green by then. In ninety-one days…' Čapek's cottage, beautifully situated by a small lake, houses today a memorial museum to him.

Six kilometres south of Dobříš, Road 4 passes the village of **Obořiště**, where the former Pauline convent (now an agricultural college) has a church designed by Christoph Dientzenhofer; built in 1702–11, it was this architect's first work in Bohemia and, with its concave façade and undulating interior, one of the earliest examples in this country of the influence of the Italian architect Guarino Guarini.

After a further 6km along Road 4, the dual carriageway comes to an end, and you should turn right to the industrial town of **Příbram**, a 6km detour to the west. Silver was mined here from the 14C to the 16C, and more recently the town became notorious for its uranium mines, where thousands of Czech political prisoners were forced to work in dangerous and appalling conditions in the 1950s. Now that all mining activity has finally ceased, the town has acquired a **Mining Museum** (Hornické muzeum) excitingly installed in an elaborate old pit head in the southwestern suburb of Březové Hory. Guided tours hourly, Apr–Oct Tues–Sun 09.00–15.00; Nov–Mar Tues–Fri 09.00–15.00.

But the main reason for coming to the town is to visit the hill that rises above its eastern suburbs. Known as **Holy Mountain** (Svatá Hora), this is crowned by the oldest and most famous **Marian shrine** in Bohemia. Originally a modest 14C church, the shrine was later taken over by the Jesuits, who constructed the present church—one of the largest pilgrimage churches in Bohemia—between 1658 and 1675. The ascent to the shrine from Příbram is by way of a covered stairway that begins at the end of Dlouhá street. This magnificent 'Scala Santa', with its terraces decorated with statues of angels and saints by Matyáš Hueber (d. 1702), dates back to 1658 but was significantly altered in 1727–28 by Kilian Ignaz Dientzenhofer. The church itself was designed by two of the leading architects associated with the early Baroque in Bohemia, Carlo Lurago and Domenico Orsi; inside there are frescoes by the first Baroque painter to employ this technique in Bohemia, Jan Jakub Steevens. **Open** daily 08.30–17.00.

Head south from Příbram along Road 30, and after 5km (just before regaining Road 4), turn right to **Březnice**, a further 12km away. The town's church (1637–42), attached to a former Jesuit college, is a large and forbidding work by Carlo Lurago; the interior contains altars by Škréta and Franz Xavier and Ignaz Raab. More interesting is the château, situated in a wooded public park on the edge of town, and creating beautiful reflections in the small lake below it. The original medieval castle was transformed into a Renaissance residence in the mid-16C, at around the time that Ferdinand, the son of the Emperor Ferdinand I, was married here to Philippine Welser of Augsburg. In front of the building is a sculpture by the locally born artist Ludvík Kuba (1863–1956), more of whose works can be seen in the gallery installed inside.

Leave Březnice on Road 19, which heads in a southeasterly direction towards Tábor, crossing Road 4 after 11km, and, 7km later, the Vltava. On the western shores of the river—which widens here into a wide and long lake created by the largest of this river's dams—stands the castle of **Orlík nad Vltavou**. Huddled between water and forest, this former Schwarzenberg property dates back to a 13C castle, built strategically near what was once a ford across the Vltava; altered and extended at the end of the 16C, it was reconstructed after a serious fire in 1802, and then remodelled in a neo-Gothic style by B. Grueber between 1849 and 1860. The interior includes a well-preserved series of Empire rooms filled with furniture of that period, and a second-floor gallery crammed to capacity with hunting trophies and a collection of arms dating from the 17C to 19C. Also on the second floor is the Teska Hall, so-called on account of a remarkably elaborate and deeply carved coffered ceiling executed in 1882–84 by Jan Teska, a relative of the painter Mikoláš Aleš. **Open** June–Aug Tues–Sun 09.00–18.00; May, Sept till 17.00; Apr, Oct till 16.00.

Numerous canoeists and a summer boat service ply the Vltava in between Orlík and Zvíkov. The journey between the two places is rather less easy by car, and involves a short detour away from the river: the quickest route is to drive due south from Orlík, past Starý Sedlo and Nevězice, then turn right towards Smetanova, and finally left and left again.

The castle of **Zvíkov**, one of Bohemia's most important medieval sights, occupies a magnificent isolated position, thrust up high on a wooded spit of land at the confluence of the Vltava and the Otava; forests extend as far as the eye can see.

History of the castle

Built for the Přemyslid kings, it was begun in around 1234, and its walls completed by 1270; though never taken by force, it was mortgaged in the 14C to the Rožmberks, who in later years were badly to neglect it. Unlike most other Czech castles it was not added to or remodelled in later centuries, and the parts that survive today, scattered around their sylvan setting, give a good idea of how the former royal residence originally looked.

You enter through a gate adjoining a tall round tower comprising the oldest part of the complex. North of here—to the east of a large courtyard—is the royal palace itself, centred around an unusual hexagonal courtyard comprising two superimposed rows of arcading, the upper of which is decorated by simple tracery. A room on the ground floor has exhibits relating to the construction of the castle, while upstairs is a terrace with a superb panorama over the Vltava.

On the upper floor are also to be found the **Royal Chapel** and the so-called **Bridal Chamber**, the two most exciting remaining parts of the palace interior. Both places are decorated with fascinating if over-restored wall-paintings by an anonymous master of c 1480 (the restoration was carried out at the end of the 19C). One of the walls in the Bridal Chamber shows courting couples in contemporary dress being entertained by a jester and musicians; above, keeping a watch on the proceedings, are the figures of four Bohemian kings. The entrance to the Royal Chapel has a tympanum with sculpted fragments (restored in 1977) representing the *Adoration of the Magi*. A row of blind trefoiled arcading runs round the lower walls of the chapel, each arch containing paintings of saints by the anonymous master of c 1480; the same artist was also responsible for the paintings above, among which are an *Adoration of the Virgin* and one of the earliest representations in Western art of Purgatory. On the high altar is a fine woodcarving of the *Deposition of Christ* by an anonymous artist of c 1520. **Open** July, Aug Tues–Sun 09.00–17.00; June 09.00–12.00 and 13.00–17.00; May, Sept 09.00–12.00 and 13.00–16.00; Apr, Oct Sat, Sun 09.00–12.00 and 13.00–15.30.

After 9km the road south from Zvíkov joins Road 33, where you turn right to **Písek** a further 7km away. Attractively situated on the Otava, Písek is both a holiday resort and a small industrial town which rose to prosperity in the Middle Ages through the sifting of gold-bearing sand from its river (the word *písek* means sand). The old centre of the town is best seen from the opposite side of the Otava, from where it presents a little-spoilt profile of 13C to 18C structures rising directly above the water. In the foreground is a late 13C bridge claimed to be the oldest in the Czech Republic and adorned in the middle with anonymous Baroque statues of 1754–57. The most prominent of the riverside buildings is the former royal castle, commissioned by Otakar II in 1254 but much altered in later centuries. The outstanding feature of the interior is the 13C Knight's Hall, decorated with anonymous wall-paintings dated 1479. The paintings, like those at Zvíkov, are in a fanciful and decorative late medieval manner, and feature battle and tournament scenes, as well as over-lifesize figures of George of Poděbrady and of his predecessor Ladislav the Posthumous. By this date the castle had for 20 years been the property of George of Poděbrady's brother-in-law, Leo of Rožmitál (d. 1485). **Open** Tues–Sun 09.00–18.00.

At Písek you join up with the E49, which you can follow 52km to České Budějovice, affording on the way a distant view to the east of the controversial nuclear power station at Temelín, the largest in the world.

B. Via Tábor and Bechyně

Total distance 149km: Prague (leave by the D1/E55) • 36km Benešov • 43km Tábor • 18km Opařany • 10km Bechyně • 42km České Budějovice.

Tábor

Take the D1 motorway to V. Popovice (21km), then head south on the E55 past Benešov and Konopiště (see Chapter 2B) until eventually, 43km later, you approach Tábor from its northwestern suburbs. The old centre is seen from this part of town looming above a large lake, which was created in 1492 by the oldest dam in Bohemia, and given the biblical name of Jordan. To the south Tábor rises above luxuriant slopes falling steeply down to the river Lužnice. The beauty of Tábor's situation, its numerous Renaissance buildings, and its strong associations with the Hussite movement, make the town one of the great tourist attractions in South Bohemia.

The Táborites

Following the martyrdom of Jan Hus in 1416, his followers came to be divided into two distinct groups, the 'Calixtines' being the more aristocratic of the two, and the 'Utraquists' having both a more popular appeal and a more radical outlook. Later a third and yet more radical party came into being, which rejected the Mass, and indeed all but two of the Sacraments, and insisted on the Bible as the sole authority in all matters of belief. This new party held open-air meetings throughout Bohemia, but their main centre was at Ústí, a small town to which they gave the name of the mountain where Christ was transfigured, Tábor. In 1420 the charismatic leader of the so-called Táborites, Jan Žižka, founded the present Tábor, 4km to the north of the former one, and on a site occupied by a castle built in the 14C over a Celtic oppidum. The blind Žižka died of the plague in 1424, and his supporters henceforth called themselves the 'Orphans', feeling that they would be unable to find a new leader equal to him. The Táborite movement died out in the 1430s, but the town which Žižka had founded lived on as a royal town after 1437. The castle was later converted into a brewery, and the visionary settlement of the Táborites is today a small industrial town known for its manufacture of sparking plugs for cars.

Surrounded on three sides by its defensive walls, the old centre of Tábor has been remarkably little spoilt. From the Jordan Lake (jezero Jordán) follow Palackého třída into its continuation Pražská, the town's main commercial street, but picturesquely narrow and lined with old buildings; the finest of these are at Nos 12 and 13 on the left-hand side, which are covered with lively sgraffito decorations of battle scenes (1570).

Pražská leads into the town's main square, which is named after Jan Žižka, who is commemorated by a memorial on the square's north side. The square, **Žižkovo náměstí**, which recent restoration has given a bright and cheerful look, is the town's main showpiece, and contains most of Tábor's more interesting monuments. In the centre is a Renaissance fountain, while all around are houses crowned with a remarkable variety of gables. One of the more fantastical of these gables belongs to a popular tourist restaurant on the north side of the square (adjoining the old U Lichvičů ale house); it comprises elaborately intertwined blind arcading, and open-work motifs on the sides.

Occupying the northwestern corner of the square is the now glisteningly white **Church of the Transfiguration of Our Lord on Mount Tábor** (kostel Proměnění Páně na Hoře Tábor), begun in 1440 on the site of a Hussite church and largely completed by 1512. You enter through the south side, with its three Renaissance gables, and find yourself in a a bright and spacious three-aisled structure, the nave of which was given cross- and net-vaulting by Master Staněk in 1512. Of slightly later date, and more remarkable, is the 'cellular' or diamond-vaulting in the chancel, the effect of which, in the words of Brian Knox, is like standing 'inside some huge intricately pleated white skirt'.

The west side of the square is dominated by the Old Town Hall, a triple-gabled structure flanked by a tall tower. The heavily restored building, built between the late 15C and early 16C, contains an excellent **museum** (Husitské muzeum) devoted to the history of the Hussite Movement, featuring medals, manuscripts, armoury and applied arts objects connected with the movement, as well as more recent works of art of Hussite subject-matter. The beautifully vaulted and starkly impressive hall contains the model of Bohumil Kafka's dynamic equestrian portrait of Žižka (1935) which now crowns Prague's Žižkov Hill. From the museum you can undertake a tour of the extensive series of **tunnels** that extend underneath the square. Begun after 1420 and completed 100 years later, they were used at first to store beer, but later acted as shelters during the frequent fires that swept through the town in the 16C; subsequently they were used for prisoners. **Open** Tues–Sun 08.30–11.00 and 11.30–16.00.

Behind the Town Hall lies an empty and neglected part of town with roughly cobbled streets leading to the attractive náměstí Mikuláše, on which stands a 17C former Augustinian monastery. The 14C **Kotnov castle** (300m from Žižka náměstí along Klokotská) is on the southwestern corner of the town, and has functioned as a brewery since the 18C; it is attached to the 15C Bechyně Gate, which has a high-pitched roof of toy-like appearance. The view from the other side of the gate down to the river is over trees and hanging gardens.

Leave Tábor on Road 33 in the direction of Písek. On the outskirts of the town take a turning to the left to **Klokoty**, a tiny pilgrimage church and cloister (1710–30) given an exotic oriental profile through a series of eight onion domes. The place stands above a particularly wooded stretch of the river

Lužnice, and commands an excellent view towards Tábor. Continue on Road 33 to **Opařany**, which has a remarkable Jesuit church built in 1732–35 by K.I. Dientzenhofer. The interior, with a complex and dynamic plan based on two interconnected tranverse ovals, features tangential three-dimensional ribs and the broken segmental pediments so characteristic of this architect's work.

At Opařany leave Road 33 and head south to **Bechyně** (10km), after 5km passing the ruins of Dobronice castle. Bechyně, which is linked to Tábor by the oldest narrow-gauge railway in Bohemia (built by František Křižík in 1903), is a small town and peat spa impressively situated above a wooded gorge thrust above the river Lužnice. The sloping and very attractive main square is a quiet and shaded place, more appropriate to a village than a town.

Off a street near the top of the square is the former **Franciscan church** and cloister, built in the late 15C, but revaulted in the late 16C: the 'cellular' vaulting in the nave is perhaps the most extraordinary of its kind in Bohemia, and seems less an example of late medieval architecture than a German expressionistic fantasy of the 1920s. The former Franciscan monastery hangs directly above the gorge, as does the other important monument in the town—the **castle**. This, at the bottom of the main square, is a building of 13C origin which was given its present look in the late 16C. The slightly shabby interior, now used for conferences organised by the Czech Academy of Sciences, has a hall decorated c 1590 with Old Testament figures and representations of Virtues and Vices; these amusing works, surrounded by a fictive framework in a North Italian style, are comparable to paintings produced at the court of Rudolph II. Bechyně has a long-standing ceramics tradition, and a good collection of locally produced ceramics can now be seen in the South Bohemian Aleš Gallery (Alšova jihočeská galerie), which is installed in a former brewery. **Open** May–Oct Tues–Sun 09.00–12.00 and 12.30–17.00.

Spanning the Lužnice gorge below the castle is a pioneering parabolically arched concrete bridge. On the other side of the river head south to the pretty village of Týn nad Vltavou (10km) where there is a small museum with archaeological, numismatic and ceramic collections.

After crossing the Vltava here drive south for 21km to **Hluboká nad Vltavou**, a sprawling village at the foot of a wooded hill crowned by one of the most famous and spectacular country houses in the Czech Republic.

History of Hluboká

The origins of Hluboká are in a castle probably founded by Wenceslas I in the early 13C; it remained officially a royal property until 1562, when it was sold to the Lords of Hradec, who had it entirely rebuilt. The work was no sooner over than it was sold again, this time to the Malovec family, who were to be its last Czech owners, keeping it until 1622. In 1661 it became one of the several southern Bohemian properties owned by the Bavarian Schwarzenbergs, whose official architect, P.I. Bayer, was to remodel the building in a Baroque style between 1707 and 1728. Only after 1830 did the Schwarzenbergs decide to make this their principle Bohemian residence, and at the same time to create a new building which would amply reflect their high standing at the Viennese court, their vast wealth and the progressive outlook which they had recently shown in a series of imaginative industrial and agricultural enterprises. The fantastical turreted showpiece which you see today is due to the rebuilding campaign carried out after 1841 by the Viennese architect F. Beer, and completed in 1871 by F.D. Deworecky.

The house at Hluboká is frequently described as in an English Gothic style, and W.S. Monroe, in his *Bohemia and the Czechs* (1902), even makes the curious assertion that the building is 'a replica of Windsor Castle in England'. In fact, the house bears as much relation to a real English building as Mad Ludwig of Bavaria's Neuschwanstein bears to German medieval architecture. The enormously tall white-stoned structure looks like the work of a demented pastry chef, and all that it has in common with Windsor are its machicolated towers, which are here piled up in profusion to create purely decorative effects: it is a vision of England as experienced by someone with the imagination of a Walt Disney. As you pass through the main entrance note the bronze handles on the doors, which represent a crow pecking at the eye of a Moor—the grotesque heraldic symbol of the Schwarzenberg family and a motif to be repeated constantly throughout the house. Around the larger of the two courtyards inside are a series of stag heads carved in stone.

The entrance hall beyond overwhelms by the sheer quantity of intricate wood-carvings (by local artists), and indeed the hallmark of the whole interior is the abundance of decorative woodwork. Almost everywhere there are marquetry floors, and elaborate wood panelling, both on the walls and ceilings. Crammed with characteristically Victorian *horror vacui* into this already congested setting is a wealth of furniture and other applied arts objects, including Czech Baroque glass, Italian Renaissance tables, Bohemian 18C porcelain, Kreussen jugs, an outstanding collection of 17C to 18C tapestries, and an inlaid Baroque wardrobe left by the writer A. Stifter. The paintings, featuring several dubious attributions, are less impressive, though among them are many interesting family and other portraits, including one by Joshua Reynolds. **Open** July, Aug daily 09.00–12.00 and 12.30–17.00; May, June Tues–Sun 09.00–12.00 and 12.30–17.00; Apr, Sept, Oct 09.00–12.00 and 12.30–16.30.

If the lover of fine arts is less than satisfied by a visit to the house at Hluboká, there is always the consolation of the **South Bohemian Aleš Gallery** (Alšova jihočeské galerie), which was transferred in 1956 from České Budějovice to the former riding stables adjoining the house; it bears the name of Mikoláš Aleš (1852–1913), one of this region's greatest painters. The building itself, also designed by F. Beer (1845–47), is entered through a magnificent and very innovative iron-and-glass construction in an elaborate Gothic style. The collections largely originate from the former diocesan and municipal museums at České Budějovice, and from the monastery at Vyšší Brod. The works include 20C Czech masters such as Václav Špála, Josef Čapek and Antonín Hudeček, and the largest collection of Dutch paintings in the Czech Republic (the latter comprises mainly minor works, but note the portraits by Cornelis van der Voort and Paulus Morelsee, and the still-lifes by Pieter Claesz). By far the most distinguished aspect of the gallery is the large collection of Bohemian paintings and sculptures of the 14C and 15C, most notably a series of characteristically sweet Madonnas and Child, including the sculpted *Rudolvov Madonna* (c 1300, the oldest work in the gallery), the painted *Madonna of the Trinity of České Budějovice* (before 1410) and the charming *Hluboká Adoration* (c 1380), a work generally attributed to the

Master of Třeboň, one of the finest Bohemian artists of the 14C. **Open** Tues–Sun 09.00–18.00.

Within the extensive grounds of Hluboká are various lakes and canals, and much statuary. Two kilometres southwest of the house, by the edge of the Munický Lake, is the **Ohrada Hunting-Lodge**, built by Bayer for the Schwarzenbergs in 1709–15. The interior, featuring a large ceiling painting of the *Enthroned Diana*, has been a Museum of Hunting and Forestry since 1842 and is oppressively decorated with hunting trophies, some of the antlers even being used for table legs and candelabra. **Open** Apr–Oct Tues–Sun 08.30–18.00.

South of Ohrada you join the E49, which will lead you 6km to České Budějovice.

16 · Prachatice to Jindřichův Hradec via Vyšší Brod

Total distance 189km: Prachatice • 18km Volary • 68km Vyšší Brod • 9km Rožmberk nad Vltavou • 18km Český Krumlov • 24km České Budějovice • 24km Třeboň • 28km Jindřichův Hradec.

Instead of driving directly from Prachatice to České Budějovice you can make a detour through the southern half of the forested Šumava Mountains, ending up at Vyšší Brod, from where you can begin one of the most exciting architectural itineraries in the Czech and Slovak Republics.

Head 18km due south of Prachatice to **Volary**, where you can see some of the last surviving examples of the traditional Alpine-style folk architecture of the Šumava, featuring wooden galleries and wide saddle roofs. Eleven kilometres west of Volary is the glass-making village and holiday resort of **Lenora**, where there is a 19C covered wooden bridge across the Vltava. The place makes a good centre for excursions up **Mt Boubín** (1362m), on the slopes of which is a primeval forest which has been protected since 1858. The trees are mainly spruce, and include bizarrely shaped fir and beech trees; a nature trail has been set up along the edge of the forest. Lenora is also exceptionally popular with canoeists, who can start from here a memorable trip along the Vltava, the source of which is nearby to the west.

Continuing south from Volary you follow the river all the way to Vyšší Brod. After Želnava, 12km from Volary, the river turns into an artificial lake, the largest in the Czech Republic, and much frequented by holiday makers. The dam is at Lipno, 36km further south. From Lipno the journey to Vyšší Brod is completed by winding along the river's banks through dense forest.

Vyšší Brod

The village of Vyšší Brod, in forested surroundings only 7km to the north of the Austrian frontier, grew up around its Cistercian monastery, one of the most famous in the Czech and Slovak republics.

History of Vyšší Brod

In 1259 Vok of Rožmberk, high officer at the Royal Court, summoned 12 monks from the Cistercian monastery at Wilhering in Austria to found a monastery in the vicinity of his residence at Rožmberk nad Vltavou; the idea of creating such an institution here was part of an attempt to colonise the south Bohemian borderland. The foundations of the monastery church were laid in the 1260s, but the chancel was not begun until 1292; the nave was commenced in the 1360s and vaulted in 1385. At the time the nave was conceived, a member of the Rožmberk family, Petr Vok of Rožmberk, was serving under Charles IV in Prague as Dean of the Chapter of the royal chapel of All Saints, and it is likely that through this connection the royal architect Peter Parléř came to influence the construction of the Vyšší Brod church.

When completed the church was one of the largest in Bohemia, an indication of the wealth and prestige which the monastery then enjoyed. Heavily fortified owing to its position on the Bohemian border, Vyšší Brod survived two sieges during the Hussite Wars in the early 15C, but then was severely damaged in 1526 by fire. After the death in 1611 of the last of the Rožmberks, another Petr Vok, the monastery came under the protection first of the Eggenbergs, and then, after 1719, of the Schwarzenbergs. The monastery was not to be dissolved until 1950.

The former **monastery** at Vyšší Brod, though still surrounded by its fortifications, has suffered greatly over the years, not only on account of the fire of 1536, but also because of drastic restoration over the centuries, and the taking away of most of its important art treasures. A visit here is largely of historical rather than of architectural or artistic interest.

The official guided tour of the monastery begins with the **church**, which was much altered during the Baroque period and given a modern look as a result of restoration carried out in the 19C and 20C. The painting on the high altar is a poor and late imitation of Titian's *Assumption* in the Frari in Venice, but it has a magnificent Baroque framework of 1644–46. In the course of 19C restoration, medieval frescoes on either side of the high altar were damaged irreparably, and in their place were put oil paintings representing the same subject-matter: one, painted in 1840 by Josef Hellich, shows the monastery's founder being miraculously saved from the flooded Vltava river; the other, a work of 1879 by Bartoloměj Čurn, is of Vok of Rožmberk and his wife Hedvika of Schaumburg consecrating the church to the Virgin Mary and St Wenceslas. In the second chapel on the west side of the south transept is a copy of the famous *Vyšší Brod Madonna* (now in the National Gallery of Prague), one of the major works of Czech medieval art: the painting's donor, Vok of Rožmberk, is shown kneeling in the left-hand corner.

Off the cloister is the **chapter house**, the oldest surviving part of the monastery. Built between 1280 and 1285, though heavily restored in recent times, it is a unique example in Czech medieval architecture of vaulting being supported by a single central sheaf pillar; the tracery of the central rosette window is original, but the stained glass dates from the 19C. Afterwards you are taken to see the library, which was founded at the same time as the monastery and contains 70,000 volumes, as well as an important collection of manuscripts and incunabula.

The present building dates from 1757, and constitutes the highpoint of the tour. You are first shown the **Small Library Hall**—with a ceiling of the *Judgement of Solomon* by Lukáš Vavra—where you will find displayed the first official map of Bohemia (by Jan Kryštof Müller); later comes the **Large Library Hall**, dazzlingly gilded, filled with furniture made by one of the monks (Josef Raffer), and with a ceiling fresco by Vávra of *Christ in the Temple*. The tour ends with the small **art gallery** founded by Abbot Valentin Schoper in 1838, and containing a largely dismal collection of paintings, with the exception of a beautiful head by the Bolognese painter Mauro Gandolfi (1764–1834), and some landscapes by Norbert Grund. **Open** Tues–Sun 09.00–12.00 and 13.00–17.00.

Separate to the tour is a museum installed in the former residential part of the monastery. It is difficult to conceive of the prosaic mind who had the idea of establishing here, in one of the more sacred spots in Bohemia, a museum devoted to the Czech Postal Service.

Entering the Rose Country

From Vyšší Brod to Jindřichův Hradec stretches a land known frequently as the 'Rose Country', after the symbol of the former lords of the area, the Rožmberks. The first important member of the family, Vítek z Prčic, was chamberlain to Vladislav II, and had a son called Jindřich who founded in 1220 the castle later named after him at Jindřichův Hradec; the last of the Rožmberks, Petr Vok (1539–1611), lies buried at his ancestral monastery at Vyšší Brod. The land over which the family ruled is virtually unrivalled in the Czech Republic for its concentration of outstanding towns and monuments. It is also a region of great natural beauty: up to České Budějovice you follow a narrow, wooded and little-spoilt stretch of the Vltava valley, while afterwards you travel through a haunting area of lakes and marshes.

From Vyšší Brod follow the Vltava for 9km to **Rožmberk nad Vltavou**, an exceptionally pretty village with crumbling old houses and a 15C–16C deanery church standing directly above the mossy, tree-lined banks of the river. This quiet, semi-abandoned place was once the main residence of the Rožmberks, whose **castle** stands imposingly in the wooded upper slopes of the village. Approached from Vyšší Brod, you will notice to the right of the castle, and at a higher level to it, an isolated round tower almost lost among the trees. This is all that survives of the original castle founded here by the Rožmberks in the mid-13C.

History of the castle

The 13C castle lost its importance after 1302, when the Rožmberk family decided to transfer their main residence from here to Český Krumlov. Nevertheless the Rožmberks by no means entirely neglected their ancestral seat, and later in the 14C built here a two-storeyed lower palace with a square tower. When the upper castle burned down in 1522, the family devoted all its attention to the lower building, which they transformed into a Renaissance residence. In around 1600 Petr Vok had part of the palace magnificently redecorated for his nephew and heir Jan Zrinský, whose death in 1612 spelt the end of the Rožmberk succession. The castle passed first into the hands of the Schwarzenbergs, and then into those of the Boucquoys, who were awarded the building for the part which they played in the Battle of the White Mountain. Under the Boucquoys—who were to keep the building until 1945—the castle was subjected to extensive alterations, first in a Baroque style and then in a neo-Gothic one.

The tour of the castle begins with the neo-Gothic Crusader's Gallery, a long panelled space lined with romantic historical portraits; afterwards comes the so-called **Bower of the White Lady**, filled with mementoes of the Rožmberk family, and of the legendary woman known as the White Lady, who had a monster of a husband, and whose ghost is still said to haunt Jindřichův Hradec.

A subsequent room, devoted to the military commander Charles Bonaventura (the father of Albert Bucquoy), has an interesting painting by Jacob Grimer of the *Feeding of the Five Thousand* (1560), in which Ferdinand I and his wife Anne of Austria are represented. After the bedroom, with its 16C Dutch bed and chandelier, comes the Picture Gallery, where there are paintings by Václav Reiner, Johann Kupecký and Škréta.

By far the most distinguished room is the following one, the **Banqueting Hall**, which formed part of the redecoration programme commissioned by Petr Vok for Jan Zrinský c 1600. Zrinský had spent much time with his mother and step-father in Mantua, and the artists who worked for him in this room were either Italian or at least well acquainted with North Italian art of the late 16C. Almost every part of the room is painted, including the wooden ceiling, which has panels covered with grotesques. In the recesses of the windows there are curious frescoes of the *Ten Stages in Human Life*, while between the windows hang seven paintings of the Planets; by the sides of the doors are *trompe-l'oeil* figures as in Veronese's frescoes in the Villa Maser. At the end of the hall, and separated from it by a Renaissance grille, is a small space reserved for the musicians. Here, in an illusionistic setting featuring a ceiling supported by caryatids, is the most extraordinary of all the castle's frescoes, a representation of musicians which incorporates actual jewels (the real jewels were stolen in the Thirty Years War and have been replaced by copies). The remaining rooms include an armoury and rooms in an early Baroque style devoted to later members of the Bucquoy family. **Open** June, Aug Tues–Sun 09.00–17.00; May, Sept 09.00–16.00; Apr, Oct Sat, Sun 09.00–16.00.

Český Krumlov

From Rožmberk nad Vltavou to České Budějovice you drive alongside the Vltava for a further 24km, passing through wooded countryside with hardly a single house. Český Krumlov sits crammed in and around a dramatic loop of the Vltava, above which rises a castle complex rivalled in size only by Prague's Hradčany. The town makes a sensational first impression on the visitor and, unsurprisingly, has emerged in recent years as the Czech Republic's most popular tourist destination outside Prague. Anyone coming here for the first time will certainly not be disappointed, even if they find themselves battling with the huge crowds of tourists that now congest the narrow streets for most of the year. Those relatively few visitors who

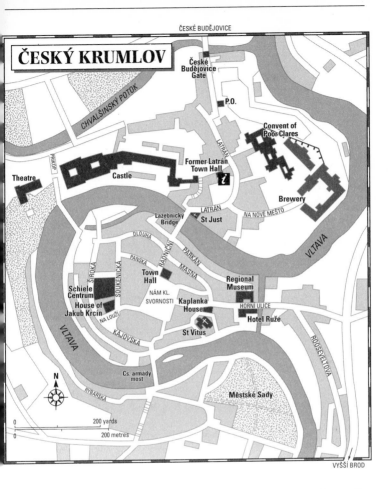

ČESKÝ KRUMLOV

ČESKÉ BUDĚJOVICE

ČESKÉ BUDĚJOVICE
Gate

P.O.

CHVALŠINSKÝ POTOK

PŘÍKOP

Theatre

Castle

LATRÁN

Former Latrán
Town Hall

Convent of
Poor Clares

Brewery

Lažebnický
Bridge

LATRÁN

St Just

NA NOVÉ MĚSTO

VLTAVA

DLOUHÁ

PANSKÁ

RADNIČNÍ

PARKÁN

ŠIROKÁ

SOUKENICKÁ

Town
Hall

MASNÁ

Regional
Museum

Schiele
Centrum

House of
Jakub Krcín

NÁM KL.
SVORNOSTI

NA LOUŽI

Kaplanka
House

HORNÍ ULICE

KÁJOVSKÁ

St Vitus

Hotel Ruže

VLTAVA

ROOSEVELTOVA

N

Cs. armády
most

RYBÁŘSKÁ

Městské Sady

0   200 yards
0   200 metres

VYŠŠÍ BROD

remember the town from before 1989, when the place had remained virtually
unchanged (and unrestored) since the 18C, cannot help but be saddened by the
way in which the romantic decay of old has now given way to brightly coloured
renovation that has given to the whole an artificial, Disneyland appearance.

History of Český Krumlov

The history of Český Krumlov is inseparable from that of its castle, which
was first mentioned in a document of 1253, when it belonged to the Vítek
family. The Lords of Krumlov, as the Víteks are often known, died out in
1302, and their estate was inherited by their distant relatives, the
Rožmberks. The Rožmberks turned Český Krumlov into the administrative
and cultural centre of their vast domains, and extended and radically
altered the castle. To the 13C lower castle they added an upper castle in the
14C, and then remodelled the entire complex in the 16C. The last of the

Rožmberks, Petr Vok, sold the castle in 1602 to Rudolph II, but the place was only to remain in Habsburg hands until 1622, when it was resold to the Eggenbergs. In 1715, on the extinction of the Eggenberg family, the castle was inherited by the Schwarzenbergs, who remained the owners until 1947. Much building work was carried out here in the 17C and 18C, but little was done subsequently either to the castle, or indeed to the increasingly somnolent small town which had grown up at its feet.

The Austrian painter Egon Schiele—whose mother was a native of the town—provided the place with some of its livelier later moments when he came here from Vienna in 1911, bringing with him his model and mistress Wally Neuzil, and two of his bohemian companions, Erwin Osen and Moa Mandu. They bought a dilapidated riverside cottage as a studio, but were soon expelled from the town, partly for hiring local girls as nude models, and for painting Wally naked in the orchard. Little else seemed to stir the town until the collapse of Communism, when the inhabitants were able to gain large sums of money through the renovation and sale of their properties. Being declared in 1992 a UNESCO-protected town only hastened the rapid commercialisation of the place, and today an astonishing 250 old houses have been sold off to Austrian, German and other foreign businesses.

A tour of Český Krumlov is best begun at the **České Budějovice Gate**, which stands at the northern edge of town, on the left bank of the Vltava: next to the gate is a lane leading down to the town's main car park, which stands between the river and the largest surviving section of the town's medieval ramparts. The gate itself is an impressive structure of 1598, designed by the Italian architect Domenico Cometa and copied almost directly from an engraving after Serlio; it is painted on its inner side. Once through the gate you find yourself in a world of narrow streets squeezed between tall, irregularly shaped houses with high-pitched roofs, some of which cluster like limpets around the rock on which the castle is built.

The street due south of the gate leads into **Latrán**, the town's picturesque main thoroughfare, which curls around the foot of the castle rock and down to the river. Half-way down Latrán on your right is a lane leading to the Red Gate (1861), through which you enter a large courtyard forming the outer bailey of the **castle**. Among the buildings here are a former salt house first mentioned in 1511, to the right of the gate, and on the left-hand side of the courtyard a former residence of the chief officer of the castle.

Looming in front of you is the lower castle, above which a **round tower** rises to a height of 72m, creating the most prominent landmark on the Český Krumlov skyline. The base of the tower is the main survival of the original 13C castle, but what gives the structure its distinction is the arcaded upper gallery and elaborate crowning-piece, a 1580s addition which makes the tower resemble some 16C astronomical instrument.

Joining the outer bailey to the lower castle is a bridge spanning a moat where bears have been kept since the 16C. Across the bridge and through the gate on the other side you enter a second courtyard, adorned with cannons and lined with walls that were given painted rustication in the 16C (restored in 1842). The buildings here include a former mint and agricultural college, the latter (founded in 1800 and dissolved in 1850) being one of the first of its kind in

Bohemia. A passage of the late 16C will take you from the second into the third courtyard, where the obligatory guided tours of the main and upper castle begin.

After such a spectacular build-up, the building's interior might come as a slight disappointment. Although thoroughly restored in recent years, the rooms continue to have a generally sparse, forbidding look, the result of years of neglect; furthermore, to see as many of the rooms as possible you now have to take no less than two guided tours, one of which concentrates on the earlier interiors, and the other on the Baroque and Rococo ones.

Near the entrance is the **Chapel of St George** (sv. Jiří), which dates back to 1334 but was given a stucco facing between 1750 and 1753 by a Viennese craftsman called Matthias André. Afterwards comes a Renaissance hall (a remodelling of 1574–77 of the upper castle's 14C hall), and a further series of rooms decorated in the late 16C, all containing portraits and other souvenirs of the Rožmberk family. The Renaissance grand hall was destroyed in the late 17C to make way for the present staircase, up which you climb to the second landing, from where there is an excellent view of the town.

The upper rooms are all of the Baroque and Rococo periods, and include an early 18C dining room containing two tapestries after cartoons by Rubens, and a Rococo cabinet of 1755 with pastel-blue chinoiserie decorations. The last upstairs room which you visit is the castle picture gallery, founded in 1733, and featuring a good portrait by Gerhard Seghers, rather lost among a host of lesser Flemish and Dutch works of the 17C, including numerous contemporary copies and studio pictures.

Finally you descend to the **ball room**, by far the most appealing room of the castle. In 1748 an artist of Swabian origin, Josef Lederer, decorated the long room with among the most entertaining Rococo frescoes to be seen anywhere in Central Europe. These comprise a Venetian-inspired illusionistic framework of balustrades and theatre boxes, behind and in front of which parade a whole series of colourful musicians, spectators in contemporary dress, masked figures, musicians, harlequins, and other types taken from the *commedia dell'arte*; the artist himself makes an appearance, drinking a cup of coffee.

At the end of the tour you should make a visit to the **castle gardens** (now a public park), situated to the west of the castle's fourth courtyard, and reached by a long covered bridge suspended high between the castle rock and a wooded hill. The view at the end of the bridge looking back towards the castle is one of the finest to be had of the town, with only some modern buildings in the distant wooded hills interrupting a scene virtually unchanged since the 18C. The large gardens, laid out in the 18C, are themselves a great treat, and contain a terrace and balustrade covered with mythological figures, and several fine buildings, including the dainty Bellaria Summer Palace, and a garden pavilion with an illusionistic Rococo ceiling. Best of all is the building which you come to immediately after entering the gardens from the castle, the **castle theatre**. The present structure, commissioned by Josef Adam of Schwarzenberg, was built in 1766–67, and has been left untouched since then, complete with all its original stage mechanism, including a set of 12 backcloths in the style of the Bibienas. As an intact 18C theatre it is rivalled in Europe only by Drottningholm in Sweden; unfortunately, owing to its fragile state, it is only irregularly open to the public, and is rarely used for performances.

Guided tours May–Aug Tues–Sun 08.00–12.00 and 13.00–17.00; Sept 09.00–12.00 and 13.00–16.00; Apr, Oct 09.00–12.00 and 13.00–15.00.

Leaving the gardens it is best to retrace your long way back through the castle's four courtyards and down to the Latrán. On the opposite side of the street to the castle is the Pivovarská ulice, a lane leading past the former convent of the Minorites and the Poor Clares (a mid-14C foundation almost completely rebuilt in the Baroque period and now partially used as an old people's home), and down to a brewery which has been created out of the former armoury of the Rožmberks, a work by the Italian architect Antonio Cometa. Back on the Latrán continue walking down to the river, noting to your right the medieval wall-paintings at No. 15 and, to your left on the riverside, the late medieval **Church of St Just** (sv. Jošta).

Crossing the river by the Lazebnický Bridge, you enter the part of town which is squeezed into the near circular loop of the Vltava. The main street here, Radniční, connects the bridge with the town's main square, where you will find a plague column of 1716, the Renaissance Town Hall (with an attic of 1580), and a 19C art school and music academy.

From the eastern side of the square the Horní ulice climbs steeply up to the **Kaplanka House** at No. 139, which has been virtually unchanged since 1520. Immediately behind it, almost at the highest point of the town, is the **Parish Church of St Vitus** (sv. Víta) of 1407–39, with terraces on its southern side falling directly down to the river. The graceful triple-aisled interior boasts the remarkable sepulchre of William of Rožmberk, which extends to the height of the vaulting, and is surmounted by a statue of the Rožmberk rider; made out of marble, terracotta and copper, it was executed between 1593 and 1597 by the sculptor Georg Bendel and the goldsmith Jan Dorn. Continuing east along Horní ulice you will pass on your right a former Jesuit college built in 1586 by Maio da Vomio, and housing since the 19C the *Hotel Růže*; on the other side of the street, in the former Jesuit seminary, is the well-displayed **Regional Museum** (Okresní muzeum), with archaeological and historical collections, and much Gothic to Baroque statuary. **Open** Tues–Fri 09.00–12.00 and 12.30–16.00; Sat, Sun 13.00–16.00.

You can return to the Lazebnický Bridge by following the semi-circular line of streets to the west of the main square; among the fine buildings that you will pass are the House of Jakub Krčín of Jelčany, at No. 54 Na Louži, and the House of the alchemist Michael of Ebersbach on Široká. In between the last two buildings is a former 15C brewery housing the town's most popular new attraction, the **Schiele Centrum**, posters for which are papered on every street: though largely taken up by changing exhibitions of contemporary art, it has a small permanent collection of Shiele's own works, notably his deeply-felt abstract-like renditions of the town at a time when its russet-red roofs were still expressive of pathos and poignancy. **Open** daily 10.00–18.00.

Four kilometres west of Český Krumlov is the notable pilgrimage church of **Kájov**, which was largely rebuilt in 1471–85: the plainly vaulted chancel contrasts with the two-aisled hall nave, the ceiling of which is a veritable forest of delicate ribs.

Leaving Český Krumlov on the road to České Budějovice, turn off after 5km to visit the quiet village of **Zlatá Koruna**, which is famous for its former Cistercian monastery. This walled complex, standing in isolation between fields and the beautiful verdant banks of the Vltava, was founded by King Přemysl Otakar II in 1263 and given the name 'Golden Crown'. Ruined by the Hussites in 1420, the building was restored after 1609, and extended in the 18C; further restoration work was carried out after the Second World War. The oldest surviving part of the complex is the severely vaulted chapter house of c 1280. The church interior, despite Baroque additions and a glistening coat of white paint, is essentially that which was built between c 1340 and c 1360; Parler at work here in 1359, and the nave shows clearly the influence of Prague's Cathedral, being one of the first spaces in Europe where the vaulting springs directly from the walls and piers instead of from capitals. Of the 18C additions the great jewel is the gilded and frescoed library of c 1770. **Open** Apr–Oct Tues–Sun 08.30–16.30.

České Budějovice

At the confluence of the rivers Vltava and Malše, 19km north of Zlatá Koruna, stands the regional capital of South Bohemia, České Budějovice. Though much rebuilt in the 19C and early 20C, and surrounded now by extensive industrial suburbs, the old centre of České Budějovice has retained its original medieval town plan, and has a spacious and solemnly impressive character.

History of České Budějovice

Founded by Otakar II in 1265, and laid out by Otakar's engineer Hrz of Zvíkov, České Budějovice boasted a town plan which for sheer scale and ambitiousness was not to be rivalled until the creation of Plzeň 30 years later. The manufacturing of beer and the storing of salt transported from Austria contributed to the town's early prosperity, which reached its highpoint in the 16C with the revenue derived from the exploitation of the nearby fish-ponds. Devastated during the Thirty Years War, and by a serious fire in 1641, the town subsequently stagnated, and its fortunes were not to improve until the 19C, when it developed into a major industrial centre. The town today has an important engineering industry, and large enamelware and pencil factories, the latter founded in 1847. But its best known institution is the Budweis Brewery, which has been functioning since 1894, and produces one of the finest of Czech beers (the original 'Budweiser' or 'Bud', as it is known to its American enthusiasts).

The medieval grid-plan of České Budějovice is contained within an oval area encircled by rivers and a long canal. At its centre is the Přemyslid Otakar II Square (náměstí Přemysla Otakará II), one of the largest not only in the Czech Republic but also in Europe. This vast and traffic-free quadratic space is empty save for the impressive **Samson's Fountain** (Samsonova kašna) at the centre: executed by Josef Dietrich in 1727, it comprises a statue of Samson rising above a large basin supported by struggling atlantes. The arcaded buildings lining the square are mainly of the 18C and 19C, the finest being the **Town Hall** in the southwest corner: crowned by three Baroque steeples, this originally Gothic structure was rebuilt in 1727–30 by Antonio Martinelli, who had come from Vienna to Bohemia to replace Bayer as the Schwarzenberg architect at Český Krumlov; note, on the left-hand side of the façade, a metal stick used for checking the length of materials.

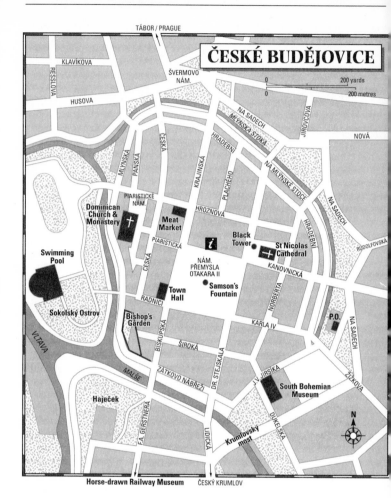

ČESKÉ BUDĚJOVICE

Horse-drawn Railway Museum   ČESKÝ KRUMLOV

The town's **Cathedral of St Nicholas** (sv. Mikuláš), off the northeastern corner of the square, is a 13C foundation which was rebuilt in 1641–49 and has been heavily restored since then. Of greater interest is the **Black Tower** (Černá věž) next to it, a structure 72m in height which was designed by Vincenz Fuggeral in the early 16C; you can climb up to its gallery, from where you can best appreciate the medieval layout of the town. **Open** July, Aug daily 10.00–19.00; Mar–June Tues–Sun 10.00–18.00 and Sept–Nov 09.00–17.00.

The oldest monument in České Budějovice lies off the northwestern corner of the square and can be reached by walking east along Piaristická. This, the former **Dominican Monastery of St Mary** (Panny Marie), was founded at the same time as the town, but was extensively remodelled at the end of the 18C when it passed into the hands of the Piarists; the dreary late Baroque interior of the church retains fragments of medieval frescoes. The street leading north off the northwestern corner of the square, Krajinská, will take you after 50m to the former **Meat Market** (Masné krámy), a curious long structure dating back to 1554 and now functioning as a tourist-loved beer-hall serving basic food.

Running south from the Town Hall is Biskupská, where at No. 132 is the late 18C Bishopric, with a very plain exterior. Turn right into Široká to see at No. 39 a private house containing traces of wall-decorations painted in 1653; at the end of the street, in a squalid alley adjoining the neglected Bishop's Garden, is one of the towers from the medieval fortifications. Continue south along Biskupská and cross the river Malše. Off the gardens at the end of this street is the **Regional Museum** (Jihočeské muzeum), a pompous eclectic building of the turn of the century housing extensive historical, numismatic and archaeological collections. **Open** Tues–Sun 09.00–12.00 and 12.30–17.30.

Further south, near the junction of General Svoboda and the main road to Český Krumlov, is a tiny **Museum of the Horse-drawn Railway** (Památník koněspřežní železnice) commemorating the first horse-drawn railway in continental Europe. Built in 1827–30, it linked České Budějovice with the Upper Austrian town of Linz, and functioned up to 1832; the museum is installed in the original station. **Open** May–Sept Tues–Sun 09.00–12.00 and 12.30–17.00. Return to the north side of the Malše and turn right down Zátkovo nábřeží.

Třeboň and the South Bohemian lakes

One of the most distinctive features of the South Bohemian landscape is its chain of some 270 artificial lakes or fish-ponds, which extends to the west and east of České Budějovice. The best base for exploring this lakeland scenery is the charming small town of Třeboň, which lies on the northern shore of Lake Svět, 24km east of České Budějovice along Road 34/E49.

History of the lakes

The channelling of water from the marshy expanses of South Bohemia dates back to at least the 12C, though the present sophisticated system of interlocking lakes held by dams and linked by narrow canals and conduits was essentially the creation of the Rožmberks in the 16C. The first engineer whom they employed, Štepánek Netolický, was responsible for the construction in 1506–20 of the Zlatá Stoka, or Golden Canal, which feeds water to most of the large ponds around Třeboň; in the second half of the century Jakub Krčín of Jelčany built a number of new ponds, as well as the Nová Řeka canal, which diverted flood waters from the Lužnice to Nežárka rivers. The ponds have always been used for the breeding of carp, a statutory Christmas dish in Czechoslovakia, as well as one of the staples of Jewish cuisine. Every three years the ponds are drained and the fish brought in by a wide sweep of dragnets. The Rožmberks, and later the Schwarzenbergs, employed a 'waterbailiff' or 'fish-master' to protect each of the main ponds from poachers and to regulate the water level; these men lived in log cabins near the ponds.

The maternal grandfather of the writer Jaroslav Hašek was the water bailiff of a lake near Protivín, some 40km northwest of České Budějovice. His life inspired Hašek's *Stories from the Water-bailiff's Lodge at Ražice*, which were published in 1908 in the humorous weekly, *Merry Prague*; an English translation appears in Sir Cecil Parrot's Hašek anthology, *The Red*

Commissar (London, 1981). The last of these stories tells how one day, when the grandfather was out fishing on another lake, a miscreant opened the sluices of his pond, leaving the carp high and dry. With great presence of mind the grandfather revived the fish by bringing in horse-drawn tanks of water. However, his superior continued to blame him for the incident, whereupon the grandfather flung his fishing-boots on the ground at the man's feet, thus losing his job and showing a disregard for authority which was to be inherited by Hašek himself.

Another writer associated with the lakes of South Bohemia is Ivan Klíma, who spent childhood holidays near Lomnice, just to the north of Třeboň; the idyllic if rather haunting calm of the area is memorably captured in his short story, *My Country*, which appeared in the semi-autobiographical collection, *My First Loves* (1985).

Třeboň, a quiet town and small spa, has a tiny but beautifully preserved old centre, bordered by parkland and water and encircled by its medieval fortifications. Acquired by the Rožmberks in the mid-14C, the town was extensively developed in the 16C, at the same time that the South Bohemian fish-ponds were being created; the last of the Rožmberks, Petr Vok, made the castle here his permanent home from 1602 to his death in 1611.

Enter the town through the impressive 16C **Svinenská Gate**, on the other side of which and to the right is an old brewery installed in a former store house belonging to the Rožmberks (beer has been made at Třeboň since 1379). To the left of the gate is the entrance to a complex of 15C–18C buildings comprising the **castle**. The main building here, standing in a shaded courtyard, dates back to 1379, but was rebuilt several times, including in 1599, when the Rožmberk architect Domenico Cometa gave it a white Renaissance facing. The interior, containing a number of 16C rooms, now houses a small history museum, with interesting displays relating to the local fishing industry. **Open** May–Sept Tues–Sun 09.00–12.00 and 13.00–17.00; Apr, Oct 10.00–12.00 and 13.00–17.00.

The northern gate of the castle complex will take you out on to the narrow and exceptionally attractive **Masarykovo náměstí**, where there is a fountain of 1569 and a plague column of 1780. Among the 16C–18C buildings that line the square is a Town Hall of 1566 and, on the north side of the square, the house belonging to the 16C water engineer Josef Štěpánek Netolický.

Behind the square, adjoining the town's northwestern fortifications, is the former Austin canons' **Convent of St Giles** (sv. Jiljí), which was founded in 1369. The convent buildings, which are of the late Baroque period, have been converted into offices and apartments but the church and cloister are the original late 14C structures. The church, begun in 1370, has an outstanding interior, divided into two by a line of very slender columns, 16 times as high as they are thick; the fresco decorations are of the 15C. Beyond the northern fortifications, on the north side of the Zlatá Stoka, is the toy-like 18C house where the dramatist J.K. Tyl briefly lived.

South of the Svinenská Gate is a landing stage from which you can make a pleasant trip by steamer around the large **Lake Svět**, which is surrounded by extensive wooded parkland. West of the landing stage, along the lakeside Světská hráz, is a sandy beach popular with bathers. Set back from the lake, a

10min walk northwest of the beach, is the **Sanatorium Aurora**, the main building of the Třeboň spa; the surroundings are delightful, but the building itself resembles a large modern factory. The treatment here, used in particular for rheumatic diseases and disorders of the spine and joints, is based on mud baths, the mud being taken from the local peat marshes.

On the southern shores of Lake Svět is a large neo-Gothic mausoleum erected by the Schwarzenbergs; nearby is an important fish-farm. Much of the land surrounding Třeboň is now a protected nature reserve, the area being of great interest both to ecologists and ornithologists. A nature trail through the peat bogs has been established at **Červené blato**, 15km to the south.

Four kilometres to the north of the town is the largest of all the Bohemian fish-ponds, **Rožmberk**, covering an area of 489ha, and constructed by Jakub Krčín of Jelčany in 1584–89; the view from its wooded northwestern shores over this vast, still expanse makes a powerful impression, and embraces a distant glimpse of Třeboň rising above trees. The hamlet of **Ruznice**, further north on the Lomnice road, has a group of traditional farm buildings in a style known as 'rustic baroque'. The nearby ponds of Velký Tisý and Malý Tisý form part of a large bird sanctuary.

Jindřichův Hradec

Jindřichův Hradec, 28km northeast of Třeboň, was a most important town in the Middle Ages, though a series of severe fires in 1435, 1773 and 1801 reduced the place to the small and run-down textiles centre of today. Its main interest is the great complex comprising its **castle**, which stands at the lower end of town on a tongue of land projecting picturesquely over a great pool formed by the river Nežárka.

History of the castle

The castle was built c 1220 by Jindřich, the son of Vítek of Prčice, Chamberlain to Vladislav II. Descended from this early member of the Rožmberk family were the powerful Lords of Hradec, under whose rule between the 14C and 16C the castle was greatly extended, and the town behind it rose to become one of the largest in Bohemia. The main additions and alterations were commissioned in the late 16C by Adam II of Hradec—Lord Chancellor of Bohemia, and nephew of Lord Zacharias, the creator of the Renaissance palace at nearby Telč. The most important architect employed by Adam was Baldassare Maggi (Maio da Vomio), who came from the village of Arogno near Lake Lugano, and entered the service of the Lords of Hradec in around 1575. The last Lord of Hradec, Jáchym Oldřich, died epileptic and deformed in 1604, only seven years before the death of the last Rožmberk, Petr Vok.

The most popular story connected with the castle is that of the so-called 'White Lady', who was born Berta of Rožmberk in 1340. Forced to marry the hard-hearted Count Liechtenstein, the beautiful Berta bade a tearful farewell to her beloved Count Sternberg on the eve of the wedding festivities at Jindřichův Hradec, but was caught by her husband-to-be, who never forgave her. Mistreated by him for the rest of his life, she returned to this castle as a widow many years later, and set about beautifying it, and making herself popular with the town's inhabitants by distributing to the poor an unappealing-sounding concoction made from warm beer, honey and oatmeal. She still regularly returns here as a ghost and, in her capacity as a distributor of gruel, is impersonated during the tourist season by a waitress at the *Bílá paní* or 'White Lady' restaurant.

The castle, grey and forbidding from the outside (like much of the town itself) gives little hint of its spectacular interiors, the full beauty of which has been revealed by painstaking restoration, recently completed. The decorations range from the medieval to the neo-Classical; but unfortunately you will not be able to appreciate their full variety unless you take all three of the guided tours on offer (a single, faster tour would surely be a better solution). Tour A concentrates on the Baroque and neo-Classical periods (including some wonderful paintings by Karel Škréta and Petr Brandl), while Tour B features a kitchen, a 13C chapel and a hall covered with gruesomely realistic wall-paintings relating the story of St George and executed in 1373. Perhaps your best option if time is short is Tour C, which begins in the main courtyard with the superlative three-tiered **Large Arcade**, which was built by Maggi between 1586 and 1591.

A gate in the arcade will then lead you through into the garden, where you are confronted with the most outstanding and original architectural feature of the castle—an extraordinary pavilion known as the **Rondel**. This rotunda, designed by Maggi but executed in 1591–93 by his assistants and compatriots, Giovanni M. Faconi and Antonio Cometa, is a bizarre mixture of Italian and Central European elements. The main ground-floor window is straight out of Palladio, while the steeply pitched conical roof ringed by gables is a flight of pure Bohemian fantasy. The interior is decorated all over with a remarkable stucco decoration carried out between c 1594 and 1600 by Georg Bendel and Giovanni P. Martinola. **Open** May–Sept Tues–Sun 09.00–12.00 and 13.00–16.15; Apr, Oct 09.00–12.00 and 13.00–15.15.

A narrow street ascends from the main castle gate up to the town square, which is lined with 18C and early 19C houses, and is dominated in the middle by Matthias Strachovský's Trinity column of 1764–68. Svatojánská leads from the square up to the **Church of St John the Baptist** (sv. Jana Křtitele), the most interesting of the town's several churches, and occupying its highest point. Built over a recently excavated Romanesque rotunda, this much-altered 14C structure, which is at present undergoing further extensive restoration, has early 14C wall-paintings.

The most enjoyable excursion to be made from Jindřichův Hradec is to the castle of **Červená Lhota**, which lies 18km to the north of the town, in between the villages of Dírná and Deštná. This pale pink gabled structure, more like a toy than a real building, stands in the middle of a lake ringed by pine trees, and is one of the more enchanting sites in South Bohemia. Of 12C foundation, it was rebuilt in 1530 for Jan Kába von Rybňany, then remodelled after 1641, and further restored in the 19C and 20C. Its main façade, reached from a 17C bridge, rises above a miniature formal garden squeezed between the masonry and the water; the interior has a mainly Empire look, and is notable for its simplicity. The composer Karl Ditters von Dittersdorf (1739–99) spent the last years of his life here, and is buried in the nearby cemetery at Deštná. **Open** July, Aug Tues–Thur, Sat, Sun 09.00–12.00 and 13.00–16.45, Fri 13.00–16.45; May, June, Sept closes 15.45; Apr, Oct Sat, Sun 09.00–12.00 and 13.00–15.45.

Moravia

In terms of its landscapes and customs, Moravia is closely similar to Bohemia, the main difference being the far greater extent of vineyards and the consequent preference for wine rather than beer. As with Bohemia, the northern half of Moravia is mountainous but heavily industrialised, while the southern half has much of the bucolic, unspoilt character of South Bohemia. The region's many cultural attractions include a particularly impressive series of 16C–18C residences, and much pioneering Modernist architecture from the 1920s and '30s.

The most direct route from Prague is following Chapter 17A, which passes near two important Bohemian monasteries set in a wooded valley (**Sázava** and **Želiv**), as well as the lowland industrial town of **Jihlava**, whose fine historical centre is closely associated with the composer Mahler; the alternative and much slower Chapter 17B (which can largely be followed by train) has as its architectural highpoint Santini-Aichel's extraordinary monastic complex at Žďár nad Sázavou, one of Europe's most original Baroque creations.

The great jewel among the small towns of Moravia is Telč, which, with its magnificent Renaissance château built by the Lords of Hradec, is the natural complement to the 'Rose Towns' of South Bohemia, to which it is joined by Chapter 18. A wonderful route from here to Brno (Chapter 19) which follows for part of the way a forested river valley dominated at one end by Fischer von Erlach's château at **Vranov**—a place whose Baroque dynamism is worthy of the highly theatrical setting; further on is the medieval town of **Znojmo** (containing the most extensive cycle of early Romanesque frescoes in the Czech Republic), and further still the castle of **Moravský Krumlov**, which displays an ambitious series of canvases by the Moravian-born Alfons Mucha.

The Moravian capital of **Brno**—a town that has played a major role in early 20C architecture—is the subject of Chapter 20, which also features such surrounding attractions as the caves of the **Moravský kras** or Moravian Karst. From here to the district capital of **Ostrava**, in North Moravia, three alternative routes are given, one of which (Chapter 21A) goes through by far the most interesting of the North Moravian towns, **Olomouc**, which has a recently restored historic centre with important monuments from the 12C up to the 18C. The attractions of Chapters 21B and 21C are concentrated in Moravia's southern half, and include the Napoleonic battle site of **Austerlitz** (Slavkov), the superb collection of Old Master paintings at **Kroměříž**, and the verdant town of **Zlín**, which was developed in the early years of the 20C as a model town of the future.

Chapters 22 and 23 are intended for those travelling from East Bohemia to North Moravia: the former passes through a largely industrial landscape comprising the heartland of Czech **Silesia**; the latter features the showpiece Bohemian town of **Litomyšl** and the slightly sinister Gothic castle at **Bouzov**.

Chapter 24, which takes you from Brno on to the Slovakian capital of Bratislava, makes a detour into an idyllic southeastern corner of Moravia, covered in vines, orchards and forested hills, and traversed by some of the trails that make up the Czech Greenways network; its highpoints are the wine-growing hill-town of Mikulov, and the two imposing Liechtenstein properties (with their entertaining folly-filled gardens) at Valtice and Lednice.

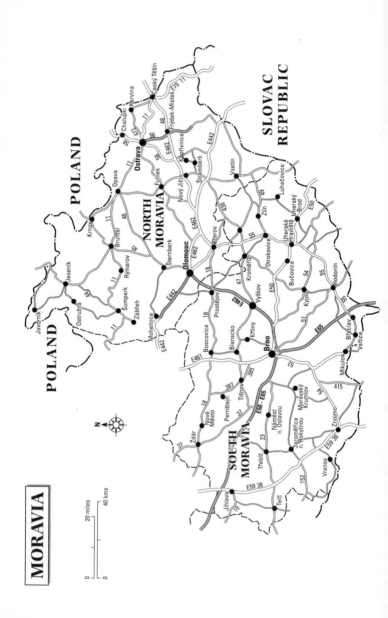

Transport
Trains
Connections with Prague: Brno (hourly; 3hr–4hr 30min); Olomouc (every 1–2hr; 3hr–3hr 30min; Ostrava (10–12 daily; 4–5hr); Žď'ár nad Sázavou (12 daily; 2hr 30min–3hr 30min).

From Brno: Blansko (10–12 daily; 25–40min); Bratislava (8 daily; 2hr); České Budějovice (4 daily; 4hr 30min); Jihlava (10–12 daily; 2hr–2hr 40min); Liberec (2 daily; 6hr 40min); Moravský Krumlov (10 daily; 45min–1hr); Olomouc (4–6 daily; 2hr); Poprad/Košice (2 daily; 7hr–8hr 20min); Slavkov/Bučovice (up to 14 daily; 25–40min/40–50min); Žď'ár nad Sázavou (hourly; 1hr–1hr 40min); Znojmo (1–2 hourly; 1hr 40min–2hr 20min).

From Lipová Lázně: Žulová/Javorník (8–10 daily; 25min/50min).

From Olomouc: Bruntál (7–9 daily; 1hr 15min–1hr 50min); Jeseník (6 daily; 2hr 25min–3hr 35min); Krnov (7–9 daily; 1hr 50min–2hr 45min); Lipová Lázně (6 daily; 2hr 10min–3hr 25min); Opava (7 daily; 2hr 20min); Ostrava (1–2 hourly; 1hr 30min–2hr 30min); Přerov (1–2 hourly; 20min); Prostějov (hourly; 15–30min); Šumperk (8 daily; 1hr 10min–1hr 30min).

From Opava: Hradec nad Moravicí (12 daily; 15min); Jeseník (4 daily; 2hr 10min); Krnov (hourly; 30–40min); Ostrava (hourly; 25–40min).

From Ostrava: Český Těšín (1–2 hourly; 50min); Frýdek-Místek/Frýdlant (1–2 hourly; 40min/1hr).

From Znojmo: Jaroměřiče nad Rokytnou (12 daily; 45min–1hr 15min); Jihlava (3 daily; 1hr 45min); Mikulov/Valtice (6–9 daily; 1hr 10min/1hr 30min); Šatov/Retz (3–6 daily; 20min).

Buses
Connections with Prague: Brno (hourly; 2hr); Olomouc/Nový Jičín/Ostrava (2 daily; 4hr/5hr/6hr); Znojmo (up to 4 daily; 3hr).

From Brno: Buchlovice/Uherské Hradiště (up to 10 daily; 1hr 10min/1hr 20min); Hodonín (up to 8 daily; 1hr 20min); Kroměříž (up to 14 daily; 1hr 30min); Křtiny/Jedovnice (up to 10 daily; 45min/1hr); Luhačovice (up to 4 daily; 2hr 10min); Mikulov (up to 14 daily; 1hr 20min); Moravský Krumlov (3–5 daily; 1hr); Zlín (up to 16 daily; 2hr–2hr 40min); Znojmo (up to 11 daily; 1hr 10min).

From Nový Jičín: Frenštát pod Radhoštěm (hourly; 40min); Frýdek-Místek (up to 8 daily; 45min); Kopřivnice (hourly; 35min); Příbor (hourly; 25min); Štramberk (1–2 hourly; 15–40min).

From Olomouc: Nový Jičín (up to 8 daily; 1hr 15min); Opava (2–4 daily; 2hr); Příbor/Frýdek-Místek (3–10 daily; 1hr 30min/1hr 50min); Rožnov pod Radhoštěm (2 daily; 1hr 15min).

From Uherské Hradiště: Buchlovice (up to 15 daily; 20min); Kroměříž (up to 6 daily; 1hr); Luhačovice (up to 5 daily; 40min); Strážnice (up to 4 daily; 45min/1hr); Trenčín (up to 6 daily; 1hr 15min); Velehrad (up to 14 daily; 25min); Zlín (up to 16 daily; 40min–1hr).

Hotels and pensions
Brno
Grandhotel Brno, Benešova 18/20, 657 83. ☎ (05) 423 212 87; Fax (05) 422 103 45. The oldest and grandest hotel in town, but uninspiringly

renovated in 1988.

U královny Elišky, Mendlovo náměstí 1a, 602 00. ☎ (05) 432 168 98. Small and homely pension installed in section of the Augustinian monastery made famous by Mendel.

Jihlava

Hotel Gustav Mahler, Křížová 4, 586 01. ☎ (066) 273 71; Fax: (066) 273 77. Unexcitingly converted monastery.

Kroměříž

Hotel Bouček, Velké náměstí 108, 76701. ☎ / Fax: (0634) 257 77. Simple, sparsely furnished hotel on attractive main square.

Mikulov

Hotel Rohatý krokodýl, Husova 8, 692 00. ☎ 0625/2692; Fax: (0625) 3695; Small, well-modernised hotel named after the horned crocodile that hangs in the billiards room.

Telč

Hotel Černý orel, náměstí Zachariáše z Hradce 7, 588 56. ☎ / Fax: (066) 962 220. Though occupying a wonderful gabled building on the beautiful main square, the ugly yellow-walled interior does not live up to the exterior.

Valtice

Hotel Hubertus, Zámek Valtice, 691 42. ☎ (0627) 945 37; Fax: (0627) 945 38. Though installed inside a wing of the Liechtenstein château, its interior is not nearly as stylish as this might suggest.

Zlín

Interhotel Moskva, náměstí Práce 2512, 762 70. ☎ (067) 836 1111; Fax: (067) 365 93. A pioneering high-rise hotel of the 1930s (by Vladimir Karfík) that unfortunately served as the model for so many of the dreary hotel blocks of the Communist era.

Znojmo

Restaurant a pension Havelka, Mikulašské náměstí 3, 669 02. ☎ / Fax : (0624) 220 138. A warm and welcoming village-style restaurant and two-roomed pension, with folkloric decorations and wooden fittings.

17 · Prague to Brno

A. By the motorway

Total distance 213km: Prague (leave by the D1) • 91km Humpolec • 29km Jihlava • 93km Brno.

The D1, the main motorway of the Czech and Slovak Republics, efficiently links the two countries' three main cities, reducing the journey from Prague to Brno to 2hr 30min, and from Brno to Bratislava to 1hr 30min. The landscape as far as Brno is remarkably unchanging, and comprises endless rolling vistas of fields interrupted by patches of dense forest. For much of the journey the road runs parallel with the narrow and wooded valley of the Sázava, along which are some of the finest sights to be seen in the vicinity of the road, including the monastery of Sázava and the castle of Český Šternberk (see Chapter 2B).

Nearer the Moravian border is the former Premonstratensian monastery of **Želiv**, which stands on a tributary of the Sázava, 10km to the south of the D1 (turn off at Koberovice, 81km southeast of Prague). Apart from the beauty of its position, impressively perched above the forested banks of the river, Želiv is notable above all for the interior of its church, a 14C hall-church remodelled in a 'Gothic-Baroque' style by the great Johann Santini-Aichel after 1712. Santini created within the nave curious projecting galleries, but his most original contribution here was his characteristically elaborate and very expressive vaulting.

You can extend your detour to Želiv by heading south from here to **Pelhřimov** (a further 13km). In the 13C this small town belonged to the Prague bishopric, which used it as a base for colonising the Moravian borderland. Two of the gates from the medieval fortifications have survived (Rynárecká and Jihlavská), but the rest of the medieval town was largely destroyed by fires between the 16C and 18C. Late Baroque and neo-Classical buildings today make up most of the old centre, which, thanks to the town's economic decline in the 19C, has been left remarkably untouched. A fascinating curiosity on the main square (Masarykovo náměstí) is Pavel Janák's 'Cubist' remodelling of a Baroque house at No. 13, which had belonged to a local doctor: the lively gable shows the extent to which Czech Cubism was in debt to the playful fantasies of traditional Bohemian architecture. Another example of Baroque influence on Janák's work is the nearby former family residence (now an estate agent) at 331 Strachovská (1912). You can regain the D1 at Humpolec (17km) by driving north from Pelhřimov along the E551.

The present-day border of Bohemia with Moravia comes near the village of Větrný Jeníkov, 12km further down the D1 from Humpolec and 10km before Pávov, where a branch of the motorway leads 7km to the large industrial town of **Jihlava**.

History of Jihlava

Founded in 1240 in the vicinity of silver deposits, Jihlava became for a short while the most important silver-mining town in Europe after Freiburg in Germany; the Royal Mint was situated here until the early 14C, when it was transferred to Kutná Hora by Václav II. In the 1730s the imperial post road from Vienna was re-routed north from Jindřichův Hradec to Jihlava, much to the detriment of the former and to the advantage of the latter. Numerous industries were established in the town in the 19C, and today the place is a major engineering and textiles centre.

The Austrian composer Gustav Mahler (1860–1911) was born in the nearby village of Kaliště (Kalischt), 5km north of the D1 exit to Želiv (see above); soon after the birth his father—a brewer and publican—moved the family to what is now Malinovského in Jihlava itself (then known as Iglau), where the future composer studied at the German Gymnasium (a previous pupil there had been Smetana).

The town's associations with Mahler have only recently begun to be exploited; the house in the Jewish quarter where he grew up has been turned into a cultural centre, while around the corner is a small museum devoted to him. You can also go and visit the Dominican Church of the Holy Cross (sv. Kříže)—a barracks church in Mahler's day—where the budding composer heard the military bands that would play such an important part in his music.

Apart from its associations with Mahler, and a small but choice gallery of 19C and 20C Czech art in the **Oblastní Galerie Vysočiny** at Komenského 10, the main interest of the town is its vast square, the equal in size if not in beauty to that of České Budějovice. The medieval houses were gutted by fire in 1523, and most of the buildings lining the square date from the late 16C to the early 19C; one of the finest (No. 58) is a late 16C building housing the **Museum of the Bohemian–Moravian Highlands** (muzeum Vysočiny), which is more interesting to visit for its courtyard and interior than its collections, which are predominantly of natural history. The appearance of the square is hardly enhanced by the prominent Prior department store, a darkly depressing block erected in the 1960s over a group of tall medieval houses where textiles had been sold. The plague column, of 1679, is a work by the Italian artist Giovanni Jacopo Brasca.

Return to the D1 at Pávov and continue for a further 87km to Brno (see Chapter 20).

B. Via Žďár nad Sázavou and Pernštejn

Total distance 218km: Prague (leave by the D1) • 68km Loket • 49km Havlíčkův Brod • 31km Žďár nad Sázavou • 37km Pernštejn • 33km Brno.

Those not wishing to rush all the way from Prague to Brno on a motorway should leave the D1 at Loket, 68km southeast of Prague, and then head north on Road 18, which after Ledeč nad Sázavou (17km) runs parallel with the D1, following the attractively wooded Sázava valley for over 60km At Světlá, 17km east of Ledeč, enthusiasts of the writer Jaroslav Hašek (1883–1923) could make a detour 10km to the south to see the village of **Lipnice nad Sázavou** by following the Humpolec road for 7.5km, then turning left at Dol. Město. In this quiet village, surrounded by woods and dominated by a 14C castle (extended in the 16C), Hašek spent the last 15 months of his life, engaged on his never-to-be-completed work, *The Good Soldier Švejk*.

The house where Hašek spent the last months of his life has now been turned into a small museum to the writer. His gravestone in the local cemetery was initially a simple one, but it has since been replaced by a granite monument in the form of an open book, bearing the gilt inscription: 'Austria, never wert thou so ripe to fall, never wert thou so damned.' In deference to Hašek's memory a Festival of Satire and Humour is held annually at the village.

From Lipnice take the side road east to Okrouhlice (8km), where you will regain Road 18. The industrial town of **Havlíčkův Brod**, 9km further east, was founded by German miners in the 13C, and is named after the 19C radical journalist Karel Havlíček Borovský (1821–56), whose house here (at No. 19 náměstí ČSLA) is now a museum to him. The town, which has retained fragments of its medieval fortifications, also has an art gallery devoted to Czech illustrations and satirical drawings from 1918 onwards, including works by Hašek's illustrator Josef Lada.

Continuing along Road 18, you will come after 31km to **Žďár nad Sázavou**,

Jaroslav Panuška

Hašek moved from Prague to Lipnice in August 1921 on the recommendation of a painter friend, Jaroslav Panuška, a well-known landscapist who came from the Bohemian–Moravian Highlands and frequently painted at Lipnice. Panuška thought that the move would be beneficial to the ailing writer, who was now reaping the consequences of a lifetime of gluttony and alcohol abuse. The two men arrived at the village together and put up at an inn called the *Czech Crown*. Despite his initial suspicion of the shabbily dressed and penniless writer, Invald, the landlord of this inn, later became totally devoted to him, and even gave him a credit of 500 crowns. Hašek was delighted with his new circumstances, and was pleased, as he put it, to be living 'bang in the middle of a pub. Nothing better could have happened to me.'

A favourite haunt of both Hašek and Panuška was the castle at Lipnice, which enjoys beautiful views over the lush Sázava valley. After befriending the custodian they were given a key to the building, and would come here of an evening to light a fire in the courtyard, grill sausages and sing old Austrian songs. Once they held a notorious drinking party here, in which the local school-teacher was left drunk in a corner. Hašek decided to play one of his characteristic pranks, and locked up the building with the teacher inside. Later that night frightened villagers claimed to have seen a ghost running along the battlements. Hašek shouted out that this was none other than the White Lady of Rožmberk, and that in her interests it would be best to shoot and 'liberate' her. The poor teacher was finally released in a trembling state.

In the summer of 1922, after securing a contract for *The Good Soldier Švejk*, Hašek bought a ramshackle house on the slope below the castle, but occupied only one of its rooms. He now weighed over 24 stones, and his health was causing serious concern. Eventually he consented to be examined by a doctor, who told him that he would never be able to complete *Švejk* unless he took greater care of himself. Hašek replied that he would have to kill off Švejk before allowing himself to die, and this would never happen as Švejk would always live on among the Czech people. He fell into a coma on the night of 3 January 1933, waking up only to beg the doctor for a sip of cognac. He was given milk instead, which prompted his last words: 'But you're cheating me.' For his funeral, attended by few of his friends and none of his family, his swollen body had to be taken out through the window rather than down the stairs. Shortly afterwards his debtors came round and loaded all that they could find onto a cart. He was buried in the local churchyard.

a small industrial town which grew up by the side of a former Cistercian monastery founded in 1252. The abbot in the early 18C was one of the most important patrons of Johann Santini-Aichel, who spent large periods at Žď'ár from 1706 almost up to his death in 1723, producing here some of the more bizarre works of a very eccentric career. His remodelling of the medieval **abbey church**—his first task here—is difficult fully to appreciate owing to the main vaults having been damaged by fire in 1784; the interest of the interior lies primarily in the transepts, which are spanned by low arches supporting dynamically-shaped organs featuring solomonic columns and curiously bent piers. The high altar (1735) is the masterpiece of Řehoř Thény, a Tyrolean pupil of Matthias Braun; he used his own features for the face of St Luke.

Santini's plans for the rest of the abbey complex were never to be fulfilled (an exhibition relating to Santini's work can be seen in the stables), though what he completed includes a number of symbolically-shaped buildings such as a court in the shape of a lyre, and outbuildings in the form of the abbot's initials. Both Santini's and the abbot's love of symbolism is further revealed in the delightful **cemetery** on the other side of the street to the monastery. Beyond the entrance pavilion, a later addition, you find yourself in an enclosure of undulating walls containing three simple chapels representing the Trinity; a statue of an angel by Thény stands in the middle, waiting to wake up the dead.

Symbolism of an unrivalled complexity in Bohemian architecture characterises Santini's last and most fascinating work at Žďár, the **Pilgrimage Chapel of St John of Nepomuk** (sv. Jana Nepomuckého) of 1720–22, which sits on top of an adjacent hill. The idea of building this chapel followed the discovery in 1719 of the miraculously undecayed tongue of Jan Nepomucký, who had been murdered supposedly for his refusal to betray the secrets of the confessional. It so happened that the finding of the tongue coincided with the fifth centenary of the coming to Žďár of a Cistercian community originating from the monastery at Nepomuk. To celebrate the two events, and to play his own part in the growing Nepomuk cult, the abbot not only commissioned the chapel from Santini, but also had the hill on which it was to be built renamed Green Hill (Zelená hora) after the hill on which the monastery's mother institution had been established. Virtually every detail of the plan and every architectural form of the chapel refers either to Nepomuk's tongue or else to the figure five, which was both an allusion to the fifth centenary and to the halo of five stars which hovered around the martyr's head after he was thrown into the Vltava.

The chapel stands at the centre of a precinct contained within a ten-pointed cloister housing five other chapels. It takes the shape of a five-pointed star, and represents Santini's most imaginative fusion of the Gothic and Baroque styles. The bizarre exterior has the angular character more typical of the former style, while the whitewashed interior makes a Baroque play of concave and convex forms. The use of Gothic lancet windows has a symbolical as well as an aesthetic significance, for they echo the tongue-shaped forms that are everywhere to be found, and allude also to the saint's tongue having been compared in its steadfastness to the Sword of the Lord. Such obsessive symbolism and complex planning are worthy of comparison with Borromini's church of San Ivo de la Sapienza in Rome, a building to which Santini may indeed have been paying homage. **Open** July, Aug daily 09.00–17.00; Apr–June, Sept, Oct 08.00–16.00.

At **Obyčtov**, 10km south of Žďár, is another work commissioned from Santini by the abbot—a chapel dedicated to the Virgin and planned in the shape of a tortoise, the symbol of constancy. To the north of Žďár extends a large area of protected forest embracing the highest point in the Bohemian–Moravian Highlands, **Devět Skal** (836m), and the large **Velké dárko Lake**; the latter, 10km due north of Žďár and near the source of the Sázava river, is used for swimming and water-sports.

Continue east from Žďár along Road 18 for 27km, until you reach the small town of Bystřice nad Pernštejnem, from where you head south on a side-road to the castle of **Pernštejn**, a further 10km away. The castle, rising over a sea of pines on a rocky spur above the river Nedvědička, has a picturesque profile rivalling that of Karlštejn (see Chapter 2C), and seems likewise to be taken straight out of a fairy-tale illustration. The seat of the Pernštejn family up to 1596, the castle was first mentioned in 1285, and soon came to be regarded as unassailable; the oldest surviving parts are the round tower and the ramparts. The building was reconstructed after a fire in 1457, and further extensive remodelling took place in the Renaissance. The Mitrovic family, who succeeded the Pernštejns and retained the building until 1945, did little to alter the castle's exterior. The cold and rather inhospitable interior, however, was largely redone in a Rococo and Empire style, and rather spoils the expectations raised by the memorable first impression of the building. **Open** May–Sept Tues–Sun 09.00–12.00 and 13.00–17.00; Apr, Oct Sat, Sun 09.00–12.00 and 13.00–16.00.

Driving east from Pernštejn alongside the Nedvědička for 2.5km (note the fine 18C wooden bridge below the castle) you will come to a main road leading southeast towards Brno. Four kilometres after the turning is the village of **Doubravník**, where there is one of the last Gothic hall-churches in the Czech and Slovak republics, constructed in 1539–57, possibly by Mert Hübel, the architect then in charge of the Church of St James in Brno.

At **Tišnov**, 10km further south, is a Cistercian convent founded in 1233; of particular interest is the west portal or Porta Coeli, an early 13C work richly adorned with carvings. The remaining 24km to Brno (see Chapter 20) continue to run through wooded hilly landscape, but with increasing signs of industrialisation.

18 · Jindřichův Hradec to Brno

Total distance 137km: Jindřichův Hradec (leave by Road 23) • 41km Telč • 36km Třebíč • 60km Brno.

Telč

Head northeast of Jindřichův Hradec on Road 23, crossing the Moravian border shortly after Studená. The landscape of marshes and chains of large fish-ponds characteristic of South Bohemia extends well into this part of Moravia and provides Telč with an enchanting setting.

The old town of Telč, one of the most beautiful and best preserved in Central Europe, floats above water like the North Italian town of Mantua. Its long western and eastern sides are lapped by water from two great ponds that are joined together at the north by a canal running through the wooded grounds of the castle. Coming from Jindřichův Hradec you should leave your car in the 24-hour security carpark just to the north of the canal, off Slavatovská. A 17C bridge, at the junction of the canal and the northern end of the Štěpnický pond, leads you to the 16C **Small Gate** (Malá brána) marking the northern entrance to the old town. On the other side of the gate unfolds before you a world which has changed little since the early 18C. Before walking around the remarkable main square which opens up to your left, turn right and enter the **castle**, the interior of which contains some of the finest Renaissance rooms in the Czech and Slovak Republics.

History of the castle

The original castle at Telč, an early 14C structure centred around a tiny court-yard, was acquired in 1339 by the Lords of Hradec from Charles IV in exchange for the strategically important castle at Bánov, situated on the former border with Hungary. The present appearance of the castle is due largely to the 16C governor of Moravia, Zachariáš of Hradec (d. 1589), who, following a stay in the Italian town of Genoa in 1552, decided to turn Telč into his principal residence. At first he limited himself largely to redecorating both the exterior and interior of the old building with sgraffito, but from the 1560s onwards he undertook ambitious architectural extensions, including the building of two new wings. His principal architect seems to have been the Italian, Baldassare Maggi (Maio da Vomio), the man responsible for the Renaissance work at Jindřichův Hradec. The building came into the hands of the Liechtenstein family after 1712.

The official tour of the castle begins with two of the rooms which Zachariáš of Hradec had decorated in the old building. The first of these rooms, the **Small Banqueting Hall,** comprises fascinating monochrome decorations after engravings by the South German artists H. Aldegrever and V. Solis; the subjects are *Orpheus Playing to the Animals*, the *Feast of Herod* and female figures person-ifying the Seven Sins. The adjoining room is the **Treasury**, covered all over with further monochrome sgraffito work, and featuring the earliest surviving exam-ples in Central Europe of fictive perspectival decorations.

Next comes the **Chapel of St George** (sv. Jiří), a tall space of Gothic proportions coated in elaborate Renaissance stucco decorations; in the centre, surrounded by an elegant Renaissance grille, is the marble tomb of Zachariáš and his wife Kateřina of Valdštejn. In the nearby former armoury is a cellular vault adorned all over with Renaissance grotesques. The long Wedding or **Theatre Hall**, opposite the armoury, has a splendid wooden coffered ceiling, and—covering what was originally a stone fireplace—a frescoed decoration with scenes representing *Judith and Holofernes* and *Hercules Capturing the Hind of Artemisia* (the freshness of these works is due to their having been hidden by plaster until 1950).

Moving from this room to the adjoining **African Hall** is like going from the sublime to the ridiculous, the latter room comprising an absurd and rather surreal display of tiger skins, ostriches, hippopotamus and zebra heads, and other gruesome trophies collected by the uncle of the castle's last owner in the course of safaris undertaken between 1903 and 1914.

An elegant Italianate loggia connects the oldest part of the castle with the **Marble Hall**, which was used by Zachariáš of Hradec as an audience chamber. The *Deeds of Hercules* are portrayed in the panels of its amusing coffered ceiling (c 1570), which bizarrely features sculpted reliefs and even real antler horns attached to a painted sky. Gilded and witty reliefs of mythological figures set against a blue background are to be found in the 30 octagonal panels comprising the magnificent coffered ceiling of the **Golden Room**. This room, originally the castle's ballroom, has walls lined with portraits of the Liechtenstein family, and a musician's gallery decorated with allegories of the Five Senses.

The last important room which you visit is the **Blue Hall**, with another splendid ceiling in gold and blue, this one comprising the coat of arms of the Hradec family flanked by four painted reliefs of the elements. Separate to the tour is a small historical museum and art gallery installed in rooms off the delightful Renaissance garden to the right of the main entrance. The gallery is dedicated to the painter Jan Zrzavý (1890–1977), who was born near the Moravian town of Havlíčkův Brod, and specialised in naïvely simplified figures in haunting settings; his art was an influence on both the naïf and Surrealist painters associated with the group Devětsil. **Open** May–Aug Tues–Sun 09.00–12.00 and 13.00–17.00; Apr, Sept, Oct closes 15.00.

In between the castle and the adjacent and rather severe late 17C Jesuit college is a covered passage leading to the parish **Church of St James** (sv. Jakub), a late 14C foundation completed in 1443; there is a wonderful view of the town from its tower. Extending like a funnel to the south of the castle is the **Zacharias of Hradec Square** (náměstí Zachariáše z Hradce), one of the most beautiful squares in a country celebrated for its squares. There is not a single modern building to spoil the arcaded rows that run, like the backcloths of a stage set, the whole length of the square's immensely long sides. The houses are mainly of the 15C and 16C, though with gables dating from the Baroque period. Wholly of the Renaissance period, and the most striking of all the square's many charming buildings, is the house at No. 61, dated 1555 and today housing the tourist office, which has a most fanciful gable and comparably playful sgraffito decorations. The former Town Hall (now the *Hotel černý orel*), on the opposite side of the square, is distinguished by a giant order of pilasters. Beyond a plague column of 1716–17, near the top of the square, is Palackého, a street leading to the so-called **Big Gate** (Velká brána), which forms part of the extensive surviving stretch of fortifications on the town's southern side.

Abbeys and castles east of Telč

The next important town along the main road to Brno is **Třebíč** (36km), today a centre of engineering, footwear and other industries, and boasting—next to the parish Church of St Martin—a tower with the largest clock in the Czech Republic; the diameter of its dial is 7.1m. Of greater interest is its former **Benedictine abbey**, around which the town had originally grown. Founded in 1101, it stands on a hill above the town, and has a church which is potentially one of the more important early medieval monuments in Moravia. Sadly this mid-13C structure, in a transitional Romanesque style, has suffered badly from a combination of neglect and heavy-handed 18C restoration and remodelling. Of the exterior the finest surviving parts are the powerfully carved north portal, the Porta Paradisi, and the galleried apse; the best-preserved part of the interior is the chancel, the nave having been spoilt by lifeless, unimaginative revaulting by Kaňka in the 18C. The adjoining monastic building was converted into a private residence in the 16C, and today houses the West Moravian Museum, of interest largely for its collection of traditional cribs or 'Bethlehems'. **Open** Tues–Sun 08.00–11.30 and 13.00–17.00.

For anyone interested in Baroque architecture an almost obligatory detour from Třebíč is to the magnificent château and park standing in the middle of the village of **Jaroměřice nad Rokytnou**, 15km due south on the road leading to Moravské Budějovice.

History of the château

This overwhelmingly large structure in red and white stone stripes dates back to a 14C castle built for the Lords of Lichtenberg. Transformed later into a grand Renaissance château by the Italian architect Giovanni Battista

Erna, it was then given its present Baroque appearance in the course of drastic remodelling commissioned in 1708 by Count Adam Questenberg. The architect originally approached was the celebrated Viennese master, Johann Lukas von Hildebrandt, whose plans for the building were even more ambitious than the ones actually executed, and had eventually to be scrapped for financial reasons. In the end Questenberg supplied his own designs, which were carried out between 1711–37 by the Italian Domenico d'Angeli, aided (for the interiors) by Konrad Adolf Albrecht von Albrechtsburg.

The principle façade, facing the main square, and approached across a massive cour d'honneur, shields a splendid series of ornate rooms that include a whimsically decorated music room and ball room, a scarlet-and-lacquer chinoiserie chamber of 1731, and a ball room frescoed on the ceiling with a *Glorification of Jaroměřice*. Questenberg, a great lover of music who turned Jaroměřice into an important centre of Baroque music (a music festival is still held here in July and August), had also a charming small **theatre** built on the eastern side of the cour d'honneur: in 1730 his valet, František Václav Miča (1694–1744)—who arranged the château's musical life and directed an orchestra made up of its servants—wrote for this the work always considered as the first Czech opera, *L'origine de Jarmeritz en Moravie*, which was translated into Czech one year later.

On the opposite side of the cour d'honneur a short passage leads to the château's **chapel**, which is dedicated to St Margaret (sv. Markéty). This dynamic elliptical stucture, decorated inside with exuberant frescoes by Karel Tepper, was the only one of Hildebrandt's designs to be executed at Jaroměřice. Visitors unwilling to follow the obligatory guided tour around the château itself are allowed at least to wander freely into the chapel (which serves also as the parish church), and from here walk into the extensive formal gardens, which were laid out by the French designer Jean Trehet. **Open** May–Sept Tues–Sun 09.00–12.00 and 13.00–17.00; Apr, Oct Sat, Sun 09.00–12.00 and 13.00–16.00.

After seeing the château and its gardens, the architectural enthusiast should go into the village itself to see the **villa of Dr Pick**, which was built in 1920–21 by the pioneering architect Pavel Janák: this curious structure is like a 'Cubist' interpretation of Britain's William-and-Mary style. Literature lovers might care to pay their homage to the Symbolist poet Otokar Březina (1868–1929), who lived in the house at No. 46/40, where there is a plaque and a memorial room: Březina, a solitary reclusive figure obsessed by Plato, medieval mystics and Indian philosophy, spent much of his life as a schoolteacher in Jaroměřice, refusing a university chair and giving up writing altogether at the age of 35.

Returning to Třebíč and continuing east for 21km, you will reach **Náměšt' nad Oslavou**, a small town with a long-established tradition in carpet-weaving. It stands on the banks of the river Oslava, which is here spanned by an 18C bridge decorated with 20 Baroque statues dating from 1730 to 1740. Rising high on a steep hill above the river is an important Renaissance castle, commissioned in around 1573 for Lord Chief Justice Jan of Žerotín and completed in the 1580s by his son Karel the Elder.

The castle at Náměšt' has been tentatively attributed to the Italian architect Leonardo Garvi and is at any rate one of the main Moravian buildings in an Italianate Renaissance style. Especially notable is the Bramante-inspired double flight of steps on the exterior, and the arcaded courtyard inside; the interior has

The Žerotíns

The Žerotíns, the most prolific builders in Moravia, were a leading Protestant family. Karel the Elder, in the course of his remarkably extensive travels around Europe, had actively supported the French king Henry IV and had befriended some of the more important personalities of the Protestant courts, as well as the Swiss reformer and successor to Calvin, Theodor de Bèze. Both Karel and his father Jan were members of the Unity of Bohemian Brethren, one of the printing centres of which was established at Náměšt˘ in the 16C and published here in 1533 the first Czech grammar book.

been much altered, and now contains a collection of 16C to 18C tapestries. **Open** July, Aug Tues–Sun 09.00–12.00 and 13.00–18.00; May, June, Sept closes 17.00; Apr, Oct Sat, Sun 09.00–12.00 and 13.00–16.00.

The architect of Náměšt˘ might also have worked for the Žerotíns at their castle at **Rosice**, a further 20km along Road 23, where you will find one of the most elegant of Moravian Renaissance courtyards. Built c 1580, this courtyard comprises three superimposed arcades, the spandrels and balustrades of which are covered all over with delicate Renaissance reliefs: this extensive use of sculptural decoration is one of the hallmarks of Moravian architecture of this period. Four kilometres east of Rosice, Road 23 joins up with the D1 motorway, leading a further 14km to Brno.

19 · Telč to Brno via Vranov and Znojmo

Total distance 163km: Telč • 12km Dačice • 12km Slavonice • 32km Bítov • 22km Vranov • 18km Znojmo • 28km Moravský Krumlov • 39km Brno.

The most rewarding route from Telč to Brno involves making a large loop south through the quiet unspoilt countryside bordering with Austria. Leave Telč on Road 406, which heads due south to **Dačice** (12km), where you will find an uninspired cube-shaped memorial on the sloping main square. This is not a provincial attempt at abstract art but rather a work commemorating Dačice's main claim to fame as the village which in 1843 introduced the world to the sugar cube. The inventor was a man of distant Swiss origin called Jakub Kryštof Rad, who manufactured the cube in a building on the square now occupied by the House of Culture.

If you descend to the bottom of the square and cross the river, you will come on the other side to a former Franciscan monastery, the 18C building of which has been drably converted into a museum and art gallery. The collections, unsurprisingly, deal in part with Krystof and his crystal sugar, but there is also a small group of erotic engravings by the turn-of-the-century Moravian artist Max Švabinský, and a room devoted to the locally born F. Bilkovský, a sugary sweet artist working in a Dufy-like style.

Return to the main square and head west for 3km on the road to Jindřichův Hradec, then head due south to **Slavonice**, a further 9km away. The town of

Slavonice, once part of the fiefdom of the Lords of Hradec, was founded in 1277, and reached the height of its prosperity in the mid-16C after it had been chosen as a staging-post on the imperial road to Vienna. The Thirty Years War left 73 of its 164 houses deserted, and its fate was finally sealed in the 1730s with the re-routing to the north of the imperial road. Slavonice has preserved much from its days of 16C glory, but in a sad, decayed state.

There are two market squares, both of which are lined with arcaded, gabled houses dating back to the Renaissance. The western and larger of the two has at No. 46 (on the north side) a house featuring a ground-floor room with a quite extraordinary cellular vault which has been likened to a cluster of half-opened fans; this plasterwork was executed in the 1540s by Master L.O. (Leopold Öster-reicher). The western end of the square is bordered by a plain and much-restored Town Hall of 1599, rising behind which is the parish church; the latter, founded in the late 14C and completed in 1521, adjoins a tall bell-tower of 1549. To the east of the church extends the smaller and more appealing of the town's two squares, this one boasting on its southern side a beautifully sgraffitoed house of the late 16C. At the far end of the square is the medieval Jemniče Gate.

Leave Slavonice on the Jemnice road, and then turn almost immediately right to Písečné. The 32km journey east from Slavonice to Bítov is on a series of tiny mean-dering roads across rolling agricultural countryside, spoilt until 1989 by the sinister fencing marking the Austrian border. After Písečné (9km) turn left and then imme-diately right to Dešná (6km), which you cross and continue to head eastwards for a further 7km. Turn right on to the road marked Police and Vysočany and continue driving east. Shortly before Bítov (8km) you enter a dense forest encasing the long and winding Vranov reservoir, a popular place for swimming, fishing and water sports. The road follows the reservoir for 2km and, after passing underneath the ruins of the medieval castle of Cornštejn (abandoned in the 17C), crosses the water just in front of Bítov. The castle of **Bítov**, towering over the reservoir, was built in the 13C for the Dukes of Lichtenberg, who remained the owners until 1576; its present romantic appearance is due to neo-Gothic remodelling in the 19C.

Vranov

Vranov lies at the eastern end of the reservoir, and can be reached from Bítov by boat. The journey by car is more circuitous and involves driving north for 7km, then turning right and following the road east to Šumná (8km). Two kilometres beyond Šumná turn left through forest to Vranov (5km), which, when approached from this direction, offers an outstanding view of its **castle**, a vast and dramatic Baroque edifice poised in sublime isolation above trees and sheer cliffs that rise high above the deep and narrow valley carved by the river Dyje.

History of the castle

The castle at Vranov, first mentioned in 1100, was once a royal castle guarding the southern borders of Přemysl territory. Following a long succession of subsequent owners, and a troubled history including devas-tation by fire in 1665, the castle was acquired in 1680 by Michal Jan II of Althann. In 1688 Michal Jan made the inspired and enlightened decision to employ at Vranov an up-and-coming Viennese architect who had spent 16 years with Bernini in Italy and of whom the Liechtensteins had spoken very highly. The man was Johann Bernard Fischer von Erlach (1656–1723), one of the most brilliant architects of the Central European Baroque. Fischer, with great boldness, did away with the original castle chapel and replaced this with an enormous oval hall, The Hall of the Ancestors.

In 1698, three years after the latter's completion, Fischer designed a family tomb for Michal Jan II, and in the following year began work on a chapel to house it. This was largely finished in time for Michal's death in 1702, though the two belfry towers of the west front were not to be added until 1710. Plans for rebuilding the rest of the castle were suspended for many years and it was not until 1723, when Vranov came into the hands of Jan Michal's ambitious and highly cultured daughter-in-law, Marie Anna Althann, née Pignatelli, that they were to be finally resumed.

The re-construction was entrusted to one of Fischer's sons, Josef Emmanuel (1693–1742), and was still incomplete by the time of Marie Pignatelli's death in 1755. Her son, Michal Antonín Althann, inherited her castle and estate, but not her cultural interests, and neglected all work at Vranov in favour of a passion for hunting; by stocking the estate with deer and boar to satisfy this passion he succeeded in destroying many of the crops, and reducing greatly the value of the land. A new interest in the house was shown by his successor, Michal Josef, whose particular contribution was the sumptuous neo-Classical decoration of the second-floor rooms; however his excessive spending on the house, combined with a passion for gambling and high living, eventually forced him to put the house up for auction in 1793.

The new owner—Josef Hilgartner of Lilienborn, Attorney of Bohemia—pulled down some of the remaining parts of the medieval castle, reconstructed the stables, and landscaped the surroundings in a Romantic style. His principle contribution, however, was to set up a pottery in the castle grounds in 1799. This pottery, later specialising in what came to be called Vranov Wedgeware, was enormously successful, and by 1839 was employing 80 workers to create products that were exported to different parts of the world; it continued to function until 1882. The castle, owned by a variety of families after Josef Hilgartner, was seized by the Nazis in 1942 and by the Czech State in 1945. Meticulous restoration work was undertaken in the 1980s.

After crossing the bridge which leads to the main entrance of the castle, you will pass on your left steps descending to Fischer von Erlach's **Trinity Chapel**, a small oval construction clinging dramatically right above the cliff face. Beyond the gate is a small courtyard around which are administrative buildings comprising all that remains of the old castle. You walk through a second gate into the cour d'honneur, which is bordered to the left by landscaped terraces affording magnificent views over the surrounding landscape. At the far end of the courtyard are two massive sculptural groups by Antonio Mattielli representing *Hercules fighting Antaeus* and *Aeneas saving Anchises* (c 1727). They were presented to Marie Pignatelli by her imperial admirer Charles VI in 1732, and placed on either side of a grand limestone staircase built that same year. The steps lead up into the main part of the house, where the official tour begins.

Adjacent to the entrance hall is Fischer von Erlach's dynamic **Hall of Ancestors** (Sál předků), which in its architecture, sculpture and frescoed decoration is one of the most exciting Baroque spaces to be seen anywhere in Europe. The oval, one of Fischer's most characteristic forms, is here given a particularly dramatic power not only through being spectacularly placed on a cliff edge, but also through being used on an enormous scale, a feat which required remarkable engineering skills for the vaulting: it is above all this oval which gives the castle such a dynamic and exhilarating profile when seen from a distance. Thanks to Fischer's growing fame, he was able to secure for the painted and sculptural decoration of the interior two of the leading Central European artists of the day, the painter Johann Michal Rottmayr and the sculptor Tobiáš Kracker. The former covered the ceiling with a great illusionistic representation of the *Apotheosis of the Althann Family* (1695), while the latter produced for the niches along the walls a series of over life-sized figures representing some of the ancestors of Michal Jan II of Althann (installed in 1694). As an example of self-promotion on a megalomaniac scale, the hall is rivalled only by G.B. Tiepolo's glorification of the Schönborns in the Würzburg Residenz.

The hall might be the highpoint of the castle tour, yet the other rooms that you are shown comprise a beautiful series of intimate and lavishly furnished late 18C interiors, including a Pompeian Room, an Oriental Room, a Swiss Room, a superb circular marble bathroom, two rooms adorned respectively with embroideries and coloured engravings by Anton Raphael Mengs, and a room which Josef Hilgartner used as one of the first freemasonry lodges in Moravia. **Open** July, Aug Tues–Sun 09.00–12.00 and 13.00–18.00; May, June, Sept closes 17.00; Apr, Oct Sat, Sun 09.00–12.00 and 13.00–16.00.

Znojmo
Leaving Vranov by the same road on which you entered the town, head due east to Znojmo (23km), which lies at the point where the river Dyje leaves its narrow wooded valley and enters a great plain stretching south to nearby Austria. Znojmo, which rises on rocky ground above the river, has had a long and distinguished history.

History of Znojmo
The original settlement in the area was the Great Moravian citadel of St Hippolytus, situated 2km west of the present town, and founded as far back as the 9C. A later citadel was established at present-day Znojmo by Prince Břetislav I in the 11C, and occupied an important position on an international trade route. The apanage Přemyslid princes made it their seat, and the Přemyslid king Otakar II was buried in its Minorite monastery; the Emperor Sigismund died here in 1437, and a Diet proclaimed in the town in 1628 strengthened the position of the Habsburg family on the Czech throne. Znojmo's subsequent history is less glamorous: the place developed into a quiet market town and centre of light industries; today it is known less for its royal and imperial associations than for the fame of its pickled cucumbers (*kyselá okurka*), a speciality introduced here from Hungary in 1571.

Much of the old town has survived, including extensive sections of its 14C–16C fortifications, but Znojmo as a whole has a run-down, untidy quality. The life of the town is concentrated in the upper square, Horní náměstí, where late Baroque and ugly modern buildings jostle uncomfortably together. Descending south from here on Obroková, you will pass near the end of the street the **Town Hall Tower** (Radniční věž), a pinnacled and fantastical structure built in 1445 by Mikuláš of Sedlešovice. South of the tower extends the Masarykovo náměstí, the largest square in town, but with a sad and neglected character. The square slopes down the hill to the former Capuchin monastery, which has an uninspired late Baroque church.

Return to the upper town by heading west off the square on the Velká Mikulášská, at the top of which you will reach the town's well-preserved western ramparts, which enjoy an excellent view down the wooded banks of the Dyje and over the flat fertile country stretching to the south. The large and impressive hall-church which stands above the ramparts is the parish **Church of St Nicholas** (sv. Mikuláš), dating back to the 14C but largely rebuilt in the late 15C by Mikuláš of Sedlešovice; behind the building is the late Gothic **Church of St Wenceslas** (sv. Václav), which was vaulted in 1521 and has the curious feature of having its lower windows actually incorporated into the ramparts. Walking north from here along the ramparts you come to the castle, which has been converted into the Sladovna Brewery and is thus largely closed to visitors ('Better a living brewery than a dead castle', runs a curious and commendable Czech proverb).

However, access has been recently allowed into the castle's newly restored 11C round **Chapel of St Catherine** (sv. Kateřina), which dates back to before 1037, and is decorated inside with the most extensive surviving Romanesque frescoes in the Czech and Slovak Republics. Commissioned by the Přemyslids in 1134, these frescoes constitute an extraordinary blend of the secular and the spiritual: scenes from the life of the Virgin decorate the lower level, while above are two bands representing the legend of the prophetess Libuše and the Přemyslid dynasty; finally, at the very top of the vault, the donors Margrave Konrád II of Moravia and his wife Maria are shown inside a triumphal arch, surrounded by angels, cherubim and the four evangelists. **Open** Tues–Sun 09.00–16.00.

Adjoining the castle, and near a terrace with good views west over wooded hills to the Citadel of St Hippolytus, is the former Minorite monastery, which now contains the **South Moravian Museum** (Jihomoravské muzeum), featuring a small gallery of Habsburg portraits, a lapidarium, and archaeological and natural history collections. **Open** Apr–Sept Tues–Sun 09.00–16.00. Ulice Přemyslovců will lead you back from here to the Horní náměstí.

To visit the **Citadel of St Hippolytus** leave Znojmo at the northern end of town and drive for 2km on the Mašovice road; the old fortified Church of St Hippolytus was pulled down to make way for the present late Baroque edifice, the interest of which lies primarily in the eloquent dome frescoes by the expressive Austrian artist F.A. Maulbertsch (1768). By the river on the southern outskirts of Znojmo is the former Premonstratensian monastery of **Louka**, which was founded in 1190. The Baroque monastery buildings have been used as an army barracks since the time of Joseph II, and the valuable library which was once here is now in the Strahov Monastery in Prague. However you can still see Louka's much-restored and altered church, which dates back to shortly after the monastery's foundation.

The fastest way from Znojmo to Brno is along the straight and flat Road 54, but a more peaceful route through rolling countryside is by way of **Moravský Krumlov** (leave Znojmo at the southern end of town and head northeast on the road marked to Suchohrdly). The small and dusty town of Moravský Krumlov 32km away, badly damaged in the Second World War, is famous for its castle, which was rebuilt after c 1560 for Pertold of Lipá, hereditary marshal of the Kingdom of Bohemia. The unknown architect—possibly to be identified with the builder of Náměstí and Rosice—created an elegant Italianate structure centred around a three-tiered arcade courtyard, which has today something of the earthy, farmyard character of the surrounding town. A school for the training of railway workers has taken over most of the much-altered interior; but one of the outbuildings contains an important series of works by the Czech Republic's most famous artist, Alfons Mucha (1860–1939). The rustic setting of Moravský Krumlov might seem at first the most unlikely place for the display of an artist best known internationally for his sensuous and elegantly sophisticated Art Nouveau posters executed in Paris. But he was born in the nearby and equally rustic-looking town of Ivančice (which you will pass on your way to Brno), and took renewed pride in his Czech roots in the latter half of his life. The main works of his on show here are 20 huge historical canvases sponsored by an American millionaire Slavophile, Charles Richard Crane. Executed between 1909 and 1928, these overblown but gloriously entertaining examples of patriotic kitsch form a cycle known as the Slav Epic. **Open** Apr–Oct Tues–Sun 09.00–12.00 and 13.00–16.00.

At Ivančice, 10km further north, turn right to Modřice (20km), which lies on the main road to Brno from Znojmo. A detour 4km to the south along this road will take you to the former Benedictine abbey of **Rajhrad**, founded in 1048 and the oldest in Moravia. The present abbey church was begun in 1722 by Johann Santini-Aichel, and is one of his finest works in a strictly Baroque style. The surprisingly large interior is particularly splendid, and comprises three inter-connected oval spaces, the domes of which are covered in illusionistic frescoes. Typically for this architect the three spaces have a symbolic significance, as is indicated by the inscription on the arch over the altar: *Faciamus hic tria taber-nacula*, the words spoken by St Peter at the Transfiguration. On the left-hand side of the church is a tablet commemorating George James Ogilvy, who defended Brno against the Swedes in 1645. Return to Modřice, from where the remaining 9km to Brno are on dual carriageway.

20 · Brno

Brno, the capital of Moravia and the second largest town in the Czech Republic, is spaciously laid out between gentle wooded hills. Though of ancient origin, and with numerous monuments from different periods in history, its present char-acter was acquired from the late 18C onwards, with the rapid development of its textile mills and other industries. Known sometimes as the Manchester or Leeds of the Czech Republic, it is a city of a remarkably progressive character which has played an important role in the development of 20C architecture.

History of Brno
The origins of Brno are seen by some to go back to the Celtic stronghold of Eburodunon, mentioned by Ptolemy; others trace the town back to a Slavic citadel or *brniti*, established in about the 5C AD. A seat of the apanage Přemyslid princes by the 11C, Brno was raised to a town in 1243, and became the centre of the Moravian Margraves after 1349; it emerged as capital of Moravia in 1641. The town prospered initially as a result of thriving trade relations with Venice, Genoa, the Hanseatic ports and

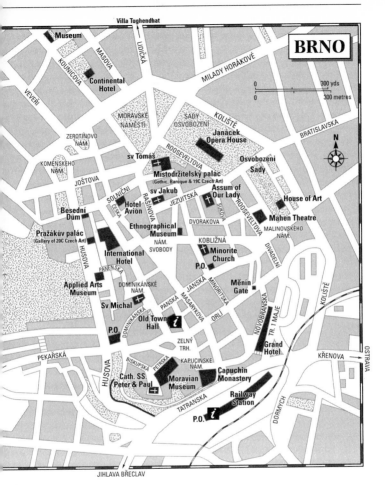

Villa Tughendhat

BRNO

Museum

KOUNICOVA
MASOVA
LIDIČKA
MILADY HORÁKOVÉ

Continental
Hotel

VEVEŘÍ
ZEROTÍNOVO
NÁM.

MORAVSKÉ
NÁMĚSTÍ

SADY
OSVOBOZENÍ

KOLIŠTĚ

Janacek
Opera House

BRATISLAVSKA

ROOSEVELTOVA

N

KOMENSKÉHO
NÁM.

sv Tomáš

Osvobození
Sady

JOŠTOVA

Mistodržitelský palác
(Gothic, Baroque & 19C Czech Art)

SOLNIČNÍ

sv Jakub

Assum of
Our Lady

House of Art

ČESKA

RAŠINOVA

Hotel
Avion

JEZUITSKÁ

SIKOVA

ROOSEVELTOVA

Mahen Theatre

Besední
Dům

Ethnographical
Museum

DVORAKOVA

MALINOVSKÉHO
NÁM.

Pražákův palác
(Gallery of 20C Czech Art)

NÁM.
SVOBODY

KOBLIŽNÁ

HUSOVA

International
Hotel

Minorite
Church

DIVADELNÍ

PANENSKÁ

P.O.

KOLIŠTĚ

Applied Arts
Museum

DOMINIKÁNSKÉ
NÁM.

JANSKÁ

Měnin
Gate

NOVOBRANSKÁ

MINORITSKÁ

Sv Michal

PANSKÁ

MASARYKOVA

TR. 1 MÁJE

DOMINIKÁNSKÁ

Old Town
Hall

ORLÍ

P.O.

ZELNÝ
TRH.

PEKAŘSKÁ

BISKUPSKÁ

PETRSKÁ

KAPUCINSKÉ
NÁM.

Grand
Hotel

KŘENOVA

OSTRAVA

HUSOVA

Cath. SS.
Peter & Paul

Moravian
Museum

Capuchin
Monastery

DORMYCH

Railway
Station

TATRANSKA

P.O.

JIHLAVA BŘECLAV

0   300 yds
0   300 metres

numerous towns in Eastern and Central Europe. Over the centuries Brno
successfully withstood sieges by the Hussites, the Swedes and the Prussian
armies of Frederick II, and was only captured once—by Napoleon in 1805.
The town's industrial development dates back to the foundation in 1766 of
a textile factory comprising 120 looms; within the space of 14 years, 19
other such factories had been established, thus earning the place the name
of 'rakouský Manchestr' (the Austrian Manchester). After 1818 locally
built machinery began to replace English imports, thanks to the creation of
the Salms ironworks at nearby Blansko. A further great boost to the town's
economy was provided in 1839, when the railway line was completed
between here and Vienna; later in the century, it developed into a considerable engineering centre, which it still remains.

One of the most outstanding periods in Brno's history followed the
creation of the Czechoslovak Republic in 1918. The local industrialists,

many of whom were Jews, were anxious that their town should reflect the progressive and revolutionary spirit of the new country, and became patrons to some of the greatest figures of the European avant-garde. It was at Brno that the German architect Ludwig Mies van der Rohe built the Villa Tugendhat, one of the pioneering Modernist constructions of this century. Less well known today outside of the Czech Republic, though no less deserving of attention than the work of Mies van der Rohe, were the achievements of the Brno-based group of artists, architects and intellectuals known as BLOK, which was founded in 1920, and included among its prominent members the painter Kalab, and the architects Bohuslav Fuchs (1895–1972) and Bedřich Rozehnal. A symbol of the new Brno was the vast trade Exhibition Ground which was opened in 1928 and designed by the city's most adventurous architects.

After suffering from the dispersal of its Jewish community in the late 1930s, Brno was then badly affected by heavy bombing in the Second World War. The architecture of post-war Brno bears little comparison to that of the inter-war years, though an active cultural life has continued to flourish here. Furthermore the Exhibition Ground, revived in 1955 after the closure of the one in Prague, has been the scene since 1959 of an International Engineering Trade Fair, an event which helps to sustain in the town a cosmopolitan and dynamic atmosphere.

Among the famous people to have been born in Brno are the botanist and founder of the modern theory of heredity, Johann Gregor Mendel (1822–84); the inventor of the Kaplan water turbine, Viktor Kaplan (1876–1934); the Austrian architect Adolf Loos (1870–1933); the pioneering Czech architect Jan Kotěra (1871–1923); and the writers Bohumil Hrabal (1914–97) and Milan Kundera (1929–).

A. Central Brno

Brno is not the best preserved of Czech towns, and its old monuments are widely scattered and enveloped by extensive 19C and 20C development. The greatest concentration of these monuments is around the **Cabbage Market** (Zelný trh), which has kept the shape of the original 13C market square. In the middle of this, the largest square in Brno, is the **Parnassus Fountain** (kašna Parnas), built in 1693–95 to a design by Fischer von Erlach.

The **Old Town Hall** (Stará radnice), the town's most important surviving secular building from the medieval period, lies off the northern side of this square, and functioned as a town hall from the 13C up to 1345. The main entrance to the building, off Radnická, is marked by a tall tower built in the 13C but heavily remodelled in later periods. At its base is a fancifully elaborate late Gothic portal executed c 1510 by the Austrian sculptor and architect Anton Pilgram. This colourful and belligerent personality spent much of his life in Vienna, where in 1513 he was to quarrel with the local mason's guild, on whom he was to take his revenge by caricaturing their leading members in the sculptural decoration of the pulpit in St Stephen's Cathedral. According to tradition he committed a comparably vindictive act at Brno: considering himself to have been underpaid for his work on the Town Hall portal, he is said to have destroyed its central pinnacle on his last night in the town and to have replaced it with the present bizarrely drooping form, a comment on the bent character of the Brno burghers.

Behind the entrance portal is the suspended corpse of a creature said to be the infamous Brno dragon, a monster which lived in the river Svratka, and terrified early travellers to the town; in fact it is the mummified remains of a crocodile presented as a gift to Matthias Corvinus by a Turkish delegation on their way to Poland. Hanging alongside it is a 16C wheel recalling the story of a young wheelwright who bet a good barrel of wine that in the space of 12 hours he would fell a tree in the forest, make a carriage wheel from it, and roll it all the way from Mikulov to Brno Town Hall. He won the wager, and the wheel has become a symbol of the town, an indication of how work is done well and quickly here; the irony is that the young wheelwright gained little from his achievement, for he was considered to be in league with the devil, and died in poverty. Exhibitions are now held in the Old Town Hall, and in the summer months you can walk up to the gallery of the entrance tower. **Open** Apr–Sept daily 09.00–17.00.

Brno

Returning from Radnická to the Zelný trh, walk round the square in an anti-clockwise direction, and you will pass at Nos 12 and 13 two reconstructed houses of medieval origin forming what is known as the Little Block (Malý Špalíček). On the southern, upper side of the square is the vast Dietrichstein Palace, a much-restored structure of the early 17C built as the palace of the Bishops of Olomouc in Brno, and taken over in 1805 by Marshal M.I. Kutuzov, Commander-in-Chief of the Russian troops fighting Napoleon; today it houses the historical, archaeological and natural history collections of the extensive **Moravian Museum** (Moravské zemské muzeum). **Open** Tues–Sat 09.00–18.00.

The elegant late 18C **Reduta Theatre** (Reduta divadlo), on the southeastern corner of the square, is the town's oldest theatre, and was where Mozart performed in 1767; today it specialises in operettas put on by the Brno State Theatre. On the southern side of the building extends the triangular-shaped Kapucínské náměstí, originally the Coal Market, and a place where charcoal was sold from the 14C onwards. The **Capuchin monastery**, which gives the square its name, is a mid-17C structure of interest largely for its crypt, where a specially designed air passage has preserved the corpses of Capuchin monks and distinguished benefactors of the monastery in a mummified state; the corpse of Brno's leading Baroque architect, Mořic Grimm, provides the crypt with one of its grim attractions, as does that of the belligerent Austrian commander Baron von Trenck, who died in Brno's notorious Špilberk prison in 1749. **Open** Tues–Sat 09.00–12.00 and 14.00–16.30, Sat 11.00–11.45 and 14.00–16.30.

From the Dietrichstein Palace the narrow Petrská climbs up to the attractive

Petrov Hill, where the town's citadel was situated before being re-sited to the Špilberk. As you climb you will pass the site intended for the **Divadlo na Provázku** (literally the Theatre on a String), a reconstruction of an avant-garde youth theatre which was founded in 1967 and named after a leading minister of the time. The **Cathedral of SS Peter and Paul** (sv. Petr a Pavel), occupying the site of the former citadel, was begun in the 14C over a Romanesque structure; partially burned in the 16C, it was remodelled by Grimm in the Baroque period, and given a neo-Gothic presbytery by A. Prokop in 1889–91, and its two tall towers and steeples in 1904–05. You enter through a neo-Gothic portal attached to a 14C–15C west façade; the main interest of the interior is to be found in the first chapel to the right, a *Madonna and Child* of c 1307, one of the most important surviving medieval statues in Moravia. The cathedral, which dominates the Petrov Hill, overlooks to the south the verdant Denis Park (Denisovy sady), in which remains of medieval and 17C walls have been preserved, as well as a Classical obelisk, erected in 1818 to commemorate the end of the Napoleonic Wars. Brno is a place where wine is drunk almost as much as beer, and on the southern slopes of the hill can also be found a number of privately owned wine cellars, where families and friends get together occasionally for wild drinking sprees.

You can descend to the lower town from the cathedral by way of the Biskupská and its continuation Dominikánská, two streets lined with much-restored 16C–18C buildings comprising the 'Big Block' (Velký Špalíček). Of especial interest is No. 9 Dominikánská, **The House of the Lords of Kunštát**, a medieval palace transformed in the Renaissance period and again at the beginning of the 18C; it is now an exhibition hall and cultural centre. The street ends up alongside the former **Dominican Church of St Michael** (sv. Michal), which rises on a terrace fringed by Baroque statuary above the small Dominikánské náměstí, the town's former fish market. The church, remodelled by J.K. Erna in the late 17C, was attached to a monastery founded in the 1330s; the Estates of Moravia used to meet in the latter's main cloister, which has retained fragments of its medieval masonry. The Baroque monastic buildings which extend north of the cloister were designed by Grimm after 1690 and now form the present Town Hall.

Panenská leads north from the Dominikánské náměstí to the unprepossessing *Hotel International* (1960–62), which overlooks to the west the verdant **Špilberk Hill**. On Husova, adjacent to the western entrance to the hotel, an imposing neo-Renaissance block built by a Jewish textile merchant in the 1880s as a museum of the applied arts; a museum to this day of the applied arts, its interior, with its classical grotesque decorations, and Italianate painted and coffered ceilings, makes an appropriate setting for the applied arts holdings of the **Moravian Gallery** (Umeleckoprumyslové muzeum). The ground and first floor rooms are used for temporary exhibitions, while those on the second floor are taken over by an old-fashioned and unimaginatively arranged display of objects ranging from Gothic tapestries to 1970's and 80's kitsch, and featuring in between some fine local Biedermier furniture in a style that seems to prefigure the Czech Cubist designers of the early 20C. Inevitably, given Brno's important role in the history of the Czech modernist movement, the most interesting holdings in the museum are those devoted to the first three decades of the 20C, including some of the original glass and tubular steel furnishings from Mies van der Rohe's Tugendhat House (see below) and a suite of Cubist dining-room furniture (a sideboard, chairs, and a coffee-table) designed by Gočar as a gift to his Cubist painter friend Emil Filla. Sadly the greying condition of these works, and their present lacklustre display, make it difficult now to appreciate their pioneering importance. **Open** Wed–Sun 10.00–18.00.

Czech Cubist painters, though lacking on the whole the originality of their architect and designer contemporaries, seem none the less more exciting in Brno thanks to the excellent display of their works to be seen just to the north of the applied arts museum in the newly restored late 19C block (known as the Pražáků palác) housing the Moravian Gallery's permanent collection of **20C Czech art**. These works, spaciously laid out in a series of pristine white rooms on the museum's second floor, include landscapes and portraits by **Kubista**, nudes by **Filla** and **Špála**, a humorous large-scale study of *Peasants in Provence* by Otakar **Kubín** (1921), an atmospheric, blue-green oil of a *Smoker* (1918–19) by **Čapek**, and a remarkably varied and lively group of canvases by the locally-based **Antonín Procházka**, who happily alternates between such styles as Cubism, Fauvism and Expressionism. Among the other works on this floor are two sensual nudes by the Art Nouveau sculptor **Jan Stursa**, expressionist carvings by **Bílek**, Cubist bronzes by **Otto Guttfreund**, and some realistic sculptures of the 1920s by **Josef Kubíček** and **Karel Pokorný**. Two wholly idiosyncratic figures of the early 20C were the little known **Grigori Musatov** (author of a powerful sunset scene of 1931 entitled *Electricity*), and **Jan Zrzavý**, whose works here include a number of linear landscapes (for instance, *San Marco*) which are like a fantastical cross between Dufy and Klee.

On the museum's first floor are numerous Surrealist and Abstract Expressionist works, among which are characteristically delicate canvases by **Šíma** and **Toyen**, and examples of the bolder and more anguished art of **František Janoušek** and **Mikuláš Medek**. Open Tues–Sun 10.00–18.00.

Adjoining the museum to the north is the late 19C **Meeting House** (Besední dům), which was once the main Czech cultural centre of the town, and is now the home of the Brno State Philharmonic Orchestra. At the junction of Husova and Solniční, on the northern side of this building, turn right and head east towards the pedestrian shopping street of Česká, where you should turn right again. As soon as you enter Česká, you will pass on the left-hand side the most distinguished-looking of Brno's modern hotels, the *Hotel Avion*, which was designed in 1927 by Bohuslav Fuchs, who created a narrow and impressively simple street front in glass and steel (the hotel has subsequently been expanded). Among the other buildings you will notice as you walk south down Česká is *Stopka's Beer Hall* (No. 5), the exterior of which was covered in sgraffito decorations by L. Novák in 1919.

The street leads into the **náměstí Svobody**, the oldest and second largest square in Brno. This square, at the heart of Brno's pedestrian district, has an overall drab and 19C character, and yet it preserves monuments from earlier periods. At its centre is a plague column of 1680 designed by J.K. Erna, while at No. 13 is the late 16C **Schwartz House** (Schwarzův palác), a Renaissance palace boasting an arcaded courtyard built in 1589–96 by A. Gabri and J. Gialdi; the building was heavily restored in 1938, and the once plain exterior given a sgraffito decoration by E. Hrbek. At the eastern end of the square, and entered at No. 1 Kobližná, is the former Foundation for Noblewomen (Ústav šlechtičen), founded in the 1670s as a home for orphaned girls from aristocratic and burgher families; the building, remodelled in the 18C and 20C, now houses the ethnographical collections of the Moravian Museum.

Brno's pedestrian district continues south and to the east of the square, but for the moment you should head north along Rašínova, reaching after a few minutes the finest of the town's medieval monuments, the **Church of St James** (sv. Jakub). Founded in the 1220s for the German burghers of Brno, it was rebuilt from the late 14C onwards, Anton Pilgram intervening in the construction around 1495; a fire in 1515 delayed the completion of the building until 1592, when the tower was erected. An amusing and curious feature of the exterior is the obscene figure placed high on the south side of the tower. It apparently shows a smirking man pointing his backside in the direction of the distant Czech Cathedral of SS Peter and Paul. Traditionally this figure has been interpreted as an indication of German attitudes towards the Czechs, but recent investigations, involving a photographer and a fireman's ladder, have revealed in fact that the man is not alone, but is accompanied by a woman with whom he is engaged in activities not normally associated with a church. Inside the building you find yourself within a hall-church of great lightness, height and elegance, and with elaborate Gothic vaulting of c 1585: at least one architectural historian has described this as the last great masterpiece of the Gothic in the Czech Republic. The high altar and other furnishings are neo-Gothic works of the 19C, but there is an outstanding pulpit of 1525, containing Baroque reliefs of the life of Christ. Among the Gothic, Renaissance and Baroque tombs in the ambulatory is the tomb of Field Marshal Count Radwit de Souches (d. 1697), the defender of Brno against the Swedes.

Further north along Rašínova, at the junction with the Moravské náměstí, is the pale yellow façade of the **Church of St Thomas** (sv. Tomáš), originally attached to a 14C Augustinian monastery. The Gothic church was remodelled in a Baroque style by J.K. Erna in the mid-17C, and further altered by M. Grimm in the following century; inside is an altarpiece by F.A. Maulbertsch.

The former monastery building, directly behind the church, was later transformed into the **Místodržitelský palác**, which served first as the residence of the governor of Moravia, and then—during the Communist period—as a museum of the working class; recently and beautifully restored, it now houses the Gothic, Baroque and 19C paintings and sculptures of the Moravian Gallery, few of which live up to the late Baroque magnificence of the setting. Among the works that stand out are four finely detailed panels of c 1420–1440 by the local master known as the **Master of the Rajhad Altar**, some vividly coloured oil sketches by **Maulbertsch**, **Ferdinand Waldmuller**'s detailed rural genre scene *Arrival of the Newly Wed* (1859), two Barbizon-inspired landscapes of the 1880s by **Antonín Chitussi**, a particulary atmospheric evening landscape of 1901 by **Antonín Hudeček**, and **Maximilián Švabinsky**'s *The Red Umbrella* (1902), a delightful half-length female portrait. **Open** Wed, Fri–Sun 10.00–17.00, Thur 10.00–19.00.

The Moravské náměstí marks the northern border of the old town, and has in its landscaped centre a large sculpture of a Red Army soldier representing *Victory over Fascism*, a work by V. Makovský of 1955. Parkland, following the line of the former medieval fortifications, takes up the whole northeast corner of central Brno. Turning right at the Moravské náměstí on to Rooseveltova, you will skirt the park Osvobození, on the edge of which stands the **Janáček Opera House** (Janáčkovo divadlo), erected in 1960–65, and specialising in both opera and ballet.

The first main turning to the right down Rooseveltova is Jezuitská, off which stands the **Church of the Assumption of Our Lady**, a Jesuit church built in 1666 and lavishly remodelled inside by M. Grimm in 1735. Back on Rooseveltova continue heading south into Divadelní, which passes alongside the **Mahen Theatre**

(Mahenovo divadlo) of 1881–82, the main dramatic theatre of Brno and apparently the first in Europe to have had electric lighting. The small building behind it—originally an Art Nouveau structure rebuilt in 1946—is the House of Art of the City of Brno, a centre for art exhibitions. After passing the Mahen Theatre, cross the Malinovského náměstí and turn right until you reach Novobranská, which leads to the **Měnín Gate**, the only remaining gate from the town's fortifications.

Heading southwest from here along Orlí, the first street which you come to is the attractive Minoritská, one of the pedestrian streets that extend south from the náměstí Svobody. At the junction of Orlí and Minoritská is the **Technical Museum** (Technické muzeum), with collections ranging from hunting weapons and mechanical musical instruments to computers, microscopes and hydro-electric generators.

Heading north up Minoritská you will come to the **Minorite church** (Minoritský kostel), a building of 14C origin which was given after 1716 a lively and richly ornamented façade by M. Grimm, who was also responsible for the attached Loreto Chapel. At the southern end of Minoritská is a former Franciscan monastery, the cellars of which have been converted into a stylish and animated wine bar. The street finishes up at the south in front of the recently renovated *Grand Hotel*, which dates back to 1870 but has an Art Nouveau annexe dominated by a splendid representation of the *Judgement of Paris*. South from here is the town's main railway station, a superb 19C ironwork construction which has recently been lovingly restored. From here you can return to the old town of Brno by walking north along the wide and animated Masarykova, the main shopping street of the town. Turning left from here into Květinářská or Orlí will take you back to the náměstí 25. Února.

B. Western Brno

West of the *Hotel International* you can climb up through parkland to the **Špilberk Citadel**, which was put up in the late 13C and reconstructed at various times in history, most notably in the 17C. A large network of underground tunnels is said to lie underneath the complex, one of which apparently led to a village 18km away, from where fresh produce was supplied to the fortress in times of siege.

History of the citadel
Gaining a reputation for being impregnable during the Thirty Years War, the Špilberk later acquired considerable notoriety on account of its prison, which was established here in the 17C. In the 18C and early 19C many of the leading miscreants of the Habsburg Empire were incarcerated here, including numerous Italian, Polish and Hungarian revolutionaries. Among the best known prisoners was Colonel Trenck, the leader of the half-savage group of Austrian soldiers known as the Pandours; he died here in 1749. But it was above all for the Italian poet and revolutionary Silvio Pellico that the prison was to be best remembered. He, together with fellow members of the secret society called the Carbonari, was a prisoner here between 1822 and 1830, an experience which left his health ruined and led him to write in 1832 *Le mie prigioni* (*My Prisons*). This moving and shocking account of conditions in the Špilberk horrified liberal Europe, and apparently inspired Chancellor Metternich to say that the book had done more damage to Austria than a lost battle; the name of Pellico is today recalled in a street underneath the citadel.

Though the main part of the fortress has been closed for restoration for many years (a museum devoted to the history of Brno will eventually be opened here), its dark and infamous dungeons can now be seen in the course of a guided tour that cannot be recommended either for claustrophobes or the squeamish: off its dank, narrow passages you will be shown numerous instruments of torture as well as the lightless cells where prisoners were chained by the neck and hands and given only bread and water (this form of punishment, instituted by the 'enlightened' emperor Josef II, was abandoned by his successor Leopold II). Pellico himself was imprisoned in the fortress's upper storey, a preferable location. **Open** June–Sept Tues–Sun 09.00–17.00.

Descending the western side of the citadel hill you reach the noisy Úvoz, at the southern end of which is Mendel Square (Mendlovo náměstí). Rising above the square is the former Convent Church of the Assumption of Our Lady, which has a Baroque high altar of 1734–35 containing an Italian-Byzantine icon. The former **Augustinian Monastery** to which the church was attached was founded in 1323 by Queen Eliška Rejčka. Of the original structure, there remains only the chapter-house and a fragment of the cloister, the rest of the convent being largely reconstructed between the 15C and 18C. Of great interest is the mid-18C library, which has elaborate Baroque shelving, and close associations with several of the best-known Moravian scientists and musicians of the 19C. The composer Křížkovský worked in the library, as did his famous pupil Leoš Janáček; the place is remembered above all for the genetician Mendel, who was a monk at the monastery and to whom is dedicated a small museum adjoining the library, the Mendelianum. **Open** Mon–Fri 08.00–17.00. The wine bar installed in the convent cellars rivals that of the Franciscan monastery as a popular and elegant place to eat and drink.

Heading west from Mendlovo náměstí along Klášterská and its continuation Vystavní, you will come to Brno's celebrated **Výstaviště Exhibition Ground**, the most important in the Czech Republic. Founded in 1928, and originally laid out by the architect Emil Králík, it has been the venue since 1959 of an International Engineering Trade Fair and, since 1965, of Intercanis Brno, an international dog show which now attracts up to 12,000 dogs to the city; these events are held respectively every September and July. But an interest in either dogs or engineering is not essential to a visit to the Exhibition Ground, which is well worth seeing for the architecture alone.

The main hall today is a vast domed structure of 1960, but of greater beauty are the original buildings of 1928, in particular **Hall A**, a pioneering white and glazed construction supported by rows of massive parabolic arches; the architects were Kalous and Valenta, working under Králík's supervision. Other fine works of this period include Bohuslav Fuchs' red-brick and glass Brno-Moravian Pavilion, and a tower by Bohumír Čermák, a stunning glass structure built around a staircase well and resembling a futuristic fantasy. Many other outstanding buildings of the 1920s are to be seen in the suburban districts of Žlutý kopec and Jiráskova čtvrtˇ, which spread over the green and shaded hill rising to the north of the Exhibition Ground: in these suburbs were once the homes of many of the more enlightened of the town's industrialists. You can ascend the hill on Lípová, where at No. 18, at the junction with Neumannova, is one of Fuchs' greatest buildings, a **nursery** designed in 1929 and having the simple, abstract qualities of a painting by a Constructivist such as Mondrian. Lípová continues into Tvrdého, which descends into Úvoz, at the foot of the Špilberk Hill.

C. Northern Brno

Head north from the Moravské náměstí along Kounicova. On the right-hand side of the road, beyond the tall block of the *Hotel Continental* (1961–64), is a neo-Classical 19C building which was formerly the School of Organists where Janáček taught; it is now the History of Music Department of the Moravian Museum, and includes a large collection of photographs, documents and other items relating to the history of music in this region; its extensive manuscript collection, founded by Professor Vladimír Heifert in 1919, has autograph works by Liszt, Brahms, Dvořák, Martinů and Beethoven. In 1910, after being appointed to the staff of the School of Organists, Janáček moved to an adjacent house at 14 Smetanova, and lived there until his death in 1918. The house, incorporated into the garden of the museum building, now forms the **Janáček Museum** (Janáčkovo muzeum), where you can see numerous photographs documenting his life, as well as listen to recordings of his music; the highpoint of the visit is the well-preserved study, in which the master's piano is to be found. **Open** Mon–Fri 08.00–12.00 and 13.00–16.00.

Continuing north you will come eventually to Bohuslav Fuchs' largest building in the city, the Provincial Army Headquarters of 1937. Further north still you come to the housing estates of Tábor and Králové Pole, where, in the middle of grim Socialist blocks of the 1950s and 1960s, can be seen innovative co-operative housing of 1928.

Villa Tugendhat

It is a modern building which provides Brno with its greatest if also most neglected attraction. This, the **Villa Tugendhat** by Mies van der Rohe, stands in the hill-side suburb of Černé Pole, a short distance northeast of the Janáček Museum. Continue until the end of Smetanova, cross the wide Lidická, and then follow Lužanecká, skirting to the south the large Lužánky Park. At Drobného turn left, and then take the first right into the steeply ascending Schodová, which you climb until you reach Černopolní, where you turn right again. The entrance to the villa is 50m down the road on the right-hand side.

History of the villa

The Tugendhats were a Jewish family who had settled in Brno in 1864, and had risen in the late 19C from being drapers to owning important textile mills. Fritz Tugendhat, the grandson of the first Tugendhat to have moved to Brno, was born on 10 October 1895 and on 30 July 1928 was married in Berlin to Greta Weis, née Löw-Beer. Greta was the daughter of another textile manufacturer, and on this, her second marriage, received as a gift from her father a plot of land on Brno's Černé Pole Hill. Even before marrying, Fritz and Greta had met Ludwig Mies van der Rohe in Berlin and had asked him to design a house for them. Mies (as he came to be known to his friends and to architectural historians) first came to Brno in September 1928 to inspect the proposed building site, and by 31 December of that year had already drawn up a project for the house. Work was begun in June of the following year and was complete by December 1930; Mies designed not only the architecture but also all the furniture of the villa. The Tugendhats lived here until 1938, when they fled from the Nazis, and eventually moved to Venezuela, where they remained after the war.

The Nazis occupied the house after 15 March 1939, and confiscated it from the family on 4 October 1939; ownership fell officially to the German Reich on 12 January 1942. After plundering the house and devastating the garden, the Germans abandoned the place in 1949. The badly damaged villa served for a short while as a private ballet school, but then was appropriated by the Czech State, who used it at first as a home for the National Institute of Physiotherapy and then, after 1955, as the department of rehabilitative physiotherapy of the Pediatric Teaching Hospital of Brno. The latter department only moved out of the building in 1969, six years after it had been declared a cultural monument, and immediately prior to a restoration campaign based partially on a report drafted by an architect from the Chicago studios of Mies van der Rohe, Dirk Lohan. Ownership of the building reverted in 1986 from the District National Health Authority to the National Committee of the City of Brno. In recent years the Brno authorities have finally opened the building to the public, but on a slightly erratic basis; and prospective visitors should contact beforehand the tourist office in the Old Town Hall behind the Cabbage Market (Zelný trh).

The Villa Tugendhat, one of the key works in the history of the Modernist movement in architecture, occupies a sloping site with magnificent views towards the old centre of Brno. From the much-altered street-side (sadly, the only part of the building which can at present be seen by the public), the villa appears as a single-storey horizontal structure; seen from the large and steeply inclined garden, however, it is a three-storey block. The main entrance is at street level, and on this level were once to be found bedrooms, bathrooms and a garage; on the floor below were the kitchen and main living quarters, while on the lowest floor were storage-rooms, service rooms and bedrooms for occasional use.

The architecture clearly reflects the ideals of the Dutch Constructivist group De Stijl, which believed that modern architecture should be based on a system of right-angled planes, perpendicular and parallel to each other. Decorative details were abolished, and space was conceived as flexible as possible, delineated by white carpets and chrome-plated cruciform columns, and with a minimum use of walls.

The main room of the house was a space of 235 square metres; it was intended as a study and library, and as a place for resting, listening to music and receiving visitors. On two sides it was bordered by great sheets of glass, and it was directly connected to a garden terrace: Mies brilliantly exploited the panoramic situation of the house and also broke down the rigid division between interior and exterior, as he did in the German Pavilion which he designed at the same time for the Barcelona Exhibition of 1929–30. The interior of the villa is now largely bare (the surviving Mies furniture being currently on show in the Moravian Gallery); and there have been a number of insensitive post-war changes to the actual structure, notably the replacement of one of the huge sheets of glass with a series of much smaller panes. However, the place has still managed to retain its serene, timeless character. **Open** Wed–Sun 10.00–15.00.

Excursion to the Moravian Karst

The Moravian Karst (Moravský kras) is a name given to the limestone area 3km to the east of Blansko (see below): 6km wide and 25km long, it is an area densely covered in forests, intercut with gorges, and pitted with caves, many of which have been formed by the underground river Punkva. Important archaeological finds have been made in a number of the caves, and in those known as Sloupsko-Šošůvské jeskyně (in the vicinity of the village of Sloup, 14km northeast of Blansko) can be seen traces of prehistoric wall-paintings.

One of the most popular excursions from Brno, a round trip to the Moravský kras is some 60km long. From the Villa Tugendhat head south down Černopolní until you reach the wide Merhautova, where you turn left, following the signs for Adamov and Blansko; much of the journey is along the Svitava river. **Blansko**, 25km away, is a small industrial town set among wooded hills and with an iron industry dating back to medieval times; many of Czechoslovakia's bronze memorials and much of the ironwork from the country's old monuments were cast in the foundries here. The local castle, remodelled in a neo-Renaissance style in the late 19C, contains the Museum of the Moravian Karst, with exhibits relating to the local iron industry. **Open** May–Sept Tues–Sun 10.00–17.00.

By far the most visited of the caves is the **Punkva Cave** (Punkevní Jeskyně) which can be reached by heading east from Blansko on the Jedovnice road, and then turning off after 2km in the direction of Sloup; at the *Hotel Skalní mlýn* (a further 2km and a popular base for those wishing to spend a long time in the Kras), the road forks, and you should take the turning to the left, continuing to drive along the bottom of a small wooded gorge formed by an overground stretch of the Punkva river. The entrance to the cave lies 1.5km further on, at the point where the Punkva disappears into the rock.

The popularity of the cave is such that there are generally large queues to get in, and in the summer months it might be necessary to book a visit several hours ahead. While waiting you might have to avail yourself of the nearby toilet complex, which is of interest in being one of the earliest examples of privatisation in Moravia (an enterprising family bought it back in 1987): as a guide was heard to say in 1989, 'In England you privatise your heavy industries; in Moravia we privatise our toilets.'

The visit to the cave lasts about an hour and a half, and is by a combination of foot and boat, an altogether claustrophobic experience. Perhaps the most enjoyable moment comes half-way through the trip when you emerge into daylight, at the bottom of the **Macocha Abyss** (propast Macocha): suddenly you are confronted with steep and rocky slopes streaked with rich vegetation of an intense green. The

In 1560 a woman from the nearby village of Vilémovice was told that her ill young son would die if she did not kill her older stepson, who was said to be draining the former's health away. Believing unquestioningly in this superstitious nonsense, she took the stepson to the Macocha Abyss, and threw him into it. Fortunately—though not for her—he managed to cling on to the vegetation on the sides, and was shortly afterwards saved by a group of foresters. When the rescuers heard of what the stepmother had done to him, they did the same to her, though she was not to be assisted by the vegetation, and was thus to become probably the first person to reach the bottom of the abyss. It was not until 1734 that a more leisurely descent was to be made into the abyss, led by a monk from the Augustinian monastery at Brno. The Punkva Cave itself was only explored after 1909, five years before part of it was opened to the public.

138m-deep abyss, one of the deepest in Europe, appears to have been created by the collapse thousands of years ago of the ceiling of an enormous domed space. This dramatic and sinister mark on the landscape has naturally given rise to many abysmal local stories, at least one of which is supported by documentary evidence.

Returning to the *Hotel Skalní mlýn*, turn left on to the Ostrov road, and you will begin climbing up the Punkva gorge; after 2km another turning to your left will take you after 1km to a forest car park and restaurant at the top of the Macocha Abyss. Back on the Ostrov road turn right after 50m to nearby Vilémovice, and from here descend to Jedovnice.

The road back to Brno heads south from here, but you could make a detour 3km to the east to visit the village of **Senetářov**, where, in 1972, all the villagers pooled their resources to build their own church; this appealing structure, rising on steps above a pool, is distantly indebted to Le Corbusier's church at Ronchamp, and has inside a painted high altar and Stations of the Cross by the Surrealist artist Mikuláš Medek, whose work reunited influences by Miro, Tanguy, Ernst, Magritte and Dalí.

The village of **Křtiny**, 8km to the south of Jedovnice and pleasantly situated among rolling meadows fringed by woods, has one of the most impressive Baroque churches in Moravia. This soaringly tall pilgrimage church, so unexpectedly large for its rural setting, has its origins in a chapel of 1237, and attracts numerous pilgrims each year on St Anne's Day. The present structure, designed c 1710 by Santini-Aichel, has the plan of a Greek cross and is an example of Santini's work in a strictly Baroque as opposed to Baroque-Gothic style. The interior, revealed by recent and still incomplete restoration to be dazzlingly bright, has domes frescoed between 1728 and 1750 by Etgens, Ignác Raab and Winterhalter. Of great ingenuity is the way in which the Greek cross is joined to an oval cloister belonging to the former convent attached to the church. Driving southwest of Křtiny by way of Babice and Bílovice you will reach Brno after 16km, entering the town on the same road on which you left it.

21 · Brno to Ostrava

A. Via Olomouc

Total distance 179km: Brno (leave by the Road 58/E462) • 36km Vyškov • 41km Olomouc • 25km Lipník nad Bečvou • 19km Bělotín • 20km Fulnek • 38km Ostrava.

Heading due east of Brno you soon reach the E462, which is now a dual carriageway to Olomouc. Almost immediately after leaving Brno you enter a chain of fertile and much built-up valleys that extend all the way to Ostrava and form the backbone of Moravia. The landscape along this, the main Ostrava road, becomes increasingly industrialised, and the towns you pass are particularly unappealing in their outskirts.

Vyškov, 36km east of Brno, has a Renaissance Town Hall of 1569–1613 (its tower can be climbed Wed and Thur, 13.00–16.00), as well as an archbishop's castle, dating back to the Gothic period but remodelled in the late 17C, that contains today a lively folk collection, and some colourful mementoes from the Arabian travels of a local professor called Alois Musil. A now uncommemorated native of the town was the first Communist president of the Czechoslovak Republic, Klement Gottwald (1896–1953), whose birthplace in the industrial northwestern suburb of Dědice was once a museum to him.

The extensive industries of **Prostějov**, 20km further on, shield a number of Renaissance monuments in and around a large and pleasant central square, the Masarykovo náměstí, that is distinguished above all by a cultural centre of 1905–7, the Národní dum: a good example of the transition in Czech architecture between Art Nouveau and Modernism, this was designed by Jan Kotěra with the help of Ludvík Kysela and the sculptor Stanislav Sucharda, who was responsible for the delightful frieze of the Three Graces in the centre's atmospheric restaurant.

Olomouc

Even more surprises await you within the grim urban sprawl of Olomouc, which had remained up to the 17C the second most important town in the Kingdom of Bohemia. Impressive even today in its scale, this polluted, heavily industrialised and much-damaged town has a fascinating if very scattered range of monuments.

History of the Olomouc

A Slavic settlement on a spur above the Morava river dates back to the 7C AD, though there is no evidence that this place was one of the main centres of the Great Moravian Empire. On the contrary, the settlement seems to have increased in importance following the collapse of the Moravian Empire in the early 10C and the annexation of Moravia by the Přemyslid king Boleslav I in 955. In the early 10C it became a seat of the apanage Přemyslid princes following the construction of a fortress here by Břetislav I. Made a bishopric in 1063, Olomouc continued to prosper, and knew one of the greatest periods in its early history under its fifth bishop, Jindřich Zdík, who had been educated in the Prague court and was a loyal supporter of the Přemyslids; holding office between 1126 and 1150, Zdík was responsible for the consecration of the unfinished Basilica of St Wenceslas (sv. Václav), and for the building of a bishop's palace, which constitutes today, even in its fragmentary state, one of the most important Central European palaces from the Romanesque period.

The capital of Moravia from 1187 to 1641, Olomouc was made a royal town in 1248. The last of the Přemyslids, Wenceslas I, was murdered here in 1306, but the town was subsequently to receive the support of the Luxembourgs, Charles IV making frequent stays in its castle. It was at Olomouc in 1469 that King Matthias of Hungary proclaimed himself king of the Czechs.

In the 16C, despite tensions between the Lutherans and the Catholics (the town had a large and powerful German minority), the economic and cultural life of Olomouc experienced a period of remarkable vitality, leading in 1573 to its Jesuit college being raised to a university, which was to survive until the mid-19C. Only during the Thirty Years War, when Olomouc suffered severe damage, was the town's importance seriously diminished. Occupied by the Swedes between 1641 and 1650, Olomouc

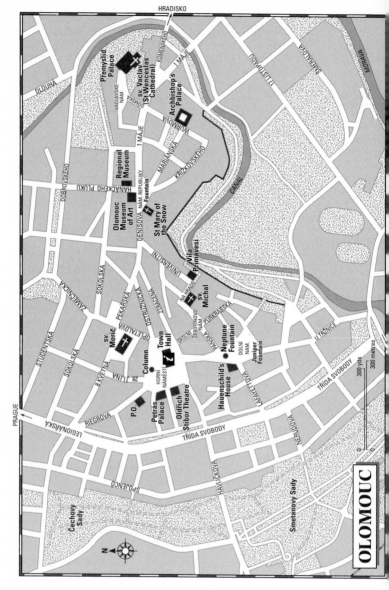

HRADISKO

Přemyslid Palace

sv. Václav (St Wenceslas Cathedral)

Archbishop's Palace

Regional Museum

Olomouc Museum of Art

St Mary of the Snow

Vila Primavesi

sv. Michal

sv. Mořic

Town Hall

Column

Neptune Fountain

Juniper Fountain

Hauenschild's House

P.O.

Petraš Palace

Oldřich Stibor Theatre

PRAGUE

DLOUHÁ

VÁCLAVSKÉ NÁM.

DOBROVSKÉHO

HANÁCKÉHO PLUKU

DENISOVA

UNIVERSITNÍ

ZÁMEČNICKÁ

SOKOLSKÁ

STUDENTSKÁ

SOKOLSKÁ

B. NĚMCOVÉ

PEKAŘSKÁ

OFIETALOVA

DSTRUŽNICKÁ

ZTRACENÁ

28. ŘÍJNA

HORNÍ NÁMĚSTÍ

RIEGROVA

LEGIONÁŘSKÁ

TŘÍDA SVOBODY

SPOJENCŮ

HÁLKOVA

ČEŠKOVA

KVĚTNA

1 MÁJE

1 MÁJE

DOMSKÁ

WURMOVA

MARIÁNSKÁ

KŘÍŽKOVSKÉHO

NÁM. REPUBLIKY

MAHLEROVA

PURKRABSKÁ

ŠKOLNÍ

ŽEROTÍNOVO NÁM.

PÁNSKÁ

DOLNÍ NÁM.

LAFAYETTOVA

NERUDOVA

U TRŽNICE

TŘÍDA SVOBODY

U TRŽNICE

KOMENSKÉHO

ŠAFAŘÍKOVA

TĚLISTOPADU

MORAVA

CANAL

Čechovy Sady

Smetanovy Sady

300 yds

300 metres

N

OLOMOUC

was replaced as the Moravian capital by Brno, and was never to regain its former supremacy.

An extensive rebuilding campaign was conducted after 1709, but the construction by Maria Theresa later that century of a large fortress not only put a halt to this, but also led to an order to pull down all buildings within a radius of 1.5km from the fortifications. The imperial court of Vienna, fleeing from the revolutions of 1848–49, took refuge at this fortress, and it was here that Emperor Ferdinand I handed over power to Franz Josef. But the fortress constituted a severe obstacle to the town's commercial development, which in consequence benefited little from the construction of a railway here in 1841. The fortress was finally abolished in 1888, and only then did industrialisation rapidly take hold, a process which has continued up to the present day. The university was revived after the Second World War and contributes to much of the liveliness of the town; it bears today the name of the great Czech historian Palacký. Despite the town's extensive industries (ironworks, a distillery, soap, chocolate, engineering factories, and so on), the place has a reputation for the fertility of the surrounding countryside, and every year since 1966 has held an important flower show.

The wedge-shaped historic centre of Olomouc is separated from the extensive surrounding development by a ring of parks, the southernmost of which, Smetana Gardens (Smetanovy sady) is the venue of the town's flower show. On the town's wide, western side the line of the old fortifications is marked by the spacious Třída Svobody, while on the other sides are to be found long stretches of the original fortifications; immediately below the fortifications, and running from the southwestern corner of the town to the northeastern spur of land where the original citadel was sited, is a canal of the Morava river.

The lively centre of Olomouc is the western side of town, where you will find the town's largest square, the vast **Horní náměstí**. This square typifies the character of the town, having numerous monuments of interest spread around an overall grey space with a predominance of tall, turn-of-the-century and modern buildings. The **Town Hall** (Radnice), a whitish free-standing structure in its centre, dates back to 1348, though it was remodelled in the late Gothic, Renaissance and Baroque periods, and was much restored after the Second World War. On its southern side there projects the apse of its late 15C chapel, while on its eastern side is a Renaissance loggia rising above a flight of steps of 1564. The building's most popular feature is the clock on its northern side, which was rebuilt by Karl Svolinský in 1945 and features a hideous mosaic of workers, peasants and intellectuals, and has figures that are supposed to move around in procession every hour. On the western side of the square are two other buildings of interest, the Baroque Petráš Palace (at No. 410) and the elegant **Oldřich Stibor Theatre**, built in 1830 by Josef Kornhäusel; Mahler was appointed Kappelmeister at this theatre in 1883, but a combination of local anti-Semitism and his own autocratic behaviour led to his dismissal three months later.

Olomouc is one of the Czech towns richest in public statuary, and it is above all the statuary on the square which holds the visitor's interest. The 35m-high **plague column**, executed by Václav Rokytský between 1716 and 1754, is the largest of its kind in the Czech and Slovak republics, and is bursting with Baroque statuary celebrating, according to a Latin inscription, 'the divine Trinity': eight rows of steps, containing eight rows each, lead up to eight doors that open into an eight-sided chapel surmounted by a mighty superstructure tapering to a column to which sculpted angels acrobatically cling; one 19C traveller wondered how such a monument could possibly have been thought suitable for 'the noble simplicity of Christianity'. Near the monument, and also to the north of the Town Hall, is a massive statue of Hercules (1688), executed by Michal Mandík to a design by V. Render; opposite the eastern steps of the Town Hall is an equestrian statue by Jiří Schaumberger of Gaius Julius Caesar (1725), who is considered by legend to have been the founder of Olomouc.

The thoroughfare called 28 října leads north of the square to another fine Baroque monument, a statue of Mercury (1727), executed by Filip Sattler, also to a design by V. Render. East of here, along the busy shopping street named 8 květná, is the Olomouc parish **Church of St Moritz** (sv. Mořic), the oldest part of which is the 13C south tower. The north tower was begun in 1412, and the whole church gradually rebuilt from west to east, the work still continuing in 1540; the furnishings inside the wide and graceful triple-naved hall are mainly of the Baroque period, including an organ of 1745, the largest in Moravia.

Returning to the Horní náměstí along Opletalova, make your way south to the adjoining **Dolní náměstí**, the second largest square in town. At its funnelling northern end is a Neptune Fountain by Michal Mandík (1683), while behind is the town's second plague column, this one executed by V. Render in 1716–23. Among the several fine houses surrounding the square are the late 16C Hauenschild's House (No. 25) and the Renaissance house at No. 22 known as Zlatý jelen (At the Golden Stag). On the southern side of the square is V. Render's Jupiter Fountain of 1707, which stands in front of the former Capuchin church of 1655–61.

Leave the square on Panská, which heads off in a northeasterly direction from the Neptune Fountain and will take you to the former Dominican **Church of St Michael** (sv. Michal), which was founded in 1230; the whole church was rebuilt by Giovanni Pietro Tencala, and all that remains of the original medieval building is the late 14C chapel of St Alexis, attached to the north aisle. Universitní heads north from here to Denisova, which forms part of the town's main axis. As you walk along Universitní, you will pass on your right the late Baroque buildings (1701–08) of the former Jesuit college, which enjoyed the status of a university from 1576 to the mid-19C. The former university **Church of St Mary of the Snow** (Panny Marie Sněžné), at the junction of Denisova and the náměstí Republiky, is the most important creation of the Czech Jesuits after the Church of St Nicholas in Prague; this heavy but dynamically planned structure was built by Josef Pirner in 1712–19, and is extensively covered inside with frescoes. On the other side of the náměstí Republiky to the church is a musical theatre incorporating on its upper floor the **Olomouc Museum of Art** (Olomoucký muzeum umění), which puts on changing exhibitions from its good permanent collection of 20C Czech art. **Open** Tues–Sun 09.00–17.00.

Next to this is a former Clarissine convent of 1773, which was converted by the Emperor Joseph in 1785 into the library and north wing of the university; the recently restored building houses today the dreary **Regional Museum** (Vlastivědné muzeum), containing archaeological, historical, applied arts and natural history collections, and a Baroque globe from the Jesuit university. **Open** Tues–Sun 09.00–17.00.

In the middle of the náměstí Republiky stands the Triton's Fountain, a work by V. Render of 1709. The continuation of Denisova north of this square is 1. Máje, another of the town's straight and very long streets, lined with shabby apartment blocks of the early years of the century. Walking to the northern end of 1. Máje will bring you almost to the Cathedral of St Wenceslas.

A longer and more interesting route to the cathedral is to turn right after the náměstí Republiky into Křížkovského, and then turn left at the end of this into Wurmova; the triangular-shaped part of the town which you are now in was laid out after the Thirty Years War, and contains Baroque buildings now appropriated by the Palacký University, as well as the vast but curiously unmonumental Archbishop's Palace designed by Filiberto Lucchese for Archbishop Liechtenstein in 1664. Wurmova will lead you back into 1. Máje, at a point directly in front of the short Domská, which ascends to the cathedral square.

The **Cathedral of St Wenceslas** (sv. Václav), standing in what was once the town's citadel, was originally a Romanesque structure consecrated during the rule of the fifth Bishop of Olomouc, Jindřich Zdík. Rebuilt after 1265, and then altered once more in 1616–19, the structure was turned by Gustav Merett into the present soaring but uninspired neo-Gothic structure in 1883–90; within the crypt is a collection of ecclesiastical bric-à-brac, including a painting of Christ by Ignáz Raab.

Of far greater interest than the cathedral is the adjoining building known as the **Přemyslid Palace**, which in fact was the bishop's palace built by Jindřich Zdík after 1141. The fragmentary but eloquent remains of the original Romanesque palace lay hidden for centuries under later medieval work, but a series of arches from this building were revealed in 1867, and more of the structure has been uncovered in the course of a recent archaeological and restoration campaign.

You enter the building through a 19C door, and will find near the entrance a model of the 12C palace. Before going upstairs and seeing the Romanesque fragments, you have to walk around a Gothic cloister of the late 14C, the north side of which has an interesting group of early 16C murals. Above the vaults of the built-in cloister runs a magnificent Romanesque arcade of paired and tripled columns belonging to the second and best-preserved floor of the former palace. The rich sculptural decoration of this arcade is unlike that of any other Romanesque building in the Czech Republic, though it can be paralleled with certain decorative details in the Holy Roman Emperor's Cathedral at Speyer in the Rhineland; it is possible that Bishop Zdík, in the course of one of his diplomatic missions to the Rhineland in the 1130s, contracted builders at Speyer to come and work with him in Olomouc. **Open** Tues–Sun 09.00–12.00 and 13.00–17.00.

The palace occupies the northeastern corner of town, and from its second-floor windows you look out over gardens and fields. Back on the 1. Máje continue walking east and you will come to Komenského, which crosses in turn first the canal of the Morava river, and then the river itself. From the wooded banks of the latter is an excellent view north towards the former Premonstratensian monastery of **Hradisko**, which was founded in 1078, and transformed after 1661 by Giovanni Pietro Tencalla, Domenico Martinelli, and others, into the largest Premonstratensian monastery in the world; since the late 19C it has served as a rather grim hospital. On this same, eastern side of the river, adjoining the bridge, is a sleek Russian Orthodox Church of the early 20C. From here you could make an excursion by car to the pilgrimage church of **Kopeček**, which can be reached by driving 3km northwest on the Šternberk road, and then turning off to the right on to the road marked Samotisky and Kopeček (a further 5km). The church, built in 1669–79, is another work by Tencalla, and dazzling above all in its scale and inflated architectural detail.

Continuing on your drive to Ostrava, head east of Olomouc on the E442. Two kilometres east of Lipník nad Bečvou (25km), you will see peering above a wooded hill on the right of the road the impressive ruins of **Helfštejn Castle**, dating back to the 13C and constituting the largest castle ruins in Moravia. You remain on the road for a further 15km, bypassing the small industrial town of Hranice, and turning off to the north on Road 47 at Bělotín. North and east of Hranice begins one the most industrialised parts of the Czech Republic, though Road 47 largely avoids the worst industries, and indeed skirts the southern edge of attractively rolling countryside.

The village of **Fulnek**, 20km north of Bělotín, is a pleasant surprise. Though damaged by bombing during the Second World War, it has been well restored, and has a charming main square surrounded on three sides by 17C and 18C buildings and backed on the fourth side by a wooded hill crowned by a Baroque castle. Steps lead from the square to an early 18C church half-way up the hill. Next to this is the rebuilt School of Lutheran Brethren, famous as the place where the great pedagogue and Czech nationalist Jan Comenius taught between 1618 and 1621 (a plaque commemorates this). From Fulnek, Road 47 heads northeast past Bílovec (11km), entering the polluted surroundings of Ostrava shortly after Klimkovice 10km further on. The centre of Ostrava (see Chapter 22) lies a further 17km northwest of here.

B. Via Kroměříž

Total distance 174km: Brno (leave by the E50) • 19km Slavkov • 52km Kroměříž • 53km Valašské Meziříčí • 17km Nový Jičín • 11km Příbor • 22km Ostrava.

The greatest attraction of the surroundings immediately to the east of Brno is the site of one of Napoleon's most famous battles, fought in 1805, and named after the nearby Baroque castle of **Austerlitz** (Slavkov in Czech). Slavkov lies 19km due east of Brno, but the battlefield itself lies 10km before this, and can be seen to your right as you drive on the dual carriageway of the E462. The battle was directed by Napoleon from the top of the hill of **Žuráň**, which you can reach by leaving the motorway just beyond the turning for Šlapanice, about 500m east of the motorway restaurant and snack-bar known unromantically as the *Non-Stop Motel*. Films re-enacting the battle have always featured a savage, densely pine-forested landscape, while in fact the eastern surroundings of Brno comprise flat countryside which has been extensively cultivated for centuries. A tiny road leads to the top of the gentle Žuráň Hill, which is distinguished by two solitary trees, next to which is a bronze plaque inscribed with a diagram indicating the respective positions of the troops that took part in the battle. From this commanding site you can see rising above fields to the north the hill which Napoleon's troops named Santon after a mountain in Egypt; to the south, meanwhile, are the distant **Pratzen Heights** (Pracký kopec), which were also to play a crucial role in Napoleon's victory.

Instead of rejoining the E462 immediately after descending from the Žuráň Hill, you should take the first turning to the right and follow for a few hundred metres the side road which runs parallel with the motorway; take the next turning to

The Battle of Austerlitz

The Battle of Austerlitz was fought between Napoleon and the combined armies of the Russians and Austrians. Whereas the French troops numbered only 35,000, the Alliance had 80,000; at the end of the battle French losses amounted to 7000 as opposed to 35,000 killed in the Alliance. The reasons for Napoleon's astonishing victory are given in Leo Tolstoy's famous description of the battle in *War and Peace*, one of the most vivid accounts of war in 19C fiction.

The battle began early on the morning of 1 December 1805. It was a foggy morning, and the confused Russian and Austrian troops made their way from the Pratzen Heights in the direction of the Santon Hill, where they imagined that the greater part of Napoleon's army was entrenched. Though unseen by them, Napoleon and his troops were able to watch their movements from the top of the Žuráň Hill, which by a great stroke of luck stood up above the fog. The scene from the hill was memorably evoked by Tolstoy: 'Napoleon, in the blue cloak he had worn throughout the Italian campaign, sat on his small grey Arab horse a little in front of his marshals. He gazed in silence at the hills which seemed to rise out of the sea of mist, and the Russian troops moving across them in the distance, and he listened to the sounds of firing in the valley. Not a muscle of his face—still thin in those days—moved; his glittering eyes were fixed intently on one spot. His forecasts were proving correct. Part of the Russian force had already descended into the valley towards the ponds and lakes, part were abandoning the Pratzen heights which he had intended to attack and which he regarded as the key to the position. He saw through the fog, in a hollow between two hills near the village of Pratzen, Russian columns, their bayonets gleaming, moving continuously in one direction, towards the valleys, and disappearing one after another into the mist.'

Napoleon was in a confident mood, not only because the weather was on his side, but also because the day of the battle happened to be the anniversary of his coronation as emperor. He bided his time, waiting for the perfect moment to attack the now dangerously extenuated Russian forces. Finally, in the words of Tolstoy, 'when the sun had completely emerged from the fog, and fields and mist were a dazzling brilliance—as though he had only been waiting for this to begin the action—he drew the glove from his shapely white hand, made a sign with it to the marshals and gave the order for battle.' After capturing the Pratzen heights, Napoleon was able to attack the remaining Alliance forces from the rear, thus achieving a swift victory. His vantage-point on the Žuráň Hill was to be used with equal success in the Second World War by the Russian Marshal Marikovsky, who directed from here a battle with the Germans.

the right marked Pracký and drive to the top of the Pratzen Heights, where there is an outstanding Art Nouveau memorial by J. Fanta (1911), which, instead of celebrating Napoleon's victory, represents a plea for peace. It is a monumental tapering structure in stone and bronze, surrounded by statues symbolising the four continents, crowned by the Crucifixion, and with a chapel at its base dedicated to peace; the idea for this '**Peace Memorial**' (Mohyla Míru), the first of its kind in the world, was that of the historian Alois Slovák (1859–1930). In the small museum adjoining the memorial is a bust of Slovák, together with mementoes of the battle and several of the numerous finds that continue to this day to be dug up in the surrounding fields; the most interesting item is the table on which Napoleon played chess with his officers shortly before the battle. **Open** Apr–Sept daily 08.00–12.00 and 13.00–17.00, Apr closed Mon; Oct–Mar Tues–Sun 08.30–15.30.

Return to the E462, which you follow for a further 3km before heading south-east on to the E50. The village of **Slavkov**, 6km east of the turning, is dominated by its imposing Baroque château, built c 1700 for the Kaunitz family. It was designed by the Italian architect Domenico Martinelli, who seems to have derived inspiration for the main façade, with its massive convex centrepiece, from Bernini's unexecuted design for the Louvre. The interior of the building has retained much of its original Baroque decoration, if in a rather shabby state, but is visited usually on account of the worthy Napoleonic Museum which is installed here; the beautiful, but rather unkempt gardens have much Baroque statuary. **Open** June–Aug Tues–Sun 08.00–17.00; Apr, May, Sept, Oct 09.00–12.00 and 13.00–16.00.

Ten kilometres further east along the E50 is the moated castle of **Bučovice**, which, despite numerous insensitive alterations, remains one of the finest of Moravia's Renaissance châteaux. Built between 1566 and 1587 for Jan Šembera Černohorský, it was executed by Pietro Gabri of Brno to designs supplied by Pietro Ferrabosco di Lagno (1512–96), a Como-born architect who worked for the Habsburgs. The outstanding feature of its exterior (which originally had battlements rather than the present high-pitched roof) is its central three-storeyed courtyard, of an elegance and lightness quite unusual for the Czech Republic, and wholly Italian in character; in the middle stands a Baroque fountain showing a man embracing the Golden Fleece, a work apparently commissioned from Paolo Materna by one of the Liechtensteins c 1635.

Of the Renaissance rooms inside special mention must be made of the extraordinary Hare Room, which features a painted world in which hares wreak their vengeance on humans and dogs (man's closest ally) and go on to re-enact the courtly, martial life of the 16C aristocracy: anthropomorphism of this kind (the attribution of human personality to animals) was an exceedingly rare subject for painters before the 19C. A more typical Renaissance decoration, albeit similarly lively and colourful, can be seen in the Imperial Room, which has a richly painted and stuccoed ceiling (dating from after 1583), comprising lunettes with gilded and richly worked statues of Mars, Diana, Europa and Charles V. **Open** May–Aug Tues–Sun 08.00–12.00 and 13.00–17.00; Sept closes 16.00; Apr, Oct Sat, Sun 09.00–12.00 and 13.00–16.00.

Kroměříž

Continue for a further 7km along the E50, and then take the side-road to the north marked Zdounky and Kroměříž. The latter, 25km from the E50 and in the middle of a very fertile district known as the Haná, is sometimes referred to as the 'Hanák Athens', a rather absurd comparison given that all that the two places have in common are their pollution. None the less this small town, the closest Czech equivalent to the former principalities of Germany, has played a vital role in the history of the arts in Central Europe.

History of Kroměříž

The origins of Kroměříž are in a fortified Slavic settlement of the 9C. The place was acquired by the Bishopric of Olomouc c 1107 and rapidly grew in importance. A key period in its early history was the mid-13C, when Bishop Bruno of Schauenburg endowed it with municipal privileges, built a large market square (on the site of the present main square), and encouraged so many settlers to move here that he is sometimes identified with the Pied Piper of Hamelin. Little survives of the medieval or indeed Renaissance town of Kroměříž, the place having been devastated by the Swedes under General Tortenson in July 1643. The bishops lavishly rebuilt the town, turning it into one of the great Baroque ensembles of Czechoslovakia. A particularly important role was played by Prince-Bishop Karl von Liechten-stein-Castelcorno, who in 1690 commissioned from Giovanni Pietro Tencala the present Bishop's Palace, and was also responsible for the Ital-ianate Flower Garden (Květná), with its breathtakingly grand colonnade by Tencalla. But the Prince-Bishop's involvement with the arts was not limited simply to patronage: he dabbled in architecture himself (one of the early plans for his palace was drawn up by him) and, more importantly, assem-bled an extraordinary collection of Old Master paintings. His 18C succes-sors maintained his enlightened interest in the arts, and when the palace was badly damaged by fire in 1752, one of the leading Rococo artists of the day, F.A. Maulbertsch, was called in to redecorate two of the rooms.

The Empress Maria Theresa and the Russian Tsar Alexander III were among the many distinguished visitors to the Bishop's Palace; more signifi-cantly, between November 1848 and March 1849, when the Austrian Imperial family were in exile in Olomouc, the Austrian Imperial Parliament held their meetings here, and drafted a famous constitution which included the statement that 'all power comes from the people'.

Kroměříž today is a sleepy small market and industrial town, with a grimy and slightly run-down look but with an undeniable charm. Its excellently preserved old centre is still encircled by extensive stretches of the original fortifications. At the northern entrance to the old town is the Masarykovo náměstí, dominated on its northern side by the twin-towered and oval-domed Piarist **Church of St John the Baptist** (sv. Jan Křtitel), a grand and harmonious Baroque structure begun in 1737 by the obscure Italian architect Cirani.

From the back of the church Pilařova leads in a northeasterly direction towards the Bishop's Palace. The first important building which you come to is the former collegiate **Church of St Maurice** (sv. Mořic), which was built by Bishop Bruno of Schauenberg after 1260; the simple, light and much-restored interior constitutes the main survival of medieval Kroměříž, and features the tombs of a number of the bishops. Running along the western side of the building is the tiny Proboštství, which is lined with elegant Baroque houses, one of which (No. 5/7) has a garden with an excellent view towards the apse of the Piarist church.

On the other side of the church is the massive 18C bulk of the former college and archbishop's seminary, which is linked by the Mill Gate of 1585 to the **Bishop's Palace**. Only part of Tencalla's monumentally proportioned palace, built over medieval and Renaissance structures, can be visited, and many of the numerous rooms centred around its grey and rather forbidding courtyard seem to have been abandoned. The surviving rooms with the finest decorations can only be seen in the course of an obligatory guided tour, and include a richly stuccoed ground-floor room of c 1700, and the first-floor Assembly Hall (Sněmovní sál), a vast Rococo hall now used for concerts and adorned with chandeliers and with gilded plasterwork set against a glisteningly white background. On the second floor is the unappealingly named Fief or Vassalage Hall (Manský sál), where the enthroned Prince-Bishops would hold meetings. The interest of this room is its spectacular and vividly painted ceiling painting by F.A. Maulbertsch representing the *Apotheosis of the Bishops of Kroměříž*; this work, which owes a clear debt to the dazzling propaganda scenes of the Venetian artist G.B. Tiepolo, features a portrait of Maulbertsch himself, standing under an umbrella. A pupil of Maulbertsch was responsible for the rather clumsier and less brightly coloured *Triumph of Bishop Egkla* adorning the ceiling of the neighbouring and beautifully panelled Library; the library has an outstanding collection of coins, as well as a musical archive containing autograph scores by Haydn and Mozart.

The famous **Picture Collection** of the Prince-Bishops is also to be found on the second floor, and can fortunately be visited without the distracting presence of a guide. Though badly displayed in large, poorly lit and depressingly decorated rooms, the collection is unquestionably the finest in the Czech Republic outside Prague, and alone justifies a visit to Kroměříž.

History of the collection

The bulk of the collection was brought together by Prince-Bishop Karl von Liechtenstein-Castelcorno, and was largely made up of works from private collections that he had acquired, including those of Provost Josef Seragli de Contis, an unknown nobleman from Prague, and the Imstenraed brothers from Cologne. The most important of the Prince-Bishop's paintings, most notably the 16C Italian works, had once formed part of the fabled collections amassed by Charles I of England, Count Arundel and the latter's brother-in-law, the Duke of Pembroke; 238 works from these collections were put on the market by Banker Jabach in 1673, and ended up not only in Kroměříž, but also in Prague Castle, the Imperial collections in Vienna and the Louvre in Paris. The collection of the Prince-Bishop was supplemented in the mid-18C by paintings amassed by Bishop Egkla.

Among the earliest paintings in the collection are a *Martyrdom of St Catherine*, a *Diptych of St Catherine*, and a superlative *Martyrdom of St John the Baptist*, all by the German artist Lucas Cranach, and commissioned in the early 16C by one of the bishops of Kroměříž; the latter painting, a richly detailed work mingling fantasy with intensely realistic observation, features the coat of arms of the Kroměříž bishops, and is signed and dated 1515. Other early Northern School works include *The Virgin and St Anne* by an anonymous Nuremberg master of 1487, a Dürer-like *Portrait of a Young Man* (1505) by Hans Kulmbach, a portrait by Quentin Matsys of King Christian II of Denmark, and a *Portrait of a Man* (1558) by Bartholomaus Brujn. The oldest of the Italian School paintings is an *Adoration* by Neri di Bicci. Among the 16C Italian paintings are a series of works by Jacopo Bassano, a *Samson and Delilah* by G.A. da Pordenone, and a work by Veronese featuring the Apostles, a fragment of a much larger painting cut down in size to make it more saleable.

The most famous of the 16C paintings, indeed the great glory of the collection, is **Titian**'s *Flaying of Marsyas*, a signed work of 1570–71, which was cleaned in 1986 prior to being shown at London's Royal Academy: dating from the artist's late period, and possibly unfinished, it is one of the artist's most personal and mysterious works, sombre in tonality, the paint boldly applied in places by the artist's fingers, and with a touch of the most grotesque black humour in the detail of the foreground dog happily lapping up the blood of the unfortunate protagonist.

Of the 17C Italian paintings, mention should be made of a dark and dramatic Annibale Carracci of *Latona and the Farmers*, and an excellent Domenico Fetti of *Christ in the Garden of Gethsemane*. The highpoint of the Northern School paintings of this period are Van Dyck's *Portrait of a Man with a Glove* and his double portrait of *King Charles I and Henrietta Maria*. Also of interest are a vivid *Vision of St Jerome* by Jan Liss, an *Alchemist at Work* by David Ruckaert III, a *trompe-l'oeil* still-life by Samuel von Hoogstraten, and a gruesome work by Johann Heinrich Schönfield showing Cato committing suicide by tearing out his entrails. **Open** May–Sept Tues–Sun 09.00–17.00; Apr, Oct Sat, Sun 09.00–17.00.

Once you have left the palace, you should visit its **gardens** (Podzámecká zahrada), which now form a public park, and can be reached by heading east of the building down Ztracená, turning left into Vodní, and then left again. Within the gardens is a Baroque colonnade adorned with mosaic lunettes (1945–51) by the locally-born artist Max Švabinský; the greater part of the gardens was relaid in the early 19C in a Romantic English style, and features among its woods a lakeside Chinese pavilion, and a Pompeian colonnade.

Returning towards the centre of the town but crossing Vodní and following the parallel street to the east, Moravcova, you will pass half-way down the street a poignant survival of the town's Jewish quarter: this, an early 17C **Jewish Town Hall** (Židovská radnice), now a cultural centre, is the only such structure outside Prague, and was left standing by the Prince-Bishop as a gesture of thanks to the Jewish community for services rendered in the Thirty Years War.

At the end of Moravcova head northwest down Farní towards the old town's main square, the **Velké náměstí**. This large and slightly decayed square, with a Marian plague column of the early 18C, retains its medieval shape, but is lined with buildings mainly of the Baroque period; the main survival from the Thirty Years War is the Town Hall of 1611, in the square's northwestern corner.

On the square's northeastern corner is the **Kroměříž Museum** (Kroměřížské muzeum), which has a large, well-arranged collection of works by one of the most celebrated Czech artists of recent times, Max Švabinský. Born in Kroměříž in 1873, Švabinský died in Prague in 1962, at the age of 89. Though in later life he received such prestigious commissions as the design of the stained-glass windows in St Vitus's Cathedral in Prague, his most striking works are nearly all from the first decade of the 20C, and are characterised by their brilliant colouring and heavy symbolism. One of the largest and most vivid works in this museum is *The Yellow Umbrella* (1909), which features two female nudes in a sensual outdoor setting painted with broad areas of pure pigment. The large *Studio* of 1914 illustrates the more conventional development of his later work, but is of interest as a psychological study of the artist. It shows him absorbed in his work, surrounded by members of his family, including his first wife Ela—who looks away from him—his brother, and his sister-in-law; the latter, whom he was shortly to marry, features also as the muse whom he is painting. **Open** Tues–Sun 09.00–12.00 and 13.00–17.00.

You can return to the Masarykovo náměstí by walking south from the square along Jánská, which is lined with elegant 18C buildings; near the end of the street, opposite the Piarist church, Švabinský's birthplace at No. 15/16 is marked by a plaque.

Leaving the old city centre and walking southwest from the Masarykovo náměstí, you will come to the broad boulevard Kojetínská; turn right along this, and then left into Gen. Svobody, passing on your right the gabled Bishop's Granary of 1711. At the end of this street is the **Flower Garden** (Květinová zahrada), a rectangular Italian garden commissioned by Karl von Liechtenstein-Castelcorno in 1665 over what had previously been the episcopal vegetable garden. Long narrow vistas converge on an oval pavilion designed by F. Lucchese in 1668; the northern end of the garden is bordered by an exciting 200m-long colonnade (1675), one of G.P. Tencalla's most successful works, and adorned with Classical busts and statues.

After seeing Kroměříž head east of the town for 6km to Hulín and from there follow the road to **Holešov** (where there is a Jewish cemetery and a 16C synagogue with 18C decorations and a small museum on the town's Jewish history), Bystřice pod Hostýnem and Valašské Meziříčí. The towns that you pass though on your way to Ostrava become increasingly industrialised, but from Holešov onwards you skirt to your right the attractive wooded hills that belong to one of the Moravian districts most famed for its folklore, **Wallachia**.

The Wallachians were shepherds who came to this part of Moravia in the 16C; their origins are disputed, and have been sought for in places as far apart as Poland, Slovakia, the Ukraine and Romania. **Valašské Meziříčí** was one of the main cultural centres of Wallachia, and it was here, in 1871, that the first grammar school in the district was founded. A centre of the cloth industry from the 16C onwards, and now with extensive chemical, electrical engineering and glass industries, it is a largely ugly town, but with a pleasant main square featuring a number of 16C–18C buildings, including an early 17C Town Hall, and, at No. 10, a former pharmacy known as At the Red Eagle; elsewhere in the town is a partially wooden church of the 16C.

Head north of the town on Road 57, after 9km passing through the village of **Hodslavice**, where there is a tiny wooden church of 1551 and the house where the historian and politician František Palacký (1798–1876) was born. The sprawling industrial town and district capital of **Nový Jičín**, 8km further north, is the main town of the Kravarsko region, which was German-speaking from the 11C until 1945, and has a name in German (Das Kuhlandchen) that recalls the cattle-farming that once flourished here. Today a well-known centre of hat production, Nový Jičín has a particularly fine main square, lined on all sides with colourful arcaded houses from the 16C to 18C; one of these is the former Post House of 1563, famous as the place where General Suvorov and Tsar Alexander I were put up in 1805. An interesting Hat Museum (Kloboučnické muzeum), said to be the only one of its kind in the world, has been installed in the town's château, and includes hats worn by such famous personages as Masaryk.

From here take the E462 dual carriageway to **Příbor**, a small town with another pleasant square, but of interest largely on account of its associations with the founder of psychoanalysis, Sigmund Freud (1857–1939).

Sigmund Freud

Sigmund Freud was born at Příbor (known in German as Freiberg) on 6 May 1856, and spent his early childhood here; he was the first son of Amalie Freud née Nathanson, the second wife of Jakob Freud, a Jewish textile manufacturer. Even during his lifetime the house of his birth was commemorated by a plaque, and in a letter of 25 October 1931 to the mayor of the town, Freud expressed his certainty that 'deep within me, although overlaid, there continues to live the happy child from Freiberg, the first-born son of a youthful mother, the boy who received from this air, from this soil, the first indelible impressions.' On another occasion he wrote: 'When I was seventeen and at my secondary school, I returned for the first time to my birthplace for the holidays ... I know quite well what a wealth of impressions overwhelmed me at that time ... I believe now that I was never free from a longing for the beautiful woods near our home, in which ... I used to run off from my father, almost before I had learnt to walk.' What Freud omitted to mention was that on this return visit as a teenager he fell in love not only with the girl whose cot he had once shared but with her mother.

The modest house of Freud's birth is at No. 117 Freudova, and though currently and appropriately a massage parlour might one day be turned into what would be the third Freud Museum in the world (the other two are in Vienna and London); for the moment visitors to the town with an interest in Freud mementoes will have to content themselves with an uninteresting small display of photographs in the town museum, which is situated in the former Piarist college on Lidická. There is also a bust of Freud that has been moved from its previous position outside a supermarket to the main square, which, like the street of his birth, has recently been renamed after him.

Another famous personality of the area, and a contemporary of Freud, is the composer Leoš Janáček (1853–1928), who was born at **Hukvaldy**, 8km to the east of Příbor (take the main road to Frýdek-Místek for 6km, and then turn right). The composer was born in what is still the village school, now marked by a plaque; in later life he often came to stay in a nearby house called Podobora, where there is a small museum to him. The latter is situated at the foot of Hukvaldy's large and impressive medieval castle, which was founded by Arnold von Hückeswagen in 1240.

Six kilometres to the south of Příbor is **Kopřivnice**, an industrial town of unmitigated ugliness, but of interest to those excited by old cars.

History of Kopřivnice

The industrial development of Kopřivnice dates back to 1812, with the foundation by Ignác Raška of a pottery works which soon began exporting earthenware to Vienna, Germany, France, and England. Of greater importance was the founding by Ignác Šustala in the summer of 1850 of what was to become the Tatra Engineering Works. In 1882, a year after the railway had come to the town, the Tatra Engineering Works began producing freight wagons, and later became one of the main world suppliers of luxury saloon cars intended for heads of state in Europe and Asia. But the real breakthrough came in 1897 with the creation of the so-called President, the first automobile of the Austro-Hungarian Empire; on 21 May of the following year this car set off on a trial journey from Kopřivnice to Vienna, a journey of 328km which it accomplished in 14hr 30min of driving time. From that time onwards car production developed as the main speciality of Tatra, though today the firm produces only lorries and the heavily built black limousines once used to transport important dignitaries of the Communist party. The research for the original edition of this guide was largely undertaken in a Tatra, kindly put at the author's disposal by the Czech government.

In a small garden adjoining the Tatra Works is a large glass-and-steel hangar housing the **Tatra Technical Museum** (Technické muzeum Tatra Kopřivnice), which is packed to capacity with old cars, including the famous President of 1897. **Open** May–Sept daily 08.00–17.00; Apr, Oct, Nov closes 16.00; Dec–Mar closes 15.00.

Incongruously tucked away on a wooded slope just to the south of Kopřivnice is the delightful village of **Štramberk**. At the top of this village, rising above trees, is the solitary round tower of its medieval castle, while the village centre below comprises a remarkable group of 18C–19C traditional Wallachian folk houses, mostly semi-timbered and featuring beautiful carving, low wooden gables and balconied fronts. Return to Příbor, and head due north to Ostrava, another 22km, passing Ostrava's airport.

C. Via Uherské Hradiště and Zlín

Total distance 252km: Brno • 71km Uherské Hradiště • 26km Luhačovice • 55km Zlín • 33km Vsetín • 17km Rožnov pod Radhoštěm • 45km Frýdlant nad Ostravicí • 31km Ostrava.

This, the longest and most complex route from Brno to Ostrava, is also scenically the most attractive, taking you to the forested heart of Wallachia; none of the towns that you will pass has the wealth of old monuments which you will find, say, in Olomouc or Kroměříž, but for enthusiasts of modern architecture there is the compensation of Zlín, the most interesting modern town in the Czech Republic.

Head due east of Brno on the E462 and continue as for Chapter 21B up to the turning for Kroměříž. East of the turning you remain on Road 50 as far as Uherské Hradiště (a further 41km), passing after 14km the early 18C château of **Buchlovice**, which is distinguished by a most lively main façade featuring a concave and balustraded central block; built for the Berchtold family, the château's architect is unknown, though there is an implausible family tradition that he was none other than the great Roman architect Carlo Fontana. **Open** July, Aug daily 09.00–18.00; May, June, Sept Tues–Sun 09.00–17.00; Apr, Oct closes 16.00.

A 3.5km uphill walk from here will take you to the top of the forested **Chřiby Hills**, where you will see an earlier Berchtold property—the austere Gothic castle of **Buchlov**. Founded as a royal seat by the Přemyslids in the 13C, this was opened to the public by the Berchtolds as early as the late 19C: its plain, sparsely furnished rooms provide a strong contrast with the family's pleasure-house at Buchlovice. **Open** May–Aug Tues–Sun 08.00–17.00; Sept closes 16.00; Apr, Oct Sat, Sun 09.00–16.00.

From Buchlovice you could also make a detour 6km northeast to the important former Cistercian abbey of **Velehrad**, which was founded in 1201 over a Slavonic site, and is dedicated to the Apostles of the Slavs, SS Cyril and Methodius (the place is sometimes identified as the site of the latter's bishopric). Romanesque crypts have been found below the church and there are remains of late Romanesque architecture in the cloister. However, the original medieval building was largely destroyed by fire in the 17C and replaced in 1684–89 with the present grandiose and exuberantly decorated building. Every year on 5 July (now a national holiday), the church is the scene of one of the most colourful and important pilgrimages in the Czech Republic. The place has gained additional popularity following the visit here—on 22 April 1990—of Pope John Paul II, who earlier had declared Cyril and Methodius as the 'Patron Saints of Europe'. **Open** daily 09.00–17.00.

Numerous finds from the period of the Great Moravia Empire have been dug up in and around the small industrial town of **Uherské hradiště**, which was founded in 1257 by Přemysl Otakar II, and retains fragments of its medieval fortifications and a number of burghers' houses of the 17C and 18C. In the Old Town district (Staré Město), on the eastern banks of the Morava, is a grim concrete building known as the **Monument of Great Moravia** (Památník Velké Moravy) sheltering the scant ruins of what is sometimes thought to have been the capital of the Great Moravian Empire, Veligrad (it is in any case the oldest Slavic settlement as yet found in the Czech and Slovak Republics). On the other side of the river, in the Smetana Gardens, is the rather more appealing **Moravian-Slovak Museum** (Moravsko-slovácké muzeum), which contains archaeological finds from the area, including Romanesque stones from the nearby monastery at Velehrad; of special interest is the folklore collection, which reflects the rich folklore traditions of the eastern borders of Moravia. **Open** Mon–Sat 09.00–12.00 and 12.30–17.00.

Next to the museum is an art gallery, largely devoted to 19C local masters. Sixteen kilometres further east on Road 50 is the smaller town of **Uherský Brod**, also with remains of its medieval walls; in the late 17C stables of the town's castle, a Renaissance structure remodelled in the 17C, is a small museum to the scholar and teacher Jan Comenius (1592–1670), who is thought by some to have been born in the vicinity. The town stands at the edge of the South Moravian Lowlands, and by the foothills of the **White Carpathians** (Biele Karpaty), which mark the border with Slovakia. The highest peak of these mountains, Velká Javorina (970m), lies only 18km to the south of the town; however, the most direct crossing into Slovakia is to continue along Road 50, which will take you after an attractive 37km drive to the outskirts of the Slovakian town of Trenčín (see Chapter 27).

From Uherské Brod turn north and drive 11km to **Luhačovice**, where you will find a charming small spa town leisurely arranged in parkland along the lush banks of a tributary of the Olšava. Though the mineral waters were known as far back as the 12C, an actual spa was not founded here until 1902. Unless you are suffering from diabetes, or respiratory and digestive disorders, the main reason for coming here is to see the remarkable buildings by the Slovakian architect Dušan Jurkovič (1868–1947), who, in combining Art Nouveau with folkloric influences from his native region, became the principal architect of what could be called the Slovakian Revival. Entering the spa's gardens and following the main path that meanders through them (named after one Dr Blaha) you will soon come to the most important of Jurkovič's buildings, the so-called Jurkovičuv dům. This large, gabled structure resembling a cross between a Tudor mansion and a deranged Swiss chalet as envisaged by a Japanese architect, has all the hallmarks of the Jurkovič style: decorative half-timbering, enormously wide eaves, and fanciful swirling motifs that culminate in a pagoda-inspired roofline.

Zlín

Thirteen kilometres north of Luhačovice you will reach Road 49, where you should turn left. Zlín (a further 10km) lies in the southwestern corner of Wallachia, an area of wooded hills and low mountains, which you will be travelling through for most of the remaining journey to Ostrava. 'Here bread ends and stone begins' was how this traditionally poor area was once characterised. Industrial and agricultural growth since the last century have radically changed this image, and the green, spacious and pleasantly situated town of Zlín was seen at one time as a projection of the ideal city of the future.

History of Zlín

The town of Zlín, which was known as Gottwaldov from 1949 to 1990, was first mentioned in the early 14C, but its importance dates from after 1894, when Tomáš Bát'a founded a footwear factory here which was to prosper during the First World War through the supplying of boots to the army; soon Bát'a footwear was to develop an international reputation, with a chain of retail outlets throughout Europe. Tomáš Bát'a was a man of vision and enlightened tastes, and his shops and factories became a hallmark for the latest in modern design, architecture and technology. During the optimistic years following the establishment in 1918 of the Czechoslovak Republic, Bát'a envisaged a model city for the workers employed at his Zlín factory. The French architect Le Corbusier was called over to draw up a plan for this city, but in the end most of the work was entrusted to the locally born architect František Gahura (1891–1958), who had gone to Prague initially to study sculpture and had subsequently become an architectural student under the celebrated 'Cubist' architect Kotěra.

The new town which Gahura built with the assistance of his two pupils Lorenz and Karfík was damaged during the Second World War. Renamed in 1949 after the Socialist president Klement Gottwald, the model town which Bát'a had seen was transformed by later architects into an example of Socialist architecture at its most drab. The town continues to develop industrially but its remaining vitality as a cultural centre is maintained largely by its well-known film studios, which specialise in animated films, and were formed by one of Czechoslovakia's most adventurous animators, Karel Zeman (1910–). The British dramatist Tom Stoppard (1937–) was born in Zlín, but his father left shortly afterwards for Singapore, and Tom and his mother ended up in England. Another native of the town is the blonde New York socialite Ivana Trump, who, as Ivana Zelníčková, was an Olymic skier in Czechoslovakia before becoming a model in Canada and later the wife (and now ex-wife) of the notorious tycoon Donald Trump.

Coming to Zlín from Luhačovice you will come first of all to the much-restored remains of the old town, notably a Renaissance château (remodelled in the Baroque period) standing in parkland and now containing natural history and orienteering museums and, on the top floor, an excellent small **art gallery** preceded by an unloved corridor with exhibits and models relating to the modern architectural history of Zlín. The gallery has a very representative selection of modern Czech art, including works by Bohumil Kubišta, Emil Filla, Václav Špála, Jaroslav Král, Jan Štursa, Otto Gutfreund and Karel Lidický. **Open** Tues–Sun 09.00–12.00 and 13.00–17.00.

Heading west from the château along a boulevard now named after Tomáš Bát˘a, you will reach the modern centre of Zlín, which, curiously, has today a rather more neglected character than the old town (this is reflected in the forlorn railway station next to the Dřevnice river). The greying remains of the visionary town dreamt up by Gahura are spaciously disposed around the Work Square (náměstí Práce) on the southern side of the Třída Tomáše Bati and the adjacent long, wide and verdant square that runs south up a forested hill (Masarykovo náměstí). On the northern side of the Work Square is the former **Bát˘a Factory** (now the Svít Corporation), which is dominated by the multi-storeyed structure in which Tomáš Bát˘a had installed for himself a moveable glass office on an elevator, so that he could inspect what was happening on every floor, and also be accountable for his own activities. Within the factory grounds is a fascinating small footwear museum that is currently closed for restoration.

Statue of Tomás Bát˘a

On the opposite side of the square are a cinema holding 2000 people, a department store and a hotel (the appropriately named *Interhotel Moskva*), all dating from 1931 and the work of Karfík; facing the store, across the lower end of the long Masaryckovo náměstí, is a school building designed by Gahura in 1926 and used by Bát˘a for the propagation of his revolutionary teaching methods. The latter square, a sloping lawn bordered by trees and four- and five-storey blocks of flats, leads up to Gahura's **House of Culture** (Dům umění) of 1932, which served once as a memorial to Tomáš Bát˘a and featured the private aeroplane in which he died in 1938 on a fog-bound trip to Dresden; today the building is both a concert hall and a place that puts on changing exhibitions of 20C art, often relating to Zlín's avant-garde traditions.

Leaving Zlín by the road on which you entered the town, continue heading east beyond the Luhačovice turning, and follow the built-up banks of the Dřevnice river for 14km all the way to **Vizovice**, which is widely known in the Czech Republic for its distillery, where one of the best plum brandies (*Jelínek slivovice)* in the country is produced. For the cultural tourist there is a Baroque château built in 1750–66 for the Brno nobleman F.A. Grimm; inside is a frescoed hall, a fine collection of china and Louis XVI furniture, and a picture gallery featuring paintings questionably attributed to masters such as Magnasco, Jan Breughel the Younger, D. Teniers and V. Liberi.

At Vizovice you should leave Road 49 and head northeast on Road 488 through forest to the small industrial town of **Vsetín**. This town, first mentioned in 1309, became in the 17C a major centre of the Wallachian resistance to the Habsburg programme of Catholicisation; today the place is sometimes referred to as Partisan Town owing to the activities in the surrounding forest of the Jan Žižka brigade during the Second World War. The history of the town and the rich folklore of the area are commemorated in the museum installed in the castle on the main square (a Renaissance building remodelled in the 18C and 19C); also on the square is the former Town Hall of 1721. Vsetín and its surroundings are popular with holiday-makers, and there are a number of attractive villages with Wallachian timber-framed houses to be seen along the narrow valley of the Vsetínská Bečva, which runs to the east of here.

Continuing your journey to Ostrava, the shortest if not the quickest route from Vsetín to Rožnov pod Radhoštěm is the side road which heads northeast of the town, climbing the western slopes of the wooded **Cáb Mountain** (842m). There are several fine walks to the summit of the mountain, where there is a tourist chalet. After 10km you descend to a small lake, and then turn right, passing after 3km the village of Valašská Bystřice. **Rožnov pod Radhoštěm**, a further 4km, is a popular holiday resort, with one of the best and most extensive of the Czech and Slovak *skansens* (open-air museums of folk architecture) in its lushly wooded outskirts. This particular *skansen* displays in its spacious forested setting a wide range of reconstructed Wallachian timber-framed buildings, including the delightful former Town Hall of Rožnov (1770), shepherds' huts, a small wooden church, a belfry, taverns, farmsteads, a forge, and so on; you can go inside most of the buildings, where appropriate furniture, utensils and garments are arranged. Open daily, times vary according to season; partially closed Oct–Apr.

Rising to the north and east of Rožnov are the **Beskyd Mountains** (Beskydy hory), which form the northwestern part of the Carpathian Massif. Sadly, pollution from the industrial developments around nearby Ostrava has taken away much of the charm of this area which once inspired the music of Janáček; the sky is often hazy, and acid rain has destroyed large parts of the forest. None the less there are pleasant walks to be had in the area, for instance from Rožnov to the summit of **Radhošt** (1129m). For those wishing to stay a while in the mountains, there is a group of fantastically shaped timber-framed tourist chalets on the ridge at Pustevny (head east out of Rožnov on Road 18, and then turn left after 7km, climbing the mountain for a further 5km); 2km further on in the direction of the ugly Frenštát pod Radhoštěm is the timber-framed *Hotel Vlčina*, a picturesque old building depressingly revamped in recent times.

The most direct route from Rožnov to Ostrava is to drive north along Road 58 past Frenštát pod Radhoštěm and Příbor (see Chapter 21B). A longer but more attractive route, taking you through the finest parts of the Beskyds, is to follow Road 18 east of the town for 19km, then turn left to Bílá. Just beyond Bílá turn left again and you will find yourself driving alongside a large reservoir and in between two of the highest of the Beskyd peaks—**Smrk** (1276m) and **Lysá hora** (1323m).

After Ostravice (13km north of Bílá), you emerge into the vast industrial area which stretches towards Ostrava. **Frýdek-Místek**, 16km further north, mainly along dual carriageway, appears from the road to be merely a featureless industrial sprawl, yet it has a pleasant old centre almost resembling that of a village. At its heart is a 17C castle with an excellently displayed museum relating to the history and folklore of Wallachia, and containing souvenirs of Janáček and the Silesian poet Petr Bezruč (1867–1958), who spent many years here. Back on the dual carriageway you are faced with a depressing 22km drive from here to the centre of Ostrava.

22 · Hradec Králové to Ostrava

Total distance 253km: Hradec Králové (leave by Road 11) • 121km Šumperk • 61km Bruntál • 38km Opava • 33km Ostrava.

Driving east from Hradec Králové along Road 11, you will approach the chain of the **Eagle Mountains** (Orlické hory), which mark the border with Poland. Châteaux and other monuments follow on from each other in rapid succession, beginning with the extraordinary museum at **Třebechovice pod Orebem** (13km), which was built to house a carved nativity scene intended as the largest in the world: begun in 1871 by a local carpenter and a woodcarving friend of his, the project was only called off after the latter's death 40 years later, by which time 400 figures had been created, many of them modelled on their friends and neighbours. **Open** May–Sept Tues–Sun 09.00–12.00 and 13.00–17.00; closes Oct–Apr 16.00.

Seventeen kilometres further on is the château of **Častelovice**, which, if lacking the artistic or architectural greatness of other Bohemian mansions, has now become a particularly rewarding place to visit. Set in an English park with tree-lined avenues, this former medieval castle was rebuilt in a Renaissance style between 1588 and 1615, and then given neo-Gothic additions in the late 19C; attempts were subsequently made to restore as much as possible its overall Renaissance character. Among its early owners was King George of Poděbrady, whose first wife was a member of the family that would later play an especially important role in the building's history—the Šternberks. The Šternberks bought the place in 1694 and remained its lords until 1948, when Count Leopold and Countess Šternberk fled to America, taking with them their only child, Diana.

The house has now been returned to the charming, energetic and drily humorous Diana Šternberk Phipps, whose strong personality has informed the house's gradual but endearing rehabilitation. A courtyard containing traces of Renaissance frescoes marks the approach to the mansion's Renaissance wing, which has now been brought alive through such personal touches as bouquets of flowers, locally-made curtains, and numerous photographs of the Countess's family and friends (among whom are Gore Vidal and President Havel). Apart from some excellent family portraits by Karel Škréta, the main artistic interest of the interior is the long Knight's Hall, which has a coffered wooden ceiling decorated with Old Testament scenes. To help meet the costs of the continuing restoration programme, the Countess hires out rooms to tourists, and organises lunches for groups, who are splendidly entertained by a local band. **Open** Apr–Oct Tues–Sun 09.00–18.00.

The next two villages to the east also have notable châteaux: the one at **Kostelec nad Orlicí** (2km away) is an elegant Empire mansion built by J. Koch in 1829–35 for a member of the Kinský family; the other one, at **Doudleby nad Orlicí** (6km further on) dates back to the late 16C and was remodelled between 1670 and 1690; it features a charming courtyard of 1585 covered with elaborate sgraffito work of flowers and hunting scenes, and a series of Baroque rooms decorated with mythological scenes.

Vamberk, 2km further on, has a long tradition in lace-making, examples of which can be seen in the local museum. From here you can make a short detour north to the small industrial town of **Rychnov nad Kněžnou**, which lies at the foot of the Eagle Mountains, and has been a centre of the cloth industry since the time the town was founded in 1258. The place is dominated by the pompous mass of its château, which was built for Karel Kolowrat in 1676–90, and remodelled in 1722, possibly by Johann Santini-Aichel, who was responsible for the undulating façade of the adjacent church. Inside the château can be seen the Kolowrats' extensive picture collection, which is particularly strong on Czech works of the Baroque period, including K. Škréta's *The Arrival of Jacob in Laban* (signed and dated 1643), a portrait by P.C. Bentum of Jan František Kolowrat (c 1730), and still-lifes by Isaac Godyn (c 1700) and J.A. Vocásek (c 1740); among the foreign school paintings are works by A. Magnasco, H. Rigaud, J.G. Hamilton, H. van Aachen, and A.R. Mengs. Twelve kilometres northeast of Rychnov is Ricky, the main winter and summer resort in the Eagle Mountains, an area which is relatively scant in tourist accommodation.

Continuing east from Vamberk, you skirt the southern slopes of the Eagle Mountains, sharply climbing a few kilometres west of Červená Voda (50km) before descending into Moravia. The district town of **Šumperk**, 33km further east, has been a textile centre since the 18C; the main square has some Baroque houses and a plague column of 1719. Šumperk lies in the southern foothills of the **Jeseníky Mountains** (Jeseníky hory), a large protected area forming a popular winter and summer resort, and featuring waterfalls, caves, curative springs and great pine forests.

Following Road 11 from Šumperk you head north for 5km and then turn sharply east, crossing the southern end of this range. If you want to spend more time in these mountains you could take the left turning at the point where Road 11 swerves to the right, and continue in a northerly direction towards the town of Jeseník. **Velké Losiny**, 3km north of the turning, is a small spa town which makes a pleasant base for mountain walks. The paper mill here dates back to 1515 and is one of only seven remaining places in the world where paper continues to be made by hand. The town is also celebrated for its castle, which was built in the 1580s for the powerful Žerotín family, and has three storeys of arcading overlooking its open courtyard; in the 17C the building became notorious as the scene of witch trials that resulted in the deaths of numerous innocent women.

Jeseník, 41km further north along a winding road through dense forest, dates back to a prosperous mining community of the 14C, and features a Town Hall of 1610 and a Renaissance castle (now a local museum) surrounded by a moat. One kilometre north of the town is a spa founded in 1826 by a local farmer, Vincenz Priessnitz, who was the first to discover the curative properties of the local waters, which he tested at first on himself and then on his family and friends. The fame of the Priessnitz-Gräfenberg cold-water cure (Gräfenberg was the German name for the town) soon spread widely, and in 1845 one of the patients here was the Russian writer N.V. Gogol. Most of the surviving buildings, including the main Spa Building, are of the early years of the 20C; the cold-water cure is still recommended for those suffering from nervous complaints, respiratory diseases and metabolical disorders, but the spa today has the faded character of a place past its heyday. Similarly pleasant and old-fashioned is the tiny spa of **Lipová Lázně**, situated 4km due west of Jeseník, cosily set between trees and lush rolling meadows; founded in 1830 by a man called Schroth, its waters have been used since then for the treatment of obesity and rheumatism.

From Jeseník you can rejoin Road 11 by going back 8km down Road 44 and then turning left in the direction of **Karlova Studánka**, a further 18km through forest. Karlova Studánka, situated at an altitude of 800m, and hidden among pines, is another small spa, but slightly earlier in date than those of Jeseník and Lipová Lázně: the waters have been used for the treatment of respiratory disorders since 1780, and the spa buildings are all of the 19C. A most enjoyable walk can be made west of here, at first following the upper reaches of the Bílá Opava river, which forms here a series of waterfalls; above the river's source are the tourist chalets of Ovčárna and Baborka, and further up is the summit of the highest peak of the Jeseníky Mountains, **Praděd** (1492m). After leaving Karlova Studánka, drive in a southeasterly direction to Bruntál, 61km east of Šumperk, where you will regain Road 11.

At **Bruntál**, an industrial district town dating back to a thriving mining community of the early 13C, you near the built-up plains that stretch towards Ostrava. The chief interest of the town is its château, which has a monumentally grand main façade designed by F.A. Neumann in 1766 and articulated by giant pilasters. Behind this, and coming as quite a surprise, is an arcaded courtyard of the 16C centred around a well which is protected by delicate Renaissance ironwork; the interior of the building, at present closed for restoration, is all of the Baroque period, and includes a main hall decorated by large landscape frescoes.

The border town of **Krnov**, 21km northeast of Bruntál, is known internationally for the making of organs. Described misleadingly in at least one guidebook as a 'charming old town', Krnov has in fact been insensitively developed since the late 19C, and has little to commend itself to tourists other than its *Hotel Morava*. In contrast to the dreary modern blocks that comprise most hotels in provincial Czech towns, the *Hotel Morava* is a place of character installed in a Minorite monastery founded in the 14C and rebuilt after 1730; the cosy dining-room of the hotel, situated off the former cloisters, is decorated with appealingly clumsy frescoes by the 18C artist Josef Sterna.

Opava, 38km east of Bruntál along Road 11, and 25km southeast of Krnov on Road 57, is a large and rapidly expanding industrial town, its architecture being characterised by the use of red brick. The main centre of Czech Silesia (the greater part of Silesia fell to Prussia in 1742 and now forms part of Poland), Opava is the birthplace both of the leading Silesian poet Petr Bezruč (1867–1958), and—more interestingly for the non-Czech tourist—of the lion-lover and author of *Born Free*, Joy Adamson (née Frederika Viktoria Gessner; 1910–80). The town has a long and important history dating back to the late 12C, but repeated raids in the Thirty Years War and heavy bombing during the Second World War have ensured that its surviving old monuments are few and scattered. Its main attraction is the excellent Silesian Museum, housed in a building of 1893–94 at Tyršova 1, and containing extensive natural history, archaeological, architectural, historical and ceramics collections. Joy Adamson's birthplace (marked by a plaque) is at Na rybníčku 48.

A popular excursion from Opava is to **Hradec nad Moravicí**, 8km due south of the town on Road 57. Here stands a large country house in the middle of a beautiful English-style park rising above the river Moravice. At the entrance to the park, and just above the village of Hradec, is a neo-Gothic red-brick building, built originally as the stables of the mansion, and now occupied by a local museum. The house itself, dating back to 1600, was rebuilt in 1795, and further altered in a neo-Gothic style after 1880. Its heyday was the early 19C, when a number of leading musicians came to stay here, including Beethoven in 1806 and 1811, and Liszt in 1846 and 1848. A Beethoven music festival is now held here every June.

The sight of smoking chimneys and coal slag 33km east of Opava welcomes you to **Ostrava**, the largest industrial town in the Czech Republic, and this country's leading source of coal and iron.

History of Ostrava

Ostrava was founded in 1267, but only began to develop its present importance after 1767, when coal deposits were discovered here. Both the Rothschilds and the Habsburg Těšín archdukes speculated in the early mining activities here, and the town received a further boost in 1828 with the opening of the Vítkovice Ironworks; the building of a railway to Vienna in 1847 consolidated the town's rapid growth. In 1980–81 the playwright and future president Václav Havel spent the worst period of a four-year term in prison at a camp near Ostrava; he described his guard here as 'a genuinely dangerous person' who once said to him that 'Hitler did things differently—he gassed vermin like you right away!'

Until recently pollution was so bad in Ostrava that a permanent black cloud seemed to hang over the town. This situation has now greatly improved, and the centre is relatively clean and with its fair share of green spaces. None the less, apart from a lively cultural life, the town has little to offer the tourist, having virtually no old monuments and few interesting modern ones. The Municipal Museum (Ostravské muzeum), with natural history, musicological, archaeological and historical collections, occupies the former Town Hall, a structure of 1556 rebuilt in 1859. The local art gallery, housed in the Palace of Culture at Jurečkova 9, has works by 20C Czech artists, including A. Slavíček, J. Preisler, B. Kubišta, O. Kubín, V. Špála and E. Filla.

23 · Hradec Králové to Olomouc

Total distance 154km: Hradec Králové (leave by Road 35/E442) • 57km Litomyšl • 19km Svitavy • 42km Mohelnice • 36km Olomouc.

For much of its length the E442 follows an ancient route from Bohemia to Moravia. Its greatest attraction, the town of **Litomyšl**, lies 57km southeast of Hradec Králové (see Route 3) and was once a great road junction. The town's declining fortunes in the 19C, when the railway was routed to the north of it, had the beneficial result that its beautiful old centre was left relatively unchanged.

History of Litomyšl

The town of Litomyšl was founded in 1260 around a 10C castle and a 12C Premonstratensian monastery; made a bishopric in 1344, it remained one until 1421 when the town was captured by the Hussite leader Jan Žižka. In the 19C the town became associated with many of the leading figures in the history of Czech culture. The scientist Jan Purkyně taught at the Piarist school here and the historical novelist Alois Jirásek worked at the local secondary school; Božena Němcová lived here in 1860–61, and Jan Neruda's *Pictures of Life* were first printed at the shop called Augusta's. The town's most famous association was with the composer Bedřich Smetana, who was born here in 1824, and in whose honour a ten-day Opera Festival (known as Smetana's Litomyšl) is held every year in June/July. Further publicity has been given to the town in recent years by the current dynamic mayor Miroslav Brýdl, who, together with his brothers Tomáš (the owner of a local advertising agency) and Jiří (mayor of neighbouring Svitavy) helped to establish here in 1993 an important School for Restoration and Conservation. More remarkably still, in 1994 they succeeded in making the town host a summit conference that brought together the presidents of seven Central European countries (including Havel and Lech Walesa).

The long main square of Litomyšl, newly repainted for the 1994 summit conference and now named **Smetana Square** (Smetanovo náměstí) after the composer, is one of the most beautiful in Bohemia, and is lined with arcaded houses dating back to medieval times, but with gables and stuccoed fronts mainly of the 16C–18C; one of the finest of the houses is No. 110, U rytířů (At the Knights), now an art gallery, which has amusing Renaissance decoration sculpted by a Master Blažek in 1546 and featuring a squat and clumsy group of knights.

Off the northern end of the square is a green avenue leading up to the remarkable **château** built for Vratislav Pernštejn by the Italian architects Giovanni B. Aostalli and Ulrico Aostalli between 1568 and 1581. A series of sgraffitoed gables crown this building's main block, which is attached to an arcaded three-storeyed courtyard; the courtyard façade of the main block is covered all over with an exuberant wealth of sgraffito decoration, featuring ancient battle scenes. Porcelain and old furniture are now displayed inside the château, which has also retained the late 18C theatre (complete with some of the original painted scenery by Josef Platzer) where the young Smetana made his debut as a pianist. The musical infant prodigy was born in the 17C living-quarters of the adjoining Litomyšl brewery, of which his father had been the director; a small memorial museum to him, the **Rodný dům Smetany**, has now been installed here. In front of this is the two-towered façade of the Piarist church, begun by Alliprandi in 1714 and attached to the college where Purkyně taught. **Open** May–Aug Tues–Sun 08.00–12.00 and 13.00–17.00; Sept closes 16.00; Apr, Oct Sat, Sun 09.00–12.00 and 13.00–16.00.

Continuing north of the church on Jiráskova and taking the first turning to the right, Terézy Novákové, you will come at No. 75 to an outwardly unremarkable-looking provincial house that contains inside Litomyšl's latest and in many ways most fascinating attraction, the so-called **Portmoneum**. The house belonged to a local civil servant, amateur printer and collector called Josef

Portman, who had a life-long obsession with one of the most idiosyncratic and eccentric Czech artists of the 20C, Josef Váchal (1884–1969). Váchal, the nephew of the famous painter Mikoláš Aleš, made his name essentially as the author of visionary book illustrations; but, thanks to Portman, was given the opportunity to extend his talents by being allowed a free hand in the decoration of the latter's Litomyšl house from the early 1920s onwards. His bizarre decorations, including numerous devils, celestial rays of light, and a portrait of himself as a rat-catcher, extend all over the walls, ceilings, and even furniture of this building, and provide a fascinating psychological portrait of this artist known for his interest in mysticism and Satanism. The house, opened to the public in 1993 after years of falling into disrepair, was the first work of renovation undertaken by the town's newly established School of Restoration and Conservation. **Open** May–Sept Tues–Sun 09.00–12.00 and 13.00–17.00.

Eighteen kilometres south of Litomyšl is the small town of **Polička**, which was founded in 1265 as the seat of the Bohemian queen. The town has a few remains of its medieval fortifications, and a main square with a Baroque Town Hall and a Marian plague column of 1727–31. As with Litomyšl, Polička boasts a celebrated composer, Bohuslav Martinů, who was born here in 1890 in surroundings even more distinctive than those in which Smetana had been born: his birth took place in the tower rooms of the neo-Gothic parish church, his father having been the town watchman. Whereas Smetana ended up in the Pantheon of Czech heroes in Prague's Vyšehrad, Martinů, after a lifetime away from his native town, was buried in the local cemetery in 1959; some of his work recollects his native region, in particular his composition, *The Opening of Wells*, a glorification of this area.

From Litomyšl, continue driving southeast on the E442 to pass after 17km the northern outskirts of the industrial town of **Svitavy**, which was the birthplace of the Nazi industrialist turned saviour of Jews Oscar Schindler (1908–74); Schindler's life was commemorated first in a novel by the Australian writer Thomas Keneally and then in Stephen Spielberg's long film *Schindler's List* (1994), after which the townspeople—who remembered him largely for his Nazi past—finally came round to erecting a memorial to him in the park opposite the house where he was born (24 Poličská).

Eighteen kilometres further on is **Moravská Třebová**, a textile centre which has kept its medieval grid plan of c 1265, stretches of its old walls, and a number of late Gothic and Renaissance buildings, most notably the Town Hall, which was remodelled between 1550 and 1565. Shortly to the east of the town the E442 enters a forest and crosses into Moravia, the first Moravian town you come to being Mohelnice (24km), from where there is a dual carriageway all the way to Olomouc (36km).

Eight kilometres to the south of Mohelnice, at Bouzov, you could turn off to the right to visit the castle of **Bouzov** a few kilometres further on. This castle, founded c 1300, came later into the possession of the 15C Bohemian king, George of Poděbrady. In 1699 it was acquired by the Grand Masters of the German Teutonic Knights, a military order which bitterly oppressed the Slavic peoples under the pretext of spreading Christianity. The appropriately sinister-looking building seems to have been created for some wicked fairy, a look which is in fact due to neo-Gothic remodelling carried out for the Grand Masters in 1895–1912.

24 · Brno to Bratislava

Total distance 154km: Brno (leave by the D2/E65) • 26km Hustopeče • 23km Mikulov • 12km Valtice • 7km Lednice • 7km Podivín • D2 • 79 Bratislava.

Southeast of Brno the D2 motorway crosses the flattest part of the Moravian Lowlands, the monotony of the landscape broken only by distant glimpses to the right of the gentle Mikulov Hills, which mark the border with Austria. By far the most interesting sights in this part of Moravia lie in the shadow of these hills, in a district closely associated with one of the most powerful families in the Czech lands, the Liechtensteins of Grand Duchy fame.

Leaving the motorway at Hustopeče 26km south of Brno, you should head southwest by way of Strachotín to the small border town of **Mikulov**, enjoying on the way a view of the hill-top ruins of the medieval castle of Dívčí Hrady. Mikulov, which lies at the centre of a well-known wine growing area, is one of Moravia's most beautiful small towns, and has—as yet—still to see the arrival of large-scale tourism, despite its famous white wines, its proximity to Austria, and its many architectural and historical attractions.

A tour of this hill-town should begin on its small and sloping main square, where you will find a Town Hall of 1606, and a number of Renaissance houses, some recently converted into cafés and restaurants. At the top of the square is the entrance to the town's large **castle**, which dates back to an early 13C castle built by the Counts of Liechtenstein, who remained the lords of Mikulov up till the end of the 16C, tolerating in 1526 the arrival in the town of a large Anabaptist community fleeing from Switzerland. Acquired subsequently by the Dietrichsteins, the castle was remodelled and extended between 1611 and 1618, and again after 1719. During the Second World War it was used for the storing of booty by the SS, who blew up the place in 1945, thus showering the town with porcelain. Reconstructed between 1948 and 1961, the castle complex now contains a wine bar and a small museum with a dully displayed collection of exhibits relating to the local wine industry, most notably a wine barrel of 1643 with the astonishing capacity of 101,000 litres. More engaging are an inner courtyard decorated with rich Baroque statuary, and the extensive views over vineyards all the way to Vienna. **Open** May–Sept Tues–Sun 08.00–17.00; Apr, Oct Sat, Sun 09.00–16.00.

Directly below the citadel's western walls, along the charming Husova, is a newly restored **synagogue** founded in the 15C. The plain exterior contrasts with the gilded interior, which dates back to the late 17C, shortly before the town's

Mikulov

former large Jewish ghetto was joined by the Supreme Rabbi for the whole of Moravia. Continuing to the northern end of Husova, you should walk up the bosky hill beyond to visit a yet more eloquent testimony of the town's Jewish past: an enormous and romantically overgrown **Jewish cemetery**, shaded by ancient oaks.

Leaving the town on the Břeclav road, continue driving southeast along the Austrian border for 12km until you come to **Valtice**, a village entirely over-shadowed by the massive Baroque bulk of one of the most important of the Liechtensteins' former properties in the Czech Republic. Built in 1668 over 13C foundations, the château was heavily depleted at the end of the Second World War, when the Liechtensteins fled from the approaching Soviet Army (the family is currently involved in a lengthy legal dispute to try and win back this and other Czech homes of theirs). Part of the interior has now been taken over by the cheaply furnished *Hotel Hubertus*, which is enormously popular with Austrian tourists. The rest can be seen in the course of a 45min guided tour that finishes up in the lavishly decorated chapel, the finest surviving testimony to the château's former glory. A Baroque Music Festival is held here in mid-August, complete with fireworks and a party. **Open** May–Sept Tues–Sun 08.00–12.00 and 13.00–17.00; Sept closes 16.00; Apr, Oct Sat, Sun 09.00–12.00 and 13.00–16.00.

The principal tourist attraction of this southeastern corner of Moravia is the Liechtensteins' former house and gardens at **Lednice**, which can be quickly reached from Valtice by a straight road running northeast across a flat land-scape skirted by lakes and a forest. But by far the most enjoyable approach from Valtice is to undertake the 3hr walk along a red-marked footpath that begins in the large forest immediately to the east of the village, and goes on to follow the southern shores of a large lake; on the way you will pass some delightful follies including a triumphal arch, a former pheasantry, a series of temples, and a neo-Gothic chapel dedicated to the patron saint of hunting, Hubert.

History of the house

The house at Lednice dates back to an early 13C estate which was acquired in 1371 by the Liechtensteins, who remained the owners until the Second World War. The medieval castle was replaced by a Renaissance one, which in turn was followed by a large Baroque structure built at the beginning of the 17C; in 1688–90 the great Austrian architect J.B. Fischer von Erlach created stables here, as well as terraces and fountains. Further remodelling of the main house took place between 1766 and 1772, and again between 1845 and 1856, the latter building campaign lending the structure its present neo-Gothic appearance.

The pinnacled and battlemented neo-Gothic skyline of the house is most picturesque, if not as grand or exciting as that of Hluboká near České Budějovice (see Chapter 14). Part of the interior, with its heavily panelled rooms, can be visited on a guided tour; another part forms a museum dedicated to agriculture, hunting and fishing; while some of the outbuildings at Lednice are at present occupied by the Institute of Agriculture and Horticulture, a department of Brno University. Among these outbuildings are Fischer von Erlach's monumentally grand **stables**, which are arranged around an enormous courtyard and articulated by giant piers and columns.

Adjoining the house is a magnificent **greenhouse**, designed by the English architect G. Devien in 1843–45, but later overlaid with filigree neo-Gothic ornamentation by the Viennese architect G. Wingelmüller. The real pleasure of a visit to Lednice comes from the vast and beautifully landscaped grounds. Three lakes to the south of the house were created c 1600, but the first major landscaping took place towards the end of the 18C, the park being laid out at that time in the shape of an enormous star, with follies and summerhouses placed along the axes; between 1805 and 1811 an Italian architect called Fanti devised a new park in an English Romantic style, its principal feature being the enormous lake to the north of the house, featuring no fewer than 15 islands.

The most celebrated of the many follies to be seen in the grounds is the 60m-high **minaret** (the largest outside the Islamic world, built to the north of the house by J. Hardmuth in 1798–1802); to the east of this, by the southern shores of Fanti's large lake, is a purpose-built ruined castle, Hansenburg Castle, designed by J. Kornhäusel in 1815. The same architect was also responsible for the Temple of Apollo (1816), which stands next to the mill pond to the south of the house. **Open** May–Aug Tues–Sun 09.00–12.00 and 13.00–18.00; Sept closes 17.00; Apr, Oct Sat, Sun 09.00–12.00 and 13.00–16.00.

Returning to the D2 motorway at Podivín, 7km north of Lednice, continue heading south, the next exit being that for **Břeclav** (8km), an important railway junction and the main town of the Podluží district, which is the part of South Moravia most renowned for its folklore. The great centre here for folk arts and traditions is the lowland town of **Strážnice**, 30km northeast of the Břeclav exit along Road 55, where even the railway station is decorated with pseudo-folk designs. The town is known for its hand-painted ceramics, but above all for its annual folk festival, which is held usually in the last week of June, and features singing and dancing in traditional costumes. Good examples of local folk art are on show at the castle here (a medieval structure rebuilt in the 19C), and there is also a large *skansen* on the outskirts of the town.

Continuing south on the motorway from the Břeclav exit you reach the Slovakian border after 10km, from where it is a 58km drive to Bratislava (see Chapter 25). As you near Bratislava, the wooded southern slopes of the White Carpathians (Lesser Carpathians) come into view to your left, and, during the last stages of your drive, rise directly above the road.

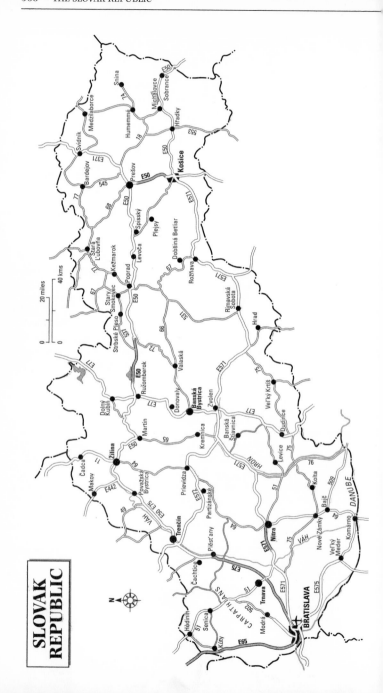

The Slovak Republic

The breaking-up of Czechoslovakia in 1993 has helped to highlight the enormous differences between the two halves of the former federation. Slovakia is poorer, cheaper, and far less visited than the Czech Republic; and its people—stereotypically viewed by some Czechs with the same patronising disdain with which the Scots or Irish are sometimes treated by the English—are predominantly conservative, church-going, and wine-loving. Though there are large pockets of post-war industrialisation, it remains an essentially rural country with a culture that is heavily folkloric and little influenced in the 20C by the strong avant-garde traditions of Bohemia and Moravia.

Unsurprisingly, for a place that has been under foreign domination for the greater part of its history, and subject to brutal Magyarisation, Slovakia is a country whose greatest artistic treasures and architectural monuments are largely the work of Austrians, Germans and, above all, Hungarians, whose legacy here—so blatantly apparent in the many abandoned feudal properties that dot the countryside—extends to other aspects of the culture such as the love of spicy, paprika-flavoured food. And whereas the Czech Republic, after the post-war expulsion of most of its remaining Germans, has a relatively unified population, Slovakia continues to be ethnically diverse, with 600,000 Hungarians, up to 150,000 Rusyns in the northeast, and 100,000 gypsies. For the foreign tourist such diversity is part of Slovakia's fascination; but, in the ever-intensifying nationalist climate of today, it is the source of growing tensions, and is already causing difficulties for those touring the country in Hungarian cars.

The least typically Slovak part of the country is West Slovakia, where the capital city of **Bratislava** is to be found. Once a popular place of residence for the Viennese aristocracy, as well as the second most important city in Greater Hungary, Bratislava (see Chapter 25) has retained an elegant old centre full of pastel-coloured Baroque palaces. Much of **West Slovakia** comprises the vast plain that is crossed in Chapter 26A, which skirts the Danube and includes places of such strong Hungarian associations as Komárno—the birth-place of both the composer Franz Lehár and the novelist Mór Jókai; the alternative Chapter 26B leaves the plain at the historically important hill town of **Nitra** (one of the main centres of the Moravian Empire) and then proceeds into the high wooded hills encasing the fascinating former mining town of **Banská Štiavnica**, which has kept numerous monuments testifying to its boomtown years in the Middle Ages and Renaissance.

The northern, Carpathian half of West Slovakia is covered in Chapter 27, which follows the Váh valley, passing the former Hungarian archbishopric at **Trnava**, the spa at **Piešt'any** (once greatly favoured by the Hungarian aristocracy), and the enormous citadel at **Trenčín**. Chapter 28 continues from Trenčín past the lively spa at **Trenčianske Teplice** and on to the Central Slovakian towns of Kremnica (the seat of the medieval Hungarian mint), **Zvolen** (whose castle contains one of the finest Old Master collections in Slovakia) and **Banská Bystrica**, a good base from which to visit the mountain ranges of the Large Fatra (Vel'ká Fatra) and Low Tatra (Nízke Tatry).

Slovak rather than Hungarian culture predominates in Chapter 29, and includes the striking painted folk architecture of Čičmany, and the town most closely associated with the growth of the Slovak nationalist movement, Martin. Slovakia's most famous feature—its mountain scenery—is seen at its most spectacular in Chapter 30, the first half of which is largely devoted to the long-established summer and winter resorts of the **High Tatras** (Vysoké Tatry), where most of Slovakia's tourism is concentrated. East of these peaks, the route continues into the rolling agricultural land known as the **Spiš**, where German settlers in the Middle Ages developed a beautiful series of towns with distinctively gabled buildings, and outstanding works of art: the district capital is the excellently preserved medieval town of **Levoča**, for which the artist Paul of Levoča created one of Central Europe's most memorable 15C altarpieces.

The whole of Slovakia east of the Tatras remains remarkably little spoilt. Chapter 31 crosses a part of the region extensively populated by the Rusyns, a people lost between cultures who speak a dialect of Ukranian and belong to a compromise religion known as the Greek-Catholic Church. One of their main centres is the enchanting medieval town of **Bardejov**, among whose nearby attractions are numerous wooden churches, and a totally idiosyncratic museum to the most internationally well-known person of Rusyn extraction—the American Pop artist Andy Warhol. Arriving via Chapter 32 at East Slovakia's fascinating main town, the bustling **Košice**, you return not only to a more metropolitan world but also to a part of Slovakia with a dominant Hungarian character: its cultural highpoint is Europe's easternmost Gothic cathedral, St Elizabeth's, a soaring, richly decorated and fabulously endowed structure dating mainly from the late 15C. From here you can follow Chapter 33 back to Central Slovakia, passing on the way the waterfalls and ravines of the '**Slovak Paradise**' (Slovenský raj).

Transport
Trains
From Bratislava main station: Banská Bystrica (2 daily; 4hr); Brno (8 daily; 2hr); Čierna nad Tisou (4 daily; 9hr 30min); Humenné (1 daily; 8hr 30min); Košice (9 daily; 5hr 10min–6hr 10min); Liptovský Mikuláš (11 daily; 3hr 30min); Piešťany/Trenčín (1–2 hourly; 1hr/1hr 30min); Poprad (9 daily; 4hr–4hr 50min); Prague (8 daily; 5hr); Prešov (1 daily; 7hr); Rožňava (2 daily; 8hr); Ružomberok (9 daily; 3hr); Štúrovo (8 daily; 1hr 20min); Trnava (14 daily; 35min); Žilina (13 daily; 2hr–2hr 45min); Zvolen (5 daily; 3hr 20min).

From Bratislava Nové Mesto station: Trnava (up to 15 daily; 35–50min); Komárno (6 daily; 2hr–3hr 20min).

From Banská Bystrica: Brezno (11 daily; 55min–1hr 30min); Červená Skala (5 daily; 1hr 40min–2 hr 30min); Martin (6 daily; 1 hr 50min); Zvolen (hourly; 20–40min).

From Košice: Čierna nad Tisou (14 daily; 1hr 10min–1hr 45min); Lučenec (4 daily; 3hr 10min); Plešivec (8 daily; 1hr 20min–1hr 50min); Rožňava (up to 10 daily; 1hr 15min–2hr).

From Kraľovany: Istebné/Dolný Kubín/Oravský Podzámok/Podbiel/ Trstená (13 daily; 16min/35min/1hr 30min/2hr).

From Poprad: Kežmarok/Stará Ľubovňa (13 daily; 35min/1hr 35min);

Košice (every 2hr; 1hr 30min); Prešov (2 daily; 1hr 20min); Spišská Nová Ves (up to hourly; 20min); Starý Smokovec/Štrbské Pleso (hourly; 45min/1hr 40min); Tatranská Lomnica (up to 15 daily; 25min).

From Prešov: Bardejov (up to 12 daily; 1hr 30min); Humenné (11 daily; 1hr 15min–2hr); Košice (up to 14 daily; 50min).

From Žilina: Liptovský Mikuláš (1–2 hourly; 1hr–1hr 30min); Poprad (1–2 hourly; 2hr 10min); Rajec (9 daily; 45min); Ružomberok (19 daily; 1hr); Strečno/Šútovo (up to 12 daily; 15min/45min); Vrútky/Kral'ovany (1–2 hourly; 30min/40min).

From Zvolen: Detva (9 daily; 40min); Kremnica (9 daily; 1hr); Lučenec (15 daily; 1hr–1hr 30min); Turčianske Teplice/Martin (10 daily; 1hr 20min–1hr 50min/1hr 40min–2hr 15min).

Buses

From Bratislava: Modra (every 30min–1hr; 35min–1hr); Komárno (up to 8 daily; 1hr 30min); Nitra (every 30–45min; 1hr 30min); Piešťany (hourly; 1hr); Senec (every 30min; 30min); Trnava (every 40min; 1hr).

From Banská Bystrica: Banská Štiavnica (up to 6 daily; 1hr 30min); Martin/Žilina (up to 6 daily; 1hr 15min/2hr); Ružomberok (up to 8 daily; 1hr 20min).

From Košice: Michalovce (1–2 hourly; 1hr 30min); Miskolcz (up to 3 daily; 2hr); Užgorod (1 daily; 4hr).

From Levoča: Poprad (up to 12 daily; 30–50min); Spišské Podhradie (up to 10 daily; 30min).

From Liptovský Mikuláš: Demänovská dolina/Jasná (hourly; 40min).

From Poprad: Prešov (up to 10 daily; 2hr); Spišské Podhradie (up to 10 daily; 45min–1hr 20min); Zakopané (4 daily; 2hr 15min); Ždiar/Lysá Pol'ana (hourly; 1hr/1hr 30min).

From Prešov: Medzilaborce (up to 2 daily; 2hr 20min); Michalovce (up to 10 daily; 1hr 45min); Užgorod (2 daily; 4hr).

From Rožňava: Krásnohorské Podhradie (up to hourly; 10min); Ochtiná (up to 6 daily; 40min); Dedinky/Poprad (up to 8 daily; 1hr/2hr).

From Stará L'ubovňa: Bardejov (up to 12 daily; 1hr 20min); Červený Kláštor (up to 10 daily; 40–50min); Prešov (up to 14 daily; 2hr); Svidník (up to 2 daily; 1hr 45min).

From Svidník: Bardejov (up to 10 daily; 1hr 15min); Prešov (up to 3 daily; 1hr 40min); Dukelský priesmyk (up to 4 daily; 35min); Medzilaborce (1 daily; 1hr 30min).

From Trnava: Nitra (hourly; 1hr–1hr 30min).

From Žilina: Čičmany (up to 6 daily; 1hr 20min); Terchová/Vrátna dolina (hourly; 45min/1hr).

Hotels and pensions
Banská Bystrica

Hotel Arcade, námestie SNP 5, 974 00. ☎ (088) 702 111; Fax (088) 723 126. Luxuriously installed within a Renaissance building on the town's beautiful main square.

Banská Štiavnica

Hotel Salamander, Palárikova 1, 969 01. ☎ (0859) 239 92. Occupying a Renaissance house in the centre of the old town, this is a wonderfully characterful establishment with spacious rooms, heavy leather furniture and shining wood floors.

Bardejov

Hotel Republika, Radničné námestie. ☎ (0935) 8605. The hotel's position on the lovely main square partly makes up for the charmless interior and lack of private bathrooms.

Bratislava

Hotel Perugia, Zelená 5, 811 01. ☎ (07) 533 1818; Fax (07) 533 1821. A luxury hotel of a rather more personal and intimate kind than the nearby *Forum* and *Danube*, and with an excellent quiet location in the middle of the old town.

Chez Dávid, Zámocká 13, 811 01. ☎ (07) 531 3824; Fax (07) 531 2642. A small pension on the site of the Jewish ghetto (at the foot of the castle), and with an excellent kosher restaurant.

Hotel No.16, Partizánska 16a, 811 03. ☎ (07) 311 672; Fax (07) 311 298. High up in a quiet residential district (near where Dubček used to live), this has good views of the castle, attractive wooden furnishings, and distinctively decorated bedrooms.

Kežmarok

Hotel Club, Alexandra 24, 060 01. ☎ (0968) 4051; Fax (0968) 4053. Small and friendly, this is the only hotel in the town centre.

Košice

Hotel Európa, Protifašistickyčh bojovníkov 1, 040 01. ☎ (095) 622 3897. A must for those who prefer atmosphere to comfort, this seedy and slightly sinister relic of the past is arranged along an echoing corridor behind a grand and glorious neo-Baroque façade.

Penzión pri Radnici, Bačíkova 18, 043 66. ☎ (095) 622 8601; Fax (095) 622 7824. A good compromise between the cheap *Hotel Európa* (see above) and the characterless *Hotel Slovan*, this is a cheerful, well-appointed small pension with a pleasant summer terrace and a restaurant specialising in venison.

Levoča

Hotel Satel, námestie Majstra Pavla 55, 054 01. ☎ (0966) 512 943; Fax (0966) 514 486. Possibly Slovakia's most beautiful hotel, this has been superlatively installed within a wonderful old house on the main square, with a painted Baroque façade, and an exquisite Renaissance courtyard complete with arcading, a small fountain, and elaborate ironwork.

Liptovský Mikuláš

Hotel El Greco, Štúrova 2, 031 01. ☎ (0849) 224 11. Art Nouveau hotel with a central location.

Malá Fatra

Hotel Boboty, Vratná Dolina 013 06 Terchová. ☎ (089) 695 227. Simple hotel with balconies enjoying good mountain views.

Nitra

Hotel Zlaý Kľúčik, Svätourbanská 27, 949 01. ☎ (087) 550 289; Fax (087)

550 293. Occupying two new houses on top of the vine-covered suburb of Zobor, this has superb views of Nitra, and a cheerful, tasteful interior.

Nízke Tatry
Mikulášska Chata, 03251 Demänovská dolina. ☎ / Fax (0849) 916 72. A homely old chalet that has recently been renovated.

Piešťany
Hotel Eden, Winterova 60, 921 01. ☎ (0838) 247 09; Fax (0838) 221 23. A white and pleasant Functionalist hotel with terrace restaurant.

Trenčín
Hotel Tatra, M.R. Štefánika 2, 911 00. ☎ (0831) 506 111; Fax (0831) 506 213. A newly and lavishly restored neo-Baroque hotel at the foot of the castle.

Vysoké Tatry
Hotel Grand, 062 01 Starý Smokovec. ☎ (0969) 2154; Fax (0969) 2157. Dating back to 1912, with some of the original panelling, and a restaurant whose moustachioed *maitre d'hôtel* seems to have stepped out of that era.
Villa Dr Szontág, 062 01 Nový Smokovec. ☎ (0969) 2061; Fax (0969) 2062. A turreted 1920s villa with a faded charm.
Grandhotel Praha, 059 60 Tatranská Lomnica. ☎ (0969) 967 941; Fax (0969) 967 891. Another of the classic Tatra resort hotels once patronised by the Hungarian aristocracy.

25 · Bratislava

The capital of Slovakia lies by the Danube, hemmed in to the north by the verdant vine-covered slopes of the Lesser Carpathians, and overlooking to the south a great plain which stretches over three countries. Bordered by both Austria and Hungary, and situated on a river which has served since ancient times as one of the great thoroughfares between Eastern and Western Europe, Bratislava is a city which has occupied literally a position of central importance in European history. The Italian writer and literary historian, Claudio Magris, in his brilliant philosophical and poetical travel book *Danube* (1986), identifies the city as 'one of the "hearts" of Mitteleuropa, with layer upon layer of centuries forever present, unresolved conflicts and lacerations, unhealed wounds and unreconciled contradictions.'

History of Bratislava
The rocky outcrops on which the castles of Bratislava and nearby Devín were built were occupied as far back as prehistoric times and became in the 1C BC the site of fortified settlements founded by the Celtic tribe of Boyes. After the 1C AD, the Romans, gradually shifting the northern frontier of their empire to Slovakia, created the settlement of Posonium, from which was to be derived the Hungarian name for Bratislava, Pozsony. The Slavs settled in the area in the 5C and 6C, and between 623 and 656 revolted against the rulers of that time, the Avarians, and founded a state of their own; this was later incorporated within the Great Moravian Empire, which came into being after the unification of the countries of Nitra and Moravia

in the 9C. The castle at Bratislava is first documented in 907, when it is referred to as Presslauspurch or 'Pressalas's castle' (hence both the Slovak name 'Bratislava' and the German one, 'Pressburg').

Nomadic Hungarian tribes had first arrived in the Danubian lowlands in 895, and by the 10C had turned the castle of Bratislava into an important stronghold on the northwestern borders of the Hungarian Empire; the Slavonic population none the less stayed on, and was to remain under foreign domination until 1918. A settlement on the eastern slopes of the castle hill grew up in the 12C and in 1291 was granted a Borough Charter by the Hungarian king Andrew III. The town developed as one of the most prosperous in Hungary, thanks to its importance as a trade and crafts centre, and also to its viniculture, which had been established here by the Romans. The growth of the town intensified in the 14C and 15C, and a second line of fortifications was put up. The Emperor Sigismund of Luxemburg had the castle rebuilt in 1423, and shortly afterwards granted the town the privilege of minting its own coins and having its own coat of arms; in 1439 Albrecht of Habsburg allowed a bridge to be built across the Danube, and in 1465, King Matthias Corvinus founded here the 'Academia Istropolitana', the first university in Slovak territory.

The heyday of Bratislava came after the defeat of the Hungarians by the Turks at the Battle of Mohács in 1526. Queen Mary, the widow of the Hungarian king Lewis II, took refuge at Bratislava, and from that time onwards the Hungarian Diet was to hold its sessions here, electing in one of its first meetings Queen Mary's brother, Ferdinand of Habsburg, as Hungarian king. The official proclamation of Bratislava as capital of Hungary, seat of the Hungarian Diet and Coronation City, came ten years later, in 1536; in the course of three centuries nine kings and eight queens were to be crowned in the city. During the 17C and 18C, the twin Hungarian townships of Buda and Pest stagnated and produced little of architectural interest, but Bratislava became one of the great Baroque cities of Central Europe and, with a population of 26,845 by 1773, emerged also as the largest city in Hungary.

A period of particular prosperity was during the reign of Maria Theresa of Austria (1740–80), who gave the title of Hungarian viceroy to her son-in-law Albert of Teschen, and designated Bratislava Castle as his seat. Maria Theresa and her court regularly took up residence at Bratislava, and in consequence the leading aristocratic families at nearby Vienna had palaces built here. Musical life flourished in Bratislava, and numerous important compositions were performed here following their premières in Vienna and Esterházy. The court orchestra of Prince Nicholas Esterházy of Eisenach gave frequent performances in the Grassalkovich Palace, and the orchestra's leading composer and conductor, Joseph Haydn, even premièred in this city his opera *La Canterina*. Mozart came several times to Bratislava, his first visit being in 1762, fresh from his triumph at the age of six at the Viennese court; this and subsequent visits were organised by an acquaintance of his family, Count Charles Hieronymus Pálffy. The librettist of Mozart's opera *The Magic Flute*, Emmanuel Schikaneder, worked in the city from 1782–84, and Mozart's widow Costanza settled here after her second marriage. The composer Johann Hummel was born in Bratislava in 1778, and was active for a short period in the most celebrated of the city's orchestras, that of Count Grassalkovich. Beethoven was also associated with Bratislava, and in 1796 met up again with a former pupil, Countess Babetta Keglevich, to whom he subsequently dedicated a number of works, including his Sonata in E sharp, op. 7.

A thriving cultural life was to persist in Bratislava long after the reign of Maria Theresa, but the city was to lose its dominant role in Hungarian affairs after 1783, when the Emperor Joseph II had the central Hungarian offices transferred to Buda and the Crown jewels to Vienna; as a result of this action, the city's population soon fell from 33,000 to only 11,000. The early 19C is marked in Bratislava by the growth of the Slovak Movement, one of its leading protagonists, Ľudovít Štúr, settling here in 1829 and issuing in 1845 the first Slovak political paper—*Slovenskie národnie noviny*. In 1848, at the last session of the Hungarian Diet held in Bratislava, Štúr successfully presented his plea for the abolition of serfdom. Two years later Emperor Franz Josef proclaimed Bratislava as district capital of the five Hungarian counties comprising West and Central Slovakia, and made Slovak the official language; he was to abrogate his decision ten years later, and the political importance of the city was to decline yet further.

After the Dual Compromise of 1867, Bratislava became the seat of a number of secondary government institutions and, like Budapest, was subject to rapid industrialisation, with many large chemical, engineering and textile works being set up here. At the same time the city continued to play a major role in the musical life of Central Europe, becoming closely associated during this period with most of the leading Hungarian composers. In between 1822 and 1885, Franz Liszt made no less than 15 visits to Bratislava, and in 1881 and 1885 performed here with the Russian composer and pianist Anton Rubinstein; the composer and pianist Ernö Dohnányi was born here in 1877, and both Ferenc Erkel and Béla Bartók were students in the city.

By the late 19C the journey between Vienna and Bratislava was reduced to little more than an hour, and the Viennese tended to look on the city as a suburb of their own and, up to 1918, would regularly come here to enjoy the good local wines. On 1 January 1919 Bratislava became part of the Czechoslovak Republic, though the district of Petržalka, on the southern side of the Danube, was to remain occupied by Hungarian troops until August of that year. In 1946 the city was joined to the surrounding communities of Petržalka, Prievoz, Vajnory, Rača, Lamač, Dúbravka and Devín to form Greater Bratislava, which had a population of 190,544. The Act of the Czechoslovak Federation was signed at Bratislava Castle on 30 October 1968, and the city was made capital of the Slovak Socialist Republic; it became the capital of the sovereign Slovak Republic on 1 January 1993.

Bratislava, the least visited of Central European capitals, has long been unfairly neglected by foreign tourists. During the days of Communist Czechoslovakia, Prague was favoured almost to the exclusion of Bratislava, despite the fact that the former had become by far the more melancholy of the two cities after 1968: 'Ever since the events of 1968,' wrote Claudio Magris in 1986, 'the splendid city of Prague has given an impression of being under the spell of neglect and death, while Bratislava, in spite of everything, is sanguine and cheerful, a vital world in an expansive phase, looking not to the melancholy of the past, but to growth and the future.' Ironically, as the capital of a now independent Slovak Republic, Bratislava has in many ways a more stagnant and provincial character than it had when Magris described it. Yet

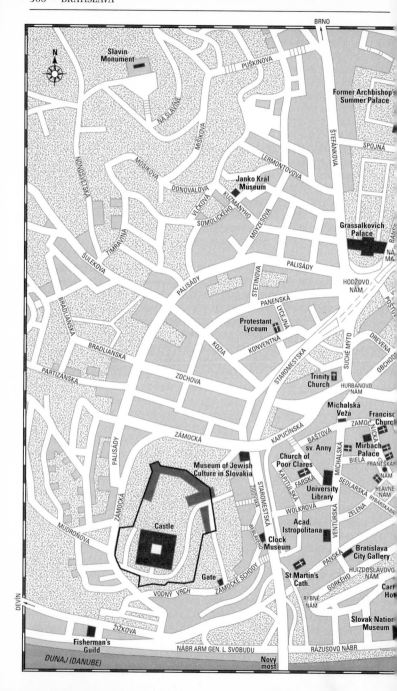

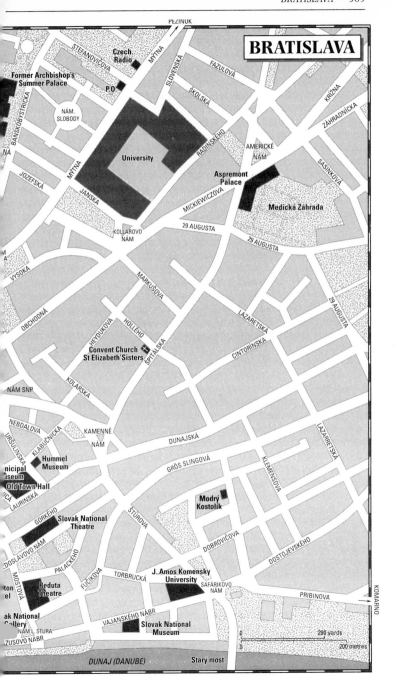

BRATISLAVA

PEZINUK

STEFANOVIČOVA

Czech. Radio

MÝTNA

SLOVENSKÁ

FAZULOVA

KRIŽNA

Former Archbishop's Summer Palace

P.O.

ŠKOLSKÁ

ZÁHRADNÍCKA

BANSKOBYSTRICKA

NÁM. SLOBODY

RADINSKÉHO

AMERICKÉ NÁM

NÁ

JOZEFSKÁ

MÝTNA

University

Aspremont Palace

ŠAŠINKOVA

JANSKA

MICKIEWICZOVA

Medická Záhrada

KOLLAROVO NÁM

29 AUGUSTA

29 AUGUSTA

MA

VYSOKA

MARKUŠOVA

29 AUGUSTA

OBCHODNÁ

LAZARETSKÁ

HEYDUKOVA

HOLLÉHO

ŠPITÁLSKA

Convent Church St Elizabeth'Sisters

CINTORÍNSKA

KOLARSKA

NÁM SNP

NEBDALOVA

KAMENNÉ NÁM

DUNAJSKÁ

LAZARETSKÁ

URSULINSKA

KLABUČNICKA

Hummel Museum

GRÖS SLINGOVÁ

KLEMENSOVA

nicipal seum

Old Town Hall

LAURINSKÁ

GORKÉHO

Slovak National Theatre

Modrý Kostolík

DOSLÁVOVO NAM

ŠTUROVA

DOBROVIČOVA

DOSTOJEVSKÉHO

ton el

MOSTOVA

Reduta Theatre

FUČÍKOVA

PALACKÉHO

TORBRUCKÁ

J. Amos Komensky University

SAFÁRIKOVO NÁM

PRIBINOVA

KOMARNO

ak National Gallery

NÁM L. STURA

ZUSOVO NÁBR

VAJANSKÉHO NÁBR

Slovak National Museum

0   200 yards

0   200 metres

DUNAJ (DANUBE)

Starý most

there are few people who would now deny the extraordinary tourist potential of Bratislava, the architectural beauty of which has been highlighted by the numerous restoration projects that have been continuing since the 1980s.

Ideally Bratislava should be included in any tour combining Vienna and Budapest, for it is a city which can boast many of the more enjoyable features of its two neighbours, but without their oppressive tourism. Its situation has some of the beauty of Budapest, and its Baroque and Rococo palaces are as elegant as any in Vienna. The local wines are excellent, and a trip to the wine-cellars on the outlying slopes of the Lesser Carpathians is as pleasurable as a visit to the Vienna Woods, particularly at the time of the autumn grape harvest, when for a period of two to three weeks the delicious young wine known as 'Burčiak' is available. Further- more, Bratislava maintains a reputation for its lively musical life, with peformances put on not only at the city's outstanding turn-of-the-century opera house (the Slovak National Theatre) and concert hall (the Reduta), but also in historic build- ings throughout the old city centre. An important international music festival (the Bratislava Music Festival) is held every October, while a pop-music festival (the Bratislava Lyre) is put on in May; additionally there is a Cultural Summer Festival every July and August, with classical, jazz and folk concerts taking place around the city. In late September and early October of every odd-numberered year the city also hosts an international biennial of children's book illustration.

At least two days are needed for a leisurely tour of Bratislava's main sights, which include the castles of both Bratislava and Devín, the Cathedral of St Martin, the Church of St Clare, the Mirbach, Pálffy and Archbishop's Palaces, the Old Town Hall, the St Michael's Tower and the neighbouring Pharmaceutical Museum, the Clock Museum 'At the Good Shepherd', the Tower of the SNP Bridge, the memorial on the Slavín Hill and the Slovak National Museum and Gallery. With the exception of Devín and Slavín, all these sights are within easy walking distance, and it is not advisable to take your car to the city centre.

A. Central Bratislava

A tour of Bratislava could begin at the Hurbanovo námestie, at the southern end of which is **St Michael's Bridge** (Michalský most), which is surmounted by Baroque statues and spans what was formerly a moat where travelling players performed in the 18C. Within the moat can be seen the main surviving section of the town's fortifications, which date back to the 13C and 14C and were pulled down in 1775 on the orders of Maria Theresa.

After crossing the bridge, you pass through a 15C gate known as the Powder Gate and enter the narrow **Michalská**, which, together with its southern continuation Ventúrská, is one of the most beautiful streets in the now wholly pedestrianised old town, and is lined its whole length with 16C–18C buildings with a burgeoning number of cafés and eateries. No. 15 on the right-hand side of the street is the narrowest house in Bratislava, while on the other side of the street at No. 28 is one of the city's oldest pharmacies, known as At the Red Cray- fish (U červeného raka), and now forming part of a fascinating **Pharmaceu- tical Museum** (Farmaceutická expozícia). In the first room of this museum can be seen the original late 18C decoration of At the Red Crayfish, comprising elegant black and gilded furnishings, and a *trompe-l'oeil* painted ceiling featuring Chronos, the god of Time. An evocative description of this room forms the opening passages of the chapter on Slovakia in Claudio Magris's book, *Danube*

(1986): 'That eighteenth-century shop ... gives the impression of a military parade in its rigid symmetry, of an unassuming yet determined art of war displayed against Chronos. The pots on the shelves, in cobalt, emerald green and sky blue, embellished with floral designs and biblical quotations are like the ranks of tin soldiers in museum reliefs of famous battles; the tinctures, balsams, balms, allopathics, purgatives and emetics are there at their battle stations, ready to intervene according to the requirements of strategy. Even the labels, with their abbreviations, are reminiscent of military contractions: Syr., Tinct., Extr., Bals., Fol., Pulv., Rad.'

Within the other rooms of the museum are objects relating to the history of pharmacy in Bratislava from the Middle Ages onwards, including a 15C Gothic mortar, Italian majolica pots of the 16C and 17C, an amusing 17C copper mortar supported by the mournful figure of a Turk, prescription books dating back to 1644, and a reconstruction of a Baroque pharmacy originally attached to the Convent of the Order of St Elizabeth's Sisters (in the middle of this is a wooden statue of St Elizabeth, the patron saint of

Central Bratislava

herbalists). The eagle eyes of Magris, always on the lookout for the culturally significant, fall on a hefty volume entitled *Taxa Pharmaceutica Posoniensis*, written by Ján Justus Torkos, and published in 1745 in four languages: Latin, Slovak, Hungarian and German. **Open** Tues–Sun 10.00–17.00

Built across Michalská, and rising high above the Pharmaceutical Museum, is **St Michael's Tower** (Michalská veža), which gives this street its name. One of the most distinctive landmarks in old Bratislava, the tower was originally connected to a church of this name, which fell into disrepair after the Battle of Mohács in 1526 and was pulled down. The lower part of the tower dates back to the 14C and features a Gothic gate which originally led through the inner walls of the city's fortifications, and is today the main surviving city gate; the upper part of the tower was added in 1511–17, and was given its onion-shaped copper steeple in 1758. The small rooms within the tower contain a well-displayed museum devoted to weaponry and the history of the town's fortifications. Bratislava was renowned for its gunsmiths, and among the objects on show— which range from medieval armour to Second World War machine guns—are firearms dating from the time of Master Heinrich, who is the earliest known of the city's gunsmiths, being first mentioned in 1414; a curiosity is a painting of fighting soldiers (1840) which is riddled with bullets and was originally used for shooting practice. From the highest room in the building you can walk outside to the gallery which encircles the tower and from which an excellent panorama can be had of the town. **Open** Wed–Mon 10.00–17.00.

Walking through the gate and heading south down Michalská, you will pass on the left-hand side of the street, at No. 8, the whitewashed façade of the small Gothic **Church of St Anne** (sv. Anny), built in 1311 and remodelled on the outside in 1845. On the other side of the street, at No. 7, is a house dating back to 1648; this was the birthplace of Johann A. Segner (1704–77), the inventor of the turbine engine and of the so-called Segner's Wheel.

Lower down on the same side, at No. 3, is a Baroque palace built in 1730 for Count Pavol Jesenák, and below this, at No. 1, is the monumental late Baroque façade of the palace now housing the university library of Bratislava, which is the largest library in Slovakia. The palace, featuring a main portal flanked by atlantes, was built to a design by the Italian architect G.B. Martinelli in 1753–56, and functioned up to 1848 as the seat of the Hungarian Diet: it was during the last meeting to be held here that Ľudovít Štúr made his impassioned plea for the abolition of serfdom in Hungary. The university library extends into the palace attached to the southern end of this building, at the entrance to the continuation of Michalská, Ventúrska. Built between 1775 and 1778 for Count Leopold de Pauli, this palace has in its courtyard a charming **Musical Pavilion**, where concerts are still given, and which bears a plaque to the composer Franz Liszt. It was here that the nine-year-old Liszt gave his début performance to a group of five magnates who, on the strength of this concert, decided to finance the prodigy's studies abroad.

Further south down Ventúrská, on the left-hand side of the street at No. 10, is another palace associated with an infant musical prodigy: this, a recently restored palace built in 1747 for the Pálffy family, was where the six-year-old Mozart gave a concert in December 1762 on the invitation of Count Charles Hieronymus Pálffy, the elder son of the court chancellor Leopold Pálffy. Facing it across the street at No. 3 is the **Academia Istropolitana**, which was founded by Matthias Corvinus in 1465 as the first university in Slovak territory.

History of the Academia

During the 25 years of its existence, the Academia Istropolitana attracted a number of internationally renowned teachers, including the astronomer, mathematician and physicist Johannes Müller Regiomontanus and his successor, the Polish astronomer Martin Bylica from Olkusz. The vice-chancellor was the Bratislava provost Schomberg, while the chancellor was the renowned humanist and archbishop of Esztergom, Ján Vítéz. Sadly, however, the institution did not outlive the death in 1490 of its founder and benefactor, Matthias Corvinus, who was not only a brilliant monarch and statesman, but also one of the great scholars of his age. In later years the building was adapted for a number of different educational institutions, and is now the drama department of the Academy of Fine Arts.

The buildings of the Academia Istropolitana, erected on a site originally occupied by the 14C Royal Mint, have been completely remodelled and restored over the centuries and retain little of their original late Gothic and Renaissance elements. At the southern end of the street, at No. 1, is the Rococo palace built in 1770 by M. Walch for Count Erdödy and, behind this, running in a northeasterly direction from the southwestern corner of the old town, is a long pedestrian and shopping thoroughfare comprising the **Panská** and its continuation, Laurinská. The former, into which the Ventúrska leads, was known originally as the Langestrasse or Long Street, and features a great number of elegant 18C palaces.

Turning left into Panská from Ventúrska you will find on the opposite side of the street, at No. 27, the Keglevich Palace, another of the important centres of musical life in the 18C: Beethoven, a teacher and protégé of Countess Babetta Keglevich, was one of the many who gave concerts here. On the same side of the street, a few houses further to the east, at No. 19, is another of the palaces belonging to the Pálffy family. This **Pálffy Palace** shields behind its austerely Classical façade fragments of a building dating back to the 13C and incorporating Roman bricks; altered extensively in the 14C, it was acquired by the Pálffys in the mid-18C, and rebuilt by them in the middle of the following century. Excellently renovated in 1981–87, the palace has housed since 1988 part of the **Bratislava City Gallery** (Galéria mesta Bratislavy).

On the ground floor are shown Slovak paintings of the late 19C and early 20C, among the most interesting of which are some landscapes by Ladislav Mednyanský (in particular the delicately coloured *A Foggy Autumn Day*, and Dominik Skutecký's much-reproduced genre scene, *Market Day at Banská Bystrica*. There are also some interesting Post-Impressionist landscapes of 1913–14 by Anton Jasusch and some early works by one of the leading Slovak painters of the 20C, Martin Benka. You pass through a medieval arch as you walk up to the first floor, where are to be found a group of minor medieval panels which had been housed until recently in the former Convent Church of St Clare. The greater part of this floor is devoted to the pioneering Slovak painters of the 20C, including characteristically Fauve-like landscapes by Ľudovít Fulla (*Piazza San Marco, Venice,* 1930, and *Madonna and Child,* 1935), a further work by Martin Benka (*In the Sliac Valley*) and paintings by Janko Alexy, Jozef Sturdiak and Cyprián Majerník. On the second floor are the gallery's rather dismal foreign school holdings, comprising dull 17C Dutch works, and 16C–18C Italian paintings that are largely school works, copies, anonymous, or wishful attributions; there is also a painting by the obscure Scottish artist William Darling Mackay, representing a ruined castle by the seashore absurdly identified as Edinburgh Castle. Temporary exhibitions are held on the third and top floor of the building. **Open** Tues–Sun 10.00–17.00.

After leaving the gallery, continue to walk along Panská in the direction of Laurinská, and you will pass on the same side of the street at No. 15 the Bállasy Palace, of 1762, at No. 13 the Esterházy Palace of 1743 and, at No. 11, the **Corpus Christi Chapel** (Kaplnka Božicho tela). The latter, now featuring a display of illuminated manuscripts and richly embellished liturgical items, was originally a Gothic chapel of 1390; damaged during the Bethlen Uprising in 1620–22 it was altered in 1627 and remodelled in 1772, when it was frescoed by followers of Maulbertsch.

Return to the junction of Panská and Ventúrská, and continue to follow the former in a southwesterly direction, gradually ascending towards St Martin's Cathedral. On the left-hand side, at No. 33, is the Csáky Palace of 1775, designed by M. Walch in a Louis XVI style and recently restored and given a vivid coat of yellow paint. Adjoining it is a splendid turn-of-the-century pharmacy, which is still functioning and features its original neo-Baroque exterior and furnishings; further on is the Bibiana, an art gallery for children, who are invited to take part in informal art classes. The street ends in Rudnayovo námestie, a small shaded square in which are to be found three commemorative busts, one of these being of Franz Liszt by V. Tilgner (1911), and another by J. Pospíšil of the priest Anton Bernolák, the author of the first standard Slovak grammar. The third bronze, unveiled in 1888 on the occasion of the 200th anniversary of the subject's birth, is of the great Austrian Baroque sculptor Georg Raphael Donner, who lived in Bratislava for ten years and executed works for **St Martin's Cathedral** (Katedrála sv Martina), which rises on steps above the square.

History of the cathedral
The first stone of St Martin's Cathedral was laid at the beginning of the 14C, on the site of the Romanesque Church of the Holy Saviour, which had been transferred here in 1221 from its position on the castle hill. Work on the cathedral continued into the 16C, when the place became the coronation church of the Hungarian kings and queens, which it was to remain until 1830. Between 1863 and 1877 the building was subject to extensive restoration and remodelling.

The cathedral, modest in size in relation to its importance, was attached on its northern side to the town's fortifications, the ruins of which can be seen below. The building's tower, which had a defensive function up to the end of the 15C, has an 85m-high steeple supporting a gilded copy of the royal crown of St Stephen. Entering the building through the early 16C south portal, which has Renaissance features, you find yourself in a three-aisled hall-church with an essentially late Gothic character. None of the medieval furnishings, however, have survived, and the stained-glass windows, the high altar, and the ceiling paintings in the long 16C chancel are all of the 19C. The outstanding work of art here is a bronze group of *St Martin Giving Away his Cape* (1733–35) by Georg Raphael Donner, one of the leading figures of the Hungarian Baroque; this dynamic work, apparently showing the saint dressed in the uniform of a hussar, stood originally on the Cathedral's high altar and was flanked by angels that are now to be found in the Hungarian National Gallery in Budapest. Further works by Donner can be seen in the Baroque St Johann Capistran Chapel, most notably the marble funerary statue of Archbishop Emmerich Eszterházy. On the wall on the left-hand side of the chancel is a list of the nine Hungarian kings and eight queens who were crowned in this building.

Today the old town is divided from the castle hill to the west by a wide flyover, Staromestská, built on what had remained as late as the 1960s of the town's Jewish ghetto, a district which had deteriorated in its later days into what was little more than a slum. Running north from the cathedral and parallel to Staromestská is the still atmospherically decayed Kapitulská, at one time inhabited largely by members of the town's clergy. At No. 26, on the left-hand side of the street, is the former Jesuit college, built in 1629–35 and housing after 1855 the law faculty at which the Slovak writer and patriot Svetozár Hurban Vajanský studied between 1867 and 1870. The building is now used as a seminary, as is the palace on the opposite side of the street at No. 19, which was built for Bishop Juraj Draškovič in 1632.

Towards the end of the street, on the right-hand side, is a small projecting stone house said to be the oldest surviving house in Bratislava. Turn right into Farská, where you will see to your right at No. 3 a well-preserved late medieval house with Renaissance sgraffito decoration. Opposite this is the former

Convent Church of St Clare (Kostol kláštora sv Kláry), built in the 14C and dominated by an elaborate early 15C steeple; the interior, occasionally opened for concerts, is a pleasingly simple single-aisled structure. At the end of the short Farská, turn left into Klariská, on which were once situated the convent buildings. The convent, founded by Cistercian nuns in the 13C and taken over by the mendicant order the Poor Clares at the end of the following century, was burnt down 200 years later, and rebuilt in the 17C to designs supplied by Jacob Rava. Following the abolition of the order of the Poor Clares in 1782, the buildings were used first as the library of Trnava University, and then as a Catholic grammar school; a plaque records that the composer Béla Bartók studied here in 1892–99. The buildings today house the library of the Faculty of Pedagogy.

At the northern end of Klariská, besides steps leading back up again to Kapitulská, turn right on to Baštová, which will take you back to the St Michael's Tower. Cross Michalská into Zámočnícka, which is the eastern continuation of Baštová, and likewise used to run below the city's northern walls; the street was lined in earlier times with locksmiths' workshops. Turn right at the end of the street into the narrow and sloping **Františkánske námestie**.

To your left, at the northeastern corner of the square, is the former **Franciscan church and monastery**. The church (kostol Zvestovania-Františkáni), consecrated in 1297 in the presence of King Andrew III, was damaged by earthquake in the 17C, and largely rebuilt; of the original Gothic building only the chancel remains, a structure which can claim to be the oldest surviving in Bratislava. Apart from a 15C stone *Pietà*, the furnishings of the church are all of the 18C, as are the nave and the adjoining monastery buildings; the medieval tower of the church can now be seen in the Janko Král Park in Petržalka. Just to the south of the church is the Chapel of St John the Evangelist, which was built as the burial chapel for the family of the powerful magistrate Jacob.

Facing the monastery on the northwestern side of the square at No. 11 is one of the city's finest Rococo palaces, the **Mirbach Palace**, which was built for Michael Spech in 1768–70, and excellently restored in the 1980s. The elegant period rooms contain a further selection of old master paintings and other works of art from the Bratislava City Gallery. Of the paintings the most striking are two large canvases of the *Annunciation* and *St Clare*, painted by the Baroque artist Franz Anton Palko for the Church of St Clare. There is a bronze bust of 1780 by the Austrian artist F.X. Messerschmidt and, in the courtyard, a bronze fountain of a Nymph and Triton, executed by a pupil of the 19C Hungarian sculptor Viktor Tilgner, and located previously in the courtyard of the Slovak National Gallery. Of the palace's original furnishings mention must be made of a panelled room covered all over with 18C French prints. **Open** Tues–Sun 10.00–17.00.

Immediately below the Mirbach Palace, at No. 10, is a house dating back to the early 15C; a drinking establishment since the Middle Ages, the place is now an appealing wine bar called the *Vel'kí Františkáni*. Further down the square, past another house of medieval origin at No. 9, is the entrance to Biela; turn left into this street to visit the house at No. 3, which was rebuilt in 1794 by the tobacco merchant Habermayer, and boasts a fire extinguisher of 1820, one of the earliest of its kind.

Return to the Františkánske námestie, and turn right into the southern half of the square, which is built around a small garden. Within this garden is a memorial (1907) by A. Strobl to the Bratislava-born Hungarian archaeologist Florián Romer and, below this, a memorial (1933) to A. Kolísek, the architect of the Slovak National Theatre. Further down still is a **Marian column** of 1675, the oldest such column in Central Europe, which was put up to commemorate the victory of Emperor Leopold over the rebellious Hungarian aristocrats. Facing the column, on the southwestern side of the square, is a small church originally built for the German Protestants in 1634–38; after being taken over by the Jesuits in 1672, it received lavish decorations and furnishings, including paintings by F.X. Palko, and a pulpit with reliefs by L. Gode, a talented pupil of G.R. Donner.

At its southern end the Františkánske námestie leads into the adjoining **Hlavné námestie**, which, despite its relatively small size, was once the main square of Bratislava, a place were markets, popular assemblies and even executions were held. The garden in its middle is dominated by the city's oldest public monument, a **fountain** executed by O. Luttringer in 1572 to celebrate the coronation of King Maximilian; this tall, tapering work is surmounted by a statue of the knight Roland, the traditional protector of municipal rights. Walk in an anti-clockwise direction around the square, which is surrounded mainly by pompous buildings of the 18C and 19C. At No. 7, adjoining Sedlárska, is a palace—built in 1762 for Count Esterházy—where the Russian pianist and composer Anton Rubinstein stayed in 1847. After crossing Sedlárska turn left into the adjacent Zelená to see the house at No. 1, where there is an elegant Baroque fountain in the 18C courtyard.

Return to the Hlavné námestie and turn right, passing after a few metres a magnificent Secessionist building in brilliant yellow (originally a bank and now the *Café Roland*), one of the finest buildings in this style in the city. On the opposite side of the square to this is the most important building on the square, the **Old Town Hall** (Staromestská radnica). Built originally as the private house of the wealthy 14C merchant and civic dignitary Jacob (whose funerary chapel stands in the Dibrovovo námestie), this was adapted after being acquired by the town authorities in the early 15C. Some of the masonry of the 14C structure survives in the façade—graced by a bay window of 1496–97—facing the square; the tower was rebuilt after a fire in 1733. A passage on the other side of the Gothic entrance portal leads into a charming courtyard, with a two-storeyed Renaissance loggia on its northern side. A number of the former civic chambers can be visited, including the Council Hall, which has a splendid coffered ceiling of 1577; next to this is a room exuberantly decorated in 1695 with stuccowork by the Italian Bastiano Orsati and frescoes by the Augsburg artist J. Drentwett. Also to be seen is a room with Pompeian-style decorations painted in 1862 by the Bratislava painter E. Engel. Most of the Old Town Hall and its adjoining annexes are now taken up by the well-displayed historical collections of the **Municipal Museum** (Mestské múzeum), which was founded in 1868 and is one of the oldest museums in Slovakia; there are also small museums devoted to Slovakian wine-making (featuring 6C–7C documents on viticulture—the oldest in existence—decorative wine barrels, old wine presses, vintners' costumes and so on) and to 'feudal justice', the latter installed in the medieval dungeons. Open Tues–Sun 10.00–17.00.

Beyond the Old Town Hall's courtyard with its neo-Gothic wing, you will come out into a quiet square, the Primaciálny námestie, dominated by the massive **Primate's Palace** (Primaciálny palác), which was built in 1777–81 as the winter seat of the Bishops of Esztergom (the Primates of Hungary); the architect of this French-style neo-Classical structure, articulated by a giant order of pilasters, was Melchior Haeferle. The building is famous as the place where the Bratislava Peace Treaty was signed by Napoleon and the Austrian Emperor Franz I in 1805, following the Battle of Austerlitz (two plaques in the courtyard commemorate the event). Functioning as a Town Hall between 1903 and 1947, it has now been fully restored inside, and houses yet more European (and indifferent) works of art from the Bratislava City Gallery. Far more impressive is a rare set of Northlake tapestries whose disputed ownership had once been the source of a heated legal battle between the Church and civic authorities. Designed in the 1630s by F. Cleyn, and representing the tragic love of Hero and Leander, they are now displayed in the palace's most magnificent room—a gilded and chandeliered Hall of Mirrors, where the Hungarian Diet would occasionally hold its assemblies. A 17C statue of St George stands in the palace's courtyard, off which is a chapel decorated with frescoes by Maulbertsch. **Open** Tues–Sun 10.00–17.00.

On the opposite side of the square to the palace is the austere and monstrous **New Town Hall**, built in 1947 over a fine Secessionist building; the original intention was simply to modernise the latter's interior and keep its façade, but the façade mysteriously fell down one night.

East of the square, on the other side of Uršulinská, runs **Klobúčnická**, where at No. 2 a plaque records the birthplace of the pianist and composer Johann Nepomuk Hummel (1778–1837). Behind the uninspired early 20C apartment block on which this is placed is a courtyard where the actual house of his birth has incongruously survived.

Johann Nepomuk Hummel

Born on 14 November 1778, Hummel moved to Vienna when still a child, but was frequently to return to Bratislava in the course of his professional life. A pupil of Mozart for two years, he was *Kapellmeister* to Prince Esterházy from 1804 to 1811, acting for the first five years for the aged Haydn. His peripatetic life led him to Brno, Prague, London, Stuttgart, Eisenstadt and, finally, Weimar, where he died on 17 October 1837. One of the great virtuoso pianists of the 19C, he was influential more on account of his piano playing and technique than for his compositions. Among the many whom he inspired were Franz Liszt and Anton Rubinstein, both of whom donated the proceeds from a dual recital which they gave in Bratislava in 1885 to the creation of the Hummel Memorial in Klobúčnická.

The enchanting small house now forming the **Hummel Memorial** (Rodný dom J.N. Hummela) dates back to the 16C, and has intimate rooms filled with 19C furniture as well as documents, photographs and paintings relating to Hummel's life and times. **Open** Tues–Sun 12.00–17.00. Return to Uršulinská, and walk south down this street to Laurinská, a lively shopping street forming the eastern continuation of Panská. Turning right on reaching this street, you will shortly pass to your right the Apponyi Palace (1761–62), which is attached to the southern end of the Old Town Hall and was acquired by the city authorities in 1867.

At the end of Laurinská turn left into Rybárska brána, which will take you to the avenue marking the southern line of the old town's fortifications, the Gorkého; this skirts the northern side of the impressively long square known as the **Hviezdoslavovo námestie**. You are now in the cultural heart of Bratislava, and to your left, at the eastern end of the square, stands one of the more flamboyant of the city's public buildings, the **Slovak National Theatre** (Slovenské národné divadlo), built between 1884 and 1886 by the ubiquitous F. Fellner and H. Helmer in replacement of an earlier, wooden structure. In front of this white neo-Renaissance building is a playful fountain executed in 1888 by the local sculptor V. Tilgner, and originally intended for the first Bratislava Savings Bank; it is surmounted by a bronze group of Ganymede being carried away by Jupiter disguised as an eagle.

Adjacent to the square, on its southern side, is the *Carlton Hotel* (now closed while awaiting new owners), which is formed out of three hotels joined together in the 1920s; its gilded neo-Baroque café was one of the most stylish of the city's few surviving traditional coffee-houses. A shaded garden lined with imposing 19C buildings comprises the western end of the Hviezdoslavovo námestie. In the middle of this garden is a commemorative statue by J. Pospíšil and V. Ihrisky (1937) of the man after whom the square is named, P.O. Hviezdoslav, a leading Slovak poet and playwright who spent much of his life in Dolný Kubín, where he worked as a lawyer.

Return to the *Hotel Carlton* and turn right down Mostová, which will take you past the **Reduta**, a neo-Baroque structure built in 1912–14 by Komor and Jakab, and intended originally as a casino, dance hall and general place of entertainment. The main hall of this building is today the concert hall of the Bratislava Philharmonic, while the former café attached to the southern side is now used, less romantically, as the head office of Czech Airlines. The Reduta looks south across the small, triangular Námestie Ľudovíta Štúra down to the Danube. This area marks the site of the so-called Coronation Hill, where the kings on horseback would swear to defend their country against its enemies. In the place where T. Bártfay's modern memorial in stone and bronze to the Slovak patriot and codifier of the Slovak language, Ľudovít Štúr, now stands, there once was a great bronze statue of Maria Theresa, executed in 1893–95 by one of the most powerful Hungarian sculptors of the last century, János Fadrusz; its artistic qualities, however, were not recognised by the Slovak patriots who in 1919 blew the work up, thus ridding the city of one of its most eloquent symbols of Habsburg oppression.

At the southern end of the Námestie Ľudovíta Štúra turn left and walk towards the Slovak National Museum, a pompous Classical-style building rising up at the eastern end of a riverside garden, at the junction of Vajanského nábrežie and Fajnorovo nábrežie. In front of the building is a memorial of a lion on a column, intended to celebrate the coming into being on 28 October 1918 of the Czecho-slovak Republic. Executed in 1938, it was originally put in front of the Reduta and was surmounted by a 4m-high statue of Milan Štefánik, shown in pilot's dress.

The original **Slovak National Museum** (Slovenské národné múzeum) was founded in the town of Martin, and only in 1924 was work begun on the one at Bratislava. The building, completed in 1928, was the work of M. Harminc and today houses only the scientific, natural history and geological collections of the museum, the historical and numismatic ones (and the bulk of the archaeological holdings) being now at Bratislava Castle. The dreary, old-fashioned display features a permanent exhibition of mushrooms, the collecting of which comprises one of the great national pastimes; as a result of numerous Slovaks falling ill from

Milan Štefánik

The son of a Slovak Lutheran pastor, Štefánik fell foul of the Hungarian authorities on account of his nationalist tendencies when he was still in his teens. Later he went to Paris and found a post at the Observatoire, which led him on astronomical expeditions to Tahiti and the Sahara. At the outbreak of the First World War he enlisted as a pilot in the French airforce, and earned a reputation for his daring exploits on the Italian and Balkan Fronts. Already he had access to leading French political circles, and through this was able to introduce his fellow Czechoslovak exile, E. Beneš, to a number of key figures in French politics such as Aristide Briand. With the creation of the Czechoslovak Republic, he joined forces with Beneš and Masaryk to form the new country's leading triumvirate. In May 1919, flying home to Slovakia from Italy, he crashed within sight of Bratislava, where a large crowd had come to greet him. This was the first great tragedy in the history of the republic, and the situation was hardly improved by vindictive rumours that he had been shot down deliberately by Czech machine-gunners. For being the bourgeois son of a clergyman, Štefánik became a *persona non grata* at the height of the Stalinist era, and the large statue to him in Bratislava was taken down. His rehabilitation had begun even before the Velvet Revolution of 1989, and it is now highly possible that he will once more be commemorated here.

poisonous mushrooms that they have gathered during their weekend break, every Monday the museum offers a useful 'mushroom consultation', a service offered in other countries by the local pharmacy. **Open** Tues–Sun 09.00–17.00.

From the pier in front of the museum you can take a boat trip along the Danube lasting 1–2hr. One of the bridges under which you will pass is that just to the east of the museum, the **Old Bridge** (Starý most); this, the oldest bridge in Bratislava and originally named the Franz Josef Bridge, dates back to 1888–89, but was rebuilt following its destruction by the Germans in 1945.

Heading east from the museum along Vajanského nábrežie, you will soon reach the Šafárikovo námestie, which marks the southeastern boundary of the old town. The main building here is the Jan Ámos Komenský University, an austere geometrical structure completed in 1938 to a design of F. Krupka. In the garden on the north side of the square is one of Bratislava's most popular fountains: executed by Robert Kühmayer in 1914, it features an exuberant scene of naked boys playfully tormenting some ducks, and is generally referred to by the people of Bratislava simply as 'The Ducks'.

Anyone interested in Hungarian architecture and the Art Nouveau generally should make a short detour from here to the **Little Blue Church** (Modrý Kostolík; continue east down the Dostojevského nábrežie, and then take the first left, Bezručova): this stunning sky-blue church with its curving walls is a work by Ödön Lechner, Hungary's answer to the Catalan architect Gaudí.

Return to the Námestie Ľudovíta Štúra along Vajanského nábrežie and continue along the Danube embankment on the Rázusovo nábrežie. Immediately to the west of the square, overlooking a narrow riverside garden containing a memorial by Fraňo Štefunko to the 19C Slovak painter Peter

Bohún, is Bratislava's most important art gallery, the Slovak National Gallery (Slovenská národná gáleria).

Slovak National Gallery

The façade of this building is most striking, consisting as it does of a bold and diagonally projecting modern frontage raised on bricks so as to afford a rectangular vista of what is in fact the remaining half of a white arcaded courtyard belonging to a former army barracks of 1775–63. Such a radical adaptation of an old building has inevitably been much criticised, but this none the less seems to be far preferable to the heavy and reverential Classical settings in which national collections are usually displayed. Furthermore, the gallery's courtyard fragment—decorated with sculptures from the gallery's collection—has been planted with grass and trees to form a most pleasant small garden, and the building's interior is light and spacious.

Founded in 1948, the Slovak National Gallery brings together a comprehensive selection of paintings and sculptures produced in Slovakia from the Middle Ages up to the present day; the collections are arranged in a roughly chronological way, the earliest works being on the ground floor, and the most recent on the second floor. By far the most distinguished of the medieval paintings are two panels of c 1480–90 representing *The Death of the Virgin* and *The Tree of Jesse*; painted by an anonymous artist known as the **Master of Spišská Kapitula**, they have something of the angular expressiveness and incisive realism characteristic of Master Pavol of Levoča, and reflect the high quality of art produced in the Spiš region in late medieval times.

Among the Baroque works are sculptures by **G.R. Donner** and his pupil **J. Gode**, oil sketches by **F.A. Palko**, **J.L. Kracker**, **F.A. Maulbertsch** and **J. Winterhalter**, a portrait by **J. Kupecký** of c 1700, and three works by **Jakub Bohdan**, an artist who is more widely known as Jakub Bogdani. Of the late 18C sculptures special mention must be made of two grimacing physiological studies in bronze (1770) by **F.X. Messerschmidt**.

Two of the best-known Slovak artists of the Romantic period are the expressive landscapist **K. Marko** and the endearingly naïve **J. Czauczik**, the former represented here by three works (including a Roman landscape of 1838), the latter by two portraits and a landscape with figures (*The Founding of the Rudnanski Spa*, 1815), generally considered to be his masterpiece. Some of the stiff and naïve qualities of Czauczik's art are to be found in the works of **Peter Michal Bohún**, whose eminence among Slovak painters of the 19C is due in part to his political activities: Bohún was one of the organisers of the Slovak Uprising of 1848–49, and one of his works in the National Gallery was actually painted during that period and features a scene from the rebellion. His other six paintings here are all portraits, including a well-known one of a woman in blue called *Davidovej-Revickej* (1853–55).

Genre scenes by the Banská Bystrica painter **D. Skutecký**, and suggestively painted landscapes and figure studies by Medňanský, feature among the turn-of-the-century works in the gallery. **Josef Hanula**, a specialist in peasant genre scenes, is represented by the much-reproduced *On Native Earth*, showing a seated peasant. There are two landscapes (including a *View of Kremnica*, 1890) by **Vojtech Angyal**, a Hungarian painter from the Spiš region who is now usually considered a Slovak artist. The works of **Gustáv Mally**, **Ľudovít Fulla** and **Martin Benka**—artists who all painted Slovak landscapes and rural scenes in vivid colours and bold compositions—feature prominently among the 20C holdings. A more original artist than any of these is **Anthon Jasusch**, by whom there is a Delaunay-like *Yellow Windmill* of 1922. Other painters include **Mikuláš Galanda**, **Konstantín Bauer** (an expressionistic, satirical work entitled *The Judged Woman*, 1927), **Josef Kollár**, **Jan Hála**, **Josef Bendík**, **Elemír Halász-Hradil**, **Zolo Palugyay**, **Janko Alexy**, **Cyprián Majerník**, **Eugen Nevan** and **Peter Matejka**. One of the more recent artists in the collection is the painter of Surreal scenes, **A. Brunovský**, who also designed the former Czech banknotes, a commission which gave rise to the joke that he was paid in his own works. Among the 19C and 20C sculptures in the museum are bronzes by **V.O. Tilgner**, **Ján Koniarek**, **Fraňo Štefunko**, **Jozef Pospíšil**, **Július Bártfay**, **Rudolf Hornák**, **Rudolf Pribiš** and **Jozef Kostka**. Open Tues–Sun 10.00–18.00.

After leaving the museum continue walking west along the Danube embankment, passing on your right two luxury hotels, the *Devín* and (immediately in front of the former SNP bridge) the newly-built, Austrian-run *Hotel Danube*, a blue-and-grey monster that successfully obliterates the beautiful view that could once be had of the castle hill from street level. From here you could work north to the nearby Hviezdoslavovo námestie, and from there regain Ventúrska, which will take you back to the Hurbanovo námestie. Alternatively, you could walk underneath the Staromestská flyover, and ascend the castle hill.

B. Bratislava Castle and Devín

The ascent to Bratislava Castle from the old town is made on the Zámocké schody, a path which begins below the Staromestská flyover, near St Martin's Cathedral. After climbing some steps you should turn to the right on Beblavého to visit the surviving houses (now a growing congestion of bars, galleries and restaurants) on the lower slopes of the castle hill. An 18C house at No. 2 Beblavého has been turned into an intimate café, *At the Golden Sun* (*U zlatého slnka*); next to this, at No. 1, an austere building of the same period houses a Crafts Museum, filled mainly with 17C–19C furniture and furnishings.

Adjacent to the museum, at No. 1 Židovská (Jew Street), is the most charming of the city's Rococo houses, a narrow yellow structure with a gabled side-façade and projecting bay windows decorated with Rococo plaster swirls. Called At the Good Shepherd (Dom U dobrého pastiera) on account of a wall chapel featuring Christ carrying a lamb, this toy-like building contains a **Clock Museum** (Múzeum Hodín), where you can see examples from over four centuries of the art of Bratislava's celebrated clockmakers, who were first documented in the 15C. **Open** Wed–Mon 10.00–17.00.

The name of the street, Židovská, is a reminder of the Jewish ghetto that once stood here: destroyed by the construction of the bridge, this ghetto is fully documented in the recently-opened **Museum of Jewish Culture in Slovakia** (Múzeum židovskej kultúry na Slovensku), which occupies at No.17 a mansion of 17C origin that was remodelled in the 18C and enlarged in the 19C. **Open** Sun–Fri 11.00–17.00.

Return to the Zámocké schody and continue your ascent, looking back occasionally to admire the ever more extensive views towards St Martin's Cathedral and the Danube. You enter the **citadel** through the early 15C Corvinus Gate, which is surmounted by a large ogee arch.

History of the citadel

The history of Bratislava Castle goes back to a fortified Celtic settlement of the 1C AD, on which was later built the Slavic hill-fort of Presslauspurch, which is first mentioned in 907. The Hungarian king Salomon rebuilt the castle in the 11C, and in the following century his great successor Stephen III lived here. In 1189 the place became an assembly point for those taking part in the Third Crusade, which was led by the Emperor Frederick Barbarossa. Between 1431 and 1434 the castle was entirely rebuilt by Sigismund of Luxemburg, who established the present square ground-plan. Further alterations and extensions were carried out between 1552 and 1570 to prepare the place as a base against the Turks and again between 1635 and 1646, following damage caused during the rebellion of Prince Gabriel Bethlen. The latter remodelling gave to the building a third storey and its distinctive corner towers; in 1673 the Emperor Leopold added three artillery embrasures and a new western gate, called today 'Leopold's Gate'.

The present look of the building, however, is due largely to the extensive work undertaken here during the reign of Maria Theresa, when the castle became the seat of the Empress' son-in-law, Albert of Saxony. After Maria Theresa, the castle fell out of favour as a Habsburg residence, and in 1783 Joseph II turned the place into a seminary. Those who worked and studied at this seminary were none too enthusiastic about the castle either, finding it cold and uncomfortable; in 1802 it was converted into a barracks which survived until 1811, when the building was severely damaged by fire.

Left slowly to decay after 1811, the castle suffered further during the Second World War, when bombing left only the outer walls standing. The restoration of the castle was begun in 1954 and completed by 1968, just in time for the signing here in October of the Act of the Czechoslovak Federation, which made Bratislava the capital of the Slovak Socialist Republic. The recently restored building now contains the historical and numismatic collections of the Slovak National Museum.

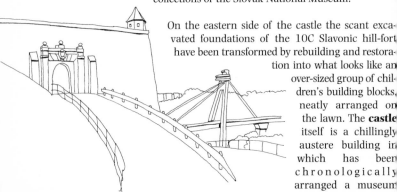

On the eastern side of the castle the scant excavated foundations of the 10C Slavonic hill-fort have been transformed by rebuilding and restoration into what looks like an over-sized group of children's building blocks, neatly arranged on the lawn. The **castle** itself is a chillingly austere building in which has been chronologically arranged a museum with objects, documents and photographs

Bratislava castle and bridge

relating to the history of Slovakia from prehistoric times onwards. The main surviving part of the medieval building is the southeast tower, which is known as the Crown Tower owing to the Hungarian Crown jewels having been kept there until 1783, when they were transferred by Joseph II to Vienna. (At the end of the Second World War they were taken by Hungarian Nazis to Germany, from where they were retrieved by the Americans and removed to Fort Knox; not returned to Hungary until 1978, they can now be seen in the National Museum at Budapest.) Though the castle no longer has these jewels there is the consolation of a **treasury** which was opened here in 1988 and contains dramatically-lit objects mainly from the period of the Great Moravian Empire; the oldest piece, displayed in a glass pyramid at the entrance, is the tiny prehistoric fertility figure known as the Venus of Věstonice, which is carved on a piece of mammoth tusk and is an estimated 25,000 years old. **Open** Apr–Sept daily 09.00–20.00; Oct–Mar 09.00–18.00.

Leave the citadel by the western Leopold's Gate, and turn left, descending down to the Danube on the steps called Schody pri st. vodárni. At the bottom of the steps, at No. 1 Žižkova, is the former Fisherman's Guild, an attractive house dating back to the Renaissance and now containing what is perhaps the city's finest fish restaurant, the *Rybársky cech*. Further down the street, at No. 12, a group of mainly Roman objects and other ancient finds from the Slovak National Museum are on show at the late 16C Kamper mansion. From here you can take Bus 29 almost all the way to Devín Castle, 10km to the west.

The journey is along the Danube, largely through a bosky suburban landscape, the idyllic properties of which had been spoilt during the Communist era by a formidable fence preventing people from jumping into the Danube and swimming across to Austria.

The suburb of **Devín**, at one time well known for its red and blackcurrant wines, has the character of a village (in contrast to the ugly modern urban sprawls of Devínska Nová Ves to the west and Dúbravka to the north). The ruins of its **castle** picturesquely crown a rocky outcrop jutting dramatically above the confluence of the Danube and Morava rivers.

History of the castle

The fortifications at Devín have their origins in a Celtic settlement, on which a Roman camp of the 14th Legion was established in the 2C AD. Although it is now known that Devín was not, as was previously thought, the capital of the Great Moravian Empire (which has been identified as being near Mikulovice in Moravia), the place was clearly an important Moravian settlement, and has a name derived from an old Slavonic word for 'maiden'. The Hungarian king Arpád is said to have come here at the end of the 10C and, recognising the strategic importance of the site, to have exclaimed 'To here and no further'; whether true or not, Devín became the westernmost point of the Hungarian empire.

The present castle was begun in the 13C and extended in the 15C, during the reign of Sigismund of Luxemburg. In the 16C, faced with a potential attack from the Turks, the then owners, the Báthorys, had the castle further strengthened and enlarged. When the Turkish threat had passed, the place lost its strategic importance and from the 18C was left to decay; in 1809 Napoleon hastened its decline by blowing up its surviving parts.

The ruins of the castle acquired great significance later in the 19C, not so much because of their obvious romantic appeal, but because of their associations with the Slavic past. The castle became a popular meeting-place for Ľudovít Štúr and many other Slovak nationalists, to whom the Great Moravian Empire represented a Golden Age.

One of the great attractions of a visit to Devín is the view from the ruins down to the wooded banks of the two rivers and across to distant fertile plains; at the point where the waters meet, the muddy browns of the Morava sharply clash with the more translucent hues of the Danube. Squeezed between the rock on which you stand and the river is an abandoned **amphitheatre** where outdoor plays and performances were put on until 1950, when it was decided that it was dangerous to bring crowds so near to the frontier of capitalist Austria; furthermore the proximity of this border meant that until 1989 taking photographs from this magnificent vantage-point was prohibited. The castle's walls have gradually been restored and in a reconstructed hall a small museum of finds from the site has been installed. Elsewhere there is a memorial plaque to Ľudovít Štúr and a monument to the legendary Moravian maiden after whom the place is named. The wooded hill behind Devín is a protected nature reserve forming part of the **Bratislava Forest Park**, which was created in 1953.

C. Northern Bratislava and the northern environs

North and east of the wide ring of boulevards encircling the old town of Bratislava you come to extensive urban development dating mainly from the post-war years. There are a number of interesting monuments to be seen here, both old and modern, yet these are scattered over a wide area. The bleakness of much of this part of Bratislava is fortunately alleviated by large areas of green and the consoling presence of the nearby wooded slopes of the Carpathian foothills.

Taking as your starting-point the Hurbanovo námestie, begin by visiting the early 18C **Trinity Church** (Kostol sv. Trojice) on the western side of the square. The interior features a spectacular illusionistic decoration commissioned in May 1744 by the Hungarian archbishop, Imre Esterházy, from the great Bolognese specialist in architectural painting, Antonio Galli Bibiena; the decoration, comprising a fictive coffered dome and completed in the remarkable space of a year, is one of the most important examples of *quadratura* or architectural painting in Central Europe.

Head due east of the church along the boulevard which marks the northern limit of the old town, and you will soon come to the unappealingly named námestie SNP, which commemorates the Slovak National Uprising. In the wooded garden in the middle of the square stands a modern memorial to the uprising—three large bronze figures executed by Ján Kulich in a setting devised by the architect Dušan Kuzma. The figures are of a distraught mother and daughter and of a man, who, with rifle at hand and at some distance from the women, stares in the other direction; for obvious reasons this absurd group is popularly referred to as the 'Angry Family'.

Continue heading east until you reach the neighbouring Kamenné námestie, and turn left on to the long and broad Špitálska. After a few hundred metres you will reach, on the left-hand side of this street (at the junction with Hollého), the former **Convent Church of St Elizabeth** (Kostol sv. Alžbety), which was built in 1734–43 by the Viennese architect A. Pilgram; the interior of this imposing building is decorated with frescoes by the great Viennese painter Paul Troger.

The walk further north up Špitálska becomes increasingly tedious, and you would be best advised to take one of the numerous buses and trams that ply its length. Get off at at the Americké námestie, which is at the junction of Špitálska and Mickiewiczova. On the southern side of this square is the enormous **Aspremont Palace** built in 1768–70 by I. Thalherr for Count Aspremont; the building today houses the dean's office and administrative staff of the medical faculty of Comenius (Komenský) University, while the large garden, laid out in a formal French style in the late 18C, is now an attractive public park called the Medical Garden (Medická záhrada). From here it is a short walk south, along the Ul. 21 augusta, to the eastern end of Cintorínska, where you will find the drinking complex known simply as *Mamut*, reputedly the largest beer-hall in the world. The small Floriánske námestie adjoins the northern side of the Americké námestie, and is dominated by a neo-Gothic church designed by V. Rumpelmayer in 1885–88 as the parish church of the once separate township of Blumenthal; more interesting than the church is the magnificent **Florian column** in front of it, a busy and dynamic Baroque work of 1732–38.

Head northwest from the church along Fazuľóvá, turn right at the end of this on to Slovenská, and then left, reaching eventually the long avenue called Mýtna. Walking south along this you will pass on the right-hand side one of Bratislava's most distinctive modern buildings, the black inverted pyramid forming the headquarters of Slovak Radio. Further south along Mýtna is the monstrous Námestie slobody, which was intended in the 1950s as a monumental new main square for Bratislava, but ended up as a grim memorial to the failure of totalitarian town planning. This singularly lifeless space is made pleasant only by its trees and greenery, which, however, have also the effect of detracting from the intended monumentality.

At the lower, southern end of the square is an exploding metallic object scattering water, known as the Fountain of Friendship, by T. Bártfay among others; Bártfay was also responsible for the more intact metal ball (representing Peace) at the top of the square, and for a third work that comprised a morose portrayal of the Communist leader Klement Gottwald apparently sprouting wings, which has now been removed. The buildings lining the southern and western sides of the square are depressing blocks belonging to the Slovak Technical College, while on the eastern side is the vast Post Office building, supposedly the largest in the world, and certainly one of the ugliest (work on this structure was begun before planning permission had been given).

At the northern end of the square, cowering behind trees from the accumulated horrors all around it, is the former **Archbishops' Palace**, the summer palace of the Bishops of Esztergom. Dating back to the 17C, but remodelled in the 18C, it was used by the bishops during the Turkish occupation of Hungary, and abandoned by them shortly afterwards. Its ownership later reverted to the state, and the building served as a garrison hospital during the First World War; heavily restored after 1968 it housed until recently the Slovak Parliament, which has now moved to a bleak modern building west of the Castle.

By the western side of the building runs Spojná, which will take you to the Štefánikova, directly in front of a splendid neo-Rococo palace at No. 25 that once housed a Lenin Museum; this has been replaced today by the similarly didactic and narrowly focused **Museum of Fellow Countrymen** (Krajanské múzeum), which is devoted to the Slovak minority in present-day Hungary, and their attempts to preserve their cultural identity. North of the museum turn left on to Puškinova, where steps will start you off on your climb through pleasant suburbia up the **Slavín Hill**. Turn left at the top of Puškinova, and then first right, and you will come finally to steps leading up to the massive monument which dominates the hill.

The **Slavín Monument**, one of the largest Soviet monuments still standing in Slovakia, commemorates the estimated 6000 Soviet soldiers who died in 1945 in the course of 'liberating' Bratislava. Much of the memorial, which was designed in the 1950s by the architect Jan Svetlík, comprises a large formal garden incorporating a cemetery; from its terraces there are wonderfully extensive views over the city and the distant Danube. At the very centre of the memorial, rising up on steps, is a Hall of Remembrance supporting a gigantic tapering pillar crowned by a bronze statue of a Soviet soldier breaking a swastika in half. This centrepiece is unquestionably one of the most powerful of its kind in Europe. The austerity of the architecture, featuring geometrical, unadorned arcading, is offset by the wealth of statuary surrounding it, executed by the leading Slovak artists of the day, including L. Snopek, J. Kulich, T. Bártfay and Rudolf Pribiš; the hall is decorated inside by the painter J. Krén, while on the outer walls are inscribed the names of the Slovak battles in which the Soviet soldiers took part. The crowning bronze of the Soviet soldier is by A. Trizuljak, who subsequently fell out of favour when it was discovered that he regularly attended Catholic Mass.

Descending the hill turn right into Mišíkova (turning left would take you back into Puškinova); Alexander Dubček lived at No. 46 during the last years of his life. Take the first street to the left, Donovalova, cross Vlčková and continue descending on Kuzmányho. On the next street which you cross, Somolického, there stands at No. 2 the charming early 20C house which belonged to the Slovak poet and translator Janko Jesenský (1874–1945); the building, which was made into a museum in 1952, has been kept exactly as it was in the writer's lifetime. Continue walking down Kuzmányho, turn right on to Moyzesova, and left on to Palisády, then first right on to Štetinova. The latter leads into Panenská, a street lined with distinguished palaces of the 19C, including, at No. 25, a building where the great Hungarian poet and revolutionary Sándor Petöfi once stayed. Lycejná leads south from here to Konventná, passing alongside the Small Protestant Church, built by Römisch in 1778 for Hungarian and Slovak Protestants. On Konventná, at Nos 13 and 15, is the **Protestant Lyceum**, a building associated with many of the leading figures of the Slovak national revival, including Ľudovít Štúr; within the Lyceum can be found the Large Protestant Church, built by M. Walch in 1776. Konventná will take you into the large and rather bleak Mierové námestie, dominated on its southern side by Bratislava's latest and most luxurious hotel, the *Hotel Forum* (1989). On the northern side of the square is the much-altered **Grassalkovich Palace**, built in 1765 by Mayerhofer and now the temporary seat of the the the youth movement known as the Pioneers; there is a bronze plaque recording Haydn's performances at the palace and, in front of the building, a modern fountain by T. Bártfay of frolicking nude women (*The Joy of Life*).

The forests and vine-covered slopes of the **Lesser Carpathians** (malé Karpaty) make for the most popular excursions in the vicinity of Bratislava; much of this gently mountainous area forms part of the vast Bratislava Forest Park, which extends north almost all the way to Modrá. The most accessible place from the city is the hill of **Kamzík**, which can be reached from the Mierové námestie on a No. 13 bus. At the end of the bus route you have a 1.5km walk to the car park adjoining the *Koliba Expo*, a wooden restaurant created for the Montreal World Exhibition of 1968; it is the prototype of the many *kolibas* throughout Czechoslovakia—places where you can eat charcoal-grilled meat in intimate and would-be primitive surroundings. There are numerous walks in the surrounding forest, but the great attraction here is the nearby television tower, which has a restaurant from which you can observe a breathtaking panorama.

A car is really needed to visit the wine-growing villages at the foot of the Lesser Carpathians' eastern slopes. Leave Bratislava on the dual carriageway which heads northeast towards Pezinok. After 15km you pass next to the pleasant small village of **Jur**, which has in its upper part a church of 13C origin commanding views down to the fertile plains to the east; the once German-dominated village has a tradition of wine-growing going back at least to the 13C, when its inhabitants supplied wine to the Hungarian kings.

Pezinok, a further 6km on, is one of the main wine centres of the area, and there are few more stylish places to try the local wines than the town's castle, a building of medieval origin remodelled in 1718: inside are a restaurant and a complex of wine bars. Pezinok was also the childhood home of the leading Baroque artist Ján Kupecký (1667–1740), who is commemorated here by a small museum in the house where he lived. The road to the west of the town takes you across the forested ridge of the Carpathians to Pernek; 13km along the road is the *Baba Hotel*, a good base for walks into the mountains.

Continuing north from Pezinok, after 8km you will reach one of Czechoslovakia's most famous wine centres, **Modra**, a small town which has retained a 17C gate-tower (within which a wine-bar has been installed) and other fragments from its original fortifications. On the main square, where there is another good wine-bar, stands a statue of Ľudovít Štúr, who lived here from 1850 until his death in 1860, staying in his last years in a house at No. 84. In 1956 the house was turned into a memorial museum containing furniture, photographs and other exhibits relating to his life and times; he is buried in the local cemetery. As well as being a wine centre, Modra is well known for its ceramics, which are characterised by colourful floral patterns set against a white background.

Northwest of Modra a small road climbs up through forest 6km to **Zochova chata**, a complex of wooden buildings comprising a hotel, a *koliba* (see above), a restaurant, and a lively small bar (*Furmanská krčma*); this is a place geared in its appeal to those with a longing for log cabins and the 'simple life' of a forester.

Eight kilometres due north of Modra is the castle of **Červený Kameň**, standing in a beautiful wooded setting at the eastern edge of the mountains. This mammoth building of medieval origin was acquired by the Fuggers of Augsburg in 1533 and converted by them into a great storehouse; it is said that the ingenious defensive system which the Fuggers installed (involving a novel way of extracting gunpowder smoke) was designed by the painter Albrecht Dürer, some of whose architectural projects feature comparable bastions.

In 1588 the place passed into the hands of the Pálffy family on the marriage of Nicholas Pálffy to Maria Magdalena Fugger. The former fortress was subsequently converted into a splendid château, featuring a *sala terrena* in the form of a grotto. The recently restored and extensively stuccoed interior is largely taken up by a collection of furniture and other applied arts objects (including some notable Renaissance and Baroque chests and cupboards) acquired during the Communist period from confiscated mansions all around Central Europe; in addition there is an exhibition relating to the building's fascinating defensive system, and an extensive collection of military items amassed by Rudolf Pálffy, among which are some wonderfully ornamented scimitars and hunting guns dating back to the Turkish occupation of Hungary. **Open** May–Aug Tues–Sun 09.00–17.00; Apr, Oct Sat, Sun 12.00–16.30.

A further 20km drive north through gently rolling, wooded countryside will take you to **Smolenice**, a former royal castle dating back to the 13C and given a most picturesque pseudo-medieval look by the Pálffys at the end of the 19C; it now belongs to the Slovak Academy of Sciences, and is used for conferences.

D. Petržalka and Rusovce

The modern **Bridge of the Slovak National Uprising** (most SNP), which spans the Danube at a point between the castle hill and the Cathedral of St Martin, is one of the most distinctive features of the Bratislava skyline. This bold yet graceful structure is held up by enormous lengths of British-made cable swung from a tall tower formed of two massive pillars supporting high above the ground an oval structure resembling a flying saucer. The latter contains a restaurant which should have been revolving had not the funds run out; the view is at any rate impressive, and worth the queue to get into the small lift which makes the vertiginous ascent.

The tower is on the southern banks of the river, in the largely residential district of **Petržalka**—a district of endless grim high-rise blocks housing a third of the city's population and claiming the highest suicide rate in Slovakia. Apart from the bridgehead the only reason why tourists might come here is to visit the large and wooded **riverside park** adjoining the bridge's eastern side. Named today after the 19C Slovak poet and revolutionary Janko Král, it was founded in the late 18C and as such is one of the oldest public parks in Europe. Among its attractions are a Gothic tower taken from the Franciscan church on the Františkánske námestie, a statue of Král executed by F. Gibala (1964) and another by A. Rigele of the singer O. Trebitsch (1922). But the most impressive of the memorials is the one to Král's Hungarian contemporary and fellow poet, Sándor Petöfi, a powerful work by J. Fadrusz, a leading Hungarian sculptor of the late 19C.

Bus 101 will take you 5km south of Petržalka to Zrkadlový háj, where a large pond forms a nudist swimming pool. Four kilometres further on is the riverside village of **Rusovce**, featuring a 19C château in an English neo-Gothic style, now used by the Slovak Folk Art Ensemble.

Nearby there was accidentally uncovered in 1961 the scant remains of the Roman trading settlement of **Gerulata**; the main interest of the site is its small museum of Roman finds, including a relief sculpture of the mid-2C AD representing Attis.

26 · Bratislava to Zvolen

A. Via Komárno

Total distance 266km: Bratislava (leave by Road 63/E575) • 100km Komárno • 44km Štúrovo • 122km Zvolen.

South and east of Bratislava extends a vast featureless plain, characterised by its ugly small towns and the endless expanses of wheatfields that give the area its reputation as the 'Granary of Slovakia'. The landscape strongly recalls that of neighbouring Hungary, and indeed this is the part of Slovakia with the largest Hungarian minority.

Leave Bratislava on Road 63, which has little of architectural let alone scenic interest for at least 100km. However, at Nové Košariská, 8km southeast of Bratislava, you can make a short detour 6km to the south to visit the tiny village of **Hamuliakavo**, which has a charming Romanesque church in a green and wooded setting. Built at the beginning of the 13C and restored in the 19C, this white-washed building has a fine Romanesque tower and an apse featuring blind arcading. Besides the nearby marshy banks of the Danube is a cormorant sanctuary.

Rejoin Road 63 at Šamorín, 6km to the east, and continue driving for a further 24km to **Dunajská Streda**. This is an ugly industrial town which has, isolated among modern buildings in its centre, a 14C church (remodelled in the 18C), with small fragments of 14C wall-painting on the left-hand side of the chancel. The flatlands north of the Danube have a number of thermal pools, around which holiday resorts have grown up; one of these, congested at week-ends in the summer, is to be found on the southern outskirts of the town. Another such resort is outside the dull small town of Cǎlovo, 21km futher south.

Road 63 finally reaches the Danube at **Komárno**, 33km southeast of Cǎlovo, and by far the most interesting town in this little-visited corner of Slovakia.

History of Komárno

The town of Komárno grew up besides a celebrated fortress, situated near the confluence of the Danube and the Váh, on the site of the Roman military camp of Kelemantia. First mentioned in 1075, the fortress successfully withstood Tartar invasions in the 13C, and became in the 16C one of the most important Hungarian centres in the struggle against the Turks. The Turks, who first besieged the town in 1529, finally destroyed the place in 1594. Between 1663 and 1673 a new fortress with a star-shaped plan was built by the Emperor Leopold alongside the old one, and at the time of the Napoleonic Wars a system of bastions and walls known as the Palatine Line was put up in between the Danube and the Váh. A thriving commercial centre in the 18C, Komárno is today a lively market and industrial town, with large shipyards. The place holds an important position in the cultural history of Hungary, being the birthplace of both the writer Mór Jókai

(1825–1904) and the composer Franz Lehár (1870–1948), who was the son of a bandmaster attached to the local garrison.

Komárno, though not the most beautiful of towns, is a place with an enormous vitality belying a faded, turn-of-the-century character. The population is mainly Hungarian, and the street-signs were in two languages until recently. On the square directly in front of the bridge which leads into Hungary is a modern bronze statue to the composer Franz Lehár, a Hungarian by birth despite attempts to claim him as Slovak, but whose charming operettas such as *The Merry Widow* (1905) belong essentially to the world of *fin-de-siècle* Vienna. West of the square, at No. 32 Gábora Steinera, is a small and dusty **museum** devoted both to Lehár and to the writer Mór Jókai, whose romantic historical novels such as *Midst the Wild Carpathians* enjoyed an international vogue in the late 19C, and were brought out in numerous English editions; the museum contains photographs and other mementoes of the two Hungarians, and even has two writing desks which belonged to Jókai.

In the 16C Serbians fleeing from the Turks formed a small Serbian community at Komárno, and in the courtyard adjoining the museum stands a fascinating **Serbian Orthodox Church** (Pravoslávny kostol). The original church, filled with 16C icons that the Serbians had taken with them from their native land, was burned down and replaced by an early 18C structure. Some of the icons from the earlier building can be seen behind the magnificent Rococo iconostasis; the Rococo stalls meanwhile are from the Camaldensian monastery of Majk in Hungary, which was dissolved by Joseph II and its furnishings sold off. The church functioned up to 1953, the services conducted by a Hungarian priest who came up once a month from the Hungarian town of Szentendre.

Returning to the riverside square head along the eastern continuation of Gábora Steinera. On the left-hand side you will come shortly to the elegant building of the local museum, in front of which stands a powerful late 19C bronze statue of the seated Jókai, at whose feet wreaths and flowers are still placed. Beyond is the late 19C Town Hall, and further along, on the right-hand side of the street, is the former Officer's Casino, a decayed and very evocative neo-Gothic monument from the last days of the Habsburg Empire (the building is now a restaurant).

On the northwestern outskirts of the town is Komárno's celebrated **fortress**, which has now been radically restored to display a large collection of Roman sculptures, including copies of Roman works from all over Slovakia. **Open** Tues–Sun 10.00–17.00.

From Komárno, Road 63 follows the Danube (Dunaj) all the way to Štúrovo, 44km away. **Patince**, 10km to the east of Komárno, has mineral springs that were known to the Romans and is today the largest of the thermal resorts in this part of Slovakia; there are two large swimming-pools fed from the springs, and numerous ungainly bungalows spread out over a large area of grass and trees. Štúrovo is in itself a place of little interest, but there are tantalising views over the Danube to the town of Esztergom, dominated by the hill on which rises the massive neo-Classical cathedral of the Hungarian primates. At Štúrovo you leave the Danube and head due north on Road 76, following for 41km the winding river Hron.

The quiet small town of **Želiezovce**, 29km north of Štúrovo, has an 18C château which belonged to the Esterházys, who invited here on two occasions the composer Franz Schubert.

Franz Schubert

Schubert, the son of a Moravian peasant schoolteacher and of a Viennese cook, was an impoverished 21-year-old living in Vienna when in 1818 he was invited to Želiezovce to teach the daughters of J.K. Esterházy. He arrived here on 7 July and remained until 19 November; six years later, in 1824, he was here again, staying from 25 May to 17 October. His best pupil was Karolina Esterházy, who accompanied him daily at the piano, and for whom he composed several works. While at Želiezovce, Schubert took a keen interest in the life of the villagers, and also made a number of important friendships, most notably with the singer K. Laczná, the actress Z. Müller and Baron Schönstein, who sang his songs. Among the numerous piano duets that he wrote here were his *German Dances* (D618), *Polonaises* (D618A), *Divertissements à la Hongroise* (D818), and two works that he dedicated respectively to Beethoven and Karolina Esterházy, *Variations* (D624) and the four-hand *Fantasy* (D 940).

The château at Želiezovce was built in 1720 but remodelled towards the end of the 18C. Schubert stayed in a small late 18C Classical building in the park; this charming place, known as the Owl's Lodge, has housed since 1970 a small commemorative museum devoted to the composer's life. Twelve kilometres north of Želiezovce, turn right on to Road 75, which crosses the Hron and passes through Demandice after 13km. Eight kilometres further east is the junction with Road 66, which heads directly to Zvolen 62km to the north (see Chapter 28), passing through progressively hillier and more wooded landscape. After 30km you will come to the unremarkable small town of **Krupina**, which was the birthplace of the Protestant clergyman and leading Slovak poet of the Štúr generation, Andrej Sládkovič (1820–72), who succesfully merged erotic and patriotic love in a famous long poem entitled *Marína*, a work inspired by an unhappy affair with a burgher's daughter from Banská Bystrica; his life and work is chronicled in a local history museum situated near the house of his birth, which is marked by a plaque.

For those with a passion for Hungarian literature, an alternative and much longer route from Demandice to Zvolen is to cross over Road 66 and continue

Kálmán Mikszáth

Mikszáth, the son of peasants descended from the lesser nobility, was a writer whose art was rooted in the oral culture of both the peasantry and the landed gentry. His greatest novels took their inspiration from his native region (known in Hungarian as Nógrád County), which, though barely 100km from Budapest, was thought of as a remote provincial backwater characterised by its sleepy conservatism, decayed estates and eccentric impoverished aristocrats. Among these novels were the two works that first established his reputation, *Slovak Yokels* (1881) and *The Good Palots* (1882), the latter's title being a reference to the *palócs* dialect spoken by the Hungarians here. His humorous and gently ironic tales of rural life gained him numerous international admirers, including Theodore Roosevelt, who made a special journey to Budapest to go and see him.

heading east along Road 75. Turn right 45km beyond the junction, on to the side road which runs a further 8km to **Sklabiňa**, the home village of Kálmán Mikszáth (1847–1910), who, with Jókai, was the most widely read Hungarian prose writer of the 19C.

Editions of Mikszáth's books in many languages, together with numerous photographs and personal objects, can be seen in the small museum installed in the house where he lived; visits to this should be arranged beforehand with the regional museum at nearby Modrý Kameň: ☎ (0854) 51103.

Another major Hungarian cultural shrine awaits you at the small village of **Dolná Strehová** (known in Hungarian as Alsósztregova), which lies 21km to the east off Road 75. Here, in a modest neo-Classical mansion set in an extensive park, the playwright, poet and essayist Imre Madách (1823–64) wrote one of the most celebrated works of Hungarian literature, *The Tragedy of Man* (1862).

The Madách mansion is now a memorial museum administered, like the one at Sklabiňa, by the regional museum at Modrý Kameň (see above). Inside, you

Imre Madách

Alsósztregova had been the family seat of the Madách family for five centuries when Madách was born there in 1823, in the present mansion, which had been built by his Catholic convert grandfather as a replacement for the 'old castle' that had dominated the village. Plagued by constant ill health and raised with strict economy (his father had died in 1834, leaving his widow to look after five children and an estate that was heavily in debt), Madách found consolation in the wide-ranging library of books that filled the family home. After training as a lawyer in Pest, Madách returned home in 1840 to become a deputy notary for the county of Nógrád. Four years later, at a country ball, he fell in love with a passionate and highly neurotic 17-year old, whom he married the following year despite heavy opposition from his mother, who objected to the bride's flirtatiousness, Protestant status and lower social rank. At first the marriage was successful, but tensions developed as Madách became increasingly involved in radical politics, which led him to play an active role in the Hungarian Revolution of 1848–49. The mood of national tragedy that befell Hungary after the unsuccessful revolution was exacerbated in Madách's case by a series of personal disasters, including the murder by bandits of one of his sisters, the death of his brother Imre, the hanging of his remaining brother's fiancée (who had served in the Ministry of Finance of the revolutionary government), and the confiscation of all the revenues from his estates, together with a period of nearly two years in prison for his having sheltered the former secretary of the defeated Hungarian leader Kossúth. Finally, returning home from prison in 1853, he discovered that his wife had been unfaithful to him during his absence; the marriage was dissolved shortly afterwards.

Unsurprisingly Madách became ever more withdrawn after all these experiences and began devoting most of his time to reading and writing in his Alsósztregova study, which he nick-named the 'Lion's Den'. It was here, in 1859–60, that he wrote *The Tragedy of Man*, a lyric drama inspired by Milton, Goethe and Byron, and featuring moments of human history from the Creation on into the future.

can see the writer's study or 'Lion's Den', as well as many personal items and pieces of furniture that belonged to him. A crypt in the large garden contains his tomb; and in the village church there is a painting by him of St Sebastian that has the features of his beloved brother Imre, who was killed while working as a dispatch-carrier during the Revolution of 1848–49.

From the village you can continue a further 45km to Zvolen by heading northwest on the side-road that follows the pleasantly verdant banks of the Tisovník river, crossing Road 75 after 7km and passing through the village of Dolný Tisovník. Ten km east of Zvolen you reach the E571, which leads 8km east to the large village of **Detva**, which in mid-July hosts one of the best-known folk festivals in Slovakia; the village cemetery has the carved wooden grave-markers resembling totem-poles that are such a feature of traditional rural Hungary.

B. Via Nitra

Total distance 196km: Bratislava (leave by Road 62/E571) • 96km Nitra • 62km Žarnovica • 15km Banská Štiavnica • 27km Zvolen.

Head east from Bratislava on the E571, passing through dull, agricultural countryside, which is unrelievedly flat until you reach **Nitra**, a large town sprawled underneath a prominent citadel, and with the pleasing sight of vine-covered slopes rising to the north.

History of Nitra
Nitra rose to prominence in the 9C AD, when it became one of the most important centres of the Great Moravian Empire. In 820 the Moravian Count Pribina made the town his seat, and founded here shortly afterwards the first Christian church in Slovakia; in 880 the town was raised to a bishopric. After the fall of the Moravian Empire, Nitra became the residence of the Hungarian apanage princes, which it was to remain until the end of the 11C. Subsequently it suffered from a brief period of subjugation to the Bohemian Přemysl king Otakar II, and was much damaged in the course of Tartar raids, the Hussite Wars, and the Hungarian rebellions led by the Zapolys, the Bethlens and Ferenc Rákóczi. The greatest damage of all was caused by the Turks, who repeatedly raided the castle in the 16C and 17C and in 1663 managed finally to conquer the town, which they afterwards destroyed. Nitra today has developed into a prosperous industrial town and a leading wine-growing and agricultural centre. The Agricultural University of Slovakia is situated here, and hosts every year an important agricultural fair with the Freudian-sounding name of AGROKOMPLEX.

The main monuments of interest in Nitra are concentrated in the town's **citadel**, the earliest surviving parts of which date back to the 11C; new fortifications were erected in the Middle Ages and again in 1603, and most of the buildings to be seen today within the walls are largely of the 17C and 18C. You enter the complex through a gate on the northern side of the Župne námestie, and climb up the Samova Pribinova until you reach a green and sloping square, the **Pribinovo námestie**. The heavy Baroque houses which line the Samova Pribinova and the southern side of the square were once used exclusively by the clergy, but today have been appropriated by local government offices and drab museums, including an Agricultural Museum. This whole part of town has an empty, forsaken character. At the upper northern end of the square stands an exuberant Marian **plague column** executed by Fogerle in 1750 and restored in 1956, and behind this rise the walls of Nitra's castle, entered through a Renaissance gate. Immediately inside the castle grounds are the **Cathedral of St Emeram** (Katedrála sv. Emerama) and the adjoining bishop's palace. The latter was built in 1732–39 above the basement of a medieval palace; it has rich Baroque decorations inside, but is not usually open to the public. The cathedral's history is a complex one, and the present building, entered through the south portal, comprises in fact three separate churches. After turning right as soon as you enter the building you will find a modern door leading to the old cathedral, which was built in 1064 over the church founded by Prince Pribina in c 833: this tiny whitewashed space was rebuilt in the 13C and 14C and renovated in the 18C, but it still retains its Romanesque apse. The main body of the cathedral features an upper and lower church, the former dating back to 1333–55 (but remodelled in the 18C), and the latter to the early 17C; these two structures, separated by a sacristy, form together a dark and oppressive whole, with gloomy Baroque frescoes.

Returning to the Župne námestie at the foot of the citadel, you should visit the large Art Nouveau building at No. 3, which was built in 1874 as the County Hall, and today houses the **Regional Gallery** (Nitrianska galéria), containing an important collection of 19C and 20C Slovak artists, including works by Jozef Kollár, Janko Alexy, Martin Benkaz, Gustáv Malý, Jozef Šturdík, Július Bártfay and Rudolf Pribiš. There is in addition a permanent exhibition of the paintings of František Studený, who was born in 1911 in the nearby village of Nová Ves nad Žitavou, and died in Bratislava in 1980; his works mainly comprise expressively painted still-lifes and landscapes. **Open** Tues–Sun 09.00–16.00.

Of the other old buildings in the uninspiring lower town of Nitra, the most prominent is the twin-towered 18C **Franciscan church**, which stands below the eastern slopes of the citadel, and has a richly frescoed interior belying a drab façade. Directly south from here, off the lower end of Farská, is a neo-Moorish **synagogue** (now serving as a concert and exhibition hall), the enormous size of which testifies to the former importance of the town's Jewish community—the subject in 1934 of a powerful novel, *Broken Branch*, by Gejza Vámoš, the son of a local Hungarian Jewish railway official. North of the citadel is the **Zobor Hill**, a pleasant suburban district with vines growing on its upper slopes; there are several popular wine-bars here, most notably the *Zoborská pivnica* on Dobšinského.

After Nitra continue driving east along Road 65/E571, after 12km passing the ruined castle of Jelenec; 2km further on is a turning to the left to the charming unspoilt village of **Kostolány pod Tribečom** 4km away, which has a whitewashed 10C church claimed to be Slovakia's oldest standing building. Return to Road 65; 16km beyond Zlaté Moravce, 25km from Nitra, the road turns sharply north and follows the narrow, wooded valley of the upper Hron, approaching ever closer to the mountains of Central Slovakia.

Banská Štiavnica

At Žarnovica, 62km northeast of Nitra, leave the main road and turn right to Banská Štiavnica 21km away, a small town lost today among high wooded hills but with a fascinating and important history, and with the potential to be one of the major tourist sights of Slovakia.

History of Banská Štiavnica

The historical importance of Banská Štiavnica is due to its silver and gold mines, which were exploited from at least the mid-13C onwards, when the place was made a royal free town. The local mining activity reached a peak in the late 15C, and then briefly declined in the following century; in 1526 what was probably the first mining strike in history was organised here. The Turkish capture of Buda in 1541 led to further anxiety in the town, and to the construction of the so-called New Castle and other fortifications. The mining industry was revived in the early 17C, and in 1627 the use of gunpowder in mines was first tried out here; a further innovation occurred in 1732 with the use of a steam engine to pump out water from the mines. By the 18C the town's population had grown to 24,000 (as opposed to only 10,000 today), making the place the third largest town in Hungary. In 1760 the world's first Mining Academy was opened here; but the seams were finally exhausted in the early 19C, and though a forestry school was founded here in 1807, the town slowly stagnated. A campaign to transform the old town into a tourist showpiece has been slowly progressing since the late 1980s, and in 1993 the place was added to UNESCO's World Heritage List.

Banská Štiavnica, a town little spoilt by modern development, is spread meanderingly along the slopes of a hill, and its layout is at first rather baffling. The place has a decayed character, but at present is undergoing major restoration, the scaffolding throughout the old centre adding to the general confusion. The main square is the narrow and sloping **Trinity Square** (Trojičné námestie), at the bottom of which is the **Church of St Catherine** (Kostol sv. Kataríny), a hall-church dating back to 1488–91 with wall-paintings of c 1500 inside; facing it is the belfried Town Hall, an originally Gothic building remodelled in the mid-18C. Half-way up the square, on the right-hand side, is the **Hellenbach House**, a 16C structure built originally as the seat of the Court of the Hungarian Mining Towns; it now houses a museum with geological finds from the mines. The adjacent building, also of the 16C, but with traces of murals on the outside, is now the **Jozef Kollár Gallery**, which has examples of local art from prehistoric times right up to the present day, some of the works being displayed in rooms with impressive Renaissance portals and carved wooden ceilings: there is a large group of landscapes by the inter-war artist after whom the gallery is named, but more memorable are the elaborated carved statues of SS Catherine and Barbara attributed to the Master M.S. **Open** Mon–Fri 08.00–16.00.

After walking back to the Town Hall and turning right you will soon reach the **Old Castle** (Starý zámok), the present appearance of which is due largely to the work carried out between 1546 and 1559 in anticipation of Turkish attacks; the building, which has been closed for many years for restoration, was once destined as a museum devoted to the history of mining in Slovakia. This museum has now been installed in the so-called Clapper Tower, a late 17C tower located south of the Town Hall, at 21 Andreja Sládkoviča (see below).

As you make your way there, you will pass, at the entrance to the street, the newly restored **Belházyho dom**, a fine Renaissance palace (now a hospital) featuring an arcaded loggia in its courtyard. Once inside the **Clapper Tower** (Klopačka), you will find atmospheric, low-ceilinged rooms housing a particularly good collection of old mining-lamps as well as the eponymous 'clapper'—a device once used to wake up the miners at five in the morning (it now 'claps' at 10.00 and 14.00, but solely for the benefit of tourists, and only in the summer months).

Continuing south along this street, you will leave the old town through the isolated 18C **Piarg Gate** (Piargska brána), the massive size of which is a reminder of the town's former importance. Nearby is the **New Castle** (Nový zámok), which stands in trees high above the town, and was built in 1564–71 as a guard tower against the Turks. This simple, harmonious structure, comprising an unadorned and whitewashed central rectangular block buttressed by round towers at each corner, has been entirely modernised inside to house an interesting museum documenting the Turkish presence in Slovakia. The upper floor, dominated by a bewildering relief map of 17C Slovakia, has excellent views from its low windows down to the town.

Further south, on the the the road leading to Štiavnické Bane, is a **Miners' Skansen** (Banské múzeum v prírode), an area of 20 acres in which numerous old mining houses and other structures have been assembled, and where you can even visit a mine—a cold and claustrophobic experience (hard hats and overcoats have to be worn) which gives you a good idea of the awfulness of the original mining conditions. **Open** May–Sept Tues–Sun 08.00–16.00; Oct–Apr Mon–Fri 08.00–16.00.

Enjoying your return into the open air, you could go back to the town centre and head northeastwards up to the imposing early 19C **Academy of Mining and Forestry**, which has delightful botanical gardens containing one of the best arboretums in Central Europe; from there you could continue up to the hilltop church of **Štiavnica kalvária**, to enjoy both its superb panorama and the exuberant Baroque statuary of the Calvary chapels leading up to it.

Another possible outlying trip is to the Baroque mansion at **Antol**, 5km southeast of the town on the road marked to Krupina (see Route 26A). The mansion, built between 1744 and 1750 for the Koháry family, has kept on the first floor much of its original furnishings and decorations (mainly by Austrian and German artists), including an illusionistically frescoed chapel, a drawing-room with paintings and mirrors set in wooden panelling, and a theatrical staircase with statues by D. Stanetti and allegorical ceiling frescoes by A. Schmidt. Other parts of the building are devoted to exhibitions of falconry and hunting, which explains why the mansion hosts annual celebrations in honour of the patron saint of hunting, St Hubert. These celebrations, featuring the off-putting spectacle of a captured stag being led around in procession, are held early in September in magnificent grounds landscaped with lakes, waterfalls, an aqueduct, an artificial grotto and a giant sequoia planted in 1878.

Twenty kilometres north of Banská Štiavnica you rejoin the E571/Road 50 and head east along dual carriageway to Zvolen (see Chapter 28). For those without a car the most enjoyable way of travelling between these two towns is to take the **scenic railway** built by youth 'volunteers' during the early Communist days (you must change trains at Hronská Dúbrava).

27 · Bratislava to Žilina

Total distance 199km: Bratislava (leave by the D61/) • E75 46km Trnava • 33km Piešt'any • 42km Trenčín • 78km Žilina.

Trnava

Drive northeast of Bratislava on the dual carriageway of the E75, passing in succession on the city's outskirts a large group of chemical works and the lake of Zlaté Piesky, a popular place for bathing and boating. The exit for Trnava is 46km beyond Bratislava. A large lowland town, Trnava has played an important role in Slovakia's ecclesiastical history, and is sometimes referred to as the 'Slovak Rome'.

History of Trnava

First mentioned in 1205, Trnava was made the first royal free town in Slovakia by Bela IV of Hungary in 1238. Only four years later the place was devastated by Tartar hordes led by Peta Khan, the nephew of the infamous Ghengis. Further royal privileges helped the town rapidly to recover and to develop as a thriving commercial and agricultural centre. Following the Battle of Mohács in 1526 the Hungarian archbishopric at Esztergom was transferred here, thus making the town the main religious centre of Hungary, a position which it was to retain for over 200 years. In 1635 Archbishop Petr Pázmány founded here a Jesuit academy, which was later raised to the status of university. The transference of this large and influential institution to Buda in 1777, and the return to Esztergom in 1820 of the archbishopric, led to the town's diminished importance in Hungarian affairs. At the same time, however, the place emerged as a major centre of the Slovak national revival, for it was here, in 1792, that Anton Bernolák, the first codifier of the Slovak literary language, founded the first Slovak Learned Society. From the mid-19C onwards the town was extensively industrialised, and in 1990 the archbishopric was re-established. The Hungarian composer Zoltán Kodály (1882–1967) spent much of his childhood here, his father being the local stationmaster.

The description of Trnava as the 'Slovak Rome' gives a misleading impression of the appearance of the town today, which has scarcely been improved either by the return of the archbishopric in 1990 or by the celebrations held two years earlier to commemorate the town's 750th anniversary: almost deserted at weekends, it remains a sprawling and decayed place where the surviving old parts are unhappily combined with tasteless modern development. The town centre, which is surrounded by extensive remains of the old fortifications, has in its northeastern corner a 17C–18C university district dominated by what is undoubtedly the most exciting building in the town—the massive **University Church of St John the Baptist** (Univerzitný kostol sv. Jána Krstitelǎ). The austere twin-towered façade of this church, built in 1637 to the designs of the Italian architect Pietro Spazzo, belies a richly stuccoed single-naved interior featuring a gilded altarpiece reaching right up to the ceiling. The surrounding university buildings are remarkable more for their scale than architectural elegance, as is also the case with the nearby 16C Archbishop's Palace, which stands to the south of here, at the eastern end of the town's main street, Hviezdoslavova. Next to the palace is the Cathedral of St Nicholas (Katedrála sv. Mikuláša), an ungainly Baroque structure which dates back to a parish church of 1380, the original form of which can be gleaned above all in the chancel.

Heading west from the cathedral along Hviezdoslavova, and passing in turn a **Book Museum** (Múzeum knižnej kultúry) chronicling the town's important intellectual history and the Ján Koniarek Gallery—named after the pompous early 20C Slovak sculptor Ján Koniarek (temporary exhibitions only)—you will come to Trnava's most attractive and best-maintained square, the newly restored **Trojičné námestie**. Centred on a dynamic 18C plague column, this square's buildings include a 16C Municipal Tower, a neo-Classical Town Hall, and a charmingly preserved salmon-pink theatre of 1831, the oldest such structure in Slovakia.

Returning to the cathedral and walking south down Kapitulská, you will pass immediately to your right a small street, Haulíka, containing a ruined neo-Moorish **synagogue**, and directly opposite this, a former Orthodox Jewish *shul* that has recently been transformed into a branch of the Ján Koniarek Gallery. Trnava's now defunct Jewish community was expelled from the city in the 16C by the Habsburg Emperor Ferdinand but allowed to return in 1862; a black marble memorial in front of the *shul* commemorates the 2000 or so local Jews who were killed in the Holocaust. Further objects from Trnava's Jewish past can be seen in the **West Slovakian Museum** (Západoslovenské múzeum), which you will reach at the southern end of Kapitulská. The museum, installed within a former Clarissine convent of the Baroque period, contains a remarkably wide range of holdings, from ethnographical displays and reconstructed old interiors to collections of bells, clocks, wine-presses and even Chinese and Japanese craft objects; but perhaps the most interesting section is the enormous group of folk pots, copper and tin utensils, Jewish ritual objects, and other miscellanea amassed by a local baker and confectioner called Štefan Cyril Parák (1887–1969). **Open** June–Sept Tues–Sun 10.00–18.00; Oct–May 11.00–16.00.

Seven kilometres northwest of Trnava is **Dolná Krúpa**, a château built for the Brunswick family in 1793–94, and now the property of the Slovak Union of Composers. Beethoven, a friend of the Brunswicks, stayed frequently in the Rococo pavilion in the château grounds and composed here in 1801 his *Moonlight Sonata*; in 1992 the pavilion was turned into a **Beethoven Memorial Museum** featuring documents relating to the composer's life and work, in particular to his stays in Slovakia and the reception of his music here.

Along the Váh

As you continue north from Trnava along the D61/E75 you join the valley of the river Váh, which you follow all the way to Žilina. After 12km there is an exit leading to the small town of **Hlohovec** (5km from the E75, on the opposite side of the Váh), which has a Jewish cemetery where the mother of the German Romantic writer Heinrich Heine is buried. The local museum has the attractive setting of a late 15C Franciscan monastery; but the holdings are of minor interest, unless you are excited by the prospect of what is reputedly 'the most extensive collection of beetles and butterflies among all the West Slovakian museums'.

Piešťany, 21km further north along the E75, stands at the northernmost edge of the plains of southwestern Slovakia, within sight of wooded foothills. It is Slovakia's largest and most famous spa town.

History of Piešťany

The earliest mention of the thermal springs at Piešťany dates back to 1113, and the fame of the waters had spread widely by the 16C, when a number of distinguished doctors began recommending them for their curative properties, including Johann Grato de Craftheim—physician to the Emperors Ferdinand I, Maximilian II and Rudolph II—and Baccius Elpidianus, physician to Pope Sixtus V. The first detailed scientific analysis of the waters was carried out in 1642 by the Benešov doctor Adam Trajanus, and a further study was included in *Taxa Pharmaceutica Posoniensis* (1745) by the renowned Ján Justus Torkos from Bratislava. The Piešťany springs, which reach temperatures of 69°C, are rich in gypsum and sulphur, and are much used by sufferers from rheumatism and other diseases of the joints; treatment today involves a combination of water and sulphuric mud baths.

The lively centre of Piešťany is situated on the west bank of the Váh, and features a number of imposing turn-of-the-century buildings, most notably the former *Hotel Slovan*, and the adjoining former **Kursalon**; the latter, designed by the Hungarian architect Alpár in 1894 and boasting an immense central hall, includes today both a tourist office and a museum documenting the history of the spa.

North of these two buildings extends the riverside Mestský Park (sady A Kmeťa), in which are to be found a cinema, an art gallery and an amphitheatre for musical and other performances. The main spa buildings are spread spaciously over a vast island park in the middle of the Váh, and can be reached by the Colonnade Bridge (Kolonádový most), just to the south of the *Hotel Slovan*. All the old buildings of interest are concentrated in the southern half of the park, beginning with the **Thermia Palace**, a huge Art Nouveau structure set among gardens coloured by decoratively shaped flower beds; the beautiful interior features a staircase well with a stained-glass decoration of a peacock, and a restaurant with a painting executed in Nice in 1932 by the daughter of the great Alfons Mucha.

Just to the east of this building are the Art Nouveau **Irma Baths** (1910–12), where a plaque to the physician Adam Trajanus can be seen, as well as a discreetly placed 19C bust of the Empress Elizabeth. Further east are the **Napoleon Baths**, a group of three neo-Classical buildings dating back to 1816–21, and as such the oldest surviving structures in Piešťany; these elegant low buildings are used today by the severely handicapped visitors to the spa. Beyond these is the Sanatorium Pro Patria of 1916.

North of here runs a wide and enormously long promenade, bordered on its eastern side by the large blocks of the modern spa. The spa is very popular today with Arab sheikhs and their families, whose robes lend an exotic quality to the park; a cultural dimension is provided by the many modern sculptures that are shown here in competition every summer.

Beyond Piešťany, the Váh valley narrows and runs between increasingly wooded and hilly countryside, the range to the west of the river being that of the **White Carpathians** (biele Karpaty), the northern continuation of the Lesser Carpathians. At Nové Mesto nad Váhom, 20km north of Piešťany, you should make a short detour to the ruined castle of **Čachtice**, which lies in the foothills of these mountains. To get there from Nové Mesto drive south for 5km to the village of Čachtice, where, next to the parish church, there is a fine Renaissance building housing a museum of local history and folklore; from the village take the Vadovce road for 2km, and walk along a ridge for the remaining 1km (an alternative and longer walk is to climb up to the castle from the village of Višňové, directly below the ruins). The castle ruins occupy an isolated hill-top site of great beauty, with extensive views over forested hills and mountains; but many of the people who come here are attracted less by the site than by the place's ghoulish reputation.

History of the castle

This border fortress dating back to the mid-13C acquired its notoriety in the 17C, when it was the home of Countess Elizabeth Báthory, who was rumoured to have tried to preserve her beauty through bathing in the blood of virgin girls. According to local gossip many of her young female servants were used for this purpose and many others were the object of sadistic rites of a kind that the much-maligned Marquis de Sade might have fantasised about but would never have indulged in. In 1611, after reputedly killing 600 women, she was finally brought to trial and sentenced to life imprisonment within her own castle. Those with a taste for 'Dracula' stories have taken a particular interest in her, and she was the subject of a book, *Dracula was a Woman*, by R. McNally; more recently, Tony Thorne, in his well-argued book *Countess Dracula: The Life and Times of the Blood Countess, Elizabeth Báthory* (1997), published new evidence suggesting that she was the victim of feudal power-brokering. In 1708 her castle was captured by soldiers of the rebellious Hungarian aristocrat Ferenc Rákóczi and burned down.

The ruins of Čachtice, though extensive, are much less decipherable than those of the nearby castle at **Beckov** 7km northeast of Nové Mesto, on the opposite side of the Váh, where Countess Báthory had another of her torture chambers. Gutted by fire in 1729, and currently undergoing major restoration, the castle rises steeply on rocks above the native village of the eccentric late 19C painter Barón Ladislav Medňanský (see Chapter 31), who is commemorated here by some photographs in the local museum; this museum, housed in an early 17C manor built for the Ambro family, also contains various exhibits tracing the history of the castle. But enthusiasts of military architecture will by now want to hurry on to **Trenčín**, a riverside town 22km north of Nové Mesto, and dominated by the second largest castle in Slovakia.

History of Trenčín

Trenčín, which is marked on Ptolemy's map of the world of the 2C AD, was the site of a battle in AD 179 between the Romans, led by Marcus Aurelius, and the Germanic tribe of the Kvads; the Roman victory is recorded in what is one of Czechoslovakia's oldest Roman inscriptions, hewn on the castle rock. The castle, first documented in 1113, was a royal property until the end of the 13C, after which it came into the possession of Matúš Čák, who was the undisputed lord of practically the whole territory of present-day Slovakia, which he governed independently of the king; in 1302 Čák began remodelling the castle and constructing within it a new residential palace. After Čák's death in 1321, the castle became once again a royal possession, and rebuilding work was carried out here both by Louis the Great and Sigismund of Luxemburg.

In the 16C the castle came into the possession first of the Zapolyas and then of the Thurzos, and the place was greatly strengthened by Italian engineers in preparation for Turkish attacks. From 1597 right up to 1835 the property belonged to the Illesházys, who between 1704 and 1708 were responsible for the last building campaign here. The castle was destroyed by fire in 1790, and was only to be restored after 1956, following over 150 years of abandonment. In the meantime the town which had grown up below developed into a prosperous industrial centre, known today for its clothes manufactures, and for the bottling plant of one of Slovakia's finest plum brandies, made from yellow plums from the nearby village of Bošáca.

The town of Trenčín extends today on both sides of the Váh, but the original settlement is on the east bank of the river, below the wooded hill on which the castle rises. Most of the many 16C and 17C buildings that once made up the old town were destroyed in the course of 19C expansion, and the present-day centre, though pleasant and cheerful, has been greatly modernised. Much of what is left of old Trenčín is concentrated around the bustling **Mierové námestie**, where you will find the early Baroque, twin-towered **Piarist Church of St Francis** (Piaristický kostol) of 1653–57, sumptuously decorated inside with early 18C frescoes by Christoph Tausch, and the adjoining former mon-astery, now an art gallery named after the prolific and uninspiring 20C Slovak painter and sculptor M.A. Pavlovský, who died in Trenčín in 1968. Off the southwestern end of the square is the town's only surviving gateway (a 16C structure) and behind this a newly restored 19C synagogue serving today as an exhibition hall.

Trenčín

Steps nearby lead up through the wooded Brezina Park to the **castle**, passing, immediately inside the citadel, a heavily remodelled 14C parish church with a Renaissance portal; the adjoining mid-15C charnel house is the only purely Gothic building in the town. Further up is a bastion dating back to 1540 (remodelled in the 17C) and now housing temporary exhibitions. At the very top of the hill stands the reconstructed castle itself, within which are the Barbara's Palace (built c 1430 and containing fragments of early 15C wall-painting) and the Matthias Tower, which has an upper wooden gallery commanding magnificent views, and from which the complex defensive system of Trenčín is best appreciated. **Open** Apr–Sept daily 09.00–17.00; Oct–Mar 09.00–16.00.

North of Trenčín, Road 61/E75 runs between the White Carpathians and the Strážov Hills and, after Považská Bystrica (44km), passes near two sites of great natural interest and beauty. Four kilometres north of Považská Bystrica, underneath the romantic ruins of a castle, turn right to drive through the nearby **Manín Gorge** (Manínska tiesňava), where giant cliffs of limestone fall down dramatically to a fast-flowing stream. Return to the E75, and 9km further north you will find another turning to the right, this one leading after 4km to the **Súľov Rocks** (Súľovské skaly), a group of bizarrely shaped rock formations thrust above the forest. As the E75 nears Žilina, 20km beyond the Súľov turning (see Route 29), the road follows the Váh as it turns sharply to the east and heads towards the range of the Little Fatra.

28 · Trenčín to Banská Bystrica

> Total distance 157km: Trenčín • 13km Trenčianske Teplice • 56km Prievidza • 37km Kremnica • 14km Žiar • 17km Zvolen • 20km Banská Bystrica.

Head north of Trenčín (see Chapter 27) on Road 61/E75, then turn right after 9km and follow the narrow Teplička valley into the Strážov Hills. **Trenčianske Teplice**, 4km east of the turning, is a delightful small spa town stretched out along the Teplička river, in between steep forested slopes.

History of Teplice

The springs at Trenčianske Teplice, first mentioned in 1247, were described at length in 1580 by the chief physician of the Moravian County, Thomas Jordanus of Klausenburg. Fourteen years later the spa was purchased by the Hungarian nobleman, Count Štefan Illesházy, whose family were to own it for two and a half centuries. In 1835 it was bought from them by Juraj Sina, a Viennese financier and banker of Greek origin who had grown rich through the importing of indigo dye. A true entrepreneur, Sina soon turned the spa into a highly profitable enterprise, which it remained under the management of later members of his family. Up to the First World War, the place proved especially popular with the Hungarians, who found that it had a rather more down-to-earth character than most of the other celebrated spas of Central Europe. The Hungarian writer Mór Jókai was a frequent guest and described the spa as the 'pearl of the Carpathians'. Other famous visitors included the brothers Čapek, whose father worked here as a doctor. As with Piešťany, the place specialises in diseases of the limbs, and has a lively cultural life, including an annual musical festival which has been held here since 1938.

The charm of Trenčianske Teplice lies both in its setting and in its cheerful, informal and exceptionally friendly character, which makes the place so different to most Bohemian spas, over which an atmosphere of gloom and decay seems perpetually to hang. The architecture is modern and largely uninteresting, but there is one jewel which no one interested in the history of 19C orientalism should miss. This, the **Hammam Bath**, is situated right in the centre of the spa, next to the Sanatorium Sina.

History of the Hammam Bath

In 1885 the then owner of the spa, Iphigenia de Castries—the grand-daughter of Juraj Sina—visited the World Exhibition in Paris and was most taken by a model of a Turkish bath (or hammam) which had been built in Egypt for the Egyptian viceroy Izmail; the court architect responsible for the building had, ironically, not been an Arab but a Czech, František Schmoranz (1845–92), who came from Prague and was later to be regarded as one of the leading Central European practitioners of the neo-Moorish style. Iphigenia subsequently set off for Egypt to ask the viceroy for permission to build such a hammam at Trenčianske Teplice; she returned not only with the permission but also with Schmoranz, who began work on the Hammam immediately and completed it by 1888. The baths attracted the wealthiest and most aristocratic elements at Trenčianske Teplice, including the Countess Paulina Metternich, grand-daughter of the Austrian chancellor, and a friend and confidante of Iphigenia.

The Hammam Bath, used today not as a bath but as a place for relaxing in after-wards and being given massages and mud packs, has a magnificent blue-tiled interior suggestively illuminated by rose-windows in the side walls and a series of glazed openings in the vaulting; built on two storeys, it has an arcade of sand-stone columns on the lower floor and, above this, a traceried gallery. The Sanatorium Sina, to which the hammam is connected, was built in the 1870s following the discovery of the warmest of all the spa's thermal springs (40.2˚C); a special feature of this sanatorium is that it is one of only two places in the world where patients are treated directly in the spring. North of the Hammam Bath extends a long riverside park, where there is a path climbing up to the left to the so-called Green Frog (Zelená žaba), a popular swimming-pool in a sylvan setting.

From Trenčianske Teplice head southeast through forest for 20km to the village of Dežerice, where you will join Road 50/E572. Turn left and follow the road for 6km to **Bánovce nad Bebravou**, which was the home town of Jozef Tiso, a priest and educationalist who served during the Second World War as president of independent Slovakia; this Fascist cleric, who was responsible for the deportation of more than 60,000 Jews from Slovakia, was later executed as a war criminal.

Memorial to Tiso

In 1990 a national outcry was caused when members of the Slovak Christian Democratic Party decided to honour Tiso's memory in Bánovce with a plaque placed above the Catholic teacher-training college which he had founded here in 1934 (the institution was the first in Slovakia). The memorial was soon splattered with paint, and was heavily condemned both by President Václav Havel and the mayor of the town, Ján Turčan, who ordered it to be removed until 'historians have decided what sort of man Tiso was'.

Beyond Bánovce turn left again to follow the side road to **Uhrovec**, a further 7km. The village of Uhrovec was the birthplace of Ľudovít Štúr (1815–56), one of the leading figures in the Slovak national revival; the son of a Protestant teacher, Štúr later codified the Slovak grammar and became the only Slovak in the Hungarian parliament after being elected deputy for the town of Zvolen in 1847. The much-restored mansion of 1613 where Štúr was born is now a small museum to him, and also contains mementoes of another distinguished native of Uhrovec, the politician Alexander Dubček (1921–92).

Alexander Dubček

One of the earliest advocates of *perestroika*, and the leader of Czechoslovakia during the heady months leading up to the Russian invasion of 1968, Dubček was subsequently demoted to being Deputy Director of State Forests, and lived thereafter in Bratislava; awarded an honorary doctorate at Bologna University in 1980, he was finally able to return in triumph to Prague in November 1989, appearing in public with Václav Havel to declare the imminent victory of the 'Velvet Revolution'. He died in a car crash in 1992.

After a few kilometres the forest road south from Uhrovec to Dol. Vestenice passes **Jankov Vŕšok**, a large memorial dedicated to the Slovak partisans who, in 1943–44, took refuge in the surrounding forests, where they gathered arms; in January 1945 they were rounded up by the Germans, who afterwards set fire to the forests to burn alive those who had remained there. The particular partisan group which was based at Jankov Vŕšok was named after the Hussite leader Jan Žižka. The main part of the memorial here comprises a large amphitheatre where on 29 August each year commemorative festivities are put on, including the occasional folkloric event; above the amphitheatre rises a great column commanding an extensive panorama of the surrounding wooded hills.

You rejoin Road 50 7km further on at Dolné Vestenice, from where a detour can be made 11km to the south to **Brodzany**, a village on the southern outskirts of Partizanské; Pushkin frequently stayed at the village's 17C château (which belonged to his sister-in-law A.M. Goncharova), inside which there has now been installed a small literary museum containing mementoes of the Russian poet, and examples of his influence on Slovakian writers.

Back on Road 50 continue east for 21km to Prievidza, and in the centre of the town turn left to **Bojnice**, which lies just beyond Prievidza's northwestern suburbs. This small spa town is dominated by the picturesque profile of its castle, a great battlemented and pinnacled structure looming above a forested park.

History of the castle

Dating back to c 1300, the castle of Bojnice was first owned by Matúš Čák of Trenčín, who kept it until 1321. From the 16C to the mid-17C it belonged to the Thurzo family, who altered the building in a Renaissance style. After coming in 1649 into the possession of the Pálffys, the residential part was extended and the fortifications strengthened. The castle withstood the Turks but was briefly held by Count Rákóczi at the beginning of the 18C. The building acquired its present appearance at the end of the 19C, when Count Ján Pálffy (1829–1908) called in the French architect J. Hubert, who had the whole place remodelled in a style inspired by the châteaux of the Loire.

Parts of the outer 14C ramparts have survived, but the essential look of the building is a pseudo-medieval one of the turn of the century. The tour of the interior is enjoyable largely on account of the eccentric old man who takes you round, but the place itself has little of intrinsic value. The heavy rooms are sparsely furnished and contain as their principal interest some badly labelled minor paintings on loan from Slovak galleries, including the East Slovak Gallery at Košice. The most impressive of the rooms is the Gold Room, which has a gilded coffered ceiling copied after one in the Accademia in Venice; in its centre is a portrait of Ján Pálffy by Francesco Silvestri. Also of interest is the chapel, which was built in the mid-17C out of one of the bastion towers, and has a Baroque stuccoed and frescoed ceiling. **Open** May–Sept Tues–Sun 08.00–17.00; Oct–Apr 09.00–15.00.

Return to Prievidza and continue along Road 50 for a further 24km; shortly after Nová Lehota, take the turning to the left marked Janova Lehota and **Kremnica** (15km). Kremnica, one of the most beautiful small towns in Slovakia, owes its former importance to the gold and silver deposits that were once to be found in the surrounding hills. Silver was mined in Kremnica as far back as the 11C, and gold from the 13C. Awarded royal privileges in 1328, the by now prosperous community of Kremnica began minting silver coins the following year and gold ones in 1335. Commemorative coins and medals are still minted here, though the town has been in gradual decline since its heyday in the 15C and 16C.

Of the fortifications built in the 15C to guard the town's wealth there are extensive remains, including, just below the main square, the town's principal gate. Around the long, green and sloping main square are arranged a number of fine houses from the 15C and 16C, including at No. 7 a building now housing a museum documenting the history of the town's mint; the mint itself, a 19C building of 14C origin, is at Nos 24/25. In the middle of the square's grassy slopes is an elaborate Baroque plague column, executed by M. Vogerle and D. Stanetti in 1765–72. Rising high above the square is the late 15C parish church, which forms the centrepiece of an excellently preserved fortified complex where there is also to be found the Romanesque rotunda of St Andrew.

Drive south of Kremnica on Road 65 and after 14km you will reach the E571, at a point just below the impressive hill-top ruins of **Šašov**, a castle which was first mentioned in 1235 and was abandoned at the beginning of the 18C; the parts that are still standing include a section built in 1424, when the castle was a royal one belonging to the Emperor Sigismund. The town of **Žiar nad Hronom**, 2km to the west, has a palace which was once a residence of the bishops of Banská Bystrica; rebuilt in 1631 on medieval foundations, it was heavily altered in the 19C and 20C and is now a school containing a memorial room to Štefan Moyses, the first chairman of the Slovak cultural association, Matica Slovenská (see Chapter 29).

The town of **Zvolen**, 17km east of Šašov on the E571, has extensive timber industries and a large and severe castle rising above the river Hron.

History of Zvolen
Built originally in 1370–82 as a grandiose hunting-lodge for Louis the Great, this four-winged block was strengthened and remodelled after 1541 in preparation for Turkish attacks; the building was a favourite residence of the 15C Hungarian king Matthias Corvinus, and was also the birthplace of

Hungary's greatest Renaissance writer, Bálint Balassi (1554–94), whose poems have been compared to the ballads of Ronsard and the sonnets of Shakespeare.

Balassi led a life that reads like the most fantastical of fictions. Though born into nobility and great wealth, and given the most privileged of educations, he was already penniless and politically suspect by the age of 24, and would later try and earn a living trading in horses and wine. In the meantime he scandalized the nobility of the day by his picaresque opportunism and continual womanising: his numerous inappropriate and often tragic affairs gave rise to extraordinarily powerful love poetry in which a courtly lyricism is balanced by a strong sense of realism. But he was also a reckless fighter (and the author of numerous poems describing the exhilaration of armed conflict) who would meet his painful death crushed by a cannon ball while battling against the Turks at the siege of Esztergom in May 1594. He was buried in the Slovak village of Hybe (see Chapter 29).

Balassi is today uncommemorated in the castle of his birth, which houses instead an art gallery largely composed of a deposit from the Slovak National Gallery at Bratislava. On the ground floor are copies of the figures from the famous altarpiece of **Master Pavol** at Levoča, and some murals of c 1452 taken from a church in Zvolen. The first floor is entirely taken over by the Slovak National Gallery's foreign school holdings. Among the Italian 15C and 16C paintings are works by **Bonifacio Veronese**, **Francesco Rondani** and **Domenico Beccafumi** (*Christ in Limbo*); the Italian 17C and 18C paintings include a version of **Annibale Carracci**'s *Laton Defending His Children* (a finer version of this is at Kroměříz), *The Taking of Christ* by **Cecco del Caravaggio**, and a *Baptism of Christ* by **Giulio Cesare Procaccini**.

The German holdings date from the 16C to 18C and feature an interesting *Christ before Pilate* by an anonymous Westphalian master of the early 16C. Of the Dutch and Flemish Schools there are still-lifes by **Joachim Beukelaer**, a *Head of Christ* from the circle of Albrecht Bouts, a *Judgement of Solomon* by **Nicolaus Knupfer**, and a beautiful river landscape by **Salomon van Ruysdael**.

A great surprise are the English holdings, which boast a portrait by **Hogarth** of Miss Collot, an excellent double portrait by **Raeburn**, and a large oil by **Sir Godfrey Kneller** showing Michael and John Richardson at the Battle of Belgrade. One of the rooms on the first floor contains also the finest survival of the castle's Baroque decorations, a panelled ceiling of 1700 adorned with quaintly provincial paintings of famous kings from ancient times up to the 17C. The second floor is taken up by 20C Slovak medals and small sculptures, including works by **Ján Koniarek**, **Ladislav Majerský**, **Rudolf Pribiš** and **František Gibala**. Open Tues–Sun 10.00–17.00.

Banská Bystrica

A dual-carriageway section of Road 66 heads north from Zvolen along the Hron to Banská Bystrica, the capital of Central Slovakia.

History of Banská Bystrica

Another of the former mining towns of Slovakia, Banská Bystrica was made a Free Royal Mining Town in 1255. Silver had been mined here since at least the 11C, but from the 14C to the 16C the town specialised in the mining of copper, and indeed briefly became the leading copper-producing centre of Europe. In 1525 the local miners went on strike, and for a while occupied the town; economic decline set in at the end of the following century. An important centre of Communism between the First and Second World Wars, Banská Bystrica later played a critical role in the Slovak National Uprising; for two months after the uprising, which broke out on 29 August 1944, the town was the seat of the Slovak National Council, and there were numerous broadcasts transmitted from here by members of the resistance. The Nazis occupied the town on 27 October 1944, and they were followed by Soviet troops on 26 March 1945. The town has been extensively industrialised since the war, and is today a centre of the timber, engineering, textile and cement industries.

Banská Bystrica, with its forested, mountainous surroundings, and views to the north of the Large Fatra and Low Tatras, often inspires nostalgic memories among older Slovaks, who remember the town for its clean, bracing air and colourful markets. The recent construction on the eastern outskirts of the town of a large cement works has rather diminished this idyllic vision, yet the place still retains a character which is both lively and pleasantly old-fashioned. The historic centre of the town lies off the námestie Štefana Moyzesa, and comprises a group of buildings which once formed the town's fortified inner citadel.

Of the actual fortifications, there remains today only three bastions and the Main Gate tower, a 15C structure to which a Baroque steeple has been added. At the centre of the citadel is the parish **Church of Our Lady** (Kostol Panny Marie Manebeuzatej)—the patron saint of miners. This originally Romanesque structure was extended and remodelled in 1478–1516, and features on its exterior a sculptural group attributed to Master Pavol of Levoča, who seems also to have been responsible for the altarpiece of St Barbara in one of the building's side chapels; on the high altar there was once a celebrated medieval painting of the *Death of the Virgin*, but this was destroyed by fire in 1761.

To the north of the church are the so-called Farni or parish bastions and a cluster of structures composed of the Miners' and Pisárska Bastions, the modest late Gothic palace built for the Hungarian king Matthias Corvinus, and the small Church of the Holy Rood (Kostol sv. Kríža), which dates back to 1479. South of the parish church, and adjoining the main gate tower, is the former Town Hall, the southern and eastern walls of which were once attached to the fortifications. Built in 1564–65, but restored and altered at various times since the 18C, this essentially Renaissance structure features an arcaded loggia on its northern and western walls. After suffering fire damage in 1761, it no longer functioned as a Town Hall, becoming a school after 1803 and a museum after 1970. Today it is one of several historical buildings (including both the Parish Bastion and the Main Gate Tower) housing the **State Art Gallery** (Štátna galéria), which as well as hosting international biennales of woodcut and wood engravings displays changing selections from a large permanent collection of 20C Slovak artists, including works by Martin Benka, Miloš Bazovský, Mikuláš Galanda, Ľudovít Fulla, Zolo Palugyay, Jozef Kollár, Július Szabó and Fraňo Štefunko. **Open** Tues–Sun 10.00–18.00, Sat, Sun 10.00–17.00.

The works of the town's principal artist, **Dominik Skutecký** (1849–1921),

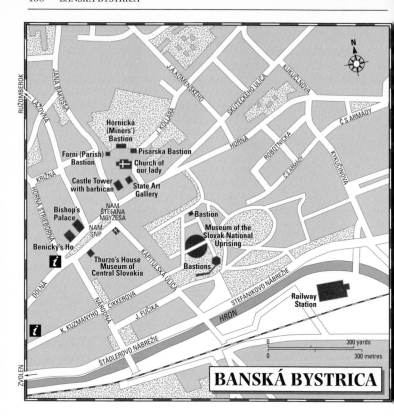

BANSKÁ BYSTRICA

are now permanently exhibited in a special branch of the gallery occupying a house designed by the artist himself at 55 Horná Str., a short walk northeast of the former Town Hall. Skutecký, after a long period spent in Vienna, Venice and elsewhere in Europe, settled permanently in Banská Bystrica in the 1880s, and painted numerous local scenes, including a series of interiors of blacksmiths' workshops and copper kilns. His main work in the gallery is his detailed and delightful *Market Scene at Banská Bystrica*, featuring a well-to-do woman and her daughter set against a background of colourfully dressed peasants.

The market which Skutecký painted used to take place on the square adjoining the southwestern side of the námestie Štefana Moyzesa, the **námestie SNP**. This long and cheerful square, the main square of Banská Bystrica, has been turned recently into a showpiece area of brightly painted houses and outdoor café tables. It features a number of buildings from the 16C to the 18C including, to your left as you enter the square, the late Baroque Jesuit church (Š. František Xavier), which is glimpsed in the corner of Skutecký's painting. Further down on the left-hand side is the 16C Thurzo's House, with a splendid yellow façade comprising rustication and a playful crowning parapet of intertwined arches; it now houses the **Museum of Central Slovakia** (Stredoslovenské múzeum), which has a worthy collection of medieval and Renaissance works, folk crafts, and archaeological pieces: note in particular the treasury of bronze objects from Vyškovce. **Open** Sun–Fri 09.00–12.00 and 13.00–17.00.

Opposite it are the sgrafittoed 16C Benický's House (now the main seat of the State Gallery mentioned above) and the former Bishop's Palace, a Baroque structure of the 18C. Head south on the street adjoining the Jesuit church and then take the first turning

Museum of the Slovak National Uprising, Banská Bystrica

to the left to come to the **Memorial and Museum of the Slovak National Uprising** (múzeum SNP). This boldly modern structure, built by Dušan Kuzma in 1969, takes the form of two large concrete segments, the appearance and meaning of which have inspired much frivolous comment. The architect's own explanation of the monument—which most closely resembles the bun of a hamburger—is that the dividing line between the two segments symbolises the great breakthrough which the Slovak National Uprising represented in the history of the Slovak People. In the middle of the monument is an eternal flame marking the tomb of an unknown soldier, while within the segments is an excitingly arranged museum which includes a reconstructed guerrilla bunker and a Soviet IL-2 aeroplane. **Open** May–Sept Tues–Sun 08.00–18.00; Oct–Apr 09.00–16.00.

The monument stands in a large formal park which comes down to the river Hron: just to the south of the monument are the scanty remains of the town's outer walls, while at the eastern end of the park is the unprepossessing modern block of the *Hotel Lux*.

Banská Bystrica is a convenient base for visiting the **Large Fatra** (veľká Fatra) and **Low Tatra** (nízké Tatry). Running between these two ranges, and following for a while a densely forested gorge, is the beautiful E77, which connects the town with Ružomberok 53km away (see Chapter 29). Seven kilometres north of Banská Bystrica along the E77 is a road to the left crossing the southern end of the Large Fatra; above it twists the railway line to Martin (see Chapter 29), one of the more spectacular stretches of railway to be found in Slovakia. Continue north along the E77 for a further 7km and, taking the turning to the left just before Staré Hory, drive 2km to **Turecká**. From here there is a chairlift up to **Mount Krížna** (1574m); at the top an exhilarating hour's walk can be made over flower-filled meadows to the summit of **Ostredok** (1592m), the highest peak in the Large Fatra. The views the whole length of the walk are quite breathtaking, and on clear days you can even see as far as the snow-capped peaks of the High Tatras. Ten kilometres north of Staré Hory along the E77 is **Donovaly**, a small but popular summer and winter resort, renowned for its wealth of flowers during the spring.

29 · Ostrava to Liptovský Mikuláš

Total distance 194km: Ostrava (leave by Road 11/E75) • 31km Český Těšín • 48km Čadca • 30km Žilina • E50 25km Martin • 39km Ružomberok • 21km Liptovský Mikuláš.

From Ostrava (see Chapter 22) drive southeast through heavily built-up land-scape, passing quickly through the Polish border town of Český Těšín, and shortly afterwards entering the wooded valley of the Beskydy Mountains; the Slovak border is just beyond the village of Mosty u Jablunkova, 40km southeast of Český Těšín. The first Slovak town which you come to is Čadca 8km further on, a small and uninteresting centre of the textile and timber industries. Beyond Čadca, however, the landscape greatly improves, and you drive through a short stretch of beautiful forest; the first turning to the left will take you to Oščadnica, a most pleasant small and little-known skiing resort lost in the woods.

Further small industries await you as you continue south along Road 11/E75 to **Žilina** (23km south of the Oščadnica turning), a town of largely modern appearance but attractively situated on the river Váh and within sight of the Little Fatra.

History of Žilina
A Slav settlement from the 5C onwards, Žilina was first mentioned in 1208 and became a town in 1312. Though the town was occupied by the Hussites from 1429–34, and devastated by fire in 1521, its prosperity was to grow right up to the end of the 16C, when some 2000 drapery workers were employed here. Repeatedly plundered and pillaged during the Thirty Years War, Žilina went into a long decline from which it was to be rescued only after the coming of the railway in the late 19C. Extensively industrialised since then, Žilina is today one of the most important railway junctions in the two republics, and a centre of forestry and the chemical and engineering industries. Discovered here this century was the oldest surviving manuscript in the Slovakian language: known as the Žilina Book, and dating back to 1370, it is a statement of the rights of citizens belonging to a free town. In 1938 the controversial Catholic priest and leader of the Slovak People's Party, Andrej Hlinka, organised a coalition that met at Žilina to sign a formal demand for Slovak autonomy.

Just before crossing the Váh and visiting the centre of Žilina, it is worth stopping off at the northern suburb of Budatín, where there is a 16C castle standing in extensive parkland and housing the charming **Považké Museum**. The interest of this museum lies in its collection of over a thousand artefacts such as baskets and naive figurines made in wire and tin by the numerous tinker craftsmen who originated from the Žilina area, in particular from the villages of Dlhé Pole and Veľké Rovné; these craftsmen once peddled their wares not only throughout Europe, but also in America and even Australia. **Open** Tues–Sat 08.00–16.00.

Žilina was badly damaged during the Second World War, and its few remaining buildings are concentrated around the arcaded Dukla námestie, which has a number of houses dating back to the 16C. Tolstoy, on visiting this square at the end of the last century, is said to have exclaimed, 'Look, Hungarian Nuremberg', though it is unlikely that visitors today will have such a reaction: heavily restored, and arranged around a small garden adorned with a modern fountain, this is a pleasant but unremarkable space. Nearby is the parish Church of the Holy Trinity, a building of medieval origin, but reconstructed on numerous occasions. In the southeastern suburb of Zavodie is the late Romanesque Church of St Stephen (take a No. 1 bus from the centre), which has traces of medieval wall-painting.

Though architecturally uninspiring, Žilina is popular as a holiday resort and makes a good base for excursions into the **Little Fatra** (malá Fatra). One such excursion is to head south down the narrow Rajčanka valley, which runs parallel to the eastern slopes of this modest range, through a beautiful landscape of meadows bordered by forests. Follow the main road to Prievidza for 7km, then take the road to the right marked Lietavská Svinná.

After 2km you will see rising above a densely wooded outcrop to your right one of the largest and most impressive of Slovakia's many ruined castles. The castle of **Lietava**, a strenuous 20min walk from the road, was built between the late 14C and early 15C, and abandoned in the 18C. Its unprotected walls, still crumbling into the forest, create a most picturesque silhouette and blend in with the surrounding pines and rock pinnacles in a way which would have greatly appealed to travellers of the Romantic generation; there are wonderful views of the valley.

Returning to the Prievidza road continue south for a further 26km, then turn right shortly after Fačkov on to the road which follows the Rajčanka river to Čičmany, a further 7km. The small village of **Čičmany** is lined with some of the most famous surviving examples of Slovak folk architecture. A village living traditionally off the raising of sheep and cattle, Čičmany was first mentioned in 1272, and later acquired a reputation for the making of felt slippers. A fire destroyed the lower half of the village in 1921, but the place was later lovingly restored by the Institute of Ethnography. The village's attractive wooden houses, featuring galleries and wide eaves, are remarkable above all for their white painted decoration: imitative of lacework, this style of decoration dates back to the 18C, and is unique to Slovakia. One of the houses (Radenov dom) is now a small and charming ethnographical museum, featuring a taped commentary in English about the history of the village, and examples of local crafts, most notably some of the village's celebrated folk costumes, which are characterised by their very sophisticated design and the predominance of white. **Open** Tues–Sun 08.00–16.00.

Another excursion from Žilina is to

Wooden church, Čičmany

Terchová and the **Little Fatra National Park**, which extends over the northern half of the range. Return to the northern suburb of Budatín, and head east for 12km along the Váh to Varín, where the road turns northeast to follow the narrow Varínka river to **Terchová** 15km further on. Terchová is famous as the birthplace of one of Slovakia's greatest heroes, Juraj Jánošík, commemorated here by a shining memorial in chrome rising prominently on a hill to the south of the village.

Juraj Jánošík

Born in 1688, Jánošík took part in the uprising against the Habsburgs led by Ferenc Rákóczi in 1707–11. He is best known, however, as a bandit chief, in which capacity he earned a reputation as the Slovak Robin Hood. According to popular tradition he embarked on a life of virtuous crime as an act of vengeance following the death of his parents. Returning to Terchová too late to see his dying mother, he had found his father to be mortally ill instead; the father had been beaten up by his employers for taking time off work to go to his wife's funeral. Arrested in March 1713 at the nearby town of Liptovský Mikuláš, Jánošík was tortured, but refused to reveal the whereabouts of his fellow bandits. Offered a royal pardon on the condition of joining the imperial army, Jánošík refused, saying, 'now that you have roasted me, you can eat me.' He was condemned to be strung up by a hook attached to one of his ribs, and took over a day to die.

From Terchová head south, passing below the statue of Jánošík and driving though the narrow **Tiesňavy Pass**. At the southern end of the pass is a landscape of dramatically projecting rocks, at the other end of which you come to an enchanting, little-spoilt valley which is popular both as a summer and winter resort. The first turning to the left will take you after a couple of kilometres to the isolated *Hotel Boboty*, the perfect base from which to explore the Little Fatra, and with good views towards the highest mountain of the range, **veľký Kriváň** (1709m). Back on the Tiesňavy road continue south for another 2km to Vrátna Chalet, where the road comes to an end and from where there is a chair-lift taking you up to to **Snilovské sedlo** (1520m), which is on the saddle of the Little Fatra range, within a short walking distance of the summit of Kriváň. Returning to Terchová you can either go back from here to Žilina or else turn right and drive for 10km to the Zázrivka river, where there is a road to your right which follows the river a further 13km all the way to the Orava valley (see below).

Back at Žilina, head east on Road 18, skirting the southern banks of the Váh. After 11km you will come to the ruined castle of **Strečno**, which rises up on a mound against a dark green background of forested mountains. Begun in the 14C on the foundations of an earlier structure, the castle has a 14C to 15C chapel, and 16C outer fortifications; burned out in 1678 to prevent its being used by rebels in an uprising against the Habsburg emperor, it has been slowly restored since 1977. **Open** June–Aug Tues–Sun 09.00–18.00; May, Sept, Oct 09.00–17.00.

Facing the castle, directly above the river, is a plinth of impressively stark simplicity commemorating the French partisans who took part in the Slovak Uprising between September and October 1944. Immediately beyond Strečno, the Váh cuts right through the middle of the Little Fatra Range, creating a beautiful wooded gorge. Rising above trees on the other side of the river to Road 18, and virtually inaccessible, are the romantic ruins of **Starý hrad**, the oldest part of which is a 13C tower. Once through the gorge, Road 18 comes out into a wide fertile valley known sometimes as the Turiec Garden, which separates the Little Fatra from the Large Fatra.

The main settlement of the valley is **Martin** (14km from Strečno), a town of uninspiring modern appearance, but with an attractive position and a central importance in the history of the Slovak nation.

History of Martin

Though dating back to 1340, Martin was an insignificant, provincial town until 1861, when there took place here a meeting at which a call was made for an autonomous Slovak nation, with Slovak rather than Hungarian as the official language. Two years later, on 4 August 1863, there came into being the Matica slovenská, an institution dedicated to the promotion of Slovak culture and education. In 1867 the first Slovak school was founded at Kláštor pod Znievom, just to the south of Martin, and in 1906 work was begun at Martin itself on the Slovak National Museum. The main branch of the museum has now moved to Bratislava, but Martin—today a centre of forestry and engineering—still retains its cultural importance. The Matica slovenská continues to function, and is now divided between three buildings, within which are the Slovak National Library and institutions dedicated to scientific and literary research.

Among the distinguished natives of Martin are Janko Jesenský (1874–1945), the poet and author of the important two-volume novel *The Democrats* (1934–37), one of the few Slovak novels translated into English; and the painter of colourful Slovak landscapes and rural scenes, Martin Benka (1888–1971).

Martin is a town of interest more for its history than its architecture, its principal monument being the pompous neo-Baroque building of 1864–65 constituting the first seat of the Matica slovenská (today the building functions as the Slovak National Literary Museum). The original National Slovak Museum, a neo-Classical building of 1906–07, is now a museum devoted to the natural history of the Turiec region. The new building of the **National Slovak Museum** (Slovenské národné múzeum), erected in 1928–32, is devoted instead exclusively to the ethnography of Slovakia, and has an extensive collection of folk objects and costumes. A branch of the museum is situated in the house and studio of the painter Martin Benka, and displays a large group of this artist's cheerful works.

More paintings by Benka can be seen in the **Turiec Gallery**, which also has works by other Slovak artists such as Ľudovít Fulla, M.A. Bazovský, Mikuláš Galanda, Z. Štefunko and Z. Palugyay. Benka's grave, together with those of other Slovak celebrities and heroes (including the leading Romantic poet Janko Kráľ' and the locally born writer Janko Jesenský) can be seen in the National Cemetery (národný cintorín), which is characterised by its drab, Lutheran headstones.

Just to the south of Martin, off Road 65 to Žiar nad Hronom, is an important and recently opened **skansen** (Múzeum slovenskej dediny) with folk buildings taken from villages throughout Slovakia. **Open** May–Oct Tues–Sun 09.00–17.00.

Due west of the town is a tiny road which winds its way up the slopes of the Little

Fatra to the modest skiing resort of **Martinské Hole**, which is renowned for its snow conditions, and lies just underneath the peak of **veľká Lúka** (1476m).

East of Martin, Road 18 continues to follow the Váh river, skirting the northern slopes of the Large Fatra. After 20km you reach the confluence of the Váh and Orava, and can make an interesting detour north up the latter's valley, following Road 59, which leads eventually into Poland.

The modern, unprepossessing town of **Dolný Kubín**, 17km north along Road 59, is the administrative capital of the Orava region and is associated with two leading figures of Slovak culture, the composer Janko Matuška, and the poet and dramatist Pavol Országh, who began writing in Hungarian before changing to Slovak and using the name of Hviezdoslav (1849–1921). Hviezdoslav, born at the nearby village of Vyšný Kubín, is commemorated at Dolný Kubín—where he spent most of his life—by a memorial museum attached to the town's important library.

One of Slovakia's most photographed buildings is 11km further north on Road 59: **Orava Castle** is perched on a rocky outcrop above the wooded banks of the Orava in a way such as you would only expect to find in the illustrations of Walt Disney. First mentioned in 1267, and enlarged and remodelled at various times between the 13C and 17C, it changed hands repeatedly, and was owned at one stage by the son of Matthias Corvinus. Destroyed by fire in 1800, it was heavily restored between 1813 and 1834 and again in the 1970s. The building has a generally pseudo-medieval character, and is best seen from below, where you can enjoy to the full its picturesque profile and spectacular position. The dreary interior has collections of armour and local history. **Open** May–Aug Tues–Sun 08.30–17.00; May, Sept, Oct 08.30–16.00.

Orava Castle

Continue along Road 59 to Podbiel and then turn right along the tiny Studený river to Zuberec 15km to the southeast. Two kilometres due east of Zuberec, in the direction of the Roháče Mountains, is the **Orava Village Museum** (Múzeum oravskej dediny), a *skansen* founded in 1965 and featuring a collection of traditional wooden buildings set in the middle of a dense pine forest.

Returning to Podbiel and continuing north along Road 59, you will come after 9km to **Tvrdošín**, where—in the local cemetery on the northern outskirts of this small town—there survives in its original setting a wooden church dating back to the late 15C. A narrow road northwest of Tvrdošín leads to a large lake which was formed after the construction of a dam over the Orava in 1954. Five villages were destroyed during the creation of the lake, though the mid-18C parish church of the former village of Slanická survives, standing in isolation on an island which can be reached by boat from Slanická osada, 10km northwest of Tvrdošín; the church has an amusing collection of Slovak folk painting and sculpture. The lake itself is a popular summer resort, and is much used for swimming and water sports.

Returning to the Váh and Road 18, continue heading east towards Ružomberok, after 7km passing **Ľubochňa**, a small and old-fashioned health resort on the wooded lower slopes of the Large Fatra. This pleasant and bosky spot was, incongruously, the place where the Slovak Communist Party was founded on 16 January 1921; the building where the critical meeting took place is a half-timbered turn-of-the-century structure known as Kollárov Dom.

The small industrial town of **Ružomberok**, 12km further east, has what claims to be the first purpose-built art gallery in Slovakia: a bold if now rather sad Functionalist structure of 1964–65, this was built as a museum devoted to one of the leading Slovak painters of the 20C, Ľudovít Fulla (1902–80), who lived and worked in the building during the last years of his life, and whose studio and study room can still be seen. But the town's main point of interest is its recently revived associations with the controversial local priest and nationalist Andrej Hlinka (1864–1938).

Andrej Hlinka

After having been out of favour during the Communist regime, Hlinka has today resurfaced as a figurehead for the more extreme nationalist tendencies in Slovakia. Born in the neighbouring village of Černová, and afterwards a Catholic pastor at Ružemberok, he was turned in 1906 into a 'Slovak martyr' after being put into prison for inciting anti-Hungarian feelings. Under a false passport he made his way to Paris in 1919 to put forward his case for Slovak autonomy; shortly afterwards he was elected leader of the newly formed Ľudová Strana (People's Party), which had as its slogan the words 'Slovakia for the Slovaks'. After his death in 1938 (soon after organising the call for autonomy at Žilina; see Chapter 29), his name lived on in Slovakia's equivalent of the SS, the Hlinka Guards, which was led by his successor in the Ľudová Strana, the Nazi puppet Jozef Tiso.

The church to which Hlinka was attached in Ružomberok stands on raised ground in the middle of a square now named after him. As a further provocation to the local Hungarian population there is also a monument honouring the British academic R.W. Seton-Watson, whose strong pro-Slovak sentiments (he is praised here for 'defending the Slovak nation') played an important part in formulating at Trianon a treaty with such disastrous consequences for Hungary.

A pleasant short excursion from Ružomberok is to drive 4km south on Road 59 to the outlying community of Biely Potok (there are also regular bus services), and from there climb up a further 2km to the tiny village of **Vlkolínec**, which offers a vision of what rural Slovakia was traditionally like: hidden from all the nearby industries, this village, though badly damaged by the Nazis in 1944 in retaliation for the Slovak National Uprising, still retains a group of two- and three-roomed logwood houses dating back to the last century, one of which, No.15, has been preserved inside as a museum.

Another interesting site in the immediate vicinity of Ružomberok is the wonderfully preserved medieval church at **Ludrová**, which can be reached by continuing east on Road 18 for 4km, and then taking the first turning to your right: standing among fields in a walled, tree-shaded enclave, this is a late 13C structure that was widened at the end of the 15C and decorated with murals in the nave and presbytery. Visits to the church must be arranged beforehand with the Liptov Museum at Ružomberok: ☎ (0848) 22468.

East of Ružomberok along Road 18 you enter a wide valley that offers your first view, to the south, of the Low Tatras (Nízke Tatry), Czechoslovakia's second highest mountain range. As you near Liptovský Mikuláš 21km away (see Chapter 30), the road turns into a dual carriageway, and you pass to your left a large reservoir; in the far distance you can make out on clear days the snow-capped peaks of the High Tatras (Vysoké Tatry).

30 · Liptovský Mikuláš to Prešov

Total distance 157km: Liptovský Mikuláš • 44km Štrbské Pleso • 17km Starý Smokovec • 12km Poprad • 26km Levoča • 15km Spišské Podhradie • 43km Prešov.

Sites in the Low and High Tatras

Liptovský Mikuláš is a small industrial town with few surviving old buildings. These few are centred around the tranquil main square, the Námestie osloboditeľov, most notably the much-restored Church of St Nicholas (Kostol sv. Mikuláša), a Gothic structure of Romanesque origin; it was on this same square that the bandit chief Juraj Jánošík met his gruesome end in 1713, condemned to be hung from one of his ribs. The garishly remodelled Baroque building at No.31 where his punishment was decided on is now a historical and literary museum named after the romantic poet Janko Kráľ (1822–76), who was born in the house at No.19. Kráľ became involved in 1849 with the pro-Habsburg, anti-Hungarian volunteers, as did the locally-born Lutheran pastor Michal Miloslav Hodža, whose parish house at Tranovského 8 is now a worthy museum documenting the Slovaks' involvement in the war of 1848–49.

Opposite this, at No.3, is a grim concrete block housing the local **art gallery** (galéria P.M. Bohúňa), which has uninspiring medieval and Baroque holdings, a large selection of the work of such ubiquitous 20C Slovak masters as Martin Benka, Gustáv Malý and Bazovský, and a particularly important 19C collection, including numerous portraits by the eponymous Bohúň, and works by such major influences on Hungarian art as the painters L. Mednánský and D. Skutecký and the sculptor A. Štróbl. **Open** Mon–Fri 08.00–12.00 and 12.30–16.30; Sat, Sun 12.00–16.00.

On the western side of the Váh is the once separate township of Paludza, where you can see the fortified late 17C **Vranovo Mansion**, which has a museum devoted to the life, times and influence of Jánošík, who was incarcerated in the building's cellar while awaiting his execution. Opposite once stood the extraordinary **Evangelical church** that can now be found at the hamlet of **Svätý Kríž**, 7km southwest of the town (take the road marked Lubela, and then turn left after 6km). Standing today isolated among pines, this large wooden structure was transferred here between 1979 and 1982 following the construction of the large Liptovská reservoir.

History of the church

In 1681 the Austrian emperor Leopold passed a law which allowed Protestants to build churches in Catholic lands but only according to strict conditions. The church had to be in open countryside, have no belfry, have its main door turned away from the township, be built within the course of a year, and so on. The church now at Svätý Kríž was built initially in the 1680s, but later proved too small for its needs, and was replaced by a much larger structure in 1774. In 1782 the Emperor Joseph II issued an edict of tolerance which did away with most of the conditions previously imposed upon the Protestants; the belfry at Svätý Kríž dates from later that year.

The interior of the church (if closed ask at the nearby pastor's house) comprises a vast galleried space covered with a depressed barrel vault, and apparently held together by not a single nail; such is the size of the building that a reputed 6000 people gathered here for the reopening ceremony in 1982. The organ, the altars, the pulpit and the choir are all from the original 17C church; the incongruous chandeliers meanwhile are from Murano, and date back to the late 18C.

The wooden Evangelical church at Svätý Kríž

The Evangelical church is by far the most interesting architectural attraction in the vicinity of Liptovský Mikuláš, a town whose appeal to tourists lies primarily in its superb position in between the Low and High Tatras. The road due south of the town climbs after 7km into the most beautiful valley of the Low Tatras, **Demänovská Dolina**, the entrance to which is marked by a landscape of pines and jagged limestone formations. Shortly after entering the valley you come to the **Ice Cave** (Demänovská ľadová jaskyňa), which is reached by a chair-lift. Discovered in August 1921, it features extensive ice formations alongside the stalagmites and stalactites (be sure to bring warm clothing); one of the early visitors was the composer Janáček, who once spent a night here listening to the 'music' of the water dripping.

Another popular and larger cave, the **Freedom Cave** (Demänovská jaskyňa slobody), is situated 4km further up the road. The road ends at the small summer and winter resort of Jasná, where there are a number of hotels and chalets shrouded by the forest, most notably the *Hotel Liptov*: within the woods surrounding the hotel is an especially attractive *koliba*. From Jasná you can ascend by chair-lift to **Chopok** (2024m), on the bleak and exhilarating ridge of the Low Tatras. Energetic walks, with magnificent views towards the High Tatras, can be made west along the ridge to **Chabenec** (1955m) or east to the summit of the highest peak of the range, **Ďumbier** (2043m). Alternatively you can descend by cable-car to the resort at Srdiečko on the southern slopes of the range, and from there join the road which heads south to Banská Bystrica (see Chapter 28).

Returning to Liptovský Mikuláš, head east on the E50. After 17km there is a forest road to the right (Road 72) which crosses the Low Tatras by way of the **Čertovica Pass**, from the top of which you can take a path to the left for a superb panorama over pines towards the snow-capped High Tatras. To visit the latter—the most spectacular area of natural beauty in the Czech and Slovak Republics—continue heading east along the E50 (bypassing the village of Hybe, where the Hungarian Renaissance poet Bálint Balassi is buried) to Tatranská Štrba 35km east of Liptovský Mikuláš; from here there is a road to the left which climbs up 9km to the popular resort of Štrbské Pleso. A rack railway constructed in 1896 also connects the two places, while a single-track electric railway—the oldest in the Czech and Slovak Republics and in operation from before the First World War—runs from Štrbské Pleso to Poprad by way of the principal resorts of the High Tatras.

The **High Tatras** (Vysoké Tatry), the highest mountain range in Czechoslovakia, are composed largely of granite, though the eastern peaks, known as the White Tatras (Belianske Tatry), are of limestone. The mountains, featuring a main ridge 26km long, are fissured by 35 valleys concealing about a hundred mountain lakes. Forests, mainly of spruce, extend up to around 1800m, after which there are alpine meadows with rich and varied high-mountain flora (especially in the Belianske Tatry, which has a number of protected areas inaccessible to tourists during the summer months). The last belt of vegetation, above 2300m, comprises isolated growths of grasses and plants in rock crevices and hollows; the highest peaks are covered in snow throughout the year. Among the wildlife are chamonix, lynx, wild cats, marmots, wolves, bears, rock eagles and grouse.

History of the Tatras

One of the first travellers to explore the Tatras was David Frölich, a student from nearby Kežmarok who came to the area in 1615. But it was not until the following century that tourism began slowly to develop here. Among 18C visitors was the Bratislava scholar Matej Bél, who, together with Jonas Andreas Czirbesz, made on 4 August 1772 the first recorded climb up the fourth highest of the Tatra peaks, Kriváň (2494m); soon afterwards Kriváň was to become a symbol of the Slovak Nationalist Movement, the theme of numerous Slovak poems, and the object of a nationalist pilgrimage, first undertaken in 1841. An extensive scientific study of the area was carried out in 1793 by the Edinburgh naturalist Robert Townson, who was also the first to climb the Tatras' second highest peak, Lomnický štít (2632m); an account of his experiences was published in his *Travels in Hungary in the year 1793* (London, 1794). Despite all this early interest in the Tatras it was only with the creation of the Košice–Bohumín railway line in 1871 that the founding of the first resorts here became a real possibility. The earliest to be established was Starý Smokovec, followed shortly afterwards by Štrbské Pleso. The clientele was at first exclusively aristocratic, but today the resorts are the most popular in the two republics, and attract great crowds of Germans.

The summer and winter resort of **Štrbské Pleso**, the highest in the Tatras, developed around its lake, on the shores of which there had grown up by 1879 a restaurant, a café and a bath-house. In the 1970s a spa was established here which is particularly renowned for the treatment of chest and breathing complaints, and has a special sanatorium devoted to children with asthma. Most of the buildings at Štrbské Pleso are modern and concentrated on the lake's southern shores. The rest of the lake is lined entirely by trees and, from the pleasant path which surrounds it, there are much-photographed views of snow-capped peaks rising above forests. Behind the *Hotel Patria*—the main building on the northern side of the lake, and the one distracting element in the mountainous backcloth—is a path leading to a large ski-jump and the neighbouring *Hotel FIS*, both built in connection with a world skiing championship which was held here in 1970; in front of the *Hotel FIS* are three pines of a type endemic to the region, the *Pinus limba*.

Near the hotel is a chair-lift which will take you up to the Solisko chalet, where refreshments are available; from here you can ascend either straight to the summit of **Predné solisko** (2093m) or take the blue-marked path to the left, which will lead you into the haunting Furkotská valley, where there are three lakes. Another excursion from the *Hotel FIS* is to head north along the red-marked path to the beautiful Poprad lake (Popradské Pleso), a 1hr 30min walk.

The energetic can continue north from here along a blue-marked path, and then turn right on to another red-marked path, this one zigzagging its way to the summit of **Rysy** (2499m) on the Polish border; on the way you will cross a snow field and pass the Chata pod Rysmi, the highest mountain hut in the two republics. From the southwestern side of the lake at Štrbské Pleso there is a red-marked path which will lead you after an hour to the Jamské lake, from where it is 2hr 30min steep climb to the summit of **Kriváň** (2494m). There are numerous other alternative walks, most of which require at least a day and are only practicable between June and November; the paths, as throughout Czechoslovakia, are extremely well-marked, but can become over-congested at the height of the summer.

Starý Smokovec, 16km due east of Štrbské Pleso along a forest road, is the oldest of the Tatra resorts (on either side are the newer resorts of Nový Smokovec and Horný Smokovec). It has a pleasantly old-fashioned character, with numerous alpine-style, half-timbered buildings of the turn of the century; the one most evocative of past splendours is the *Grand Hotel*, which was built in 1912 and has kept some of its original panelled interior, alongside Art Deco and more modern additions. A funicular of the early years of the 20C will take you from the resort to Hrebienok, where there are good views looking towards the dramatic Lomnický štít.

Among the walks you can do from here is to continue to the top of **Slávkovský štít** (2452m), a good 3hr ascent: turn left at the top of the funicular on to a red-marked path, and then after 20min turn right on to a blue-marked one. **Tatranská Lomnica**, 7km northeast of Starý Smokovec, is another old-fashioned resort, this one boasting the *Grand Hotel Praha*, which stands in extensive wooded grounds and was built between 1900 and 1914; some of the rooms are still decorated with their original heavy furnishings. A cable-car dating back to 1940 makes the dizzying climb in two stages from Tatranská Lomnica up to the summit of **Lomnický štít**, where there is an old astronomical and meteorological station; the half-way station is besides the tiny, spectacularly situated lake of Skalnaté pleso (1751m). Three kilometres southeast of Tatranská Lomnica is the Eurocamp FICC, the best-appointed campsite in Slovakia, but not a place for those who appreciate peace and intimacy.

Tatranské Matliare, 3km northeast of the resort, is the site of the sanatorium where Franz Kafka stayed between December 1920 and August 1921, when he was already in the advanced stage of turberculosis.

Continuing to drive northeast through the forest, after 6km you will come to Road 67, where you should turn left and drive 9km further on to **Ždiar**, a most attractive and little-spoilt village with beautiful views over meadows to the protected Belianske Tatry. The village, rich in folk traditions and a place which resisted the setting up of collective farms in the Socialist period, is traditionally the home of the Gorals, an ethnic group derived from the interbreeding of Poles and Slovaks, and named after the Polish word for 'mountain people'. The main street, running parallel with Road 67, is unasphalted and lined with traditional wooden farms, some with cheerful blue-and-white decoration; many of the buildings are now used as holiday homes by Germans. Adjoining a popular wooden restaurant is a small museum devoted to local ethnography.

The Spiš, Levoča and its environs

Return to Starý Smokovec and head south to the largest town of the district, **Poprad**, which lies on the western edge of rolling agricultural countryside extending east towards Prešov. This area, with its views over undulating wheat-fields to the ever more distant High Tatras, is known as the **Spiš**, and is of exceptional cultural interest, bearing the mark of many centuries of German dominance. The towns were founded in the 13C by the Hungarian King Béla, and populated with Saxons, who were offered tax exemption and other privileges in return for colonising the area, which had recently been ravaged by the Tartars; the Germans represented the majority race until the Second World War.

Poprad itself is today largely an ugly industrial town, but it is now joined in the north to the quiet and once separate township of **Spišská Sobota**, which features a most attractive if rather run-down main square, shaded by trees and lined with Renaissance and Baroque houses, some with picturesque gables. The main monument on the square is a church of mid-13C origin which was rebuilt in 1468, and given 40 years afterwards a late Gothic chapel, remodelled in the 18C. The high altar of St George (1516) was the work of pupils of the greatest artist to have worked in the Spiš region, Master Pavol of Levoča, who himself was responsible for the sculptures on the two flanking altars. The free-standing belfry adjoining the church dates back to 1598, but was reconstructed in 1728 and restored in 1956.

Drive east of Poprad on the E50, and after 14km you will see rising above fields to the right of the road the medieval church of **Spišský Štvrtok**. The main body of the church dates back to early Gothic times, but has suffered great damage over the centuries; more interesting is the large chapel attached to its southern side and built in the late 15C as the burial place of the powerful Hungarian family, the Zápolskýs. The interior of the chapel, reached through a door on the right aisle of the church, was heavily restored in the late 19C by Ladislav Steinhausz and given vivid stained-glass windows; the anonymous altarpiece, however, is original, and shows in its main panel the Virgin holding the body of the dying St John Zapolyas, who was buried at Spišská Kapitula but whose body was later transferred here. From the crypt underneath the chapel is an underground passage leading to a former Franciscan monastery, which is now a psychiatric hospital.

Levoča

Levoča, 12km further east and beautifully set among rolling fields, has an old centre wholly surrounded by its 14C–15C walls. It is the great architectural jewel of Slovakia, and a place which rivals in its little-spoilt character some of the German colonies of Transylvania.

History of Levoča

The history of Levoča goes back to a Moravian settlement which had flourished between the 5C and 9C. However, the town was destroyed in the early Middle Ages by the Tartars, and only renewed after the 13C with the arrival of German settlers. In 1231 it became the capital of the semi-autonomous Spiš region when it was made the seat of the union of the 21 Spiš towns. In 1323 it broke with this union and became a Royal Free Town allied with Bardejov, Košice, Prešov and Sabinov. Though no longer enjoying its previous tax-free status, the town prospered as a result of its position on important trade routes, and enjoyed the greatest period in its history between the 14C and 16C. Printing-works were founded here in 1624, but already the town's decline had set in, a decline which was to be compounded in the 19C, when this by now remote and out-of-the-way place was bypassed by the railway.

A quiet town for most of the year, Levoča comes alive on the first weekend of July, when up to 250,000 Catholics descend on the place to take part in Slovakia's most celebrated Marian pilgrimage. This pilgrimage to the Shrine of Mariánska hora 2km to the north is comparable to the festive pilgrimages of Spain known as *Romerías*, and is accompanied by much singing and dancing, and an enormous amount to drink. The celebrations begin with a six o'clock mass on Saturday evening, and continue all night, climaxing with a High Mass on Sunday.

A narrow ring of modern development today encircles the old town of Levoča, but once through the medieval walls you will find yourself in a slumbering, slightly decrepit place barely touched by the late 20C. Entering through the Košice Gate on the northeastern side of town, you will see to your left the **New Minorite Church** (Nový kostol Minoritov), which was built in the middle of the 18C and has a single nave articulated with elaborate altars, and a profusely rich Baroque ceiling decoration.

Head west from here along Košická until you reach the main square, where most of Levoča's monuments are concentrated. Surrounding the square are 50 merchants' houses, many with Gothic stone portals and all originally only one storey high; numerous fires led to most of the medieval houses being rebuilt between the 15C and 17C. One of the finest of the Renaissance houses is the **Thurzov dom** on the northeastern corner of the square, immediately to your left when entering the square from Košická: it has a wonderful gabled attic, though the sgraffito decoration below this dates back only to 1903.

Continuing to walk down the eastern side of the square, you will come first to the town's information office, and then, alongside this at No. 20, to the house which was used as a studio by the celebrated 16C artist Master Pavol of Levoča; inside is a small didactic museum devoted to artistic practice in Slovakia in the Middle Ages and Renaissance.

Most of Master Pavol's known work is to be found in the parish **Church of St James** (Kostol sv. Jakuba), which faces the artist's former workshop and stands in the verdant centre of the square, along with the town's other major attraction, the Renaissance Town Hall. This church, completed by 1400 though added to and much restored since then, is the largest in Slovakia after the cathedral at Košice; its exterior is dominated by a neo-Gothic tower of 1852–57.

The three-aisled interior, entered through the south portal, is remarkable above all for its wealth of polychromed statuary by Master Pavol and his workshop. Above the south door is a Crucifixion group by him, while the altarpiece of St Anne (1515), attached to the penultimate pier of the right aisle, is a studio work. Behind this, besides the entrance to the chancel, is the altarpiece of St John (1520), also by Master Pavol and with a central panel featuring both St John the Baptist and St John Chrysostom; its companion-piece on the other side of the chancel is the altarpiece of SS Peter and Paul (1500), yet another of his works.

In between is Master Pavol's most outstanding achievement, the high altar, an elaborate late Gothic structure crowned by a forest of pinnacles, and which, at 2.5m high, is reputedly the largest wing altar in the world; executed in 1508–17, it was restored in 1552–54. The four central figures are the Virgin and Child flanked by St John the Baptist and St James dressed as a pilgrim. Scenes from the lives of these saints are portrayed on the four panels executed in relief on the altar's two wings, which open up to reveal scenes from the Passion. The realism and liveliness of Master Pavol's art is shown above all in the predella of the Last Supper, a witty and unorthodox representation of the scene, with the Apostles apparently unconcerned about Christ's message, and shown instead absorbed in their eating and drinking, and even dozing off. Such is the realism of the faces that popular tradition has it that they were portraits of members of the town's council, including one particularly mean member whom Master Pavol decided to take revenge on by portraying him as Judas, an act for which the artist had to leave the town.

Continuing to walk around the church in an anti-clockwise direction you will come to another work by Master Pavol, this one placed in front of the penultimate pier of the left aisle: this, the altar of St Nicholas, was executed in 1507 but incorporated a central figure of the 14C. The walls of the left aisle have curious wall-paintings of 1370–1400, showing moralising and apocryphal scenes from the life of St Dorothy. At the western end of the left aisle, encased in a Baroque framework, is a delightful Nativity group of 1494, with a most realistically depicted kneeling shepherd on the left which is clearly by the hand of Master Pavol. **Open** July, Aug Tues–Sat 09.00–18.00, Mon, Sun 13.00–18.00; June, Sept Tues–Sat 08.30–17.00, Mon, Sun 13.00–17.00; Oct–May Tues–Sat 08.30–11.30, Mon, Sun 13.00–16.00.

In between the Church of St James and the Old Town Hall is a belfry of 1656–61. The **Old Town Hall** (Radnica) dates back to the 15C, but was rebuilt in 1550–99 and given the two-storeyed loggia on its west side in 1615; the high-pitched roof is of 1893–95. You enter the building through its eastern side, in front of which stands a late medieval cage originally used as a punishment for women. The well-preserved interior of the building features some finely sculpted doors, cellular vaulting, and a council chamber adorned with a Renaissance ceiling; the objects on display relate mainly to the history of the town.

The neo-Classical Evangelical church of 1825–37 is a free-standing building just to the south of the Old Town Hall, while on the southwestern side of the square is an exceptionally well-preserved group of Renaissance buildings comprising the Spillenberg House (Špillenbergov dom) at No. 45, built for a distinguished medical family; the Krupek House (Krupkov Dom) at No. 44, with a late 16C façade restored in 1979–80; and the former **Levoča School** at No. 40. The latter, belonging once to the Renaissance chronicler of the town, Gaspár Hain, served as the town school in the 18C and 19C; today it houses the art gallery of the Spiš Region, and includes numerous medieval works from local churches.

Leaving the square by its southwestern corner, turn immediately to the right and you will come shortly to the attractive Bernolákova ulica. Turn left down this and, beyond a neo-Baroque college of the early years of the 20C, you will pass on the right the former **Monastery Church of the Minorites** (Kostol Minoritov), which dates back to the late 15C but was completed in the 17C; inside there are late 14C murals on the north wall. Continuing south down Bernolákova, passing the Baroque buildings of the former monastery, you will end up at the Polish Gate, on the other side of which are views over gardens down to a narrow river.

Ten kilometres south of Levoča is **Spišská Nová Ves**, a former mining-town which was under Polish rule between 1412 and 1472. Encased by modern and industrial development, this bustling small town has kept little of its old centre. The main monument is the Gothic parish church, which was begun in 1395, given a tall steeple in 1771–72, and remodelled in the mid-19C; inside are carvings of the Stations of the Cross by Master Pavol of Levoča. Facing the north side of the church at Letná 57/50 is a municipal museum, housed in a building of medieval origin which received in 1765 a lively and amusing Rococo facing.

Five kilometres southeast of Spišská Nová Ves is the château of **Markušovce**, a fortified structure with corner towers built for the Mariássy family in 1643, and then remodelled during the Rococo period; after having been closed for many years for restoration, it was reopened in 1994 to house a collection of old furniture and other applied arts objects; in its terraced, French-style gardens is an especially elegant Rococo summer pavilion that has now been turned into a museum of old keyboard instruments. Southwest of the town extend the wooded ravines of the Slovak Paradise (see Chapter 33).

Heading east from Levoča on Road 18/E50, you continue driving through the fertile hills of the Spiš, and soon come to two further major attractions of this region, both of which are in the surroundings of Spišské Podhradie. Take the turning to the right 12km east of Levoča, marked Spišské Podhradie, and you will come after 2km to **Spišská Kapitula**, a completely walled township—the only one in the Czech and Slovak Republics—standing isolated among fields like an abandoned film set. Officially this citadel is the seat of the Spiš bishopric, though for many years during the period of Socialist rule there was no bishop to occupy the modest palace within. The other buildings inside once all belonged to the clergy, but now many of them are abandoned, lining cobbled lanes overgrown with grass and weeds; the ugly grey block built between the wars as a seminary has now reverted back to its original use after having served as a police college from 1948 to 1992.

Though the interior of the citadel has been much altered over the centuries and does not have the picturesque medieval appearance which the exterior would lead you to believe, it has a hauntingly run-down and deserted character, and you can only be thankful that attempts to transform the whole into a medieval theme park for tourists have so far been resisted.

The principal monument is the **Cathedral of St Martin**, the key to which can be had from the old caretaker in the bishop's palace opposite the west façade. The building dates back to the 11C, but was heavily remodelled following a fire in the 13C, and extensively restored in the 1870s. The twin-towered west façade is an unsatisfactory mixture of Romanesque, Gothic and Renaissance elements overlaid with heavy-handed 19C restoration. Inside, the main survival of the original 11C church are the Romanesque capitals underneath the organ gallery at the west end. The white-washed, three-aisled interior is otherwise in a Gothic style, the most modern-looking part being the chancel, which was redecorated in 1889 by a member of the Csáky family who was Bishop of the Spiš.

There are notable furnishings, including some locally carved pews of 1630, and various altars of the late 15C and early 16C. The main altar, which has been constantly restored over the centuries, is an anonymous work dating back to the late 15C and featuring a central panel of the Crucifixion and two side panels showing the saints of Hungary and of Western Europe. The altar at the end of the right aisle has a main panel of the *Death of the Virgin* and is by the School of Veit Stoss; a carved *Coronation of the Virgin*, surrounded by painted scenes of her life, is to be found in a chapel in the south transept and is by the School of Paul of Levoča. An anonymous late 15C carved group of the *Adoration of the Magi* is in the last chapel of the left aisle. A 14C mural of the *Coronation of Charles of Anjou* can be seen above the north portal, while the coats of arms of the Hungarians who helped in the wars against the Turks are hung on the west wall.

From Spišská Kapitula you make a short descent into Spišské Podhradie, a small town which developed from the 12C underneath **Spišský hrad**, a great ruined mass rising on a dramatic limestone spur 2km to the east (to reach the castle rejoin the E50, take the first turning to the right, and then turn right again, climbing up through a stretch of beautiful open countryside). The ruins of the castle are the largest and most impressive in Slovakia.

History of the castle

The limestone spur on which Spišský hrad is situated seems to have been inhabited as early as the 5C BC, and there is also evidence of a fortified settlement having existed here in the 2C AD. The present castle—a foundation of the Hungarian kings—dates from the early 13C, and in 1241 successfully repelled a Tartar siege; shortly afterwards a keep and palace were built here. In the late 1430s the widowed queen of King Sigismund, opposing the Polish king Vladislav's claims to the Hungarian throne, secured the help of Jan Jiskra of Brandýs, who built the lower fortifications at Spišský hrad, and transformed the place into the largest castle in Central Europe. Later in the century the castle was donated by the Hungarian throne to the Zápolský brothers, who abandoned the lower fortifications but extended and remodelled the upper ones. Further rebuilding was undertaken by the subsequent owners, the Thurzos, and again by the Csákys, who came into the possession of the castle in 1636. The Csákys were to own the castle up to 1945, but only lived here for about 100 years, moving in the early 18C to Bratislava. In 1710 the castle experienced its last military action when it was occupied by the Imperial army following the capitulation of the Rákóczi forces. Destroyed by fire shortly afterwards, and again in 1780, the castle was then left to ruin; restoration work was only begun in 1969.

Entering the castle through a Romanesque gate built in 1249, you find yourself in a reconstruction of the mid-13C palace (of which only fragments have survived). Within the reconstruction are numerous finds from the area, from prehistoric times onwards, and a large collection of torture instruments loaned from a number of local museums. There are good views of the restored walls of the lower fortifications.

After leaving the castle, you could head south for 3km to the tiny village of **Žehra**, where there is a church dating back to 1275, but much altered in later centuries. It stands on top of a small verdant hill, its cheerful white-washed exterior dominated by a black onion dome; the 17C interior contains a 13C baptismal font, some 15C carvings, and a series of 13C–15C murals in a touchingly naïf style. Return to the E50, and drive the remaining 30km to Prešov (see Chapter 32).

31 · Poprad to Svidník

Total distance 191km: Poprad • 15km Kežmarok • 45km Červený Kláštor • 24km Stará Ľubovňa • 61km Bardejov • 46km Svidník.

Road 67 north of Poprad runs at first through the northwestern corner of the Spiš region (see Chapter 30), with distant views over rolling agricultural countryside to the High Carpathians. After 8km, the road bypasses to the right the small town of Veľká Lomnica, where there is an impressive parish church (under restoration) built in 1412 over the foundations of a 13C building. **Kežmarok**, 7km further north, is one of the most interesting of the Spiš towns colonised by Germans in the 13C. Though the town has developed considerably following the introduction of textile factories in the 19C, it has kept extensive stretches of its medieval fortifications, several medieval and Renaissance houses, and an old-fashioned Germanic character. Outside the town walls, on Hviezdoslavova, is an **Evangelical Church**, one of Slovakia's finest, built entirely in wood in 1716 but plastered on the outside. The recently restored interior takes the form of a broad, aisle-less hall originally containing 1460 seats that have now been removed to make way for a local museum. **Open** daily 09.00–12.00.

Next to the building is the **New Evangelical Church** (Nový evanjelický kostol), a neo-Moorish structure of the early years of the 20C. This is a place of great emotional significance to Hungarians, for it is here that their outstanding military commander of the 17C, Imre Thököly, is buried. Duke of Transylvania and Upper Hungary, Thököly was born in Kežmarok in 1652 and died in the Turkish town of Izmid Nicomedi in 1705, his remains being subsequently taken back to his native town; his tomb stands in a chapel on the right side of the church, bedecked with garlands and other tributes left by Hungarian visitors. **Open** daily 09.00–12.00.

The quiet and tiny Námestie požiarnikov in the town centre is dominated by the parish **Church of the Holy Cross** (Kostol sv. Krížu), which was built between 1444 and 1498 and partially altered in the 16C. Entering through the finely carved south portal, you find yourself in a hall-church with late 15C vaulting; the high altar of the Crucifixion and the two side altars are all by the

School of Pavol of Levoča. Facing the church is its delightful, free-standing belfry of 1591, of a type which is very characteristic of the Spiš region: covered in white plaster, and sgraffitoed with exquisite Renaissance decoration on its upper level, it is crowned by a fanciful parapet made up of gablets (decorative forms taking the shape of small gables). The church square adjoins the town's long main square, which contains several late Gothic and Renaissance houses, though it is mainly 19C in appearance. The most prominent monument is the former Town Hall, a tall pedimented structure dating back to the Renaissance, but rebuilt in the late 18C. On the northern side of the old town, attached to the best-preserved stretch of the medieval walls, is the **town castle**, which was built in 1433 and transformed into a sumptuous residence at the end of the 16C. As with the belfry of the parish church, its architecture is unmistakably of the Spiš region, with white plastered walls and small gable-like forms acting as crenellations. Badly damaged by fire in 1787, since 1930 the building has housed a museum containing exhibits relating to the history and archaeology of the town. Hourly tours (except 12.00) Tues–Sun 09.00–16.00.

Six kilometres south of the town is the attractive village of Vrbov, with a Spiš-style belfry of 1644, and, on its outskirts, some tiny lakes popular with bathers. Continuing north of Kežmarok on Road 67, you will come after 7km to the village of **Strážky**, which has one of Slovakia's most interesting mansions. Dating back to the late 15C, for the following three centuries the building belonged to the enlightened Horváth-Stansith family, who established here in 1584 one of the richest libraries in Hungary, as well as a humanist school for the children of the Spiš nobility which functioned up to 1711. Acquired in the 19C by the Mednyanský-Czóbel family (who laid out the present English-style park), the place has recently been taken over by the Slovak National Gallery. Despite extensive rebuilding over the centuries, the mansion retains much of its late medieval character, and has a wonderful whitewashed exterior, with the characteristic gable-shaped crenellations of the Spiš region. Many of the mansion's 18C–19C furnishings survive, supplemented by paintings, furniture and other objects from the Slovak National Gallery, including highly refined examples of the work of Spiš goldsmiths of the Renaissance and Baroque periods, and some rather less sophisticated examples of 17C–19C Slovak portraiture. **Open** Tues–Sun 10.00–17.00.

An important and fascinating part of the collections is devoted to the artist known in Slovakia as the Baron Ladislav Mednanský (1852–1919), a member of the Mednyanský-Czóbel family, and a frequent visitor to the house throughout his life.

One kilometre north of Strážky is the village of **Spišská Belá**, the birth-place of J.M.Petzval (1807–91), a pioneer in photographic optics whose various inventions—including two early film apparatuses—are on show in the museum housed in his family home. From here Road 76 turns due west towards Ždiar (see Chapter 30).

Leave the road 2km west of Spišská Belá, and take the forest road northwest to Spišská Stará Ves (27km). At the crossing 2km north of the latter village turn right and follow the fast-flowing Dunajec river, which marks the border with Poland, and enters the **Pieniny National Park**. In the middle of the forests and low mountains forming this small park is a beautifully situated former monastery, **Červený Kláštor**, which looks north into Poland to the highest peak of the Pieniny range, Trzy Korony (992m), a jagged rocky outcrop densely covered with pines.

Ladislav Mednansky

Though considered a Slovak artist by the Slovaks, Mednanský is known generally by his Hungarian name of Lászlo Mednyanszký, and is thought of by the Hungarians as one of their greatest painters. In any case he was a strange, isolated and itinerant figure, deeply attracted to Buddhism and other oriental religions, and as such largely indifferent to questions of nationality. Trained in Munich and Paris, and drawn at first to the landscapes of the Barbizon School, he travelled extensively through France and Italy before acquiring a studio first in Vienna and then in Budapest. A restless traveller throughout his life, he specialised at first in sombre and expressively painted landscapes, but in his later years concentrated more on scenes of suffering humanity. His compelling journals reveal his complete rejection of the trappings of his aristocratic background, his mystical, tramp-like existence, and his morbid desire to visit parts of Europe beset by extremes of violence: the tortured faces of First World War soldiers became a particularly important source of inspiration in his later paintings.

History of the monastery

Červený Kláštor was founded as a Carthusian monastery in 1319, and appropriated by the Camuldensian Order in 1704; its name, meaning the 'red monastery', might derive from its red-tiled roof. The place acquired a great reputation for its garden of curative plants, particularly during the rule as abbot of Brother Cyprián, the 18C author of a famous *Herbarium*, and a man with a passionate interest in science. What might well have been Brother Cyprián's most extraordinary achievement—as well as one of the great breakthroughs in Western technology—is sadly unsupported by written evidence. In 1768 he is said to have invented a flying apparatus, which he used to glide from Trzy Korony to the High Carpathians.

The walled and much-restored monastery complex has a simple 14C church, and a grass-covered enclosure with a group of one-roomed hermits' dwellings; the famous herb garden can still be seen, as can the laboratory belonging to Brother Cyprián, in front of it. Most of the surviving buildings are of the Baroque period, and are used today as a catering school, the headquarters of the Pieniny National Park, and a historical and ethnographical museum. The main tourist attraction of the place is the trip by raft down a wooded gorge of the Dujanec river from a landing site just below the monastery (the return journey is by bus); the journey can also be done from the Polish side of the river, which has the added fun of raftsmen in traditional folk costume and a musical send-off. Should the trip by raft not appeal to you, you can do the same journey by walking along the beautiful riverside path.

The road which passes through Červený Kláštor continues southeast 24km to **Stará Ľubovňa**, a town on the southern banks of the river Poprad. The town itself is of little interest, but above the river's northern banks there rises in isolation an imposing castle, built in the 13C to guard the border of the Hungarian kingdom. The castle, in a state of gradual decay from the early 19C onwards, was purchased in 1883 by the Polish Zamojski family, who restored the residential quarters in the lower half of the complex but left the upper half in ruins. These residential quarters, retained by the family until 1945, now house a district museum.

At Stará Ľubovňa turn east on to Road 77, following the Poprad valley in the direction of Bardejov 51km away, after 16km passing the scant ruins of the 13C Plaveč Castle. For a slightly longer route to Bardejov, leave Road 77 13km before the town, and head south on a side road 2km to Kružlov, where you turn left to **Krivé**, a further 2km. In an exposed hillside setting just above the latter village is one of the many wooden churches that are to be found throughout East Slovakia. As with many of these churches, this one was built by Greek Catholics, a sect which combines elements of Roman Catholicism and the Greek Orthodox Church and is very widespread on the eastern confines of the former Habsburg Empire. Dating back to 1826, this small and simple structure resembling an upturned boat was dedicated to St Luke.

Continue to follow the same side road in a southeasterly direction, and turn right after 10km to come to one of the most remarkable of all Slovakia's wooden churches, that of **Hervartov**. Hidden in a densely wooded grove (high trees were generally planted next to wooden churches to serve as lightning conductors), this Catholic church built out of red spruce was originally constructed in 1593–96, and renovated at various times since then. It is fascinating above all for the painted decorations inside, which date back to 1594 and were restored in the 1660s and again in 1969–70. They are concentrated mainly on the south wall of the nave, where you will find representations of Adam and Eve, St George and the Dragon, and engagingly naïf scenes of the Wise and Foolish Virgins, the latter portrayed in contemporary costume and blissfully asleep. Returning from Hervartov to the side road south of Road 77, turn right and then almost immediately left, approaching Bardejov from the south.

Bardejov, situated in wooded, gently hilly countryside, is one of Slovakia's best-preserved medieval towns. A Royal Free Town from 1376, Bardejov reached the height of its prosperity in the 15C and 16C, thanks to its situation on an important trade route, its cloth factories, printing works and other industries. Populated at one time by numerous Armenian merchants, the town today has a large Rusyn or Ruthenian minority (non-Catholic Slavs of Ukranian origin), with the street signs in both Slovak and Rusyn Ukranian.

The old centre of Bardejov is surrounded by extensive stretches of its remarkably well-preserved 14C–15C fortifications, the northern ones having at their foot a long wooded garden containing the *Hotel Dukla*. Entering the old town from the street on the eastern side of this hotel, you will find yourself immediately in Bardejov's wide and long main square, one of the most beautiful in the two republics, and surrounded almost entirely by steeply gabled pastel-coloured houses of the 15C and 16C.

At the northern end of the square is the parish **Church of St Egidius** (Kostol sv. Egídia), built in the 14C on the site of a Cistercian foundation, and restored following a fire in 1878; inside are 11 wing-altars of the 15C and 16C, the most notable of which is that of the Nativity, situated just to the left of the neo-Gothic high altar of the early 1890s. Facing the church, in the centre of the square, is the free-standing **Old Town Hall** (Radnica), a recently restored structure dating back to 1505–11 and now contains part of the Šariš Museum (Šarišské múzeum) documenting the town's medieval history with the aid of armour, old prints, statuary and other artefacts, notably a superlative Calvary group by Master Paul of Levoča.

Two further branches of the museum are to be found in two neighbouring houses at the southern end of the square, one of them devoted to natural history, and the other housing the largest collection of icons in Slovakia (dating from the 16C–19C), as well as some fascinating models of the district's wooden churches. **Open** May–Sept Tues–Sun 09.00–18.00; Oct–Apr 08.00–12.00 and 12.30–16.00.

Between these houses, running south of the square, is the attractive Rhodyho, a street which leads to the largest surviving area of the town's fortifications, comprising two parallel lines of walls, a gate and bridge, and numerous turrets and bastions. Turning left on to Na hradbách and following the line of the inner walls will take you to the most imposing of these bastions, the **Malá bašta**, a massive structure (later converted into a granary) with a rounded eastern end and an upper gallery underneath a high-pitched roof with wide eaves. From here the sloping Veterná, with numerous fine old houses (including one which belonged to to the town's executioner), will take you uphill to the southeastern corner of the main square.

Leaving Bardejov on Road 77, you will find 2km to the north of the town a turning to the left to **Bardejovské kúpele**, a quiet small spa which in its heyday was one of the more renowned in Hungary.

History of the spa

The curative properties of the Bardejov waters were recognised in the 13C, but the springs were not exploited until the 17C. In 1767 Armenian merchants constructed a group of wooden cabins around the springs, and shortly afterwards the place developed as an exclusive and predominantly aristocratic resort, visited by, among others, Napoleon I's wife Marie Louise in 1809, Tzar Alexander I in 1821 and, in 1895, Franz Joseph's wife Elizabeth, in whose honour a row of lime trees was planted. The resort, essentially a summer one, was built mainly in wood, and was severely damaged by fires in 1910–12. Only with the construction of a series of modern buildings in the 1960s was the popularity of the spa revived, but it still remains a very modest place in comparison with others in Slovakia; the waters are used above all for the treatment of digestive disorders.

The spa is attractively and spaciously arranged alongside a narrow park bordered by gentle pine-covered slopes. There are a number of turn-of-the-century buildings, including, at the western end of the park, the *Hotel Dukla*, in front of which is a bronze statue of the Empress Elizabeth. South of this is a small museum with a rare collection of icons and, in the sloping woods behind this, Slovakia's first village museum or *skansen*: founded in 1955, its oldest and most interesting building is a wooden Orthodox Church of 1706. **Open** Apr–Sept Tues–Sun 09.00–18.00; Oct–Mar 08.00–15.30.

Return to Road 77, and continue east 34km to **Svidník**, another town with a large Ukranian minority, whose history and arts are the subject respectively of the small museums at 258 Centrálna and in the late 18C manor on Partizánska; the latter institution, the Galéria Dezidera Millyho, has 16C–18C icons, numerous folk objects, and paintings by 20C Rusyn artists such as the eponymous Milly, a painter of Expressionistic peasant scenes. The town, almost entirely rebuilt after the last war, was destroyed during the Battle of Dukla, which lasted between October and November 1944 and led to what later came to be known as the 'Soviet Liberation' of Czechoslovakia. Red Army troops, led by Ludvík Svoboda, entered Czechoslovakia on 4 October 1944 by way of the Dukla Pass, 15km northeast of Svidník along Road 73. Eighty-four thousand members of the Red Army were killed, 9000 of whom were buried at Svidník, at a site marked today by an enormous obelisk. In a field near this monument is a display of tanks, planes and other weapons used in the conflict, and there are more of these arranged at regular intervals the whole length of the wooded valley leading up to the pass.

At **Vyšný Komárnik**—3km before the pass, and the first Czechoslovak village to be liberated—is a large Monument to the Unknown Soldier, next to which is a line of bronze busts of the Czechoslovak and Soviet officers who took part in the conflict. Along the same valley is the largest concentration of wooden churches to be seen in Slovakia, including those at Ľudomírova, Hunkovce and at Vyšný Komárnik itself. Two of the finest are in the neighbouring villages of Bodruzal and Mirola (leave Road 73 at Krajná Polǎna, 9km north of Svidník, and head in a southeasterly direction): both these churches have three picturesquely shaped steeples crowned by bulbous forms.

Slovakia's most bizarre and unexpected recent attraction—a museum devoted to the American pop artist of Slovak origin Andy Warhol (1931–87)—also lies within reasonable driving distance of Svidník. Situated in the middle of the otherwise uninteresting small town of **Medzilaborce**, 45km east of Svidník by way of Stropkov, the Andy Warhol Family Museum (Múzeum moderného umenia rodiny Warholovcov) occupies a modern white building previously used by the local cultural centre, and now guarded by two gigantic concrete cans of Campbell's Soup.

More of a curiosity than a place of great artistic interest, the museum's holdings include 18 original screenprints (some on loan), as well as derivative prints by his untrained artist brother Paul, and two oil paintings by his nephew James,

Andy Warhol

Although the town's one street has been dubbed Andy Warhola, the artist's real Slovak name was Ondrej Varchola, the surname having the appropriate meaning of 'rebel'. His coal-mining family did not come from Medzilaborce but from the nearby Rusyn village of Miková (8km to the northwest, off the road from Stropkov), where his sister is buried in the local cemetery. He was not born in Slovakia but in Pittsburgh, to where his father had emigrated before the First World War: though brought up speaking both English and Rusyn Ukranian, Warhol later showed as little interest in his Rusyn roots as Walt Disney had done in his Almerian ones, and indeed preferred to promote himself as a man who 'came from nowhere'. Only after his death did his brother John, together with a group of local Rusyn artists, decide to honour his memory in this remote corner of Slovakia. When it opened in 1991, the museum was the first in the world dedicated to the artist, and remained the only such institution until the opening in 1994 of the Warhol Museum in his native Pittsburgh (a place to which he was similarly indifferent). Funded by a combination of the Slovak Ministry of Culture and a small fund from the hugely endowed Andy Warhol Foundation, the Slovakian museum, after a slow start, has been remarkably successful in attracting tourists to a previously almost unvisited area of the country.

a New York-based artist. Perhaps the most fascinating aspect of the museum is the Warhol memorabilia (such as a selection of the artist's leather jackets) and the photographs and documentary panels (in English, Slovak and Rusyn) tracing the history of the Warhol family and its emigration from Slovakia to the United States. **Open** Tues–Sun 10.00–17.00.

32 · Svidník to Košice

Total distance 93km: Svidník • 57km Prešov • 36km Košice.

Driving south of Svidník on Road 73, after 43km you come to Road 18, where you can either head west to Prešov or else head east to visit the narrow eastern-most extremity of Slovakia, driving in between gentle wooded hills to the north and agricultural plains to the south. Apart from a number of wooden churches, this area of Slovakia offers little of architectural interest, and has no spectacular scenery such as you find in the centre of the region. The principal attraction is the enormous **Zemplínska Šírava Reservoir** (70km east of Košice), the Slovak Republic's most popular water resort, and impossibly crowded during the summer months.

The large industrial town of **Prešov**, situated in flat and built-up countryside, is a bustling place of no great beauty, but with a number of fine monuments around its main square.

History of Prešov
A Slovak settlement existed on the site of present-day Prešov by the end of the 8C, but the first document mentioning the town dates only from the early 13C. Granted royal privileges in 1299, Prešov was made a Royal Free Town in 1374, and rapidly developed as an important centre of trade and commerce. The place was a centre of anti-Habsburg uprisings in the 17C and 18C, and as a result suffered badly, in particular after the suppression of Count Thököly's revolt in 1684. Made district town of Šariš County at the end of the 18C, Prešov experienced an economic revival, but this was not sufficient to prevent widespread emigration from the town in the late 19C and early 20C. On 16 June 1919 the short-lived Slovak Republic of the Proletariat was declared here, inspired by the example of Russia's October Revolution. The town, today an important centre of the food, textile and engineering industries, is also the cultural capital of the Rusyns or Ruthe-nians (see Chapter 31).

The main square of Prešov takes the form of an enormously long avenue domi-nated at its northern end by the parish **Church of St Nicholas** (Kostol sv. Mikuláša), which was begun in the late 14C, and altered in 1502; the medieval furnishings within the light and spacious interior have been replaced by late Baroque ones, including several altars and a dynamic pulpit. One of the finest of the old houses on the square is Rákocziho dom, a double-fronted Renaissance structure housing a museum documenting the Slovak Republic of the Proletariat; near this is the Town Hall of 1511–20, from the balcony of which the Republic was declared.

At the southern end of the square is the former **Monastery Church of St John the Baptist** (Kláštorný kostol sv. Jána Krstitelă), built by Gaspar Urlespacher in 1753–59, and featuring an elaborate Baroque façade; the monastery belonged originally to the Minorite order, but with the abolition of the order by Joseph II in 1787 its buildings were used as a military store before being handed over to the Greek Catholics in 1821. Walking back in the direction of the Church of St Nicholas along the western side of the square, you will come at No. 326 to an **art gallery** which puts on temporary exhibitions of Slovakian artists; the permanent collection, rarely on display, contains works by the leading Slovakian artists of the 20C, including Jozef Bendík (who was born in Prešov), Ľudovít Fulla, Ján Želibský and Jozef Fabini. An arch through the western side of the square leads into the 29 Augusta ulica, where, on the left-hand side, is the so-called **Caraffa Prison** (Caraffova väznica), built in 1624.

Heading south from Prešov on the E50, you pass alongside the southern suburb of Solivar, an old salt-mining town (the name of which means 'the place where salt is boiled'), where a number of 17C salt works have survived. Shortly afterwards the E50 turns into the D1 motorway, which speeds through flat and built-up countryside almost all the way to Košice (36km).

Košice

The second largest town in Slovakia, Košice is encircled by extensive industrial development, including the most important foundry works in the country. These unprepossessing surroundings, together with the place's relative isolation from the famed beauty spots of Slovakia, have helped to ensure that Košice is not the major tourist destination it deserves to be. An intensive restoration prgramme in recent years has turned its old centre into a glowing showpiece, and highlighted the beauty of a cathedral rivalled only by that of St Vitus in Prague as the finest in Central Europe. Furthermore, the town exudes a sense of scale and cosmopolitanism appropriate both to its history and to its continuing position as a major railway junction on the lines between Budapest and Krackow, Prague and Moscow.

History of Košice

It is not known when the original settlement at Košice was established, though German settlers moved in here following Tartar invasions in the early 13C. First mentioned in 1248, Košice received royal privileges in the 1340s, and became a Royal Free Town in 1347. Trade and commerce flourished from the 14C onwards, with the town acquiring a particular reputation for its furriers, bell-founders and goldsmiths. Enjoying a leading position within the league of East Slovak towns known as the Pentapolitana, Košice became by the 15C the third largest town in the Kingdom of Hungary. The Turkish invasion, and the re-aligning of the trade route which once went through the town, led to a great decline in the 16C that was only briefly halted towards the end of the following century. Rapid industrialisation led to renewed prosperity in the 19C, and in 1907 the first workers' newspaper in Hungary was published here. After being under Czechoslovak rule for only 19 years, Košice was handed back to the Hungarians as a result of the Munich Treaty of 1938. At the end of the Second World War it became the temporary seat of the Czechoslovak government immediately after their return from exile. The town today, known to the Hungarians as Kassa, still has a strong Hungarian minority, and attracts numerous visitors from Budapest an eight-hour drive away, particularly in mid-June when the Hungarian traditions of the region are celebrated in a lively and at times provocative folk festival. Ethnic tensions have been exacerbated by the presence in the town of a large gypsy community.

Košice has changed in recent years more radically than perhaps any other town in Slovakia, and in a way that is highly indicative both of the country's present mood and of a Europe succumbing to growing uniformity. The changes have been concentrated on the magnificent central thoroughfare known as the **Hlavná**, a long and broad avenue which swells out in the middle to form the adjoining squares of the Hlavné námestie and the námestie Slobody—respectively to the north and south of the town's cathedral. Right up to the early 1990s this monumental space had all the animation of a major city such as Budapest, with trams and a constant stream of traffic running in between the once blackened palaces and apartment blocks from the turn of the century and earlier. Today the tram-lines have been kept purely as a historical souvenir, and the whole area transformed into a vast pedestrian precinct, flanked by brightly restored buildings and decorated for its entire length with a hazardous water channel flowing into a fountain whose floodlit jets 'dance' to the continual sounds of muzack. Outside the summer months, the place is eerily quiet by night, and animated at weekends mainly by shoppers making their way to Europe's easternmost branch of Tesco's, the British supermarket chain.

The vital and pungent character of old Košice has undoubtedly been eroded by all these changes; but the still relatively few tourists who come to the town can at least count themselves lucky in being able to see in its full glory the superlative **Cathedral of St Elizabeth** (Katedrála sv. Alžbety).

History of the cathedral

Work on the cathedral, the largest in Slovakia, was begun c 1380 on the site of a former parish church which had been destroyed by fire in 1378. Sigismund of Luxemburg and later Matthias Corvinus gave much help in the construction of the building, which was supervised until 1420 by the royal architect Master Peter, and until 1477 by Master Štefan of Košice. Badly damaged in 1491, when Košice was besieged in the course of the struggle between Vladislav II and his younger brother John Albert, the cathedral was finally brought to completion c 1508. A serious fire devastated the interior in 1556, destroying most of the medieval furnishings, including 18 of the original 22 altars.

Following further damage by flood and earthquake, major repairs were carried out between 1857 and 1867, and from 1877 to 1896 neo-Gothic remodelling of the interior was undertaken by Franz Schmidt, the restorer of St Stephen's Cathedral in Vienna. Restoration work was begun in 1985 and virtually completed by 1997.

The exterior of the cathedral, with its crocketed and dramatically tapering crossing tower and steeply pitched roofs covered in coloured tiling, has a west façade framed by two towers, one tall and octagonal, the other squat, with late Gothic detailing; in the tympanum of the west portal is a carved representation of Christ in the Garden of Gethsemane, above which is a group of the Lamentation. The most elaborately shaped and richly carved of the cathedral's portals is the northern one, which has a tympanum portraying the Last Judgement. The dark interior, lit by 19C stained glass, has at its western end a raised choir supported by arches adorned with intricate late Gothic statuary, the colouring of which was renewed in the 19C. Perhaps the most striking architectural feature of the interior is the openwork and minutely carved **stone staircase** attached to the north side of the presbytery and leading up to the Royal Gallery in the triforium; executed in 1468–77 it is the masterpiece of Master Štefan of Košice. Of the furnishings, special mention must be made of the late Gothic **pulpit** (another remarkably elaborate structure, crowned by a soaring wooden canopy) and of the **high altar** of St Elizabeth of Hungary, a vast wing altar containing 48 panels painted on a gold ground, executed in 1474–77 and attributed by some to the German master Michael Wolgemut. In the **crypt** is to be found the tomb of the great Hungarian challenger to Habsburg rule, Ferenc Rákóczi II, whose remains, together with those of his fellow exiles, were brought over from Turkey in 1909.

Cathedral of St Elizabeth

In the garden on the south side of the cathedral is the late 14C Chapel of St Michael (Kaplnka sv. Michala), while in front of the cathedral's north portal is the former belfry tower known as the **Urban's Tower** (Urbanova veža), a 15C structure surrounded by arcading at ground level and remodelled in the 16C; inside you can climb up to the top for the superb view, or else enjoy a miscellaneous collection of local metalwork ranging from cannon-balls to exquisitely wrought liturgical objects. **Open** Tues–Sat 09.00–17.00, Sun 09.00–13.00.

Due west of the cathedral is the entrance to the cheerfully restored street known as Alžbetina where, on the left-hand side, there are a couple of adjoining museums: that at No.22 (a branch of the Július Jakoby Gallery described below) specialises in the artistic representation of Košice over the centuries; the other, at No.20, is the newly opened **Vojtech Löffler Museum**, which is laid out in and around the former studio of this leading local sculptor from the Communist period: his works in a Socialist Realist vein have at least a certain kitsch appeal wholly lacking in his preferred but rather dull abstract renditions of the figure. **Open** Tues–Sat 10.00–18.00, Sun 13.00–17.00.

Return to the Hlavná and head north on the avenue's western side. To your right, rising above a large landscaped area at the centre of the Hlavné námestie, is an **Opera House** (Štátne divadlo) on a scale that would seem more suited to a major capital city than to a provincial town: dating back to 1899, and now shining under its newly restored coat of honey-yellow paint, this is one of the livelier and more imposing works by that ubiquitous Viennese pair, Helmer and Fellner. In the gardens on the northern side of this building is a Marian column of 1723.

As you continue to walk north along the western side of the Hlavná, you will be confronted at No.88 with the giant columns of the late Baroque Rákóczi Palace, an 18C remodelling of a building that had served as the headquarters of the Hungarian military authorities. Today it houses the **Slovak Technical Museum** (Slovenské technické múzeum), the only museum of its kind in Slovakia, and a place whose diverse objects document such important aspects of Slovak economy as mining and metallurgy: the exhibits include mining interiors, and a large collection of wrought ironwork. **Open** Tues–Fri 08.00–17.00, Sat 09.00–14.00, Sun 12.00–17.00.

The avenue comes to an end at the námestie Maratónu mieru, on the left-hand side of which stands the enormous neo-Renaissance building of 1899 containing the main branch of the **Museum of Eastern Slovak** (Východoslovenské múzeum). Though the heart might sink at the prospect of a museum devoted to the history of East Slovakia from prehistoric to modern times, this place differs from the usual dreary institutions of its kind by displaying in its basement (in a claustrophobic walk-in safe that is unlocked at regular intervals for groups of visitors) what is claimed to be one of the largest gold hordes in the world.

The Košice Gold Treasure

The so-called **Košice Gold Treasure**, comprising 16C gold medallions minted in Kremnica, a Renaissance gold chain, and 2920 15C–18C gold coins (from 81 European mints), was amassed in the middle years of the 17C by an unknown local burgher who invested in gold at a time when the European economy had been seriously undermined by the Thirty Years War and the wars against the Ottomans. Apparently a supporter of the Habsburgs, he seems to have hidden his treasure at some time between 1680 and 1682, when the town was occupied by the Hungarian rebel Imre Thököly, a leader of the anti-Habsburg faction. Buried under the cellar floor of a house at 68 Hlavná (known today as the Spiš Chamber), the gold was uncovered accidentally in 1935 by men engaged on renovation work—appropriately enough—on the city's Financial Directorate; although entitled by law to receive one third of the value of their find, the discoverers of the treasure went completely unrewarded.

Behind the museum is a reconstructed wooden church from Kožuchovce in Carpatho-Ruthenia, while in front, on the opposite side of the square, is another branch of the Museum of Eastern Slovak, this one featuring a musty display of Gothic sculptures and panel paintings, and some charming reconstructed interiors from different periods in the town's history. **Open** Tues–Sat 09.00–17.00, Sun 13.00–17.00.

Returning to Hlavná, you should now walk down its eastern side, passing almost immediately the new branch of Tesco's (a replacement for the Prior Department Store). As you near the Opera House once more, you will see to your left the exposed stone facade of the 17C Jesuit church, beyond which is a street whose name has been significantly changed since 1992 from E. Ady (one of Hungary's greatest poets) to the less controversial Univerzitná. This will take you to the **Miklos Prison** (Miklošova väznica), a whitewashed 16C structure, inside which you can see much of the original interior, a torture chamber, and a network of secret passages. Adjoining this, at the western end of the street, is the **Executioner's Bastion** (Katova bašta), which forms part of the medieval ramparts, and is now used to display the geological and zoological sections of the East Slovak Museum. Within its verdant courtyard is a replica of the picturesque half-timbered tower where Ferenc Rákóczi lived after being exiled to the Turkish town of Tekirdag; the intriguing interior, with its small exhibition devoted to Rákóczi's life, features a richly ornamented dining-room with the original coloured wainscoting. **Open** Tues–Sat 09.00–17.00, Sun 09.00–13.00.

Back on Hlavná, continue south to pass at No. 65 the much-restored Levoča House, a building of 15C origin with an attractive whitewashed courtyard and an excellent cheap Hungarian restaurant (*Miškolc Maďarská reštaurácia*); attached to its southern side is the newly restored *Café Slavia*, a splendid Art Nouveau building with polychromed decoration on its exterior.

Further south, directly facing the cathedral's apse, is the main branch of the **Július Jakoby Gallery** (Galéria Júliusa Jakobyho), which occupies part of a pedimented palace of 1779 that had served in 1945 as the first seat of the newly returned Czechoslovak government. The spacious and recently revamped gallery, which now has a good café in the basement, puts on changing exhibitions culled mainly from an extensive permanent collection of East Slovak art from the late 18C to recent times, including works by the 18C portraitist Bogdany (who settled in England and is often considered English) and the naïf landscapist and portraitist Jozef Czauczik. Other artists in the collection include Ján Rombauer, Anton Stadler, František Klimkovič, Ladislav Medňanský, Ferdinand Katona, Jozef Hanula, Ľudovít Cordák, Max Kurth, Elemir Halász-Hradil, Anton Jasusch, Konštantín Kövári, Konštantín Bauer, Jozef Bendík and Jozef Fabini. **Open** Tues–Sat 10.00–18.00, Sun 10.00–14.00.

33 · Košice to Banská Bystrica

Total distance 214km: Košice • 69km Rožňava • 53km Švermovo • 49km Brezno • 43km Banská Bystrica.

Head south from Košice on Road 50/E571, to begin with following a short stretch of dual carriageway which comes to an end just before the industrial community of Šaca (16km), and turns sharply to the west. The road, which passes at first through flat countryside, soon enters a green and beautiful valley running between the hills of northern Hungary and the southern slopes of the Slovak **Ore Mountains** (Slovenské rudohorie).

At Moldava nad Bodvou, a turning to the right will bring you after 9km to **Jasov**, where there is a former Premonstratensian monastery, founded in the 12C. The original foundation was destroyed by Tartar invasions in the early 13C, and the present structure is an impressive late Baroque building executed in 1750–66 to designs by F.A. Pilgram (the frescoes and the high altar are by J.L. Kracker). The village stands on the eastern edge of the **Slovak Karst** (Slovenský kras), the largest karst area in Central Europe, extending well to the west of Rožňava; geographically a part of the Slovak Ore Mountains, it features numerous gorges and caves, in one of which—on the outskirts of Jasov—footprints of neo-Palaeolithic man have been discovered.

Return to the E571 and continue heading west, passing to the right after 10km the scant, hill-top ruins of Turňa castle. On the eastern outskirts of Rožňava, 26km further on, the imposing mass of one of Slovakia's most famed castles, **Krásna Hôrka**, provides a glowing white crown to a tall, steep mound ringed with wild meadows.

History of the castle
Founded in 1320, the castle was acquired in the 16C by the Andrássy family, who between 1578 and 1586 remodelled the medieval building, and at great expense extended the fortifications in preparation for a possible Turkish attack. Inhabited up to 1812, the castle was partially renovated in 1903 by its last owner, Count Dionysius Andrássy, who transformed it into a family museum opened to the public in 1910, and built at its foot an extraordinary family mausoleum. In 1989 the castle was re-opened following further extensive restoration.

Shortly before leaving the E571 and climbing up to the castle, you will pass on the right-hand side of the road the gates of the mausoleum which was built by Count Dionysius Andrássy in 1903–04. It contains the tombs both of himself and of his wife Františka Hablavcová (d. 1902), a celebrated Czech opera singer who had been rejected by her husband's family for her non-aristocratic origins. Shaded by a wooded grove it is a lavish temple-like structure in a Secessionist style, with a resplendent marbled interior, the apse of which is highlighted in gold mosaic. At the end of the long climb up to the castle you are offered an outstanding view over fields and wooded hills. In the entrance courtyard is a section of Budapest's Chain Bridge, which was founded in the Andrássy iron-works. The western part of the castle was destroyed by fire in 1817 and has recently been re-opened with a modern display of armour, portraits of the Andrássy family, 17C and 18C furniture, traditional costumes of the Hungarian aristocracy and items relating to the history of the building and of the Thirty Years War. The series of rooms created by Dionysius Andrássy in 1903 as a family museum have Baroque to Empire furnishings and decorations, and include paintings and drawings by Dionysius himself and a fine collection of old European glass assembled by Stefán Andrássy. Among the castle's other attractions are a traditional kitchen and an early 18C chapel housing the mummified and lace-covered remains of Štefán's wife, Zsofia Sereghy. **Open** May–Oct Tues–Sun, tours every 1hr 30min 08.00–17.30; Nov–Apr hourly tours 09.00–15.00 (except 12.00).

Rožňava, 5km to the west, is a medieval mining town with an early 18C bishop's palace and a main square containing a number of old buildings, most notably a tower of 1643–54. Fourteen kilometres southwest of the town is another of the well-known caves of the Slovenský kras, the **Gombasek Ice Cave**, with ice-covered stalactites as long as 3m; even larger is the **Domica Cave**, which lies 15km to the south (leave the E571 at Plešivec, and turn left), and is linked to the Aggtelek Cave in Hungary (the border between the two countries is marked by a grille).

Continuing on your journey to Banská Bystrica head north of Rožňava on Road 67, and you will come after 6km to **Betliar**, another of the many properties that belonged to the Andrássy family. The present appearance of this château, which dates back to a 16C building remodelled in the 18C, is due to drastic reconstruction carried out in 1880–86. The rather heavy interior (at present closed for restoration) has numerous hunting trophies and collections of china, ceramics, furniture and armour. More appealing are the magnificent gardens, laid out in an English style at the end of the 18C and featuring numerous waterfalls, grottoes, temples and other follies.

North of Betliar, Road 67 climbs up into the Slovak Ore Mountains, entering after the small village of Dobšiná (19km) the popular summer resort of the **Slovak Paradise** (Slovenský raj), an area of densely forested mountains intercut with deep, rocky chasms. Seven kilometres beyond Dobšiná is a turning to the right to Dedinky, where there is a small reservoir and a chair-lift leading up to the wooded plateau of Geravy, a popular place for cross-country skiers. North of the turning Road 67 descends into the narrow Stratená Gorge and is hemmed in by steep faces of rock. The first turning on the right will take you along a most beautiful if poorly surfaced road which runs through the heart of the Slovak Paradise and all the way to Hrabušice (18km).

From Hrabušice an hour's walk to the east leads to the finest place from which to explore the Paradise, **Kláštorisko**, a clearing in the forest featuring a restaurant, a group of tourist chalets and excellent views towards the snow-capped High Tatras (see Chapter 30). It was in Kláštorisko that the inhabitants of the region took refuge in the wake of the Tartar invasions of the early 13C, and in memory of this representatives of the 24 Spiš towns founded here a Carthusian monastery in 1305; conquered in the 16C by the cruel bandit Matthias Baso, and used by him as a base for his various savage forays, the place was later demolished, and now only a few scant ruins can be seen. Kláštorisko stands above the spectacular gorge of the Hornád, and a short walk can be made from here to the **Tomášov Balcony** (Tomášovský výhlăd), a dramatic overhang with a sheer drop down to the river. There are numerous other walks of a more adventurous kind to be done in the area, most notably along the gorge and up a series of interconnecting ones; these walks involve climbing up ladders along the side of waterfalls, and skirting sheer rock faces with the aid of chains and climbing irons.

Continuing to Banská Bystrica along Road 67 you will pass the **Dobšiná Ice Cave** (Dobšinská ládorá jaskyňa), 2km west of the turning to Hrabušice; the largest such cave in the Czech and Slovak Republics, it is filled with a massive iceberg 145,000 cubic metres in size.

Shortly beyond the cave you leave Road 67, and turn left on to Road 66, which descends through attractive countryside into the valley of the Hron, bordered to the south by the Slovak Ore Mountains and to the north by the Low Tatras (see Route 30). Fourteen kilometre after the turning there is a small dead-end road to the right leading 3km to one of the least-spoilt and least-visited villages in Slovakia, **Šumiac**; composed almost entirely of traditional 19C wooden houses, the villagers continue to wear the old folk costumes, particularly on Sundays and public holidays.

A further 14km west along Road 66, you pass through the large village of Helpa, a place of no great character but with a number of wooden houses on the left-hand side of the road, and with a reputation for its folk traditions; a folklore festival is held here every summer. At Brezno, another 29km west, an old Town Hall dating back to the 1780s houses a museum devoted to local history and ethnography.

Six kilometres beyond Brezno there branches off to the north Road 72, a beautiful road crossing right over the ridge of the Low Tatras. Continuing on Road 66, one of the few sites of interest before reaching Banská Bystrica 33km away (see Chapter 28) is **Nemecká**, the site of a Nazi atrocity during the Second World War. You will see on the right-hand side of the road 12km east of Banská Bystrica a lime kiln in which around 900 Slovak partisans involved in the National Uprising were killed by the Germans, a crime which was only discovered much later; a nearby small museum and a modern bronze of a woman with outstretched arms commemorate the incident.

Index

Adriaen de Vries 51, 135, 136, 146, 152
Aleš Mikoláš 59, 109, 117, 121, 129, 165, 172, 185, 191, 273, 275, 283, 288, 355
Alliprandi, G.B. 111, 133, 157, 159, 216, 217, 258, 355
Antol 396
Arcimboldo, Giuseppe 52, 100
Austerlitz 303, 338

Balšánek, Antonín 58, 108, 168
Bánovce nad Bedravou 403
Banská Bystrica 361, 406
Banská Štiavnica 361, 395
Bardejov 362, 428
Bardejovské kúpele 429
Barvitius, Viktor 59, 129, 191
Báťa, Tomáš 64, 90, 165, 348, 349
Bechyně 287
Beckov 400
Benátky nad Jizerou 222
Bendel, Georg 296, 302
Bendelmayer, Bedřich 109, 167
Bendl, Jan 120
Bendl, Petr 56, 152
Benešov nad Ploučnicí 235
Bethlehem Wood 217
Betliar 438
Bezděkov 221
Bezděz 235
Bezruč, Petr 79, 350, 353
Bílek, František 61, 127, 174, 212
Bílina 245
Bítov 316

Black Lake 269
Blansko 331
Blatná 279, 281
Bodruzal 430
Bohemian Paradise 222
Bohún, Peter Michal 61, 379, 380, 416
Bojnice 404
Boleslav II 99, 153, 177, 185
Borovský, Karel Havlíček 78, 171, 308
Boubín, Mt 289
Bouzov 303, 356
Brandl, Petr 55, 110, 132, 146, 212, 216, 218, 234, 237, 240, 247, 302
Brandýs nad Labem 222, 223
Bratislava 361, 365
  Academia Istro-politana 372
  Amphitheatre 384
  Archbishops' Palace 385
  Aspreymont Palace 384
  Citadel 381
  City Gallery 373
  Corpus Christi Chapel 373
  Grassalkovich Palace 386
  Hummel Memorial 377
  Jewish Culture in Slovakia, Museum of 381
  Koliba Expo 386
  Mirbach Palace 375
  Pharmaceutical Museum 370
  Primate's Palace 376
  Old Town Hall 376
  St Clare, Church of 374
  St Elizabeth, Church of 384

Bratislava cont.
  St Martin's Cathedral 374
  St Michael's Bridge 370
  St Michael's Tower 371
  Slavín Monument 386
  Slovak National Museum 378
  Slovak National Theatre 377
  Trinity Church 384
Braun, Matthias 52, 54, 55, 110, 118, 119, 131, 132, 136, 137, 139, 140, 152, 174, 176, 209, 216, 217, 240, 242, 243, 265, 266, 310
Brezno 439
Brno 303, 320
  Capuchin monastery 323
  Cathedral of SS Peter and Paul 324
  Divadlo na Provázku 324
  Moravian Museum 323
  Old Town Hall 322
  Parnassus Fountain 322
  Reduta Theatre 323
  St James, Church of 326
  St Michael, Dominican Church of 324
  Špilberk Citadel 327
  Villa Tugendhat 329
  Výstaviště Exhibition Ground 328
Brod, Max 81
Brodzany 404
Broumov 221
Bruntál 353
Břeclav 359
Březnice 283
Broggio, Giovanni 239,

240
Broggio, Ottavio 236, 239, 240, 243, 245
Brokoff, Ferdinand Maximilian 56, 110, 111, 127, 131, 132, 137, 140, 152, 157, 159
Brokoff, J. 56, 131, 132, 173, 175, 235, 246
Brožík, Václav 117, 172, 191
Broumov 221
Buchlov 346
Buchlovice 346
Bučovice 340
Budatín 410
Budeč 203
Bussi, Santino 118

Čachtice 399
Čadca 410
Čapek, Josef 62, 117, 189, 233, 256, 275, 288
Čapek, Karel 82, 117, 256, 282
Caratti, Francesco 53, 119, 120, 137, 159, 236
Carlone, Carlo 118
Častelovice 351
Čermák, Jaroslav 59, 129, 191
Černice 280
Čertovica Pass 418
Červená Lhota 302
Červený Kameň 387
Červený Kláštor 426
Česká Skalice 219
České 229
České Budějovice 297
Český Krumlov 293
Český ráj 208
Český Šternberk 199
Chabence 417
Charles IV 36, 48, 49, 99, 130, 142, 147, 162, 169, 175, 177, 200, 202, 206, 235,

251, 270, 290, 333
Cheb 257
Chelčický, Petr 39, 74
Chitussi, Antonín 59, 129, 211
Chlumec nad Cidlinou 209
Chochol, Josef 58, 63, 101, 179
Chod Region 249, 266
Chomutov 245
Chopok 417
Chrudim 211
Čičmany 411
Cornštejn 316

Dačice 315
Dalimil 74
Děčín 235
Dedinky 438
Demänovská Dolina 417
Demänovská jaskyňa Slobody 417
Detva 393
Devět skal 310
Dientzenhofer, Christoph 53, 133, 136, 153, 160, 185, 214, 264, 282
Dientzenhofer, K.I. 53, 109, 115, 133, 135, 136, 159, 160, 166, 175, 176, 181, 184, 185, 221, 255, 264, 265, 267, 268, 280, 281, 283, 286
Dobříš 282
Dobrovský, Josef 42, 76, 161, 164
Dobšiná Ice Cave 439
Doksany, Convent of 237
Dolná Krúpa 398
Dolná Strehová 392
Dolný Kubín 414
Domažlice 249, 266
Domica Cave 438
Donovaly 409
Donner, Georg Raphael 56, 374, 376, 380

Doubravník 311
Doudleby nad Orlicí 351
Dryák, Alois 165, 167, 174, 184
Dubček, Alexander 44, 45, 163, 404
Dubí 243
Duchcov 229, 243
Ďumbier 417
Dunajská Streda 389
Dušek, František Xaver 69, 181
Dušková, J. 181
Dvořák, Antonín 71, 176, 205, 255, 256
Dvořák, Karel 62, 147, 164, 170, 182, 190
Dvůr Králové 219

Einstein, Albert 111, 181
Erlach, J.B. Fischer von 53, 110, 118, 150, 160, 205, 209, 245, 316, 317, 322, 358

Fellner, Ferdinand 57, 377, 435
Fellner and Helmer 254, 255
Filla, Emil 62, 189, 256, 275, 349, 354
Forman, Miloš 90-91, 143
Františkovy Lázně 249, 259
Freedom Cave 417
Freud, Sigmund 80, 344, 345
Frýdek-Místek 350
Frýdlant 233
Fulla, Ľudovít 65, 373, 380, 407, 413, 415, 432
Fulnek 338

Gerulata 388
Giant Mountains 208, 221, 225
Gočár, Josef 63, 101, 110,

167, 182, 211, 214
Godyn, Abraham 55, 191
Gombasek Ice Cave 438
Gutfreund, Otto 62, 167,
  170, 183, 189, 219, 349

Hamuliakavo 389
Harrachov 226
Hašek, Jaroslav 81, 176,
  299, 308, 309
Havel, Václav 43, 44, 45,
  47, 74, 89, 92, 93,
  102, 109, 118, 143,
  145, 163, 165, 172,
  180, 282, 351, 354,
  403
Havlíčkův Brod 308
Helpa 438
Heřmánkovice 221
Hervartov 428
High Tatras 362, 418
Hlohovec 398
Hluboká nad Vltavou
  279, 287
Hodslavice 344
Holub, Miroslav 92
Horšovský Týn 266
Hostinné 228
Hrabal, Bohumil 65, 88,
  90, 322
Hradec Králové 207, 211
Hradec nad Moravicí 353
Hrádek U Nechanic 210
Hronov 221
Hrubá skála 224
Hrubý Rohozec 223
Hukvaldy 345
Hummel, Johann
  Nepomuk 68, 366, 377
Husinec 270
Hus, Jan 37, 74, 100,
  112, 113, 122, 270,
  285
Hynais, Vojtěch 59, 129,
  164, 172

Ivančice 320

Jablonec 232

Jäckel, Matěj Václav 56,
  131
Janáček, Leoš 71, 256,
  328, 329, 350
Janák, Pavel 63, 156,
  159, 165, 170, 185,
  233, 307, 314
Jankov Vršok 404
Jánošík, Juraj 79, 412
Janské Lánzě 228
Jaroměř 214
Jasov 437
Jasusch, Anthon 373,
  380, 436
Jeseník 352
Jesenský, Janko 413
Jičín 225
Jihlava 303, 307
Jilemnice 227
Jindřich, Jindřich 267
Jindřichův Hradec 300
Jirásek, Alois 59, 78, 185,
  221
Jizera Mountains 229
Jókai, Mór 389, 390, 402
Jungmann, Josef 42, 76,
  171, 234
Jur 387
Jurkovič, Dušan 347

Kačina 197
Kadaň 245
Kafka, Bohumil 61, 109,
  148, 183, 286
Kafka, Franz 80, 111,
  115, 143, 165, 182,
  420
Kájov 296
Kaliště 307
Kaňka, F.M. 119, 120,
  123, 153, 159, 179,
  209, 247
Karlova Koruna 209
Karlova Studánka 353
Karlovy Vary 249, 250
  Art Gallery 256
  Castle 254
  Diana's tower 256
  Findlater Chapel 256

Karlovy Vary cont
  Grand Hotel Pupp 255
  Haus Zawojski 254
  Kaiserbad 255
  Mill Colonnade 253
  Moser Glassworks 256
  Mühlbrunnen 253
  Museum 255
  Sadová Colonnade 253
  St Luke, church of 256
  SS Peter and Paul,
    church of 256
  St Mary Magdalene,
    church of 255
  Thermal Sanatorium
    253
  Tržní Colonnade 254
  Vřídelní Colonnade 254
Karlštejn 200
Kašperské Hory 270
Kdyně 268
Kepler, Johannes 40, 119,
  100, 159
Kežmarok 425
Kisch, Egon Erwin 81,
  123, 183
Kladbury 264
Kladruby nad Labem
  211
Klášterec nad Ohří 246
Kláštorisko 438
Klatovy 268
Klenčí pod Čerchovem
  267
Klíma, Ivan 93, 238, 300
Klokoty 286
Klouček, C. 166
Kodály, Zoltán 397
Kohl, Ludvík 128
Kolín 197
Komárno 389
Konopiště 199
Kopeček 337
Kopřivnice 345
Košice 362, 432
Kostelec nad Orlicí 351
Kostolány pod Tribečom
  394
Kotěra, Jan 58, 63, 64,

124, 127, 165, 167, 170, 211, 213, 214, 322, 333, 348
Kracker, Johann Lucas 55, 133, 380, 437
Kracker, Tobiáš 318
Král', Janko 79, 388, 413, 416
Kralupy 197
Krásna Hôrka 437
Krásńy Dvůr 229, 247
Kratochvíle, summer palace of 271
Kremnica 405
Křinice 221
Krivé 428
Křivoklát 202
Krkonoše Mountains 208
Krnov 353
Kroměříž 303, 340
Křtiny 332
Krupina 391
Kuba, Ludvík 283
Kubišta, Bohumil 62, 189, 233, 256, 275, 349, 354
Kuks 207, 209, 215, 243
Kundera, Milan 34, 44, 88, 89, 91, 322
Kunětická Hora 211
Kupecký, J. 55, 146, 152, 206, 209, 292, 380, 387
Kupka, František 61, 189
Kutná Hora 191, 192
Kysela, František 147, 148, 166, 167, 213

Labská bouda 227
Lány 203
Large Fatra 409
Latrán 294
Lázně Bohdaneč 210
Lázně Kynžvart 263
Lázně Libverda 234
Lednice 303, 358

Lehár, Franz 390
Lenora 289
Levoča 362, 421
Levý Hradec 205
Lhoták, Kamil 64, 190
Liberec 233
Libochovice 236
Lidice 203
Lietava 411
Lipnice nad Sázavou 308
Lipová Lázně 353
Liptovský Mikuláš 412, 416
Liška, Jan 55, 152, 206, 209, 244
Litoměřice 229, 239
Litomyšl 303, 354
Little Fatra 411
Lnáře 280
Loket 257, 261-262
Lomnický štít 418
Loos, Adolf 184, 322
Louka 319
Louny 246
Löw, Rabbi 124
Low Tatra 409
Lubenec 247
Ľubochňa 415
Ludrová 415
Luhačovice 347
Lurago, Anselmo 114, 119, 133, 145, 154, 166
Lurago, Carlo 53, 120, 137, 167, 178, 212, 246, 283
Lysá hora 350

Máchás Region 234
Machek, Antonín 58, 128, 211
Macocha Abyss 331
Maggi, Baldassare 51, 301, 312
Mahler, Gustav 80, 307, 335
Maisel, Markus 124, 126

Mandl, M.B. 131
Mánes, Antonín 58, 128, 240
Mánes, Josef 58, 109, 116, 121, 128
Manín Gorge 402
Mařák, Julius 59, 129, 188
Mařatka, J. 61, 118
Mariánské Lázně (Marienbad) 249, 261
Markušovce 423
Martin 413
Martinola, G.P. 302
Martinské Hole 414
Martinů, Bohuslav 72, 138, 356
Masaryk, Jan 44, 159
Masaryk, President Tomáš 43, 64, 78, 85, 143, 145, 203, 214
Mascharino, Ottaviano 52
Master of the Litoměřice Altarpiece 50, 148, 152
Mathey, Jean Baptiste 53, 54, 135, 120, 190, 243, 277
Matuška, Janko 414
Maulbertsch, Franz Anton 55, 152, 161, 319, 326, 341, 342, 373, 377, 380
Max, Emmanuel 60, 120, 131
Max, Josef 60, 121, 150
Mayer, J.O. 131
Medňanský, Baron Ladislav 61, 373, 380, 400, 416, 426, 436
Medzilaborce 430
Mělník 206
Menzel, Jiří 91, 93
Mezná 235
Mikulov 303, 357
Mirola 430
Mladá Boleslav 223
Mnichov Hradiště 223

Mocker, Josef 57, 105,
  120, 147, 148, 169,
  201, 202
Modra 387
Moravian Karst 330
Moravská Třebová 356
Moravský kras 303
Moravský Krumlov 303,
  319
Most 245
Mucha, Alfons 59, 108,
  109, 129, 139,
  150, 240, 320, 399
Myslbek, Josef Václav
  60, 109, 150, 164,
  165, 172, 174, 178,
  182

Náchod 220
Náměšť nad Oslavou 314
Navrátil, Josef 58, 234,
  240, 275
Nelahozeves 205
Němcová, Božena 267
Nemecká 439
Nepomucký, Jan 52, 54,
  100, 131, 280, 310
Nepomuk 280
Neruda, Jan 78, 109,
  140, 171, 355
Neumann, Balthasar 53,
  258, 259
Němcová, Božena 77,
  109, 172, 219, 234,
  260, 267, 355
Nitra 361, 393
Novák, K. 108
Nové Město 220
Nový Jičín 344

Obořiště 282
Obrovský, Jakub 109,
  183, 209
Obyčtov 310
Ohrada Hunting-Lodge
  289
Ohře to Klášterec nad
  Ohří 245
Olomouc 303, 333

Opařany 287
Opava 353
Opočno 221
Orava Castle 414
Ore Mountains 229, 437
Orlík nad Vltavou 283
Osek 245, 281
Ostrava 303, 354
Ostrov 246

Pacassi, N. 145
Palach, Jan 44, 102,
  163, 182
Palacký, František 42,
  76, 164, 171, 335
Palko, F.X. 55, 133, 376
Palliardi, I.J. 141, 161
Parléř, Peter 49, 100,
  113, 130, 146, 147,
  150, 193, 197, 290
Pardubice 210
Paštiky 281
Patince 390
Pec pod Sněžkov 228
Pelhřimov 307
Pernštejn 310
Pešánek, Zdeněk 64, 190
Piepenhagen, August 128
Pezinok 387
Pieniny National Park
  426
Piešťany 361, 398
Pilgram, Anton 322,
  326, 384
Pinkas, Soběslav 59, 129
Písek 281, 284
Plasy, monastery of 277
Platzer, Ignác František
  56, 133, 143, 282
Plečnik, Josip 64, 143,
  145, 155, 156, 182
Plzeň 249, 272
  Brewery Museum 276
  Franciscan church and
    monastery 275
  Great Synagogue 274
  Meat Hall 276
  náměsti Republiky 273
  Pilsner Urquell Brewery

Plzeň cont
  276
  St Anne, Dominican
    Church of 273
  St Bartholomew,
    Cathedral of 273
  St George, Church of
    277
  Škoda Museum 275
  Town Hall 273
  West Bohemian Gallery
    275
Ploskovice 240
Poděbrady 209
Poděbrady, George of 39,
  100, 111, 113, 132,
  148, 209, 284, 356
Police nad Metují 221
Polička 356
Polívka, Osvald 58, 108,
  118, 171, 212
Poprad 420
Popradské Pleso 419
Poříčí nad Sázavou 200
Postl, Karel 58, 128
Prachatice 270
Prachner, Richard 199
Prachner, Václav 60, 118
Prachovské Skály 224
Prague
  Adria Palace 170
  Astronomical Clock
    116
  At the Painter's 137
  Barrandov 101
  Báťa Department Store
    165
  Bertramka 180
  Bethlehem Chapel 122
  Bethlehem Square 122
  Břevnov 184
  Břvnov 184
  Bubeneč 186
  Café Arco 167
  Café Slavia 171
  Carolinum 123
  Castle Steps 139
  Cathedral, St Vitus 146
  Celetná 109

Prague cont
  Central Station 168
  Ceremonial Hall 126
  Charles Bridge 100,
    130
  Chotěk Park 156
  City Transport Museum
    184
  Church of
    Our Lady before Týn
      113
    Our Lady Na Slupi
      175
    Our Lady of Loreto
      160
    Our Lady of the
      Snows 169
    Our Lady under the
      Chain 136
    Sacred Heart 182
    St Castullus 129
    St Catherine 176
    St Clement, 119
    SS Cyril and
      Methodius 174
    St Gall 123
    St Giles 122
    St James 110
    St John at the Wash-
      House 138
    St John of Nepomuk
      159
    St John on the Rock
      175
    St Margaret 185
    St Mary the Victorious
      138
    St Nicholas 101, 114,
      130, 133
    St Peter na Poříč 168
    St Thomas 135
  Clam-Gallas Palace 118
  Clementinum 101, 119
  Convent of St Agnes
    128, 188
  Convent of St Anne 121
  Convent of St George
    151
  Customs House 105

Prague cont
  Czech Museum of Fine
    Arts 110
  Černín Palace 137, 159
  Emmaus Monastery
    175
  Estate Theatre (formerly
    Tyl) 123
  Faust House 174
  Golden Lane 153
  Goltz-Kinský Palace 114
  Grand Hotel Europa
    165
  Grand Prior's Mill 138
  Grand Prior's Palace
    137
  Hanavský Pavilion 186
  Hibernians, The 105
  High Synagogue 125
  Historical Museum 154
  Hlubočepy 180
  Holešovice 186
  Hotel Intrercontinental
    127
  House at the Stork's
    121
  House at the Two Suns
    140
  House of the Black
    Virgin 110
  Hradčany Square 157
  Hrzán Palace 137
  Hunger Wall 141
  Husova 117
  Hybernská 167
  Jan Hus Monument
    112
  Jewish Museum 124
  Jewish Town Hall 125
  Jungmann Square 169
  Kampa Island 138
  Karlín 184
  Karlov 175
  Karlova 117
  Kaunic Palace 132
  Ke Karlovu 176
  Kinský Palace 167
  Kinský Villa 181
  Klárov 136

Prague cont
  Klaus Synagogue 126
  Kluks 136
  Kolowrat-Černín Palace
    134
  Komárov 186
  Koruna Palace 166
  Ledebour-Trautt-
    mansdorf Palace 134
  Legio Bank 167
  Leopold Gate 178
  Letenská 135
  Letná Park 186
  Little Quarter Square
    132
  Lobkowicz Palace 141,
    154
  Loreto Square 159
  Magic Lantern 171
  Magic Lantern Theatre
    102
  Maisel Synagogue 126
  Maison Muller 184
  Malá Strana 130
  Malé Náměstí 117
  Malta Square 137
  Mánes Gallery 172
  Mánes Hall 128
  Martinic Palace 162
  Masaryck Railway
    Station 167
  Melantrich House 165
  Michna of Vacínov
    Palace 138
  Military Museum 158,
    183
  Modern Art, Museum of
    187
  Morzin Palace 140
  Mostecká 132
  Mozart Museum 181
  Municipal House 105
  Municipal water tower
    121
  Museum of Czech
    Literature 162
  Museum of Decorative
    Arts 127
  Museum of the City of

Prague cont
Prague 168
Na Příkokě 101
Na Příkopé 166
Náprstek Museum 122
National Gallery 151,
157
National Monument
183
National Museum 163
National Technical
Museum 186
National Theatre 171
Nerudova 139
New Archbishop's
Chapel 150
New Jewish Cemetery
182
New National Theatre
171
New Town Hall 118,
173
New White Tower 153
Nostitz Palace 137
Nový Svět 159
Old Castle Steps 143
Old Jewish Cemetery
126
Old Royal Palace 154
Old Town Hall 115
Old Town Square 111
Old-New Synagogue
125
Olšanské Cemetery 102
Ošany Cemetery 182
Palace Gardens Below
Prague Castle 134
Palace Hotel 169
Palace of the Lords of
Hradec 139
Palacký Bridge 174
Palacký Momument
174
Palacký Square 174
Pálffy Palace 134
Pařížská 123
Petřín Gardens 141
Petřín Hill 141
Philosophical Hall 161

Prague cont
Pinkas Synagogue 125-
126
Platéýz House 170
Pohořelec 160
Portheimka 181
Powder Bridge 156
Powder Gate 105
Powder Tower 151
Prague Castle 101,
130, 142
Prague Castle Gallery
146
Rotunda of St Longinus
176
Rotunda of St Martin 178
Rotunda of the Holy
Rood 121
Royal Riding School 156
Rudolfinum 126
Schönborn-Colloredo
Palace 140
Schwarzenberg
Lobkowicz Palace 158
Slavonic Island 172
Smetana Embankment
121
Smíchov 180
Smiřický Montág Palace
132
Sněmovní 134
Spanish Synagogue
127
Spartakiáda Stadium
184
Sports Museum 138
Square of the Grand
Priory 137
St Wenceslas
Monument 164
Star Castle 185
Strahov Art Gallery 162
Strahov Monastery 160
Straka Palace 137
Střešovice 184
Summer Palace 156
Sylva-Taroucca Palace
166
Šternberk Palace 157

Prague cont
Šverma Park 168
Tábor Gate 178
Teacher's Co-operative
127
Theatre on the
Balustrade 121
Three Ostriches 136
Thun Palace 139
Thun-Hohenstein
Palace 140, 159
Tomášská 135
Tower of the Old Town
Bridge 120
Town Hall 132
Toy Museum 154
Trade Fair Palace 187
Troja 101
Troja Château 117,
190
Třeboň 152
Turba Palace 137
U Fleků 173
U kalicha 176
U mecenáše 133
U Tomáše 135
Urbánek House 170
Vikářská 151
Villa America 176
Vinohrady 181
Vladislav Hall 100,
154, 155
Vojanovy Gardens 136
Vrtba Palace 139
Vyšehrad Cemetery 178
Vyšehrad Citadel 177
Wallenstein Palace 134
Wencelas Square 102,
162
Works Mill 138
Zbraslav 179
Žižkov 183
Pratzen Heights 338
Pravčická brána 235
Predné Solisko 419
Preisler, Jan 60, 188,
191, 256, 275, 354
Prešov 431
Příbor 344

Příbram 281, 282
Procházka, Antonín 62, 128, 164, 189
Prostějov 333
Protivín 299
Průhonice 198
Punkva Cave 331
Purkyně, Karel 59, 129, 275
Pustevny 350

Rabí 270
Radhošť 350
Radok, Alfréd 90
Rajčanka Valley 411
Rajhrad 320
Ratibořice 220
Reid, Benedikt 245
Reiner, V.V. 55, 110 120, 122, 123, 135, 139, 152, 159, 160, 181, 186, 206, 209, 243, 292
Rejsek, Matěj 113,114, 116, 117, 193, 195
Ricky 352
Ried, Benedikt 50, 100, 147, 148, 153, 154, 155, 193, 194, 266, 269, 270, 281
Rilke, Rainer Maria 80, 183
Říp Mountain 236
Rohe, Mies van der 64, 322, 329
Rosice 315
Rottmayr, Johann Michal 318
Roudnice nad labem 236
Rožmberk nad Vltavou 291
Rožnov pod Radhoštěm 350
Rožňava 438
Roztoky 205
Rudolph II 40, 51, 66, 100, 124, 136, 145, 146, 158, 162, 202, 221, 287, 294
Ruprechtice 221

Rusovce 388
Ruznice 300
Ružomberok 415
Rychnov nad Kněžnou 352

Sadská 209
Šafařík, Pavel Josef 42, 76
St Wenceslas 148
Šaloun, Ladislav 60, 108, 109, 164, 166, 171
Santini-Aichel, Johann 53, 54, 140, 151, 157, 175, 197, 209, 214, 265, 307, 309, 310, 320, 332, 352
Šašov 405
Sázava 198
Schikaneder, Jakub 60, 128, 129, 183, 188, 191, 256
Schnirch, Bohuslav 127, 172, 209,
Schubert, Franz 390, 391
Schulz, Josef 57, 127, 164, 171
Sedlec 197
Seifert, Jaroslav 85, 86, 92, 110, 183, 205, 219
Senetářov 332
Šic, Jiří 137
Silesia 303
Sklabiňa 392
Škoda, Emil 277
Škréta, Karel 54, 134, 135, 137, 152, 206, 209, 240, 244, 247, 265, 283, 292, 302, 351, 352
Skutecký, Dominik 61, 373, 380, 407, 416
Škvorecký, Josef 34, 73, 87, 90, 91, 141
Slavíček, Antonín 60, 198, 240, 236, 256, 275, 354
Slavkov 338, 340
Slavkovský štít 419
Slavonice 315

Slovak Karst 437
Slovak Paradise 362
Slovenskí rudohorie 436
Smetana, Bedřich 70, 109, 117, 171, 235, 255, 273, 307, 355
Smiřice 214
Smolenice 388
Smrk 350
Snilovské Sedlo 412
Sobotka 224
Šonov 221
Špála, Václav 62, 189, 198, 256, 275, 288, 349, 354
Špičák 269
Špindlerův Mlýn 227
Spiš 362
Spiš Region 420
Spišská Belá 426
Spišská Kapitula 423
Spišská Nová Ves 423
Spišská Sobota 420
Spišské Podhradie 424
Spišský hrad 424
Spišský Štvrtok 420
Šporck, Count F.A.G. 56, 217, 218
Spranger, Bartolomaeus 52, 100, 146, 152, 162, 244
Stará Boleslav 222
Stará Ľubovňa 427
Starý Plzenec 280
Starý Smokovec 419
Starýhrad 413
Štefánik, Milan 378
Stella, Paolo della 50, 156
Strakonice 279, 281
Štramberk 346
Strážky 426
Strážnice 359
Strážov Hills 401
Štrbské Pleso 418
Strečno 412
Střekov 241
Strž 282
Střekov 241
Studený, František 394

Štúr, Ľudovít 79, 367, 378, 383, 386, 387, 387, 403
Štúrovo 390
Štursa, Jan 61, 127, 148, 164, 167, 170, 189, 212, 349
Sucharda, Stanislav 60, 118, 165, 168, 174, 312, 333
Súľov Rocks 402
Šumava Mountains 249, 268
Šumiac 439
Šumperk 352
Sušice 268-269
Švabinský, Max 60,108, 109, 148, 150, 167, 183, 191, 315, 343, 344
Svatopluk 35
Svätý Kríž 416
Svidník 429
Švihov 269
Svitavy 356
Švýcarsko 229

Tábor 279, 285
Tatranská Lomnica 419
Tatranské Matliare 420
Teige, Karel 63, 65
Telč 301, 311
Teplá 261, 264
Tencalla, Giovanni Pietro 336, 337, 341, 344
Teplice 229, 241
Terchová 412
Terezín 229, 237
Thököly, Imre 425, 431, 435
Tiesňavy Pass 412
Tišnov 311
Tiso, Jozef 34, 43, 403
Tkadlík, František 128
Tomášov Balcony 439
Tomec, Josef 109
Třebechovice pod Orebem 351
Třebíč 313
Třeboň 299, 300

Trenčianske Teplice 361, 402
Trenčín 361, 400
Troger, Paul 244, 384
Trnava 361, 397
Troskovice 224
Trutnov 228
Turecká 409
Turnov 223
Tvrdošín 414
Tyl, Josef Kajetán 77, 171, 272, 273, 277, 281, 300
Týn nad Vlatou 287

Uherské Hradiště 347
Uherský Brod 347
Uhrovec 403
Újezd 267
Ústí nad Labem 241

Valašské Meziříčí 344
Valdštejn 224
Valtice 303, 358
Vamberk 351
Vančura, Vladislav 84, 88
Velehrad 347
Veľké dárko lake 310
Veľké Javorina 347
Veľká Lomnica 425
Veľké Losiny 352
Veľka lúka 414
Veľký Kriváň 412
Veltrusy 206
Verneřovice 221
Vimperk 270
Višnové 400
Vizovice 349
Vižnov 221
Vlkolínec 415
Volary 289
Vosecká bouda 226
Vosmík, Č. 168
Vranov 303, 316
Vrbatova bouda 227
Vrbov 426
Vrchlabí 227
Vsetín 349
Vsetínská Bečva 350
Vyškov 333

Vyšňy Komárník 430
Vyšší Brod 279, 290

Wallachia 344
Wallenstein, Albrecht von 52, 134, 234, 243, 251, 257
Warhol, Andy 430
Weil, Jiří 86, 138, 184
Wenceslas I 128, 272, 287, 333
White Carpathians 347
Wiehl, A. 165
Willman, Michael Leopold 55, 206, 209
Wohlmut, Bonifác 51, 147, 150, 155, 156, 175

Záhel, Antonín 109
Zákupy 234
Zamojski family 427
Žatec 246
Žďár nad Sázavou 308
Žebrák 272
Žehra 425
Železná Ruda 269
Želiezovce 390
Želiv 303, 307
Želivský, Jan 38 111, 169, 174, 432
Zemplínska Šírava Reservoir 431
Ženíšek, František 59, 121, 129, 164, 172, 191
Žerotíns 315
Žiar 420
Žiar nad Hronom 405
Žilina 410
Zítek, Josef 57, 127, 171
Zívr, Ladislav 65, 190
Žižka, Jan 38, 61, 285, 286, 355
Zlatá Koruna 297
Zlín 303, 348
Znojmo 303, 318
Zochova chata 387
Žurán 338
Zvíkov 279, 284
Zvolen 361, 405